D0744193

THE PAPERS OF ALEXANDER HAMILTON

Alexander Hamilton
Miniature by James Peale, 1789

Collection of Mrs. Alfred I. DuPont, Nemours, Wilmington, Delaware

THE PAPERS OF
Alexander Hamilton

VOLUME XVII

AUGUST 1794–DECEMBER 1794

HAROLD C. SYRETT, EDITOR

Associate Editors

BARBARA A. CHERNOW   PATRICIA SYRETT

COLUMBIA UNIVERSITY PRESS

NEW YORK AND LONDON, 1972

FROM THE PUBLISHER

The preparation of this edition of the papers of Alexander Hamilton has been made possible by the support received for the work of the editorial and research staff from the generous grants of the Rockefeller Foundation, Time Inc., and the Ford Foundation, and by the far-sighted cooperation of the National Historical Publications Commission. To these organizations, the publisher expresses gratitude on behalf of all who are concerned about making available the record of the founding of the United States.

International Standard Book Number: 0-231-08916-3
Library of Congress Catalog Card Number: 61-15593
Printed in the United States of America

PREFACE

THIS EDITION of Alexander Hamilton's papers contains letters and other documents written by Hamilton, letters to Hamilton, and some documents (commissions, certificates, etc.) that directly concern Hamilton but were written neither by him nor to him. All letters and other documents have been printed in chronological order. Hamilton's legal papers are being published under the editorial direction of Julius Goebel, Jr., George Welwood Murray Professor Emeritus of Legal History of the School of Law, Columbia University. Two volumes of this distinguished work, which is entitled *The Law Practice of Alexander Hamilton*, have been published by the Columbia University Press.

Many letters and documents have been calendared. Such calendared items include routine letters and documents by Hamilton, routine letters to Hamilton, some of the letters or documents written by Hamilton for someone else, letters or documents which have not been found but which are known to have existed, letters or documents which have been erroneously attributed to Hamilton, and letters to or by Hamilton that deal exclusively with his legal practice.

Certain routine documents which Hamilton wrote and received as Secretary of the Treasury have not been printed. The documents that fall within this category are warrants or interest certificates; letters written by Hamilton acknowledging receipts from banks, endorsing margins of certificate of registry, and enclosing sea letters; letters to Hamilton transmitting weekly, monthly, and quarterly accounts, or enclosing certificates of registry and other routine Treasury forms; and drafts by Hamilton on the treasurer. Statements of facts from the judges of the District Courts on cases concerning violations of the customs laws and warrants of remission of forfeiture issued to Hamilton have generally been omitted unless they pertain to cases discussed in Hamilton's correspondence.

The notes in these volumes are designed to provide information concerning the nature and location of each document, to identify Hamilton's correspondents and the individuals mentioned in the text, to explain events or ideas referred to in the text, and to point out textual variations or mistakes. Occasional departures from these standards can be attributed to a variety of reasons. In many cases the desired information has been supplied in an earlier note and can be found through the use of the index. Notes have not been added when in the opinion of the editors the material in the text was either self-explanatory or common knowledge. The editors, moreover, have not thought it desirable or necessary to provide full annotation for Hamilton's legal correspondence. Perhaps at this point it should also be stated that arithmetical errors in Hamilton's reports to Congress have not been corrected or noted. Finally, the editors on some occasions have been unable to find the desired information, and on other occasions the editors have been remiss.

GUIDE TO EDITORIAL APPARATUS

I. SYMBOLS USED TO DESCRIBE MANUSCRIPTS

AD	Autograph Document
ADS	Autograph Document Signed
ADf	Autograph Draft
ADfS	Autograph Draft Signed
AL	Autograph Letter
ALS	Autograph Letter Signed
D	Document
DS	Document Signed
Df	Draft
DfS	Draft Signed
LS	Letter Signed
LC	Letter Book Copy
[S]	[S] is used with other symbols (AD[S], ADf[S], AL[S], D[S], Df[S], L[S]) to indicate that the signature on the document has been cropped or clipped.

II. MONETARY SYMBOLS AND ABBREVIATIONS

bf	Banco florin
V	Ecu
f	Florin
₶	Livre Tournois
medes	Maravedis (also md and mde)
d.	Penny or denier
ps	Piece of eight

£	Pound sterling or livre
Ry	Real
rs vn	Reals de vellon
rdr	Rix daller
s	Shilling, sou or sol (also expressed as /)
sti	Stiver

III. SHORT TITLES AND ABBREVIATIONS

Albert, *History of the County of Westmoreland*	George Dallas Albert, ed., *History of the County of Westmoreland, Pennsylvania, with Biographical Sketches of Many of Its Pioneers and Prominent Men* (Philadelphia, 1882).
Annals of Congress	*The Debates and Proceedings of the Congress of the United States; with an Appendix, Containing Important State Papers and Public Documents, and All the Laws of a Public Nature* (Washington, 1834–1849).
ASP	*American State Papers, Documents, Legislative and Executive, of the Congress of the United States* (Washington, 1832–1861).
Baldwin, "Orders Issued by General Henry Lee"	Leland D. Baldwin, ed., "Orders Issued by General Henry Lee during the Campaign against the Whiskey Insurrectionists," *The Western Pennsylvania Historical Magazine*, XIX (June, 1936).
Baldwin, *Whiskey Rebels*	Leland D. Baldwin, *Whiskey Rebels: The Story of a Frontier Uprising* (Pittsburgh, 1939).
Bee, *Reports of Cases Adjudged in the District Court of South Carolina*	Thomas Bee, *Reports of Cases Adjudged in the District Court of South Carolina by the Hon. Thomas Bee, Judge of That Court* (Philadelphia, 1810).
Brackenridge, *Incidents*	Hugh H. Brackenridge, *Incidents of the Insurrection in the West-*

	ern Parts of Pennsylvania, in the Year 1794 (Philadelphia, 1795).
Brackenridge, *Insurrection*	Henry M. Brackenridge, *History of the Western Insurrection in Western Pennsylvania, Commonly Called the Whiskey Insurrection, 1794* (Pittsburgh, 1859).
Calendar of the General Otho Holland Williams Papers	*Calendar of the General Otho Holland Williams Papers in the Maryland Historical Society* (Baltimore, 1940).
Calendar of Virginia State Papers, VI	Sherwin McRae, ed., *Calendar of Virginia State Papers and Other Manuscripts, from August 11, 1792, to December 31, 1793, Preserved in the Capitol at Richmond*, VI (Richmond, 1886).
Calendar of Virginia State Papers, VII	Sherwin McRae and Raleigh Colston, eds., *Calendar of Virginia State Papers and Other Manuscripts, from January 1, 1794, to May 16, 1795*, VII (Richmond, 1888).
Carter, *Territorial Papers*	Clarence E. Carter, ed., *The Territorial Papers of the United States* (Washington, 1934–).
Correspondence of the French Ministers with the United States Government	*Correspondence of the French Ministers, Joseph Fauchet and P. Adet; with the United States Government during the Years 1794–1796* (n.p., 1797?).
Domett, *History of the Bank of New York*	Henry W. Domett, *A History of the Bank of New York, 1784–1884* (New York, 1884).
Executive Journal, I	*Journal of the Executive Proceedings of the Senate* (Washington, 1828), I.
Findley, *History of the Insurrection*	William Findley, *History of the Insurrection, In the Four Western Counties of Pennsylvania: In the Year M.DCC.XCIV. With a Recital of the Circumstances Specially Connected Therewith: And an Historical Review of the*

	Previous Situation of the Country (Philadelphia, 1796).
Freeman, *Washington*	Douglas Southall Freeman, *George Washington* (New York, 1948–1957). Volume VII of this series was written by John Alexander Carroll and Mary Wells Ashworth.
GW	John C. Fitzpatrick, ed., *The Writings of George Washington* (Washington, 1931–1944).
GW Diaries	John C. Fitzpatrick, ed., *The Diaries of George Washington* (Boston and New York, 1925).
Hamilton, *History*	John C. Hamilton, *Life of Alexander Hamilton, a History of the Republic of the United States of America* (Boston, 1879).
Hamilton, *Intimate Life*	Allan McLane Hamilton, *The Intimate Life of Alexander Hamilton* (New York, 1910).
HCLW	Henry Cabot Lodge, ed., *The Works of Alexander Hamilton* (New York, 1904).
JCC	*Journals of the Continental Congress, 1774–1789* (Washington, 1904–1937).
JCH Transcripts	John C. Hamilton Transcripts, Columbia University Libraries.
JCHW	John C. Hamilton, ed., *The Works of Alexander Hamilton* (New York, 1851–1856).
"Journal by Major William Gould"	"Journal by Major William Gould, of the New Jersey Infantry, During an Expedition into Pennsylvania in 1794," *Proceedings of the New Jersey Historical Society*, III (1849).
Journal of the House, I, II, III	*Journal of the House of Representatives of the United States* (Washington, 1826), I, II, III.
JPP	"Journal of the Proceedings of the President," George Washington Papers, Library of Congress.

Knopf, *Wayne*	Richard C. Knopf, ed., *Anthony Wayne: A Name in Arms; Soldier, Diplomat, Defender of Expansion Westward of a Nation; the Wayne-Knox-Pickering-McHenry Correspondence* (Pittsburgh, 1960).
Miller, *Treaties*, II	Hunter Miller, ed., *Treaties and Other International Acts of the United States of America* (Washington, 1931), II.
Pennsylvania Archives, 2nd ser., IV	*Pennsylvania Archives*, 2nd ser., IV (n.p., 1876).
Pennsylvania Archives, 9th ser., I, II	*Pennsylvania Archives*, 9th ser., I, II (n.p., 1931).
PRO: F.O., or PRO: C.O.	Transcripts or photostats from the Public Record Office of Great Britain deposited in the Library of Congress.
PRO: F.O. (Great Britain)	Public Record Office of Great Britain.
1 *Stat.*	*The Public Statutes at Large of the United States of America* (Boston, 1845).
6 *Stat.*	*The Public Statutes at Large of the United States of America* [Private Statutes] (Boston, 1856).
Wharton, *State Trials*	Francis Wharton, *State Trials of the United States During the Administrations of Washington and Adams* (Philadelphia, 1849).

IV. INDECIPHERABLE WORDS

Words or parts of words which could not be deciphered because of the illegibility of the writing or the mutilation of the manuscript have been indicated as follows:

1. ⟨-----⟩ indicates illegible words with the number of dashes indicating the estimated number of illegible words.
2. Words or letters in broken brackets indicate a guess as to what the words or letters in question may be. If the source of

the words or letters within the broken brackets is known, it has been given a note.

V. CROSSED-OUT MATERIAL IN MANUSCRIPTS

Words or sentences crossed out by a writer in a manuscript have been handled in one of the three following ways:

1. They have been ignored, and the document or letter has been printed in its final version.
2. Crossed-out words and insertions for the crossed-out words have been described in the notes.
3. When the significance of a manuscript seems to warrant it, the crossed-out words have been retained, and the document has been printed as it was written.

VI. TEXTUAL CHANGES AND INSERTIONS

The following changes or insertions have been made in the letters and documents printed in these volumes:

1. Words or letters written above the line of print (for example, 9th) have been made even with the line of print (9th).
2. Punctuation and capitalization have been changed in those instances where it seemed necessary to make clear the sense of the writer. A special effort has been made to eliminate the dash, which was such a popular eighteenth-century device.
3. When the place or date, or both, of a letter or document does not appear at the head of that letter or document, it has been inserted in the text in brackets. If either the place or date at the head of a letter or document is incomplete, the necessary additional material has been added in the text in brackets. For all but the best known localities or places, the name of the colony, state, or territory has been added in brackets at the head of a document or letter.
4. In calendared documents, place and date have been uniformly written out in full without the use of brackets. Thus "N. York, Octr, 8, '99" becomes "New York, October 8, 1799." If, how-

ever, substantive material is added to the place or date in a calendared document, such material is placed in brackets. Thus "Oxford, Jan. 6" becomes "Oxford [Massachusetts] January 6 [1788]."

5. When a writer made an unintentional slip comparable to a typographical error, one of the four following devices has been used:
   a. It has been allowed to stand as written.
   b. It has been corrected by inserting cither one or more letters in brackets.
   c. It has been corrected without indicating the change.
   d. It has been explained in a note.
6. Because the symbol for the thorn was archaic even in Hamilton's day, the editors have used the letter "y" to represent it. In doing this they are conforming to eighteenth-century manuscript usage.

THE PAPERS OF ALEXANDER HAMILTON

1794

From Tench Coxe[1]

Treasury Department, Revenue Office, August 1, 1794. Requests "a payment to be made to John J. Feach & Co.[2] of the sum of five thousand Dollars on a/count of a contract made with them for the casting of a quantity of Kentledge or Iron Ballast & Cannon ball."[3]

LC, RG 75, Letters of Tench Coxe, Commissioner of the Revenue, Relating to the Procurement of Military, Naval, and Indian Supplies, National Archives.

1. Coxe, who was commissioner of the revenue, had been made responsible for procuring military, naval, and Indian supplies. See H to Coxe, April 4, 1794.
For background to this letter, see Henry Knox to H, March 29, April 21, 1794.

2. John Jacob Feasch, who had come to the United States from Switzerland in 1764, was a well-known ironmaster in Morris County, New Jersey. In 1787 he was a member of that state's ratifying convention. Feasch's Mount Hope Furnace in Rockaway township supplied shot, shell, and cannon for the Continental Army during the American Revolution.

3. See Coxe to John J. Feasch and Company, July 18, 1794 (LC, RG 75, Letters of Tench Coxe, Commissioner of the Revenue, Relating to the Procurement of Military, Naval, and Indian Supplies, National Archives).

To Tench Coxe[1]

[Philadelphia, August 1, 1794]

Dr. Sir

Sundry papers were sent to you to day by Judge Wilson to get the hand writing proved. Did you get them? Has the needful been done? Have they been returned? Pray be in Town tomorrow Morning at seven oClock.[2]

Yrs A Hamilton

ALS, Tench Coxe Papers, Historical Society of Pennsylvania, Philadelphia.

1. Coxe wrote on the back of this letter that he had received it on August 1, 1794. The "Sundry papers" which James Wilson, associate justice of the Supreme Court, had sent to Coxe obviously concerned the Whiskey Insurrection in western Pennsylvania. See "Conference Concerning the Insurrection in Western Pennsylvania," August 2, 1794, note 9. For background information on the Whiskey Insurrection, see "Deposition of Francis Mentges," August 1, 1794.

2. Coxe endorsed this letter "ansd." Letter not found.

To Tench Coxe

[*Philadelphia, August 1–15, 1794.*] "It will be proper to instruct Mr. Carrington to give facility to a legal decision in any case where it may be desired—taking care to secure an appeal in the last resort to the Supreme Court." [1]

AL, RG 58, General Records, 1791–1803, National Archives.

1. This note appears on an envelope addressed to H and attached to an "Extract of a letter from the Supervisor of Virginia to the Commissioner of the Revenue, dated July 28th: 1794." The extract from Edward Carrington's letter reads as follows:

"I am apprehensive we shall meet with a pacific, or what will be called a legal, opposition to the Collection of the Duties on Carriages. A very general idea prevails in this district, that the act is unconstitutional, and numbers of very respectable Characters have signified their determination to try the point by legal decision. This circumstance renders it of material consequence, that the Officers should proceed strictly under the provisions contained in the Act, that, in a legal contest, there may be no confusion of principles, and a decision may turn fairly on the constitutionality of the Act, if that is made a point of.

"Should my Construction of the Act be right as the legal provision for recovering the duties in cases of non-entry or non-payment, and the contemplated opposition be persevered in, the institution of suits will rest with the United States, and the defence of individuals will be calculated to try the point set up."

The tax on carriages had been provided for in "An Act laying duties upon Carriages for the conveyance of Persons" (1 *Stat.* 373–75 [June 5, 1794]).

On August 26, 1794, Coxe wrote to Carrington: ". . . I have to request that you will give every facility in your power to a legal decision relative to the question as to the constitutionality of the duty on carriages in any case where it may be desired, taking care to secure an appeal, in the last resort, to the Supreme Court" (LC, RG 58, Letters of Commissioner of Revenue, 1794–1795, National Archives).

Deposition of Francis Mentges [1]

[Philadelphia, August 1, 1794]

Philadelphia (to wit) Francis Mentges at present of the City of Philadelphia maketh oath That he arrived at Pittsburgh in the County of Alleghanny on the 22 of July last past and continued

DS, in the handwriting of H and signed by Francis Mentges, Connecticut Historical Society, Hartford.

1. Mentges was a colonel in the Pennsylvania militia.

Many inhabitants of the four western counties of Pennsylvania (Allegheny, Fayette, Washington, and Westmoreland) actively opposed the laws imposing duties on spirits distilled within the United States ("An Act repealing, after

there until the 25 of the same month. That it was there matter of public notoriety and general conversation that several collections of armed men had on the seventeenth of the same month successively made repeated attacks upon the house of General John Neville [2] In-

---

the last day of June next, the duties heretofore laid upon Distilled Spirits imported from abroad, and laying others in their stead; and also upon Spirits distilled within the United States, and for appropriating the same" [1 *Stat.* 199–214 (March 3, 1791)]; "An Act concerning the Duties on Spirits distilled within the United States" [1 *Stat.* 267–71 (May 8, 1792)]). By September, 1792, opposition to the excise duties had become so pronounced that the President was forced to issue a proclamation denouncing "certain violent and unwarrantable proceedings [which] have lately taken place tending to obstruct the operation of the laws of the United States for raising a revenue upon spirits distilled within the same" and enjoining all citizens to obey the laws. For George Washington's proclamation, see "Draft of a Proclamation Concerning Opposition to the Excise Law," September 7, 1792, note 1. For information on the 1792 disturbances, see H to Tench Coxe, September 1, 1792; H to Washington, September 1, 8, first letter of September 9, September 11, 22, 26, 1792; H to John Jay, September 3, 1792; Washington to H, September 7, two letters of September 17, September 21, October 1, 1792; Jay to H, September 8, 1792; Edmund Randolph to H, September 8, 1792; Rufus King to H, September 27, 1792; George Clymer to H, September 28, October 4, 10, 1792; Washington to Thomas Mifflin, September 29, 1792; Coxe to H, October 19, 1792.

During the succeeding months fewer inflammatory addresses against the excise were made and acts of violence against collectors of the tax decreased. But inhabitants of western Pennsylvania continued to oppose the excise. Attempts by the Government to conciliate opponents of the excise through legislation ("An Act making further provision for securing and collecting the Duties on foreign and domestic distilled Spirits, Stills, Wines and Teas" [1 *Stat.* 378–81 (June 5, 1794]) proved unavailing. Early in July, 1794, spasmodic and scattered violence broke out culminating in what came to be known as the Whiskey Insurrection.

2. John Neville, Revolutionary War veteran and a former member of the Supreme Executive Council of Pennsylvania, was inspector of the revenue for Survey No 4. in Pennsylvania. As such, he was both a symbol and a target for those who opposed the excise laws in western Pennsylvania. In addition, he was a man of considerable wealth and the head of the so-called "Neville connection" (Brackenridge, *Insurrection*, 31). His son Presley, also a Revolutionary War veteran, was a member of the Pennsylvania Assembly, surveyor in Allegheny County, and brigadier inspector of the militia for Allegheny County. John Neville's daughter Amelia was married to Major Isaac Craig, the deputy quartermaster general of the United States Army, and his sister-in-law was married to Abraham Kirkpatrick, another Revolutionary War veteran, who had settled in Pittsburgh and had become wealthy through speculation.

On July 17, 1794, the insurgents attacked Neville's house for the second consecutive day. Neville described this attack in a letter to Tench Coxe, dated July 18, 1794: ". . . I applied to Major [Thomas] Butler commandant in Pittsburg for some assistance he sent me twelve men, I also made application to the Judges of our Court, the Generals of Militia [John Wilkens, Jr., and John Gibson] and to the Sheriff of the County [Samuel Ewalt], but had no hopes of Assistance from these quarters. Thus circumstanced I had certain information about ten OClock yesterday that a large party were again advancing. I imspector of the Revenue for and on account of his holding and exercising the said Office and to oblige him to relinquish the same in the course of which attacks one of the Assailants was killed [3] and several of them wounded and some persons who assisted in defending the house were also wounded and the said house with the adjoining

---

mediately wrote to my friends to come to my assistance, a very few of them attempted it, but were too late, about 5 OClock 500 men in regular order properly appointed, made their appearance; . . . I quitted the House . . . leaving a friend aided by the 12 Soldiers to capitulate for the property—my Servants rendered timid by their Numbers had disappeared—several Flags and Messages pass'd between the parties—but the Assailants not offering Terms sufficiently implicative of Safety, an Engagement once more commenced the numbers in the house were reduced to Twelve, who kept up a small fire about one house, which was returned many hundred fold from without, when they were obliged to surrender, during the Skirmish they had fired the Barn, Stables and different out-Houses, and immediately on the Surrender a large and well furnished dwelling house with all its appurtenances shared the same fate, the fences all destroyed, and two whole crops of Grain consumed what was yesterday an elegant and highly cultivated farm with every convenience is now a melancholy waste. The party in the House had three badly wounded, all Soldiers in the U.S. Service, the Loss without is not ascertained, one of their Leaders fell, an old officer and a Man of respectability & we know of some wounded" (LS, Neville Papers, Carnegie Library of Pittsburgh, Pennsylvania). For the first attack on Neville's house, see H to Washington, August 5, 1794, note 77.

In a letter to Henry Knox on July 18, 1794, Isaac Craig described these same events as follows: ". . . And yesterday a large number of Armed Men Amounting it is said to seven hundred Assembled & Attacked his [John Neville's] house, defended only by himself Major Kirkpatrick and ten Soldiers, during the attack General Nevill seeing it impossible, to defend the House, against such numbers, took an Opportunity of escaping and Concealing himself in a Thicket, Major Kirkpatrick Continued to defend the House, till One of his men was Killed and four wounded having killed two and Wounded several of the Insurgents, as soon as the Major surrendered the Enemy set fire to the House, which is Consumed to ashes with all the Property it Contained, not a single Article saved. . . . Major [David] Lenox Coll Nevill, Myself & two others in Attempting to get into the House, with a supply of Ammunition, were made Prisoners, disarmed & Confined, till the Action was Over, and then Carried several Miles to their Rendezvous, treated Major Lenox with the Utmost Indignity, and all of Us with Insult in the night, I was happy enough to make my escape, and to find General Nevill & to Escort him to my House, where he now is. . ." (LS, Connecticut Historical Society, Hartford).

For additional accounts of this attack, see Abraham Kirkpatrick to Washington, July 25, 28, 1794 (ALS, Connecticut Historical Society, Hartford); "Statement of Thomas Williams as published in the Beaver Argus in 1855" (copy, Neville Papers, Carnegie Library of Pittsburgh, Pennsylvania); Thomas Butler to Knox, July 18, 1794 (*Pennsylvania Archives*, 2nd ser., IV, 74–75).

3. James McFarlane. During the American Revolution McFarlane had served as a lieutenant in the 1st Pennsylvania Regiment. In 1794 he was a major in the Pennsylvania militia.

The *Pennsylvania Archives* states that the assailant was Major Abram MacFarlane (*Pennsylvania Archives*, 2nd ser., IV, 793).

barn & stables were burnt down by the said Assailants—moreover that David Lenox Marshall of the District had been taken into custody by some of the said armed collections in consequence of his having been there for the service of certain processes in relation to laws of the United States laying duties on distilled spirits and on stills but was afterwards released and that the said Marshall together with the said Inspector of the Revenue had descended the Ohio in a Boat to avoid personal violence or the being compelled by force to enter into engagements or do acts contrary to the duties of their respective Offices and also by reason of the difficulty and danger which would probably have attended an attempt on their part to pass by any of the usual routes to the seat of Government. And the said Deponent further saith that on the twenty fourth of the same month of July he saw & conversed at Pittsburgh aforesaid with Hugh Brackenridge [4] who informed him that he had been the day preceding at a Meeting of sundry persons about One hundred and forty in number at Mingo Creek Meeting House [5] in the County of Washington consisting generally of the most respectable people of that County including sundry Magistrates & principal Officers of Militia and the Recorder who were assembled to consider the propriety of ratifying and supporting the measures which had been taken towards obstructing the execution of the Excise law by the proceedings on the seventeenth as above mentioned—that it was there proposed that the Meeting should approve the said proceedings and pledge themselves to stand by each other until the Excise law was repealed and an Act of Oblivion passed—which proposition was not agreed to but instead of it it was proposed and agreed to that the four Western Counties of Pensylvania and the neighbouring counties of Virginia should be invited to assemble by delegates in a Convention to be holden on the fourteenth of this present

4. Brackenridge was a playwright, lawyer, and a leading citizen of Pittsburgh. He helped to establish Pittsburgh's first newspaper, academy, and bookstore, and he was a member of the state assembly in 1786–1787. He described and defended his role—which was somewhat ambiguous—in the Whiskey Insurrection in detail in Brackenridge, *Incidents*. His son, Henry M. Brackenridge, performed the same task in Brackenridge, *Insurrection*.

5. At the Mingo Creek meeting described in Mentges's deposition, Brackenridge had urged the opponents of the excise to avoid illegal acts. An account of the Mingo Creek meeting is printed in Brackenridge, *Insurrection*, 57–65, and Brackenridge, *Incidents*, I, 29–36.

Month of August in Mingo Creek aforesaid at Parkinson's [6] in the county of Washington to take into consideration the situation of the Western Counties and adopt such measures as should appear suited to the exigency. And this Deponent further saith that from the general state of affairs in the said Western Counties of Pensylvania as they came under his observation he doth verily believe that it is intirely impracticable to execute the laws aforesaid by the means of civil process and Judiciary proceeding. And further this Deponent saith noth. F Mentges

Sworn this first Day of August 1794 at the City of Philadelphia before me. [The Subscriber One of The Alderman of the said City.] [7] Reynold Keen

6. Parkinson's Ferry on Mingo Creek. For the minutes of this meeting, see *Pennsylvania Archives*, 2nd ser., IV, 159–61.

7. The material within brackets is not in H's handwriting.

From William Ellery [1]

Newport [*Rhode Island, August 1–6*] *1794.* "On the 9th. day of May last the Schooner Harmony of Somerset whereof Preserved Pierce now is master or commander, an enrolled and licensed vessel arrived in this Port from Somerset in the District of Dighton laden with the produce and manufacture of the United States and desired to be endorsed master of said Vessel. I asked him for his papers, upon which he produced her Enrollmt. & License. I then asked him for his Manifest he told me he had none. I informed him that he had incurred the penalty of 20 dollars, shewed him the Law [2] & told him that it was my duty to enforce it. As he lived out of this State I issued a Writ against him. Whereupon . . . I was told that he had determined to stand trial . . . and it appeared from conversation . . . the Defendent meant to rely principally on this point, that the Defendt. could not be considered as master or commander of the Vessel until he was endorsed as such; and to endeavour to influence the Jury by representing the hardship of the case—that no fraud was intended, &c. &c. It will be proved that the Defendt. reported the change of master & exhibited the papers of the Vessel to the Collector desired to be endorsed master of her, and that he declared he had no manifest of her lading. The District Attorney[3] is clear that the cause is a good law cause, but is under some apprehensions that the Jury may be disposed to favour the defendt. as there doth not appear to have been any intention to defraud the Revenue, and that if the United States should loose the Cause it may encourage others to transgress the Law and to pass from District to District without manifest. . . . Please to favour me with your directs. in this Cause. . . ."

LC, Newport Historical Society, Newport, Rhode Island.

1. Ellery was collector of customs at Newport, Rhode Island.

2. "An Act for enrolling and licensing ships or vessels to be employed in the coasting trade and fisheries, and for regulating the same" (1 *Stat.* 305–18 [February 18, 1793]). See Ellery to H, March 18–25, 1794, note 4.

3. Ray Greene.

To Joseph Nourse[1]

Treasury Department, August 1, 1794. Sends a list of acts of Congress making appropriations "for the service of the year 1794, and for making good deficiencies, the sums following."[2]

Copy, RG 53, Register of the Treasury, Estimates and Statements for 1794, Vol. "136-T," National Archives.

1. Nourse was register of the Treasury

2. This list constituted Nourse's warrant for making the payments authorized by Congress. The warrant is countersigned by Oliver Wolcott, Jr., comptroller of the Treasury.

To Joseph Nourse

Treasury Department, August 1, 1794. "In consequence of a new arrangement of the General accounts of appropriations and expenditures, you are hereby directed to make the following entries, for warrants drawn on the Treasurer[1] from the first of January 1794, to the 31st of July following. . . ."[2]

DS, RG 39, Appropriation Warrants, Treasury Proper, August 1, 1794–January 2, 1795, National Archives.

1. Samuel Meredith.

2. The warrants totaled $5,064,734.89.

This document is countersigned by Oliver Wolcott, Jr.

From Wilhem and Jan Willink, Nicholaas and Jacob Van Staphorst, and Nicholas Hubbard[1]

TRIPLICATE. ORIG: PR. SHIP PEGGY. ELLIOT.
DUPL. PR. SHIP ADRIANNE. FITZPATRICK.

Amsterdam 1 August 1794

Sir!

Being deprived of your esteemed favors, since We had the pleasure to address you the 15th Ultimo, We have now chiefly to transmit you the Account Current of the United States with us, up to 31 Ultimo, The Balance whereon due by us Holland Currency f 1,481,-729. 3.— We transfer to their Credit in a new Account.

Mr. Jay, having wrote us, that his Powers not extending to the case upon which We asked his directions, He did not consider himself authorized to give us any advice or opinion on the subject:[2] But at same time favoring us with his opinion as a private Citizen, that the United States ought to be prepared for every Event, whether more or less probable, We have taken ye most strong and efficacious measures, to have Your Order for Saltpetre executed:[3] In consequence of which We hope, in a short time, to be able to forward You Bill of Lading for the parcel We purchased in Hamburgh, and to advise the final purchase in Copenhagen, of the remainder of the Quantity to compleat the One Hundred Tons you desired to be shipped on account of the United States.

We are respectfully Sir! Your most obedient and very humble servants

Wilhem & Jan Willink
N & J Van Staphorst & Hubbard

Five per Cent Bonds of the U.S. 98¼ a 98½ p Ct.

Alexr. Hamilton Esqr. Secretary of the Treasury of the U.S.

LS, Connecticut Historical Society, Hartford.

1. Willink, Van Staphorst, and Hubbard were the bankers for the United States in Amsterdam.

2. See Willink, Van Staphorst, and Hubbard to H, July 15, 1794, note 4.

3. See H to Willink, Van Staphorst, and Hubbard, May 8, 1794; Willink, Van Staphorst, and Hubbard to H, July 1, 15, 1794.

Conference Concerning the Insurrection in Western Pennsylvania[1]

[Philadelphia, August 2, 1794][2]

The President opened the business by stating that it was hardly necessary to prepare the subject of the conference, as it was generally understood, and the circumstances which accompanied it were such as to strike at the root of all law & order; that he was clearly of opinion that the most spirited & firm measures were necessary to rescue the State as well as the general government from the impending danger, for if such proceedings were tolerated there was an end to our Constitutions & laws. He then observed that there were some papers besides those already communicated to the Gov'r which would throw additional light on the subject, and he presented them to the Secretary of State who read them aloud.

The papers consisted of letters from Gen'l Nevil,[3] Presley Nevil,[4] Maj. Lenox[5] and Capt. Butler,[6] a Deposition of Col. Menges[7] and a deposition of the Post Rider whose mail had been stopped.[8] In some

Pennsylvania Archives, 2nd ser., IV, 144–46.

1. For background to this document, see "Deposition of Francis Mentges," August 1, 1794.

Those present at this conference were George Washington, Edmund Randolph, H, Henry Knox, William Bradford, and the following officials from Pennsylvania: Thomas Mifflin, governor; Thomas McKean, chief justice; Jared Ingersoll, attorney general; Alexander J. Dallas, secretary of the Commonwealth.

2. In the *Pennsylvania Archives* this document is dated "the 9th [2d?] August, 1794." Internal evidence indicates that August 2 is the correct date.

3. John Neville. See "Deposition of Francis Mentges," August 1, 1794, note 2.

4. See "Deposition of Francis Mentges," August 1, 1794, note 2.

5. David Lenox was United States marshal for the District of Pennsylvania.

6. This is a reference to Major Thomas Butler, commander of Fort Fayette, Pittsburgh, who wrote to Knox concerning the insurgents on July 18, 1794 (*Pennsylvania Archives,* 2nd ser., IV, 74–75).

7. See "Deposition of Francis Mentges," August 1, 1794.

8. This is a reference to the interception of the mail between Pittsburgh and Philadelphia. The intercepted letters were described by Hugh Henry Brackenridge as follows: ". . . these letters were from colonel Presly Neville, to his father-in-law, General [Daniel] Morgan; General [John] Gibson to the governor of Pennsylvania; James Brison, prothonotary, to the governor; Major [Thomas] Butler, to the secretary at war; and Edward Day [a clerk in Pittsburgh], to the secretary of the treasury" (Brackenridge, *Incidents,* I, 45). Day's letter to H has not been found.

According to Henry M. Brackenridge, the mail was intercepted on July 26 by John Mitchell, acting on orders from the leaders of the insurgents (Bracken-

of the letters were inclosed sundry extracts from the Pittsburgh *Gazette* which had been published in the papers of Phila.

The President declared his determination to go every length that the Constitution and Laws would permit, but no further; he expressed a wish for the co-operation of the State Government, and he enquired whether the Governor could not adopt some preliminary measures under the State Laws, as the measures of the Gen'l Gov't would be slow, and depended on the certificate of Judge Wilson, to whom the documents had been delivered for his consideration.[9]

---

ridge, *Insurrection,* 80). In describing the incident Hugh H. Brackenridge wrote: "The post was interrupted on the 26th of July, on the way from Pittsburgh, and near Greensburgh. The packet from Washington and Pittsburgh was taken out. It was carried by Benjamin Parkinson to Washington, and from thence it was accompanied, by [David] Bradford and [James] Marshall, and others, to Cannonsburgh, a village seven miles distant. It was there opened. No letter, on the late affairs, from any individual of Washington: There were letters from individuals of Pittsburgh; these letters gave great offence, and made the writers objects of resentment" (Brackenridge, *Incidents,* I, 39). See also Alexander Addison to Hugh H. Brackenridge, January 18, 1795 (*Pennsylvania Archives,* 2nd ser., IV, 522); Daniel Morgan to Washington, January 19, 1795 (LS, RG 59, Miscellaneous Letters, 1790–1799, National Archives).

9. In addition to this conference with the Pennsylvania officials, the cabinet apparently held at least one meeting on the disturbances in western Pennsylvania before August 2. In a letter of August 5 to Washington, Randolph stated: "At our first consultation, in your presence, the indignation, which we all felt at the outrages committed, lead us to advise, that the information received should be laid before an associate justice or the district judge to be considered under the act of May 2d, 1792. This step was urged by the necessity of understanding without delay all the means, vested in the President for suppressing the progress of the mischief. A caution however, was prescribed to the attorney-general, who submitted the documents to the judge; not to express to him the most distant wish in the President that the certificate should be granted" (ALS, George Washington Papers, Library of Congress). Randolph's letter is printed in Wharton, *State Trials,* 156. See also H to Tench Coxe, August 1, 1794.

Randolph was referring to Section 2 of "An Act to provide for calling forth the Militia to execute the laws of the Union, suppress insurrections, and repel invasion" (1 *Stat.* 264–65 [May 2, 1792]), which reads as follows: "That whenever the laws of the United States shall be opposed, or the execution thereof obstructed, in any state, by combinations too powerful to be suppressed by the ordinary course of judicial proceedings, or by the powers vested in the marshals by this act, the same being notified to the President of the United States, by an associate justice or the district judge, it shall be lawful for the President of the United States to call forth the militia of such state to suppress such combinations, and to cause the laws to be duly executed. And if the militia of a state, where such combinations may happen, shall refuse, or be insufficient to suppress the same, it shall be lawful for the President, if the legislature of the United States be not in session, to call forth and employ such numbers of the militia of any other state or states most convenient thereto, as may be necessary, and the use of the militia, so to be called forth, may be continued,

The Secretary of State read the act of Congress under which the Gen'l Gov't were proceeding[10] and repeated the enquiries, whether some more expeditious, preliminary course, could not be pursued, referring to a particular act of the state.

The officers of the State Government remaining silent for some time, the Att'y Gen'l of the U.S. turned to the act of the 22d Sept., '83, authorizing calls of the Militia on sudden emergencies,[11] but the Secretary of the Comm'th referred him to a note in the index, subjoined to title militia, and suggested his opinion that the law referred to was repealed,[12] whereupon the Att'y Gen'l of the U.S. asked the Sec'y of the Com'th, what was his opinion respecting the power of

---

if necessary, until the expiration of thirty days after the commencement of the ensuing session."

On August 4, 1794, Justice James Wilson of the Supreme Court submitted the following opinion to the President: "From Evidence, which has been laid before me, I hereby notify to you, that, in the Counties of Washington and Allegany in Pennsylvania, Laws of the United States are opposed, and the Execution thereof obstructed by Combinations too powerful to be suppressed by the ordinary Course of judicial Proceedings, or by the Powers vested in the Marshal of that District" (ALS, Pennsylvania Miscellany, Whiskey Rebellion, Vol. I, Library of Congress; copy, Historical Society of Pennsylvania, Philadelphia). Wilson's opinion is printed in *ASP, Miscellaneous*, I, 85, and *Pennsylvania Archives*, 2nd ser., IV, 82–83.

In his letter of August 5 to Washington Randolph wrote concerning Wilson's statement: "The certificate has been granted, and altho' the testimony is not, in my judgment, yet in sufficient legal form to become the groundwork of such an act; and a judge ought not *a priori* to decide, that the marshall is incompetent to suppress the combination by the posse comitatus; yet the certificate, if it be minute enough, is conclusive. . . . But the certificate specifies no particular law, which has been opposed. This defect I remarked to Judge Wilson, from whom the certificate came, and observed, that the design of the law being, that a judge should point out to the executive where the judiciary stood in need of military aid, it was frustrated if military force should be applied to laws, which the judge might not contemplate. He did not yield to my reasoning, and therefore I presume, that the objection will not be received against the validity of the certificate" (ALS, George Washington Papers, Library of Congress).

Washington quoted Wilson's opinion in his proclamation of August 7, 1794 (*GW*, XXXIII, 457–61).

10. "An Act to provide for calling forth the Militia to execute the laws of the Union, suppress insurrections, and repel invasions" (1 *Stat.* 264–65 [May 2, 1792]). See note 9.

11. "An Additional Supplement to an Act, Entitled 'An Act for the Regulation of the Militia of the Commonwealth of Pennsylvania'" (*Pennsylvania Laws*, 7th Sess., Ch. LXXXIII).

12. The act of September 22, 1783, was repealed by Section XXXIV of "An Act for the Regulation of the Militia of the Commonwealth of Pennsylvania," which was passed on April 11, 1793 (*Pennsylvania Laws*, 1793 Sess., Ch. CLXXVI).

the Governor to call out the Militia on such occasions, to which the secretary replied, that as an individual he had no objection to give a private opinion—that independent of the law referred to, or any other special law, the executive Magistrate was charged with the care of seeing the laws faithfully executed, and that upon the requisition of the civil authority declaring it incompetent to the task, the very nature of the Executive Magistrate's duty and obligations, required that he should aid the civil authority by an exertion of the military force of the Government.

The intention of proceeding against the Rioters in Allegheny co., being declared by the President, the Chief Justice expressed it as his positive opinion, that the judiciary power was equal to the task of quelling and punishing the riots, and that the employment of a military force, at this period, would be as bad as anything that the Rioters had done—equally unconstitutional and illegal.

The opinion of the Secretary of the Treasury was introduced by argument upon the general necessity of maintaining the Government in its regular authority. He referred to the various co-operating sources of opposition to the Constitution and laws of the U.S., (The Judiciary,[13] excise,[14] Mississippi navigation,[15] erecting a new State,[16]

13. This is a reference to the case of *Chisholm* v *Georgia,* in which the Supreme Court ruled on February 18, 1793, that a citizen of one state (in this case South Carolina) could bring suit against another state (Georgia) for breach of contract (A. J. Dallas, *Reports of Cases Ruled and Adjudged in the Several Courts of the United States and of Pennsylvania, Held at the Seat of the Federal Government. Second Edition. Edited, with Notes and References to Later Decisions, By Frederick C. Brightly* [New York, 1914], II, 419). Georgia reacted first (in 1792) by attempting unsuccessfully to secure the adoption in the state legislature of a resolution declaring that the state would not be bound by the decision of the Court. After the Court rendered its decision, the legislature again tried—once more unsuccessfully—to pass a bill providing that any official who tried to execute the process issued by the Court should be "guilty of felony and shall suffer death. . ." (Herman V. Ames, *State Documents on Federal Relations: The States and the United States* [Philadelphia, 1906], 10). For the opposition in Massachusetts to a similar suit in *Vassall* v *Massachusetts,* see Fisher Ames to H, August 31, 1793, note 3.

14. For the early opposition to the excise duties on distilled spirits, see "Draft of a Proclamation Concerning Opposition to the Excise Law," September 7, 1792, note 1; H to Tench Coxe, September 1, 1792; H to Washington, September 1, 8, first letter of September 9, September 11, 22, 26, 1792; H to John Jay, September 3, 1792; Washington to H, September 7, two letters of September 17, September 21, October 1, 1792; Jay to H, September 8, 1792; Randolph to H, September 8, 1792; Rufus King to H, September 27, 1792; George Clymer to H, September 28, October 4, 10, 1792; Washington to Mifflin, September 29, 1792; Coxe to H, October 19, 1792.

15. This is a reference to the dissatisfaction of the citizens of Kentucky with

&c., &c.,) and insisted upon the propriety of an immediate resort to Military force. He said that it would not be sufficient to quell the existing riot to restore us to the state in which we were a few weeks back; for, before the present outrages, there was equal opposition to the laws of the U.S.,[17] though not expressed in the same manner; but that now the crisis was arrived when it must be determined whether the Government can maintain itself, and that the exertion must be made, not only to quell the rioters, but to protect the officers of the Union in executing their offices, and in compelling obedience to the laws.

The Secretary of the Com'th stated, as information, that in a conversation with Judge Addison,[18] the Judge had declared it as his opinion that if the business was left to the courts, the rioters might be prosecuted and punished, and the matter peaceably terminated; but that a resort to military force, would unite in the resistance, the peaceable as well as the riotous opponents of the excise, upon the Idea that the military was intended to dragoon them equally into submission. He also stated that similar riots against the excise had been punished in the State courts.[19]

The secretary of the Treasury observed, that the Judge alluded was among those who had most promoted the opposition in an insidious manner, that perhaps it would lead to a disagreeable animadversion to point out the particulars of the Judge's conduct; but that they were stated at large in a report to the President, which the President said was the case.[20]

---

the Government's efforts to negotiate with Spain for the free navigation of the Mississippi River. For information on the Kentucky resolutions of May 24, 1794, see Randolph to Bradford, H, and Knox, July 11, 1794, note 1; H to Washington, July 13, 1794.

16. This is a reference to the attempt by Elijah Clark, major general in the Georgia militia, and citizens of Georgia to erect a new state on lands reserved for the Creek Indians. See Randolph to Bradford, H, and Knox, July 11, 1794; H to Washington, July 13, 1794.

17. See notes 13, 14, 15, and 16.

18. Alexander Addison was presiding judge of the County Court of the western district of Pennsylvania. See Bartholomew Dandridge to H, April 19, 1794, note 1; Washington to H, second letter of May 29, 1794.

19. This is presumably a reference to "the conviction of Samuel Wilson, and the submission of the other rioters in Allegheny county. . ." (Addison to Mifflin, March 31, 1794 [*Pennsylvania Archives,* 2nd ser., IV, 60]).

20. This document ends with the following statement: "Here the minutes of the conference suddenly terminate."

Presumably the cabinet met on August 9, 1794, to discuss the insurrection in western Pennsylvania, for on August 8, 1794, Washington wrote to Randolph:

". . . I request also, that all the information that can be obtained from the Inspector Nevill, & the Marshall, may be had as soon as they shall have arriv'd in the City, & wish it to be delivered before your self & the other Gentlemen, that all of you being thoroughly possessed of the facts—and digesting them well—may be ready to meet me at my Ho. in the City tomorrow morning with your opinion on the propriety of changing any measure already resolved on, or for adding others thereto according to the information which shall be received from them. . ." (ALS, RG 59, Miscellaneous Letters, 1790–1799, National Archives).

From Tench Coxe[1]

Treasury Department, Revenue Office, August 2, 1794. ". . . from the best opinion which can be formed at present, it appears, that five thousand Dollars will be sufficient to be placed in the hands of each of the Naval Agents. . . ."[2]

LC, RG 75, Letters of Tench Coxe, Commissioner of the Revenue, Relating to the Procurement of Military, Naval, and Indian Supplies, National Archives.

1. This letter concerns the naval armament for 1794. See Henry Knox to H, April 21, 1794.

2. See Knox to H, June 25, third letter of July 9, 1794.

From John Fitzgerald[1]

Alexandria [Virginia] August 2, 1794. "A violent Rheumatic complaint, by which I am afflicted without intermission, obliges me to have recourse to the Berkley Springs. . . . Mr Gray[2] will superintend the business of my Office during my absence. . . ."

Copy, RG 56, Letters to and from the Collector at Alexandria, National Archives; typescript furnished by the National Society, Daughters of the American Revolution, Washington, D.C.

1. Fitzgerald was collector of customs at Alexandria, Virginia.

2. Vincent Gray was surveyor for the District of Alexandria and inspector of the revenue for the port of Alexandria.

To Elizabeth Hamilton[1]

Philadelphia Aug 2
1794

I have had the happiness to receive one letter from my beloved Eliza[2] and I need not tell her how much consolation was given to me by whatever was flattering in the situation of my darling Johnny nor how much alarm I felt at the unfavourable change which happened on the day she wrote. Alas my Charmer great are my fears—poignant my distress. I feel every day more & more how dear this Child is to me & I cease not to pray heaven for his recovery. I hope the plan of exercise has been continued & that in the attention to Diet he has not been refused a moderate portion of pork if he continued anxious for it. But a course has now been tried & Experience & the Physician must direct.

Our dear Children here continue well & the City is unusually healthy but it begins to be very hot & I intend this week to send them into the Country. Yet they seem very unwilling to go from me & it is a great satisfaction to have them with me.

I hope My Dear Eliza's health has mended. Remember, My Love, you have a husband & other Children than the little sick one whose happiness depends on you. Pray exert yourself to preserve & better your health at all events. Adieu My Angel

Yr. ever Affect. AH

Give my love to all. Tell your father [3] I shall shortly write him but that I am so engaged with my Western insurgents [4] & other matters that I have scarcely a moment to spare.

Mrs. Hamilton

ALS, Hamilton Papers, Library of Congress.

1. For background to this letter, see H to George Washington, July 11, 23, 1794; Washington to H, July 11, 1794; H to Elizabeth Hamilton, July 31, 1794.

2. Letter not found.

3. Philip Schuyler.

4. This is a reference to the opposition to the excise laws in western Pennsylvania. See "Deposition of Francis Mentges," August 1, 1794; "Conference Concerning the Insurrection in Western Pennsylvania," August 2, 1794.

To George Washington [1]

Treasury Department August 2d. 1794

Sir

In compliance with your requisition I have the honor to submit my Opinion as to the course which it will be adviseable for the President to pursue in regard to the armed Opposition recently given

LS, George Washington Papers, Library of Congress; copy, Hamilton Papers, Library of Congress.

1. For background to this letter, see "Deposition of Francis Mentges," August 1, 1794, and "Conference Concerning the Insurrection in Western Pennsylvania," August 2, 1794.

in the four Western Counties of Pennsylvania to the execution of the laws of the U. States laying duties upon Spirits distilled within the United States and upon Stills.[2]

The case upon which an Opinion is required is summarily as follows. The four most Western Counties of Pennsylvania since the Commencement of those laws a period of more than three Years, have been in steady and Violent Opposition to them. By formal public meetings of influential individuals, whose resolutions and proceedings had for undisguised objects, to render the laws odious, to discountenance a compliance with them, and to intimidate individuals from accepting and executing Offices under them—by a general Spirit of Opposition (thus fomented) among the Inhabitants—by repeated instances of armed parties going in disguise to the houses of the Officers of the Revenue and inflicting upon them personal violence and outrage—by general combinations to forbear a compliance with the requisitions of the laws by examples of injury to the Property and insult to the persons of individuals who have shewn by their conduct a disposition to comply and by an almost universal noncompliance with the laws—their execution within the Counties in question has been completely frustrated.

Various Alterations have been made in the laws by the Legislature to obviate as far as possible the objections of the Inhabitants of those Counties.[3]

The executive, on its part has been far from deficient in forbearance lenity or a Spirit of Accomodation.

But neither the Legislative nor the Executive accomodations have had any effect in producing compliance with the laws.

The Opposition has continued and matured, till it has at length broke out in Acts which are presumed to amount to Treason.[4]

Armed Collections of men, with the avowed design of Opposing

2. H is referring to "An Act repealing, after the last day of June next, the duties heretofore laid upon Distilled Spirits imported from abroad, and laying others in their stead; and also upon Spirits distilled within the United States, and for appropriating the same" (1 *Stat.* 199–214 [March 3, 1791]), "An Act concerning the Duties on Spirits distilled within the United States" (1 *Stat.* 267–71 [May 8, 1792]), and "An Act making further provision for securing and collecting the Duties on foreign and domestic distilled Spirits, Stills, Wines and Teas" (1 *Stat.* 378–81 [June 5, 1794]).

3. H is referring to the act of June 5, 1794. See note 2.

4. See "Deposition of Francis Mentges," August 1, 1794.

the execution of the laws, have attacked the house of the Inspector of the Revenue, burnt and destroyed his Property and Shed the blood of Persons engaged in its defence [5]—have made Prisoner of the Marshall of the District and did not release him till for the Safety of his life he stipulated to execute no more processes within the disaffected counties [6]—have compelled both him and the Inspector of the Revenue to fly the Country by a circuitous route to avoid personal injury perhaps Assassination—have proposed the Assembling of a Convention of delegates from these Counties and the Neighbouring ones of Virginia probably with a view to systematise [7] measures of more effectual Opposition—have forcibly seized Opened & Spoliated a Mail of the United States.[8]

What in this State of things is proper to be done?

The President has with the advice of the heads of the Departments and the Attorney General, caused to be submitted all the evidence of the foregoing facts to the Consideration of an Associate Judge [9] under the Act intitled "An Act to provide for calling forth the Militia to execute the laws of the Union Suppress Insurrection and repel Invasion." [10]

If the Judge shall pronounce that the case described in the second section of that Act exists [11]—it will follow that a competent force of Militia should be called forth and employed to suppress the insurrection and support the Civil Authority in effectuating Obedience to the laws and the punishment of Offenders.

It appears to me that the very existence of Government demands this course and that a duty of the highest nature urges the Chief Magistrate to pursue it. The Constitution and laws of the United States, contemplate and provide for it.

What force of Militia shall be called out, and from What State or States?

5. John Neville. See "Deposition of Francis Mentges," August 1, 1794, note 2.

6. David Lenox. See "Deposition of Francis Mentges," August 1, 1794, note 2.

7. This word is in H's handwriting.

8. See "Conference Concerning the Insurrection in Western Pennsylvania," August 2, 1794, note 8.

9. James Wilson. See H to Tench Coxe, August 1, 1794; "Conference Concerning the Insurrection in Western Pennsylvania," August 2, 1794, note 9.

10. 1 *Stat.* 264–65 (May 2, 1792). See "Conference Concerning the Insurrection in Western Pennsylvania," August 2, 1794, note 9.

11. See "Conference Concerning the Insurrection in Western Pennsylvania," August 2, 1794, note 9.

The force ought if attainable to be an imposing one, such if practicable, as will deter from opposition, save the effusion of the blood of Citizens and secure the object to be accomplished.

The quantum must of course be regulated by the resistance to be expected. Tis computed, that the four opposing Counties contain upwards of sixteen[12] thousand males of 16 years and more, that of these about seven thousand may be expected to be armed. Tis possible that the union of the nieghbouring Counties of Virginia may augment this force. Tis not impossible, that it may receive an accession from some adjacent Counties of this state on this side of the Alleghany Mountain.

To be prepared for the worst, I am of opinion, that twelve thousand Militia ought to be ordered to assemble; 9000 foot and 3000 horse. I should not propose so many horse, but for the probability, that this description of Militia, will be more easily procured for the service.

From what State or States shall these come?

The Law contemplates that the Militia of a State, in which an insurrection happens, if willing & sufficient shall first be employed, but gives power to employ the Milita of other States in the case either of refusal or insufficiency.

The Governor of Pennsylvania in an Official conference this day, gave it explicitly as his opinion to the President, that the Militia of Pennsylvania alone would be found incompetent to the suppression of the insurrection.

This Opinion of the Chief Magistrate of the State is presumed to be a sufficient foundation for calling in, in the first instance, the aid of the Militia of the Neighbouring States.

I would submit then, that Pennsylvania be required to furnish 6000 men of whom 1000 to be horse, New–Jersey 2000 of whom 800 to be horse, Maryland 2000 of whom 600 to be horse, Virginia 2000, of whom 600 to be horse.

Or perhaps it may be as eligible to call upon each State for such a number of Troops, leaving to itself the proportion of horse and foot according to convenience. The Militia called for to rendezvous at Carlisle in Pensylvania & Cumberland Fort in Virginia on the 10th of September next.[13]

12. This word is in H's handwriting.
13. This sentence is in H's handwriting.

The law requires that previous to the using of force a Proclamation shall issue, commanding the Insurgents to disperse and return peaceably to their respective abodes within a limited time.[14] This step must of course be taken.

The application of the force to be called out and other ulterior measures must depend on circumstances as they shall arise.[15]

With the most perfect respect I have the Honor to be Sir Your Most Obedient Servant Alexander Hamilton

The President of the
United States

14. This is a reference to Section 2 of "An Act to provide for calling forth the Militia to execute the laws of the Union, suppress insurrections, and repel invasions," which reads as follows: ". . . whenever it may be necessary, in the judgment of the President, to use the military force hereby directed to be called forth, the President shall forthwith and previous thereto, by proclamation, command such insurgents to disperse, and retire peaceably to their respective abodes, within a limited time" (1 *Stat.* 264).

15. H reinforced the views expressed in this letter in a letter to Washington dated August 5, 1794, which is a historical account of opposition to the excise laws in western Pennsylvania. For the opinions of the other members of the cabinet on the policies the Government should pursue in western Pennsylvania, see William Bradford to Washington, n.d. (ALS, George Washington Papers, Library of Congress); Henry Knox to Washington, August 4, 1794 (LS, George Washington Papers, Library of Congress); Edmund Randolph to Washington, August 5, 1794 (ALS, George Washington Papers, Library of Congress).

From Tench Coxe[1]

Treasury Department
Revenue office, August 5th 1794

Sir,

The state of things in the western country[2] raises some doubts whether it will be practicable to procure in that quarter Spirits *lawfully distilled* for the military supply of 1795. It remains to be considered therefore, whether that point (the spirits having been lawfully distilled) shall be adhered to as indispensible.

Your letter of the 31st July[3] relative to Mr. Wiats[4] agency, was not received until my letter had gone. The cause of my not recurring to the Supervisor of Virginia[5] was that I had not the necessary antecedent information of any arrangement by which such agencies were to be under his direction in the state of Virginia. The case was emergent, and as I have conceived that the Treasury business for the War department; (as designated in the 5th Section of the act making alterations in the Treasury and War departments) [6] was the duty transferred to my office, I did not hesitate to employ a suitable person. I could not recur to you having learned that you were absent,[7] and being unable to procure information of the time of your return.

My confidence in the Supervisor of Virginia and my wish to promote his interests would have led me to apply to him, but Fredericksburg can be reached by letter from hence several days sooner than thro' Richmond, and the case appeared to require dispatch. I confess I was very uneasy at finding that an extensive arrangement had been requested on the 16th. June by the Secretary at War,[8] of the receipt of whose requisition by you I had no information. I supposed that the letter had by some unfortunate accident miscarried between the Offices.

I have the honor to be, with great respect, Sir Your most Obedient Servant

Tench Coxe
Commissr. of the Revenue

P.S. The postmaster general [9] on a previous enquiry, personally made by me, spoke in terms inspiring the necessary degree of confidence, concerning Mr. Wiat.

The Secretary
of the Treasury

LC, RG 58, Letters of Commissioner of Revenue, 1794–1795, National Archives.

1. For background to this letter, see Coxe to H, July 29, 30, 1794.
2. For information on the Whiskey Insurrection, see "Deposition of Francis Mentges," August 1, 1794; H to George Washington, August 2, 5, 1794.
3. Letter not found.
4. William Wiatt. See Coxe to H, July 30, 1794.
5. Edward Carrington.
6. 1 *Stat.* 279–81 (May 8, 1792). See H to Coxe, April 4, 1794.
7. See H to Washington, July 11, 23, 1794; Washington to H, July 11, 1794.
8. Henry Knox's letter to H has not been found. See Coxe to H, July 29, 1794.
9. Timothy Pickering.

From Tench Coxe

Treasury Department, Revenue Office, August 5, 1794. "I have the honor to request that you will place the sum of eight thousand eight hundred forty nine Dollars & 25 cents in the hands of Benj. Lincoln

Esqr.[1] for the purpose of enabling him to comply with the terms of the contract made by him with M. M. Hays on the 6th. day of June last for 19561 & ½ gallons Sperma Oil, for the use of the Light houses of the United States." [2]

LC, RG 75, Letters of Tench Coxe, Commissioner of the Revenue, Relating to the Procurement of Military, Naval, and Indian Supplies, National Archives; LC, RG 26, Lighthouse Letters, Vol. I, National Archives.

1. Lincoln was collector of customs at Boston.
2. See Coxe to H, April 30, July 9, 1794.

Alexander Hamilton and Henry Knox to George Washington[1]

Philada. August 5, 1794.

Sir,

The draft of a proclamation [2] and that of an instruction to the Commissioners [3] being both prepared,[4] we take the liberty to suggest that we think a meeting tomorrow morning at such hour as may be convenient to the President, may be adviseable. The Secretary of State & Attorney General being out of town we cannot consult them, but we will engage the attendance of the Attorney General provisionally by Nine o'Clock & if the President concludes on the Meeting at that hour, he can have the Secy. of State apprised of it.

We have the honor to be &c. A Hamilton

H Knox.

LC, George Washington Papers, Library of Congress.

1. For background to this letter, see "Deposition of Francis Mentges," August 1, 1794, "Conference Concerning the Insurrection in Western Pennsylvania," August 2, 1794, and H to Washington, August 2, 5, 1794.

2. In his proclamation of August 7, 1794, Washington recapitulated the events in western Pennsylvania which had culminated in the attack on the house of John Neville, inspector of the revenue, and warned the insurgents that measures necessary to call out the militia had been undertaken. The proclamation concluded with a warning to "all persons, being insurgents . . . and all others whom it may concern, on or before the 1st day of September next, to disperse and retire peaceably to their respective abodes. And I do moreover warn all persons whomsoever, against aiding, abetting, or comforting the perpetrators of the aforesaid treasonable acts. . ." (*GW*, XXXIII, 457–61). The proclamation is also printed in *Pennsylvania Archives*, 2nd ser., IV, 123–27, and *ASP*, *Miscellaneous*, I, 85–86.

3. In a final effort to secure the compliance of the residents of western Pennsylvania with the excise laws, Washington appointed James Ross, Jasper Yeates, and Attorney General William Bradford as Federal commissioners to confer with the representatives of the insurgents in western Pennyslvania. Ross was a lawyer in Washington County, Pennsylvania, and a Federalist member of the

United States Senate. Yeates had been appointed associate justice of the Pennsylvania Supreme Court in 1791 by Thomas Mifflin and held that position until his death in 1817.

The instructions to the commissioners, which are dated August 7, 1794, were written by Edmund Randolph and read as follows:

"The recent events in the neighborhood of Pittsburgh, have called the attention of the President to the formation of some plan by which the insurrection may be suppressed.

"The intelligence which has been transmitted, having been laid before Judge [James] Wilson, he has granted a certificate, declaring that the opposition to the laws of the United States in the Counties of Washington and Allegany, cannot be suppressed by the ordinary course of judicial proceedings, or the power of the marshal. A copy of that certificate is enclosed (No. 1).

"You or any one or more of you are therefore authorized and appointed forthwith to proceed to the scene of the insurrection and to confer with any bodies of men or individuals with whom you shall think proper to confer, in order to quiet and extinguish it. There is reason to believe that a collection of discontented individuals, will be found at Mingo Creek on the fourteenth instant, and as the object of their assembling, is undoubtedly to concert measures relative to this very subject, it is indispensably necessary, that you should press thither with the utmost expedition. It is uncertain whether they will remain together for a long or short time—therefore the being on the ground on the day first named for their meeting is necessary to prevent a miscarriage.

"These are the outlines of your communication.

"1. To state the serious impressions which their conduct has created in the mind of the Executive, and to dilate upon the dangers attending every Government where laws are obstructed in their execution.

"2d. To inform them that the evidence of the late transactions has been submitted to a Judge of the Supreme Court, and that he has granted the abovementioned certificate whence a power has arisen to the President to call out the militia to suppress the insurrection (see the act of May 2. 1792 No. 2).

"3d. To represent to them, how painful an idea it is, to exercise such a power, and that it is the earnest wish of the President, to render it unnecessary by those endeavors which humanity, a love of peace and tranquility, and the happiness of his fellow citizens dictate.

"4th. You will then explain your appointment as Commissioners in a language and with sentiments most conciliatory, but reconcileable to the self respect which this Government ought to observe.

"5th. Whether you are to proceed further, and in what manner must depend upon your judgment and discretion at the moment, after an estimate of the characters with whom you are conversant, their views, their influence &c. &c.

"6th. Whensoever you shall come to the point at which it may be necessary to be explicit, you are to declare that with respect to the excise law, the President is bound to consider it as much among the laws which he is to see executed, as any other. That as to the repeal of it, he cannot undertake to make any stipulation; that being a subject consigned by the Constitution to the Legislature from whom alone a change of Legislative measures can be obtained. That he is willing to grant an amnesty and perpetual oblivion for every thing which has past—and cannot doubt, that any penalty to which the late transactions may have given birth, under the laws and within the jurisdiction of Pennsylvania may be also wiped away—but upon the following conditions.

"That satisfactory assurances be given that the laws be no longer obstructed in their execution by any combinations directly or indirectly, and that the offenders against whom process shall issue for a violation of, or an opposition to the laws shall not be protected from the free operation of the law. Nothing

will be inforced concerning the duties of former years if they will fairly comply for the present year.
"7th. If they speak of the hardship of being drawn to the federal Courts at a distance, to that no other reply can be made than this—that the inconvenience whatsoever it may be, was the act of their own representatives, and is continued as being still their sense—that however on all occasions which will permit the State Courts to be used without inconvenience to the United States or danger of their being frustrated in the object of the suits and prosecutions the State Courts will be resorted to—but the choice of Jurisdictions must always depend upon the discretion of the United States and therefore nothing more specific can be said at present.
"8th. Whensoever you shall choose to speak of the ulterior measures of the Government, you will say that orders have already issued for the proper militia to hold themselves in readiness, and that every thing is prepared for their movements, as will be seen by the Proclamation (No. 3) and is known to yourselves from the communications of the Government, but that these movements will be suspended until your return.
"9th. These are said to be the *outlines:* you will fill them up and modify them so as most effectually to prevent if possible the last dreadful necessity which the President so much deprecates, and you may in particular assure any individuals of pardon who will expiate their offence by a compliance with the laws.
"10th. You will keep the Executive minutely and constantly informed of all your proceedings and will use expresses whensoever you think proper at the public expense.
"11th. You will be allowed eight dollars per day and your expenses, and may employ a proper person to act as your Clerk, who shall be paid whatsoever you may certify him to deserve. The sum of one thousand dollars is advanced to you on account.
"12th. William Bradford is empowered to add the name of Thomas Smith or any other proper person if either James Ross, or Jasper Yeates shall refuse or be unable to attend." (LS, Historical Society of Pennsylvania, Philadelphia; Df, with insertions in Randolph's handwriting, Pennsylvania Miscellany, Whiskey Rebellion, Vol. I, Library of Congress; copy, Pennsylvania Miscellany, Whiskey Rebellion, Vol. I, Library of Congress.)

At the bottom of the draft in the Library of Congress Henry Knox wrote "Approved" and H wrote the following: "It seems to be intended that the measure of calling out the Militia be kept back until the case of failure in compromise. This appears to me neither candid nor dignified. They should be apprised exactly of what has been done & left to act accordingly.

"Perhaps a question may arise about the *duties* of former years. I think they may be told on this point that the Executive will forbear to enforce any thing concerning the former years if they will fairly comply for the present year. This compliance ought to be an unequivocal condition of any promise on the part of the Govt.

"But on further & mature reflection any judgment is against the measure of commissioners till the force called out has rendezvoused. A Hamilton."

Randolph inserted H's suggestions in points 5 and 8 in the draft.

In *ASP, Miscellaneous,* 86–87, these instructions are dated August 5, and in *Pennsylvania Archives,* 2nd ser., IV, 137, they are dated August 8.

In addition to his instructions to Ross, Yeates, and Bradford, Randolph also wrote a letter to them on August 8, 1794, notifying them of their appointment and stating that "In Pursuance of instructions from the President of the United States, you, or any one or more of you, are hereby authorized and impowered forthwith to repair to the Counties on the Western Side of the Alleghany Mountain in the State of Pennsylvania, there to confer with such Bodies or

Individuals as you may approve, concerning the Commotions. . ." (two copies, Pennsylvania Miscellany, Whiskey Rebellion, Vol. I, Library of Congress). At the conclusion of the second copy of Randolph's letter to the commissioners H wrote "approved A. Hamilton." Knox signed his name after H's. Randolph's letter is printed in *ASP, Miscellaneous*, 87, and *Pennsylvania Archives*, 2nd ser., IV, 136–37.

4. Some historians have construed the first sentence of the letter printed above to mean that H and Knox drafted the proclamation and the instructions to the commissioners (see, for example, Freeman, *Washington*, VII, 189). No draft, however, of either document in H's or Knox's handwriting has been found. On the contrary, Randolph apparently wrote the draft of the instructions and later incorporated H's suggestions. See note 3. Moreover, a note signed with the initials of George Taylor, Jr., State Department chief clerk, states: "E Randolph says that these instructions enclosed were drawn by him, not as his own sentiments but as those of the President, there being some things in them which do not accord with his opinion. 5 Augt. 1794" (ADS, Pennsylvania Miscellany, Whiskey Rebellion, Vol. I, Library of Congress).

To George Washington [1]

Treasury Department
[August 5] 1794

Sir

The disagreeable crisis at which matters have lately arrived in some of the Western counties of Pensylvania, with regard to the

ADf, Hamilton Papers, Library of Congress; copy (incomplete), Hamilton Papers, Library of Congress; copy, RG 46, Third Congress, 1793–1795, Messages from the President, National Archives; [Philadelphia] *Dunlap and Claypoole's American Daily Advertiser*, August 21, 1794.

1. The copy in the National Archives was transmitted by the President in his speech to both houses of Congress on November 19, 1794 (*ASP, Miscellaneous*, I, 83–85, 106–12).

On August 6 and 16, 1794, H wrote to Washington for permission to publish the letter printed above. Permission was granted (Bartholomew Dandridge to H, August 19, 1794), and the letter appeared in *Dunlap and Claypoole's American Daily Advertiser* on August 21, 1794. It was subsequently published in other newspapers (see, for example, *Greenleaf's New York Journal, & Patriotic Register*, August 27, 30, September 3, 6, 1794).

In the draft of this letter H crossed out words, sentences, and paragraphs. When such deletions are substantive, they have been noted below. At the same time there are differences between the draft of this letter and both the copies and the newspaper version. When these differences are substantive, they have been noted below.

For background to this letter, see H to Tench Coxe, September 1, 1792; H to Washington, September 1, 8, 9, 11, 22, 26, 1792, August 2, 1794; H to John Jay, September 3, 1792; Washington to H, September 7, two letters of September 17, September 21, October 1, 1792; "Draft of a Proclamation Concerning Opposition to the Excise Law," September 7, 1792; Jay to H, September 8, 1792; Edmund Randolph to H, September 8, 1792; Rufus King to H, September 27, 1792; George Clymer to H, September 28, October 4, 10, 1792; Washington to Thomas Mifflin, September 29, 1792; Coxe to H, October 19, 1792; "Deposition of Francis Mentges," August 1, 1794; "Conference Concerning the Insurrection in Western Pennsylvania," August 2, 1794; H and Henry Knox to Washington, August 5, 1794.

This letter has been the standard—and often the only—source for those who have written about opposition in western Pennsylvania to the excise laws in the period before August, 1794. William Findley, who in 1796 published a defense of his own activities under the guise of a history of the insurrection, follows H's account closely (with certain notable exceptions) and on one occasion states: "I have taken this enumeration from the Secretary's report" (Findley, *History of the Insurrection*, 60). Henry M. Brackenridge also used H's letter as a major source for information in the early pages of his book (Brackenridge, *Insurrection*, 21–30). The introduction to the appropriate volume in the *Pennsylvania Archives* (*Pennsylvania Archives*, 2nd ser., IV, 5–18) often reads like a paraphrase of H's letter, and much the same can be said of the opening pages of the "Statement of Facts" preceding the account of the "Trials of the Western Insurgents" in Wharton, *State Trials*, 103–11. Finally, Leland D. Baldwin in his relatively recent study of the insurrection, while using a wide variety of sources, on more than one occasion relies either on H's letter or on those who had used it in their earlier studies (Baldwin, *Whiskey Rebels*). In fact, the only writer who did not turn to H's letter for information was Hugh H. Brackenridge (Brackenridge, *Incidents*), whose account was an attempt at a personal vindication and as such deals almost exclusively with his own activities.

This letter as well as seven documents relating to the Whiskey Insurrection is printed in *The Proceedings of the Executive of the United States, Respecting the Insurgents, 1794* (Philadelphia: John Fenno, 1795).

Before H's letter was printed in *Dunlap and Claypoole's American Daily Advertiser*, August 21, 1794, Edmund Randolph wrote to Washington suggesting changes that he thought should be made in H's letter before its publication. Randolph's letter, dated August 18, 1794, reads as follows: "The following remarks occur upon the statement of Colo. Hamilton, which you did me the honor of communicating to me this morning.

"1. In what manner is it to be exhibited to the public? or in other words, is it to be introduced under the known or allowed countenance of the President? As I do not see, how the one or the other can be avoided, it seems proper to call his attention to these points.

"The specifying of names in the third page, and the omission of all names, except Cannon and *Gallatin* in the 16th page, when the names of the other persons assembled at Pittsburg are known, will be interpreted into a kind of warfare waged by the President against individuals in the former case, and a desire of selecting for odium *Gallatin*, whose hostility against the Secretary of the Treasury is well known. May it not be better to pass over names? They are sufficiently notorious already, and if such an idea, as I have suggested would be endangered, it would be an inconvenient thing without any profit.

"In the 4th page it is objected to these men, that they criticize the salaries of the public officers. This does not absolutely belong to the subject, and the President will readily see, why, if it be not necessary, it may be more delicate to leave out the remark.

"In page 5th I repeat the remark as to names, as well as the last remark about salaries.

"It will occur, on reading the marshal's letter in page the 8th. that he ought to have tried a posse comitatus, and that it never has been tried; and this will be urged, as an insinuation of eagerness to get at military force. The like observation will arise, upon reading the close of the first paragraph in the 19th page.

"The affair of the maniac in the 11th. page will be exposed to some shafts of

laws laying duties on spirits distilled within the UStates and on Stills,[2] seems to render proper a review of the circumstances which have attended those laws in that scene, from their commencement to

---

ridicule, inserted as it is among the ⟨–⟩ criminations of the insurgents in the appeal of the President to the understanding of the people; which this statement will be considered.

"In page 18th, the reasoning on the terms *legal measures to obstruct the operation of a law* savours more of the acuteness of a lawyer, than the gravity and solid reasoning of the President. Suppose for instance, they had associated against drinking excised liquors, & keeping stills; would not this have been a legal measure, and would it not have obstructed the operation of a law?

"In page 19th. the supervisor is said to have been sent up with certain objects. Was it known to the President, that he went to obtain evidence of those, who composed the meeting at Pittsburg? This circumstance would be pregnant with many remarks; especially as the attorney general is afterwards said to have been of opinion, that they were not indictable. For why send to enquire into the conduct of men, who were not liable to prosecution? The supervisor and his report will be treated, as they have been, with much contempt.

"The opinion of the attorney general, as stated in page 21st. is not now recollected; but a great doubt is entertained whether there be not an inaccuracy, at least so far as this, that the statement is not as strong as the opinion.

"In page 22d. the representations referred to are, I believe more favorable to government, than as they are quoted.

"In page 37th. an opportunity is offered to rectify, what major Lenox complained of; and besides, it will be considered as uncandid not to notice, that he had served all the processes, except one.

"2. These observations result from the examination, which I have been able to give the paper. There may be more, deserving attention than I have pointed out. But under the possibility of your becoming responsible for what nothing but a repeated examination can secure you: under the facility, with which the facts may be communicated to the public, without your intervention; and after your having given the essence and summary of these facts in your proclamation; I wish that the paper should be communicated to the world, in some other manner than under your auspices. I confess that I never can approve the drawing forth of your name and character without necessity.

"3. If on the other hand, you should be of opinion, that your being supposed to have authorized the publication does not commit you, and that the whole affair rests upon the responsibility of the Secretary of the treasury alone, it may be still expedient to recommend to his notice, such of the preceding remarks as may have any weight, and the word '*the*' instead of these in the 14th. line of the first page, and the word '*if*' instead of '*of*' in the 10th. line of the 27th. page; both of which effect the sense." (ADfS, RG 59, Miscellaneous Letters, 1790–1799, National Archives; LC, George Washington Papers, Library of Congress.)

Randolph is referring to the pagination of the copy in the Hamilton Papers, Library of Congress, which is apparently the letter H sent to Washington.

2. "An Act repealing, after the last day of June next, the duties heretofore laid upon Distilled Spirits imported from abroad, and laying others in their stead; and also upon Spirits distilled within the United States, and for appropriating the same" (1 *Stat.* 199–214 [March 3, 1791]), "An Act concerning the Duties on Spirits distilled within the United States" (1 *Stat.* 267–71 [May 8, 1792]), and "An Act making further provision for securing and collecting the Duties on foreign and domestic distilled Spirits, Stills, Wines and Teas" (1 *Stat.* 378–81 [June 5, 1794]).

the present time and of the conduct which has hitherto been observed on the part of the Government, its motives and effect; in order to a better judgment of the measures necessary to be pursued in the existing emergency.

The opposition to those laws in the four most Western Counties of Pensylvania (Alleghany Washington Fayette and Westmoreland) commenced as early as they were known to have been passed. It has continued, with different degrees of violence, in the different counties, and at different periods. But Washington has uniformly distinguished its resistance by a more excessive spirit, than has appeared in the other Counties & seems to have been chiefly instrumental in kindling and keeping alive the flame.

The opposition first manifested itself in the milder shape of the circulation of opinions unfavourable to the law & calculated by the influence of public disesteem to discourage the accepting or holding of Offices under it or the complying with it, by those who might be so disposed; to which was added the show of a discontinuance of the business of distilling. These expedients were shortly after succeeded by private associations to *forbear* compliances with the law. But it was not long before these more negative modes of opposition were perceived to be likely to prove ineffectual. And in proportion as this was the case and as the means of introducing the laws into operation were put into execution, the disposition to resistance became more turbulent and more inclined to adopt and practice violent expedients.

The officers now began to experience marks of contempt and insult. Threats against them became frequent and loud; and after some time, these threats were ripened into acts of ill-treatment and outrage.

These acts of violence were preceded by certain Meetings of malcontent persons who entered into resolutions calculated at once to confirm inflame and systematize the spirit of opposition.

The first of these Meetings was holden at a place called Red Stone Old Fort, on the 27 of July 1791 where it was concerted that county committees should be convened in the four Counties at the respective seats of Justice therein.[3] On the 23 day of Aug following

3. According to Henry M. Brackenridge, it "was resolved at this meeting, that it be recommended to the several counties to appoint delegates, at least three for each elective district, to meet at the seat of justice, and having col-

one of these committees assembled in the County of Washington[4] consisting (as appears by their proceedings published in the Pittsburgh Gazette) among others of James Marshall Register & Recorder of the County—David Bradford Deputy Atty. General for the State—Henry Taylor & James Edgar now Associate Judges—Thomas Crooks[5] & William Parker then or shortly before Magistrates & Militia Officers, Thomas Sedgwick and Alexander Wright Magistrates and Peter Kidd an officer of the Militia. This Meeting passed some intemperate resolutions, which were afterwards printed in the Pittsburgh Gazette, containing a strong censure on the law, declaring that any person *who had accepted or might accept an office under Congress in order to carry it into effect should be considered as inimical to the interests of the Country; and recommending to the Citizens of Washington County to treat every person who had accepted or might thereafter accept any such office with contempt, and absolutely to refuse all kind of communication or intercourse with the Officers and to withold from them all aid support or comfort.*[6]

---

lected the sense of the people in each county, from each of these delegates choose three to form a committee. These were to meet at Pittsburgh, on the first Tuesday of September, and there draw up and pass resolutions expressing the sense of their constituents respecting the excise law" (Brackenridge, *Insurrection*, 22). William Findley, who attended the Redstone meeting, wrote: "How this meeting could have been ranked by the secretary of the treasury, in his report to the President, preparatory to calling out the militia, among the causes of the insurrection, and given as one of the instances of unlawful combination, I know not. Surely such a meeting may be held, and such resolves passed, in Great Britain, even after the sedition bills, which have thrown that nation into such a flame, are enacted into laws. I never knew that a meeting to petition government respectfully, was esteemed criminal in any country that had the least pretensions to freedom" (Findley, *History of the Insurrection*, 42).

4. The remainder of this sentence was crossed out in the copy in the Hamilton Papers and does not appear in the copy in the National Archives or in the newspaper version. See Randolph to Washington, August 18, 1794, quoted in note 1.

5. In the draft under Thomas Crook's name H listed and crossed out fourteen names. The names are the same as those who attended the Washington County meeting on August 23, 1791. For these names, see note 6.

6. The resolutions are contained in the following account of the Washington County meeting, which has been taken from a clipping dated August 23, 1791, from an unidentified newspaper; the clipping was enclosed in a letter from John Neville to George Clymer, September 8, 1791 (LS, Connecticut Historical Society, Hartford):

"PURSUANT to resolutions entered into at Redstone Old Fort the 27th of July last, by a number of respectable citizens, recommending to the citizens of Westmoreland, Washington, Fayette, and Allegheny counties to choose county committees to meet at the seat of justice in their respective counties on the 4th Tuesday in August, to collect the sense of the people on the act of Congress impressing a duty on spirits distilled within the United States, the following gentlemen met: Washington district, James Marshal, David Bradford, Henry Taylor. Hill's district, Thomas Crooks, Eli Jenkins, Joseph Hill. Blazler's district, David Drennon, James Edgar, Henry Graham. M'Candless's district, Peter Kidd, Samuel Scott, Alexander Wright. Hamilton's district, David Philips, John Baldwin, William Parker. Cline's district, John Flanagan, Thomas Sedgwick, John Badollet. After producing the credentials of their election they proceeded to appoint a chairman, when James Edgar, Esquire, was unanimously elected to the chair. David Bradford was appointed clerk.

"The different members were called upon by the chair to make report of the sense of their respective constituents on the act of Congress under deliberation; when each member seemed to find less difficulty in expressing the indignation and just resentment of his constituents against said act, than to conceal his own.

"Resolved, That in the opinion of this committee the duty laid by Congress on spiritous liquors distilled from the produce of the United States, is a tax not in proportion to property, and if carried into effect will be partial in its operations and inconsistent with that protection which the laws of all nations, even the most savage, but our laws especially, give to the repositories of a man's house: and that any person or persons whatever, who have or may accept of any office under Congress, in order to carry into effect said act, shall be considered as inimical to the interests of that country.

"Resolved, That it be recommended to the citizens of Washington county, to treat all such persons who have or may hereafter accept any such office or appointment with that contempt they deserve, and that they absolutely refuse all kind of communication or intercourse with them, and that they will withhold all aid, support or comfort from such officer or officers.

"Resolved, That in the opinion of this committee the salaries allowed by Congress to the different officers on the civil list establishment, are far beyond that moderation that ought to have been observed in the disposition of public money taking into view our present circumstances, or indeed any possible affluent circumstances to which the United States might arrive. That such enormous per diem and per annum allowances to officers as estab'shed by said act have a tendency to beget habits of inattention to duty and swell to insolence, men appointed to serve the public and not to roll in affluence, forgetful of duty and obligation.

"Resolved, That this committee will delegate three of their members to meet other delegates from the counties of Westmoreland, Fayette, and Allegheny on the first Tuesday in September next, for the purpose of expressing the sense of the people of these counties in an address to the Legislature of the United States upon the subject of the excise law and other grievances.

"Then the committee, proceeded to the appointment of their members, as agreeable to the forgoing resolution, and James Marshall, Esq, David Bradford. Esq. and the Revd. David Philips, were appointed.

"Resolved, That the aforegoing resolutions be forwarded to the Printer at Pittsburgh for publication."

"James Edgar, Chairman."

In describing the Washington County meeting of August 23, 1791, Henry M. Brackenridge wrote: "At the preparatory meeting for the county of Washington, some resolutions of a violent character were adopted by way of instructions for the delegates who were to attend at Pittsburgh. They were modeled after those passed before the Revolutionary War in relation to the stamp act and other excises" (Brackenridge, *Insurrection,* 22).

Not content with this vindictive proscription of those, who might esteem it their duty, in the capacity of Officers, to aid in the execution of the constitutional laws of the land—The Meeting proceeded to pass another resolution [7] on a matter essentially foreign to the object, which had brought them together, namely the salaries & compensations allowed by Congress to the Officers of Government generally, which they represent as enormous; manifesting by their zeal, to accumulate topics of Censure that they were actuated not merely by the dislike of a particular law, but by a disposition to render the Government itself unpopular and odious.[8]

This Meeting in further prosecution of their plan deputed three of their Members to meet Delegates from the counties of Westmoreland Fayette and Alleghany on the first Tuesday of Sepr. following for the purpose of expressing the sense of the people of those counties, in an address to the Legislature of the UStates, upon the subject of the Excise Law and *other grievances;* [9] naming for that purpose James Marshall David Bradford & David Philips.[10]

Another Meeting accordingly took place on the 7th of September 1791 at Pittsburgh in the County of Alleghany, at which there appeared persons in character of delegates from the four Western counties; [11] from Westmoreland Nehemiah Stokely & John Young, from

7. See the third resolution quoted in note 6.

8. In the two copies and in the newspaper version of this letter this paragraph reads as follows: "Not content with this vindictive proscription of those who might esteem it their duty, in the capacity of officers, to aid in the execution of the constitutional laws of the land, the meeting proceeded to accumulate topics of crimination of the government, though foreign to each other; authorising, by this zeal for censure, a suspicion that they were actuated, not merely by the dislike of a particular law, but by a disposition to render the government itself unpopular and odious." In the copy in the Hamilton Papers, Library of Congress, the words "accumulate topics of crimination of the Government, though foreign to each other; authorising by this zeal for censure a suspicion" are in H's handwriting. See Randolph to Washington, August 18, 1794, quoted in note 1.

9. The remainder of this paragraph was crossed out in the copy in the Hamilton Papers, Library of Congress, and does not appear in the copy in the National Archives or in the newspaper version. See Randolph to Washington, August 18, 1794, quoted in note 1.

10. David Phillips. In the margin opposite the end of this paragraph H wrote and crossed out in the draft: "B Were there not at this time other county Meetings?" Apparently the Washington County meeting was the only county meeting before the Pittsburgh meeting of September 7, 1791 (Findley, *History of the Insurrection*, 43).

11. The remainder of this paragraph was crossed out in the copy in the

Fayette Edward Cook Nathaniel Breaden[12] & John Oliphant, from Alleghany Thomas Moreton[13] John Woods & Wm. Plume,[14] from Washington, the three persons above named.

This Meeting entered into resolutions more comprehensive in their objects & not less inflammatory in their tendency, than those which had before passed the Meeting in Washington. Their resolutions contained severe censures not only on the law which was the immediate subject of objection; but upon what they termed the exorbitant salaries of Officers, the unreasonable interest of the public debt, the want of discrimination between original holders & transferrees and the institution of a national Bank.[15] The same unfriendly temper towards the Government of the UStates which had led out of their

---

Hamilton Papers, Library of Congress, and does not appear in the newspaper version or in the copy in the National Archives. See Randolph to Washington, August 18, 1794, quoted in note 1.

12. H is referring to Nathaniel Bradly, delegate from Fayette County.

13. Thomas Morton.

14. William Plummer.

15. The delegates at the Pittsburgh meeting of September 7, 1791, "*Resolved,* That having considered the laws of the late Congress, it is our opinion that in a very short time hasty strides have been made to all that is unjust and oppressive. We note particularly the exorbitant salaries of officers, the unreasonable interest of the public debt, and the making no discriminations between the original holders of public securities and the transferees, contrary to the ideas of natural justice in sanctioning an advantage which was not in the contemplation of the party himself to receive, and contrary to the municipal law of most nations and ours particularly, the carrying into effect an unconscionable bargain where an undue advantage has been taken of the ignorance or necessities of another. . . . What is an evil still greater, the constituting a capital of nearly eighty millions of dollars in the hands of a few persons who may influence those occasionally, in power, to evade the Constitution. As an instance of this, already taken place, we note the act establishing a National Bank on the doctrine of implication, but more especially we bear testimony to what is a basic offspring of the funding system, the excise law of Congress. . . .

"*Resolved,* That the said law is deservedly obnoxious to the feelings and interests of the people in general. . . . It operates on a domestic manufacture, a manufacture not equal through the States. It is insulting to the feelings of the people to have their vessels marked, houses painted and ransacked, to be subject to informers, gaining by the occasional delinquency of others. . . .

"*Resolved,* That there appears to be no substantial difference between a duty on what is manufactured from the produce of a country and the produce in its natural state. . . . The excise on home-made spiritous liquors, affects particularly, the raising of grain, especially rye, and there can be no solid reason for taxing it more than any other article of the growth of the United States.

"*Resolved,* That the foregoing representations be presented to the Legislature of the United States.

"*Resolved,* That the following remonstrance be presented to the Legislature of Pennsylvania. . ." (*Pennsylvania Archives,* 2nd ser., IV, 20–22).

way the Meeting at Washington produced a similar wandering in that at Pittsburgh.[16]

A representation to Congress and a remonstrance to the Legislature of Pensylvania against the law more particularly complained of were prepared by this Meeting—published together with their other proceedings in the Pittsburgh Gazette & afterwards presented to the respective bodies to whom they were addressed.[17]

These Meetings composed of very influential Individuals and conducted without moderation or prudence are justly chargeable with the excesses, which have been from time to time committed; serving to give consistency to an opposition which has at length matured to a point, that threatens the foundations of the Government & of the Union; unless speedily & effectually subdued.

On the 6th of the same Month of September, the Opposition broke out in an act of violence upon the person & property of Robert Johnson Collector of the Revenue for the Counties of Alleghany & Washington.

A party of men armed and disguised way-laid him at a place on Pidgeon Creek in Washington county—seized tarred and feathered him cut off his hair and deprived him of his horse, obliging him to travel on foot a considerable distance in that mortifying and painful situation.

The case was brought before the District Court of Pensylvania out of which Processes issued against John Robertson John Hamilton & Thomas McComb: three of the persons concerned in the outrage.[18]

16. In the copy in the Hamilton Papers, Library of Congress, this sentence reads as follows: "The same unfriendly temper which [seemed to have] led out of their way the meeting at Washington [appears to have] produced a similar wandering in that at Pittsburgh." The words within brackets are in H's handwriting. The newspaper version and the copy in the National Archives are similar to the copy in the Hamilton Papers.

17. On November 22, 1791, the House of Representatives received and referred to H "A memorial of the Committee of the counties of Washington, Westmoreland, Fayette, and Allegheny, in the State of Pennsylvania . . . stating their objections to an act, passed at the last session, imposing a duty on spirits distilled within the United States, and praying that the same may be repealed" (*Journal of the House*, I, 458). See H's "Report on the Difficulties in the Execution of the Act Laying Duties on Distilled Spirits," March 5, 1792. The remonstrance to the Pennsylvania legislature has not been found.

18. In a letter to Edmund Randolph on July 30, 1794, William Rawle, United States attorney for the District of Pennsylvania, wrote: "The first instance of open resistance to the law imposing duties upon distilled Spirits occurred in the case of Robert Johnson in September 1791. On the 29th. Sept. he made an

The serving of These processes was confided by the then Marshall Clement Biddle to his Deputy Joseph Fox, who in the month of October went into Alleghany County for the purpose of serving them.[19]

The appearances & circumstances which Mr. Fox observed himself in the course of his journey, & learnt afterwards upon his arrival at Pittsburgh, had the effect of deterring him from the service of the processes and unfortunately led to adopting the injudicious and fruitless expedient of sending them to the parties by a private Messenger [20] under cover.

The Deputy's Report to the Marshall states a number of particulars evincing a considerable fermentation in the part of the country, to which he was sent, and inducing a belief on his part that he could not with safety have executed the processes. The Marshall transmitting this report to the District Atty makes the following observations upon it "I am sorry to add that he (the Deputy) found the people in general in the Western part of the State, and particularly beyond the Alleghany Mountain, in such a ferment, on account of the Act of Congress for laying a duty on distilled spirits & so much opposed to the execution of the said Act, and from a variety of threats to himself personally, although he took the utmost precaution to conceal his errand, that he was not only convinced of the impossibility of serving the process, but that any attempt to effect it would have occasionned the most violent opposition from the greater part of the Inhabitants, & he declares that if he had attempted it, he believes he

---

affidavit of this violence before W. L. Esquire [William Lewis] Judge of the District Court which was transmitted to me with directions to take such measures as the Law required" (ADf, Pennsylvania Historical Society, Philadelphia).

John Neville gave the following account of the attack on Johnson in a letter to Clymer, dated September 15, 1791: "The bearer of this is mr. Johnson one of the collectors of the revenue for the counties of Allegheny and Washington, as he will be before you I shall refer you to him altogether for the loss & abuse he suffered by a number of men in disguise (some in womens cloathes) on the 6th of this month, we have been able to find out sixteen of them, a list of which is enclosed." Neville listed "Col John Hamilton, John Robinson, Thos. McComb (in Womans cloathes), Colo. Wm Parker, Capn Jas. Parker, Danl Hamilton, Docr. Jas. Robinson, Joseph McClary (alias woman), Thos. Hill, Arthur Gardner, McCall, David Hamilton, Saml Scott, John Johnston, Robt. Morrisan, and Jas. Langwell" (ALS, Connecticut Historical Society, Hartford). To this list H added "John Woods." H endorsed this letter as follows: "abuse of Collector Johnson Meeting at Pittsburgh resolution."

19. See H to Tench Coxe, September 1, 1792, note 1.

20. John Connor. See H to Coxe, September 1, 1792, note 1.

should not have returned alive. I spared no expence nor pains to have the process of the Court executed & have not the least doubt that my Deputy would have accomplished it, if it could have been done."

The reality of the danger to the Deputy was countenanced by the opinion of General Neville,[21] the Inspector of the Revenue, a man who before had given & since has given numerous proofs of a steady and firm temper. And what followed, announced in a letter of that officer of the 27th of October 1791 [22] is a further confirmation of it. The person who had been sent with the processes was seized whipped tarred & feathered, and after having his money & horse taken from him was blind folded and tied in the woods, in which condition he remained for five hours.

Very serious reflections naturally occurred upon this occasion. It seemed highly probable, from the issue of the experiment, which had been made, that the ordinary course of civil process would be ineffectual for enforcing the execution of the law in the scene in question—and that a perseverance in this course might lead to a serious concussion. The law itself was still in the infancy of its operation and far from established in other important portions of the Union. Prejudices against it had been industriously disseminated—misreprepretentations diffused, misconceptions fostered. The Legislature of the UStates had not yet organised the means by which the Executive could come in aid of the Judiciary, when found incompetent to the execution of the laws.[23] If neither of these impediments to a decisive exertion had existed, it was desireable, especially in a republican Government, to avoid what is in such cases the ultimate resort, till all the milder means had been tried without success.

21. John Neville.

22. In the copy in the Hamilton Papers, Library of Congress, this letter is dated October 27, 1791, and the phrase "as announced in a letter of that Officer of the 27 of October 1791" is crossed out. The phrase does not appear in the newspaper version or in the copy in the National Archives.

Neville wrote to H on October 27, 1791, but that letter does not deal with the Whiskey Insurrection. The Neville letter to which H is referring was presumably to George Clymer, supervisor of the revenue for the District of Pennsylvania. It has not been found.

23. H is referring to "An Act to provide for calling forth the Militia to execute the laws of the Union, suppress insurrections and repel invasions" (1 *Stat.* 264–65 [May 5, 1792]).

Under the united influence of these considerations, it appeared adviseable to forbear urging coercive measures, 'till the law had gone into more extensive operation, till further time for reflection & experience of its operation had served to correct false impressions and inspire greater moderation, and till the Legislature had had an opportunity, by a revision of the law to remove as far as possible objections, and to reinforce the provisions for securing its execution.

Other incidents occurred from time to time, which are further proofs of the very improper temper that prevailed among the inhabitants of the refractory counties. Mr. Johnson was not the only officer who about the same period experienced outrage. Mr. Wells Collector of the Revenue for Westmoreland & Fayette was also illtreated at Greensburgh & Union Town.[24] Nor were the outrages perpetrated confined to the Officers. They extended to private citizens, who only dared to shew their respect for the laws of their country.

Sometime in October 1791 an unhappy man of the name of Wilson, a stranger in the county, and manifestly disordered in his intellects imagining himself to be a Collector of the Revenue, or invested with some trust in relation to it, was so unlucky as to make inquiries concerning the Distillers who had entered their stills; giving out that he was to travel through the UStates to ascertain & report to Congress the number of Stills &c. This man was pursued by a party in disguise, taken out of his bed, carried about five Miles back to a Smith's Shop, stripped of his Cloaths which were afterwards burnt,

24. Benjamin Wells. Findley, who disagreed with H concerning the events at Greensburgh and Uniontown, wrote: ". . . I have passed one instance mentioned by him [H], viz. that Wells the collector was injuriously treated at Greensburgh, in Westmoreland, in 1792. I passed it, because I was convinced it was without foundation. On the most minute enquiry, I have not found the smallest trace of any injury or insult that he received there. . . .

"The account of his being ill treated at Greensburgh, is connected by the secretary with a similar assertion respecting the treatment he received at Union Town, in Fayette county. This, however, also appears to have but little foundation. On the first day appointed for entering the stills, a number of distillers attended; but the collector did not appear. On the second day, for he was to have attended one day in the week, a greater number of distillers appeared; but the collector was not to be found, though called and diligent enquiry made for him. He was known to be a timid man, and very probably was afraid of their numbers, and this might have been the reason why a greater number attended the second day; but they were neither armed with weapons nor threats. When he undertook the office he ought to have discovered more boldness and less apprehension. . . ." (Findley, *History of the Insurrection*, 60–61.)

and after having been himself inhumanly burnt in several places with a heated Iron was tarred and feathered—and about day light dismissed—naked wounded and otherwise in a very suffering condition. These particulars are communicated in a letter from the Inspector of the Revenue of the 17th of November,[25] who declares that he had then himself seen the unfortunate maniac, the abuse of whom, as he expresses it, exceeded description and was sufficient to make human nature shudder. The affair is the more extraordinary, as persons of weight and consideration in that county are understood to have been actors in it, and as the symptoms of Insanity were, during the whole time of inflicting the punishment apparent—the unhappy sufferer displaying the heroic fortitude of a man, who conceived himself to be a martyr to discharge of some duty.[26]

Not long after a person of the name of Roseberry underwent the humiliating punishmt of tarring & feathering with some aggravations; for having in conversation hazarded the very natural and just, but unpalatable remark, that the inhabitants of that County could not reasonably expect protection from a Government, whose laws they so strenuously opposed.[27]

The audacity of the perpetrators of these excesses was so great that (as appears by a letter from Mr. Nevil of the 22 of December) [28] an armed banditti ventured to seize and carry off two persons, who were witnesses against the rioters in the case of Wilson;

25. H's description of the attack on Robert Wilson is based on a letter which John Neville wrote to Clymer on November 17, 1791 (ALS, Connecticut Historical Society, Hartford). For the indictment against the men who attacked Wilson, see James Brison to Thomas Mifflin, November 9, 1792 (*Pennsylvania Archives,* 2nd ser., IV, 44–45). Brison was prothonotary of Allegheny County.

26. In the copy in the Hamilton Papers, Library of Congress, H changed this phrase to read: "who conceived himself to be a martyr to the discharge of some important duty." The newspaper version and the copy in the National Archives are similar to the copy in the Hamilton Papers.

27. On December 11, 1791, John Neville wrote to Clymer: ". . . a Person of the name of Roseberry, among many Others was giving his oppinion of the Law, and hapend to Say the People Could hardly Expect protection from Congress Since they were So much opposed to their Laws, upon Which he was imediately Branded as they term it With Tar and Feathers one half of his head Close Shaved and otherwise much Abused, and Let him go. . ." (ALS, Connecticut Historical Society, Hartford). H endorsed this letter "Tarring & feathering of one Rosebery."

28. In the copy in the Hamilton Papers, Library of Congress, the words "(as appears by a letter from Mr. Nevil of the 22 of December)" were crossed out, and they are not in the newspaper version or the copy in the National Archives.

in order, as was inferred, to prevent their giving testimony of the riot to a Court then sitting or about to sit.[29]

Designs of personal violence against the Inspector of the Revenue himself, to force him to a resignation, were repeatedly attempted to be put in execution by armed parties, but by different circumstances were frustrated.[30]

In the session of Congress, which commenced in October 1791, the law laying a duty on distilled spirits and on stills came under the revision of Congress as had been anticipated. By an act passed the 8th of May 1792,[31] during that session, material alterations were made in it. Among these, the duty was reduced to a rate so moderate, as to have silenced complaint on that head—and a new and very favourable alternative was given to the Distiller, that of paying a monthly, instead a yearly rate, according to the capacity of his Still, with liberty to take a license for the precise term which he should intend to work it, and to renew that license for a further term or terms.

This amending Act, in its progress through the Legislature, engaged the particular attention of members who themselves were interested in distilleries, and of others who represented parts of the Country in which the business of Distilling was extensively carried on. Objections were well considered and great pains taken to obviate all such as had the semblance of reasonableness.

The effect has in a great measure corresponded with the views of

29. On December 22, 1791, Neville wrote to Clymer: "The Same opposition to our law Continues or rather increases. The two persons who gave testimony against the rioters that burnt or abused Willson, was on Saturday and Sunday nights last, taken by a banditty of Armed men, and carryed off, one of them has not been heard of since, the other got from a part of them on Monday last, but can give No Account of the other, this has been our Court Week, and it is Supposed they have taken him over the river to prevent his appearing as a witness against them. . ." (ALS, Connecticut Historical Society, Hartford). H endorsed this letter "Wilson."

30. Neville described one such incident in his letter of December 22, 1791, to Clymer: ". . . on Saturday the 3rd. of this month a party gathered on the road leading to my house and waited till after dark to Ketch me, but luckily I did not go home that night, nor have I Ventured their since, by which means I have escaped their Vengeance. I have now armed my negros and shall go home tomorrow, If I am Attacked I must defend myself in the best manner I can" (ALS, Connecticut Historical Society, Hartford).

31. H is referring to "An Act concerning the Duties on Spirits distilled within the United States" (1 *Stat.* 267–71).

the Legislature.[32] Opposition has subsided in several districts where it before prevailed; and it was natural to entertain and not easy to abandon a hope that the same thing would by degrees have taken place in the four Western Counties of this State.

But notwithstanding some flattering appearances at particular junctures, and infinite pains by various expedients to produce the desireable issue the hope entertained has never been realized, and is now at an end, as far as the ordinary means of executing laws are concerned.

The first Law had left the number and positions of the Offices[33] of Inspection, which were to be established in each District for receiving entries of Stills, to the discretion of the Supervisor.[34] The second, to secure a due accommodation to Distillers, provides peremptorily that there shall be one in each County.[35]

The idea was immediately embraced, that it was a very important point in the scheme of opposition to the law to prevent the establishment of Offices in the respective Counties. For this purpose, the intimidation of well disposed inhabitants was added to the plan of molesting and obstructing the Officers by force or otherwise, as might be necessary. So effectually was the first point carried, (the certain destruction of property and the peril of life being involved)

32. On April 1, 1794, the House of Representatives received petitions from the inhabitants of Washington County, Maryland, and Chester and Lancaster counties, Pennsylvania, requesting revision of "An Act concerning the Duties on Spirits distilled within the United States" (*Journal of the House*, II, 109; 1 *Stat.* 267–71). The petitions were referred to a committee consisting of Andrew Moore of Virginia, John Smilie of Pennsylvania, Joseph McDowell of Virginia, John Beatty of New Jersey, and Thomas Sprigg of Maryland, with instructions to "report to the House, the general operation and effect of the excise in the United States, and the nett amount of revenue arising therefrom" (*Journal of the House*, II, 109). The committee's report, presented to the House by Andrew Moore on May 16, 1794, stated that opposition to the excise law still existed "in two western surveys of South Carolina, in the survey of Kentucky, and the western survey of Pennsylvania" (*ASP*, *Finance*, I, 279).

33. In the copy in the Hamilton Papers, Library of Congress, and in the newspaper version this word is "officers." In the copy in the National Archives it correctly reads "offices."

34. See Section 7 of "An Act repealing, after the last day of June next, the duties heretofore laid upon Distilled Spirits imported from abroad, and laying others in their stead; and also upon Spirits distilled within the United States, and for appropriating the same" (1 *Stat.* 200–01 [March 3, 1791]).

35. See Section 2 of "An Act concerning the Duties on Spirits distilled within the United States" (1 *Stat.* 268 [May 8, 1792]).

that it became almost impracticable to obtain suitable places for Offices in some of the Counties—and when obtained, it was found a matter of necessity in almost every instance to abandon them.

After much effort The Inspector of the Revenue succeeded in procuring the house of William Faulkner a captain in the army for an Office of Inspection in the County of Washington. This took place in August 1792. The office was attended by the Inspector of the Revenue in person, till prevented by the following incidents.

Capt Faukner, being in pursuit of some Deserters from the troops, was encountered by a number of people in the same neighbourhood, where Mr. Johnson had been ill treated the preceding year, who reproached him with letting his house for an Office of Inspection—drew a knife upon him, threatened to scalp him, tar and feather him, and reduce his house and property to Ashes, if he did not solemnly promise to prevent the further use of his House for an Office.

Capt Faulkner was induced to make the promise exacted—and in consequence of the circumstance wrote a letter to the Inspector dated the 20th of August countermanding the permission for using his house—and the day following gave a public notice in the Pittsburgh Gazette that the Office of Inspection should be no longer kept there.[36]

At the same time, another engine of opposition was in operation. Agreeable to a previous notification, there met at Pittsburgh on the 21st of August a number of persons stiling themselves "A Meeting of sundry Inhabitants of the Western Counties of Pensylvania"[37] who appointed JOHN CANON Chairman and ALBERT GALLATIN Clerk.

This Meeting entered into resolutions[38] not less exceptionable than those of its predecessors. The preamble suggested that a tax

36. This incident was described by Neville in a letter of August 23, 1792, to Clymer (LS, Connecticut Historical Society, Hartford). See H to Coxe, September 1, 1792, note 3. Faulkner's deposition describing these events is dated September 28, 1792 (DS, Pennsylvania Miscellany, Whiskey Rebellion, Vol. I, Library of Congress). See also Clymer to H, October 4, 1792.

37. The remainder of this sentence was crossed out in the copy in the Hamilton Papers, Library of Congress, and does not appear in the newspaper version or in the copy in the National Archives. This was a correction which Randolph suggested to Washington in his letter of August 18, 1794. See note 1.

38. For these resolutions and an account of the meeting, see H to Coxe, September 1, 1792, note 5. These resolutions are also printed in *Pennsylvania Archives*, 2nd ser., IV, 30–31.

on *spirituous liquors* is unjust in itself and oppressive upon the poor—that *internal taxes upon consumption* must in the end destroy the liberties of every country in which they are introduced—that the law in question, from certain local circumstances which are specified, would bring immediate distress & ruin upon the Western Country, and concludes with the sentiment, that they think it their duty to persist in remonstrances to Congress, and in every other LEGAL measure, that may *obstruct* the *operation* of the LAW.

The Resolutions then proceed, first, to appoint a Committee to prepare and cause to be presented to Congress an address, stating objections to the law and praying for its repeal—secondly to appoint Committees of correspondence for Washington Fayette, and Alleghany, charged to correspond together and with such Committee as should be appointed for the same purpose in the County of Westmoreland, or with any Committees of a similar nature, that might be appointed in other parts of the UStates, and also if found necessary to call together either general Meetings of the people, in their respective Counties, or conferences of the several Committees: And lastly to declare, that they will in future consider those who hold Offices for the collection of the duty as unworthy of their friendship, that they will have no *intercourse nor dealings with them*, will *withdraw* from them *every assistance*, *withhold* all the *comforts of life which depend upon those duties that as men and fellow Citizens we owe to each other, and will upon all occasions treat them with contempt; earnestly* RECOMMENDING IT TO THE PEOPLE AT LARGE TO FOLLOW THE SAME LINE OF CONDUCT TOWARDS THEM.

The idea of pursuing *legal* measures to *obstruct* the *operation* of a *Law* needs little comment. Legal measures may be pursued to procure the repeal of a law, but to *obstruct its operation* presents a contradiction in terms. The *operation*, or what is the same thing, the *execution* of a *law*, cannot be *obstructed*, after it has been constitutionally enacted, without illegality and crime. The expression quoted is one of those phrases which can only be used to conceal a disorderly & culpable intention under forms that may escape the hold of the law.

Neither was it difficult to perceive, that the anathema pronounced against the Officers of the Revenue placed them in a state of virtual outlawry, and operated as a signal to all those who were bold enough to encounter the guilt and the danger to violate both their lives and their properties.

The foregoing proceedings as soon as known were reported by the Secretary of the Treasy to The President.[39] The President on the [40] issued a proclamation [41]

and likewise directed that prosecutions might be instituted against the Offenders, in the cases in which the laws would support and the requisite evidence could be obtained.

Pursuant to these instructions, the Atty General [42] in cooperation with the Attorny of the District [43] attended a Circuit Court which was holden at York Town in October 1792 for the purpose of bringing forward prosecutions in the proper cases.

Collateral measures were taken to procure for this purpose the necessary evidence.

The Supervisor of the Revenue was sent into the opposing survey [44] to ascertain the real state of that survey—to obtain evidence of the persons who were concerned in the riot in Faulkeners case—and of those who composed the Meeting at Pittsburgh—to uphold the confidence and encourage the perseverence of the Offi-

39. H to Washington, September 9, 1792.

40. Space left blank in MS. In the copy in the Hamilton Papers, Library of Congress, H inserted "15th of September 1792." These words also appear in the newspaper version and in the copy in the National Archives.

41. At this point in the draft H left a blank space and wrote in the margin "D Proclamation." In the copy in the Hamilton Papers, Library of Congress, a blank space was also left at this point in which H inserted the following quotation from Washington's proclamation of September 15, 1792: "earnestly admonishing and exhorting all persons whom it might concern, to refrain and desist from all unlawful combinations and proceedings whatsoever, having for object or tending to obstruct the operation of the laws aforesaid inasmuch as all lawful ways and means would be put in execution for bringing to Justice the infractors thereof and securing obedience thereto; and moreover changing and requiring all Courts, Magistrates and Officers whom it might concern according to the duties of their several Officers to exert the powers in them respectively vested by law for the purposes aforesaid; thereby also enjoining and requiring all persons whomsoever as they tendered the welfare of their Country, the just and due authority of Government and the preservation of the public peace to be aiding and assisting therein according to law." The quotation from the proclamation appears in the newspaper version and in the copy in the National Archives. For the proclamation, see "Draft of a Proclamation Concerning Opposition to the Excise Law," September 7, 1792, note 1.

42. Edmund Randolph.

43. William Rawle.

44. See Clymer to H, September 28, October 1, 4, 10, 1792.

cers acting under the law—and to induce if possible the inhabitants of that part of the survey, which appeared least disinclined, to come voluntarily into the law, by arguments addressed to their sense of duty and exhibiting the eventual dangers and mischiefs of resistance.

The mission of the Supervisor had no other fruit than that of obtaining evidence of the persons who composed the Meeting at Pittsburgh—and of two who were understood to be concerned in the riot[45]—and a confirmation of the enmity, which certain active and designing leaders had industriously infused into a large proportion of the inhabitants, not against the particular laws, in question, only, but of a more antient date, against the Government of the UStates itself.

The then Attorney General being of opinion,[46] that it was at best a doubtful point, whether the proceedings of the Meeting at Pittsburgh contained indictable[47] matter, no prosecution was attempted against those who composed it; though if the ground for proceeding against them had appeared to be firm, it is presumed, that the truest policy would have dictated that course.

Indictments were preferred to the Circuit Court and found against the two persons[48] understood to have been concerned in the Riot, & the usual measures were taken for carrying them into effect.

But it appearing afterwards from various representations supported by satisfactory testimony, that there had been some mistake as to the

45. Alexander Berr and William Kerr.

46. See Randolph to H, September 8, 1792.

47. In the draft H put dashes under the word "indictable" and in the margin wrote: "examine opinion." In the copy in the Hamilton Papers, Library of Congress, the word is underlined. See Randolph to Washington, August 18, 1794, quoted in note 1.

48. The following account of the activities of Berr and Kerr in the Faulkner riot in Washington County is in Peter Myer's deposition, dated September 29, 1792: ". . . And farther this Deponant saith that a Certain Alexander Berr said it would be well done if the house [Faulkner's] was burnt, for as it stood at some distance from the other houses it might be burnt without Injuring any other house in Town—& farther this Deponant saith that a Certain William Kerr said it would be well done if the house was undermined & thrown down. . ." (D, Pennsylvania Miscellany, Whiskey Rebellion, Vol. I, Library of Congress). See also Clymer to H, October 4, 1792, notes 9, 10, and 12.

According to Williame Rawle, "the indictment against . . . [Berr and Kerr] was ordered by the President to be withdrawn upon exculpating affidavits without subjecting them to the trouble & expence of a trial" (Rawle to Randolph, July 30, 1794 [ADf, Pennsylvania Historical Society, Philadelphia]).

persons accused—justice and policy demanded that the prosecutions should be discontinued, which was accordingly done.

This issue of the business unavoidably defeated the attempt to establish examples of the punishment of persons who engaged in a violent resistance to the laws—and left the officers to struggle against the stream of resistance, without the advantage of such examples.[49]

The following plan, afterwards successively put in execution, was about this time digested for carrying if possible the laws into effect, without the necessity of recurring to force.

1 To prosecute delinquents in the cases in which it could be clearly done for non compliances with the laws 2 to intercept the markets for the surplus produce of the distilleries of the non complying counties, by seizing the spirits in their way to those markets, in places where it could be effected without opposition 3 by purchases through Agents for the Government[50] for the use of the army (instead of deriving the supply through contractors as formerly) confining them to spirits in respect to which there had been a compliance with the laws.

The motives to this plan speak for themselves. It aimed, besides the influence of penalties on delinquents, at making it the general interest of the distillers to comply with the laws, by interrupting the market for a very considerable surplus, and by, at the same time, confining the benefit of the large demand for public service, to those who did their duty to the public, and furnishing through the means

49. At this point in the draft H wrote and crossed out the following: "Two circumstances in the laws conspired to embarrass the success of measures, short of force, for overcoming this resistance—one the necessity towards incurring the penalties of non compliance of having an office of inspection in each County which was prevented in all the opposing counties but one by the means of intimidation which were employed—the other the questionableness of the right of seizure of casks under twenty gallons upon which the duties might not have been paid." H is referring to Section 9 of "An Act concerning the Duties on Spirits distilled within the United States," which provided that "casks and vessels of the capacity of twenty gallons and upwards, containing distilled spirits, which shall be found in the possession of any distiller or dealer in spirits, except at a distillery where the same were made, or in going from one place to another, without being marked according to law, or without having a certificate from some proper officer, shall be liable to seizure and forfeiture. . ." (1 *Stat.* 269 [May 8, 1792]).

50. In the two copies and in the newspaper version the words "for the Government" are omitted.

of payments in Cash that medium for paying the duties, the want of which, it was alleged, was a great difficulty in the way of compliance.

But two circumstances conspired to counteract the success of this plan—one, the necessity towards incurring the penalties of non compliance of there being an office of Inspection in each County, which was prevented in some of the counties by the means of intimidation practiced for that purpose—another,[51] the non extension of the law to the territory N West of the Ohio [52]—into which a large proportion of the surplus beforementioned was sent.

A cure for these defects could only come from the legislature. Accordingly in the session which began in November 1792, measures were taken for procuring a further revision of the laws. A bill containing amendments of these [53] defects was brought in; [54] but it so happened that this object, by reason of more urgent business, was deferred 'till towards the close of the session and finally went off, through the hurry of that period.

The continuance of the embarrassments incident to this state of things naturally tended to diminish much the efficacy of the plan which had been devised. Yet it was resolved as far as legal provisions would bear out the Officers to pursue it with perseverance. There was ground to entertain hopes of its good effect—and it was certainly the most likely course which could have been adopted, towards obtaining the object of the laws by means short of force;

51. In the draft and in the copy in the Hamilton Papers, Library of Congress, the following material was crossed out at this point: "the questionableness of the right of seizure of casks or vessels containing less than 20 Gallons, the general usage of the country being to employ casks of less capacity for sending spirits to Market—a third." These words do not appear in the newspaper version or in the copy in the National Archives. See note 49.

52. Section 4 of "An Act repealing, after the last day of June next, the duties heretofore laid upon Distilled Spirits imported from abroad, and laying others in their stead; and also upon Spirits distilled within the United States, and for appropriating the same" divided the United States into fourteen districts, one for each state. No provision was made for extending the law to the territories (1 *Stat.* 200).

53. In the copy in the Hamilton Papers, Library of Congress, H inserted "and other" at this point. These words appear in the newspaper version and in the copy in the National Archives.

54. On March 2, 1793, the final day of the session, "The House resolved itself into a Committee of the Whole House on the bill marking farther provision for securing and collecting the duties on Foreign and Domestic distilled spirits, stills, wines, and teas; and after some time spent therein, the Committee rose, and were discharged from the further consideration of the said bill" (*Annals of Congress*, III, 966).

evincing unequivocally the sincere disposition to avoid this painful resort and the steady moderation, which have characterised the measures of the Government.[55]

In pursuance of this plan, prosecutions were occasionally instituted in the mildest forms—seizures were made, as opportunities occurred—and purchases on public account were carried on. It may be incidentally remarked, that these purchases were extended to other places, where though the same disorders did not exist, it appeared adviseable to facilitate the payment of the duties by this species of accommodation.

Nor was this plan, notwithstanding the deficiencies of legal provision, which impeded its full execution, without corresponding effects. Symptoms from time to time appeared which authorised expectation, that with the aid, at another session, of the desired supplementary provisions, it was capable of accomplishing its end, if no extraordinary events occurred.

The opponents of the laws, not insensible of the tendency of that plan, nor of the defects in the laws which interfered with it, did not fail from time to time to pursue analogous modes of counteraction. The effort to frustrate the establishment of offices of Inspection in particular was persisted in and even increased. Means of intimidating officers and others continued to be exerted.

In April 1793 a party of armed men in disguise made an attack in the night upon the house of a Collector of the Revenue, who resided in Fayette-County,[56] but he happening to be from home, they contented themselves with breaking open his house threatening terrifying and abusing his family.

Warrants were issued for apprehending some of the rioters upon this occasion by Isaac Mason and James Finley assistant Judges of Fayette County,[57] which were delivered to the Sheriff[58] of that

55. In the margin opposite the end of this paragraph H wrote and crossed out the following: "Instances still continued to influence the non acceptance of the law—Additional opposition."

56. Similar accounts of the attack on Benjamin Wells's house may be found in a letter, dated May 24, 1793, from Neville to Clymer (ALS, Connecticut Historical Society, Hartford) and in Findley, *History of the Insurrection*, 59. For events which occurred after the attack, see Neville to ———, June 7, 1793 (LS, Connecticut Historical Society, Hartford), and Rawle to Randolph, July 30, 1794 (ADf, Pennsylvania Historical Society, Philadelphia).

57. Isaac Meason and James Findley.

58. Joseph Huston. For the indictment against Huston, see Rawle to Randolph, July 30, 1794 (ADf, Pennsylvania Historical Society, Philadelphia).

County who it seems refused to execute them, for which he has been since indicted.

This is at once an example of a disposition to support the laws of the Union and of an opposite one in the local officers of Pensylvania within the disaffected [59] scene. But it is a truth too important to be unnoticed and too injurious not to be lamented, that the prevailing spirit of those Officers has been either hostile or lukewarm to the execution of those laws—and that the weight of an unfriendly official influence has been one of the most serious obstacles with which they have had to struggle.

In June following, the Inspector of the Revenue was burnt in Effigy in Alleghany County at a place & on a day of some public election with much display,[60] in the presence & without interruption from Magistrates and other public officers.[61]

59. In the copy in the Hamilton Papers, Library of Congress, H crossed out the word "disaffected" and inserted the word "non complying." This change appears in both the newspaper version and the copy in the National Archives.

60. In describing this incident, Neville wrote the following account to an unidentified correspondent on June 21, 1793: ". . . it is now the period of electing Militia Officers I had attended some of those Elections, Yesterday there was one in the forks between Mononga. & Yohga. in this County. I had thoughts of being there but was disappointed, my son from the Nature of his Office (being an Inspector) was obliged to be there. There were present about 100 people who had mounted an Effigy with labels purporting it to be 'Genl. Neville the excise man' and a great deal of illiberal Stuff against me & the law. They exposed it during the day and in the Evening consigned it to the flames, regretting it was not me instead of an Effigy" (LS, Connecticut Historical Society, Hartford). H endorsed this letter "appearances of compliance deceitful, Effigy."

61. At this point in the draft H wrote and crossed out the following paragraphs: "Yet notwithstanding particular excesses, there appeared during the latter periods of this year symptoms in different parts of the discontented Counties of a decrease of the spirit of opposition & of a growing disposition to comply with the laws. The appearances for some time were such as to strengthen the hope that a perseverance in the plan which had been adopted especially when fortified by the additional legal provisions which were contemplated would ultimately procure success.

"The idea of giving time for the laws to go into more full operation in other quarters where they had met with obstructions continued to have weight during all this time in regulating the measures which were pursued towards the Counties in question—and cooperated with the occasionally favourable symptoms there to induce an adherence to the plan of endeavouring by forbearance moderation & collateral expedients to promote the gradual establishment of the authority of the laws.

"But the encouraging symptoms were not of long duration. It began soon to appear, that the probability of success in the plan, which was in execution, had excited alarm with those who were determined at all events to prevent

On the night of the 22d. of November, another party of men, some of them armed and all in disguise, went to the house of the same Collector of Fayette which had been visited in April—broke and entered it and demanded a surrender of the officer's Commission and Official books. Upon his refusing to deliver them up, they presented pistols at him, and swore that if he did not comply they would instantly put him to death. At length, a surrender of the Commission & books was enforced. But not content with this, the rioters before they departed required of the officer, that he should within two weeks publish his resignation, on pain of another visit & the destruction of his house.[62]

---

the quiet establishment of the laws—and that they had resolved to renew and increase their efforts to counteract it.

"To make the danger of compliance so great, as completely to deter from it, and absolutely to oblige all the Officers of the revenue to relinquish their Offices appear to have become the fixed objects of the opposition. And they seem to have been for some time determined to bring matters to this issue at every hazard, expecting by it to strike at the root of the laws."

62. Wells's deposition concerning this incident is dated January 29, 1794, and reads in part as follows: ". . . on the night of the 22d. day of November last past, about two o clock, this deponents dwelling house in Franklin township Fayette County was forcibly attacked, the doors broken open and six men, two of them armed with pistols entered the room in which the deponent lay. That they were all disguised by having their faces blacked and four of them had handkerchiefs tied over their mouths. That they advanced to the deponent and required him to deliver up his commission and also his books relative to Excise business, which the deponent refused. They then presented two pistols to the deponent and swore that if he did not produce his said Commission and books they would instantly put him to death. That the deponent being in fear of his life and under the necessity of submitting to superior force told them his commission & books were in another room and that if furnished with a light he would get them. That a light was brought & he went in to the other room followed by one of the said men who had a cocked pistol in his hand which he kept presented towards him and having found the commission & books he returned & laid them on the table. That some of the six men insisted in his delivering the commission into their hands but he refused saying it is there on the table. That they then took the said commission & books and went away first requiring the said deponent to publish his resignation in two weeks other wise they would pay him another visit and would not leave one log upon another at his house.

"That four of the said assailants were wholly unknown to the deponent, that the day after the outrage aforesaid happened this deponent was at Isaac Meason Esquire Iron works where he saw a man whose features instantly struck his attention and upon approaching him to take a nearer view the man endeavored to conceal his face, but from the sight of it which the deponent was able to get he is well satisfied in his own mind that this person whose name is John M'Culloch was one of the six persons guilty of the assault aforesaid. That he is equally well satisfied that Robert Smilie son of John Smilie Esquire was another of the said persons as well from having been able to distinguish his features tho'

Notwithstanding these excesses, the laws appeared, during the latter periods of this year,[63] to be rather gaining ground. Several principal distillers, who had formerly held out, complied; and others discovered a disposition to comply, which was only restrained by the fear of violence.

But these favourable circumstances served to beget alarm, among those who were determined at all events to prevent the quiet establishment of the laws. It soon appeared, that they meditated by fresh and greater excesses to aim a still more effectual blow at them—to subdue the growing spirit of compliance, and to destroy intirely the organs of the laws, within that part of the country, by compelling all the officers to renounce their offices.

---

blacked as from his tone of voice during part of the time while in the deponents house." (DS, Connecticut Historical Society, Hartford.) Wells's deposition was sworn to before Richard Peters, judge of the United States District Court for the District of Pennsylvania.

Washington issued a proclamation, which was published in *The Pittsburgh Gazette* on March 15, 1794. The proclamation reads as follows: "WHEREAS by information given on oath, it appears that in the night time of the twenty second day of November a number of armed men having their faces blackened and being other wise disguised, violently broke open and entered the dwelling house of Benjamin Wells collector of the revenue arising from spirits distilled within the United States, in and for the counties of Westmoreland & Fayette in the district of Pennsylvania, and by assaulting the said collector and put[t]ing him in fear and danger of his life, in his dwelling house aforesaid, in the said county of Fayette did compel him to deliver up to them his commission for collecting the said revenue, together with the books kept by him in the execution of his said duty, and did threaten to do further violence to the said collector, if he did not shortly thereafter publicly renounce the further execution of his said office:

"AND WHEREAS several of the perpetrators of the said offence are still unknown, and the safety and good order of society require that such daring offenders should be discovered and brought to justice so that infractions of the law may be prevented, obedience to them secured, and officers protected in the due execution of the trusts reposed in them, therefore I have thought proper to offer and hereby do offer a reward of TWO HUNDRED DOLLARS for each of the said offenders that shall be discovered and brought to justice for the said offence, to be paid to the person or persons who shall first discover and give information of the said offenders to any judge, justice of the peace, or other magistrate.

"And I do hereby strictly charge and enjoin all officers and ministers of justice according as their respective duties may require, to use their best endeavors to cause the offenders to be discovered, apprehend[ed] and secured, so that they may be speedily brought to trial for the offence aforesaid."

For information on the earlier attack on Wells's house, see note 56.

63. At this point in the copy in the Hamilton Papers, Library of Congress, H put an asterisk and at the bottom of the page wrote "1791." In the newspaper version and in the copy in the National Archives "(1791)" appears at this point.

The last proceeding in the case of the Collector of Fayette was in this spirit. In January of the present year further violences appear to have been perpetrated. William Richmond who had given information against some of the rioters in the affair of Wilson had his barn burnt with all the grain & hay which it contained—and the same thing happened to Robert Shawhan a distiller who had been among the first to comply with the law and who had always spoken favourably of it. But in neither of these instances (which happened in the County of Alleghany) though the presumptions were violent was any positive proof obtained.

The Inspector of the Revenue in a letter of the 27 of February[64] writes, that he had received information that persons living near the dividing line of Alleghany & Washington had thrown out threats of tarring and feathering one William Cochran, a complying Distiller, and of burning his distillery—and that it had also been given out, that in three weeks there would not be a house standing in Alleghany County of any person who had complied with the laws; in consequence of which he had been induced to pay a visit to several leading individuals in that quarter, as well to ascertain the truth of the information as to endeavour to avert the attempt to execute such threats.

It appeared afterwards, that on his return home, he had been pursued by a collection of disorderly persons threatening, as they went along, vengeance against him. In their way, these men called at the house of James Kiddoe, who had recently complied with the laws, broke into his Still-house, fired several balls under his still and scattered fire over and about the house.[65]

Letters from the Inspector in March announce an increased activ-

64. No letter from Neville of this date has been found.

65. In an undated and unaddressed letter, which is endorsed as having been received on March 21, 1794, Neville stated: "In my last I informed you Mr. Johnson and myself had paid a Visit to Some of the most Obstinate distillers, about the line of Washington and this County, and that We had not been interrupted, but we Soon after found that they had Collected after us, to the Number of Sixty or upwards, and followed us Swearing Vengeance against us, Called at one Kildoes who had first entered his Stills, broke into his Still house, fired Several Guns under his Still, Threw the fire over the House and out of the door, and then pursued us who had Luckily got out of their reach, when first hearing of the news we flattered our selves that they Suffered us to Get out of the Way before they began to assemble, but from What has Since happened I believe it was not the Case" (ALS, Connecticut Historical Society, Hartford). H endorsed this letter: "purposed outrage to him. plan of compelling him to renounce his Com∼."

ity in promoting opposition to the laws—frequent meetings to cement and extend the combinations against it—and among other means for this purpose a plan of collecting a force to seize him, compel him to resign his commission and detain him prisoner—probably as a hostage.[66]

In May and June, new violences were comitted. James Kiddoe the person abovementioned & Wm. Cochran another complying Distiller met with repeated injury to their property. Kiddoe had parts of his Grist mill at different times carried away, and Cochran suffered more material injuries. His still was destroyed his saw Mill rendered useless by the taking away of the Saw and his Grist Mill so injured as to require to be repaired at considerable expence. At the last visit, a note in writing was left, requiring him to publish what he had suffered in the Pittsburgh Gazette, on pain of another visit in which he is threatened, in figurative but intelligble terms, with the destruction of his property by fire; thus adding to the profligacy of doing wanton injuries to a fellow Citizen, the tyranny of compelling him to be the publisher of his own wrongs.[67]

June being the month for receiving annual entries of Stills, endeavours were used to open offices in Westmoreland & Washington, where it had been hitherto found impracticable. With much pains and difficulty places were procured for the purpose.

That, in Westmoreland, was repeatedly attacked in the night by armed men, who frequently fired upon it, but according to a report which has been made to this Department it was defended with so much courage and perseverance by John Wells an auxiliary officer & Philip Ragan the owner of the house—as to have been maintained during the remainder of the Month.[68]

That, in Washington, after repeated attempts was suppressed. The first attempt was confined to pulling down the signs of the office &

66. In an undated and unaddressed letter, endorsed as having been received on March 21, 1794, Neville wrote: "On Monday morning, Last . . . a Carpenter . . . who has Worked for me better than a year, came to me and told me to take care of myself, that a Wm Smith had Informed him that day that all the Militia Captains had been Sent to by a Number of distillers to raise 4 or 500 men at once, and finish the business, to Come and Seize me and Make me Give up my Commission, and keep me a prisoner. . ." (ALS, Connecticut Historical Society, Hartford).

67. See Findley, *History of the Insurrection*, 59–60.

68. John Wells was a collector of the revenue for Westmoreland County; Philip Reagan was a deputy collector (Baldwin, *Whiskey Rebels*, 165).

threats of future destruction. The second effected the object in the following mode. About twelve persons armed & painted black, in the night of the 6th of June, broke into the house of John Lynn,[69] where the office was kept, and after having treacherously seduced him to come down stairs & put himself in their power, by a promise of safety to himself and his house—they seized and tied him, threatened to hang him—took him to a retired spot in the neighbouring wood & there after cutting off his hair, tarring and feathering him, swore him never again to allow the use of his house for an Office, never to disclose their names and never again to have any sort of agency in aid of the excise; having done which, they bound him naked to a tree and left him in that situation 'till morning when he succeeded in extricating himself. Not content with this, the malcontents some days after made him another visit, pulled down part of his house—and put him in a situation to be obliged to become an exile from his own home & to find an asylum elsewhere.[70]

During this time several of the Distillers who had made entries & benifitted by them refused the payment of the duties; actuated no doubt by various motives.

Indications of a plan to proceed against the Inspector of the Revenue in the manner which has been beforementioned continued. In a letter from him of the 10 of July [71] he observed that the threatened visit had not yet been made, though he had still reason to expect it.

In the session of Congress which began in December 1793 a bill for making the amendments in the laws, which had been for some-

69. A different view of this incident by a contemporary reads as follows: "About the last of June or first of July, 1794, John Lyn, a Deputy Inspector, residing in Canonsburg, Washington county, was taken from his bed, carried into the woods and received a coat of tar and feathers, and he was left tied to a tree but so loosely that he could easily extricate himself. He returned to his house, and after undergoing an ablution with grease and soap and sand and water, he exhibited himself to the boys in the Academy and others, and laughed and made sport of the whole matter" (James Carnahan, "The Pennsylvania Insurrection of 1794, Commonly Called the Whiskey Insurrection," *Proceedings of the New Jersey Historical Society*, VI [1853], 120). For an account that agrees with H, see Findley, *History of the Insurrection*, 60.

70. At this point in the draft H wrote and crossed out: "These particulars are contained in three letters from the Inspector of the Revenue of the 6th 13 & 20th of June." See Neville to Clymer, June 13, 20, 1794 (LS, Connecticut Historical Society, Hartford). Neville's letter of June 6, 1794, has not been found.

71. Neville's letter has not been found.

time desired, was brought in, and on the 5th of June last became a law.[72]

It is not to be doubted, that the different stages of this business were regularly notified to the malcontents, and that a conviction of the tendency of the amendments contemplated to effectuate the execution of the law had matured the resolution to bring matters to a violent crisis.

The increasing energy of the opposition rendered it indispensable to meet the evil with proportionable decision. The idea of giving time for the law to extend itself in scenes, where the disatisfaction with it was the effect not of an improper spirit, but of causes which were of a nature to yield to reason reflection & experience (which had constantly weighed in the estimate of the measures proper to be pursued) had had its effect, in an extensive degree. The experiment too had been long enough tried to ascertain, that where resistance continued the root of the evil lay deep; and required measures of greater efficacy than had been pursued. The laws had undergone repeated revisions of the legislative representatives of the Union; & had virtually received their repeated sanction, with none or very feeble attempts [73] to effect their repeal; affording an evidence of the general sense of the community in their favour. Complaints began to be loud from complying quarters, against the impropriety & injustice of suffering the laws to remain unexecuted in others.

Under the united influence of these considerations, there was no choice but to try the efficiency of the laws in prosecuting with vigour delinquents and Offenders.

Processes issued against a number of non complying distillers in the Counties of Fayette & Alleghany; and indictments having been found at a Circuit Court holden at Philadelphia in July last against Robert Smilie & John McCulloch two of the rioters in the attack, which in November preceding had been made upon the house of a Collector of the Revenue in Fayette County, processes issued against

72. See *Annals of Congress,* IV, 437, 560, 715, 720, and "An Act making further provision for securing and collecting the Duties on foreign and domestic distilled Spirits, Stills, Wines and Teas" (1 *Stat.* 378–81).

73. In the copy in the Hamilton Papers, Library of Congress, H crossed out this phrase and above it wrote: "without even an attempt, so far as is now recollected or can be traced." This correction appears in the newspaper version and in the copy in the National Archives.

them, also, to bring them to trial and if guilty to punishment.[74] The Marshall of the District[75] went in person to serve these processes. He executed his trust without interruption, though under many discouraging circumstances, in Fayette County; but while he was in the execution of it in Alleghany County being then accompanied by the Inspector of the Revenue (to wit) on the 15th of July last he was beset on the road by a party of from thirty to forty armed men who after much previous irregularity of conduct finally fired upon him but as it happened without injury either to him or the Inspector.[76]

This attempt on the Marshall was but the prelude of greater excesses.

About break of day the 16th of July, in conformity with a plan which seems to have been for some time entertained, and which probably was only accelerated by the coming of the Marshall into the survey, an attack by about 100 persons armed with guns & other weapons was made upon the house of the Inspector in the vicinity of Pittsburgh. The Inspector though alone vigorously defended himself against the assailants and obliged them to retreat without accomplishing their purpose.[77]

74. See note 62.
75. David Lenox.
76. In describing this incident, Hugh H. Brackenridge wrote: "I had supposed they [the insurgents] would have considered the marshal in the light of a sheriff, or a judicial officer, and would not molest him. However, it so happened, that I was mistaken in my confidence of his security; for the evening of the next day [July 15], having been out in company with the inspector of revenue for the district, John Neville, serving some remaining writs upon distillers, in the county of Alleghany, he returned with an unfavorable account of his reception. He had served the last writ he had to serve, in that quarter, and had just quitted the house of a distiller, of the name of [William] Miller, when a number of men were observed to be in pursuit of them and a gun was discharged. The marshal conceiving it not to be with a view to injure, but intimidate, turned and expostulated. But observing a sullenness of countenance, and advised by the inspector, who knew their disposition better, he thought proper to ride off, and escape from them. . ." (Brackenridge, *Incidents*, I, 6).
77. In a letter to Tench Coxe, dated July 18, 1794, Neville gave the following account of this attack on his house: "On Wednesday Morning the 16th about day light, my Servants having just gone out to their employments, I discovered my House was surrounded with men, supposed about 100, Sixty of whom was well armed, the others with Sticks and clubs—tho alone being well provided with Arms and Ammunition, I determined to defend myself to the last, knowing that extreeme Insult would be the consequence of my falling into their Hands—An Action accordingly commenced and to make good the old adage 'that Victory is not always to ye Strong' after a firing of 25 Minutes, I obliged

Apprehending that the business would not terminate here he made application by letter to the Judges Generals of Militia & Sheriff of the county for protection. A reply to his application from John Wilkins Junior & John Gibson Magistrates & Militia officers [78] informed him, that the laws could not be executed, so as to afford him the protection to which he was intitled, owing to the too general combination of the people in that part of Pensylvania to oppose the Revenue law; adding that they would take every step in their power to bring the Rioters to Justice & would be glad to receive information of the individuals concerned in the attack upon his house, that prosecutions might be commenced against them and expressing their sorrow, that should the POSSE COMITATUS of the County be ordered out in support of the civil authority, very few could be gotten who were not of the party of the Rioters.

The day following, the Insurgents reassembled with a considerable augmentation of numbers amounting as has been computed to at least 500 and on the 17th of July renewed their attack upon the house of the Inspector; who in the interval had taken the precaution of calling to his aid a small detachment from the garrison of Fort Pit which at the time of this attack consisted of 11 Men, who had been joined by Major Abraham Kirkpatrick a friend & connection of the Inspector.[79]

---

them to retire having wounded at least five of them, one or two supposedly dangerously—they did me no other damage than firing about 50 Balls into my house, Mrs. Neville, a young lady, and a little girl, the only companions of my danger narrowly escaping" (LS, Neville Papers, Carnegie Library of Pittsburgh, Pennsylvania).

Isaac Craig, in a letter to Henry Knox dated July 18, 1794, describes this incident as follows: "About day break in the Morning of the 16th Instant a number of Armed Men Attacked General Nevilles House, he himself only defending it, he however dispersed the party having wounded six or seven, One of whom it is said Mortally. . ." (LS, Connecticut Historical Society, Hartford).

78. Gibson was a judge of the Court of Common Pleas of Allegheny County and a major general of the Pennsylvania militia. Wilkins was a brigadier general of the militia and a justice of the peace. See "Deposition of Francis Mentges," August 1, 1794, note 2.

79. The contents of this paragraph and those immediately following it closely parallel two letters which Kirkpatrick wrote to Washington on July 25 and 28, 1794 (ALS, Connecticut Historical Society, Hartford). Kirkpatrick, a major in the American Revolution, was at this time engaged in speculation in Pittsburgh and was a member of the "Neville connection." See "Deposition of Francis Mentges," August 1, 1794, note 2.

In his letter of July 28 to Washington, Kirkpatrick wrote: "Last post I wrote

There being scarcely a prospect of effectual defence against so large a body, as then appeared, and as the Inspector had every thing to apprehend for his person, if taken, it was judged adviseable that he should withdraw from the house to a place of concealment—Major Kirkpatrick generously agreeing to remain with the[80] 11 men, in the intention if practicable to make a capitulation in favour of the property if not to defend it as long as possible.

A parly took place, under cover of a flag, which was sent by the Insurgents to the House to demand, that the Inspector should come forth, renounce his office and stipulate never again to accept an office under the same laws. To this it was replied, that the Inspector had left the house upon their first approach, and that the place to which he had retired was unknown. They then declared that they must have whatever related to his office. They were answered that they might send persons not exceeding six to search the house and take away whatever papers they could find appertaining to the Office. But not satisfied with this, they insisted unconditionally, that the armed men who were in the house for its defence should march out & ground their arms; which Major Kirkpatrick peremptorily refused; considering it and representing it to them as a proof of a design to destroy the property. This refusal put an end to the parley.

A brisk firing then ensued between the insurgents and those in the House, which it is said lasted for near an hour; 'till the assailants having set fire to all the neighbouring & adjacent buildings, Eight in number, the intenseness of the heat & the danger of an immediate communication of the fire to the house obliged Maj Kirk: & his small party to come out & surrender themselves. In the course of the

---

the Sec. of the Treasury respecting the Attack on the house of Genl. Nevill Supt. of the Revenue Law, this morning we have heard the post was rob'd. As I seemed to have acted a principal Character in the Transactions of this day—some gentlemen thought it would be proper for me to State such facts as come more particularly under my View & am as follows" (ALS, Connecticut Historical Society, Hartford).

Kirkpatrick's letter to H has not been found. The possibility exists, however, that the letter dated July 25, which Kirkpatrick sent to Washington, was a copy of that which he sent to H and which had been lost when the mail was robbed. In any event, the contents of Kirkpatrick's two letters addressed to Washington (with the exception of the paragraph quoted above from the letter of July 28) are virtually identical.

For this second attack on Neville's house, see "Deposition of Francis Mentges," August 1, 1794, note 2.

80. The copy in the Hamilton Papers, Library of Congress, ends at this point.

firing, one of the insurgents was killed & several wounded and three of the persons in the house were also wounded. The person killed is understood to have been the leader of the party of the name of James McFarlane,[81] then a Major in the Militia formerly a Lieutenant in the Pensylvania line.

The dwelling house after the surrender shared the fate of the other buildings the whole having been consumed to the ground. The loss of property to the Inspector upon this occasion, is estimated and as is believed with great moderation at not less than 3000 pounds.

The Marshall, Col Presly Neville [82] & several others were taken by the insurgents going to the Inspector's House. All except the Marshall and Col Neville soon made their escape; but these were carried off some distance from the place, where the affray had happened, and detained till one or two oClock the next morning. In the course of their detention, the Marshall in particular suffered very severe and humiliating treatment—and was frequently in imminent danger of his life. Several of the party repeatedly presented their pieces at him, with every appearance of a design to assassinate, from which they were with difficulty restrained by the efforts of a few more humane & more prudent.

Nor could he obtain safety or liberty, but upon the condition of a promise guaranteed by Col Neville, that he would serve no other process on the West side of the Alleghany Mountain. The alternative being immediate death extorted from the Marshall a compliance with this condition; notwithstanding the just sense of official dignity and the firmness of character, which were witnessed by his conduct throughout the trying scenes he had experienced.

The insurgents on the 18th sent a deputation of two of their number (one a Justice of the Peace) to Pittsburgh [83] to require of the Marshall a surrender of the processes in his possession, intimating that his compliance would satisfy the people & *add to his safety*—and also to demand of General Neville in peremptory terms the resignation of his Office, threatening in case of refusal to attack the

81. See "Deposition of Francis Mentges," August 1, 1794, note 3. In the newspaper version this name is incorrectly given as "McTarlane."

82. See "Deposition of Francis Mentges," August 1, 1794, note 2.

83. David Hamilton and John Black. Hamilton was the justice of the peace.

place & take him by force: demands which both these officers did not hesitate to reject as alike incompatible with their honor & their duty.

As it was well ascertained, that no protection was to be expected from the Magistrates or inhabitants of Pittsburgh, it became necessary to the safety both of the Inspector & the Marshall to quit the place—and as it was known that all the usual routes to Philadelphia were beset by the insurgents, those officers concluded to descend the Ohio & proceed by a circuitous route to the seat of Government, which they began to put in execution on the night of the 19th of July.

Information has also been received of a Meeting of a considerable number of persons at a place called Mingo Creek Meeting House in the County of Washington, to consult about the further measures which it might be adviseable to pursue: [84] That at this Meeting a motion was made to approve and agree to support the proceedings which had taken place, until the Excise law was repealed and an Act of oblivion passed. But that instead of this it had been agreed, that the four Western Counties of Pensylvania & the neighbouring Counties of Virginia should be invited to meet in a Convention of Delegates on the 14th of the present Month, at Parkinson's on Mingo Creek in the County of Washington,[85] to take into consideration the situation of the Western Country & concert such measures as should appear suited to this occasion.

It appears moreover that on the 26 of July [86] last the Mail of the UStates on the road from Pittsburgh to Philadelphia was stopped by two armed men, who cut it open & took out all the letters, except those contained in one packet.[87] These armed men, from all the circumstances which occurred, were manifestly acting on the part of the Insurgents.

The declared object of the foregoing proceedings is to obstruct the execution and compel a repeal of the laws, laying duties upon

84. This meeting was held on July 23, 1794. For a detailed account of its proceedings, see Brackenridge, *Insurrection*, 57–65, and Brackenridge, *Incidents*, 29–36. See also "Deposition of Francis Mentges," August 1, 1794, note 5.

85. See "Deposition of Francis Mentges," August 1, 1794, note 6.

86. In the newspaper version and in the copy in the National Archives this date is incorrectly given as "25th of July."

87. See "Conference Concerning the Insurrection in Western Pennsylvania," August 2, 1794, note 8.

spirits distilled within the UStates and upon Stills. There is just cause to believe, that this is connected with an indisposition too general in that quarter to share in the common burthens of the community—and with a wish among some persons of influence to embarrass the Government. It is a fact of notoriety, that the revenue laws of the State itself have always been either resisted or defectively complied with in the same quarter.[88]

88. In the draft H wrote and crossed out five additional paragraphs. The final paragraph is incomplete. This additional material reads as follows:

"The very serious and dangerous nature of these transactions need not be dilated upon. The immediate Question is whether the Government of the U States shall ever raise revenue by any internal tax on articles of consumption; the ultimate one whether a small minority of the community shall controul & defeat the will of the majority declared through its constitutional representatives? in other words whether anarchy shall take place of Government?

"Whatever declamation may be indulged on the subject, the practical truth is that without a capacity to exercise the power in question a Government cannot provide for the exigencies of a nation. That of the UStates would feel particular embarrassment from such a privation; if the ideas generally entertained are well founded of peculiar difficulties in laying by its authority taxes on real property. To deprive the Government then of that capacity is in fact, whatever it may be in form, to destroy it.

"Still more manifest is it that to permit a small portion of the community successfully to resist the execution of a law by an armed force is to sacrifice the authority of the laws and to prostrate Government? Who can say when & in what corner resistance to other laws will arise?

"The sacredness of the laws is inculcated by considerations of peculiar obligation upon all true friends to free government. Tis by that alone that the necessity of force as the ordinary instrument of civil obedience is superseded.

"Viewing the subject in the limitted and subordinate light of finance nothing can be more agreeable than the actual situation of"

From Tench Coxe[1]

Treasury Department, Revenue Office, August 6, 1794. "I have the honor to request you will place the sum of four thousand & forty seven dollars & 22 cents in the hands of Nathaniel Gorham Esquire of Boston for the purpose of paying for a quantity of copper & tin, necessary for making ten eight inch Howitz, and for a small advance upon the workmanship, agreeably to a contract with Paul Revere for that purpose."[2]

LC, RG 75, Letters of Tench Coxe, Commissioner of the Revenue, Relating to the Procurement of Military, Naval, and Indian Supplies, National Archives.

1. For background to this letter, see Henry Knox to H, March 29, April 21, 1794; H to Coxe, April 4, 1794.

2. A draft of the contract between Revere and Coxe on behalf of the United States, dated July, 1794, may be found in RG 58, Records of the Bureau of Internal Revenue, General Records, 1791–1803, National Archives.

On August 6, 1794, Coxe wrote to Gorham, supervisor of the revenue for Massachusetts: "You are hereby authorized to purchase such quantity of copper as may be wanted by Mr. Paul Revere for the casting of the ten Howitzers for the United States. . . . I shall immediately take the necessary measures for having the money . . . for the advance to Mr. Revere placed in your hands. . ." (LC, RG 75, Letters of Tench Coxe, Commissioner of the Revenue, Relating to the Procurement of Military, Naval, and Indian Supplies, National Archives). On August 7, 1794, Warrant No. 3932 for $4,047.22 was issued to Gorham for the advance to Revere (D, RG 217, Miscellaneous Treasury Accounts, 1790–1894, Account No. 7701, National Archives).

To George Washington

[Philadelphia, August 6, 1794]

The Secretary of the Treasury presents his respects to the President, sends him the statement of facts promised.[1] The date is proposed to be two or three days before the Proclamation,[2] when it was in fact begun. There is a blank to be filled with a quotation from a former proclamation which is not immediately at hand; but the blank will be filled before it goes to the press.[3] If the President thinks the publication proper & will be pleased to return the enclosed, the original draft being too much obliterated for the purpose, it shall be immediately begun in Dunlap's paper.[4]

6 Augt. '94.

LC, George Washington Papers, Library of Congress.

1. H to Washington, August 5, 1794.
2. See H and Henry Knox to Washington, August 5, 1794, note 2.
3. See H to Washington, August 5, 1794, note 41.
4. H's letter to Washington of August 5 appeared in [Philadelphia] *Dunlap and Claypoole's American Daily Advertiser* on August 21, 1794.

To Thomas Willing[1]

Treasury Department, August 6, 1794. "I request that you will furnish William Bradford Esquire with Eight hundred Dollars for a matter relative to the public service. . . ."[2]

ALS, Connecticut College Library, New London, Connecticut.

1. Willing was president of the Bank of the United States.
2. This money was for the expenses of the United States commissioners—of

which Bradford was one—appointed to confer with representatives from western Pennsylvania. See H and Henry Knox to George Washington, August 5, 1794, note 3. Documents itemizing the expenses of the commissioners may be found in RG 217, Miscellaneous Treasury Accounts, 1790–1894, Account No. 6562, National Archives.

At the bottom of this letter Bradford wrote: "Recd the above Wm. Bradford."

To Tench Coxe

[Philadelphia, August 7–8,[1] 1794]

Mr. Hamilton requests Mr. Coxe agreeably to the wish of the President to have the contents of the inclosed Letters published omitting and altering such things as disclose the Writers. Dunlaps Paper will be a good channel for this purpose.[2]

The sooner the better.

AL, RG 58, General Records, 1791–1803, National Archives.

1. H did not date this letter. At the bottom of the letter Coxe wrote: "recd. Augt. 7 or 8th 1794."

2. The letters which H enclosed in his letter to Coxe have not been found, but see [Philadelphia] *Dunlap and Claypoole's American Daily Advertiser*, August 22, 1794, in which are printed the extracts of two letters dated June 19 and 25, 1794, "from a very respectable Mercantile House in London . . . to their Correspondent in New York." The first letter commends "The moderation and wisdom of America in sending a man of Mr. Jay's known and high character, to settle the differences between us by fair representation and negociation" and predicts that John Jay's mission "will be completely successful." The second letter, after stating that the British ministry in reply to a request from British merchants and manufacturers believed that "there would be little doubt that the matters in dispute would be all amicably arranged," added that "the [British] Ministers disclaim any responsibility for the error [in their prediction] should it unexpectedly hereafter happen, that the influence of any party in America should overrule the dispositions of her government, and prevent the negociation terminating, as was expected."

From Elizabeth Hamilton

[*Albany, August 7, 1794.* On August 12, 1794, Hamilton wrote to Elizabeth Hamilton: "Your letter of the 7th alarms me." *Letter not found.*]

To Benjamin Lincoln

Treasury Department, August 7, 1794. "A warrant has issued this day in your favor . . . for Eight Thousand, Eight hundred and forty nine dollars and twenty five Cents . . . for Spermiceti Oil for the use of the Light Houses in the United States. . . ." [1]

LS, RG 36, Collector of Customs at Boston, Letters and Papers re Lighthouses, Buoys, and Piers, 1789–1819, Vol. 3, National Archives.

1. See Tench Coxe to H, July 9, August 5, 1794.

[*Proclamation by the President of the United States*] [1]

[Philadelphia, August 7, 1794]

1. Although this proclamation concerning opposition to the excise laws in western Pennsylvania has been attributed to H in *HCLW*, VI, 389, and Hamilton, *History*, VI, 73, no manuscript of this document in H's handwriting has been found, and there is no conclusive evidence of H's authorship. See H and Henry Knox to George Washington, August 5, 1794, note 4. The proclamation is printed in *GW*, XXXIII, 457–61.

Edmund Randolph to Thomas Mifflin [1]

Philadelphia Aug. 7. 1794

Sir

The President of the UStates has directed me to acknowlege the Receipt of your letter of the 5th instant [2] and to communicate to you the following reply.

Df, in the handwriting of H, Hamilton Papers, Library of Congress.

1. For background to this letter, see "Deposition of Francis Mentges," August 1, 1794; "Conference Concerning the Insurrection in Western Pennsylvania," August 2, 1794; H to George Washington, August 2, 5, 1794; H and Henry Knox to Washington, August 5, 1794.

This letter is the same as that which Randolph actually sent to Mifflin. Randolph's letter to Mifflin is printed in *Pennsylvania Archives*, 2nd ser., IV, 112–22, and *ASP, Miscellaneous*, I, 99–101.

2. Mifflin's letter to Washington of August 5, 1794, reads in part as follows: "The important subject, which led to our conference on Saturday last, and the interesting discussion that then took place, having since engaged my whole attention, I am prepared, in compliance with your request, to state with candor the measures which, in my opinion, ought to be pursued by the commonwealth of Pennsylvania. The circumstances of the case evidently require a firm and energetic conduct on our part, as well as on the part of the General Government; but as they do not preclude the exercise of a prudent and humane policy, I enjoy a sincere gratification in recollecting the sentiment of regret, with which you contemplated the possible necessity of an appeal to arms. . . . I cannot hesitate to declare on the part of Pennsylvania, that the incompetency of the Judiciary Department of her Government, to vindicate the violated laws, has not at this period been made sufficiently apparent; and that the military power of the Government ought not to be employed, until its Judiciary au-

In requesting an interview with you, on the subject of the recent disturbances in the Western parts of Pensylvania, the President, besides the desire of manifesting a respectful attention to the Chief Magistrate of a State immediately affected, was influenced by the hope, that a free conference, guided by a united & comprehensive view of the constitutions of the UStates and of Pensylvania, and of the respective institutions authorities rights and duties of the two Governments—would have assisted him in forming more precise ideas of the nature of the *cooperation,* which could be established between them and a better jugment of the plan, which it might be adviseable for him to pursue, in the execution of his trust, in so important and delicate a conjuncture. This having been his object, it is matter of some regret, that the course, which has been suggested by you, as proper to be pursued, seems to have contemplated Pensylvania in a light too separate and unconnected.[3] The propriety of that course, in most, if not all respects, would be susceptible of little question; if there were no Fœderal Government, Fœderal laws, Fœderal Judiciary, or Fœderal officers; if important laws of the UStates, by a series of violent as well as of artful expedients, had

---

thority, after a fair experiment, has proved incompetent to enforce obedience, or to punish infractions of the law. . . . I propose issuing a Proclamation, in order to declare (as far as I can declare them) the sentiments of the Government; to announce a determination to prosecute and punish the offenders; and to exhort the Citizens at large to pursue a peaceable and patriotic conduct: I propose engaging three respectable Citizens to act as Commissioners for addressing those who have embarked in the present combination, upon the lawless nature, and ruinous tendency of their proceedings; for inculcating the necessity of an immediate return to the duty which they owe their Country, and for promising (as far as the State of Pennsylvania is concerned) a forgiveness of their past transgressions, upon receiving a satisfactory assurance, that, in future, they will submit to the laws: and I propose, if all these expedients should be abortive, to convene the Legislature, that the ultimate means of subduing the spirit of insurrection, and of restoring tranquility and order, may be prescribed by their wisdom and authority" (LS, Pennsylvania Miscellany, Whiskey Rebellion, Vol. I, Library of Congress; Df, Division of Public Records, Pennsylvania Historical and Museum Commission, Harrisburg). This letter is printed in *Pennsylvania Archives,* 2nd ser., IV, 105–09, and *ASP, Miscellaneous,* I, 97–99.

In his letter to Washington, Mifflin ignored the July 18, 1794, report of John Gibson, major general in the Pennsylvania militia, who, in describing the attack on John Neville's house, wrote to Mifflin: "I am sorry to have to inform your Excellency that a civil war has taken place in this county. . ." (Copy, Connecticut Historical Society, Hartford).

3. See note 2.

not been frustrated in their execution for more than three years; if officers immediately charged with that execution, after suffering much and repeated insult, abuse personal ill treatment, and the destruction of property, had not been compelled for safety to fly the places of their residence and the scenes of their official Duties; if the service of the processes of a Court of the UStates had not been resisted and prevented, the Marshall of the District[4] made and detained for some time prisoner & compelled, for safety also, to abandon the performance of his duty, & return by a circuitous route to the seat of Government: if, in fine, a judge of the UStates[5] had not in due form of law notified to the President, that in the Counties of Washington & Alleghany, in Pensylvania, laws of the UStates are opposed and the execution thereof obstructed, by combinations too powerful to be suppressed by the ordinary course of Judicial proceedings, or by the powers vested in the Marshal of that District. It is true Your Excellency has remarked that in the plan suggested, you have only spoken as the Executive Magistrate of Pensylvania, charged with a general superintendance and care, that the laws of the commonwealth be faithfully executed, leaving it implicitly to the judgment of the President to chose on such evidence as he approves, the measures for discharging the analogous trust, which is confided to him in relation to the laws of the Union. But it is impossible not to think that the current of the observations in your letter, especially as to the consequences which may result from the employment of coercive measures,[6] previous to the preliminary course which is indicated in it, may be construed to imply a virtual disapprobation of that plan of conduct, on the part of the General Government, in the actual stage of its affairs, which you acknowlege would be proper on the part of the Government of Pensylvania if arrived at a similar stage. Let it be assumed here (to be more particularly shewn hereafter) that the Govert. of the UStates is now at that point, where it is admitted, if the Govert. of Pensylvania

4. David Lenox. See "Deposition of Francis Mentges," August 1, 1794.

5. This is a reference to a statement made by James Wilson, associate justice of the Supreme Court. See H to Tench Coxe, August 1, 1794; "Conference Concerning the Insurrection in Western Pennsylvania," August 2, 1794, note 9.

6. H is referring to questions which Mifflin asked in his letter to Washington of August 5, 1794. See note 2. H quotes these questions in the last part of this paragraph.

was, the employment of force, by its authority, would be justifiable—and Let the following extracts be consulted for the truth of the inference which has been just expressed. "Will not the resort to force inflame and cement the existing opposition? Will it not associate in a common resistance those who have hitherto peaceably, as well as those who have riotously, expressed their abhorrence of the Excise? Will it not collect & combine every latent principle of discontent, arising from the supposed oppressive operations of the Fœderal Judiciary, the obstruction of the Western Navigation & a variety of other local sources? [7] May not the magnitude of the opposition on the part of the ill disposed, or the dissatisfaction of a *premature resort to arms*, on the part of the well disposed, citizens of this state, eventually involve the necessity of employing the Militia of other States? And the accumulation of discontent, which the jealousy engendered by that movement may produce—who can calculate or who will be able to avert?"

These important questions naturally give birth to the following serious reflections.

The issues of human affairs are in the hands of Providence. Those entrusted with them in society have no other sure guide than the sincere and faithful discharge of their duty, according to the best of their judgments. In emergencies great and difficult, not to act with an energy proportioned to their magnitude and pressure is as dangerous as any other conceivable course. In the present case, not to exert the means, which the laws prescribe for effectuating their own execution, would be to sacrifice those laws and with them the Constitution, the Government, the principles of social order and the bulwarks of private right and security. What worse can happen, by the exertion of those means?

If, as cannot be doubted, the great body of the Citizens of the UStates are attached to the Constitution, which they have established for the management of their common concerns—if they are resolved to support their own authority in that of the constitutional laws, against disorderly and violent combinations of comparitively small portions of the community—if they are determined to protect each other in the enjoyment of security to person and property—if

7. See "Conference Concerning the Insurrection in Western Pennsylvania," August 2, 1794, notes 13–16.

they are decided to preserve the character of republican Government, by evincing that it has adequate resources for maintaining the public order—if they are persuaded, that their safety and their welfare are materially connected with the preservation of the Union, and consequently of a Government adequate to its exigencies—in fine, if they are disposed to continue that state of respectability and prosperity, which is now deservedly the admiration of Mankind—the Enterprise to be accomplished, should a resort to force prove inevitable, though disagreeable and painful, cannot be arduous or alarming.

If in addition to these dispositions in the community at large—the officers of the Governments of the respective States, feeling it to be not only a patriotic, but a constitutional duty (inculcated by the oath enjoined upon all the officers of a State, legislative Executive & Judicial) to support in their several stations, the Constitution of the UStates—shall be disposed, as occasion may require (a thing as little to be doubted as the former) with sincerity and good faith to cooperate with the Government of the UStates, to second with all their influence and weight, its legal & necessary measures, by a real and substantial concert; then the enterprise to be accomplished can hardly even be deemed difficult.

But if contrary to the anticipations which are entertained of these favourable dispositions—the great body of the people should be found indifferent to the preservation of the Government of the Union, or insensible to the necessity of vigorous exertions to repel the danger, which threatens their most important interests—or if an unwillingness to encounter partial inconveniences should interfere with the discharge of what they owe to their permanent welfare—or if either yielding to the suggestions of particular prejudices, or misled by the arts which may be employed to infuse jealousy & discontent, they should suffer their zeal for the support of public order to be relaxed by an unfavourable opinion of the merits & tendency of the measures, which may be adopted,—if above all, it were possible, that any of the State Governments should instead of prompting the exertions of the Citizens assist directly or indirectly in damping their ardor, by giving a wrong byass to their judgment—or by disseminating dissatisfaction with the proceedings of the General Government—or should counteract the success of those proceedings by any sinister influence whatever—then indeed no one can calculate, or may be able to avert, the fatal evils with which such a state of things would be pregnant. Then indeed the foundations of our political happiness may be deeply shaken, if not altogether overturned.

The President however can suppose none of these things. He cherishes an unqualified confidence in the virtue & good sense of the people, in the integrity and patriotism of the Officers of the State Governments—and he counts absolutely on the same affectionate support, which he has experienced upon all former occasions, and which he is conscious that the goodness of his intentions now, not less than heretofore, merits.

It has been promised to shew more particularly hereafter, that the Government of the UStates is now at that point where it is confessed if the State Government was, the employment of force on its part would be justifiable. This promise remains to be fulfilled.

The facts already noted establish the conclusion; but to render it palpable, it will be of use to apply them to the positions which Your Excellency has been pleased to lay down.

You admit, that as the offences committed respect the State, the military power of the Government ought to be employed, where its judiciary authority, after a fair experiment, had proved incompetent to enforce obedience or to punish infractions of the law—that if the strength and audacity of a lawless combination shall baffle and destroy the efforts of the Judiciary Authority, to recover a penalty or inflict a punishment, that authority may constitutionally claim the auxiliary intervention of the Military Power—that in the last resort, at the requisition, & as an auxiliary, of the Civil Authority, the Military force of the State would be called forth. And you declare, that the circumstances of the case evidently require a firm and energetic conduct on the part both of the state and General Government.

For more than three years, as already observed, certain laws of the UStates have been obstructed in their execution by disorderly combinations. Not only officers, whose immediate duty it was to carry them into effect, have suffered violent personal outrage and injury and destruction of property, at different times, but similar persecution has extended to private citizens, who have aided countenanced or only complied with the laws. The violences committed have been so frequent and such in their degree as to have been matters of general notoriety and alarm—and it may be added, that they have been abundantly within the knowlege and under the notice of Judges and Magistrates of Pensylvania of superior as well as of inferior jurisdiction. If in particular instances, they have been punished by the exertions of those Magistrates, it is at least certain, that their efforts have been in the main ineffectual. The spirit has continued, and with some intervals of relaxation has been progressive, manifesting itself in reiterated excesses. The Judiciary authority of the ustates has also, prior to the attempt, which preceded the late crisis, made some fruitless efforts. Under a former Marshall,[8] an officer sent to execute process[9] was deterred from it by the manifest danger of proceeding. These particulars serve to explain the extent, obstinacy & inveteracy of the evil.

But the facts which immediately decide the complexion of the existing crisis are these. Numerous delinquencies existed, with regard to a compliance with the laws laying duties on spirits distilled within the UStates and upon Stills.[10] An armed banditti in disguise had recently gone to the house of an officer of the Revenue in the night, attacked it, broken open the doors; and by menaces of instant death enforced by pistols presented at him had compelled a surrender of his Commission and books of office.[11] Cotemporary Acts of violence had been perpetrated in other quarters. Processes issued out of a Court of the UStates to recover the penalties incident to non compliance with the laws and to bring to punishment the violent infractors of them, in the abovementioned case against two of whom indictments had been found. The Marshall of the District went in person to execute these processes. In the course of his duty, he was actually fired upon on the high road by a body of armed men. Shortly after, other bodies of armed men (in the last instance amounting to several hundred persons) repeatedly attacked the

8. Clement Biddle.

9. Joseph Fox. See H to Tench Coxe, September 1, 1792, note 1. See also H to Washington, August 5, 1794.

10. For the legislation regulating the excise, see H to Washington, August 5, 1794, note 2.

11. For this incident and others mentioned in this paragraph, see H to Washington, August 5, 1794.

house of the Inspector of the Revenue with the declared intention of compelling him to renounce his office, and of obstructing the execution of the laws. One of these bodies of armed men made prisoner of the Marshall of the District, put him in jeopardy of his life, and did not release him till for safety & to obtain his liberty, he engaged to forbear the further execution of the processes with which he was charged. In consequence of further requisitions and menaces of the insurgents, the Marshall, together with the Inspector of the Revenue, have been since under the necessity of flying secretly and by a circuitous route from the scene of these transactions towards the seat of Govérnt. An associate Justice, pursuant to the provisions of the laws for that purpose, has in the manner already stated officially notified the President of the existence of combinations in two of the Counties of this State, to obstruct the execution of the laws, too powerful to be suppressed by the Judiciary authority or by the powers of the Marshal.

Thus then, is it unequivocally, and in due form, ascertained, in reference to the Government of the UStates—That the judiciary authority, after a fair and full experiment, has proved incompetent to enforce obedience to or to punish infractions of the laws—that the strength and audacity of certain lawless combinations have baffled & destroyed the efforts of the Judiciary Authority to recover penalties or inflict punishment, and that this authority, by a regular notification of this state of things, has in the last resort, as an auxilliary of the Civil Authority, claimed the intervention of the Military Power of the UStates. It results from these facts, that the case exists when according to the positions advanced by Your Excelly in reference to the State Govt, the Military power may with due regard to all the requisite cautions be rightfully interposed: And that the interposition of this power is called for, not only by principles of a firm and energetic conduct, on the part of the General Government, but by the indispensable duty, which the constitution & the laws prescribe, to the Executive of the UStates.

In This conclusion, Your Excellency's discernment on mature reflection cannot it is presumed, fail to acquiesce: nor can it refuse its concurrence in the opinion which The President entertains, that he may reasonably expect, when called for, the zealous cooperation of the Militia of Pensylvania—that as citizens, friends to law and order, they may comply with the call without anything that can be properly denominated "a *passive* obedience to the *mandates* of Government," and that as freemen, judging rightly of the cause & nature of the service proposed to them, they will feel themselves under the most sacred of obligations to accept & to perform it with alacrity. The theory of our political institutions knows no difference between the obligations of our Citizens in such a case, whether it relate to the Govermt. of the Union or of a State—and it is hoped & confided that a difference will be as little known to their affections or opinions.

Your Excellency it is also presumed will as little doubt on the like mature reflection, that in such a case the President could not, without an abdication of the undoubted rights and authorities of the UStates & of his duty, postpone the measures for which the laws of the UStates provide to a previous experiment of the plan, which is delineated in your letter.

The People of the UStates have established a Government for the management of their general interests. They have instituted Executive Organs for administering that Government and their Representatives have established the rules by which those Organs are to act. When their authority in that of their Government is attacked, by lawless combinations of the citizens of part of a state, they could never be expected to approve, that the care of vindicating their authority, of enforcing their laws should be transferred from the Officers of their own Government to those of a State—and this to wait the issue of a process so indeterminate in its duration, as that which it is proposed to pursue; comprehending a further and full experiment of the Judiciary authority of the State, a proclamation "to declare the sentiments of its Government, announce a determination to prosecute and punish offenders, and to exhort the Citizens at large to pursue a peaceable & patriotic conduct"—the sending of Commissioners "to address those who have embarked in the present Combinations, upon the lawless nature & ruinous tendency of their proceedings, to inculcate the necessity of an immediate return to the duty, which they owe their Country & to promise, as far as the state is concerned, forgiveness of their past transactions, upon receiving a satisfactory assurance that in future they will submit to the laws"—and finally a call of the Legislature of Pensylvania, "that the ultimate means of subduing the spirit of Insurrection and of restoring tranquillity and order may be prescribed by their wisdom & authority." [12]

If there were no other objection to a transfer of this kind, the very important difference, which is supposed to exist in the nature and consequences of the Offences that have been committed in the contemplation of the laws of the UStates & of those of Pensylvania—would alone be a very serious obstacle.

The paramount considerations, which forbid an acquiescence in this course of proceeding—render it unnecessary to discuss the probability of its success; else it might have been proper to test the considerations, which have been mentioned as a ground of hope, by the inquiry what was the precise extent of the success of the past experiment—& especially whether the execution of the Revenue laws of Pensylvania within the scene in question was truly & effectually accomplished by them—or whether they did not rather terminate in a tacit compromise, by which appearances only were served.

You are already, Sir, advised, that The President yielding to the impressions which have been stated, has determined to take measures for calling forth the Militia; and that These measures contemplate the assembling a body of between twelve & thirteen thousand men from Pensylvania & the neighbouring States of Virginia Maryland & New Jersey. The recourse thus early to the Militia of the neighbouring States proceeds from a probability of the insufficiency of that of Pensylvania alone to accomplish the object; your Excellency having in your conference with the President confirmed the conclusion, which was deducible from the known local and other circumstances of the State, by the frank and explicit declaration which you made of your conviction of that insufficiency, in reference to the number which could be expected to be drawn forth for the purpose.[13]

But while the President has conceived himself to be under an indispensable obligation to prepare for that eventual resort, he has still consulted the sentiment of regret, which he expressed to you, at the possible necessity of an appeal to arms; & to avert it, if prac-

12. The quotations in this paragraph are from Mifflin's letter to Washington of August 5, 1794. See note 2.

13. See "Conference Concerning the Insurrection in Western Pennsylvania," August 2, 1794.

ticable, as well as to manifest his attention to the principle, that "a firm and energetic conduct does not preclude the exercise of a prudent and humane policy" [14] he has (as you have been also advised) concluded upon the measure of sending himself Commissioners to the discontented counties to make one more experiment of a conciliatory appeal to the reason, virtue & patriotism of their Inhabitants,[15] and has also signified to you how agreeable would be to him your cooperation in the same expedient, which you have been pleased to afford. It can scarcely be requisite to add, that there is nothing he has more at heart, than that the issue of this experiment, by establishing the authority of the laws, may preclude the always calamitous necessity of an appeal to arms. It would plant a thorn in the remainder of his path through life to have been obliged to employ force against fellow Citizens, for giving solidity and permanency to blessings, which it has been his greatest happiness, to cooperate with them in procuring for a much loved Country.

The President receives with much pleasure the assu[r]ance you have repeated to him, that whatever requisition he may make, whatever duty he may impose, in pursuance of his constitutional and legal powers, will on your part be promptly undertaken and faithfully discharged; and acknowleging, as an earnest of this and even more, the measures of cooperation which you are pursuing, he assures you in return, that he relies fully on the most cordial aid and support from you in every way, which the constitutions of the UStates & of Pensylvania shall authorise and present or future exigencies may require.

And he requests that you will construe, with a reference to this assurance of his confidence, whatever remarks may have been made in the course of this Reply to your letter, if it shall have happened that any of them have erred through a misconception of the sentiments and views which you may have meant to communicate.[16]

14. This is a quotation from Mifflin's letter to Washington of August 5, 1794. See note 2.

15. For information on the appointment of the commissioners, see H and Knox to Washington, August 5, 1794, note 3.

16. On a page attached to this letter H wrote the following note to George Taylor, Jr., Department of State chief clerk: "The Secretary of State desired that this Letter might be sent to Mr. Taylor for copying. As from its conditions mistakes will be easy Mr. Taylor after copying will please to sent it with the draft to Mr. H for examination. AH."

With perfect respect & esteem I have the honor to be Sir Your Excellency Most Obedient & most humble servant

His Excellency Thomas Mifflin Esq
Governor of Pensylvania

To John Quincy Adams[1]

Treasury Department August 8th. 1794

Sir,

You will find herewith sundry Documents marked A, B, C, D, E, F, G, & H—A being a copy of the Presidents Power to me to conduct certain loans, directed by two Acts of Congress therein referred to,[2] B a Copy of a power from me to Messrs. Wilhem and Jan Willinks & Nicholas & Jacob Van Staphorst & Hubbard predicated upon that of the President to me,[3] C a copy of a power from me to Mr. Short founded also upon the Presidents power to me,[4] D a copy of my general instructions to Mr Short transmitted with that power,[5] E a list of the Loans which have been effected under these powers,[6] F a Power from me to Messrs. Wilhem & Jan Willinks & Nicholas & Jacob Van Staphorst & Hubbard authorising them to make a Loan not exceeding one Million of Dollars for the purposes of an Act entitled "An Act making further provision for the expenses attend-

LS, Adams Family Papers, deposited in the Massachusetts Historical Society, Boston.

1. Adams had been appointed United States Minister Resident at The Hague on May 30, 1794 (*Executive Journal*, I, 159), replacing William Short, who had also been in charge of the negotiations of United States loans abroad. Short had been transferred to Madrid. Adams did not leave the United States for his new post until September 15, 1794.

2. For this power, dated August 28, 1790, see George Washington to H, first letter of August 28, 1790.

3. This power, dated August 28, 1790, is printed as an enclosure to H to Willink, Van Staphorst, and Hubbard, August 28, 1790.

4. See "Commission to William Short," September 1, 1790, enclosed in H to Short, September 1, 1790.

5. H to Short, September 1, 1790.

6. The document originally enclosed as "E" has not been found. In it H had inadvertently omitted one of the Holland loans (see H to Adams, August 9, 1794). The corrected statement is entitled "Schedule of Monies borrowed in Holland and at Antwerp, on Account of the United States, pursuant to two Acts of Congress of the 4th. and 12th. of August 1790" (copy, Adams Family Papers, deposited in the Massachusetts Historical Society). According to this schedule, the amount borrowed through the various Holland loans and the Antwerp loan was 23,550,000 guilders.

ing the intercourse of the United States with foreign Nations and further to continue in force the Act entitled "An Act providing the means of Intercourse between the United States and foreign Nations" [7] G a copy of my instructions respecting the execution of that power,[8] H a power from me to you to make such further Loans as are authorised by those Acts and as the public Service does or shall require.[9]

These papers are intended to give you a general outline of the business. The instruction to Mr Short will serve to communicate ruling ideas which appeared to me proper to regulate the course of it. But subsequent circumstances have rendered many of the suggestions there inapplicable to the actual posture of things. In fact no Loan is to be made without further special instruction except that to which the Documents F & G relate.

This as well as the future ones which may be directed, you will consider as subject to your superintendence, as our Commissioners at Amsterdam will be informed. The instruction to them will in this particular be your guide. In the situation in which this object has been placed, you will easily appreciate what propriety towards those Gentlemen demands. And in general I may observe respecting them, that while you ought not to lose sight of the possibility of their having sometimes a personal interest, different from that of the Government, you ought to consider them as men who have established a well founded Claim to its confidence.

In the future progress of things it is probable that the subject here by committed to you will again become of great importance and delicacy & you will of course take pains to possess yourself of all requisite and useful information.

With the truest Wishes for your Success & happiness & with much personal consideration and Esteem,

I have the honor to be Sir, Your most Obedient Servant

Alexander Hamilton
Secy of the Treasy

John Q Adams Esquire
Minister Resident from the United States
at the Hague

7. 1 *Stat.* 345 (March 20, 1794). This power is enclosed in H to Willink, Van Staphorst, and Hubbard, July 7, 1794.

8. See H to Willink, Van Staphorst, and Hubbard, July 7, 1794.

9. See enclosure.

[ENCLOSURE][10]

[Philadelphia, August 8, 1794]

To all to whom these Presents shall come.

Whereas by an Act passed the fourth day of August in this present year, intitled "An Act making provision for the debt of the United States"[11] it is among other things enacted that The President of the United States be authorised to cause to be borrowed on behalf of the United States a Sum or Sums not exceeding in the whole Twelve Millions of Dollars, and that so much of that Sum as may be necessary to the discharge of the said Arrears and Installments and (if it can be effected upon terms advantageous to the United States) to the paying off the whole of the said foreign debt, be appropriated solely to those purposes, and that the President be moreover further authorised to cause to be made such other Contracts respecting the said debt as shall be found for the Interest of the said States; provided nevertheless That no engagement nor Contract shall be entered into, which shall preclude the United States from reimbursing any sum or sums borrowed within fifteen years, after the same shall have been lent or advanced. And whereas by another Act passed the Twelfth day of August in the present year, intitled "An Act making provision for the reduction of the public debt"[12] it is also among other things enacted that the President of the United States be authorised to cause to be borrowed on behalf of the United States a sum or sums not exceeding in the whole Two Millions of Dollars at an Interest not exceeding five per Cent.

And Whereas by Virtue of the said several Acts The President of the United States of America hath been pleased by a certain Commission or Warrant under his hand to authorise and empower the Secretary of the Treasury for the time being, by himself or any other Person or Persons to borrow on behalf of the United States within the said States or elsewhere, a sum or sums not exceeding in the whole Fourteen Millions of Dollars, and to make or cause to be

10. Copy, Adams Family Papers, deposited in the Massachusetts Historical Society.

11. This act was passed August 4, 1790 (1 *Stat.* 138–44).

12. This act was passed August 12, 1790 (1 *Stat.* 186–87).

made for that purpose such Contract or Contracts as shall be necessary and for the Interest of the said States; subject to the restrictions and limitations in the said several Acts contained.[13]

And Whereas by an Instrument under my hand and the seal of the Treasury bearing date of the Twenty eight day of August One Thousand Seven hundred and Ninety reciting as above recited, I did by Virtue of the Commission, power or Warrant aforesaid, Authorise and empower Messrs. Wilhem & Jan Willink and Nicholas and Jacob Van Staphorst and Hubbard to borrow on behalf of the United States, a sum or sums not exceeding in the whole Three Millions of Florins subject to the restrictions and limitations in the said several Acts contained and above recited.[14]

And Whereas by another Instrument under my hand and the Seal of the Treasury bearing date the first of September One Thousand Seven hundred and Ninety and reciting as above recited. I did likewise by Virtue of the said Commission, Power or Warrant Authorise and empower William Short Charge des Affaires of the United States at the Court of France, to borrow on behalf of the United States in any part of Europe a sum or Sums not exceeding in the whole fourteen Millions of Dollars and to make or cause to be made for that purpose such Contract or Contracts as shall be necessary and for the Interests of the said States; subject to the restrictions and limitations in the said Several Acts contained.[15]

And Whereas sundry loans amounting together to Twenty Three Millions five hundred & fifty Thousand Current Guilders have been effected pursuant to the Powers aforesaid.

And whereas the said William Short is no longer in a Situation to execute the Power and Authority to him given as aforesaid, but John Q Adams Esquire hath been appointed Minister Resident of the United States at the Court of the Hague, and it hath pleased the President of the United States, that he should be charged with the business of superintending and making such further loans as the public service may require, pursuant to the Acts aforesaid.

Now therefore know ye that I Alexander Hamilton Secretary of the Treasury of the United States for the time being, by Virtue of

13. See note 2.
14. See note 3.
15. See note 4.

the said Commission, Power or Warrant of the President of the United States of America have authorised and empowered, and by these presents do authorise and empower John Q Adams Esquire Minister Resident of the United States at the Court of the Hague to borrow on behalf of the United States in any part of Europe a sum or sums which together with the sum or sums heretofore borrowed by Virtue of the Powers and Authorities heretofore given pursuant to the said Acts, shall not exceed on the whole fourteen Millions of Dollars and to make or cause to be made for that purpose Such Contract or Contracts as shall be necessary and for the Interests of the said States; subject to the restriction and limitations in the Said Several Acts contained.

And for so doing this shall be your sufficient Warrant.

In Testimony whereof I have caused the seal of the Treasury to be affixed to these presents and have hereunto subscribed my hand the Eighth day of August in the year of our Lord 1794

Alexander Hamilton
Secretary of the Treasy

In presence of
Edward Jones

To William Bradford[1]

Philadelphia Aug 8. 1794

My Dear Sir

Your letter by express duly came to hand.[2] The separate power[3] has I understand been dispatched.

General Nevil[4] suggests that if a disposition to comply should appear, the best proof of it would be a request from the parties to Mr. Johnson to resume the exercise of his Office with assurances of support from them.[5] This idea is well worth your attention; though I do not expect you will approach that point.

The repeal of the law[6] is out of the question. The expectation of it can in no event be encouraged but if any alterations are suggested tending to render it in any respect more convenient assurances of the favourable consideration of these may be given as far as it is safe for the Executive to go & with the due guards. For in truth every admissible accommodation in this way would accord with the wishes of this Department.

With prayers for your health & success I remain truly Yrs

A Hamilton

Wm. Bradford Esqr

ALS, Historical Society of Pennsylvania, Philadelphia.

1. For background to this letter, see H and Henry Knox to George Washington, August 5, 1794, note 3. See also "Deposition of Francis Mentges," August 1, 1794; "Conference Concerning the Insurrection in Western Pennsylvania," August 2, 1794; H to Washington, August 2, 5, 1794; Edmund Randolph to Thomas Mifflin, August 7, 1794.

2. Bradford to Randolph, August 8, 1794 (ALS, Pennsylvania Miscellany, Whiskey Rebellion, Vol. I, Library of Congress).

3. In his letter to Randolph of August 8, 1794, Bradford requested a "separate [that is, separate from the instructions which had been sent] & general power to confer with any bodies of men or individuals for the purpose of allaying discontents and restoring order & the authority of the laws. . . ." On the same day, Randolph sent to Washington a copy of Bradford's request, urging that "The separate powers, which he asks, tho' they cannot with propriety be demanded by insurgents, will be forwarded by a special messenger, to gratify him, if the two other Secretaries approve of them" (LS, RG 59, Miscellaneous Letters, 1790–1799, National Archives). Washington responded affirmatively to Randolph on the same date (ALS, RG 59, Miscellaneous Letters, 1790–1799, National Archives). On August 10, 1794, Bradford wrote to Randolph that he had received the powers he had requested, and as a result the insurgents could not question the authority of the commissioners (ALS, Pennsylvania Miscellany, Whiskey Rebellion, Vol. I, Library of Congress).

4. John Neville, inspector of the revenue for Survey No. 4 in Pennsylvania. See "Deposition of Francis Mentges," August 1, 1794, note 2.

5. Robert Johnson, collector of the revenue for the counties of Washington and Allegheny in Pennsylvania, had resigned his office on July 20, 1794. Johnson's resignation reads as follows: "Finding the opposition to the revenue law more violent than I expected, regreting the mischief that has been done, and may from the continuation of measures—feeling the opposition changed from dignified rabble to a respectable party, think it my duty and do resign my commission" (*Pennsylvania Archives*, 2nd ser., IV, 71). For Johnson's earlier experiences with the insurgents, see H to Washington, August 5, 1794, note 18.

6. For legislation concerning the excise, see H to Washington, August 5, 1794, note 2.

From Tench Coxe

T: D: R O August 8th 1794

Sir

In the present deranged state of things, there appears little probability of obtaining a timely supply for 1795 of spirits lawfully distilled in the western survey of Pennsylvania, and there is a manifest possibility that like causes may prevent such a supply from Kentucky & the Western Survey of Virginia. It therefore becomes a matter of importance, that such eventual arrangements should be made as will *ensure* to the Western Army the necessary quantity of distilled spirits. The point to be considered is whether the whole shall be procured from the places in which spirits are permitted to be lawfully distilled Vizt. Virginia & Kentucky.

I have the honor to be your mo obedt. Servt.

Tench Coxe Commissr.

The Secy. of the Treasy.

LC, RG 75, Letters of Tench Coxe, Commissioner of the Revenue, Relating to the Procurement of Military, Naval, and Indian Supplies, National Archives.

To Elizabeth Hamilton[1]

Philadelphia Aug 8. 1794

I just take up my pen My Dear Eliza to assure you of all our health & of our continual & fervent prayers for you & those with you. Your last letter[2] and one from Doctor Stringer[3] have been received. The latter gave me hopes; though I shall tremble as often as I open a letter from Albany till My Darling boys situation has become more decided. God of his infinite mercy grant that he may be preserved to us.

Adieu My Love

Thank the Doctor for his kind letter.

AL, Hamilton Papers, Library of Congress.

1. For background to this letter, see H to George Washington, July 11, 23, 1794; Washington to H, July 11, 1794; H to Elizabeth Hamilton, July 31, August 2, 1794.

2. Letter not found.

3. Dr. Samuel Stringer was an Albany physician. His letter to H has not been found.

From Henry Knox

[*Philadelphia, August 8, 1794.* On August 12, 1794, Tench Coxe wrote to Samuel Hodgdon:[1] "I have just received from the secy. of the Treasy a letter to him of the 8th. inst. from the Secy. at War, containing a requisition of certain articles." [2] *Letter not found.*]

1. Hodgdon was commissary of military stores. See Knox to H, June 20, 1794.
2. LC, RG 75, Letters of Tench Coxe, Commissioner of the Revenue, Relating to the Procurement of Military, Naval, and Indian Supplies, National Archives.

From Henry Knox

War Department, Accountant's Office, August 8, 1794. "I have the honor to inclose you an abstract of pay due the dismounted Infantry for the defensive protection of the Territory south west of the Ohio . . . in 1793 and part of 1794, an estimate of expenses and for pay of the Federal troops in that Quarter, also an estimate of the ordinary expenses of Government for Governor Blount [1] for the year 1794. . . ."

LC, RG 93, Letter Book, 1794, National Archives.
1. William Blount was governor of the Territory South of the Ohio River.

To John Quincy Adams

Treasury Department August 9th. 1794

Sir,

Upon a revision of the Loans, which have been made under the Acts of Congress of the 4th. & 12th. of August 1790,[1] I have discovered, that a loan for One Millions of Guilders, made the 1st. of June 1793, is not upon the list marked E, accompanying the other papers, mentioned in my letter to you of the 8th. Instant.[2]

In consequence of this omission, the sum already borrowed in pursuance of the said Acts, will amount to twenty three millions five hundred & fifty thousand Guilders, in place of Twenty two millions five hundred & fifty thousand as stated in the list and as inserted in the power [3] from me to you. To give accuracy therefore, to the documents respecting this business I have transmitted to you herewith, a correct list of the Loans already made with a new power executed in form upon the receipt of which you will be pleased to cancel the other power and return it with the imperfect list under cover to me.

I have the Honor to be with great respect Sir Your Most Obedient Servant A Hamilton

John Q. Adams Esquire
Minister Resident from
the United States
at the Hague.

LS, Adams Family Papers, deposited in the Massachusetts Historical Society, Boston.

1. "An Act making provision for the (payment of the) Debt of the United States" (1 *Stat.* 138–44 [August 4, 1790]); "An Act making Provision for the Reduction of the Public Debt" (1 *Stat.* 186–87 [August 12, 1790]).

2. See H to Adams, August 8, 1794, note 6.

3. See the enclosure to H to Adams, August 8, 1794.

From Tench Coxe

Treasury Department, Revenue Office, August 9, 1794. Calls attention to his letters of May 24, February 18, March 11, and April 19, 1794, "which have been transmitted or communicated to you for the purpose of obtaining the Decision of the President."

LC, RG 26, Lighthouse Letters, Vol. I, National Archives; LC, RG 75, Letters of Tench Coxe, Commissioner of the Revenue, Relating to the Procurement of Military, Naval, and Indian Supplies, National Archives.

From Tench Coxe[1]

Treasury Department, Revenue Office, August 9, 1794. "Brown & Francis & Co. having agreed to make one hundred & twenty eight pieces of Iron cannon,[2] I have to request that you will possess the supervisor of Rhode Island[3] of the sum of 5400 Dollars which is to be paid them in advance."[4]

LC, RG 75, Letters of Tench Coxe, Commissioner of the Revenue, Relating to the Procurement of Military, Naval, and Indian Supplies, National Archives.

1. For information concerning the fortifications and the naval armament, see Henry Knox to H, March 29, April 21, 1794. See also H to Coxe, April 4, 1794.

2. A copy of the articles of agreement between Coxe on behalf of the United States and "John Brown, John Francis, and Rufus Hopkins, Nicholas Power, Obadiah Brown, Brown, Benson, and Ives, and Jabez Bowen, being the owners of the furnace Hope," dated August 8, 1794, may be found in the Massachusetts

Historical Society, Boston. The contract is printed in *ASP, Naval Affairs*, I, 53–54. See also Coxe to H, June 27, 1794.

3. John S. Dexter.

4. On August 9, 1794, Coxe wrote to Dexter: "I enclose to you a contract . . . with Brown Francis and others, owners of and agents for the Furnace Hope, for one hundred & twenty-eight pieces of Iron cannon, executed by me. . ." (LC, RG 75, Letters of Tench Coxe, Commissioner of the Revenue, Relating to the Procurement of Military, Naval, and Indian Supplies, National Archives). On the same day he notified Brown and Francis that the "sum of 5400 dollars will be lo[d]ged in Mr. Dextors hands. . ." (LC, Letters of Tench Coxe, Commissioner of the Revenue, Relating to the Procurement of Military, Naval, and Indian Supplies, National Archives).

From Jonathan Dayton[1]

Elizabethtown [*New Jersey*] *August 9, 1794.* "Will you be so obliging as to turn your attention immediately to the subject of Judge Symmes's purchase between the Miamis, in order to have the different writings prepared for executing upon his arrival in Philadelphia, which will be in four or five days? . . ."[2]

ALS, Hamilton Papers, Library of Congress.

1. Dayton was a member of the House of Representatives from New Jersey.

For information concerning John Cleves Symmes's purchase of western lands, see H to William Rawle, January 6, 1793; March 13, June 21, 1794; Dayton to H, June 26, 1794.

2. Symmes arrived in Philadelphia in August, and on September 30, 1794, he wrote to Dayton: "I was last week several times with Mr. Secretary Hamilton and Atty. Genl. Bradford on the subject of the Miami patent. Some parts of the proposed form I do not fully approve, but rather than state objections which might work delay, I agree to waive every thing that might retard. I expected to have heard of the signing of the patent yesterday or to-day, but have not heard a word tho' I have been several times at the office" (Beverley W. Bond, Jr., *The Correspondence of John Cleves Symmes, Founder of the Miami Purchase* [New York, 1926], 166). On the same date, George Washington signed a patent for the 311,682 acres for which Symmes had paid (Carter, *Territorial Papers*, II, 496–98).

On October 1, 1794, William Bradford wrote to Edmund Randolph: "Judge Symmes having stated certain objections to the following words introduced into the draught expressing his consent to the alteration of his Contract with the Board of Treasury viz 'in & to the first mentioned contract so as aforesd. made with the said Samuel Osgood Walter Livingston & Arthur Lee Commissioners of the said Board of Treasury.'

"I am of opinion that they may safely be struck out and that the residue will be a substantial compliance with instructions given, & with the intention of the President." (ALS, RG 60, General Records of the Department of Justice, Letters from and Opinions of Attorneys General, 1791–1811, National Archives.) On October 2, 1794, Randolph informed Washington of the contents of Bradford's letter of October 1 (LS, RG 59, Miscellaneous Letters, 1790–1799, National Archives).

From Isaac Holmes[1]

[*Charleston, South Carolina, August 9, 1794.* On September 4, 1794, Hamilton wrote to Holmes acknowledging "the receipt of your letter of the 9th of August." *Letter not found.*]

1. Holmes was collector of customs at Charleston, South Carolina.

To Tench Coxe

[*Philadelphia*] *August 10, 1794.* "Mr. Hamilton wishes to see Mr. Coxe at his house tomorrow Morning as early as may be not exceeding 9 oClock."

AL, RG 58, General Records, 1791–1803, National Archives.

From Jeremiah Olney[1]

Custom House
District of Providence 11th Augt. 1794.

Sir.

On the 24th April last I had the Honor of Transmitting for your information Sundry Documents relative to the Suits of Messrs. Arnold and Dexter[2] against me: my not hearing from you, Since, on that Subject, and as the Court meets in this Town on the 15th Septr. next, when Damages are to be assessed—I am induced to enclose a letter from Mr. Barnes[3] to me, relative to his Idea of the Future Management of those Suits and respectfully to ask your advice & Instructions as to the Ultimate mode of Defence thereof, and to say *with Deference*, that I am in Sentiment with Mr. Barnes (Since a favourable Change in the Court has taken place) of Petitioning the Genl. Assembly for a New Trial. As there Seems to be no new points to be Stated before the Court in the assessment of Damages, I have deemed it inexpedient for the United States to be at any Further Expence for Counsil in the Defence of these Suits, than what will accrue in the employment of Messrs. Barnes & Eddy,[4] but whatever instructions (in respect to this, or the ultimate modes of Conducting the Suits) you may please to Communicate shall attentively be carried into Execution.

I have the Honor to be &c. Jereh. Olney Collr.

Alexander Hamilton Esqr.
Secretary of the Treasury.

ADfS, Rhode Island Historical Society, Providence.

1. For background to this letter, see Olney to H, November 7, 15, 28, December 10, 13, 27, 1792, March 14, 25, April 15, 25, September 23, October 7, 21, November 21, 1793, February 17, March 31, April 14, first letter of April 24, May 5, 1794; H to Olney, November 27, 1792, November 7, 1793, March 19, April 24, 1794.

2. Welcome Arnold and Edward Dexter.

3. David Leonard Barnes.

4. Samuel Eddy had served as clerk of the Rhode Island Supreme Court from 1790 to 1793.

From John Quincy Adams[1]

New York August 12 1794

Sir

I have just received your favor of the 9th inst. with the inclosures, and agreeable to your directions, herewith return the former power cancelled, and the previous Schedule marked E.

The word "your" instead of "his" sufficient Warrant, used at the close of the present, as well as the former power, is I presume not sufficiently material to need an alteration.

I have the honor to be with the highest Respect Sir your very humble & obedient Servant

LC, Adams Family Papers, deposited in the Massachusetts Historical Society, Boston.

1. For background to this letter, see H to Adams, August 8, 9, 1794.

From Tench Coxe[1]

Treasury Department, Revenue Office, August 12, 1794. "Mr. Coxe . . . will be glad to have the remittance of 5000 Dolls. transmitted to each of the Naval agents, who have not had that sum. Mr. Blagge[2] of N York & Messr. Sterret[3] of Baltimore have applied so lately as this day & yesterday for a payment on account. Mr. Coxe's reply to the Secrys enquiry[4] was sent the 2d instant."

LC, RG 75, Letters of Tench Coxe, Commissioner of the Revenue, Relating to the Procurement of Military, Naval, and Indian Supplies, National Archives.

1. For background to this letter, see Henry Knox to H, April 21, June 25, July 19, 1794.

2. John Blagge.

3. Samuel and Joseph Sterett.

4. Letter not found.

To Tench Coxe

[*Philadelphia*] *August 12, 1794.* "Mr. Hamilton requests Mr Coxe to call at his house as soon as he comes in this Morning."

AL, RG 58, General Records, 1791–1803, National Archives.

To Elizabeth Hamilton[1]

[Philadelphia, August 12, 1794]

Your letters, my beloved Eliza, have been regularly received[2] & I thank you much for your punctuality fatigued as you are with our precious infant. Would to heaven I were with you but alas 'tis impossible. My fervent prayers are not wanting that God will support you & rescue our loved Child.

I believe the course you are pursuing is as good a one as can be pursued—though I am somewhat afraid of the relaxing effect of the laudanum. I think well of the lime water but I count most on exercise and nourishment. Your letter of the 7th[3] alarms me, in which you say he does not gain strength & that he was not so well as he had been. Yet I hope something from the favourable change of the weather.

You wish to hasten your return to me. Alas My Betsey how much I wish you with me. But I really hope more from the climate you are in than from this. Besides how could you without assistance make such a journey with our dear lamb without exposing him & yourself too much. I pray heaven that he may grow better & that you may be so far relieved as to benefit by your native air. My anxiety on your account is little less than for our dear Child.

Receive my most tender and affectionate wishes for you both. They are all I can now offer—Hard hard situation. A Hamilton

I can advise you nothing better than to pursue the Doctor's advice.

Aug. 12. 1794

ALS, Hamilton Papers, Library of Congress.

1. For background to this letter, see H to George Washington, July 11, 23, 1794; Washington to H, July 11, 1794; H to Elizabeth Hamilton, July 31, August 2, 8, 1794.

2. Letters not found.

3. Letter not found.

To Elizabeth Hamilton[1]

[Philadelphia] August 12, 1794

I wrote to you my beloved Eliza by the post of to day. My heart cannot cease to ach till I hear some more favourable account from you. I sit down to write such further thoughts as have occurred.

If my darling child is better when this reaches you persevere in the plan which has made him so. If he is worse—abandon the laudanum & try the cold bath—that is abandon the laudanum by degrees giving it over night but not in the morning—& then leaving it off altogether. Let the water be put in the Kitchen over night & in the morning let the child be dipped in it head foremost wrapping up his head well & taking him again immediately out, put in flannel & rubbed dry with towels. Immediately upon his being taken out let him have two tea spoons full of brandy mixed with just enough water to prevent its taking away his breath.

Observe well his lips. If a glow succeeds continue the bath. If a chill takes place forbear it. If a glow succeeds the quantity of brandy may be lessened after the first experiment.

Try the bark at the same time in tincture about mid day, but if this disagrees discontinue it.

When you exercise him, if he can bear it, give him eight or ten Miles at a time.

Shew this letter to your father & tell the Doctor of the advice I have given. But if the child be certainly worse do not easily be persuaded from the course I advise.

May heaven direct you & bless the means which shall be used. My love to all the family.

Yrs. ever Affect A Hamilton

Mrs E Hamilton

ALS, Hamilton Papers, Library of Congress.

1. For background to this letter, see H to George Washington, July 11, 23, 1794; Washington to H, July 11, 1794; H to Elizabeth Hamilton, July 31, August 2, 8, first letter of August 12, 1794.

From Joseph Howell, Junior

War Department, Accountant's Office, August 12, 1794. Requests the Treasury to provide five thousand dollars for various expenses of the War Department.

LC, RG 93, Letter Book, 1794, National Archives.

To George Washington[1]

[Philadelphia, August 12, 1794]

The Secretary of the Treasury presents his respects to the President & sends him two letters which were received last night from Pittsburgh.[2]

Would it not be adviseable to put the Garrison of Fort Franklin[3] in the power of Major Butler, so that if he deems it advisable he may draw a part of it to his aid?

An attack from the Indians appears at present improbable,[4] & an attack from the Insurgents probable enough.

The bearer[5] of the letters waits orders to return. Will The President suggest anything?

August 12. 1794

LC, George Washington Papers, Library of Congress.

1. For background to this letter, see "Deposition of Francis Mentges," August 1, 1794; "Conference Concerning the Insurrection in Western Pennsylvania," August 2, 1794; H to Washington, August 2, 5, 1794; H and Henry Knox to Washington, August 2, 1794.

2. On August 12, 1794, John Stagg, Jr., chief clerk in the War Department, wrote to Knox: "An express arrived here last night from Pittsburg with letters from Col [Thomas] Butler and Major [Isaac] Craig dated the 3d. instant. . . . Col Butler is threatened with proscription, and that if the President does not remove him and his garrison, that they [the insurgents] will burn the Fort" (ALS, Henry Knox Papers, Massachusetts Historical Society, Boston). Butler's letter to Knox has not been found. Craig's letter, which was written at Fort Fayette, Pittsburgh, reads as follows: "On the 1st Instant a numerous body of armed men assembled on Bradock's Fields about nine miles from this place, and Continued there til yesterday morning, their numbers increasing it is asserted, to four thousand five hundred, being Joined by a number of the Inhabitants of Pittsburg, commenced their march about nine OClock, & it was Confidently reported with a design of attacking the Fort, but some of their leaders being informed that every possible means had been adopted for its defence, they Prudently concluded to postpone the attack to some more favourable Oppertunity, & Sent a flag to inform the Commandant that they intended to march Peaceably past the Fort into Pittsburg, & then cross the monongahela & Return

home. Major Butler intimated to the flag that their peaceable intentions would be evinced by their Passing the Fort at a proper distance; they therefore took another road into Town, (Having as they asserted accomplished the object of their assembling Viz forming a union with the inhabitants of Pittsburg, Banishing some Gentlemen inimical to their Cause and proscribing several Others who are also Obliged to leave this Country in a few days.) When there Committed several excesses Crossed the River, Burned a barn & a large quantity of Grain in stacks the property of Major [Abraham] Kirkpatrick, whom they have Banished. Colo [Presley] Neville and Genl [John] Gibson are under proscription and to leave Pittsburg immediately. I am told that I am allowed till the 12 of this month to settle my affairs at Pittsburg and then to disappear.

"On the 14th instant, an other Genl. meeting is to take place the result of which God only Knows.

"Every possible pains has been taken & is now pursued to protect the property & Support the Honor of the arms of the United States. I feel particularly happy that Major Butler Commands at this Crisis.

"The bearer Edwd OHara leaves this on foot to Prevent a suspicion of Conveying intelligence be pleased to direct means for his returning on horse Back. The arms and ammunition is all Safely Come to hand in good time." (LC, Isaac Craig Papers, Carnegie Library of Pittsburgh, Pennsylvania.)

At a town meeting held at Pittsburgh on July 31, 1794, residents of the town of Washington, Pennsylvania, had demanded that three friends of the excise (Abraham Kirkpatrick, James Brison, and Edward Day) be banished from Pittsburgh (*Pennsylvania Archives,* 2nd ser., IV, 79, 80). See "Extract from the Affidavit of William Meetkirk" in Brackenridge, *Insurrection,* 120–21, and Gabriel Blakeney to H. H. Brackenridge in Brackenridge, *Incidents,* 97–99. See also "Conference Concerning the Insurrection in Western Pennsylvania," August 2, 1794, note 8; H to Washington, August 5, 1794, note 79. The proscription of Presley Neville and John Gibson had been voted at a meeting at Braddock's Field on August 2, 1794 (*Pennsylvania Archives,* 2nd ser., IV, 158).

The reasons for the proscription of Kirkpatrick, Neville, and Gibson are explained as follows in the "Resolves of the Committee of Pitsburg respecting Genl. Gibson and Colo. P Neville": "At a meeting of the Committee (of twenty one) of the Town of Pittsburg on Monday morning 4th. Augt. 1794 Report was made to them by the Committee of four who were a part of the Committee of Battallions on Braddocks fields on 2d. Inst. Vizt. That in Committee on Braddocks fields it was stated on the part of the Committee of four that the three prescribed persons of the Town of Pittsburg Vizt. Abraham Kirkpatrick, James Brisson and Edward Day were expelled the Town and had Disappeared.

"It was then taken into view what other persons were obnoxious as being suspected of being friendly to the Excise Law as might appear from Letters by them written or otherwise, and on Certain letters being read which had been intercepted in the Mail from Pittsburg to Philadelphia Vizt. One from Colo. Presley Neville to his Father containing in a certain paragraph words unfavourable to the opposers of the Excise Law tho' no persons in particular were mentioned, but this being considered a sufficient Evidence of his enmity to the cause it was resolved that he should be expelled the Country within ten days.

"Also one letter from Genl. John Gibson to the Governor of Pennsylvania which in a certain paragraph evinced a like disposition by a mistatement made by him in information which information was thought not to be exact and which he had too hastily credited, it was resolved that he should be subject to the like sentence and that the Committee of Pittsburg should carry into effect these measures necessary for the public safety.

"Resolved therefore that notice of their respective sentences be forthwith given to these persons and they depart accordingly and that a Guard be ordered for each of them to conduct them to a proper distance.

"Resolved also that a Copy of this minute be given to each of those present as a passport from the Country." (Copy, RG 59, Miscellaneous Letters, 1790–1799, National Archives; copy, Connecticut Historical Society, Hartford.) This document is printed in *Pennsylvania Archives,* 2nd ser., IV, 158–59.

Gibson enclosed the resolves in a letter to Edmund Randolph, dated August 14, 1794, which reads: "At the request of Judge [Jasper] Yates and Mr. [William] Bradford I do myself the honour of informing you, that I met them on Tuesday Morning ten Miles East of Bedford. They desired me to inclose the written papers which I recd. from the Committee of Pitsburg, and to give you every other Information respecting the Western Country which I might possess.

"I left Pitsburg on Friday last, and had a guard of three of the Committee to the Border of Westmoreland County. They then returned, and on my arrival at Greensburg, I found a number of people collected there, in order to Choose delegates to attend the Genl. Meeting this day at Parkinsons on the Monangohela River. They Surrounded the house, and told me that they would allow me half an hour to refresh myself and that I must quit the town or abide the Consequences. I then left them and came a short distance on this side the town.

"I had some hopes of Being able to remain there a day or two in order to Wait for Colo. P. Neville who was to have overtaken me there, and to have learned the disposition of the people of that County, But was prevented as Before mentioned. I am sorry to have to add, that from the Choice the people have made to represent them at the General Meeting, little good is to be Expected, the men that have Been chosen are generally the most violent of any in the Country. I wish they may Even treat the Commissioners with Common decency. The[y] say Nothing less than a repeal of the Excise Law will Satisfy them, and that unless they can obtain that they will join the British or the Savages. I shall remain here until I know the Result of the Genl. Meeting, as I have left my family and everything Dear to me at Pitsburg. Should anything offer in which I can render any Service to my Country at the Risque of my Life and Fortune you may Command me. [David] Bradford, who headed the Column that Marched thro the town of Pitsburg, harangued the people, and informed them that he woud Write to Washington to remove Butler, and that if he did not Comply with his request he would remove him and take the Fort. . . ." (LS, RG 59, Miscellaneous Letters, 1790–1799, National Archives.)

3. Fort Franklin was located at the confluence of the Allegheny River and French Creek and was approximately thirty-five miles northeast of Pittsburgh.

4. Additional forces had been ordered to Fort Franklin in June, 1794, because of the threat of an Indian attack, which, however, had not materialized (*ASP, Indian Affairs,* I, 508–16).

5. Edward O'Hara. See note 2.

From George Washington

[Germantown, Pennsylvania, August 12, 1794]

The Secretary of the Treasury (acting for the Secy. of War).[1]

Your letter of the 12. did not get to my hands until my return from Philada. about an hour ago.

The Letters from Majors Butler [2] and Baif,[3] make it necessary, in my opinion, to vest discretionary orders with the former, to reinforce the Garrison at Pittsburgh with as many men from Fort Franklin, as can be drawn from it without hazarding that post too much; provided the hazard (on account of the Insurgents) may not be too great for the proposed advantage of the measure.

I sent you through the Secry. of State, two letters (of the 14 & 16 ulto.) with enclosures from Govr. Blount, which you will consider & report on.[4] Go: Washington

German town Augt. 12, 1794.

Tuesday 4 o'Clock

LC, George Washington Papers, Library of Congress.

1. In the summer of 1794, Secretary of War Henry Knox decided that it was necessary for him to go to Maine to look after his land interests there. Because the crisis over the insurrection in western Pennsylvania was reaching a climax, Knox informed Washington that he would delay his journey "or even renounce it altogether if your view of the subject should render my continuing here of public importance, although permanent pecuniary ruin or something very like it attends either the one or the other" (Knox to Washington, August 8, 1794 [ALS, George Washington Papers, Library of Congress]). Washington permitted Knox to go to Maine, and the responsibility for the administration of the War Department fell upon H until Knox's return to Philadelphia on October 5, 1794.

2. Thomas Butler.

3. Either Washington or the copyist made a mistake, for the letter in question was not from "Baif," but from Isaac Craig. See H to Washington, August 12, 1794, note 2.

4. William Blount was governor of the Territory South of the Ohio River. His letters of July 14 and 16, 1794, have not been found.

To the President, Directors, and Company of the Bank of the United States [1]

Treasury Department, August 13, 1794. "I have to request that you will be so obliging as to pay to Thomas Cumming, Attorney for Fanny Forsyth, the sum of Two thousand Dollars; being so much granted to the Widow and Children of Robert Forsyth, late Marshall for the District of Georgia, by an Act of Congress of the 7th. of June 1794. . . ." [2]

LS, Mr. Malcolm Curry, Flanders, New Jersey.

1. Thomas Willing was president of the Bank of the United States.

2. "An Act to make provision for the widow and orphan children of Robert

Forsyth" reads as follows: "That the sum of two thousand dollars be allowed to the widow of Robert Forsyth, late marshal of the district of Georgia, for the use of herself and the children of the said Robert Forsyth, to be paid in equal proportions, out of any moneys in the treasury of the United States not heretofore appropriated" (6 *Stat.* 17 [June 7, 1794]).

The following receipt appears at the bottom of this letter: "Recd the above from the Bank of the United States Aug 13th. 1794. Thos. Cumming."

To Tench Coxe

[*Philadelphia*] *August 13, 1794.* "Mr. Hamilton requests Mr. Coxe to send him the letter from Coll Neville [1] with the inclosures to complete his statement." [2]

AL, RG 58, General Records, 1791–1803, National Archives.

1. H was apparently mistaken in his reference to "Coll Neville," for the letter in question was undoubtedly that which General John Neville (rather than his son Colonel Presley Neville) wrote to Coxe on July 18, 1794. For this letter, see "Deposition of Francis Mentges," August 1, 1794, note 2, and H to George Washington, August 5, 1794, note 77.

2. H is referring to his letter to Washington of August 5, 1794. In the margin of the draft of that letter H had written several questions, and he was presumably requesting Neville's letter at this time from Coxe in order to complete his letter to Washington for publication. See H to Washington, August 6, 16, 1794.

At the bottom of this letter Coxe wrote "Sent."

To Isaac Craig [1]

Philadelphia August 13
1794

Sir

In consequence of an arrangement of the Secretary at war, who is absent,[2] your letter of the 3d. instant [3] has been communicated to me.

It is satisfactory to receive exact intelligence of the movements of the insurgents.

Your care of the interests confided to you is in every event depended upon, according to circumstances. The keeping the arms and stores out of the hands of the Insurgents is a matter of great importance. It is hoped that you will personally in the worst issue of things, find safety in the Fort.

The friends of Government may depend, that it will not be wanting to its duty and interest upon this occasion. And can there be any doubt of the sufficiency of its means?

With much esteem I am Sir Your obedient servant

Alexander Hamilton

Isaac Craig Esqr. D Q M G
Pittsburg

ALS, Isaac Craig Papers, Carnegie Library of Pittsburgh, Pennsylvania.

1 For background to this letter, see H to George Washington, August 12, 1794; Washington to H, August 12, 1794.

2. See Washington to H, August 12, 1794, note 1.

3. See H to Washington, August 12, 1794, note 2.

To William Ellery

[*Philadelphia, August 13, 1794.* On August 25, 1794, Ellery wrote to Hamilton and referred to "Your letter of the 13th. of this month." [1] *Letter not found.*]

1. Although this letter has not been found, it was similar in content to H to Jeremiah Olney, August 13, 1794. See Ellery to H, August 25, 1794, and Olney to H, August 25, 1794.

To Jeremiah Olney [1]

Treasury Department, August 13, 1794. "As great inconveniences have arisen from your discontinuing to endorse the name of your Office on your letters of a public nature; as heretofore directed [2] I have to request, that you will in future be more punctual in conforming to a regulation so necessary to the dispatch of business in my Department."

LS, Rhode Island Historical Society, Providence; copy, RG 56, Letters to the Collector at Providence, National Archives; copy, RG 56, Letters to Collectors at Small Ports, "Set G," National Archives.

1. Olney was collector of customs at Providence.

2. See "Treasury Department Circular to the Collectors of the Customs," May 10, 1792.

From Nathaniel Appleton

Boston, August 14, 1794. Requests payment of his salary as commissioner of loans in Massachusetts for the second quarter of 1794, amounting to three hundred seventy-five dollars.[1]

ALS, RG 217, Miscellaneous Treasury Accounts, 1790–1894, Account No. 5879, National Archives.

1. On August 23, 1794, Warrant No. 3878 was issued to Appleton for this amount (RG 217, Miscellaneous Treasury Accounts, 1790–1894, Account No. 5879, National Archives).

To the Executors of the Estate of Otho H. Williams[1]

[*Philadelphia, August 14, 1794.* On August 14, 1794, Hamilton wrote to Robert Purviance: "I have Judged it most adviseable to address a letter to . . . [Williams's] executors." *Letter not found.*]

1. For the executors of Williams's estate, see H to Robert Purviance, August 14, 1794, note 2. Williams had been collector of customs at Baltimore.

To Henry Jackson[1]

[*Philadelphia*] *August 14, 1794.* "A Warrant has this day issued in your favor on the Treasurer of the United States for five Thousand Dollars, which he has been directed to pay, by remitting to you a draught for a Similar amount on the Office of Discount and Deposit at Boston. This money being on account of the Frigate, intended to be built at Boston, you will receive the necessary information with respect to the application thereof from the Commissioner of the Revenue."[2] *Letter not found.*]

LS, sold at American Art Association, March 12, 1920, Lot 382.

1. Jackson was naval agent at Boston.

For information concerning the naval armament, see Henry Knox to H, April 21, 1794. See also Knox to H, second letter of June 25, July 14, 1794; Tench Coxe to H, August 2, 12, 1794.

2. On August 15, 1794, Coxe wrote to Jackson: "Your favor of the 9. instant is duly received. On the 2d inst. the Secy. of the Treasury was requested to place in the hands of each of the naval agents, the sum of five thousand dollars for present purposes. It is presumed you will have received that sum before this reaches you. When farther sums are likely to become necessary in the course of this business, You will be pleased to make a requisition to that purpose" (LC, RG 75, Letters of Tench Coxe, Commissioner of the Revenue, Relating to the Procurement of Military, Naval, and Indian Supplies, National Archives).

Text taken from extract in dealer's catalogue.

To Robert Purviance[1]

Treasury Department
August 14th 1794

Sir,

As I am at a loss to determine into whose hands the monies, Bonds and other property belonging to the United States have fallen, in consequence of the death of General Williams your predecessor in Office, I have Judged it most adviseable to address a letter to his Executors on the subject[2] and another to the Deputy Collector,[3] both of which you will find inclosed.

I have therefore to request, that immediately upon the receipt of this, you will take the necessary measures for getting into your possession all the monies and other property of the United States as aforesaid—observing to give me the earliest information thereof.

I am with consideration Sir Your most Obedient Servant

Alexander Hamilton

Robert Purviance Esquire
Collector Baltimore

LS, Columbia University Libraries.

1. Purviance had been naval officer of the port of Baltimore when Otho H. Williams was collector of customs at Baltimore. Williams died at Miller's Town, Virginia, on July 15, 1794. George Washington appointed Purviance collector on August 9, 1794 (JPP, 307). The Senate confirmed the appointment on December 11, 1794 (*Executive Journal*, I, 165).

2. Letter not found. In his will, dated June 5, 1794, Williams designated his wife, his brother Elie Williams, William Smith, and Dr. Philip Thomas as his executors (*Calendar of the General Otho Holland Williams Papers in the Maryland Historical Society* [Baltimore, 1940], 341).

3. The letter to Christopher Richmond has not been found.

From William Rawle[1]

[*Philadelphia, August 14, 1794.* The endorsement on a letter that Hamilton wrote to Rawle on July 17, 1794, reads as follows: "recd Augt. 14. answd same day." *Letter not found.*]

1. Rawle was United States attorney for the District of Pennsylvania.

To Christopher Richmond

[*Philadelphia, August 14, 1794.* On August 14, 1794, Hamilton wrote to Robert Purviance: "I have Judged it most adviseable to address a letter to . . . the Deputy Collector . . . which you will find enclosed." *Letter not found.*]

To George Washington

Treasy. Dept. August 14. 1794.

Sir,

The Attorney for the District of Virginia[1] has presented to the accounting officers of the Treasury Department, a claim against the United States for his services in attending at Norfolk by direction from the Secy. of State, in order to take depositions respecting a british vessel alledged to have been taken by a french privateer within the limits of the United States; which claim has been accordingly adjusted and the sum of sixty four dollars found due to the said Attorney.[2]

As I know of no other fund out of which this money can be paid, and as it is highly probable that similar charges for preserving the neutrality of the United States, may be presented at the Treasury, I would beg leave to suggest to the President, whether they ought not to be discharged out of the fund of twenty thousand dollars appropriated the last session of Congress, to defray the contingent charges of Government.[3] If the President should be of this opinion, he will be pleased to signify his approbation, as it relates to the Attorney for Virginia, upon the Comptroller's certificate transmitted herewith.[4]

I have also further to observe that Mr. Higginson, late Agent for the United States in the british West India Islands[5] has in pursuance of his instructions from me, approved by The President, drawn upon the Treasurer of the United States, three bills, amounting to Three thousand nine hundred & fifty Dollars, on account of the expenses attending his mission. It will be necessary therefore, in order to honor these drafts, that the President should also authorize me to pay them out of the said fund of twenty thousand Dollars.[6] This will be conformable with the course pursued in regard to the money advanced to him previous to his departure.

With the most perfect respect I have the honor to be &c.

Alexander Hamilton

LC, George Washington Papers, Library of Congress.

1. Alexander Campbell.

2. On November 11, 1793, Thomas Jefferson had written to the United States district attorneys requesting them to take depositions in cases of foreign vessels captured within United States territorial waters (LC, RG 59, Domestic Letters of the Department of State, Vol. 4, February 4, 1792–December 31, 1793, National Archives). In January, 1794, Campbell had traveled from Richmond to Norfolk, Virginia, to take depositions in the case of the British brig *Conyngham*. See "Cabinet Meeting. Opinion on Restoring the Brigs *Conyngham* and *Pilgrim* to the British," March 27, 1794, and Edmund Randolph to H, July 2, 1794.

3. "An Act making appropriations for certain purposes therein expressed" (1 *Stat.* 394–95 [June 9, 1794]).

4. On August 16, 1794, Washington "Approved the paymt. of 64 dolls. out of the Contingent fund, . . . as due by an a/c settled at the Treasury, with the Dist: Atty. of Virginia" (JPP, 308).

5. Nathaniel C. Higginson had died of yellow fever in July, 1794, while he was in the West Indies as a special agent for the United States. For Higginson's mission to the West Indies, see H to Higginson, April 16, 1794. See also "Cabinet Meeting. Opinion on a Request for a Passport," April 2, 1794; H to Washington, April 2, 1794; "Conversation with George Hammond," April 15–16, 1794.

6. On September 29, 1794, the President "Authorised the Secy. of the Treasury to pay out of the Contingent fund, the sums of 3950 Dollars, & 1863 dollars, to defray the expenses of mr. Higginson's mission" (JPP, 310).

From Jeremiah Wadsworth[1]

Hartford, August 15, 1794. "I have taken a mortgage of Col Timothy Seymour as I proposed[2] dated this day for the better security of his debt due Wadsworth & Church[3] of a good tract of Land in this Town of One & twenty acres more or less fully sufficient I believe to keep our debt which is . . . £ 800 0 0 Lawfull Money."

ALS, Connecticut Historical Society, Hartford.

1. Wadsworth, a resident of Hartford, was a member of the House of Representatives from Connecticut from 1789 to 1795.

2. See Wadsworth to H, April 25, 1794; H to Wadsworth, June 4, 1794.

3. John B. Church had been Wadsworth's partner during the American Revolution and was married to Angelica Schuyler, H's sister-in-law. H managed Church's business affairs in the United States.

To George Washington

[Philadelphia, August 15, 1794]

The Secretary of the Treasury presents his respects to The President—incloses him a letter which Mr. Coxe has just brought to him for his perusal.[1]

It is conceived that a reply may be given to this Letter, by Mr Coxe, which being published with the letter, may do good. If the President sees no objection, the idea will be pursued.[2]

Augt. 15, 1794.

It is said that papers have been received from England down to the 26. of June, which announce that the duke of york[3] & general Clairfait[4] have received a new & total defeat, their army cut to peices & the duke of york missing.[5] This was in an attempt to relieve Ypres. It is added that in consequence the Emperor has offered to purchase peace by a relinquishment of all the Low Countries.

LC, George Washington Papers, Library of Congress.

1. The letter to which H is referring was one which Hugh H. Brackenridge, a resident of Pittsburgh and a prominent figure in western Pennsylvania politics, sent to Tench Coxe on August 8, 1794. Brackenridge stated: ". . . the United States cannot effect the operation of the law in this country. It is universally odious in the neighboring parts of all the neighboring States, and the militia under the law in the hands of the President cannot be called out to reduce an opposition" (Brackenridge, *Insurrection*, 144–45). The letter is also printed in *Calendar of Virginia State Papers*, VII, 251–53.

2. On September 15, 1794, Brackenridge acknowledged receipt of Coxe's response to his letter of August 8 and wrote: "Suppressing your name, I have just given your letter to the printer of the *Gazette* of this place, conceiving that it will be of service in composing the minds of the people of this country" (Brackenridge, *Insurrection*, 146–47). Coxe's letter, dated August 26, 1794, appeared in *The Pittsburgh Gazette* of September 20, 1794. The heading states that "The following is a letter from a Citizen of Philadelphia to an Inhabitant of Pittsburgh, in answer to one giving some account of the late Transactions." Coxe's letter reads in part as follows: ". . . My intentions in replying to your letter do not extend to an examination of the several laws, the nature, operation & provisions of which you consider as either injurious to our western brethren or disagreeable to all the philosophic men and the Yeomanry of America. I shall confine myself on the one hand to some remarks upon the danger to our free governments, and to the peace and safety of the United States, which such means of opposition and relief tend to produce—and on the other to a statement of certain reasons, which appear to render it improbable that the desired relief will be attained by those means" (ADfS, Tench Coxe Papers, Historical Society of Pennsylvania, Philadelphia). Coxe's draft of this letter is dated August 20, 1794.

3. Frederick, Duke of York, was a general of the English forces in the United Provinces from April, 1793, until November, 1794. He was the second son of George III.

4. François Sebastien Charles Joseph de Croix, Comte de Clerfayt, was a member of a family prominent in the Austrian Netherlands and a field marshal in the Austrian army.

5. This is presumably a reference to the Battle of Turcoing, fought on May 18, 1794, in which the allied armies lost a total of fifty-five hundred men. The report that the Duke of York was missing was incorrect.

To Isaac Craig

[*Philadelphia, August 16, 1794.* John C. Hamilton states that on this date Hamilton wrote to Craig.[1] *Letter not found.*]

1. Hamilton, *History*, VI, 90.

From John Jay

London 16 Augt. 1794

Dear Sir

I am happy to find by a New York paper, that the Result of the late Inquiry into your official Conduct is perfectly consistant with the Expectations of your Friends.[1] It is there represented as being voluminous, and in a variety of Respects interesting. Be so good as to send me a copy. I wrote to you lately a confidential Letter, under Cover to the President.[2] My Dispatches to Mr Randolph were under the same cover. I presumed that if the Vessel should be examined by some rude privateer, more Respect would be paid to a Letter directed to the President, than to others.

Nothing very important has since occurred. Things are in a Train that *looks* promising; but the Issue is of Course uncertain. The Resolutions from Kentucky [3] and N. Carolina [4] are here; and make disagreable Impressions. Incivilities as often produce Resentment as Injuries do.

Affairs in Europe wear a serious aspect. The french continue Succesful, and the English decided—it is thought the Dutch will resign to their Fate without very strenuous opposition.[5] Geneva is undergoing another Revolution.[6] News of Robertspiere's ⟨vio⟩lent Death,[7] has arrived, and gains Credit. If true, the ⟨impo⟩rtance of it to France or the Allies cannot yet be calculated. ⟨–⟩ Events have hitherto been more common than influencial.

Yours sincerely John Jay

⟨– Hamil⟩ton

ALS, Hamilton Papers, Library of Congress; ADfS, Columbia University Libraries.

1. See Stephen Higginson to H, June 17, 1794, note 5.

2. Jay to H, July 18, 1794.

3. For information on the Kentucky resolutions, see Edmund Randolph to William Bradford, H, and Henry Knox, July 11, 1794, note 1; H to George Washington, July 13, 1794.

4. This may be a reference to "a respectable meeting of the citizens of Halifax county, State of N. Carolina, for the purpose of taking into consideration the conduct of Great Britain towards the United States," which sent "the following address to the Representatives in Congress from that County": ". . . We take occasion to declare to you our warmest indignation at the insults and robberies exercised on the person property of our fellow-citizens, unaccountably seized carried to the West-Indies, and other parts of the British dominions, and condemned by the minions of George of Britain, without even the formality of trial, farther than by adding insult to injury. We, your constituents, avow our highest approbation of the spirited measures adopted by the General Government, in remedy of those insufferable wrongs; We are pleased to see the harmony and consonance of temper, pervailing between the constituents and representatives of our country at large; but especially to find our immediate representatives, think with us, having discernment enough to discover, thro' the mist of false colouring and mean subterfuges, for which that haughty and contemptible nation, is particularly distinguished—and spirit to resent their insults and injuries.

"Be ye sure, fellow-citizens, that in this you meet our warmest applause, and most hearty concurrence, readily and cheerfully to support you at the risque of life and everything dear on earth. We highly commend your peremptory and decided demand, that they go instantly into a strict observance of the treaty of peace: THAT PEACE! purchased by the sword and the richest blood of our countrymen—and above all, that they without delay surrender the Western-posts, the asylum of brutal, bloody savages, and source of their destructive invasions, attended with robberies and murders, with circumstances of cruelty surpassing the powers of description; Convinced, that on our part there prevails every disposition to fulfil the treaty. We highly commend the policy of sequestrating debts, that are due to their subjects in this country, that we may be enabled to do ourselves that justice, which they dishonorably withhold. We highly approve the principles producing the embargo laid upon exports, however great the temporary inconveniences attending thereon; the greatest of which is the derangement of revenue; this, and all other inconveniences incident to the measure, we cheerfully undergo, rather than feed the carcasses of those insatiable wolves. Having opposed the principles of passive obedience and non-resistance when LIBERTY was only an idea, we are by no means tempted to yield it at this day of our political manhood, invigorated by the sweets of a Free Republican Government. . . .

"In addition to other grievances, the sufferings of our fellow-citizens in Algiers, claim our warmest sympathy. The calamities of our fellow-citizens in the West Indies, invite our pity, and command our resentment. . . .

"We cannot forebear some remarks upon the situation of our magnanimous allies and republican brethren, the FRENCH PEOPLE; we see in them the lustre of republican and patriotic virtues unequalled; a spirit caught from us, highly improved on by them; We are therefore highly gratified in being informed of the manly career, to bring down their corrupt opposers wherever they meet them; We conceive that the present European war, is a war of human notice, and the issue in trial is, whether mankind may govern themselves by their own laws and consent, or shall be governed by the sceptre of arbitrary power, arrogated by those self-created monsters, called Kings, Priests and Lords. . . .

"Tell John Bull from us, that if he does not relinquish his infamous system of cruelty, oppression, theft, intrigue, low cunning, breach of faith, and innumerable other corruptions that particularly distinguish him the worst of tyrants! and if he does not instantly surrender the Western posts, and abolish his mean traffic, with his savage brethren, we will pursue him with vengeance, will in a furious march stride from lake to lake, and level to dust, post by post: Demand from him a release of our fellow-Citizens, detained in his infamous isles and a restitution of their plundered property, or we will wade the ocean to their relief. . . ." ([Philadelphia] *General Advertiser*, June 21, 1794.)

5. After the French victory in the Battle of Fleurus on June 26, 1794, the French military operations in the Low Countries continued to be successful.

6. The impact of the French Revolution created dissension and turmoil in Geneva. In December, 1792, those citizens of Geneva who considered themselves oppressed by their government allied themselves with the peasants and returning exiles from Paris and forced governmental changes. In July, 1794, the revolutionists took possession of the city, executed many prominent citizens, and imprisoned others.

7. Maximilien François Marie Isidore de Robespierre, the French revolutionist, was executed on July 28, 1794.

From Edmund Randolph

Philadelphia, Saturday afternoon
August 16th 1794

Dear Sir,

I have just seen Mr. Fauchet. He says, that La Carmagnol was ordered by him to sail eight or ten days ago, and is probably gone; but that she came in hither, pursued by a vessel of war, now waiting for her at the mouth of the Delaware.[1] I informed him, that his answer was desired in writing: [2] He promised to send it to the Office this afternoon, and I have directed it to be sent to you. He will perhaps place the thing in such a point of view, as to require some consideration and perhaps modification. I wish therefore, that you would send the letter out, if after reading it you think that something must be immediately done.

Yours with respect and esteem Edm: Randolph.

LC, RG 59, Domestic Letters of the Department of State, Vol. 7, June 27–November 30, 1794, National Archives.

1. On August 14, 1794, Randolph wrote to Jean Antoine Joseph Fauchet, French Minister to the United States: "Information has been given to the President . . . that the privateer, called La Carmagnol [or Columbia], which has always been considered as one of those fitted out in opposition to the sense of our government, is now in the river Delaware. This Vessel is represented, to retain still her warlike apparatus. It is probable, that you have not been informed, that she was ordered to quit our ports, or to be dismantled. . . . The readiness with which you complied with the wish of the Government on a similar occasion, induces me to hope, that you will issue orders for dismantling her, and prevent the President from taking on this subject, those measures which he wishes to avoid" (LC, RG 59, Domestic Letters of the Department of State, Vol. 7, June 27–November 30, 1794, National Archives). This letter is printed in *ASP, Foreign Relations,* I, 600.

At the request of the President, Henry Knox on May 23 and May 24, 1793, had sent circular letters to the governors of the states asking for information on armed vessels of the European belligerents in American ports (LS, to Thomas Sim Lee, Hall of Records of Maryland, Annapolis; Knox to Henry Lee [*Calendar of Virginia State Papers,* VI, 377, 379]). After several months of deliberation on this question the cabinet drew up a list of rules which Knox sent in a circular letter to the governors of the states on August 7, 1793. See "Cabinet Meeting. Opinion on the Fitting Out of Privateers in the Ports of the United States," August 3, 1793, note 3. For H's draft of these rules, see "Cabinet Meeting. Proposed Rules Governing Belligerents," August 3, 1793.

2. On August 16, 1794, Fauchet wrote to Randolph: "Je vous préviens que les inquiétudes que témoigne le Governement des États Unis, relativement à la Columbia que l'on prétend être dans la Délaware, sont sans fondement. Ce bâtiment a reçu de moi l'ordre de mettre à la mer *sur le champ* le 4 du présent mois; s'il ne l'avait point exécuté, c'est qu'il en aurait été empêché par les forçes Anglaises, ou par la nécessité de faire quelques réparations indispensables avant le voyage qu'il va entreprendre" (*Correspondence of the French Ministers with the United States Government,* part 1, 4). A translation of this letter is printed in *ASP, Foreign Relations,* I, 600.

Randolph's answer to Fauchet on August 20, 1794, reads in part as follows: "I should have done myself the honor, before this day of transmitting to you a copy of certain rules, instituted by the President of the United States in relation to the belligerent powers, if I had not taken it for granted, that your intercourse with your predecessor had rendered it unne[ce]ssary. But I take the liberty of now inclosing them, as having a direct connection with my letter to you of the 14th. instant, and with your reply of the 16th. . . .

"But the Carmagnol (or Columbia) has been the subject of particular letters from Govr. [George] Clinton to Mr. [Edmond Charles] Genet and the French Consul at New York [Alexandre Maurice Blanc de Lanautte, Comte d'Hauterive], and the result has been an assurance, that she should no longer offend those rules. This assurance has produced a great degree of anxiety, that she should not now enter our ports. . . .

"It is very far from the wish of the President, that your dispatches should be at any time interrupted. The step of dismantling which is desired, is merely to fulfil an engagement, which has been frequently made.

"Whether the Carmagnol be *at present* in the Delaware, we cannot at this place ascertain. If she has sailed, I have only to communicate to you the hope and expectation of the President, that you will by your orders prevent her from returning to our ports in her military equipment. If she has not sailed, we must repeat our confidence, that you will cause her to be dismantled. The rules above referred to will not permit an illicit privateer, as she has been deemed to be, to make any reparations within the United States. . . ." (LC, RG 59, Domestic Letters of the Department of State, Vol. 7, June 27–November 30, 1794, National Archives.) This letter is printed in *ASP, Foreign Relations*, I, 600.

To George Washington[1]

Treasy Departmt. Aug: 16. 1794.

Sir,

It appears probable that advantages will result from giving to the Citizens at large information on the subject of the disturbances which exist in the Western parts of Pennsylvania.

With this view, if no objection to the measure should occur to you, I would cause a publication to be made of the Report which I had the honor to address to you, dated the 5th. instant.[2]

With the most perfect respect &c. A Hamilton

LC, George Washington Papers, Library of Congress.

1. For background to this letter, see H to Washington, August 6, 1794.
2. H's letter to Washington of August 5, 1794, was printed in [Philadelphia] *Dunlap and Claypoole's American Daily Advertiser*, August 21, 1794. It was subsequently published in other papers.

To Elizabeth Hamilton[1]

[Philadelphia, August 17, 1794]

My loved Eliza

I wrote you two or three times last week.[2] But since my last I have received another letter from you[3] which does not remove my anxiety. The state of our dear sick angel continues too precarious. My heart trembles whenever I open a letter from you. The experiment of the Pink root alarms me—But I continue to place my hope in Heaven.

You press to return to me. I will not continue to dissuade you. Do as you think best. If you resolve to come I should like best your coming by land & I wish you could prevail on Doctor Stringer[4] to accompany you. It would be matter of course & pleasure to make him a handsome compensation. If you want money, you may either get it from your father or draw on Mr. Seton[5] at New York for it.

But let me know before hand your determination that I may meet you at New York with an arrangement for bringing you or rather write to Mr. Seton who I will request to have things ready. All you will have to do will be to inform him that you leave Albany on a certain day. All here are perfectly well & join in love to you

Adieu My Angel AH

Aug 17
Mrs. Hamilton

ALS, Hamilton Papers, Library of Congress.

1. For background to this letter, see H to George Washington, July 11, 23, 1794; Washington to H, July 11, 1794; H to Elizabeth Hamilton, July 31, August 2, 8 two letters of August 12, 1794.

2. H to Elizabeth Hamilton, August 8, two letters of August 12, 1794.

3. Letter not found.

4. Samuel Stringer was an Albany physician.

5. William Seton had resigned as cashier of the Bank of New York in June to devote his time to his mercantile interests. See Seton to H, June 16, 1794.

To Abraham Hunt[1]

Treasury Department
Aug 17. 1794

Sir

In the event of a detachment of Militia assembling in New Jersey to march against the insurgents in the Western parts of Pensylvania[2] it is my wish that it may be convenient to you to undertake to procure supplies for them of every kind transportation included until they get into Pensylvania, for which a Commission of 5 ℔ Cent on the amount of expenditures would be allowed.

If it shall be agreeable to you to undertake, I request that you will without delay confer with the Governor,[3] as to the places of rendezvous, in the first instance, and routes of the corps which may be called out, so as to digest beforehand the necessary ideas respecting the execution, when the final order shall go from hence, which if not prevented by a submission of the insurgents (of which there is too little probability) cannot I presume be long delayed.

You may take as a guide that the Militia of Pensylvania and Jersey are to be assembled at Carlisle.

The public has already contracts in New Jersey [at Elizabeth Town[4] & New-Brunswick[5] for supplying the Troops of the United

States. The price of the ration at the first mentioned place is 12¼ Cents and at the last place fourteen Cents, including Medical aid.] [6] You will judge whether it is its interest to avail itself of any supplies which may be wanted under these contracts or whether they can otherwise be obtained on better terms; for the contracts only fix the rates which shall be paid for any supplies that *may be* required.

It will be agreeable to me to hear from you without delay.

With much esteem I am Sir Your obedient ser AH

Abraham Hunt Esq
Trenton

ADfS, Connecticut Historical Society, Hartford.

1. Hunt, a resident of Trenton, New Jersey, was a contractor furnishing supplies for the United States Army.

2. In his proclamation of August 7, 1794, concerning opposition to the excise laws in western Pennsylvania, George Washington stated that it was necessary "to take measures for calling forth the militia" (*GW*, XXXIII, 460). On August 7, 1794, Henry Knox sent a circular letter to the governors of New Jersey, Pennsylvania, Maryland, and Virginia, which reads in part as follows: "It is desired that the Corps should consist of Four thousand five hundred Infantry, Five hundred Cavalry and Two hundred Artillery. . . .

"The force to be called out will be according to the following Schedule:

	Infantry	Cavalry	Artillery	
New Jersey	1,500	500	100	
Pennsylvania	4,500	500	200	
Maryland	2,000	200	150	
Virginia	3,000	300	—	
	11,000	1,500	450	12,950."

(LC, Hall of Records of Maryland, Annapolis.) This circular is printed in *Pennsylvania Archives*, 2nd ser., IV, 123.

3. Richard Howell, who had served in the American Revolution as a major, in September, 1788, became clerk of the New Jersey Supreme Court, and on June 3, 1793, following the resignation of William Paterson, was elected governor by the New Jersey legislature.

Howell issued general orders to the New Jersey militia on August 23, 1794 (D, Anthony Walton White Papers, Rutgers, The State University, Library, New Brunswick, New Jersey).

4. William Shute was the contractor for Army rations at Elizabeth, New Jersey.

5. John Bray was the contractor for Army rations at New Brunswick, New Jersey.

6. The words within brackets are not in H's handwriting.

From John Davidson[1]

Annapolis August 18, 1794

Sir

I have always with cheerfulness obeyed your Mandates, and to keep up a proper Republican System, I have in my turn to request that you will be pleased to obey mine; it goes to your providing Funds for the improvement of an high eligible Lot in our Presidents City convenient to his House,[2] over which you may look as to position only, which I mean to convey to you in Fee, on Condition that you improve it to your own liking by the year 1800; for your choice of the Lot I will locate my property there, and if you approve not of my choice you may roam over the whole and perch where you please; my choice lays on the north edge of K Street No. 284 east or west of it the highest situations in the City. Hambugh heights excepted, upon the plan of that City published at Boston[3] you will please to cast your Eye from South G Street to North N Street and from East 9 Street to West 15 Street, you will perceive the limits to which I must confine you: K Street divides the City North & South, and the first Circle on Vermont Avenue from the Presidents Square ranging with K Street Eastward are the highest and in my Opinion the most desireable Situations, but should you wish to be nearer the Presidents House on either side of New York Avenue you shall be accomodated by

Sir Your most respectfull & very Obedient Servt. John Davidson

Mr. Secretary Hamilton

ALS, Hamilton Papers, Library of Congress.

1. Davidson, who had served as collector of customs and inspector of the revenue for Annapolis, was one of the original owners of sizable tracts of land on the site of the present city of Washington.

2. The building of the White House was begun in the summer of 1793, after the laying of the cornerstone on October 13, 1792.

3. This is a reference to Pierre Charles L'Enfant's plan of the Federal City. When L'Enfant, despite the urging of George Washington, failed to have the plan engraved, it was turned over to Andrew Ellicott, a surveyor. Ellicott then sent the plan to Samuel Blodgett, Jr., in Boston, who had it engraved there in 1792 by Samuel Hill (John Stewart, "Early Maps and Surveyors of the City of Washington, D.C.," *Records of the Columbia Historical Society, Washington, D.C.* [Washington, 1899], II, 48–71; *GW*, XXXI, 499).

From Stephen Moylan[1]

[*Philadelphia*] *August 18, 1794.* "On the 5th of this month I received from the Secretary of War an order to pay Invalid Pensioners the Sum of 8752 dollars & 1 cent being for the amount of their annual pension up to the 4th day of Sepr. 1794 inclusively. You will please to issue a Warrant for that Sum." [2]

LC, RG 53, Pennsylvania State Loan Office, Letter Book, 1793–1795, Vol. "616-P," National Archives; LC, RG 217, First Comptroller's Office, Pennsylvania Loan Office, Letter Book "A," National Archives.

1. Moylan was commissioner of loans for Pennsylvania.

2. On August 29, 1794, Warrant No. 3986 was issued to Moylan for $8,752.01 (D, RG 217, Miscellaneous Treasury Accounts, 1790–1894, Account No. 6018, National Archives).

To Robert Purviance

Treasury Department August 18th 1794

Sir,

I have to request that you will furnish me with a Statement of the circumstances relating to the Schooner Martha belonging to Messrs. Munnickhuysen & Sadler of Baltimore which sailed for Hispaniola during the Embargo [1] and conditioned to return in Ballast.[2]

It appears from a Letter of her Owners to me [3] that she brought back some Molasses and Taffia, the latter of which was contained in Casks of less than Ninety Gallons.[4]

I am with consideration Sir your most obedient Servant

A Hamilton

Robert Purviance Esquire
Collector of Baltimore

LC, Columbia University Libraries.

1. On March 26, 1794, a joint resolution of Congress provided "That an embargo be laid on all ships and vessels in the ports of the United States . . . for the term of thirty days" (1 *Stat.* 400). A joint resolution of April 18, 1794, provided "That the present embargo be continued . . . until the twenty-fifth day of May next" (1 *Stat.* 401).

2. Section 1 of "An Act to provide for mitigating or remitting the forfeitures and penalties accruing under the revenue laws, in certain cases therein mentioned" (1 *Stat.* 122–23 [May 26, 1790]) provided in part that "whenever any person who now is, or hereafter shall be liable to a fine, penalty or forfeiture

. . . shall prefer his petition to the judge of the district in which such fine, penalty or forfeiture may have accrued . . . the said judge shall inquire in a summary manner into the circumstances of the case . . . and shall cause the facts which shall appear upon such inquiry, to be stated and annexed to the petition, and direct their transmission to the Secretary of the Treasury of the United States, who shall thereupon have power to mitigate or remit such fine, penalty or forfeiture, or any part thereof, if in his opinion the same was incurred without wilful negligence or any intention of fraud."

The petition of Munnickhuysen and Sadler, dated September 12, 1794, to William Paca, United States judge for the District of Maryland, reads as follows:

"That agreeable to a permission obtain'd in May last by our Friend Mr. John Vochez, then in Philadelphia, Our Schooner Martha sailed from this Port with a number of French Passengers for Hispanjola, two days previous the raising of the Embargo. We did conformably to Law, give Security in Six Thousand Dollars, that the Schooner Shou'd return in Ballast. We advised a French Gentleman to whom we had charter'd the Vessel of this obligation and of the necessity to comply therewith.

"She sailed from our Capes on the 26th. of May last, and on their arrival at Hispanjola those Gentlemen did not find the Island in the situation they had expected, the Person who had freighted the Schooner therefore determined to return to this Country. Persuaded by some Friends, who wished to take Shelter in America from the oppressions they experienced at St. Marc's, he consented in giving them a Passage in the Schooner. and to receive also on board the only affects they had left to Secure for a little time their existence in this Country, namely Six Tierces of Taffia and Eleven Tierces of Molasses. The Captain conscious of the difficulties that might arise from such proceedings, resisted for a long time their United Sollicitations, however at length, on their assurances that by a representation of their Situation, lenity might be shewn, feeling himself interested in the safety of two of the Passengers, whose Political principles indanger'd their liberty, he assented to take them on board, and set sail for this Port, where he arrived on the 29th of July.

"As soon as we were made acquainted with the circumstances we Waited on the Collector, whom we found already informed of the fact by the Manifest delivered, and who told us that however sorry of this Event he cou'd not avoid consistently with his duty to order a prosecution against us, which has been since commenced, and is now depending.

"We beg leave to observe, and we hope our observation will have some Weight, that our conduct in the expedition, has evinced no mark of design to have a back freight, for as we had a certain intelligence that the Embargo wou'd be discontinued two days after the departure of the Vessell, we wou'd either have detained her two days longer here, and sent her with a common permit, or have directed the Captain to call at Hampton & take his clearance from that Port. The Goods taken at Hispanjola are in themselves of so inconsiderable a Value, and the frieght to which they might be subjected, so very trifling, that we are confident their Shipment will not even Warrant a Suspicion of designed contravention on our part, to the Laws of the Country, we therefore feel a confidence that we not only will be cleared of the charge but also from the Penalty incurred.

"Your Petitioners therefore pray that your Honor will cause an enquiry to be had in the facts above stated, and that your Honor will make a representation to the Secretary that your Petitioners may be released from the Pains & Penalties in such case made & provided." (Copy, RG 59, Miscellaneous Letters, 1790–1799, National Archives.)

On September 12, 1794, Paca stated: "Upon inquiring into the facts Stated in the within Petition I find them to be true" (copy, RG 59, Miscellaneous Letters, 1790–1799, National Archives).

3. Letter not found.

4. Section 10 of "An Act concerning the Duties on Spirits distilled within the United States" (1 *Stat.* 279 [May 8, 1792]) states: "That, from and after the last day of April, one thousand seven hundred and ninety-three, no distilled spirits except arrack and sweet cordials, shall be brought into the United States from any foreign port or place, except in casks or vessels of the capacity of ninety gallons and upwards."

In addition, Munnickhuysen and Sadler incurred penalties and forfeitures under "An Act repealing, after the last day of June next, the duties heretofore laid upon Distilled Spirits imported from abroad, and laying others in their stead; and also upon Spirits distilled within the United States, and for appropriating the same" (1 *Stat.* 199–214 [March 3, 1791]) and "An Act for enrolling and licensing ships or vessels to be employed in the coasting trade and fisheries, and for regulating the same" (1 *Stat.* 305–18 [February 18, 1793]).

War Department Circular to the Governors of the States

Philadelphia August 18th 1794

Sir,

The Secretary at War being absent from the Seat of Government,[1] I am directed by the President to write to you [2] on the Subject of those French privateers, fitted out in our ports which you have been heretofore informed were to be denied asylum within the United States, except upon the condition of being dismantled of their military equipments.[3]

The subsequent conduct of some of these Vessels is a matter of real embarrassment and dissatisfaction.[4] By running from one port to another, they have in effect enjoyed the asylum, which it was intended to deny them, and have thereby placed the Government in the unpleasant situation not only of seeing itself trifled with but of being liable to the suspicion of connivance in an evasion of its positive assurances to Foreign powers.

It is inadmissible that such a state of things should continue. And therefore the President has come to a resolution to cause every such Vessel which since the promulgation of his instruction to refuse them asylum shall have been in a port of the United States so as to have had an opportunity to acquire a knowledge of that instruction and which shall hereafter be found in any Port or District of the United states to be deprived of her military equipments.

I have it in instruction from him to communicate this resolution to you and to request your effectual cooperation in carrying it into execution within the state of [Massachusetts].[5]

While the reasons which have been assigned beget a solicitude in the President that the measure may be punctually and completely executed, there are weighty considerations which induce him to wish that it may be found practicable to accomplish it in each case without bloodshed. To this end it will be useful that any force which may be employed for the purpose should be such as will controul a disposition to resist.

With perfect respect, I have the honor to be Sir Your most obedient and humble servant Alexander Hamilton

LS, to Samuel Adams, The Sol Feinstone Collection, American Philosophical Society, Philadelphia; LS, to Joshua Clayton, The Free Library of Philadelphia; LS, to Arthur Fenner, Rhode Island State Archives, Providence; LS, to John Taylor Gilman, sold by Goodspeed's Book Shop, Boston, Catalogue No. 496, Item 271; LS, to Samuel Huntington, Connecticut Historical Society, Hartford; LS, to Henry Lee, Historical Society of Pennsylvania, Philadelphia; LS, to Thomas Sim Lee, Hall of Records of Maryland, Annapolis; LS, to George Mathews, courtesy of the Trustees of the Boston Public Library; LS, to Richard Dobbs Spaight, Mr. Albert M. Greenfield, Philadelphia; LC, to Samuel Adams, Massachusetts State Archives, Boston; LC, to Thomas Sim Lee, RG 56, Miscellaneous Letters Sent, "Set K," National Archives; LC, to Thomas Mifflin, Division of Public Records, Pennsylvania Historical and Museum Commission, Harrisburg; copy to Thomas Sim Lee, RG 56, Letters 2d Comptroller, 2d Auditor, Executive of Maryland and Georgia, 1789–1833, Maryland, National Archives; copy, Hamilton Papers, Library of Congress.

1. See George Washington to H, August 12, 1794, note 1.

2. See H to Washington, August 18, 1794.

3. This is a reference to a War Department circular which Henry Knox had sent to the governors of the states on August 7, 1793. See "Cabinet Meeting. Opinion on the Fitting Out of Privateers in the Ports of the United States," August 3, 1793, note 3.

4. See Edmund Randolph to H, August 16, 1794.

5. The material within brackets varies according to the governor to whom the circular was addressed.

To George Washington

Philadelphia Aug: 18. 1794.

The Secretary of the Treasury submits to the President the draft of a letter on the subject of the proscribed privateers.[1] Would it not be adviseable to communicate the matter to the French minister,[2] & to request his cooperation in causing our ports to be no longer ⟨–⟩ by those vessels? [3]

The appointments of Collectors for the Districts of Hampton & Snow-Hill is become urgent, the present incumbents[4] having reiterated their requests that they might be relieved. Names have been placed before the President by letter in the first place,[5] & in the last verbally.

The enclosed papers will remind the President of the state of the business in each case. The Secretary wishes it may appear to him expedient to name Mr Jones for Hampton.[6]

He has been able to obtain no light as to Mr Randolph's suggestion respecting Mr Selby,[7] but he imagines the present Collector would not recommend a person really obnoxious to his fellow Citizens. There are some other vacancies to be filled, which the Secretary will shortly have the honor of conferring with The President concerning.

A Hamilton

LC, George Washington Papers, Library of Congress.

1. See "War Department Circular to the Governors of the States," August 18, 1794.

2. Jean Antoine Joseph Fauchet.

3. In accordance with H's suggestion, Edmund Randolph wrote to Fauchet on August 20, 1794. See Randolph to H, August 16, 1794, note 2.

4. George Wray was collector of customs in Hampton, Virginia, and John Gunby was collector at Snow Hill, Maryland.

5. See H to Washington, June 24, 1794; Washington to H, June 30, 1794.

6. On August 23, 1794, Washington commissioned "Thos. Jones to be Collector for Hampton Dist. in Virginia" (JPP, 308). On December 10, 1794, Washington nominated Jones "to be Collector for the District of Hampton, and Inspector of the Revenue for the Port of Hampton," and on the following day the Senate approved the nomination (*Executive Journal*, I, 165).

7. On August 23, 1794, Washington commissioned "William Selby to be Collector of the District of Snow hill in Maryland; & Inspector of the revenue for the sevl. ports within the sd. District" (JPP, 308). On December 10, 1794, Washington sent Selby's nomination to the Senate, and on the following day it was approved (*Executive Journal*, I, 165).

From Wilhem and Jan Willink, Nicholaas and Jacob Van Staphorst, and Nicholas Hubbard

Quadruplicate Or: pr. Sh. Adrianae. Fitzpatrick. Dupl. pr. Br. Union Leader to New York Tripl: pr. Br. Harriot Holland.

Amsterdam 18 August 1794.

Sir!

Conformable to our last respects of 1 Instant We have now the pleasure to transmit You inclosed Bill of Lading and Invoice of 89

Casks Salpetre,[1] consigned to You by our order, by David Henry Rowohl of Hamburgh per the Bacchus bound to Philadelphia, Richard George Master, amounting to Holland Currency f 42,579.14. 8

f 46,000. Insurance upon ditto, at

6 percent	f 2,760.—	
Policy	3.12–	
Our Commission ½ per Cent	230.—	2,993.12. —
To debit of the United States in		Hd. Cy. f 45,573. 6. 8

Which Salpetre We wish soon and safe to you in perfect good condition.

We are yet without, but hourly expect to receive intelligence of the remainder of your order for this article having been purchased and shipped at Copenhagen, in consequence of the positive and strong directions We gave to that effect.

We are respectfully Sir! Your most ob. hb. Servants

Wilhem & Jan Willink
N & J Van Staphorst & Hubbard

Alexd. Hamilton Esqr. Secretary of the Treasury

LS, Connecticut Historical Society, Hartford.

1. See also H to Willink, Van Staphorst, and Hubbard, May 8, 1794, and Willink, Van Staphorst, and Hubbard to H, July 1, 15, August 1, 1794.

From Tench Coxe

Treasury Department, Revenue Office, August 19, 1794. "I have the honor to request of you, that a Warrant may issue for three hundred Dollars in my favor intended to make a payment to the workman who is doing the copper work of the Lantern for the Tybee Light House."

LC, RG 26, Lighthouse Letters, Vol. I, National Archives.

From Tench Coxe[1]

T:D: R:O. August 19th. 1794

Mr. Coxe has the honor to inform the secy. of the Treasy. that he is only waiting for a return from the War Departmt. of the places and numbers, at, & for which, the Rations will be wanted.[2] As a document which might have served the purpose, he applied at the Secy. of the Tresys. office, for a sight or a copy of the notification for supplies of the last year, which he understands cannot be found. As soon as either of the two papers shall be received, Mr. Coxe will proceed in the business.

LC, RG 75, Letters of Tench Coxe, Commissioner of the Revenue, Relating to the Procurement of Military, Naval, and Indian Supplies, National Archives.

1. Within the Treasury Department Coxe was responsible for procuring supplies for the Army. See H to Coxe, April 4, 1794.

2. On August 16, 1794, Coxe wrote to John Stagg, Jr., chief clerk in the War Department, requesting information "concerning the garrisons, detachments, and army in the field in the Western parts of Pennsylvania Virginia and the N. W. Territory & of their situations as will enable me to make arrangements for Rations, and Quarter masters supplies for 1795" (LC, RG 75, Letters of Tench Coxe, Commissioner of the Revenue, Relating to the Procurement of Military, Naval, and Indian Supplies, National Archives).

From Bartholomew Dandridge[1]

[*Philadelphia*] *August 19, 1794.* "I am directed by the President to inform you, in reply to your letter of the 16. instant, that relying that the facts contained in the Report have been stated with due care, & from authentic sources, he perceives no objection to the publication of it as proposed."

LC, George Washington Papers, Library of Congress.

1. For background to this letter, see H to George Washington, August 6, 16, 1794.

Dandridge was Washington's secretary.

From William Ellery

Newport [*Rhode Island*] *August 19, 1794.* "Since my last[1] have arrived here the Schooner St. George of Montego Bay . . . captured on the High Seas by the Frigate La Concorde; also the Brig Perserverance of St. John New Brunswick . . . bound last from Turks Island for Newyork and captured on the high Seas, by the Privateer Sans Pareille. . . .[2] Inclosed are copies of the papers produced to me. . . . I wrote a letter to the Governor of this State . . . inclosing . . . a copy of that part of your instructs. which relates to Privateers *originally fitted out* in the United States, and prizes brought or sent in by such Privateers. . . .[3] Jean Baptiste Bernard the Prize master of the Perseverance has been apprehended on a charge of having murdered a man in Charlestown last June . . .[4] and he has been confined in Gaol. . . ."

LC, Newport Historical Society, Newport, Rhode Island.

1. Ellery to H, August 1–6, 1794.

2. Soon after its arrival in Newport, the French frigate *Concorde* sailed for Boston, where it stopped an American ship and seized both letters and money which that ship was carrying. (Stephen Higginson and others to Edmund Randolph, September 8, 1794 [LS, RG 59, Miscellaneous Letters, 1790–1799, National Archives]). On the other hand, the *Sans Pareil* and its prize, the English brig *Perseverance,* remained at Newport because of a protracted dispute between France and the United States. On orders from Governor Arthur Fenner of Rhode Island, acting under the authority granted by George Washington in a circular letter to the governors of the states, which Henry Knox had written on August 7, 1793 (See "Cabinet Meeting. Opinion on the Fitting Out of Privateers in the Ports of the United States," August 3, 1793, note 3), both vessels were detained at Newport, and the *Perseverance* was seized on the ground that the *Sans Pareil* had been armed in ports of the United States (Jean Antoine Joseph Fauchet to Randolph, August 26, 1794 [*Correspondence of the French Ministers with the United States Government,* part 1, 7–8]; Randolph to Fenner, September 3, 1794 [LC, RG 59, Domestic Letters of the Department of State, Vol. 7, June 27–November 30, 1794, National Archives]). On August 26, 1794, Fauchet protested to Randolph that the charge was false and that the seizure was an obvious form of harassment, and on September 18, in a letter to Randolph, Fauchet described in detail his side of the story: ". . . Le bricg Anglais la Persévérance, prise du corsaire le Sans Pareil, commissionné au Cap Français, isle de St. Dominque, est arrivé à . . . [Newport] le 13 Août dernier. Le Vice Consul d'Angleterre [Thomas William Moore] suggère immediatement que le Sans Pareil avait été commissionné à Charleston; le Collecteur de la douane envoye à l'instant saisir la prise, en expulse les capteurs, en fait prendre possession, et en enlève tous les papiers.

"Le Capitaine de prise Français veut réclamer. Deux matelots Anglais, excités sous main, déposent sous ferment, que cet officier a tué un homme à Charleston; on l'emprisonne de suite. Heureusement le Consul de la République à Boston [Thomas Dannery] instruit de cette étrange persécution, envoye son chancelier à Newport.

"Le chancelier trouve, que de justes soupçons contre les deux matelots Anglais, et l'impossibilité où ils avaient été de donner caution pour leur comparation au procès criminel commencé contre le Capitaine de prise, les avait fait mettre en prison eux mêmes; que se voyant abandonnés, inquiets des conséquences, peut-être repentans, ils avaient avoués que leur dépositions étaient fausses; qu'enfin ils s'étaient retractés judiciarement, en confessant qu'ils n'avainet agi que par malice, et avaient été mis en liberté; que cependant on ne poursuivait pas ces deux parjures, et qu'on différait d'élarger définitivement le Capitaine de prise.

"Le Chancelier demande en arrivant au Collecteur communication des papiers de la prise; il le prie de la faire passer à Providence pour plus de sûreté; parceque la veille une tentative avait été faite par le propriétaire et des matelots Anglais pour l'enlever. Il n'obtient ni l'un ni l'autre, est obligé de protester, et se transporte à Niewport pour réclamer justice du Gouverneur. Le Gouverneur tient séance le 25 Août. Le Vice Consul Anglais obtient renvoi de l'affaire à une époque plus éloignée et paraît chercher gagner du tems. Enfin la prise est finalement rendue aux capteurs, mais dans l'intervalle elle se détériore, des frais judiciares en absorbent une partie de la valeur, les corsaires se découragent." (*Correspondence of the French Ministers with the United States Government*, part 1, 7–8, 21–22.)

On September 27, 1794, Randolph informed Fauchet "that the Governor of Rhode Island has decided, that the Perseverance, a prize of the Sanspariel, shall be restored to the Captors" (LC, RG 59, Domestic Letters of the Department of State, Vol. 7, June 27–November 30, 1794, National Archives), and on October 4, 1794, he sent to George Hammond "the proceedings of the Governor of Rhode Island, relative to the Brigantine, Perseverance" (LC, RG 59, Domestic Letters of the Department of State, Vol. 7, June 27–November 30, 1794, National Archives). At this point, however, the British instituted court proceedings to recover the *Perseverance*, and Fauchet wrote to Randolph demanding that the United States Government intervene (Fauchet to Randolph, October 17, 1794 [*Correspondence of the French Ministers with the United States Government*, part 1, 29–30]). In refusing Fauchet's request, Randolph wrote: ". . . the extent of the United States imposes the necessity of substituting the agency of the Governors in the place of an instantaneous action by the federal executive, and therefore general rules alone can be provided.

"Under these rules, formed in the last year the Governor of Rhode Island operated on the prize of the Sans Pariel, and discharged her. If however individuals conceive, that they have a legal claim upon her, and draw her before a Court of law, the Executive of the United States cannot forbid them. The plea, . . . that the Court has no cognizance of French prizes, will be admitted *if it applies*, and the person, by whom the process is instituted, will be liable to a judgment for costs and damages, if he fails in his proof." (Randolph to Fauchet, October 22, 1794 [LC, RG 59, Domestic Letters of the Department of State, Vol. 7, June 27–November 30, 1794, National Archives].)

This complex and prolonged dispute did have one positive result, for it produced a modification, or at least a clarification, of United States policy. On October 22, 1794, Randolph sent a circular letter to the governors of the states, which reads in part as follows:

". . . Mr. Fauchet, the minister plenipotentiary of the French Republic, believes that he has reason to complain of the treatment, which French prizes have too often received in our ports.

"He represents, that by the machinations of the enemies of his country, the Captors are harrassed by seizures, arrests and detentions, the most vexatious and cruel: that as soon as the claimants are foiled in one attempt they betake themselves to another. . . .

"A late circumstance has . . . brought to view the practicability of oppression, unless precautions be adopted by the Executives. The claimants may often pursue a double chance by first procuring a trial before the Governors; and if defeated, by next resorting to the Courts of law. It is desirable therefore, that whensoever an application shall be made to your Excellency with respect to a prize, you should cause it to be examined well, whether the Courts have jurisdiction to inquire into the affair. If they have, then it seems proper that your Excellency should not interpose. If the Courts have not jurisdiction, and you are convinced *that there is good ground for detaining the prize, in order to comply with the rules established by the President last year, then and then only* your Excellency will so proceed. . . ." (LC, RG 59, Domestic Letters of the Department of State, Vol. 7, June 27–November 30, 1794, National Archives.)

3. "Treasury Department Circular to the Collectors of the Customs," August 4, 22, 1793.

4. For an account of the circumstances surrounding this alleged murder, see Fauchet's letter to Randolph of September 18, 1794, which is quoted in note 2.

From William Ellery

Newport [*Rhode Island*] *August 19, 1794.* "The Sloop Aurora Hersey Bradford of Bristol master arrived not long since at the Port of Bristol in this District from the Port of Boston without a Register, or Enrollment and License, but with a Certified manifest from the Custom house there. By said proceeding both the Vessel and her cargo became subject to seizure and forfeiture;[1] and upon Notice being given to me of this transactn. by the Surveyor of the Port of Bristol[2] I directed him to take the Vessel into his Custody until the District Attorney[3] could be consulted in the Case. . . . The District Attorney has been applied to, and inclosed is a copy of his Advice. . . ."

LC, Newport Historical Society, Newport, Rhode Island.

1. This is a reference to "An Act for enrolling and licensing ships or vessels to be employed in the coasting trade and fisheries, and for regulating the same" (1 *Stat.* 305–18 [February 18, 1793]).
2. Samuel Bosworth.
3. Ray Greene.

From Joseph Howell, Junior

War Department, Accountant's Office, August 19, 1794. ". . . I have . . . in the absence of the Secretary of War[1] to request you will be pleased to place in the hands of the Treasurer the sum of Thirty six thousand four hundred and fifty dollars for the pay and Subsistence of the Troops under the immediate command of General Wayne,[2] the further sum of Two thousand five hundred dollars and 90 Cents for the Troops at Fort Pitt and its dependencies and also a further sum of Sixty Thousand dollars for the Kentucky Volunteers. . . ."

LC, RG 93, Letter Book, 1794, National Archives.

1. See George Washington to H, August 12, 1794, note 1.
2. Major General Anthony Wayne was commander of the United States Army, which at this time was preparing for a campaign against the western Indians. Wayne defeated the Indians at the Battle of Fallen Timbers on August 20, 1794.

From Henry Lee[1]

[*Richmond, August 19, 1794.* On August 27, 1794, Hamilton wrote to Lee: "I have . . . received your letter to me of the 19th." *Letter not found.*]

1. Lee was governor of Virginia.

To Benjamin Lincoln

Treasury Department, August 19, 1794. "A temporary absence from the seat of Government[1] added to a great pressure of public Business since my return has prevented me from replying sooner to your favor of the 8th July last.[2] As it was not in my power to do anything in the case stated by you untill it came properly before me—I have in consequence of an application from the parties themselves, pointed out to them the only mode that can be pursued under similar circumstances."

Copy, RG 56, Letters to Collectors at Small Ports, "Set G," National Archives; copy, RG 56, Letters to the Collector at Boston, National Archives.

1. See H to George Washington, July 11, 23, 1794; Washington to H, July 11, 1794; H to Elizabeth Hamilton, July 31, 1794.
2. Letter not found.

From Robert Purviance

[*Baltimore, August 19, 1794.* On August 22, 1794, Hamilton wrote to Purviance: "I am to acknowledge the Receipt of your Letter of the 19th Instant, with the inclosures therein mentioned." *Letter not found.*]

Treasury Department Circular to the Naval Agents[1]

Treasury Department August 19th 1794

Sir,

There has been furnished to you as Agent for the Frigate to be built at Boston the sum of five Thousand Dollars.[2]

The laws respecting the Treasury and War Departments, direct that all supplies for the latter shall be procured under the direction of the former.[3] This part of the business of the Treasury Department has been confided by me to the Commissioner of the Revenue, who is Tench Coxe Esquire [4] and who will accordingly communicate with you respecting the Supplies which you are to provide.

With Esteem I am Sir, Your very Obedient Servant A Hamilton

LS, to Henry Jackson, The Darlington Collection of the University of Pittsburgh Library.

1. For information concerning the naval armament, see Henry Knox to H, April 21, 1794. See also Knox to H, second letter of June 25, July 14, 1794; Tench Coxe to H, August 2, 12, 1794; H to Henry Jackson, August 14, 1794.

2. As the words "Boston" and "five thousand Dollars" were inserted in this letter, it may be assumed that the town and sum differed in each circular.

3. Section 5 of "An Act making alterations in the Treasury and War Departments" reads as follows: "That all purchases and contracts for supplying the army with provisions, clothing, supplies in the quartermaster's department, military stores, Indian goods, and all other supplies or articles for the use of the department of war, be made by or under the direction of the treasury department" (1 *Stat.* 280 [May 8, 1792]).

4. See H to Coxe, April 4, 1794.

To George Washington

Treasy. Dept. Augt. 19. 1794

Sir,

A temporary absence from the seat of Government,[1] & the extra avocations which have occupied me since my return have delayed my submitting to you the inclosed communication of the 15 of July from the Commissioner of the Revenue.[2]

The arrangement proposed is the result of a previous consultation between the Commissioner of the Revenue & myself, and appears to me proper.[3]

If adopted, it will remain to appoint the requisite officers to which the power of the President is competent. On this head I will have the honor of submitting personally the result of my reflections & enquiries.

I have the honor &c. A Hamilton

LC, George Washington Papers, Library of Congress.

1. See H to Washington, July 11, 23, 1794; Washington to H, July 11, 1794; H to Elizabeth Hamilton, July 31, 1794.

2. Tench Coxe to H, July 15, 1794.
3. H is referring to "An Act of the President of the United States erecting the Revenue Districts of Ohio & Tennasee" enclosed in Coxe to H, July 15, 1794.

From Tench Coxe

Treasury Department, Revenue Office, August 20, 1794. "The enclosed three counterfeit notes of the Bank of North America, with the affidavits accompanying them, were transmitted to this office by the Supervisor of Virginia.[1] Col. Carrington wishes . . . that the amount of these notes . . . will be placed to his Credit by the United States."

LC, RG 58, Letters of Commissioner of Revenue, 1794–1795, National Archives.
1. Edward Carrington.

From Benjamin Lincoln

Boston August 20th 1794

Sir

Captain Magee[1] returned here a few days since from a long voyage to the Northwest shores of America Canton &c. He has been absent about three years during which time he has sailed about fourteen thousand leagues. He left Boston in a new ship with two new suits of sails one of Boston manufactured cloth and one foreign. I asked him particular respecting the Boston duck and had for answer that none could be better.[2] It is impossible for a man to express himself in strong terms in favour of any thing than he did in favour of this Cloth.

On the 17th of May last I addressed a line to you covering a complaint from Mr. Tisdale[3] and others respecting the value we put on the goods they imported from France. What gave rise to the discontent was the estimate made in New york & Philadelphia on like goods imported at the same time. They as is represented put the value of a liver much lower that we did. Their first bonds have been paid; their second are now due. Your decision on the question will probably prevent an action being brought on them. What ever you shall say on the subject will I doubt not put an end to the business. This leads me to wish your early attention to this complaint.[4]

Secy of the Treasury

LC, Massachusetts Historical Society, Boston; LC, RG 36, Collector of Customs at Boston, Letter Book, 1790–1797, National Archives; two copies, RG 56, Letters from the Collector at Boston, National Archives.

1. James Magee, a Boston ship captain, had left Boston on the ship *Margaret* on December 24, 1791, on a voyage to the northwest coast of North America and to Canton.

2. In a letter, dated August 27, 1794, Magee wrote: "It is unquestionably the duty of every citizen to render that justice to the *Manufactures* of his country which truth and experience will justify. It is therefore that I request you to inform the public, That in August, 1791, I purchased a quantity of SAIL CLOTH, made at the Manufactory in *Boston*, for the use of the ship *Margaret*, on a voyage to the Northwest coast of America; that the sails made of the sail cloth, were on the yards, and in constant wear, *thirty-four months*, and are now in good condition. I feel happy in being able to make this declaration, and farther to say, that I never sailed with better *cloth*, and that I think it equal if not *superior* to any imported" [Philadelphia] *Gazette of the United States and Daily Evening Advertiser*, September 8, 1794). See also H to Lincoln, June 28, 1794; Lincoln to H, July 5, 1794; Stephen Higginson to H, July 12, 1794.

3. James Tisdale was a Boston merchant.

4. On October 28, 1794, Oliver Wolcott, Jr., wrote to Tisdale and other Boston merchants: "Your letter of the 30th of Sept. has been rec'd. . . .

"Your application relates to a subject which is of an embarrasing nature, the value of assignats to the price of Exchange being continually fluctuating in consequence of causes which have no effect upon the value of Merchandize. A variety of practice within a certain extent, appears therefore to be unavoidable.

"It may be inferred from your letter that the rate of Exchange between France & London was considered by you as affording a rate for estimating the value of assignats.

"This has however been deemed by the Treasury a very imperfect criterion. . . . It cannot therefore be certainly inferred from what you have stated, that the duties have been erroniously estimated by the Collector.

". . . I take the liberty to request that copies of your Invoices as far as they relate to articles subject to ad valorum duties may be made out & certified by the Collector, & transmitted to this Department. . . ." (ADf, Connecticut Historical Society, Hartford.)

On January 19, 1795, Wolcott wrote to Lincoln: "I have recd. your favour of the 9th. instant & consent to a postponement of the demand of the public upon Mr. Tisdale untill his claim for a drawback of the duties can be brought forward in a form which will admit of an official decision.

"Instead of the unauthenticated copies of letters which have been transmitted, the originals or notarial Copies, ought to be lodged with you, and Mr. Tisdales representation should be confirmed by his Oath. Any information or evidence which the officers of the Customs can afford ought also to be transmitted to this Office.

"In cases where the formal proofs of delivery abroad, cannot be exhibited to substantiate a claim for a drawback of duties, it is deemed reasonable to require the most authentic evidence which the nature of the case will admit." (ADf, Connecticut Historical Society, Hartford.)

From Jeremiah Olney

Providence, August 20, 1794. "The public Scale-beam, now in use at this Port, being in want of repairs, and too small for weighing Hemp and large hhds of Sugar . . . I ask your permission to procure another Beam . . . necessary for the convenience and dispatch of public business in this District. . . ."

ADfS, Rhode Island Historical Society, Providence.

To the President and Directors of the Bank of the United States[1]

Treasury Department August 21 1794

Gentlemen,

The President of the United States having empowered me by an instrument, (of which the inclosed is a Copy) to make the loan authorised by the Second Section of the Act intitled "An Act making appropriations for certain purposes therein expressed"[2] a Copy of which is also herewith sent—

I have the honor to propose to the Bank of the United States a Contract for the loan therein contemplated, namely to the amount of One Million of Dollars, upon the same rate of Interest,[3] with former loans to be advanced in the following proportions and at the following epochs—Viz.

200,000 Dollars on the first of September
400,000 Dollars on the first of October
200,000 Dollars on the first of November, and
200,000 Dollars on the first of December of the

present year to be reimbursed severally within Six Calendar Months after each advance.

With great respect & consideration I have the honor to be Gentlemen Your Obedient Servant Alexander Hamilton
Secy of the Treasy

The President & Directors of the Bank of the United States

LS, from the original in the New York State Library, Albany.

1. Thomas Willing was president of the Bank of the United States.

2. 1 *Stat.* 394–95 (June 9, 1794). Section 2 of this act authorized the President to borrow a sum not exceeding one million dollars.

3. The loan of one million dollars was "agreed for the 27th August as per Contract a 5 ℔ Cent ℔ Annum from the time of advance. . ." (D, RG 217, Miscellaneous Treasury Accounts, 1790–1894, Account No. 6336, National Archives).

To William Ellery

Treasury Department August 21st 1794

Sir,

I have directed the Treasurer of the United States to remit to you on account of the fortifications [1] erecting at Newport the further Sum of Two thousand five hundred Dollars in bills to be drawn payable to yourself or order.

These draughts having blanks for the directions are to be filled up on yourself provided the funds in your hands are adequate to the purpose. If that however should not be the case, you will draw upon the Cashier of the Bank of Providence for the deficiency.

I shall Just add, that in the expenditure of this money, you will strictly conform to the instructions & regulations contained in my letter to you of the 3d of April 1794.[2]

I am with consideration Sir, Your most obedient Servant

A Hamilton

As the remittance now made completes the whole sum allotted for the fortifying of Newport you must take care, that the expenditures including your Commission thereon does not exceed the amount of the remittances.

William Ellery Esquire
Collector of Newport
Rhode Island

LS, The Sol Feinstone Collection, American Philosophical Society, Philadelphia.

1. For information concerning the fortifications, see Henry Knox to H, March 29, 1794; "Treasury Department Circular to the Collectors of the Customs," April 3–June 4, 1794.

2. "Treasury Department Circular to the Collectors of the Customs," April 3–June 4, 1794.

To Elizabeth Hamilton[1]

[Philadelphia, August 21, 1794]

Your last letter, My beloved Eliza, gave me inexpressible pleasure.[2] It tells me that my precious boy was fast recovering. Heaven Grant that the favourable appearances may have continued.

If you have not already left Albany write to me the precise day you will certainly leave it; so that I may meet you at *New Ark.* When you get to New York apply to Col Fish[3] to make an arrangement for carrying you & the Child to New Ark & when there, go to Mr. Boudinot's[4] till I come.

Philip & Alexander are gone to Trenton.[5] Angelica[6] is in good health.

Adieu my sweet. Love to all with you & best blessings on you & My dear boys.[7]

Aug 21. 1794

Mrs. Hamilton

AL[S], Hamilton Papers, Library of Congress.

1. For background to this letter, see H to George Washington, July 11, 23, 1794; Washington to H, July 11, 1794; H to Elizabeth Hamilton, July 31, August 2, 8, two letters of August 12, August 17, 1794.

2. Letter not found.

3. Nicholas Fish, who had known H since they were students together at King's College and who had been H's second in command at Yorktown, was a prominent resident of New York City. In 1794 he was supervisor of the revenue for the District of New York.

4. Elisha Boudinot, a lawyer and businessman in Newark, New Jersey, was a director of the Society for Establishing Useful Manufactures.

5. Philip A. Hamilton (born January 22, 1782) and Alexander Hamilton, Jr. (born May 16, 1786) were H's two oldest sons. Both studied under William Frazer, the Episcopal rector of St. Michael's Church in Trenton, New Jersey.

6. Angelica Hamilton, who was born on September 25, 1784, was H's second child and at this time his only daughter.

7. James Alexander Hamilton (born April 14, 1788) and John Church Hamilton (born August 22, 1792) were H's two youngest sons at this time.

To Henry Lee[1]

[*Philadelphia, August 21, 1794.* "In the absence of The Secretary at War,[2] I have the honor to acknowledge the Receipt of your letter to him of the 13th instant. The contents of it are such as were expected from your patriotism, from the steady zeal you have manifested for the support of the Government of the Union, and from the Chief Magistrate of a State, where the laws resisted are executed in a manner that does honor to the character of its Citizens. The President to whom it has been communicated instructs me to acknowledge on his part this new proof of your good dispositions & to say to you that he counts implicitly on the efficacious and affectionate support of the Government and People of Virginia.[3] When the requisition for the marching of the Militia shall be made, which it is feared cannot be avoided, measures will be announced for supplying the deficiency of arms from the magazines of the United States." [4] *Letter not found.*]

ALS, sold by The Rosenbach Company, 1937, Item 182.

1. For background to this letter, see H to Abraham Hunt, August 17, 1794, note 2.
2. See George Washington to H, August 12, 1794, note 1.
3. On August 16, 1794, Lee issued general orders calling up the militia of Virginia. Lee's orders are printed in *Pennsylvania Archives*, 2nd ser., IV, 161–62.
4. Extract taken from dealer's catalogue.

To Thomas Sim Lee

Philadelphia August the 21st
1974

Sir

I have the honor to acknowlege the Receipt of your letter to the Secretary at War [1] of the 15 instant.

The President, to whom it has been communicated, considers the determination of the Council to furnish the detachment of Militia called for from your State [2] with Musquets Bayonets and Cartouch-boxes as a new proof of their zeal for the support of the Government and laws of the United States.[3] It is understood that all other articles are to be provided and furnished by the United States.

With perfect respect & esteem I have the honor to be Sir Your most Obedient & humble servant Alexander Hamilton

His Excellency
Thomas E. Lee esq
Governor of Maryland

ALS, Hall of Records of Maryland, Annapolis.

1. See George Washington to H, August 12, 1794, note 1.

2. See H to Abraham Hunt, August 17, 1794, note 2.

On August 14, 1794, Thomas Sim Lee issued general orders calling up the militia of Maryland. His orders are printed in *Pennsylvania Archives*, 2nd ser., IV, 155–57.

3. In his letter to Henry Knox of August 15, 1794, Lee wrote: ". . . the Gentlemen of the Council have determined to furnish the whole detachment of Militia ordered from this State . . . with Musquetts Bayonets and Cartouch boxes. . . . I have to repeat that the detachment will stand in need of every other Article of equipment and I have no doubt that the necessary provisions will be made by the General Government to complete the equipment. . ." (LC, "Council Letter Book, 1793–1796," Hall of Records of Maryland, Annapolis). John Stagg, Jr., chief clerk in the War Department, informed Knox of the decision of the Maryland Council on August 23, 1794 (LS, Henry Knox Papers, Massachusetts Historical Society, Boston).

From Robert Purviance

Baltimore, August 21, 1794. "I am to Acknowled[g]e the receipt of your favor of the 14 Instant, covering a Letter to the Exec[u]tors of General Williams [1] and another to Mr. Richmond [2] his late Deputy. . . . The backward state in which the late Collectors Books stand at this moment, leaves me at a loss to Judge when I shall be enabled to pass a receipt for the Bonds and other property of the United States. . . . I must Observe, that ever since Mr. Delozier left the Collectors office,[3] the Accts have gradually fallen behind, occasioned from a want of Clerks and a proper person to conduct so important a trust. . . ."

ADfS, RG 53, "Old Correspondence," Baltimore Collector, National Archives.

1. Letter not found. In his will, dated June 5, 1794, Otho H. Williams had designated his wife, his brother Elie Williams, William Smith, and Dr. Philip Thomas as his executors (*Calendar of the General Otho Holland Williams Papers*, 341).

2. Letter to Christopher Richmond not found.

3. Daniel Delozier had been deputy collector of customs at Baltimore.

To George Washington

Philada. Augt. 21. 1794.

Sir,

The Secretary of War [1] contemplated the sending about this time two months pay to the troops & mounted volunteers under General Scott.[2] A law directs that the payments to the troops may be so regulated as that there shall be at no time in arrears more than two months pay.[3] The requisite Treasury arrangements are made & every thing is ready for making the contemplated remittance to the army. But a question (adverted to by the Secretary at War before he left this) presses—shall the sending of the money be hazarded, under the actual circumstances of the Western Counties of Pennsylvania? This question involves not only the possible evil of the loss of the money, but that of throwing a pecuniary aid into the hands of the Insurgents. It is true that the money will be almost wholly in Bank Post Notes in favor of the Pay Master Mr Swan,[4] and requiring, to be negotiable, his indorsement. Yet if taken, and the parties are bold enough to put his name upon them, they may possibly give them circulation & turn them to account. On the other hand if no use is made of them, if they are not recovered, difficulties may arise with the Bank. They will have paid the Warrant in bank notes, obtained a credit for it, & their notes will be outstanding.

In this situation there is no doubt that the public interest recommends a suspension of the remittance. But delay will risk a non compliance with the law, the remittances heretofore only extending to the end of July. To take the one or other kind of responsibility on me in a case which respects another Department, without first consulting you, not appearing either prudent or required by the situation, I have concluded to trouble you with the subject & ask your direction or opinion.

With perfect respect I have the honor to be &c.

Alexander Hamilton

P.S. If money is sent immediately it may suffice to confine it to one months pay for the troops. Can the idea of a circuitous route be embraced with advantage?

LS, George Washington Papers, Library of Congress.

1. Henry Knox was in Maine. See Washington to H, August 12, 1794, note 1.

2. Charles Scott, a native of Virginia, had served during the American Revolution as an officer of the 2nd, 3rd, and 5th Virginia Regiments. When this letter was written, he was a major general of the Kentucky Volunteers under the command of Anthony Wayne in the campaign against the western Indians, which culminated in the Battle of Fallen Timbers on August 20, 1794.

3. H is referring to "An Act in addition to the 'Act for making further and more effectual provision for the protection of the frontiers of the United States'" (1 *Stat.* 390 [June 7, 1794]).

4. Caleb Swan.

To George Washington[1]

[Philadelphia] Augt. 21. 1794

The Secretary of the Treasury presents his respects to The President. The letter written to the President on the 16. respecting the publication of the Report of the 5.[2] was written at the Secry. of State's Office, where Mr H. expected a copy of it had been taken previous to its delivery. But when Mr. H. sent to enquire for a copy in order to the publication of it, he found none had been taken—which, it being then too late to obtain a copy in time from the President, left him the dilemma, either of suffering the Report to go out without the letters,[3] or to draft one as a substitute for that which had been sent. The latter appeared to him to be most likely to be agreeable to the President, & he drew one accordingly a copy of which appears in Dunlap's paper of today,[4] corresponding with the enclosed original, which the President will find perfectly the same in substance with the former.

Another circumstance may require explanation. The letters follow, instead of preceding the Report. This happened from the report having been immediately sent to promote dispatch, & the President's answer not having been received 'till the day following, so that it went to the printer too late for insertion in the first instance without too great a derangement of his types.

LC, George Washington Papers, Library of Congress.

1. For background to this letter, see H to Washington, August 6, 16, 1794.
2. H to Washington, August 5, 1794.
3. H to Washington, August 16, 1794, and Bartholomew Dandridge to H, August 19, 1794.
4. [Philadelphia] *Dunlap and Claypoole's American Daily Advertiser*, August 21, 1794.

From George Washington

[Germantown, Pennsylvania, August 21, 1794]

Sir,

To your note of this date (in behalf of the Department of War) asking my opinion or direction respecting the advisability of sending (under the existing circumstances of the western counties of

Pennsylvania) two months pay to the army under the immediate orders of General Wayne, I answer, that under my present impressions the measure had better be delayed—at least until the Commissioners who were sent into those counties, make their report.[1] It certainly would from all the information that has been received from that quarter be too hazardous to send a sum of money by the way of Pittsburgh, thro' counties that are in open rebellion; & besides the circuitousness of the route through what is called the Wilderness,[2] & the length of time required to send it by a messenger that way, there would be, in my opinion, no small risk in the attempt. But as I shall be in the City tomorrow, I will converse with you on this subject.

German town 21 Augt. 1794.
Go Washington.

LC, George Washington Papers, Library of Congress.

1. Washington had appointed James Ross, Jasper Yeates, and Attorney General William Bradford as Federal commissioners to confer with representatives from western Pennsylvania. See H and Henry Knox to Washington, August 5, 1794, note 3.

2. The route through the Wilderness connected with the roads from Maryland and Pennsylvania.

From William Bradford

[*Pittsburgh, August 22, 1794.* On August 23, 1794, Bradford wrote to Hamilton: "Yesterday I wrote to you." *Letter not found.*]

To Robert Purviance

Treasury Department August 22d 1794

Sir,

I am to acknowledge the Receipt of your Letter of the 19th Instant,[1] with the inclosures therein mentioned, excepting the Copy of the letter from the Grand Jury to you.

I am pleased with your compliance with the request of the Grand Jury as to Stationing the Cutter and I shall be so with every other practicable co-operation on the part of the Custom House in a case, in which consideration of public policy and humanity so eminently coincide.[2] But as it cannot be forseen how long the occasion for precautions of this sort may continue, and as the establishments connected with the Custom House, cannot durably be diverted from their destination, it will be right to observe to the proper persons, that your cooperation can only be for a moderate period of time and that if there is a probability that the necessity for such precautions may be prolonged, it will be requisite that a substitute should be thought of.

I am with consideration Sir. Your most obedient Servant

A Hamilton

Robert Purviance Esquire
Collector of Baltimore

LS, Columbia University Libraries.

1. Letter not found.

2. This is a reference to the fear of the Baltimore authorities that yellow fever might be imported into the city by vessels from the West Indies. As a consequence, a quarantine was established to check ships from the West Indies, and vessels were needed for maintaining the quarantine (*The Maryland Journal, and the Baltimore Advertiser*, August 15, 29, September 5, 1794). The revenue cutter was used to help enforce the quarantine (*Baltimore Daily Intelligencer*, August 14, 25, 26, 1794). This was done in accordance with Section 8 of a Maryland statute, passed December 28, 1793, entitled "An Act to appoint a health officer for the port of Baltimore-town in Baltimore county," which reads: "That the assistance of the custom-house tender or boats is hereby requested to aid the said physician to carry this law into effect, whenever the same can be done consistently with their orders from the United States or their officers" (*Maryland Laws*, November, 1793, Sess., Ch. LVI).

To Robert Purviance

Treasury Department
August 22d. 1794

Sir

It has been represented to me that notwithstanding the Law prohibiting the exportation of arms and military stores from the United States [1] that business goes on from the Port of Baltimore with nearly as little restraint as if there were no such law.[2]

I cannot credit this information as it would imply so culpable a negligence in the Officers of the Customs—yet it comes to me with a degree of positiveness that I cannot disregard it, and am perplexed what to think.

I request to hear speedily & explicitly from you on this head, and I must urge that it is expected the Officers of the Customs will increase their vigilence to discover and prevent the practice, if it exists. Could it be possible to suppose that any officer of the United States would wink at such a breach of the Laws, from whatever motive, I should think it my duty to observe that the discovery of such a delinquency would be deemed and treated as inexcuseable.

With great consideration & Esteem I am Sir Your obedient Servt. Alexander Hamilton

P.S. It has also been mentioned to me that there are Vessels equipping themselves in the Port as for Armed Vessels.[3] What can this mean?

The Collector of Baltimore

LS, Columbia University Libraries; ADf, Connecticut Historical Society, Hartford.

1. "An Act prohibiting for a limited time the Exportation of Arms and Ammunition, and encouraging the Importation of the same" (1 *Stat.* 369–70 [May 22, 1794]).

2. On August 16, 1794, George Hammond, the British Minister to the United States, wrote to Lord Grenville: "I farther learn that notwithstanding the provisions of an act of Congress, prohibiting the exportation of arms and ammunition for the space of one year, a large quantity of gunpowder and lead is also preparing to be shipped from Baltimore for either Guadeloupe or Port de paix. . ." (PRO: F.O., Series 5, Vol. 5.1). On August 29, Hammond again wrote to Grenville: ". . . I have received additional testimony, relative to the French republicans assembled at Baltimore (under the direction of the French minister) of whom the number continue to increase, and to the noctural and clandestine shipments of gunpowder, and other military stores, for either Guadeloupe or Port de paix, which are still carrying on from that port to a very alarming extent. I farther learn that additional privateers have recently been surreptitiously fitted out at Charleston, under the expectation of falling in with part of the Jamaica homeward bound fleet. . ." (PRO: F.O., Series 5, Vol. 5.1).

3. On September 5, 1794, Hammond wrote to Grenville: "There appears to be no diminution of the *active* hostile disposition of the *people* of this country towards Great Britain. At Baltimore, exclusively of the proceedings above recited, several privateers are fitting out, and one, a schooner *carrying ten guns and ready for sea,* is openly advertised for sale in the newspapers of that city" (PRO: F.O., Series 5, Vol. 5.1). This advertisement, dated August 20, appeared in the *Baltimore Daily Intelligencer* on August 21, 22, 1794.

On December 1, 1794, Hammond again wrote to Grenville: "I have frequently adverted to the clandestine shipments of military stores from Baltimore; And I learn from Mr. [Edward] Thornton, his Majesty's Vice Consul there, that intelligence, has reached that place, of the capture, by the Solebay frigate, of a vessel belonging to, and bound from Baltimore, to Point a petre, and laden with five hundred barrels of gunpowder, which must have been shipped subsequently to the prohibitory act alluded to above. That Gentleman (Mr. Thornton) farther acquaints me that, having received information that a British prize, formerly named the Lively Lass, was equipping and arming as a privateer, he had represented to the Collector of the Customs at Baltimore the necessity of instituting a rigid enquiry into the situation of that vessel, from the result of which it appeared that she had been armed with fourteen cannon, furnished in the port of Baltimore. The vessel was immediately seized, and a legal process commenced against her, that will, I trust ensure her condemnation. . ." (PRO: F.O., Series 5, Vol. 5.1).

To William Rawle [1]

Treasury Department August 22d 1794

Sir

I am to acknowledge the receipt of your favor of the 14th Instant [2] in reply to my letter to you of the 17th of July last on the subject of the bad quality of the Hats and Shoes furnished for the use of the Army for 1793.

As in the event of instituting suits against the Contractors,[3] it will be adviseable to go upon sure grounds. I have thought it proper to inform you, that the Inspectors [4] under whose inspection the cloathing was received, were persons appointed by the public. I shall submit it therefore to you to determine how far this circumstance could operate in exoneration of the Contractors.

I am with great consideration Sir Your most Obedient Servant

A Hamilton

William Rawle Esquire
Attorney for the District
of Pennsylvania

LS, Historical Society of Pennsylvania, Philadelphia.

1. For background to this letter, see Henry Knox to H, May 1, 1794.
2. Letter not found.
3. William Young and George Dannacker.
4. Nathaniel Waters and Peter Cooper.

From William Bradford [1]

Pittsburgh, August 23. 1794

My dear Sir,

Yesterday I wrote to you pretty fully [2]—to day I have little to add beyond what is contained in the official communication.

Whatever may be the declarations of a determination to submit, or exertions on the part of those whose indemnity depends upon a general acquiescence in the execution of the acts of Congress—there seems to be a necessity for some force being stationed here, to overawe the disaffected individuals & protect the officers in the execution of their duty. This idea was perfectly agreeable to most of the Committee of Conference;[3] but they were apprehensive that any public declarations of it, might give rise to an idea that they were stipulating for their own protection. We therefore declared it in the letter which inclosed the articles.[4] But it deserves consideration, whether such protecting force would not be more advantageously furnished by the States, at least untill Congress can make some permanent provision for it.

I am not sorry for the opportunity we have had of terrifying the Ohio-men by discovering a disposition to leave them out.[5] They were individually the principal leaders of the opposition: & it is said have been the authors of some outrages on the Collector there.[6] I hope the State of Virginia will take some measures with them that may tend to suppress this spirit. If we have a conference with them, the first preliminary of our recommendation shall be that they will not interfere in any future consultations respecting our propositions to the Pennsylvanians. We shall also take measures to secure the restoration of bonds taken from the Collector, by some of these people in Ohio County.

We have evidently gained much ground in the three last days & if we can but inspire the moderate men with firmness & decision I hope all will be well. The more I see of this country and of the tempers of the people the more sollicitous I am that any contest with them should be avoided unless there were troops who could be kept in the field longer and act with more energy than the militia.

I forgot to enclose in my letter of yesterday the handbill I mentioned, & send it to you now.

I regret the death of poor Higgonson [7]—but am exceeding pleased with the prospects that Mr Jay seems to have. The opinion, that we are likely to be at peace with the British will aid us in our endeavors to restore order.

I am my dear Sir very truly yours W. Bradford

P.S. All the precipts served by the Marshall [8] are safe in the hands of Major Craig.[9] I shall take the first perfectly safe conveyance to send them down, or will take them with me. W.B.

ALS, Pennsylvania Miscellany, Whiskey Rebellion, Vol. I, Library of Congress.

1. Bradford wrote this letter in his capacity as one of the three commissioners (along with James Ross and Jasper Yeates) appointed by George Washington to confer with representatives from western Pennsylvania. See H and Henry Knox to Washington, August 5, 1794, note 3.

2. Letter not found.

3. On August 14, 1794, there was a meeting attended by "delegates duly elected by the respective counties of Westmoreland, Fayette, Allegheny, Washington and that part of Bedford county lying west of the Allegheny mountain, in Pennsylvania, and by the county of Ohio in Virginia, convened at Parkinson's Ferry on Monongahela river, in order to take into consideration the situation of the Western Country" (*Pennsylvania Archives,* 2nd ser., IV, 159). This meeting appointed a "committee of conference," consisting of three members from each county, "to meet any commissioners that have been, or may be appointed by the government" (*Pennsylvania Archives,* 2nd ser., IV, 160–61). In addition to the Federal commissioners, there were two commissioners from the Commonwealth of Pennsylvania appointed by Thomas Mifflin: Thomas McKean, who was chief justice of Pennsylvania from 1777 to 1799, and William Irvine, who had been a brigadier general of the 2nd Pennsylvania Regiment during the American Revolution and was a member of the House of Representatives from Pennsylvania from 1793 to 1795. The committee of conference was composed of the following delegates from western Pennsylvania: David Bradford, James Marshall, and James Edgar from Washington County; Thomas Morton, John Lucas, and Hugh Henry Brackenridge from Allegheny County; John Kirkpatrick, George Smith, and John Powers from Westmoreland County; Edward Cook. Albert Gallatin, and James Lang from Fayette County. Ohio County in Virginia sent William McKinley, William Sutherland, and Robert Stephenson.

The committee of conference, the United States commissioners, and the Pennsylvania commissioners met on August 21–23 at Pittsburgh, with most of the negotiations being conducted in writing. The upshot of these negotiations was that the committee finally agreed to advise the people to submit to the laws and accept an amnesty. Copies of the records of these negotiations may be found in Pennsylvania Miscellany, Whiskey Rebellion, Vol. I, Library of Congress, and the records are printed in *Pennsylvania Archives,* 2nd ser., IV, 182–206. For a report of these negotiations by a member of the committee of conference, see H. H. Brackenridge, *Incidents,* 100–07.

4. United States commissioners to the committee of conference. August 22, 1794 (copy, Pennsylvania Miscellany, Whiskey Rebellion, Vol. I, Library of Congress). This letter is printed in *Pennsylvania Archives,* 2nd ser., IV, 190–93.

5. This is a reference to a dispute between the members of the committee from Ohio County in Virginia and the members of the United States commission as to whether the amnesty proposed for western Pennsylvania should include Virginia. Despite the protests of the delegates from Ohio County, the commissioners refused to have the amnesty include those who had interfered with the collection of the excise tax in Virginia. Copies of the correspondence between the Ohio County delegates and the commissioners may be found in Pennsylvania Miscellany, Whiskey Rebellion, Vol. I, Library of Congress. The letters are printed in *Pennsylvania Archives,* 2nd ser., IV, 201–03.

6. On August 23, 1794, the commissioners wrote to the delegates of Ohio County: "But as certain Bonds have been lately taken by Force from Zacheus Biggs the Collector of the said Revenue in Ohio County, it is to be clearly understood, that said Pardon shall not extend to prevent any civil Remedy against those who have destroyed the said Bonds, or are Parties to them" (copy,

Pennsylvania Miscellany, Whiskey Rebellion, Vol. I, Library of Congress). This letter is printed in *Pennsylvania Archives*, 2nd ser., IV, 202.

7. Nathaniel C. Higginson. See H to Washington, August 14, 1794, note 5.

8. David Lenox.

9. Isaac Craig.

From George Gale[1]

[*Baltimore, August 23, 1794.* On August 27, 1794, Hamilton wrote to Gale: "I have received your letter of the 23d. instant." *Letter not found.*]

1. Gale, who was supervisor of the revenue for the District of Maryland, was in charge of supplying the Maryland militia.

Tully No. I[1]

[Philadelphia, August 23, 1794]

For the American Daily Advertiser.
To the PEOPLE *of the* UNITED STATES.

LETTER I.

It has from the first establishment of your present constitution been predicted, that every occasion of serious embarrassment which should occur in the affairs of the government—every misfortune which it should experience, whether produced from its own faults or mistakes, or from other causes, would be the signal of an attempt to overthrow it, or to lay the foundation of its overthrow, by defeating the exercise of constitutional and necessary authorities. The disturbances which have recently broken out in the western counties of Pennsylvania furnish an occasion of this sort. It remains to see

[Philadelphia] *Dunlap and Claypoole's American Daily Advertiser*, August 23, 1794.

1. This is the first of four "Tully" letters. The other three letters are dated August 26, 28, September 2, 1794.

The authority for H's authorship of the "Tully" letters is John C. Hamilton (*JCHW*, VII, 157–69). The letters which John C. Hamilton printed are not organized in the same way as those which appeared in the newspapers. Thus, "Tully No. III" in *JCHW* included the last half of the letter printed as "Tully No. IV" in *Dunlap and Claypoole's American Daily Advertiser*. In addition, "Tully No. IV," which was printed in the newspaper, is approximately twice as long as the letter printed in *JCHW*.

whether the prediction which has been quoted, proceeded from an unfounded jealousy excited by partial differences of opinion, or was a just inference from causes inherent in the structure of our political institutions. Every virtuous man, every good citizen, and especially EVERY TRUE REPUBLICAN must fervently pray, that the issue may confound and not confirm so ill omened a prediction.

Your firm attachment to the government you have established cannot be doubted.

If a proof of this were wanting to animate the confidence of your public agents, it would be sufficient to remark, that as often as any attempt to counteract its measures appear, it is carefully prepared by strong professions of friendship to the government, and disavowals of any intention to injure it. This can only result from a conviction, that the government carries with it YOUR affections; and that an attack upon it to be successful, must veil the stroke under appearances of good will.

It is therefore very important that YOU should clearly discern in the present instance, the shape in which a design of turning the existing insurrection to the prejudice of the government would naturally assume. Thus guarded, you will more readily discover and more easily shun the artful snare which may be laid to entangle your feelings and your judgment, and will be the less apt to be misled from the path by which alone you can give security and permanency to the blessings you enjoy, and can avoid the incalculable mischiefs incident to a subversion of the just and necessary authority of the laws.

The design alluded to, if it shall be entertained, would not appear in an open justification of the principles or conduct of the insurgents, or in a direct dissuasion from the support of the government. These methods would produce general indignation and defeat the object. It is too absurd and shocking a position to be directly maintained, that forcible resistance by a sixtieth part of the community to the representative will of the WHOLE, and its constitutional laws expressed by that will, and acquiesced in by the people at large, is justifiable or even excusable. It is a position too untenable and disgustful to be directly advocated—that the government ought not be supported in exertions to establish the authority of the laws against a resistance so incapable of justification or excuse.

The adversaries of good order in every country have too great a share of cunning, too exact a knowledge of the human heart, to pursue so unpromising a cause. Those among us would take upon the present occasion one far more artful, and consequently far more dangerous.

They would unite with good citizens, and perhaps be among the loudest in condemning the disorderly conduct of the insurgents. They would agree that it is utterly unjustifiable, contrary to the vital principle of republican government, and of the most dangerous tendency—But they would, at the same time, slily add, that excise laws are pernicious things, very hostile to liberty, (or perhaps they might more smoothly lament that the government had been imprudent enough to pass laws so contrary to the genius of a free people) and they would still more cautiously hint that it is enough for those who disapprove of such laws to submit to them—too much to expect their aid in enforcing them upon others. They would be apt to intimate further, that there is reason to believe that the Executive has been to blame, sometimes by too much forbearance, encouraging the hope that laws would not be enforced, at other times in provoking violence by severe and irritating measures; and they would generally remark, with an affectation of moderation and prudence, that the case is to be lamented, but difficult to be remedied; that a trial of force would be delicate and dangerous; that there is no forseeing how or where it would end; that it is perhaps better to temporize, and by mild means to allay the ferment and afterwards to remove the cause by repealing the exceptionable laws. They would probably also propose, by anticipation of and in concert with the views of the insurgents, plans of procrastination. They would say, if force must finally be resorted to let it not be till after Congress have been consulted, who, if they think fit to persist in continuing the laws, can make additional provisions for enforcing their execution. This too, they would argue, will afford an opportunity for the public sense to be better known, which (if ascertained to be in favor of the laws) will give the government a greater assurance of success in measures of coercion.

By these means, artfully calculated to divert YOUR attention from the true question to be decided, to combat by prejudices against a particular system, a just sense of the criminality and danger of violent resistance to the laws; to oppose the suggestion of misconduct on the part of government to the fact of misconduct on the part of the insurgents; to foster the spirit of indolence and procrastination natural to the human mind, as an obstacle to the vigor and exertion which so alarming an attack upon the fundamental principles of public and private security demands; to distract YOUR opinion on the course proper to be pursued, and consequently on the propriety of the measures which may be pursued. They would expect (I say) by these and similar means, equally insidious and pernicious, to abate YOUR just indignation at the daring affront which has been offered to YOUR authority and YOUR zeal for the maintenance and support of the laws to prevent a competent force, if force is finally called forth, from complying with the call—and thus to leave the government of the Union in the prostrate condition of seeing the laws trampled under foot by an unprincipled combination of a small portion of the community, habitually disobedient to laws, and itself destitute of the necessary aid for vindicating their authority.

Virtuous and enlightened citizens of a now happy country! ye could not be the dupes of artifices so detestable, of a scheme so fatal; ye cannot be insensible to the destructive consequences with which it would be pregnant; ye cannot but remember that the government is YOUR OWN work—that those who administer it are but your temporary agents; that YOU are called upon not to support their power, BUT YOUR OWN POWER. And you will not fail to do what your rights, your best interests, your character as a people, your security as members of society conspire to demand of you. TULLY

Minutes of a Meeting Concerning the Insurrection in Western Pennsylvania[1]

[Philadelphia, August 24, 1794]

At a Meeting at the Presidents House
City of Philadelphia Aug 24. 1794

Present

The President of The United States.
The Secretary of State
The Secretary of the Treasury.

The President proposed for the opinion and advice of The Secretary of State & the Secretary of the Treasury the following questions.

1 Shall orders issue for the immediate convening of the whole or any part of the Militia ordered to hold themselves in readiness [2] to be called forth for suppressing the Insurrection in the Western parts of Pensylvania?

Answer

It appears adviseable to send immediate orders to the Governor of Virginia [3] to assemble those of that State—recommending to him not to issue his public orders for the purpose 'till the first of September.

Question 2 Shall an additional number of Militia be called for?

Answer

It appears adviseable to call for a further number sufficient to complete the whole to fifteen thousand non Commissioned Officers and privates. That of these fifteen hundred be called for from Virginia and that in the call for the purpose it be suggested to the Governor as eligible to endeavour to obtain as many riflemen as may be practicable under Major General Morgan [4] and as near the scene of action as they can be had. Five hundred to Maryland with a like intimation as to Riflemen and five hundred to New Jersey.

Question 3 What will be the proper places and time of rendezvous?

Answer

The place of general rendezvous to be—For New Jersey, Carlisle; for Pensylvania Carlisle & Chambersburgh. These to have reference to Bedford as an interior point. For Maryland; Williamsport and such other place more Westerly as the Governor of Maryland [5] may deem adviseable for the more western Militia of that State. For Virginia; Winchester & the vicinity of Old Fort Pleasant with such other place as The Governor of Virginia may think eligible for the Militia of that State lying beyond the Alleghany. These places (except the one which shall be appointed by the Governor of Virginia for the Militia beyond the Alleghany) in Maryland & Virginia to have reference to Fort Cumberland as an ulterior point.

The supplies to be directed towards the points of rendezvous and the Governors to be left at liberty to make duration for local convenience having regard to the places of supply. The time to be aimed at for reaching the ulterior points Bedford & Cumberland to be the first of October.

Question 4th What communication shall be made to The Commissioners in answer to their letter of the 17th instant? [6]

Answer

The Commissioners to be informed [7] of what further has been done with regard to the Militia—and to be advised explicitly to remain in that Country till after the proposed Meeting of the 2d. of September and also to be advised to continue there as much longer as may in their opinion promise any public utility & be consistent with their personal safety not exceeding the last of September, as their stay beyond that day can not be supposed necessary for the beneficial purpose of their Meeting and can only be prolonged by a plea of delay on the part of the Insurgents—to instruct them to announce with frankness and explicitness the determination of the Executive Government to exert all the means with which it is invested to produce a compliance with the laws—to encourage the well-disposed to cooperate in their support under a full assurance of the decision & perseverance of the Government; acting under the Conviction that the question concerns the very being of Government of law and order—& to communicate the substance of the information received with regard to the disposition of the Citizens to cooperate effectually with the Government.

D, in the handwriting of H, Pennsylvania Miscellany, Whiskey Rebellion, Vol. I, Library of Congress.

1. For background to this document, see "Deposition of Francis Mentges," August 1, 1794, note 1; H to George Washington. August 2, 5, 1794. See also H and Henry Knox to Washington, August 5, 1794; Edmund Randolph to Thomas Mifflin, August 7, 1794.

2. See H to Abraham Hunt, August 17, 1794, note 2.

3. Henry Lee.

4. Brigadier General Daniel Morgan of the Virginia militia. Morgan, who was commissioned a captain in a company of Virginia riflemen in 1775, was captured at Quebec on December 31, 1775, and upon his release became a colonel in a Virginia regiment. On October 13, 1780, he was made a brigadier general in the Continental Army and served in that capacity until the end of the war. His daughter Nancy was married to Colonel Presley Neville.

5. Thomas Sim Lee.

6. On August 17, 1794, James Ross, Jasper Yeates, and Attorney General William Bradford, Federal commissioners appointed to confer with representatives from western Pennsylvania, reported to the Secretary of State: "We think it of Importance to take the earliest Opportunity of stating to you the present Situation of the Western Part of Pennsylvania, & to request some *eventual* Instructions on certain Points which are likely to arise in the Prosecution of our Mission. . . . We have great Doubts whether we ought to stay in this Country after the 1st September, or confer with any Bodies assembled in this Manner, after that Day; But at the same Time, if the Committee [of insurgents] should deny their Power to call the Body, or refuse to do it, we wish to be instructed, whether we ought to wait the Meeting on the 2d. September" (LS, Pennsylvania Miscellany, Whiskey Rebellion. Vol. I, Library of Congress). This letter is printed in *Pennsylvania Archives,* 2nd ser., IV, 163–66.

7. Randolph sent the Federal commissioners these instructions on August 25, 1794 (LC, RG 59, Domestic Letters of the Department of State, Vol. 7, June 27–November 30, 1794, National Archives).

From Edward Carrington

Richmond Aug. 25. 1794

My dear Sir

You have upon sundry occasions done me the favor to request my opinions upon the public Sentiment in Virginia. Conceiving that there can never have been an occurrence giving you greater anxiety than the present Insurgency in the Western parts of Pensylvania, or upon which a knowledge of the public opinions and dispositions here could be more interesting, I anticipate your request, and proceed to give you that information in which I feel myself confident. Virginia will do her duty. The requisition of the President,[1] and as many more as he shall find it necessary to make, will be complied with, with alacrity. It is a case which goes home to the people themselves; and they will act according to their own principles—it is not one of those cases in which they remain silent while Democratic societies, British debtors & other Factions presume to declare, in Resolutions & Toasts, opinions for them. The great Body of the People of Virginia are independant planters & Farmers, much attached to liberty, property, and domestic happiness, & busy themselves but little about public concerns, unless they feel that these blessings are brought into danger. Hence it is, that factious Men, for a time, succeed in giving a complection to the conduct of the country, very different from the real temper of the People; and this is a misfortune under which Virginia has been placed for several years. Virtuous Men have been cried down under a ding of Monarchy, Aristocracy, british influence, & French Republicanism, terms to which no rational significations have been applied, because they have seriously recollected that we had a Country & government of our own, and, in Congress & elswhere, voted to preserve and prosper them. These clamors have been set up & propagated with a degree of industry which none have, with equal zeal, opposed. Investigations for the truth have been beyond the reach of the Multitude, which has of course gone with the clamor. But the people of Virginia mean to be right when they can be in possession of the truth. The Insurgency is a case in which the truth cannot be veiled. The great Body of our Country know that the government they have chosen for themselves is a republican one, to be directed by a Majority; and when a Minority openly resists the Laws passed by a Majority, and thus counteracts the most essential principle of republicanism, the truth stands too fully exposed to be perverted. Pretended republicans are compelled to support the government, or to exhibit themselves in their true character of Anarchists. Taking the first turn they may not do us much good, but taking the latter, they lose their power of doing evil. These are my reflections on the subject, and the accounts received from the different parts of the State assure me that the real state of the opinions & conduct of the Country, are in concord with them.

I hope & trust that a radical extirpation will be effected in the instance. A patched up reconciliation will only leave the embers of sedition to be rekindled with greater violence at a future day. There must be a compleat conquest and serious examples of the leaders in the business.

I am with great regard yr. Freind & st. E. Carrington

Should you be of opinion that a publication without names, of this letter, or any part, will be of service, you have my consent thereto.

ALS, Hamilton Papers, Library of Congress.

1. See George Washington's proclamation of August 7, 1794, concerning the insurgents in western Pennsylvania. The part of this proclamation to which Carrington is referring reads as follows: "And whereas it is, in my judgment, necessary, under the circumstances of the case, to take measures for calling forth the militia, in order to suppress the combinations aforesaid, and to cause the laws to be duly executed, and I have accordingly determined so to do, feeling the deepest regret for the occasion, but withal the most solemn con-

viction that the essential interests of the Union demand it; that the very existence of Government, and the fundamental principles of social order, are materially involved in the issue, and that the patriotism and firmness of all good citizens are seriously called upon, as occasion may require, to aid in the effectual suppression of so fatal a spirit" (*GW*, XXXIII, 460).

To Isaac Craig[1]

War Department August 25th 1794

Sir,

Your letter of the 17th Instant to the Secretary at War[2] has been received and duly attended to.

The suggestions respecting additional measures of defence have been considered, but the danger of the means falling into the hands of the insurgents, appears at present an objection.

It is hoped that every thing at Pittsburgh or which shall come there, not necessary for the Post itself, has been forwarded down the river & will continue to be so as long & as fast as it can be done with safety.

The friends of Government at Pittsburgh ought to rally their confidence and if necessary manifest it by Acts. They cannot surely doubt the power of the U. States to uphold the authority of the laws, and they may be assured that the necessity of doing it towards preserving the very existence of Government so directly attacked will dictate & produce a most rigorous and persevering effort; in which the known good sense and love of order of the quiet body of the people and all the information hitherto received of their sentiments & feelings with regard to the present emergency, authorise a full expectation of their hearty cooperation—with esteem

I am Sir Your Most Obedient Servant Alexander Hamilton
for the Secy at War

Isaac Craig Esquire
D Q M G

LS, Isaac Craig Papers, Carnegie Library of Pittsburgh, Pennsylvania.

1. For background to this letter, see H to George Washington, August 12, 1794; Washington to H, August 12, 1794; H to Craig, August 13, 1794.

2. On August 17, 1794, Craig wrote to Henry Knox: ". . . Messr. [Jasper] Yeats, [William] Bradford & [James] Ross are now here. I do beleave they are by what they have seen and heard *Pretty well Convinced that the powers they are Vested with will have but a small effect in bringing the Misguided multitude to a sence of their duty as Citizen of the United States* and although

I have no Doubt but Proper measures will be adopted, I must beg leave to Offer as my Opinion that Something ought to be done immediately to excite Confidence in those that remain well effected to Government.

"Several of the inhabitants of Pittsburg say that they submitted to the Humiliating Condition imposed on them by the multitude on Bradocks Field only with a view of saving their Property & that if the Town Could have been protected it would have been Otherwise. Therefore as the Works & Troops at this post is not adequate to the protection of the Town on all Sides, I presume another work ought to be errected on the points of Grants hill Mounted with two 12 pounders & two three pounders & also that two 12 pounders & two three pounders & a 5½ inch Howitzer with Proper apparatus ought to be added to Fort Fayette. A Company of Artillery I presume will Also be necessary. I have mentioned my Opinion on the above Particulars to Colo. [Thomas] Butler who fully Approves of it." (LC, Isaac Craig Papers, Carnegie Library of Pittsburgh, Pennsylvania.)

Craig wrote to Knox on August 29, 1794, requesting permission to provide additional barracks in case the garrison at Fort Fayette was augmented (LC, Isaac Craig Papers, Carnegie Library of Pittsburgh, Pennsylvania). On September 6, 1794, John Stagg, Jr., chief clerk in the War Department, wrote to Craig: ". . . as there is no positive arrangement at present, for a permanent augmentation of force, to the garrison at Fort Fayette, the erecting of additional barracks therein, as suggested in your letter, is a matter that must be governed by existing circumstances on the spot" (LS, Isaac Craig Papers, Carnegie Library of Pittsburgh, Pennsylvania). On September 26, 1794, Craig informed Knox that ". . . I am Accordingly agreeable to the Orders of Coll Butler, Enlarging the Barracks & building a Store House" (LC, Isaac Craig Papers, Carnegie Library of Pittsburgh, Pennsylvania).

From William Ellery

Newport [*Rhode Island*] *August 25, 1794.* "Your letter of the 13th. of this month [1] expressing that great Inconveniences have arisen from my *discontinuing* to endorse the name of my office on my letters as heretofore directed [2] surprized me very much. Whatever *interruption*, or *omission* of that kind has taken place must have been occasioned by a hurry of business, not an intention to forbear a compliance with your direction. . . ."

LC, Newport Historical Society, Newport, Rhode Island.

1. Letter not found, but see H to Jeremiah Olney, August 13, 1794.

2. "Treasury Department Circular to the Collectors of the Customs," May 10, 1792.

From Samuel Hodgdon

[*Philadelphia, August 25, 1794.* On August 25, 1794, Hamilton wrote to Hodgdon and referred to "your letter to me of this date." *Letter not found.*]

To Samuel Hodgdon

Treasury Department, August 25, 1794. "I have to request, that you will purchase for the use of the Quarter Masters Department, the horses with their necessary trappings, to be employed as Post Horses and to be stationed at the several places, mentioned in your letter to me of this date." [1]

LS. Mr. Pierce Gaines, Fairfield, Connecticut.

1. Letter not found.

To Samuel Hodgdon

War Department, August 25, 1794. "It is expected, that there will be shortly assembled at Williamsport in Maryland a body of 2850 Militia and at and near Winchester in Virginia a body of 4800 Militia.[1] It is of the most urgent importance that you should forward without delay to those places respectively all sorts of Military Stores and tents and other Camp Equipage proportioned to the number to be assembled at each. . . . The articles ought to arrive at their destination by the 20th. of September at furthest. . . ."

ADf, Connecticut Historical Society, Hartford.

1. See "Minutes of a Meeting Concerning the Insurrection in Western Pennsylvania," August 24, 1794.

To Henry Lee[1]

War Department
August 25. 1794

Sir

In place of The Secretary at War, who is absent,[2] I am instructed by The President to signify to you his wish and request that you will come forth in the command of the Militia, which is to be detached from Virginia against the Insurgents in the Western parts of Pensylvania;[3] in which case You will have the command of the whole force that may be employed upon that Enterprise.

The President anticipates, that it will be as painful to you to execute, as it is to him to direct, measures of coertion against fellow citizens however misled. Yet he needed not the assurance you have already given him of the sense you entertain of their conduct and its consequences to be convinced that he might count ever on your zealous personal service,[4] towards suppressing an example fatal in its tendency to every thing that is dear and valuable in political society.

With the greatest respect & attachment I have the honor to be Your Excellency's Most Obedt & humble servant Alex Hamilton

His Exellency Henry Lee Esqr
Governor & Commander in Chief
of Virginia

ALS, Historical Society of Pennsylvania, Philadelphia.

1. For background to this letter, see "Deposition of Francis Mentges," August 1, 1794, note 1; H to George Washington, August 2, 5, 1794.

2. See Washington to H, August 12, 1794, note 1.

3. See "Minutes of a Meeting Concerning the Insurrection in Western Pennsylvania," August 24, 1794.

4. On August 17, 1794, Lee wrote to Washington: "Your late orders for a detachment of militia & proclamation give birth to a variety of sensations & opinions. All good citizens deplore the events which have produced this conduct on your part, & feel but one determination to maintain inviolate our happy government at the risk of their lives & fortunes. There are some among us from the influence of party spirit & from their own ambitious views who rejoice in national adversity & gladden when they hear of governmental embarrassments.

"I am gratified in telling you that the great body of this State will excel themselves in whatever way you may direct to the utmost of their power & I am persuaded that you may count with certainty on their zeal & determination. The awful occasion demands united efforts & I beg leave to offer to you my services in any way or station you may deem them proper. . . ." (ALS, George Washington Papers, Library of Congress.)

On August 26, 1794, Washington replied to Lee's letter as follows: "Your favor of the 17th. came duly to hand. . . . it gives me sincere consolation amidst the regret with which I am filled, by such lawless & outrageous conduct, to find by your letter above mentioned, that it is held in general detestation by the good people of Virginia; and that you are disposed to lend your *personal* aid to subdue this spirit, and to bring those people to a proper sense of their duty" (ALS, George Washington Papers, Library of Congress).

To Henry Lee[1]

Philadelphia August 25
1794

Sir

In consequence of information just received from the Commissioners sent to confer with the Insurgents in the Western parts of

Pensylvania,[2] who appear resolved to dictate a repeal of the laws,[3] to which they object, and an act of amnesty and oblivion—and concerning whom The Commissioners give an express opinion that nothing but an exertion of the Physical strength of the Union will bring them to a submission to the laws—

I am directed by The President of the U States to communicate to you his desire That the Militia of the State of Virginia which by a letter from the Secretary at War of the 7th instant [4] You were requested to hold in readiness may be called forth and assembled at the places and within the time hereinafter mentioned.

The places of rendezvous which appear eligible for the Militia on this side the Alleghany Mountain are Winchester & old Fort Pleasant or its Vicinity. It is desired that their assemblings at those places may be so regulated as that they may be able to reach Fort Cumberland on the last day of September. The Militia of Maryland will be directed to assemble at Williamsport and some convenient place more Westerly so as to be able to form a junction at Fort Cumberland on the same day. With regard to such Militia of your state, being beyond the Alleghany Mountain, as may be called out, it is left to your Excellency to appoint such place of rendezvous as may appear to you most proper; having regard to the time abovementioned and to the best cooperation which the nature of the case will admit.[5]

In addition to the number heretofore required The President requests that the further number of Fifteen hundred non Commissioned officers and Privates with a due proportion of commissioned Officers may be called forth. It is his wish that as many of these as possible may be drawn from places near the scene of action and may be riflemen. It is represented that the insurgents are impressed with more respect for a force of that kind and from that quarter, than for any other, which they expect to come against them. General Morgan [6] whom it is understood to be your intention to employ can it is believed be very useful in carrying this particular object into effect.

Your orders for assembling the Militia cannot well issue before the first of September. For particular reasons, it is wished they may be dated on that day.[7]

Col Carrington is requested to undertake the arrangement for all supplies in the Quarter Master and Commissary lines,[8] and for that purpose to confer with you without delay. I have sent him an order upon Mr. Holt Keeper of the public Magazines at New London[9] for whatever he can furnish; and I have instructed the Commissary of Stores to forward without delay to Winchester, Artillery, Ammunition, tents and whatsoever else may be requisite to be sent from hence.[10] I understand there are now at New London fifteen hundred stands of arms ready for service & that 100 more per week can be got ready there.

I request to be particularly informed of the deficiencies if any which you may expect will exist in the articles of arms and accoutrements.

No expence will be spared necessary to an effectual equipment. Too much depends upon the event not to give in every way a vigorous support to the undertaking. Yet a just œconomy is always precious in public operations. The one in train will involve no trifling bill of Costs with the utmost possible care—and therefore I trust that the Patriotism of all concerned will adopt as a principle to add nothing needlessly to it. With the greatest respect and attachment I have the honor to be Your Excellency's most Obedient & humble servant Alexander Hamilton

P.S. It seems there was a person appeared as a delegate from Ohio County in Virginia.[11] It is said he was sent by a very feeble & partial suffrage. But it is very important that the disease should not be suffered to spread in that scene. The addition of 1500 now called for is part of 2500 determined to be added to the original number so as to make the whole 15000.

His Excellency Henry Lee Esqr
Governor of Virginia

ALS, Mr. Lucius S. Ruder, Clearwater, Florida.

1. For background to this letter, see "Minutes of a Meeting Concerning the Insurrection in Western Pennsylvania," August 24, 1794. See also H to Abraham Hunt, August 17, 1794; H to Lee, August 21, 25, 1794.

2. On August 17, 1794, James Ross, Jasper Yeates, and William Bradford wrote to Edmund Randolph that at the Parkinson's Ferry meeting of the representatives of the insurgents, held on August 14, ". . . there appears to us to have been three parties . . . one of which was at that time disposed to renounce all connection with the Government and to maintain their present opposition by violence without further appeals to Congress. This was not

numerous, nor open. . . . A second party is disposed to remain a part of the nation, but at the same time to resist at all hazards, the execution of the excise acts. These were numerous and violent, and evidently overawed the third or moderate party, which consisted of men of property, who whatever might be their opinions of the excise, are disposed to submit to the national will, rather than hazard the convulsions of a civil contest. . . . One of them [the moderate party] had prepared resolves demanding a repeal of the excise acts, an act of oblivion, and a suspension of all measures of coercion untill the sense of Congress was known, as the most moderate measure that could have been carried" (copy, Pennsylvania Miscellany, Whiskey Rebellion, Vol. I, Library of Congress). This letter is printed in *Pennsylvania Archives,* 2nd ser., IV, 163–66.

3. H to George Washington, August 2, 1794, note 2.

4. See H to Hunt, August 17, 1794, note 2.

5. For the rendezvous points of the militia, see "Minutes of a Meeting Concerning the Insurrection in Western Pennsylvania," August 24, 1794.

6. Daniel Morgan.

7. See "Minutes of a Meeting Concerning the Insurrection in Western Pennsylvania," August 24, 1794.

8. On September 1, 1794, Edward Carrington wrote to Lieutenant Governor James Wood of Virginia: "The Secretary of the Treasury requests me to obtain from the Executive an accurate idea what arms and accoutrements, if any, are wanted . . ." *Calendar of Virginia State Papers,* VII, 288). H's letter to Carrington has not been found.

9. In his letter of September 1, 1794, to Wood, Carrington also wrote: "I have an order on Capt. [Thomas] Holt, the store-keeper at New London, for all the arms, ammunition, and accoutrements, and camp equipage in his possession, or so much thereof as shall be necessary; and shall take measures for their being delivered to your officer as soon as I am informed what will be wanted" *Calendar of Virginia State Papers, VII,* 288).

10. See H to Samuel Hodgdon, August 25, 1794.

11. In their letter of August 17, the commissioners reported that at the meeting at Parkinson's Ferry on August 14 "there was a feeble and partial deputation from Ohio County, in Virginia" (copy, Pennsylvania Miscellany, Whiskey Rebellion, Vol. I, Library of Congress). This letter is printed in *Pennsylvania Archives,* 2nd ser., IV, 163. According to the minutes of this meeting, dated August 14, 1794, William Sutherland represented Ohio County (*Pennsylvania Archives,* 2nd ser., IV, 161).

To Henry Lee

[*Philadelphia, August 25, 1794.* On September 2, 1794, Lee wrote to Hamilton: "I am extremely chagrined on finding from your private letter accompanying your public letter [of August 25, 1794] that the intended secrecy is entirely baffled." *Private letter not found.*] [1]

1. On August 26, 1794, George Washington wrote to Lee: ". . . . I shall refer you to letters from the War office, and to a private one from Colo. Hamilton (who in the absence of the Secretary of War, superintends the *military* duties of that department) for my sentiments on this occasion" (ALS, George Washington Papers, Library of Congress).

From Jeremiah Olney

Custom House,
Providence 25th. August 1794.

Sir.

I was much hurt by your Letter of the 13th. instant, until it occurred to me that it might, by mistake, have been misdirected; which I am persuaded must have been the case: For on every official Letter from this Office, addressed to "the Secretary of the Treasury," since the receipt of your circular directions of the 10th. of May 1792 (excepting Two or Three in that Year, omitted thro forgetfulness) have been invariably endorsed the name of "my *Office*, and the *Place* where it is kept."

As a Servant of the Public, it is my Intention to "conform to *all* the regulations" prescribed by my Superiors, with such *promptitude*, as not to merit the censure of want of "punctuality." Among the great variety of Instructions from the Treasury, some one *may* slip my Memory; and I beg of you to believe Sir, that the omission of *any* will not be *intentional*.

I have the Honor to be, Very respectfully, Sir, Your Most Obedt. & Hume. Servant Jereh. Olney Collr.

A. Hamilton Esquire,
Secy. of the Treasury.

ADfS, Rhode Island Historical Society, Providence.

To Samuel Hodgdon

[Philadelphia, August 26, 1794]

Mr. Hamilton requests Mr. Hodgsdon to have ready an express to go tomorrow Morning to cumberland County in this State.

Tuesday. Aug 26

AL, Miss Barbara Chernow, New York City.

From Robert Purviance

Baltimore, August 26, 1794. Encloses "the report of Joseph Farland, Master of the Schooner Martha." [1]

L[S], RG 56, Original Letters to the Collector at Baltimore, National Archives.
1. See H to Purviance, August 18, 1794.

Tully No. II[1]

[Philadelphia, August 26, 1794]

For the American Daily Advertiser.
To the PEOPLE *of the* UNITED STATES.
LETTER II.

It has been observed that the means most likely to be employed to turn the insurrection in the western country to the detriment of the government, would be artfully calculated among other things "to divert your attention from the true question to be decided."

Let us see then what is this question. It is plainly this—shall the majority govern or be governed? shall the nation rule, or be ruled? shall the general will prevail, or the will of a faction? shall there be government, or no government?

It is impossible to deny that this is the true, and the whole question. No art, no sophistry can involve it in the least obscurity.

The Constitution *you* have ordained for yourselves and your posterity contains this express clause, "The Congress *shall have power* to lay and collect taxes, duties, imposts, and *Excises,* to pay the debts, and provide for the common defence and general welfare of the United States." You have then, by a solemn and deliberate act, the most important and sacred that a nation can perform, pronounced and decreed, that your Representatives in Congress shall have power to lay Excises. You have done nothing since to reverse or impair that decree.

Your Representatives in Congress, pursuant to the Commission derived from you, and with a full knowledge of the public exigencies have laid an excise. At three suceeding Sessions they have revised that act,[2] and have as often, with a degree of unanimity not common, and after the best opportunities of knowing your sense, renewed their sanction to it, you have acquiesced in it, it has gone into general operation: and *you* have actually paid more than a million dollars on account of it.

But the four western counties of Pennsylvania, undertake to rejudge and reverse your decrees, you have said, "The Congress *shall have power* to lay *Excises.*" They say, "The Congress *shall not have* this power." Or what is equivalent—they shall not exercise it:—for a *power* that may not be exercised is a nullity. Your Representatives have said, and four times repeated it, "an excise on distilled spirits *shall* be collected." They say it *shall not* be collected. We will punish, expel, and banish the officers who shall attempt the collection. We will do the same by every other person who shall dare to comply with your decree expressed in the Constitutional character; and with that of your Representative expressed in the Laws. The sovereignty shall not reside with you, but with us. If you presume to dispute the point by force—we are ready to measure swords with you; and if unequal ourselves to the contest we will call in the aid of a foreign nation. We will league ourselves with a foreign power.*

If there is a man among us who shall affirm that the question is not what it has been stated to be—who shall endeavour to perplex it, by ill timed declamations against excise laws—who shall strive to paralise the efforts of the community by invectives, or insinuations against the government—who shall inculcate directly, or indirectly, that force ought not to be employed to compel the Insurgents to a submission to the laws, if the pending experiment to bring them to reason [3] (an experiment which will immortalize the moderation of the government) shall fail; such a man is not a good Citizen; such a man however he may prate and babble republicanism, is not a republican; he attempts to set up the *will* of a part against the *will* of the whole, the *will* of a *faction,* against the *will* of *nation,* the pleasure of a *few* against *your* pleasure; the violence of a lawless combination against the sacred authority of laws pronounced under your indisputable commission.

Mark such a man, if such there be. The occasion may enable you to discriminate the *true* from *pretended Republicans; your* friends from the friends of *faction.* 'Tis in vain that the latter shall attempt to conceal their pernicious principles under a crowd of odious invectives against the laws. *Your* answer is this: "*We* have already in the

* *Note*—Threats of joining the British are actually thrown out—how far the idea may go is not known.

Constitutional act decided the point against you, and against those for whom you apologize. *We* have pronounced that *excises* may be laid and consequently that they are not as you say inconsistent with Liberty. Let our will be first obeyed and then we shall be ready to consider the reason which can be afforded to prove our judgement has been erronious: and if they convince us to cause them to be observed. We have not neglected the means of amending in a regular course the Constitutional act.[4] And we shall know how to make our sense be respected whenever we shall discover that any part of it needs correction. But as an earnest of this, it is our intention to begin by securing obedience to our authority, from those who have been bold enough to set it at defiance. In a full respect for the laws we discern the reality of our power and the means of providing for our welfare as occasion may require; in the contempt of the laws we see the annihilation of our power; the possibility, and the danger of its being usurped by others & of the despotism of individuals succeeding to the regular authority of the nation."

That a fate like this may never await *you*, let it be deeply imprinted in your minds and handed down to your latest posterity, that there is no road to *despotism* more sure or more to be dreaded than that which begins at *anarchy*. TULLY.

[Philadelphia] *Dunlap and Claypoole's American Daily Advertiser*, August 26, 1794.

1. The other "Tully" letters are dated August 23, 28, September 2, 1794.
2. See H to George Washington, August 2, 1794, note 2.
3. This is a reference to the appointment of Federal commissioners to treat with the insurgents of western Pennsylvania. See H and Henry Knox to Washington, August 5, 1794, note 1.
4. See "An Act making further provision for securing and collecting the Duties on foreign and domestic distilled Spirits, Stills, Wines and Teas" (1 *Stat.* 378–81 [June 5, 1794]).

To George Gale

Treasury Department
Aug 27. 1794

Sir

I have received your letter of the 23d. instant.[1]

I expect that the next post will carry to the Governor instructions for assembling and marching the Militia with all practicable expedition.[2] You may therefore proceed to put in motion the means for supplying them without further delay. It is understood that you will appoint the requisite Agents and settle the allowances by way of compension; doing as much by contract as the nature of the service will admit with advantage and as far as shall consist with dispatch.

The Governor has informed that arms and accoutrements will be furnished by the State.[3] Artillery Military Stores tents and other Camp Equipage will go from hence to the place of general rendezvous which shall be named by The President. He has thought of Williamsport which I understand is within six miles of Hagars Town. But he will, no doubt, leave it optional to prefer Hagars Town if there shall appear to The Governor reasons for that preference. You will therefore confer with the Governor and act upon this Idea. A conductor of stores will accompany them from hence, who will be instructed to take the orders of yourself or your Agent at Hagars Town or Williamsport. An arrangement for their reception and safe keeping ought to be made.

From what has been said you will perceive that provisions forage fuel & transport are the objects for which you are to provide. Whiskey of course falls under the article provisions which leaves you at liberty to consult the consideration of policy you hint at.

The Treasurer has been directed to remit you for this service blank drafts for fifteen thousand Dollars which you may fill up upon the Bank of the United States & the Offices of Discount & Deposit at New York & Baltimore. These will go by the next post.

You speak of appointments by the Governor of Quarter Masters & Commissaries. As the service to be executed will involve a great expenditure, Characters of this description will be appointed for the whole army by this Government. The appointment of the Governor therefore need not go beyond Regimental Quarter Masters. You may notice this to him.

The affair of the Arms at Frederick is of the greatest importance. Nothing ought to be left to hazard. The insurgents are of an enterprising character & would make the attempt if they thought there was a prospect of success. But the practicability of execution must depend on the temper of the inhabitants and other local considerations which I here cannot appreciate. I intend to write a line by this post to the Governor on the subject.[4]

With consideration & esteem I am sir Your obedt ser

George Gale esq
Maryland

ADf, Connecticut Historical Society, Hartford.

1. Letter not found.
2. See H to Thomas Sim Lee, first letter of August 29, 1794.
3. See H to Thomas Sim Lee, August 21, 1794.
4. There is no indication that H wrote to Lee "by this post," but see H to Thomas Sim Lee, September 6, 1794, note 3.

To Samuel Hodgdon

Philadelphia Aug 27
1794

Sir

You will procure without delay the number of horses you mention for the Artillery.

I am of opinion that it is adviseable to appoint Conductors of stores here, which I request you to do with such compensations as are usual. When arrived at Winchester, they will take the orders of Edward Carrington Esquire or the person who may appear as his Agent.[1]

You will send me the names of the Conductors for the several destinations.

With consideration I am sir Your obedient servant

Samuel Hodgsdon Esq

ADf, Connecticut Historical Society, Hartford.

1. See H to Henry Lee, second letter of August 25, 1794.

To Abraham Hunt

Treasury Department
Aug 27. 1794

Sir

I have received your letter[1] in answer to mine,[2] concerning the supply of the Militia about to assemble in New Jersey. I should think what you mention for a ration at Trenton too high. It appears to me that ten Cents, for so considerable a supply in a short time, would be sufficient. If you are not willing to undertake at this rate, I will request you to conduct the business upon commission as heretofore proposed.[3]

But it appears to me that a person having some general superintendence of the business of supplying the militia in the course of their march through the State may be necessary; for the contractors at Brunswick & Trenton are only to supply on the spot & some intermediate halts will be necessary for which an arrangement should be made. Besides I can never think of allowing the present contract price of the Ration at New Brunswick & if Mr Bray[4] to whom I have written[5] does not agree to a price which appears moderate I shall prefer purchases there also on Commission.

It is this kind of general direction which I wished you to undertake and for which a suitable compensation would be made according to the trouble it might occasion. In other words I want a person who will adjust with the Governor[6] the course to be pursued and will undertake to see it executed. That the Treasury may have but one point to look to.

I request your answer by return of Post, as I expect the Post of tomorrow will convey an instruction for the assembling of the Militia.

With esteem, I am Sir Your Obedient serv

Abraham[7] Hunt Esquire
Trenton

ADf, Connecticut Historical Society, Hartford.

1. Letter not found.
2. H to Hunt, August 17, 1794.
3. In his letter to Hunt on August 17, 1794, H had proposed "a Commission of 5 ℔ Cent on the amount of expenditures."
4. John Bray was the contractor for Army rations at New Brunswick, New Jersey.
5. Letter not found.
6. Richard Howell.
7. "Abraham" is not in H's handwriting.

To John Kean[1]

[*Philadelphia*] *August 27, 1794.* Encloses "two draughts of a Contract, for the Loan of One million of Dollars, agreed to be made to the United States by the Bank [2]—one of which draughts is already signed in due form by the Secretary on the part of the United States—the other is intended to be executed by the President of the Bank." [3]

L, Historical Society of Pennsylvania, Philadelphia.

1. Kean was cashier of the Bank of the United States.

2. See H to the President and Directors of the Bank of the United States, August 21, 1794.

3. Thomas Willing.

To Henry Lee

Philadelphia August 27th. 1794

Sir

Inclosed are duplicates of two letters which went by the last Post.[1] I have since received your letter to me of the 19th.[2] and I have seen one to the War Office which came by the last Post but which having been sent to the President, I have not now before me. If there should be any thing in it requiring an answer more than I have said in mine of the 25th. and may say in this—the next post will convey it.

You are informed that an order has been sent to Col: Carrington upon the Keeper of our Magazine at New London for whatever he may have.[3] Among the articles which will go from hence to Winchester will be a compleat set of accoutrements for the Cavalry which is required from Virginia. But as you specify nothing about the number of Arms you may want for the infantry I am at some loss to judge whether those at New London will suffice. I shall expect to hear from you if they do not. There were 1500 ready by the last return. I hereby authorise you to cause to be purchased on behalf of the United States the necessary land for the fortifications going on,[4] so as the cost do not exceed One thousand Dollars—which is the sum reserved by the Secretary at War. On receiving information of the purchase I will remit the money through the Collector of Norfolk.[5]

With great respect and attachment I have the honor to be Sir Your Excellencys Obedient Servant Alexander Hamilton

Henry Lee Esquire
Governor of Virginia

LS, University of Virginia; ADf, Connecticut Historical Society, Hartford.

1. See the first two letters from H to Lee, August 25, 1794.

2. Letter not found.

3. Edward Carrington. See H to Lee, first letter of August 25, 1794, note 9.

4. For information on the fortifications, see Henry Knox to H, March 27, 1794.

5. William Lindsay. Lindsay's account with the United States for the purchase and survey of the land for Fort Norfolk may be found in RG 217, Miscellaneous Treasury Accounts, 1790–1894, Account No. 7376, National Archives.

From Benjamin Lincoln

Boston, August 27, 1794. "I called a few days since for the settlement of a number of Bonds a collection of the money due on which had been suspended as the duties arose on goods which afterwards were exported.[1] Many of the people come and say that they have not yet received their certificates of the landing of the Goods in a foreign port the reason of which arises from the detention the vessels have experienced in France that they are now liberated and will probably be at home in a very short time.[2] Will their late detention in a foreign port justify a farther delay in collecting the money due on the bonds?" [3]

LC, Massachusetts Historical Society, Boston; LC, RG 36, Collector of Customs at Boston, Letter Book, 1790–1797, National Archives; two copies, RG 56, Letters from the Collector at Boston, National Archives.

1. See "An Act for extending the Benefit of a Drawback and Terms of Credit in certain cases, and for other purposes" (1 *Stat.* 372–73 [June 4, 1794]).

2. This is a reference to a French embargo on foreign ships at Bordeaux and the lifting of this embargo in March, 1794. See Stephen Girard to H, February 26, 1794, note 2.

3. On October 28, 1794, Oliver Wolcott, Jr., wrote to Lincoln on behalf of H, who was with the troops opposing the Whiskey Insurrection: ". . . In cases where relief is sought under the Law, it will be proper to recommend to the Merchts. the exhibition of Bills of Sale, Invoices, or affidavits of respectable characters, tending to establish the fact of a delivery in a foreign port" (ADf, Connecticut Historical Society, Hartford).

To George Washington

[Philadelphia, August 27, 1794]

The Secretary of the Treasury presents his respects to the President incloses a recommendation of persons for officers of the Revenue Cutter in South Carolina.[1] Capt. Cochran [2] who is now here expresses an opinion that as the person recommended for third Mate is very young, it will be adviseable to defer his appointment 'till some further trial of him.

Augt. 27. 1794.
A Hamilton

LC, George Washington Papers, Library of Congress.

1. On August 29, 1794, Washington "Signed commissions appointing . . . James Christian to be 2d. mate of the So. Carolina Revenue Cutter" (JPP, 309).

2. Robert Cochran, master of the South Carolina revenue cutter.

To Tench Coxe

[Philadelphia, August 28, 1794]

Mr. Hamilton requests to see Mr Coxe this Morning at his House.

Thursday Aug 28

AL, Tench Coxe Papers, Historical Society of Pennsylvania, Philadelphia.

From Tench Coxe

[Philadelphia, August 28, 1794]

If Mr. Hamilton has recd. the letters from & *to* Mr. Brackenridge [1] Mr Coxe will thank him for them *by the Bearer*. It will require some part of this day & to Morrow to copy the latter.[2]

Col. Miller [3] is not expected for several Days.

Thursday 7 o'Clk

AL, Tench Coxe Papers, Historical Society of Pennsylvania, Philadelphia.

1. Coxe is referring to a letter, dated August 8, 1794, which Hugh H. Brackenridge wrote to him and his answer to Brackenridge of August 26, 1794. For this correspondence, see H to George Washington, August 15, 1794.

2. At the bottom of Coxe's letter printed above H wrote the following: "I requested by a note to see you this morning at my house. The above letter was one subject. Yrs AH. Augt 28 94." See H to Coxe, August 28, 1794.

3. Henry Miller, supervisor of the revenue for the District of Pennsylvania. See H to Coxe, June 28, 1794.

From Joseph Howell, Junior

War Department, Accountant's Office, August 28, 1794. Encloses "copies of the Contracts for Clothing for the Year 1787, 88 & 89 which governed me in the settlement of those accounts. . . ."

LC, RG 93, Letter Book, 1794, National Archives.

From Thomas Sim Lee

In Council Annapolis August 28th 1794.

Sir

By an act of the General Assembly of this State passed at their last Session, a Copy whereof is enclosed, certain arrangements are provisionally made for preventing, the Introduction of malignant contagious diseases into the Town of Baltimore.[1] The Consent of the Legislature of the United States being necessary to the imposition and collection of the Tonnage duty contemplated by this Act as the means of its Execution, a Law was passed at the last Session of Congress by which the Operation of the above-mentioned Act of Assembly is assented to "so far as to enable this State to collect a duty of one cent per Ton on all Vessels coming into the District of Baltimore from a Foreign Voyage for the purpose in the said Act intended."[2]

The Act of Assembly, the operation of which is thus assented to, directs the duty to be paid to such person as may be appointed by the Governor with the advice of the Council to receive the same, and it is presumed that in virtue of these two laws a Collector appointed by us will be justified in demanding and receiving the duty imposed. But as neither the Laws of the United States nor that of this State contains any particular provision for securing or compelling the payment of the duty the demand of which is authorized; and as any person appointed by this Government for the purpose of making the collection would have considerable difficulties to encounter unless aided by the Revenue Officers of the General Government: We take the liberty of requesting, that, if nothing exceptionable is discovered in it, directions may be given to the proper officers of

Revenue at Baltimore to afford their assistance to the person to be appointed by this Board so as to enable him to gratify the views of the Laws before alluded to in securing and enforcing the said duty.

We beg leave also to point out to you the request of our General Assembly contained in the 8th Section of the enclosed Act,[3] and to solicit as speedy and effectual a compliance as possible both with their requisition and ours as the establishments to which they have reference cannot with propriety be longer delayed.

We have the honor to be with respectful consideration Sir, your most obt Servt Thos S. Lee

The Honorable
Alexander Hamilton Esq
Secretary Treasury.

Copy, RG 56, Letters of the 2d Comptroller, 2d Auditor, Executive of Maryland and Georgia, 1789–1833, Maryland, National Archives.

1. Lee is referring to "An Act to appoint a health officer for the port of Baltimore-town in Baltimore county," which was passed December 28, 1793 (*Maryland Laws,* November, 1793, Sess., Ch. LVI).

2. "An Act declaring the consent of Congress to an act of the state of Maryland, passed the twenty-eighth of December one thousand seven hundred and ninety-three, for the appointment of a Health Officer" (1 *Stat.* 393–94 [June 9, 1794]).

3. See H to Robert Purviance, August 22, 1794, note 2.

From Edmund Randolph

Philadelphia, August 28, 1794. ". . . it is the wish of the President of the United States, that General Miller[1] should be sent into the counties of Pennsylvania, west of the Susquehannah, to ascertain their real temper, in case they should be called upon to quell the insurrection in the West. This idea arose from the suggestion in Mr. Bradford's private letter,[2] and is certainly important. The office of Supervisor does not perhaps include such a duty, but the object and the fitness of the man would at least render his expences a *contingent* charge."

LC, RG 59, Domestic Letters of the Department of State, Vol. 7, June 27–November 30, 1794, National Archives.

1. Henry Miller.

2. In an undated letter William Bradford wrote to George Washington: "Other circumstances may arise that may make it unnecessary to march the Militia. It would therefore be very desirable—if not indispensible—to obtain

accurate, full & faithful accounts of the conduct, intentions and temper of the inhabitants of these Counties, especially after they know of the call of the Militia. This may be obtained from some persons resident among them to whom a messenger, not likely to be suspected, might be immediately dispatched" (ALS, George Washington Papers, Library of Congress).

From Daniel Stevens[1]

[*Charleston, South Carolina, August 28, 1794.* On September 18, 1794, Tench Coxe wrote to Stevens: "The Secretary of the Treasury has transmitted to me your letter of the 28 Ulto."[2] *Letter not found.*]

1. Stevens was supervisor of the revenue for South Carolina.
2. LC, RG 75, Letters of Tench Coxe, Commissioner of the Revenue, Relating to the Procurement of Military, Naval, and Indian Supplies, National Archives.

Tully No. III[1]

[Philadelphia, August 28, 1794]

For the American Daily Advertiser.
To the PEOPLE *of the* UNITED STATES.
LETTER III.

If it were to be asked, What is the most sacred duty and the greatest source of security in a Republic? the answer would be, An inviolable respect for the Constitution and Laws—the first growing out of the last. It is by this, in a great degree, that the rich and powerful are to be restrained from enterprises against the common liberty—operated upon by the influence of a general sentiment, by their interest in the principle, and by the obstacles which the habit it produces erects against innovation and encroachment. It is by this, in a still greater degree, that caballers, intriguers, and demagogues are prevented from climbing on the shoulders of faction to the tempting seats of usurpation and tyranny.

Were it not that it might require too lengthy a discussion, it would not be difficult to demonstrate, that a large and well organized Republic can scarcely lose its liberty from any other cause than that of anarchy, to which a contempt of the laws is the high road.

But, without entering into so wide a field, it is sufficient to present to your view a more simple and a more obvious truth, which is this—that a sacred respect for the constitutional law is the vital principle, the sustaining energy of a free government.

Government is frequently and aptly classed under two descriptions, a government of FORCE and a government of LAWS; the first is the definition of despotism—the last, of liberty. But how can a government of laws exist where the laws are disrespected and disobeyed? Government supposes controul. It is the POWER by which individuals in society are kept from doing injury to each other and are bro't to co-operate to a common end. The instruments by which it must act are either the AUTHORITY of the Laws or FORCE. If the first be destroyed, the last must be substituted; and where this becomes the ordinary instrument of government there is an end to liberty.

Those, therefore, who preach doctrines, or set examples, which undermine or subvert the authority of the laws, lead us from freedom to slavery; they incapacitate us for a GOVERNMENT of LAWS, and consequently prepare the way for one of FORCE, for mankind MUST HAVE GOVERNMENT OF ONE SORT OR ANOTHER.

There are indeed great and urgent cases where the bounds of the constitution are manifestly transgressed, or its constitutional authorities so exercised as to produce unequivocal oppression on the community, and to render resistance justifiable. But such cases can give no colour to the resistance by a comparatively inconsiderable part of a community, of constitutional laws distinguished by no extraordinary features of rigour or oppression, and acquiesced in by the BODY OF THE COMMUNITY.

Such a resistance is treason against society, against liberty, against every thing that ought to be dear to a free, enlightened, and prudent people. To tolerate were to abandon your most precious interests. Not to subdue it, were to tolerate it. Those who openly or covertly dissuade you from exertions adequate to the occasion are your worst enemies. They treat you either as fools or cowards, too weak to perceive your interest and your duty, or too dastardly to pursue them. They therefore merit, and will no doubt meet your contempt.

To the plausible but hollow harangues of such conspirators, ye cannot fail to reply, How long, ye Catilines, will you abuse our patience.[2]

TULLY.

[Philadelphia] *Dunlap and Claypoole's American Daily Advertiser*, August 28, 1794.

1. The other "Tully" letters are dated August 23, 26, September 2, 1794.

2. In *JCHW*, VII, 163–67, "Tully No. III" included several additional paragraphs which were printed at the end of "Tully No. IV" in the newspaper version of September 2, 1794.

To Thomas Sim Lee [1]

Philadelphia August 29th. 1794

Sir

I am directed by the President of the United States to communicate to you his desire.

That such part of the Militia of the State of Maryland which by a Letter from the Secretary at War of the [2] instant You were requested to hold in readiness, as may have been allotted by you to the Eastern Shore of the State, may be assembled and marched without delay to the Town of Baltimore, there to receive further orders. The detachments from the other parts of the State will wait for future direction.

From the nature of the co-operation intended, Williamsport has appeared an eligible place of general Rendezvous for the Militia of Maryland. But if there are any reasons of weight which lead to a preference of Hagers Town the difference is not considered here as material.

If the local situation of any of the Militia called for shall require a more Westerly rendezvous, it is with your Excellency to appoint it as well as any other place or places of particular Rendezvous in the way to the general ones which may appear expedient.[3]

The intention is to send to Williamsport or Hagars Town, as the one or the other shall be preferred by you, the Artillery, Ammunition, Tents and other Camp equipage and whatsoever else is necessary to go from hence. If an alteration in this plan should appear to you adviseable it is requested that it may be notified without delay. Your orders for assembling the Militia cannot well issue before the first of September. For particular reasons it is wished that they may be dated on that day.

George Galc Esquire has been requested [4] to undertake the arrangement for all supplies both in the Quarter Master & Commissary lines; and for that purpose to confer with you.

Your Excellency will oblige by advising frequently of the progress of the operation and of any thing which may occur requiring attention here.

With great respect & Esteem I have the Honor to be Your Excellencys Most Obedient Servant A Hamilton

His Excellency
Thom S Lee Esqr.
Governor of Maryland

LS, Hall of Records of Maryland, Annapolis.

1. For background to this letter, see "Deposition of Francis Mentges," August 1, 1794, note 1; H to George Washington, August 2, 5, 1794; "Minutes of a Meeting Concerning the Insurrection in Western Pennsylvania," August 24, 1794.

2. Space left blank in MS. For Henry Knox's letter to the governors of New Jersey, Pennsylvania, Maryland, and Virginia, dated August 7, 1794, see H to Abraham Hunt, August 17, 1794, note 2. See also H to Thomas Sim Lee, August 21, 1794.

3. For the places of rendezvous, see "Minutes of a Meeting Concerning the Insurrection in Western Pennsylvania," August 24, 1794.

4. H to Gale, August 27, 1794.

To Thomas Sim Lee

Philad Aug 29. 1794

Dear Sir

We have received by the last Pittsburgh Mail advices which give a hope that the disturbances there may terminate without bloodshed.[1] Yet the symptoms thus far are too equivocal to be relied upon and may be a mere trick to produce a relaxation of efforts. Hence the President has concluded to proceed as if they might prove fallacious. I thought this hint might not be unacceptable to you.

It is very important in its example & consequences that even if the Militia are not [to] be used a zeal for the support of Government should appear amongst them. It may save the necessity of using force now & at future periods.

With great respect & esteem I have the honor to be Dr Sir Your obed ser A Hamilton

His Exellency Governor Lee
Maryland.

ALS, Massachusetts Historical Society, Boston.

1. H is referring to the correspondence between the Federal commissioners and the committee of conference appointed by the insurgents in western Pennsylvania at their meeting at Parkinson's Ferry on August 14, 1794. See William Bradford to H, August 23, 1794, note 3.

After a meeting between these two groups, it was agreed that all further negotiations should be carried on in writing. On August 22, 1794, the committee of conference wrote to the Federal commissioners that "we are impowered to give you no definitive Answer with Regard to the sense of the People on the great Question of acceding to the Terms of Accommodation; but that in our own Opinion, it is the Interest of the Country to accede to them, & that we shall make this Report to the Committee, to whom we are to report, & state to them the Reasons of our Opinion, that so far as they appear to have Weight, they may be regarded by them. It will be our Endeavor not only to conciliate them, but the public Mind in general to our Sense on this Subject" (copy, Pennsylvania Miscellany, Whiskey Rebellion, Vol. I, Library of Congress). This letter is printed in *Pennsylvania Archives,* 2nd ser., IV, 190.

Edmund Randolph to Thomas Mifflin[1]

Philadelphia Aug 30 1794

Sir

I am directed by the President to acknowlege the Receipt on the 17th. of Your Excellency's letter dated the 12th instant.[2]

The President feels with you the force of the motives which render undesireable an extension of correspondence on the subject in question. But the case being truly one of great importance and delicacy, these motives must yield, in a degree, to the propriety and utility of giving precision to every part of the transaction, and guarding effectually against ultimate misapprehension.

To this end, it is deemed adviseable, in the first place, to state some facts which either do not appear, or are conceived not to have assumed an accurate shape in Your Excellencys Letter. They are these—

Df, in the handwriting of H, Massachusetts Historical Society, Boston.

1. For background to this letter, see "Deposition of Francis Mentges," August 1, 1794; "Conference Concerning the Insurrection in Western Pennsylvania," August 2, 1794; H to George Washington, August 2, 5, 1794; H and Henry Knox to Washington, August 5, 1794; Randolph to Mifflin, August 7, 1794.

2. LS, RG 59, Miscellaneous Letters, 1790–1799, National Archives; copy, Pennsylvania Miscellany, Whiskey Rebellion, Vol. I, Library of Congress. This letter is printed in *Pennsylvania Archives,* 2nd ser., IV, 148–54, and *ASP, Miscellaneous,* I, 102–03.

1 You were informed at the Conference,[3] that all the information which had been received had been laid before an associate Justice,[4] in order that he might consider and determine whether such a case as is contemplated by the second section of the Act, which provides for calling forth the Militia to execute the laws of the Union, suppress insurrections and repel invasions,[5] had occurred; that is, whether, combinations existed too powerful to be suppressed by the ordinary course of Judicial proceedings, or by the powers vested in the Marshal by that act—in which case, The President is authorised to call forth the Militia to suppress the combinations and to cause the laws to be duly executed.

2 The idea of a preliminary proceeding by you was pointed to [as] an eventual cooperation with the Executive of the UStates, in such plan as upon mature deliberation should be deemed adviseable in conformity with the laws of The Union. The inquiry was particularly directed towards the possibility of some previous accessory step, in relation to the Militia, to expedite the calling them forth; if an acceleration should be judged expedient & proper, and if any delay on the score of evidence should attend the notification from a judge, which the laws make the condition of the Power of The President to require the aid of the Militia and turned more especially upon the point, whether the law of Pensylvania of the 22d. of September 1783 was or was not still in force.[6] The Question emphatically was—Has the Executive of Pensylvania power to put the Militia in Motion, previous to a requisition from the President under the laws of the Union, if it shall be thought adviseable so to do? Indeed it seems to be admitted by one part of your letter, that the *preliminary* measure contemplated did turn on this question, and with a particular eye to the authority and existence of the act just mentioned.

3 The information contained in the papers read at the confer-

3. See "Conference Concerning the Insurrection in Western Pennsylvania," August 2, 1794.

4. James Wilson. See H to Tench Coxe, August 1, 1794; "Conference Concerning the Insurrection in Western Pennsylvania," August 2, 1794, note 9.

5. 1 *Stat.* 264–65 (May 2, 1792). See "Conference Concerning the Insurrection in Western Pennsylvania," August 2, 1794, note 9.

6. See "Conference Concerning the Insurrection in Western Pennsylvania," August 2, 1794, notes 11 and 12.

ence, besides the violence offered to the Marshall,[7] while in company with the Inspector of The Revenue,[8] established, that the Marshall had been afterwards made prisoner by the Insurgents, put in jeopardy of his life—had been obliged to obtain safety and liberty by a promise guaranteed by Colonel Presly Neville, that he would serve no other process on the West-side of the Alleghany Mountain—that in addition to this, a deputation of the Insurgents had gone to Pittsburgh to demand of the Marshall a surrender of the processes in his possession, under the intimation that it would satisfy the people and *add to his safety;* which necessarily implied that he would be in danger of further violence without such a surrender—That under the influence of this menace he had found it necessary to seek security by taking secretly & in the night a circuitous route.

This recapitulation is not made to invalidate the explanation offered in your last letter of the view of the subject, which you assert to have led to the suggestions contained in your first, and of the sense which you wish to be received as that of the observations accompanying those suggestions. It is intended solely to manifest, that it was natural for the President to regard your communication of the 5th instant in the light under which it is presented in the Reply to it.

For, having informed you that the matter was before an associate Justice, with a view to the law of the UStates which has been mentioned, and having pointed what was said respecting a *preliminary* proceeding on your part to a call of the Militia under the authority of a State-law, by anticipation of a requisition from the General Government and in cooperation with an eventual plan to be founded upon the laws of the Union—it was not natural to expect, that you would have presented a plan of conduct intirely on the basis of the State-Government, even to the extent of resorting to the Legislature of Pensylvania, after its judiciary had proved incompetent, "to prescribe by their wisdom and authority the means of subduing the spirit of insurrection and of restoring tranquility and order";[9] a plan, which being incompatible with the course marked out in the

7. David Lenox. See H to Washington, August 5, 1794.

8. John Neville. See H to Washington, August 5, 1794.

9. Mifflin had made this recommendation in his letter to Washington of August 5, 1794. See Randolph to Mifflin, August 7, 1794.

laws of the UStates evidently could not have been acceded to without a suspension, for a long & indefinite period, of the movements of the Fœderal Executive pursuant to those laws. The repugnancy and incompatibility of the two modes of proceeding at the same time cannot it is presumed be made a question.

Was it extraordinary then, that the plan suggested should have been unexpected, and that it should even have been thought liable to the observation of having contemplated Pensylvania in a light too separate and unconnected?

The propriety of the remark, "that it was impossible not to think that the current of the observations in your letter might be construed to imply a virtual disapprobation of that plan of conduct on the part of the general Government, in the actual stage of its affairs, which you acknowleged would be proper on the part of the Government of Pensylvania, if arrived at a similar stage" [10] must be referred to the general tenor and complexion of those observations and to the inference they were naturally calculated to inculcate. If this inference was, that under the known circumstances of the case, the employment of force to suppress the insurrection was improper without a long train of preparatory expedients—and if in fact the Government of the UStates (which has not been controverted) was at that point, where it was admitted that the Government of Pensylvania being arrived, the resort to force on its part would be proper—the impression which was made could not have been effaced by the consideration, that the forms of referring what concerned the Government of the Union to the judgment of its own Executive were carefully observed. There was no difficulty in reconciling the intimation of an opinion unfavourable to a particular course of proceeding with an explicit reference of the subject, officially speaking, to the judgment of the officer charged by the constitution to decide, and with a sincere recognition of the subjection of the individual authority of the State to the national jurisdiction of the Union.

The disavowal by Your Excellency of an intention to sanction the inference, which was drawn, renders what has been said a mere explanation of the cause of that inference and of the impression, which it *at first* made.

It would be foreign to the object of this Letter to discuss the

10. See Randolph to Mifflin, August 7, 1794.

various observations, which have been adduced to obviate a misapprehension of your views and to maintain the propriety of the course pursued in your first communication. It is far more pleasing to the President to understand you in the sense you desire,[11] and to conclude, that no opinion has been indicated by you inconsistent with that which he has entertained of the state of things & of his duty in relation to it. And he remarks with satisfaction the effect which subsequent information is supposed calculated to produce favouring an approximation of sentiments.

11. In his letter to Washington of August 12, Mifflin wrote: "That the course which I have suggested as proper to be pursued, in relation to the recent disturbances in the western parts of Pennsylvania, contemplates the State, in a light too separate and unconnected, is a position, that I certainly did not intend to sanction, in any degree, that could wound your mind with a sentiment of regret. In submitting the construction of the facts, which must regulate the operations of the General Government, implicitly to your judgment, . . . I thought that I had manifested the strongest sense of my Federal obligations, and that, so far from regarding the State in a separate and unconnected light, I had expressly recognized the subjection of her individual authority, to the national jurisdiction of the Union" (LS, RG 59, Miscellaneous Letters, 1790–1799, National Archives).

George Washington to Lord Lansdowne[1]

Philadelphia Augt. 30th. 1794[2]

My Lord

I have had the pleasure of receiving your Lordship's letter introducing to me Mr. Taillerand Perigord.[3]

It is matter of no small regret to me that considerations of a public nature, which you will easily conjecture, have not hitherto permitted me to manifest towards that Gentleman the sense I entertain of his personal character and of your Lordship's recommendation. But I am informed that the reception he has met with, in general, has been such as to console him, as far as the state of society here will admit of it, for what he has relinquished in leaving Europe. Time must naturally be favourable to him every where, and may be expected to raise a man of his talents and merit above the temporary disadvantages, which in revolutions result from differences of political opinion.

It would be painful to me to anticipate that the misfortunes of Europe could be the cause of an Event, which on every personal account would give me the truest satisfaction—the opportunity of welcoming you to a country, to the esteem of which you have so just a title, and of testifying to you more particularly the sentiments of respect and cordial regard with which I have the honor to be

Your Lordship's Most Obedient servant.

The Right Honorable
Lord Lansdown

Df, in the handwriting of H, George Washington Papers, Library of Congress.

1. William Petty, second Earl of Shelburne, had been created first Marquis of Lansdowne in 1784. For background to this letter, see H to Washington, May 5, 1794; Washington to H, May 6, July 11, 1794.

2. The place and date are in Washington's handwriting.

3. Charles Maurice de Talleyrand-Perigord. See H to Washington, May 5, 1794; Washington to H, May 6, July 11, 1794.

Note on the Funding System

[Philadelphia, August, 1794] [1]

The funding system (says a correspondent) as much abused, as if it were *criminal* in a Government *to provide for the payment of the Debts of a Nation* or as if it had *created* the debt for which it *but provides*, has not only produced all the advantageous effects which were promised from it (that is) contributed, by an increase of *active* or *negotiable* capital, to extend commerce and industry in every branch and to raise the value of lands, but it is at this moment promoting a very important advantage of another sort which was not predicted, namely the transfer to this Country of foreigners of property *with their property*. Every body knows that the difficulty of transferring property from one country to another without loss or risk of loss is not among the least of the impediments to emigration. But the funds of the U States, which have been carried to Europe, obviate this difficulty, and offer at once a mode of investment and transfer altogether convenient and even profitable; a circumstance which it is known has had its influence and is likely to have still greater. Thus the U States receive a double compensation for their funds by the first price which was given for them, and by their return with the additional advantage of an acquisition of citizens who come to this country from a mode of thinking congenial with our political establishments. Those who think accessions of Capital to a young Country, which has more to improve, than capital for improvement, beneficial, will not undervalue the advantage which has been mentioned. At any rate, they will see in it a diminution of what has been supposed by some as evil, the transfer of our funds to foreigners.

ADf, Hamilton Papers, Library of Congress.

1. It is impossible to date this document with any degree of accuracy. At the top of the first page of the MS someone (not H) has written: "[1791?]." This date, which has been accepted by Broadus Mitchell (Mitchell, *Alexander Hamilton* [New York, 1957–1962], II, 590, note 11), appears to be too early, for on the back of this document H wrote the following notes for his own use: "Enquire of Mr. Frances if he is in the way of procuring the needful supplies. Note Contractors for Cloathing. Proscribed Privateers." Tench Francis was the agent for military purchases in Philadelphia. Although H's remarks concerning supplies and clothing could apply to either 1793 or 1794, it seems more likely that he was referring to the problem of supplying the militia army used against the opponents of the excise tax in 1794 in western Pennsylvania. In addition, and perhaps more important, while the proscribed privateers were an issue in both 1793 and 1794, on August 18, 1794, H wrote to George Washington: "The Secretary of the Treasury submits to the President the draft of a letter on the subject of the proscribed privateers."

To George Washington

[Philadelphia, August, 1794] [1]

The Secretary of the Treasury presents his respects to the President. He sent yesterday for the papers necessary to furnish the particular instances of misconduct in certain officers of Pennsylvania,[2] but on examination they prove not to be the right ones. There is probably not time to correct the error today; but the President may mention the circumstance to the Governor [3] & inform him that he will direct me to communicate particulars.

LC, George Washington Papers, Library of Congress.

1. In the George Washington letter book this letter is dated March 13, 1794. The contents, however, indicate that it was written in late August, 1794.

2. For "instances of misconduct in certain officers of Pennsylvania," see H to Washington, August 5, 1794.

3. On August 22, 1794, Thomas Mifflin wrote to Washington requesting details on the charges which H had made in his letter to Washington of August 5, 1794 (LS, RG 59, Miscellaneous Letters, 1790–1799, National Archives).

To John Bray[1]

[*Philadelphia, September 1, 1794.* On February 1, 1795, Bray presented to the Treasury Department his "Account with the United States" for "provisions and forage furnished various parties of the division of the New Jersey Militia . . . pursuant to instructions from the Secretary of the Treasury as contained in his letter of the 1st Septr 1794."[2] *Letter not found.*]

1. Bray was the contractor at New Brunswick, New Jersey, for provisions for the militia.
2. D, RG 217, Miscellaneous Treasury Accounts, 1790–1894, Account No. 6432, National Archives.

To Tench Coxe

[Philadelphia, September 1–2, 1794]

Mr. Hamilton requests Mr. Coxe to examine the Draft herewith sent—to make the parts which are taken from Mr. Coxe's report such as the examination he was to make shall render correct—to note whether the inquiry of Mr. Dallas ought to make any alteration in what is said about prosecutions for offences in the last paragraph but one—& to ascertain whether Col Nevill has any scruples about what is stated on his authority.[1]

The business is urgent & ought not to be delayed more than is unavoidable. AH

ALS, Tench Coxe Papers, Historical Society of Pennsylvania, Philadelphia.
1. See H to George Washington, September 2, 1794.

From William Ellery

Collector's Offe. Port of Newport [Rhode Island]
Sept. 1st. 1794

Sir,

I am informed that a Statemt. of the Case of James Smith master and owner of the Schooner Fox of and from Halifax in Nova Scotia burthen about 18 tons will by direction of the District Judge[1] be transmitted to you by this Post.

The Schooner Fox arrived at Bristol in this District on the 9th. day of the last month about eight or nine o'clock in the morng. without any Cargo. On the same day the master purchased and took on board a quanty. of Onions and Apples. By some mismanagement the Vessel oversat, sank, and the goods floated out of her and were lost. He did not report to the Surveyor of the Port [2] in twenty four hours, nor at the Custom House until Seventy two hours after his arrival at Bristol. Whether this neglect, and this delay was occasioned in the manner represented in his petition I cannot say, nor whether he inquired for the Custom house and received the information therein mentioned. It appeared to the District Atty.[3] and to me that he is a person of small property, that he had offered to sell his Schooner after she had sunk for one hundred Dollars, and that he would not be able to procure bail and must go to Gaol if he were prosecuted, the District Atty. therefore advised that he should apply to you and deposit his vessel as a pledge to abide your determination. He readily consented to this measure, and as he is at expence here, which I believe he can illy sustain, he earnestly wishes that you would be pleased to decide upon his case as soon as you can make it convenient.

I am with great Consideration Sir, Yr. most obedt. servant

Wm. Ellery Colle

Alexr Hamilton Esqr
Secry of the Treasy

LC, Newport Historical Society, Newport, Rhode Island.

1. Henry Marchant.
2. Daniel Lyman.
3. Ray Greene.

From Wilhem and Jan Willink, Nicholaas and Jacob Van Staphorst, and Nicholas Hubbard

Triplicate ORIG: PER BR. HARRIOT HOLLAND DUPL. PR. BR. UNION LEADER TO NEW YORK

Amsterdam 1 September 1794.

Sir!

We had the pleasure to address you our last respects the 18th ultimo since when We have not received any of your esteemed favors.

With satisfaction do We announce to you, the delivery of all the Bonds of the Loan of Three Millions of Florins dated the 1 January 1794.[1]

Inclosed you have the Account Current of the United States with us up to this day, the Balance whereon due by us Holland Currency f 972,676.12. 8 We transfer to their Credit in a new Account.

No further news yet arrived from Copenhagen. We shall therefore write again and press all possible the purchase of the salpetre You ordered.[2]

With great regard and esteem We are Sir! Your most obed. hb. servants

Wilhem & Jan Willink
N & J. Van Staphorst & Hubbard

Bonds of the U: S: at 5 percent. 99 pr. ct.
Do. . . . . . . 4 ″ do. . 88½ ″ ″.

Alexr. Hamilton Esqr. Secretary of the Treasury

LS, Connecticut Historical Society, Hartford.

1. For a description of the January, 1794, Holland loan, see Willink, Van Staphorst, and Hubbard to H, December 27, 1793.

2. See H to Willink, Van Staphorst, and Hubbard, May 8, 1794, and Willink, Van Staphorst, and Hubbard to H, July 1, 15, August 1, 18, 1794.

From ——————[1]

York County, Virginia, September 2, 1794. "As diffidence, distant modesty, and great Secrecy, hinders me from avowing myself, and not having the Honour of Knowing you, with a wish of gratitude to serve your cabinet, and if necessary to aid your field, in a Country, which I have had both experience in and friendship from, occasions now, that doubtfulness, which a surety of my intentions being received, would counteract & prevent; from & under these impressions, I trust, my signature being absent, will be readily excused. The resources of this Country being manifold and efficient—The view is to point out the elegibility and necessity of improving the Public Taxes, from these resources, with the smallest ease, and least appearance of Burthen: a number of new Laws, their utility &c—A Seine Tax, propriety of—Lottery Tax—Mile Tax, Stamp Tax on Receipts—Bonds, Mortgages &c—moderate—it will answer; and it may be observed, that what has been unpopular at one time, may yet meet the opinion of the public at another. . . ."

ALS, Hamilton Papers, Library of Congress.

1. Although this letter is written in the first-person singular, it is signed "Eleven Friends." A postscript to this letter reads as follows: "Inclose yr. letter, without any direction Sealed up—unto my friend Mr. William Dalley, Northampton County, Eastern Shore, Virginia."

From William Ellery

[*Newport, Rhode Island, September 2, 1794.* In Ellery's letter book below his letter to Hamilton on September 1, 1794, the following notation appears: "Wrote a letter to the Secry of the 2nd. of Sept. 1794." [1] *Letter not found.*]

1. LC, Newport Historical Society, Newport, Rhode Island.

To Samuel Hodgdon [1]

[*Philadelphia*] *September 2, 1794.* Requests "an Inventory of intrenching tools to be procured for the Militia force destined against the insurgents if it should become necessary to march them formed upon a moderate scale with an estimate of the probable Cost."

AL, The Indiana Historical Society Library, Indianapolis.

1. For background to this letter, see H to Hodgdon, second letter of August 25, 1794.

From Henry Lee

Norfolk [Virginia] 2d. Sept. 94

dear Hamilton.

I am extremely chagrined on finding from your private letter accompanying your public letter that the intended secrecy is entirely baffled as it respected the call on me to take care of the insurgents.[1]

Being absent from Richmond on a visit to the forts at Norfolk, the public letr. was opened by the Lt. Govenor [2] & there being no injunction of secrecy on it, The purport was divulged without ceremony & before I received my letters the report reached me of my late appointment.

I do not believe that any thing but good will result from this accident in this state for I am persuaded it will accelerate the readiness of the troops & I am confident G. Morgan[3] will prefer me to any other—nor can he consider his former relative claim[4] slighted in as much as he is in the habit of obeying me as commander in chief of the militia, in which character I shall act if sad necessity so decrees. However knowing his value & anxious to prevent any disturbance of harmony I wrote yesterday to him in terms suitable for the object I contemplated, & I hope my letr. will have its designed effect.

When I return to Richmond which will be very soon, I will see Carrington.[5]

I love him dearly & should prefer him to any other in the character you suggest. But you ought to weigh well the objection you mention, for such is the temper of the people & such the eventful crisis that no measure however wise ought to be adopted which furnishes fuel for the discontentist political declaimers in which the U S abound.

The honor you propose as possible I receive with every respect due to your goodness & friendship & I well know the extensive good I should derive from your wisdom zeal & sincerity but really when you talk of acting in a station so inferior, you add to the awkwardness of my feelings which I assure you are too much so already for that tranquillity of mind indispensible for the conducting of business great & difficult—a good adjutant general may secure & save Mifflins[6] feelings.

God bless you: H: Lee

ALS, Hamilton Papers, Library of Congress.

1. On August 25, 1794, H wrote two letters to Lee, both of which were public letters. The private letter to which Lee is referring has not been found.

2. James Wood.

3. Daniel Morgan.

4. During the American Revolution Morgan was a brigadier general, and Lee was a lieutenant colonel.

5. Edward Carrington, supervisor of the revenue for the District of Virginia. See H to Lee, second letter of August 25, 1794.

6. Thomas Mifflin, governor of Pennsylvania.

Tully No. IV[1]

[Philadelphia, September 2, 1794]

For the American Daily Advertiser.
To the PEOPLE *of the* UNITED STATES
LETTER IV.

The prediction mentioned in my first letter[2] begins to be fulfilled. Fresh symptoms every moment appear of a dark conspiracy, hostile to your government, to your peace abroad, to your tranquility at home. One of its orators dares to prostitute the name of FRANKLIN, by annexing it to a publication as insidious as it is incendiary.[3] Aware of the folly and the danger of a direct advocation of

[Philadelphia] *Dunlap and Claypoole's American Daily Advertiser,* September 2, 1794.

1. The other "Tully" letters are dated August 23, 26, 28, 1794.
2. "Tully No. I," August 23, 1794.
3. In criticizing the policies of the Federal Government "Franklin" wrote: "The period is at hand when you will be called upon to exercise the right of freemen, the right to declare who shall be your lawgivers. The magnitude of this right must appear to every reflecting mind, but its importance has additional energy when the present state of our country is considered—a state at which the manly and independent soul revolts, and which the friend of humanity sincerely deprecates. Scorned, injured and insulted by that nation which has no claim to humanity or civilization but what the few philosophers among them give, we have borne them with a meekness that seemed to give birth to a question of the purity of the motives which led to such submission. The common rights of nations have been denied us, and the manly and pacific means of redress within our power have been shamefully abandoned. That spirit, that elevation of soul which prompted us to resist a British tyrant's will, and bore us triumphantly through one of the most glorious revolutions in the annals of mankind, seems to have slumbered in shameful apathy or to have yielded to considerations of sordid calculation. When the bold tone of freedom ought to have animated every heart to a resistance of a despotic nation's decrees; when every arm ought to have been nerved against a bloody and barbarous foe, we have slept over our wrongs, and have rather kiss'd the rod of chastisement. Shall we then, fellow-citizens, continue our confidence to men who have reduced us to such a state of degradation? Shall we continue to delegate a trust the most important in a freeman's gift to men who are absorbed in their own calculations, and who appear to consider their country's interest as a secondary thing? Shall we foster agents at the expence of the vital principle of the body politic, and neglect an exertion that shall restore our lost dignity and honor?

"Not only is our situation abroad critical and humilating, but intestine divisions are taking place among us, and the sword of civil war is about to be unsheathed. An odious excise system, baneful to liberty, engendered by corrup-

the cause of the Insurgents, he makes the impudent attempt to inlist your passions in their favour—by false and virulent railings against those who have heretofore represented you in Congress. The fore ground of the piece presented you with a bitter invective against that wise, moderate, and pacific policy, which in all probability will rescue you from the calamities of a foreign war, with an increase of true dignity and with additional lustre to the American name and character. Your Representatives are delineated as corrupt pusylanimous and unworthy of your confidence; because they did not plunge headlong into measures which might have rendered war inevitable; because they contented themselves with preparing for it, instead of making it, leaving the path open to the Executive for one last and solemn effort of negociation—because they did not display either the promptness of gladiators, or the blustering of bullies—but assumed that firm, yet temperate attitude which alone is suited to the Representatives of a brave, but rational People—who deprecated war, tho' they did not fear it—and who have a great and solid inter-

---

tion, and nurtured by the *instrumentality* of the enemies to freedom, has taken root among us. A resistance to this system by force of arms has been made, and if the intemperate spirit which dictated the system should prompt to its execution, a civil war, the consummation of human evil, will be the consequence. When men who understand the principles of freedom, and know the horrors and distresses of anarchy rise in hostility to laws, a radical defect must either exist in their government, or in those who are entrusted with its administration. A defect, and a very serious one too, no doubt exists, and this consists in men being appointed to legislative trusts, who represent their *own feelings* and their *own interests*. Those men are so generally led by their immediate interests, that when the great interests of the United States come in competition with theirs, no doubt can be entertained which will have the preponderance. Let me refer you, fellow-citizens, to the Journals of Congress, and you will there see congressional stockholders marshalled in an impenetrable phalanx of opposition whenever their property is to contribute towards the general good. You will see the warmest contention to secure themselves from any part of the national burthen, when the detestable and corrupt plans of indirect taxation, shall be enforced by them by every exertion of subtlety and persuasion. You will see human ingenuity on the rack to discover ways and means to draw money out of the pockets of the deserving and industrious parts of the community, while wealth, luxury and indolence shall have every contrivance played off to prevent a portion of their means from flowing into the national treasury. Listen to the congressional debates and you will hear the man possessing thousands endeavour to exempt himself from paying a shilling towards the support of government, and at the same time plan[n]ing systems that shall drain the laborer of his hardearned pittance, who has not a shilling beyond his daily earnings. Are these things right, are they just follow-citizens? Are the authors of such inequality and injustice entitled to your confidence? . . ." ([Philadelphia] *Independent Gazetteer*, August 30, 1794.)

est in peace which ought only to be abandoned when it is unequivocally ascertained that the sacrifice is absolutely due to the vindication of their honor and the preservation of their essential rights—because in fine, your Representatives wished to give an example to the world that the boasted moderation of republican governments was not (like the patriotism of our political barkers) an empty declamation, but a precious reality.

The sallies of a momentary sensibility, roused and stung by injury were excusable. It was not wonderful that the events of war, were under the first impressions heard from good, and even prudent men. But to revive them at this late hour, when fact and reflection unite to condemn them; to arraign a conduct which has elevated the national character to the highest point of true glory—to hope to embark you in the condemnation of that conduct, and to make your indignation against it useful to the cause of Insurrection and Treason, are indications of a wrong-headedness, perverseness, or profligacy, for which it is not easy to find terms of adequate reprobation.

Happily the plotters of mischief know ye not. They derive what they mistake for your image, from an original in their own heated and crooked imaginations and they hope to mould a wise, reflecting and dispassionate people, to purposes which presuppose an ignorant unthinking and turbulent herd.

But the declamations against your Representatives for their love of peace is but the preface to the main design. That design is to alienate you from the support of the laws by the spectre of an "odious excise system, baneful to Liberty, engendered by corruption and nurtured by the INSTRUMENTALITY (favoured word, fruitful source of mountebank wit) of the enemies of Freedom." [4] To urge the execution of that system would manifest it is said an intemperate spirit; and to excite your disapprobation of that course, you are threatened with the danger of a civil war, which is called the consummation of human evil.

To crown the outrage upon your understandings; the Insurgents are represented as men who understand the principles of freedom & know the horrors and distresses of anarchy, and who therefore must have been tempted to hostility against the laws by a RADICAL DEFECT

4. The remainder of this letter was published in *JCHW* as the concluding part of "Tully No. III" (*JCHW*, VII, 165–67).

EITHER in the government, or in those entrusted with its administration. How thin the partition which divides the insinuation from the assertion, that the government is in fault, and the insurgents in the right.

Fellow-Citizens; a name, a sound has too often had influence on the affairs of nations; an EXCISE has too long been the successful watch-word of party. It has even sometimes led astray well meaning men. The experiment is now to be tried, whether there be any spell in it of sufficient force to unnerve the arm which it may be found necessary to raise in defence of law and order.

The jinglers who endeavor to cheat us with the sound, have never dared to venture into the fair field of argument. They are conscious that it is easier to declaim than to reason on the subject. They know it to be better to play a game with the passions and prejudices than to engage seriously with the understanding of the auditory.

You have already seen, that the merits of excise Laws are immaterial to the question to be decided—that you have prejudged the point by a solemn constitutional act, and that until you shall have revoked or modified that act, resistance to its operation is a criminal infraction of the social compact, an inversion of the fundamental principles of Republican Government, and a daring attack upon YOUR sovereignty, which you are bound by every motive of duty, and selfpreservation to withstand and defeat. The matter might safely be suffered to rest here; but I shall take a future opportunity to examine the reasonableness of the prejudice which is inculcated against excise laws—and which has become the pretext for excesses tending to dissolve the bands of Society.

Fellow Citizens—You are told, that it will be intemperate to urge the execution of the laws which are resisted—what? will it be indeed intemperate in your Chief Magistrate, sworn to maintain the Constitution, charged faithfully to execute the Laws, and authorized to employ for that purpose force when the ordinary means fail—will it be intemperate in him to exert that force, when the constitution and the laws are opposed by force? Can he answer it to his conscience, to you not to exert it?

Yes, it is said; because the execution of it will produce civil war, the consummation of human evil.

Fellow-Citizens—Civil War is undoubtedly a great evil. It is one that every good man would wish to avoid, and will deplore if inevitable. But it is incomparably a less evil than the destruction of Government. The first brings with it serious but temporary and partial ills—the last undermines the foundations of our security and happiness—where should we be if it were once to grow into a maxim, that force is not to be used against the seditious combinations of parts of the community to resist the laws? This would be to give a CARTE BLANCH to ambition—to licentiousness; to foreign intrigue; to make you the prey of the gold of other nations—the sport of the passions and vices of individuals among yourselves. The Hydra Anarchy would rear its head in every quarter. The goodly fabric you have established would be rent assunder, and precipitated into the dust. You knew how to encounter civil war, rather than surrender your liberty to foreign domination—you will not hesitate now to brave it rather than surrender your sovereignty to the tyranny of a faction—you will be as deaf to the apostles of anarchy now, as you were to the emissaries of despotism then. Your love of liberty will guide you now as it did then—you know that the POWER of the majority and LIBERTY are inseparable—destroy that, and this perishes. But in truth that which can properly be called a civil war is not to be apprehended—Unless, from the act of those who endeavour to fan the flame, by rendering the Government odious. A civil war is a contest between two GREAT parts of the same empire. The exertion of the strength of the nation to suppress resistance to its laws by a sixtieth part of itself, is not of that description.

After endeavouring to alarm you with the horrors of civil war—an attempt is made to excite your sympathy in favour of the armed faction by telling you that those who compose it are men, who understand the principles of freedom, and know the horrors and distresses of anarchy, and must therefore have been prompted to hostility against the laws by a radical defect EITHER in the government or in its administration.

Fellow Citizens! For an answer to this you have only to consult your senses. The natural consequence of radical defect in a government, or in its administration is national distress and suffering—look around you—where is it? do you feel it? do you see it?

Go in quest of it beyond the Alleghaney, and instead of it, you will find that there also a scene of unparralleled prosperity upbraids the ingratitude and madness of those, who are endeavouring to cloud the bright face of our political horizon, and to mar the happiest lot that beneficent Heaven ever indulged to undeserving mortals.

When you have turned your eyes towards that scene—examine the men whose knowledge of the principles of freedom is so emphatically vaunted—where did they get their better knowledge of those principles than that which you possess? How is it that you have been so blind or tame as to remain quiet, while they have been goaded into hostility against the laws by a RADICAL DEFECT in the government, or its administration?

Are you willing to yield them the palm of discernment, of patriotism or of courage? TULLY.

To George Washington[1]

Treasury Department September 2nd. 1794

Sir,

The state of my health since you were pleased to refer to me the letter from Governor Mifflin of the 22 of August[2] has been such

Copy, Lloyd W. Smith Collection, Morristown National Park, Morristown, New Jersey.

1. For background to this letter, see "Deposition of Francis Mentges," August 1, 1794; "Conference Concerning the Insurrection in Western Pennsylvania," August 2, 1794; H to Washington, August 2, 5, 1794, August, 1794; H and Henry Knox to Washington, August 5, 1794; Edmund Randolph to Thomas Mifflin, August 7, 30, 1794.

2. Mifflin's letter to Washington of August 22, 1794, reads in part as follows: "In the Secretary of the Treasury's Report, dated the 5th instant, and published with your assent, relatively to the opposition, which has been given to the execution of the laws, for laying duties on spirits distilled within the United States, and upon Stills, the following passage occurs:

" 'This is at once an example of a disposition to support the laws of the Union, and of an opposite one, in the local officers of Pennsylvania, within the non-complying scene. But it is a truth, too important not to be noticed, and too injurious not to be lamented, that the prevailing spirit of those officers has been either hostile or lukewarm to the execution of those laws; and that the weight of an unfriendly official influence has been one of the most serious obstacles with which they have had to struggle.'

"Desirous of manifesting in every way a zealous co-operation in the views of the General Government, permit me to request, that you will direct the evidence, on which the above charge is founded, to be communicated to me, in order that I may take the proper steps to vindicate the honor of the State Government, and to remove the delinquent officers. If any officer . . . has

as to delay the necessary previous examination in order to a reply—and prevents now its being as full and particular as I had wished it to be.

I premise for greater clearness that by official influence, I understand, that influence which is derived from *Official situation*, whether exerted directly in the line of Office, or collaterally and indirectly in other ways.

It will readily be concurred, that a spirit, like that which has been stated to have prevailed would frequently discover itself in forms so plausibly disguised and with so much duplicity of aspect as not to be capable of being rendered palpable by precise specification and proof. It appeared, for example, among other shapes, in observations on the exceptionable nature of the Laws [3] tending to foment dissatisfaction with them; in recommendations of what has been called legal or constitutional opposition, in a disrespectful and disparaging demeanor towards the Officers charged with their execution and in severe strictures on what were denominated rigorous and irregular proceedings of those Officers, calculated to foster public contempt and hatred of them—in ambiguous hints susceptible of different interpretations, but easily applied by the passion of those to whom they were addressed to purposes of opposition. To enter into an exhibition of these instances would require a long detail an appeal to persons now within the discontented Scene whose apprehensions would restrain them from becoming voluntarily witnesses—and would after all be liable to specious controversy about their true import and nature.

I therefore confine myself to those instances of opposition and discountenance to the Laws by persons in Office, which are unequivocal.

---

evinced '*a spirit hostile to the execution of the laws*' . . . I do not hesitate to promise the severest animadversion upon so criminal a conduct. . . . In its present form, however, the charge is so indiscriminate that those Citizens who may be involved in its obloquy, do not enjoy a fair opportunity for defence, nor does the Government possess the means to discover the proper objects for its indignation and censure." (LS, RG 59, Miscellaneous Letters, 1790–1799, National Archives.) This letter is printed in *Pennsylvania Archives*, 2nd ser., IV, 193–94. For "the Secretary of the Treasury's Report," see H to Washington, August 5, 1794.

3. For the excise laws to which H is referring, see H to Washington, August 5, 1794, note 2.

Among those who composed the meeting noticed in my report to you of the 5th. of August referred to by the Governor in his Letter—which was holden on the 23 of August 1791,[4] in the County of Washington were the following public Officers of Pennsylvania (vizt) James Marshall Register and Recorder, David Bradford Deputy to the Attorney General of the State, Henry Taylor and James Edgar Associate Judges Thomas Crooks, William Parker, Eli Jenkins, and Thomas Sedgwick Justices of the Peace and Peter Kidd a Major of the Militia.

Among those who composed the second meeting noticed in the same report which was holden on the second of September 1791,[5] at Pittsburgh, were, besides James Marshall and David Bradford above mentioned—the following public Officers of Pennsylvania (vizt.) Edward Cooke and Nathaniel Braden [6] Associate Judges Nehemiah Stokely and Thomas Moreton [7] Colonels of Militia, the last a member of the Legislature of Pennsylvania John Cannon and Albert Gallatine Members of the Legislature of Pennsylvania, the former since a Justice of the peace.

Among those who composed the third meeting noticed in the same Report and which was holden at Pittsburgh on the 21 of August 1792,[8] were, besides John Cannon, David Bradford, Albert Gallatine, James Marshall and Edward Cook before mentioned the following public Officers of Pennsylvania (vizt.) John Smilie Member of the State Senate, Thomas Wilson, and Samuel Giddes Colonels of the Militia William Wallace, then Sheriff now Colonel of the Militia John Hamilton Sheriff and Colonel of Militia and Basil Bowel Captain of Militia.

It may happen in some instances that the Offices annexed to particular names may not have been holden at the specified times of

4. For the resolutions agreed to at this meeting, see H to Washington, August 5, 1794, note 6.

5. The date of this meeting was actually September 7, 1791. For the resolutions of this meeting, see H to Washington, August 5, 1794, note 15.

6. Nathaniel Bradly, delegate from Fayette County.

7. Thomas Morton.

8. See H to Tench Coxe, September 1, 1792, note 5. The minutes of the meeting, in which the names of those who attended are listed as well as the resolutions which were adopted, are printed in *Pennsylvania Archives,* 2nd ser., IV, 29–31.

meeting. But this cannot materially affect the consequence to be drawn, as well because it is believed that the instances which may have been omitted to be noticed as very few—as because the conduct of the persons concerned has continued in a uniform Tenor of opposition.

The circumstance has been noted in the cases in which it was known to exist. These are John Cannon and William Wallace. It is understood, that the former was appointed by the Governor a Justice of the peace in May last. The time of the appointment of the latter as a Colonel of Militia is not particularly known.

The evidence to which immediate reference may be made of the Agency of the foregoing persons at the meetings alluded to, maybe found in the cotemporary public Gazettes of Pittsburgh and Philadelphia which contained the proceedings at large of those meetings with the names of the persons of whom they were respectively composed. The Governor can be at no loss to obtain more legal evidence of the fact if he desire it—and of the identity of the persons.

The following cases present other instances of opposition to the Laws by Officers of Pennsylvania. John Hamilton before mentioned Sheriff of a County and Colonel of Militia, is affirmed by Jacob Forwood and Robert Johnston Collector of the Revenue to have been one of a party who seized the said Johnson when travelling about his duty tarred and feathered him.[9]

Caleb Mount then a Captain since a Major of Militia stands charged before Isaac Meason and James Finley[10] Assistant Judges by information upon Oath of Benjamin Wells Collector of the Revenue and his Wife with being of a party that broke into the House of the said Collector sometime in April 1793.[11]

Andrew Robb a Justice of the peace stands charged by information upon Oath before Jacob Beason another Justice of the peace with having offered a reward of Ten pounds for killing the Excise man meaning as was understood Wells the Collector. This fact is stated on the information of the said Collector.[12]

9. See H to Washington, August 5, 1794, note 18.
10. James Findley.
11. See H to Washington, August 5, 1794, note 56.
12. Wells's deposition has not been found.

James McFarlane who commanded the Rioters in the second attack upon the House of the Inspector of the Revenue on the 17th. of July[13] last was a Major of Militia.

David Hamilton a Justice of the peace was the person who previous to that attack went to the House with a summons to surrender.

William Meetkirk a Justice of the peace, Gabriel Blakney[14] a Colonel of Militia and Absolom Beard[15] Inspector of Brigade were three of four persons who went as a Committee from the Rioters assembled at Braddocks field on the [16] to demand of the Inhabitants of Pittsburgh the expulsion of Kirkpatrick, Brison and Day as friends to the Laws.[17]

Edward Cooke the Associate Judge already mentioned was the Chairman of a Committee at the same place, which ordered the expulsion of John Gibson and Presly Neville for the same cause.

Satisfactory testimony of these several last mentioned facts can be had from Abraham Kirkpatrick and Presly Nevill now in this City and well known to the Governor.

The following cases are instances of *conduct* in Office denoting an unfriendly temper towards the Laws.

James Wells a Justice of the peace and an Associate Judge upon information of an Assault committed upon John Webster Collector of the Revenue, in the execution of his duty in an attempt to sieze some Whisky illegally distilled, told the Collector that he had never read so worthless a Law as the Revenue Law of Congress—that he expected no person in the County would have been rascal enough to take a Commission under it, that if the Whisky had been siezed he would have thrown it into the road, and he was sorry the person who made the assault had not knocked down the Collector. No measures were taken to cause a redress for the Assault. This statement is made on the information of the said Webster.[18]

13. For the attack on John Neville's house, see "Deposition of Francis Mentges," August 1, 1794, note 2.

14. Gabriel Blakeney.

15. Absalom Baird.

16. Space left blank in MS.

17. For the expulsion of Abraham Kirkpatrick, James Brison, and Edward Day, see H to Washington, August 12, 1794, note 2.

18. William Findley wrote the following concerning Webster: "Threatening letters were sent into the center and southern parts of Westmoreland to excite

Jacob Stewart and William Boyd Justices of the peace severally declined to issue process against Jacob Snyder a Distiller who was charged before them with having threatned another Distiller named Stoffer with burning of his House or some other injury, if he should enter his Still at an Office of Inspection. This statement is made on the information of Benjamin Wells the Collector, who affirms to have received it from Stoffer.[19]

them to go against Webster, collector of Bedford, and many poor people in those parts had cause of complaint against him, which did not exist against other excise officers. He had made a practice of seizing liquors on the road from poor people, who were carrying it to procure salt, or other necessaries; some instances of this might be mentioned that were very inhumane; sometimes he was contented with receiving the excise tax and letting the liquors pass, but generally he kept all, and sometimes detained the horses for a time, restoring them again as a matter of favour. This hardship fell generally on the poor, for he let others pass, even though they called and drank at his tavern, with their loads. It was believed he did not account with the public for the proceeds. That his conduct was not agreeable to law was asserted by the inspector, when he was applied to, but no redress was given, nor was the practice relinquished. The law authorising seizure was not made till June immediately preceding the insurrection. . . .

"Webster made no resistance, but brought out his papers, and tore and trod on them. The party differed among themselves. Some were for tarring, feathering, &c. Fire was set to his hay stacks and stables, but the more moderate party were the majority. They extinguished the fire and protected the man from any other injury than insulting language. Not agreeing how he should be treated they took him along with them some miles, and apprehensions being entertained by himself and some others, of the outrageous party falling back and treating him ill when the others were gone, he was taken into Westmoreland and there being lodged in safety that night, he was permitted to return home the next day without further injury. . . ." (Findley, *History of the Insurrection*, 107–08.)

On August 23, 1794, Webster wrote to William Rawle concerning his deposition on James Wells: "In some Conversation with James Wells Esqr. yesterday he Says he has been Informed that A Summons from the Federal Court Was found among Mr [David] Lennox papers When he was made prissoner by the Ryoters of Washington, I did not expect my deposition was Taken, with an intent to Commence a prosecute. I Mentioned in Conversation to Mr [Tench] Cox, that I had Reason to believe that Mr Wells Since his Apointment of Asst Judge had done All in his power with the distillers to Induce them to Comply. I am now Fulley Convinced that it has been the Case & On the Late meetings to Opose Government he has not been at One—Should thear have been A Action Commenced I Request it as A Favour that you will have it with drawn. The Westmoreclaner peeple About One hundred & Fiftey have paid me a Vissit and Used me Verritrey Ill. destroyed my papers—plundered my house dragd me A prissoner Twenty Miles . . ." (ALS, Historical Society of Pennsylvania, Philadelphia).

19. John Stouffer's deposition reads as follows: "On the Evening of the 12th Day of November 1792 Being a few Days after I Enterd Some Whiskey with Benj Wells I had my Ferry Boat Sot a Drift and Damage to the Amount of Three pounds. Being in formd, that a near Neighbour of Mine had then At-

Joseph Huston Sheriff of the County of Fayette stands indicted at a Circuit Court for having refused or declined the service of Warrants and Suppœnas issued by Isaac Measan and James Finley assistant Judges of that County in the Case of the Riot which was committed at the House of a Collector of the Revenue in April 1793.[20] This is the same with the instance mentioned in my Report.

The following is a case of peculiar and rather of a mixed complexion relating both to conduct in office and conduct out of Office—and including in it a specimen of that species of discountenance to the Laws which I have thought it most adviseable as a general rule to forbear entering into, but which being in this instance ascertainable by the acknowledgements of the party and by respectable testimony at hand, seems proper to form an exception to that rule, which may be useful, by way of example and illustration.

It is mentioned in my Report, that the supervisor of the Revenue[21] in September 1792, was sent into the refractory Counties—among other things to collect evidence of the persons concerned in the Riot in Faulkners case.[22] When at Pittsburgh, he applied by letter to Alexander Addison President of the Court of Common pleas—who resided at the Town of Washington to engage his Assistance, in taking the depositions of persons who were named to him by the Supervisor as able to testify concerning infractions of the Laws, and in causing some of the best informed Witnesses to attend a Circuit Court of the United States about to be holden at York Town.

The Judge not content with declining an Agency in the business, in his answer to the application[23] digresses into a Censure on the

tempted To Burn my house if I did Enter my Whiskey I made Application To Jacob Steoart Esqr And he told me he did not like to do any thing in the matter As he wanted to git the man I Suspected to Still him some Whiskey But he told me to Go to William Boyd Esqr And When I went To Boyd he told me to go to Steward As Witness my hand this 15th Day of January 1793" (ADS, Historical Society of Pennsylvania, Philadelphia).

20. For a discussion of the Huston affair, see John Neville to George Clymer, June 7, 1793 (LS, Connecticut Historical Society, Hartford), and Neville to Clymer, May 24, 1793 (ALS, Connecticut Historical Society).

21. George Clymer.

22. For William Faulkner's case, see Neville to Clymer, August 23, 1792, quoted in H to Tench Coxe, September 1, 1792, note 3. Faulkner's deposition is dated September 28, 1792 (DS, Pennsylvania Miscellany, Whiskey Rebellion, Vol. I, Library of Congress).

23. For Addison's letter to Clymer of September 29, 1792, see Clymer to H, October 4, 1792, note 5.

Judiciary System of the United States which he represents as impracticable, unless it be intended to sacrifice to it the *essential principles of the liberty* of the Citizens and the *Just authority* of the State Courts—and afterwards declares, that were it his duty to do what was requested of him (which however he states in a manner different from what the Supervisor seems to have intended) he should do it *with reluctance* because he should be serving a cause which he thought unfavorable to liberty and the Just authority of the State Courts.

Without examining the sufficiency of the reasons which led to declining the Agency proposed to him—without commenting upon the observations which seek to derive a part of the justification for it from the resentment of the people against the Laws and the danger of loosing their confidence by a compliance with what was desired of him; topics the propriety of which in the mouth of a Magistrate might well be contested—it cannot admit of a doubt, that there was a great unfitness in a JUDGE of Pennsylvania indulging himself with gratuitous invectives against the Judiciary system of the Government of the Union:—pronouncing it to be impracticable—unfavorable to liberty and to the just authority of the *State Courts.* It is difficult to perceive in such a digression the evidence of a temper cordial to the institutions and arrangements of the United States. The particulars of this affair have been long since in possession of the Governor.

Judge Addison in a letter, an extract from which was lately transmitted by the Governor to you—acknowledges in terms that he "had endeavoured to inculcate constitutional resistance" to the particular Laws in question.[24] Here is proof by his own confession that the weight of his influence was exerted against those Laws.

It is not easy to understand what is meant by the terms "constitutional resistance." The Theory of every constitution presupposes as a *first principle* that the *Laws are to be obeyed.* There can therefore be no such thing as a "constitutional resistance" to Laws constitutionally enacted.

24. For an extract of Addison's letter to Thomas Mifflin, dated March 21, 1794, see Bartholomew Dandridge to H, April 19, 1794, note 1. Addison's letter is printed in *Pennsylvania Archives*, 2nd ser., IV, 59–61. See also H to Coxe, April 19, 1794; H to Washington, April 19, 1794; Washington to H, May 29, 1794.

The only sense, which I have been able to trace as that intended by these terms, and the equivalent ones "legal resistance" "legal opposition" which have been frequently used by the opposers of the Laws is that every thing should be practiced to defeat the execution of the Laws short of actual violence or breach of the peace; accordingly that endeavours should be used to prevent the accepting or holding Offices under them by making it matter of popular contempt and reproach to do so and by a humiliating and insulting treatment of those who should accept or hold those Officers—that non compliances with the Laws by persons having Stills should be countenanced and promoted—that means of intimidation, guarded so as to escape legal animadversion, should be superadded, to discourage compliances to obstruct the establishment of Officers of Inspection and to deter from attempts to coerce delinquents, in fine that every obstacle which was supposed not to amount to an indictable Offence should be thrown in the way of the Laws.

The conduct of Judge Addison in particular instances as it has been represented, will perhaps afford no ill comment upon his expressions.

Benjamin Wells Collector declares that the said Judge then attending a Session of a Circuit Court as president at a public House, in the presence of Isaac Measan an Assistant Judge expressed himself, to him Wells in strong terms of disapprobation of the Laws laying duties on spirits distilled within the United States, saying they were "unjust and unequitable—that the money to be raised was unnecessary and that there was no use for it"—and afterwards at the same place and during the same Session of the Circuit Court, sitting at dinner with a mixed company, spoke in terms of contempt of the Officers of the Inspector and Collectors of the Revenue, and of disrespect towards the Officers themselves. At the next term of the Court, Wells went to the same Tavern, but was informed by the Tavern keeper and his Wife that he could not be received there, assigning for reason that Judge Addison had declared that if they took him in again he would leave the House.

Mr. Stokely[25] a Member of the Pennsylvania Legislature for Washington, states that Judge Addison wrote a letter or letters in opposition to his election to the Legislature, and among other ob-

25. Thomas Stokely.

jections to him mentioned his having applied for or having had an intention to obtain an Office in the Excise.

General Nevill[26] Inspector of the Revenue mentions a circumstance of a light but of an unequivocal nature to evince the prejudices against the Revenue Officers which were manifested by Judge Addison even from the Bench. It seems that it was a practice not unfrequently for the Judges then sitting in Court to invite within the Bar such persons who came into the Hall as they deemed of respectability. Judge Addison as General Neville affirms, repeatedly since the time of the meeting at Pittsburgh in August 1792, has given such invitations openly from the Bench, to those who were supposed to be of that discription within view, omitting a similar call or invitation to that Officer though present.

He adds that his own son Colonel Nevill[27] standing by his side in conversation with him has been thus invited, while the like attention was withheld[28] from him in a manner too marked to leave any doubt of the motive.

As the call of the Governor is for particular cases I forbear to adduce confirmations of the prevailing spirit of Officers alluded to from their extensive non compliance with the Laws in their capacity of distillers and from the neglect to bring to Justice offenders against them who were at the same time breakers of the peace of Pennsylvania. I observe indeed on this point the Governor entertains a different impression from that which I have; but after the most diligent inquiry, I am not able to discover a single case of the punishment of any such offender. There were indeed indictments foun⟨d⟩ against persons supposed to have been concerned in the violence upon the Maniac Wilson,[29] and against others supposed to have been concerned in an assault upon one John Corner an old man who had been unknowingly the bearer of the letters containing processes which were sent by the Deputy Marshall as stated in my Report:[30] but it is not understood that any of these were prosecuted to Judgment. The only cases known of actual punishment are

26. John Neville.
27. Presley Neville.
28. In MS, "With led."
29. Robert Wilson. See H to Washington, August 5, 1794, note 25.
30. Daniel Hamilton was indicted in April, 1792, for assault and battery on John Connor (*Pennsylvania Archives*, 2nd ser., IV, 46–47).

of persons concerned in forcibly carrying off certain Witnesses in the case of Wilson. But this was on a Collateral point; and the cases of indictment respected transactions where humanity had been too much outraged to leave an option and where even punishment might have been inflicted upon Ground distinct from that of suppressing opposition to the Laws. I can learn no instance of the conviction and punishment of any person for a violence committed upon Officers or private Citizens clearly on account of their Agency under a friendly disposition towards the Laws; which is the more remarkable as the Rioters in Faulkeners case are asserted to have passed in open day through the Town of Washington, to have parleyed there with Inhabitants of the Town and to have been afterwards entertained at two or three Houses.

I have contented myself in the first instance with indicating particular cases and the sources of information without a formal exhibition of the evidence, because I could not fore see what cases in the view of the Governor would be proper for that animadversion which he seems to contemplate because considerable delay would have attended the collection of formal evidence in all the cases; and because in many of them the evidence is as accessible to the Governor as to myself: But I stand ready to afford the aid of this Department, in bringing forward testimony in any Cases in which the Governor may specifically desire it.[31]

With the most perfect respect I have the honor to be sir, Your most obedient and humble Servant Alexander Hamilton

The President of the United States

31. On September 12, 1794, Randolph sent H's letter to Thomas Mifflin (*Pennsylvania Archives,* 2nd ser., IV, 286).

To the President, Directors, and Company of the Bank of the United States

Treasury Department September 3d 1794

Gentlemen,

There being reason to apprehend that the monies belonging to the United States, in the Office of Discount and Deposit at Baltimore, may not be adequate to the urgent wants of the public, in that quarter during the present Month I have to request that you will be so obliging as to give the United States a Credit at the said Office of Discount and Deposit for Twenty Thousand dollars. The mode which I should wish to be adopted would be for you to direct the Officers of the said Bank to honor all such draughts (not exceeding the sum already mentioned) as may be drawn by the Treasurer of the United States on that institution over and above the amount of the public monies in their hands. The sums so advanced to be repaid in this place to the Bank of the United States, upon the draughts being presented at the Treasury.

I am with great respect Gentlemen, Your most Obedient Servant Alexander Hamilton

The President Directors
and Company of the Bank of the United States

LS, Mr. Hall Park McCullough, North Bennington, Vermont.

To Henry Lee[1]

War Department, September 3, 1794. "As it will be highly necessary that the Militia called out by order of the President, agreeably to the Secretary of War's letter of the 7. of August last, should be mustered and inspected at their respective rendezvous, I have to request the favor of your Excellency to appoint some suitable character in your State to perform that service. . . ."

LS, Archives Division, Virginia State Library, Richmond.

1. For background to this letter, see H to Abraham Hunt, August 17, 1794, note 2; "Minutes of a Meeting Concerning the Insurrection in Western Pennsylvania," August 24, 1794; H to Henry Lee, second letter of August 25, 1794.

To Edmund Randolph

[*Philadelphia, September 3, 1794.* On September 5, 1794, Randolph wrote to Hamilton "in answer to his letter of the 3d instant." *Letter not found.*]

From George Washington

[Germantown, Pennsylvania, September 3, 1794]

Dear Sir,

As I know nothing that calls me to the City to day, I shall not be there until tomorrow—which will be in time for common occurrances.

The contents of the enclosed are agreeable.

Yours always Go: Washington

Wednesday
3d Septr. 1794

ALS, Hamilton Papers, Library of Congress.

To Isaac Holmes[1]

Treasury Department
Sepr. 4. 1794

Sir

A temporary absence from the seat of Government,[2] an extreme press of still more urgent business since my return and ill health have conspired to delay an answer to your letter of the 30th of June last.[3] My regret at this delay has become extreme since the

ADf, Connecticut Historical Society, Hartford.

1. This letter concerns the equipping of a vessel in Charleston about which Holmes had apparently written to H in a letter which has not been found. The *Cygnet,* an American brig, which had originally been an American privateer that had been converted to a merchant ship, was purchased by Abraham Sasportas and Jean Gaillard, both of Charleston. In May and June, 1794, Sasportas supervised her reconversion to a privateer. She was then sold to an American citizen and renamed *le Général Laveaux.* Before she could sail, Holmes detained her, removed her guns, and compelled her owner to reseal her gun ports. She then put to sea, where it was charged that she received her guns from another vessel. After she eventually returned to Charleston with a British prize, the *Mermaid,* the British consul, Benjamin Moodie, filed a libel charging that she had been illegally fitted out. For this case, see *British Consul* v *Ship Mermaid,* April 3, 1795 (Bee, *Reports of Cases Adjudged in the District Court of South Carolina,* 69–73). See also Moodie to Phineas Bond, December 17, 1794 (PRO: F.O. [Great Britain], 5/6); Melvin H. Jackson, *Privateers in Charleston, 1793–1796* (Washington, 1969), 69–72.

2. See H to George Washington, July 11, 1794; Washington to H, July 11, 1794.

3. Letter not found.

receipt of your letter of the 9th of August,[4] which shews the continuance of a most unfortunate & mischievous error—contrary to what I had hoped considering the very plain tenor of the Act of Congress entitled "An Act in addition to the Act for the punishment of certain Crimes against the UStates" passed the 5th of June last.[5]

The construction that expressions "Equipments of a doubtful nature as being applicable either to Commerce or War are deemed lawful" which occur in the 4th & 5th of the rules transmitted in my letter of the 4th of Aug 1793 [6]—were intended to tolerate the fitting and arming of vessels for *defence* or for *merchandize* and war is wholly erroneous, and as far as I know peculiar to Charlestown.

It is to the last degree embarrassing to conceive how such a construction could have been reconciled to the clear terms of the first rule which declare that "The original *arming* and *equipping* of vessels in ports of the UStates by any of the belligerent parties for *military service*, offensive or *defensive* is deemed unlawful."

Now *all arming* is for military service offensive or defensive. It is for *war*, for *combat*, which is *military* service, to *commit* or to *repel* hostility, the first being *offensive* the last *defensive*. A letter of Marque, armed for the protection of her Merchandize, is as unequivocally a vessel armed for military service as a frigate, though the object be primarily and principally self-defence. Indeed the having or being without a commission can make no difference in the case—tis the *arming* 'tis the *warlike* nature of an equipment that is the criterion of its destination for military service.

4. Letter not found.

5. Section 3 of this act prohibited "any person . . . within any of the ports, harbors, bays, rivers or other waters of the United States" from the fitting out and arming "of any ship or vessel with intent that such ship or vessel shall be employed in the service of any foreign prince or state to cruise or commit hostilities upon the subjects, citizens or property of another foreign prince or state with whom the United States are at peace" (1 *Stat.* 383). Section 4 of the same act prohibited the increasing or augmenting the force of "any ship of war, cruiser or other armed vessel in the service of a foreign prince or state or belonging to the subjects or citizens of such prince or state the same being at war with another foreign prince or state with whom the United States are at peace, by adding to the number or size of the guns of such vessel prepared for use, or by the addition thereto of any equipment solely applicable to war" (1 *Stat.* 383).

6. For the rules which H is discussing, see "Cabinet Meeting. Proposed Rules Governing Belligerents," August 3, 1793. H enclosed the rules in "Treasury Department Circular to the Collectors of the Customs," August 4, 1793.

I observe with surprise the idea that a Commission was deemed to be within the meaning of the word "equipping" in the first rule. It is repugnant to the familiar and obvious sense of the term; which includes only those things which are done to the Vessel herself as a machine, and perhaps articles of furniture & supply; but was never before (I believe) understood to comprehend a military Commission. If this had been intended, the expression would naturally have been "arming equipping and commissioning" the stopping at the second term was a manifest exclusion of the last.

It follows that every thing which has been permitted under this unfortunate construction of the rules has been a contravention of them and of the Neutrality of the Ustates.

What then it may be asked was intended by the terms "Equipment, of a doubtful nature as being applicable either to commerce or War?" I will answer by stating a case or two that occurred. A vessel had her waste board raised considerably higher than is usual & strengthened with additional timber & plank which was understood to be preparatory to the opening of Port Holes. This was considered as an equipment of a doubtful nature. 'Till *port holes* were actually opened it could not be pronounced with certainty that the object was a military one. But *port holes* themselves have been determined to be a military equipment, being foreign to mere navigation, and solely adapted to *combat* or *war*.[7]

Again—A French Privateer procured at Baltimore an *extra* number of oars. It was suggested, that this must have been for military service, as it was intirely unusual to have so great a number for mere navigation. The determination was that it was an equipment of a doubtful nature & therefore permitted. An oar is purely an

7. The following notice appeared in *The* [Charleston] *City Gazette & Daily Advertiser*, July 22, 1794: "*The following is the explanation, from the secretary of war, of the circumstances of equipment in any vessels belonging to the bel*[*l*]*igerent nations.*

"The mounting additional guns, or changing or altering the calibre of the guns in any manner whatever; the making of new gun carriages, or the cutting of new port-holes in any part of a vessel, are each adjudged to be an unlawful augmentation of force, and is therefore to be prevented.

"The United States being a neutral nation, the vessels of their citizens, in most cases, do not require to be armed. To guard against any abuse, no vessel belonging to any citizen of the United States is to be permitted to be armed and sail, until after all circumstances concerning her shall have been transmitted to the President, and his decision thereon be made known."

instrument of navigation—the having an extra number did not clearly alter the nature of the Equipment. There was no certain criterion by which to determine what excess should change the nature of the thing.

But how could it have been imagined for a moment that *arms* were an equipment of a *doubtful* nature? Their peculiar & appropriate use is war *offensive* or *defensive*. The first rule proves that defensive equipments was as much intended to be prohibited as offensive ones. It is manifest too that any difference in this particular was liable to a degree of evasion that would intirely defeat the regulations.

I feel myself compelled to ask how it has happened, that a construction of this kind, about the justness of which doubts must certainly have been entertained, defeating in its operation the manifest intention of the Executive Government could have been adopted & so long acted upon without resorting for an explanation to this Department?

As to the construction which the District Attorney [8] has given to the Act, I must acknowlege that it intirely confounds me. After what has been said, I need scarcely add that it must not govern your conduct.

You are to consider all arming or augmentation of force by or for any of the belligerent parties as absolutely prohibitted, & you are to act accordingly. I request too that you will communicate the substance of this letter both to the Governor [9] & to the District Attorney.

It is my duty to lay before The President the correspondence to which this is a reply. His chagrin, I may anticipate, will not be less than mine.[10]

With consideration I am sir Your obed ser

The Collector of Charles Town

8. Thomas Parker.
9. William Moultrie.
10. On October 6, 1794, Oliver Wolcott, Jr., sent the following circular to the collectors of customs: "It appears from communications to this Department that the expressions '*Equipments which are of a doubtful nature as being applicable either to commerce or war*' which occur in the 4th and 5th rules adopted by the President of the United States, which were communicated to you by the Secretary of the Treasury on the 4th of August 1793, have been in

some instances understood to tolerate the *fitting* and *arming* of Vessels for *defence* or for *Merchandize and War*.

"As this construction is manifestly irreconcileable with the first of the rules referred to, and with the plain tenor of the supplementary act of Congress passed on the fifth of June 1794 for defining and punishing certain crimes against the United States, it is of importance immediately to correct an error, the operation of which is to defeat the intentions of the Government and contravene the neutrality of the United States.

"You will therefore be pleased to understand that the *arming* and *equipping* of vessels in the Ports of the United States for *military service* whether *offensive or defensive*, by any of the belligerent parties, is unlawful, and that the prohibition as effectually extends to *military equipments* destined for the *protection* and *defence of a vessel and her merchandize*, as to those equipments the object of which is *combat* or *offensive hostility*.

"The equipments of a 'doubtful nature as being applicable either to commerce or war' which were intended by the rules of the President and which are deemed lawful, will be best exemplified by stating certain cases which have occurred.

"1st. The *Waste Boards* of a vessel had been raised considerably higher than usual and strengthened with additional timber and plank, which was understood to be preparatory to the opening of *Port Holes*.

"In this case it was determined that the equipment was of a 'doubtful nature' for until *Port Holes* were actually opened it could not be pronounced that there existed a military object. Port Holes have however been determined to be a *military equipment*, their use being foreign to *navigation* and being merely applicable to *combat or war*.

"2d. A French Privateer procured an *extra* number of *Oars* and it was suggested that this must have been for *military service*, as it was intirely unusual to have so great a number for mere navigation.

"It was however decided that this equipment was also of a 'doubtful nature' an oar being merely an instrument of navigation and there being no criterion by which to determine what extra number should change the nature of the Equipment.

"It is an established principle that we cannot without a contravention of our Neutrality, permit either of the belligerent parties, to increase their force or means of *annoyance* or *military defence* within the Ports of the United States, and it is essential that this principle be maintained with good faith and according to the dictates of impartiality and reason.

"A temporary absence of the Secretary of Treasury on public business, is the cause of my addressing you on this subject—it is proper that I should add, that the principles of this communication are conformable to his opinion." (LS, Connecticut Historical Society, Hartford.)

From Thomas Sim Lee

Annapolis Sept. 4th 1794

Sir.

I have the honor to acknowledge the receipt of your letter dated the 29th of August intimating the Presidents desire that the Eastern Shore part of the detachment of Militia required from this State should be immediately marched to Baltimore Town. I have also received and beg you to accept my thanks for your private letter of the same date.[1] In conformity to the President's direction I have issued orders dated the 1st Instant for the assembling of the Troops at the places most convenient for their embarkation for Baltimore; and have engaged the several Brigadiers of Militia on the Eastern Shore to be active in the execution of these orders.[2] I have likewise sent to Baltimore a number of Tents belonging to this State, sufficient for the accommodation of the men during their stay at that place and shall forward some to George Town and perhaps to Frederick Town for the use of those who in the event of further orders may be assembled at those places. Presuming that the advantage of water Carriage and possibly an early junction with the Virginia Detachment may be Contemplated in the fixing on William's Port as a point of rendezvous for the militia of this State, I think it a very proper place except as to those of Allegany and the Upper part of Washington Counties. These according to the arrangement hereto subjoined, you will perceive, I propose to assemble at Cumberland. If any objection lies against this plan I hope to receive timely information of it.

I see no reason to propose any further alteration to the arrangements suggested, except that knapsacks, Canteens and Camp Kettles will be requisite for the Troops on their march from Baltimore and from George Town (if that place should eventually become a place of partial rendezvous) to Williams Port; and that provision should be made for the accommodation of those who may assemble in the first instance at Cumberland. Perhaps Mr Gale may have received directions on this head, if not I presume you will weigh the expediency of the measure and instruct him accordingly.

It remains to observe that although a disposition to condemn the Conduct of the Insurgents, and to support the Government in its measures to seduce them to a sense of duty may with great truth be ascribed generally to the people of Maryland, this disposition has hitherto produced effects very unequal at different places and at different points of time since the requisition was made. I have however no reason to doubt that it will be complied with, at least so far as respects the Infantry. I am less able to ascertain what number of Artillery and Cavalry will be obtained. From the very recent organization of our Militia[3] the whole number now in training will not much exceed the amount of the requisition, and of these it may be supposed that a considerable portion cannot without great injury to their affairs serve in person. With respect to Cavalry in particular, which cannot be replaced by substitutes, notwithstanding a considerable shew of alacrity at the Commencement, the ultimate collection of the number required is very doubtful. This arises from Some circumstances for which it is difficult to find a remedy. It seems certain that no one Troop will furnish Volunteers sufficient for a distinct Command, of course an incorporation of persons belonging to different Troops will be requisite; and I am apprehensive that the necessity of passing under the command of new officers and of mixing with Horsemen in a great variety of Uniforms will deduct greatly from their ardour, and of course from the number to be obtained. Besides the inconveniences already stated, these Corps are hitherto but partially equipped, and in order that no means may be neglected of encouraging them to serve, I would recommend that swords and pistols for one hundred Horsemen (or as many as can be spared) be forwarded immediately to Baltimore directed to Brigadier General Smith[4] who will Command the detachment from this State. This will destroy a ground of excuse, which otherwise would be conclusive and will I think greatly strengthen our means of Complying with the requisition.

I am &c Tho S Lee

The Honorable
Alexander Hamilton Esq
Secretary Treasury.

Copy, RG 56, Letters 2d Comptroller, 2d Auditor, Executive of Maryland and Georgia, 1789–1833, Maryland, National Archives.

1. This is a reference to H's second letter to Lee, August 29, 1794.

2. See George Gale to Thomas Sim Lee, September 1, 1794 (ALS, Hall of Records of Maryland, Annapolis).

3. "An Act to regulate and discipline the militia of this state" was passed on December 28, 1793 (*Maryland Laws,* November, 1793, Sess., Ch. LIII).

4. Samuel Smith had served during the American Revolution from January, 1776, until he resigned as a lieutenant colonel in the 4th Maryland Regiment on May 22, 1779.

Smith was United States Representative from Maryland from March 4, 1793, to March 3, 1803.

From Christopher Richmond

Baltimore, September 4, 1794. "The Treasurer of the United States having on the 17th July remitted to me four Bills drawn by him on Otho H Williams Collector of this Port to be applied to the expence of fortifying the Port of Baltimore and having paid but one of them over to Samuel Dodge the Contractor of the Works,[1] I have thought proper, in order to close the Account erected against me. . . , to deliver over to Robert Purviance Esqr the present Collector the remaining three Bills. . . ."

ALS, RG 53, "Old Correspondence," Baltimore Collector, National Archives; ADf, RG 53, "Old Correspondence," Baltimore Collector, National Archives.

1. See H to Williams, June 9, 1794; Richmond to H, July 26, 1794.

To George Washington

[*Philadelphia*] *September 4, 1794.* "The Secretary of the Treasury requests the favor of the President to send him the communication from the Governor,[1] on which he not long since reported,[2] containing imputations on the conduct of the officers of the UStates employed in the Western Counties. They will be useful in forming the reply to his last letter, in which a considerable progress has been made."

LC, George Washington Papers, Library of Congress.

1. Thomas Mifflin to Washington, August 12, 1794 (LS, RG 59, Miscellaneous Letters, 1790–1799, National Archives). See also H to Washington, August, 1794.

2. See H's draft of Edmund Randolph to Mifflin, August 30, 1794.

From Edmund Randolph

Philadelphia, September 5, 1794. "The Secretary of State has the honor of informing the Secretary of the Treasury, in answer to his letter of the 3d. instant,[1] that Mr. Higginson's [2] papers have been withheld from the Department of State, at the desire of Mr. Ralston,[3] who is supposed to be one of the health Committee.[4] As soon as they are delivered, whatsoever appears respecting payments to Mr. Lemaigre [5] shall be communicated."

LC, RG 59, Domestic Letters of the Department of State, Vol. 7, June 27–November 30, 1794, National Archives.

1. Letter not found.

2. See H to Higginson, April 16, 1794; H to George Washington, August 14, 1794.

3. Robert Ralston was a Philadelphia merchant.

4. In an effort to prevent the entrance of yellow fever into Philadelphia, the legislature on March 11, 1794, had passed "An Act to revive part of the act entituled 'A Supplement to an act, entituled "An Act to prevent infectious diseases being brought into this province"'" (*Pennsylvania Laws*, December, 1793, Sess., Ch. CXCIX). This act provided that health officers could prevent "any person or thing" from landing in the city.

5. Peter Le Maigre was a Philadelphia merchant.

To John Langdon[1]

Philadelphia September 6th. 179[4] [2]

Dear Sir.

Permit me to recommend to your civilities General Walterstoff, Governor of the Island of St. Croix; [3] a Gentleman of real merit, possessing all the requisites to render an acquaintance with him valuable. He is accompanied by my particular friend Doctor Stevens.[4] They are upon an excursion through the Northern States.

With esteem and regard I have the honor to be D. Sir

Your Obed. Servt A Hamilton

John Langdon Esq.
Portsmouth.

Magazine of American History, XXI (January–June, 1889), 279.

1. Langdon, a merchant in Portsmouth, New Hampshire, was United States Senator from 1789 to 1801.

2. This letter is dated "1796," but the date is almost certainly a mistake, for in early September, 1796, H was in New York City. See H to George Washington, September 5, 8, 1796. It is more likely that the letter was written in 1794 when H lived in Philadelphia and when Walterstorff visited the United States. See note 3.

3. Ernst Frederich von Walterstorff was governor general of the Danish West Indies from 1787 until July 25, 1794. On leaving office he went to the United States and traveled there until he returned to Denmark in 1796.

4. Edward Stevens, a physician educated in Edinburgh, was H's boyhood friend in St. Croix. See H to Stevens, November 11, 1769. In addition, Stevens was H's doctor during the yellow fever epidemic in Philadelphia in 1793. See Washington to H, September 6, 1793, note 1; H to the College of Physicians, September 11, 1793.

To Thomas Sim Lee

War Department
September 6th. 1794

Sir

I am directed by the President to notice to your Excellency that information has been received that some riotous proceedings have taken place, in the upper part of Baltimore County [1] and in the neighbourhood of Hagers Town,[2] connected with the Insurrection in the Western Counties of Pennsylvania.[3]

He instructs me to observe that it appears to him of the highest importance that efficacious measures should be pursued to suppress the first beginnings of this Spirit in your State and thereby to check the progress of an evil, which radically threatens the order, peace and tranquility of the Country.

Much depends in such a crisis, as the present, on an early display of energy under the guidance of due legal precaution.

It is understood that the magazine of Arms of the State is at Frederick.[4] Adequate means no doubt will be used to prevent the possibility of these falling into bad hands.

With great Respect I have the honor to be, Your Excellencys, most obedient & Humble Servant A Hamilton

His Excellency
Thomas S. Lee Esquire
Governor of Maryland

LS, Hall of Records of Maryland, Annapolis.

1. No record has been found of "riotous proceedings" in Baltimore County.

2. When the militia in Hagerstown, Maryland, was called into service early in September, the militiamen rebelled against their officers and erected a liberty pole in the courthouse square. When the officials had the liberty pole removed, the militiamen put up another and threatened reprisals against anyone who disturbed it (Thomas Sprigg to Thomas Sim Lee, September 11, 1794 [ALS, Hall of Records of Maryland, Annapolis]). See also the *Baltimore Daily Intelligencer*, September 8, 1794.

3. The alleged connection between the Maryland riots and the insurrection in western Pennsylvania is described in the following letter from Lieutenant John Lynn to General John Davidson, September 1, 1794: ". . . We are Constantly threatened with an invasion from Pennsylvania, the Friends to that Party among us Not being sufficient to accomplish their infernal Designs, on Saturday Evening Last in Consequence of the Draught that Party in this Town [Fort Cumberland, Maryland] & its Vicinity took many Improper Steps in

giving insult to those who are well Disposed & finally Declared they would Erect A Liberty Pole Which the Friends of Government Conceived Improper as they meant thereby to Insult Not only Government and its Officers but Every person Inclined to keep peace, and this being Considered in fact only a prelude to farther Outrage, the volunteer Company Commanded by Capt. [John C.] Beatty were Ordered to prepare to put a Stop to It" (ALS, Hall of Records of Maryland, Annapolis). See also the *Baltimore Daily Intelligencer*, September 20, 1794.

4. On September 11, 1794, Colonel Thomas Sprigg wrote as follows to Thomas Sim Lee regarding the magazine at Frederick: ". . . I have been this day well informd that a Number of their recruiting Officers are beating up for Volunteers both in this city [Hagerstown] and in the adjacent Citys in Pennsylvania for the purpose of raising a pole on Fredk. Town and to plunder the Magazine, in consequence of this informtn. I set out this eveng for Fredk. to warn them of the danger and get them to increase the Guards. I met Genl. [Mountjoy] Bailey . . . Comg. here for information, . . . [who] will Set out before day and I hope do every thing necessary. I am pleased to hear they are well effected there" (ALS, Hall of Records of Maryland, Annapolis).

From Edmund Randolph[1]

[Philadelphia, September 6, 1794]

The Secretary of State presents his Compliments to the Secretary of the Treasury and incloses to him by direction of the President sundry letters and other papers received from Mr. Seagrove[2] respecting the Creek nation and the Governor of Georgia.[3] The President is anxious that the whole of this business should be reviewed and brought into one summary. For this purpose he thinks that Mr. Stagg[4] should be directed to collect all the documents, belonging to the affairs of Georgia in her contest with the Insurgents and the Invaders of the Creek Territory. If the State of Coll Hamilton's health will not permit him to undertake the business, and he will instruct Major Stagg to bring the papers to E. Randolph, he will endeavour to assist Coll. Hamilton.

Philadelphia, Septemr. 6th 1794.

LC, RG 59, Domestic Letters of the Department of State, Vol. 7, June 27–September 30, 1794, National Archives.

1. For background to this letter, see "Cabinet Meeting. Opinion on the Depredations of the Creek Indians Upon the State of Georgia," May 29, 1793.

2. James Seagrove was United States agent to the Creeks. The "papers" included three letters: Seagrove to Henry Knox, May 16, 1794; George Mathews to Seagrove, May 12, 1794; Seagrove to Mathews, May 16, 1794 (*ASP, Indian Affairs*, I, 486–87). See also Randolph to William Bradford, H, and Knox, first letter of July 11, 1794; H to George Washington, July 13, 1794.

3. George Mathews.

4. John Stagg, Jr., was chief clerk in the War Department.

From David Lenox[1]

Philadelphia Septr. 8th. 1794

Sir

As I find my name brought into public view respecting the transactions which have taken place to the Westward, my feelings demand that I should come forward & state facts as they respect myself, leaving it to you to make what use you may think proper of the information.

In the Month of May last the Attorney of the District[2] informed me that certain process were about to be issued against persons in several of the Counties for noncompliance with the Revenue laws[3] of the United States, it therefore became my duty to make preparation for an execution of them. As difficulties had occured on former occasions of a similar kind I came to the determination of doing the duty in person, accordingly on the 22d. day of June, I left this City and proceeded through the Counties of Cumberland Bedford & Fayette without encountering much difficulty, indeed in the County of Fayette I met many instances of personal respect & attention from some of the persons on whom I had served process. On my entering the County of Allegheny I waited on General Nevill[4] who very kindly offered to accompany me rather than put me to the trouble of looking out for a guide. We left his House on Tuesday Morning the 15th. July and in the course of a few hours I served process on four persons all of whom shewed much contempt for the Laws of the United States, we proceeded to the House of a certain William Miller between the hours of eleven and twelve O'Clock in the forenoon who in much agitation refused to receive a Copy of the process against him, but it was legally served. During a conversation with him in which I pointed out the folly of his conduct, we perceived a number of Armed Men approaching us to appearance about thirty or forty. As my mind had been previously made up

ALS, Connecticut Historical Society, Hartford.

1. For background to this letter, see "Deposition of Francis Mentges," August 1, 1794; H to George Washington, August 5, 1794.
2. William Rawle was United States attorney for the District of Pennsylvania.
3. See "Deposition of Francis Mentges," August 1, 1794, note 1.
4. John Neville.

on the business it was not my wish to avoid them in which I was seconded by my companion. Soon after we left the House and were proceeding on our route we were fired upon at the distance of forty or fifty yards. I immediately reined in my Horse and upbraided them with their conduct, but was answered in a language peculiar to themselves. Having finished my business in that quarter excepting the service of a process against a certain John Shaw who was on my way down the Country, I parted with General Nevill who took the road to his Home and I proceeded to Pittsburgh with the intention of prosecuting my journey to places where I had further business. The morning following Colonel Presley Nevill entered my Chamber & put into my hands a letter from his father in which he mentioned that about sun rise that Morning he had been attacked by a considerable body of Men (which I afterwards learnt from good information Amounted to about One hundred) that after a considerable conflict they retreated with three or four Wounded, one of whom I was informed died of his Wounds. On receiving this information I determined to remain in th⟨is⟩ Country to see the issue. An application was made to Major Butler[5] who very readily ordered a detachment of sixteen Men under the command of Captain Howe[6] as a guard to protect General Nevill from further insult. They arrived at his House that Evening & as nothing happened during the Night, Captain Howe returned to town the next morning accompanied by Colonel Nevill leaving a Serjeant and eleven Men at the ⟨–⟩. In the forenoon of the same day (vizt Thursday 17th) General Nevill dispatched a person through the Woods with a letter in which he ment⟨ioned⟩ that he had certain information that about ⟨–⟩ hundred Men would Attack him that Night. He added that if he had any freinds in Pittsburgh they would shew themselves on this occasion. On receiving this information I accompanied Col Nevill to Messrs. Gibson & Wilkin's[7] in whom were united the rank of Generals of Militia and Diginitys of Associate Judges under the State Government. After a conversation of some length & after deliberation on their part they gave their opinion in writing which

5. Thomas Butler was commandant at Fort Fayette.

6. Richard Howe.

7. Major General John Gibson and Brigadier General John Wilkins, Jr. Gibson was a judge of the Court of Common Pleas of Allegheny County. Wilkins was associate judge of the Allegheny County Court.

I am informed has been transmitted to you.[8] As this opinion was such as to afford no protecti⟨on⟩ to General Nevill it became extremely natural for his Son to endeavour to obtain for him all the assistance in his power. I very chearfully offered my services and we were joined by Major Craig[9] Lieut. Semple[10] of the Army and Mr. John Ormsby.[11] We left Pittsburgh about three O'Clock in the afternoon and proceeded to within about half a Mile of General Nevills House where we were all made Prisoners by the insurgents. Soon after the firing commenced and continued with some intermission for about an hour when we perceived the buildings on fire. About eight O'Clock the main body collected where we were which consisted of about five hundred men as they themselves asserted and which I believe. They called a Council and it was determined that I should march to a place called Couch's fort[12] where my fate should be determined. Major Craig Mr Semple & Mr Ormsby got off in the course of the March but Colonel Nevill & myself were obliged to proceed in the most painful and humiliating situation. Here however candor obliges me to express the obligations I am under for the personal protection I frequently met with from several of the party whose names I forbear at present to mention for reasons respecting themselves. On my arriving at the place of Rendezvous and being announced four or five of a large party there fired towards me without injuring me, tho' by the light of the moon my person was plainly exposed to them at ⟨but⟩ few yards distance. I will not pretend to say they meant to injure me but the Men who had before protected me immediately interfered and upbraided them with their conduct. Soon after this and while their Committee were deliberating on my fate two fellows advanced from among the Croud towards me with their Knives drawn. On my mentioning publickly that I hoped I was not to be assassinated in that way, they were driven from my side, tho not before they had cut my Coat in several places. I was then desired to dismount and walk into the House as a place of greater

8. Letter not found.
9. Isaac Craig was deputy quartermaster general at Pittsburgh.
10. Presumably William Semple of Pittsburgh.
11. Ormsby was the son of John Ormsby of Pittsburgh.
12. Couch's Fort, designed for protection against the Indians, was located four miles southeast of John Neville's house at Bower Hill in Washington County, Pennsylvania.

safety. Here I found Colonel Nevill who had arrived half an hour before me. At length, it was determined that I should be released on my promising that I would serve no more processes on the West side ⟨of the⟩ Allegheny Mountain which was consent⟨ed to on⟩ my part and guaranteed by Colonel N⟨evill⟩. We then requested that some persons might accompany us a short distance to protect us from further insult as men were constantly coming in much in liquor. Three persons were accordingly named by their Committee & we had not proceeded more than half a Mile before we were met by a Number of Men much intoxicated. On finding who we were they instantly presented at us and as instantly our escort through themselves between us which in all probability saved us at that time. We were ordered back to the Rendezvous and on the way I was a little ahead of the party accompanied only by one of their principals. On considering what I had already suffered and the danger I should again be exposed to I determined on attempting my escape. Accordingly watching my opportunity I gave my Horse the Spur & rode into the Woods. After riding a short distance I stoped to listen ⟨if⟩ I was persued but hearing no noise, I ⟨give the⟩ credit to the humanity of my companion. I proceeded on and attempted to gain the road leading from Washington to Pittsburgh in which I succeeded and Continued my rout to the River Monongahela. Having reconnoitred the landing and finding everything quiet I led my Horse into a Boat, rowed myself across the River and arrived at Pittsburgh about three O'Clock in the Morning of Friday the 18th. July. The same day ⟨–⟩ men made their appearance in town to demand certain terms of General Nevill & myself. They delivered me a paper writing signed Hugh Scott Junr. Chairman, in which they demanded that I should send all the Summon's (as they called them) in my possession and expected that I should make no returns of the processes I had served to Court, which they said would satisfy the people & add to my safety. To this I replied verbally in presence of Mr. Brakenridge[13] & others that I should send them no Papers & that the processes which I had served should be returned as was my duty. This answer they said would not satisfy the People and

13. Hugh H. Brackenridge. See "Deposition of Francis Mentges," August 1, 1794, note 4.

after taking the opinion of Mr. Brakenridge [14] how far the process would affect their property and after receiving their answer from General Nevill (which was not very favorable to their views) they left the Town. By this time the Inhabitants began to be much alarmed & it was mentioned to Genl. Nevill & myself that some persons were whispering how far it might be justifiable to give us up rather than have the town destroyed. In such a situation it behoved us to keep a good look out and to think of our personal safety. Major Thomas Butler very kindly offered his protection and we are much indebted to him for his manly & decided conduct on the occasion, but as our presence could be of no further use in the Country it was our wish to proceed to the seat of Government as soon as possible. We had good information both by letter & otherwise that it was not practicable for us to proceed with any kind of safety by the direct road as Parties would intercept us. We therefore determined by the advice of a few friends to descend the Ohio river and a Barge was provided accordingly. On an application to Major Butler he very chearfully ordered an Officer and ten Men for this service and we embarked about ten O'Clock in the night of Saturday the 19th. July. We reached Wheelen the following Evening where we declined the further service of the Officer & two of the Men and proceeded on to Marietta where we arrived on Tuesday Morning. Much attention was paid us by the Inhabitants but we are particularly indebted to Colonel Sproat [15] who supplied us with

14. Brackenridge describes this incident as follows: "The marshal conceived it, from what he understood, to be but an initiatory process; and that judgment could not be taken; that there must be another writ, and service of it, in order to found a judgment: He referred them to my opinion, which he conceived must be to that effect. . . . It appeared to me, as the marshal had conceived, to be but in the nature of a summons, to shew cause why process should not issue. I presume, it had been devised by the court, for the greater mildness in carrying into operation the excise law. It was analagous to the subpœna from the court of chancery; in disobedience of which an attachment issues. My answer therefore, which I gave in writing, and which I gave to serve the marshal, for it was without fee from any one, was to this effect, viz. That the marshal was on oath to make return of his writs; but that judgment could not be taken on these returns . . ." (Brackenridge, *Incidents*, I, 23–24).

15. During the American Revolution Ebenezer Sproat was a lieutenant colonel in the 12th Massachusetts Regiment. He was appointed inspector of the revenue for Survey No. 2 in the District of Ohio on December 11, 1794 (*Executive Journal*, I, 164, 165).

every thing we stood in need of and to Lieutenant Miggs[16] of the Militia who offered to March through the Wilderness with the men under his command. However this we declined as it would have been a fatiguing tour to them and would have been attended with delay to us. We proceeded by Clarksburgh accompanied by two faithful guides who had been recommended to us by Colonel Sproat and arrived here on the 8th. day of August. In addition to this statement of facts, I beg leave to notice some points in Governor Mifflin's speech to the Legislature, that I entered the Western Country at a time "peculiarly inauspicious."[17] If any thing here is meant respecting me it would imply that the time was in my choice but it should be recollected that it was my duty to execute the processes previous to the day of return which was the 12th. August. That I met *some* difficulties and encountered *some* opposition is very true and I shall make no comments on these with respect to what the Commissioners appointed by the Governor now to the Westward have said in their communication to him of the 22d August.[18] I think it proper for me to observe that I knew nothing of Dr. Baird[19] or his meeting and I differ very materially with them where they say that it was on the night of the 15th. July thirty of my men instantly flew to Arms and marched towards Nevills House.[20] Now I do again assert that

16. This is presumably a reference to Return Jonathan Meigs, a Revolutionary War veteran, who was a leading promoter of the Ohio Company.

17. Lenox is referring to Governor Thomas Mifflin's message to the Pennsylvania Assembly on September 2, 1794. This message is printed in *Pennsylvania Archives*, 2nd ser., IV, 247–58.

18. On August 6, 1794, Mifflin named Thomas McKean and William Irvine commissioners of the Commonwealth of Pennsylvania to accompany the commissioners appointed by the United States to confer with representatives of the insurgents in western Pennsylvania. Lenox is referring to a report which the Pennsylvania commissioners made to Mifflin on August 22, 1794 (*Pennsylvania Archives*, 2nd ser., IV, 149–99). For the United States commissioners' report of September 24, 1794, see *Pennsylvania Archives*, 2nd ser., IV, 348–59.

19. Dr. Absalom Baird was the brigade inspector of the Washington County militia. See also note 20.

20. Lenox is referring to the following section from the Pennsylvania commissioners' report: "On Monday we endeavored to ascertain the facts that led immediately to the Riots in this county on the 16th & 17th of last month at General Nevil's Estate, and the result is as follows: The Marshal for the District of Pennsylvania had process to serve upon divers persons residing in the counties of Fayette and Allegheny, and had executed them all (above thirty) without molestation or difficulty, excepting one, which was against a Mr. [John] Shaw; he, or some other person went to the place where Doctor [Absalom] Beard, the Brigade Inspector for Washington county, was hearing

it was between the hours of eleven & twelve O'Clock in the forenoon of the same *day* that about the same number assembled at Millers House & fired upon Genl Nevill & myself. The inference from this mistatement of facts is that the proceedings were influenced by a sudden gust of passion excited by intoxication common enough in the Evening, but the truth is that the hour mentioned in the forenoon neither a gust of passion nor heat of Liquor are probable circumstances. I beg Sir you will pardon me for stating facts in a more particular manner than perhaps the subject required, but I esteem it necessary to my own Honor and for public satisfaction that the truth and *whole* truth relative to my Official conduct should be known. If it has met the approbation of the Executive I am fully compensated for the difficulties I have encountered. I have the honor to be

With every sentiment of esteem & respect Sir Your Obedient & very hume servt.

D Lenox
Marshall for the Pennsylvania District

The Honble.
Alex Hamilton Esquire

Appeals made by some of the Militia of a Battalion, who had been called upon for a proportion of the quota of this State of the eighty thousand men, to be in readiness agreeably to an Act of Congress; there were upwards of fifty there with their fire-arms, to whom it was related, that the Federal Sheriff (as they stiled the Marshall) had been serving writs in Allegheny county & carrying the people to Philadelphia for not complying with the Excise laws and that he was at General Nevil's house. It was then in the night of the 15th of last month, between thirty & forty flew instantly to their arms and marched towards Mr. Nevil's, about twelve miles distant, where they appeared early next morning . . ." (*Pennsylvania Archives*, 2nd ser., IV, 195–96).

The act of Congress the Pennsylvania commissioners are referring to is Section 1 of "An Act directing a Detachment from the Militia of the United States," which reads: "That the President of the United States be, and he is hereby authorized to require of the executives of the several states, to take effectual measures, as soon as may be, to organize, arm and equip, according to law, and hold in readiness to march at a moment's warning, the following proportions, respectively, of eighty thousand effective militia . . ." (1 *Stat.* 367 [May 9, 1794]).

From William Ellery

[*Newport, Rhode Island*] *September 9, 1794.* "I acknowledge the receipt of your letter of the 21st. of the last month[1] with the Treasurer's draughts . . . and shall attend to the directions therein contained. . . ."

LC, Newport Historical Society, Newport, Rhode Island.

1. Letter not found.

To Samuel Hodgdon

[*Philadelphia*] *September 9, 1794.* Requests Hodgdon to furnish a return of what accoutrements and arms for the cavalry are in the public stores and to specify those which have been lately sent forward.

Typescript furnished by an anonymous donor.

To Thomas Mifflin

War department, Sept. 9th 1794.

Sir.

The last intelligence from the Western Counties of this State, which has been communicated to you, leaves the issue of measures for an amicable accommodation, so very doubtful, and the season for military operation is wearing away so fast, that the President, with great reluctance, finds himself under a necessity of putting in motion, without further delay, all the militia which have been called for.

I am therefore instructed by him to request, that your Excellency will immediately cause the quota of this State to assemble. The general rendezvous appointed by the President, for all those who may not lie westward of it, is Carlisle, where also the Jersey Militia will be ordered to repair without delay. Particular places of rendezvous for local convenience will be regulated by your Excellency. I was glad to understand from you, in conversation, that Philadelphia, Reading, and Lancaster, were intended, as at these places, the United States have already contracts.[1] Will it not be most convenient for the militia to bring with them their own supplies from their own homes, or neighbourhoods, to the places of first rendezvous, to be compensated for them by the public?

The Superintendent of military Stores, Mr: Hodgdon,[2] will wait upon you, to ascertain what proportions of tents, camp equipage, ought to be sent to the different places of rendezvous, in order that the Militia may be accommodated in the most convenient manner.

I shall in the course of the day call on your Excellency to adjust in a personal conference anything further that may occur.

The President, in making this final call entertains a full confidence that Pennsylvania will upon an occasion which so immediately affects herself, as well as the general interests, display such zeal and energy as shall maintain unsullied her character for discernment, love of order, and true patriotism. It is unnecessary to add, that the part she shall act is of peculiar consequence to the welfare and reputation of the whole Union.

With the highest respect, I have the honor to be, Your Excellency's Most obedt: Servt. Alexander Hamilton
on behalf of the Secry at War [3]

His Excellency Governor Mifflin.

LS, Mr. George L. Tait, Dallas, Texas.

1. Jacob Bower was the Army contractor at Reading, and Matthias Slough was the contractor at Lancaster.

2. Samuel Hodgdon.

3. The words "on behalf of the Secry at War" are in H's handwriting. For Henry Knox's absence from Philadelphia, see George Washington to H, August 12, 1794, note 1.

On September 12, 1794, in answer to this letter from H, Mifflin wrote to Washington and informed him that he was complying with Washington's request (*Pennsylvania Archives,* 2nd ser., IV, 296–97).

To Jeremiah Olney

Treasury Department, September 9, 1794. "In answer to your favour of the 11th. of August last on the subject of the Suits brought against you by Arnold & Dexter,[1] I shall just observe, that if an application to the General Assembly for a new Trial, can be effected in time, without precluding the right of ultimately resorting to the Court of the United States, there can be no objection to your adopting that mode in the first instance."

LS, Rhode Island Historical Society, Providence; LC, RG 56, Letters to the Collector at Providence, National Archives; LC, RG 56, Letters to Collectors at Small Ports, "Set G," National Archives.

1. For information on the case involving Welcome Arnold and Edward Dexter, see Olney to H, November 7, 15, 28, December 10, 13, 27, 1792; March 15, 25, April 15, 25, September 23, October 7, 21, November 21, 1793; February 17, March 31, April 14, first letter of April 24, May 5, August 11, 1794; H to Olney, November 27, 1792; November 7, 1793; March 19, April 24, 1794.

From Edmund Randolph[1]

Philadelphia September 9th 1794

Sir,

The President of the United States instructs me to request, that you will cause an inquiry to be immediately made, through some of the Officers of the Customs, into the damage sustained by the detention of the Brig William of Glasgow, a prize to a French Cruiser, while She was detained by Government for examination, whether she was not captured within the protection of our coast. It may perhaps be important to ascertain the *time*, when the damage accrued and through what means. You will be pleased to direct the persons, who shall be employed to inform the French Consul in Philadelphia[2] of the time and place of their proceeding; in order that the persons interested in behalf of the Captors may be present, if they think proper.

These measures are adopted by the President, that he may have the whole subject before him, when he shall decide on the application made by the French minister,[3] for compensation, and not because he has already decided in its favor. Those therefore who shall be appointed to inquire, will not give any intimation to the Consul or others, that the President has in the smallest degree prejudged the matter.

I have the honor, Sir, to be with great respect & esteem Your most obedient Servant Edm: Randolph

The Secretary of the Treasury

LS, Free Library of Philadelphia; LC, RG 59, Domestic Letters of the Department of State, Vol. 7, June 27–November 30, 1794, National Archives.

1. For background to this letter, see "Opinion on Compensation for Captured Vessels," June 22, 1794; H to George Washington, June 22, 1794. For the *William*, see H to Rufus King, June 15, 1793; Thomas Jefferson to H and Henry Knox, June 25, 1793, note 1; "Cabinet Meeting. Opinion on Vessels Arming and Arriving in United States Ports," July 12, 1793; "Cabinet Meetings. Opinions Concerning Relations of the United States with Several European

Countries," November 1–22, 1793; Randolph to William Bradford, H, and Knox, April 5, 1794; Randolph to H and Knox, May 20, 1794; Randolph to H, June 9, 17, 1794.

2. Antoine René Charles Mathurin de La Forest had been appointed French consul general for the states of New York, New Jersey, Pennsylvania, and Delaware on March 2, 1792, and was recalled on May 18, 1793. He was reappointed on February 22, 1794.

3. On August 26, 1794, Jean Antoine Joseph Fauchet wrote to Randolph: ". . . Cette réflexion que la justice me suggère, me rappelle qu'une lettre que je vous ai écrite en demande d'indemnités pour le navire le William qu'on a laissé déperir dans le port de Philadelphie, en lui faisant attendre une détermination pendant plus d'une année, est restée sans résponse. J'aime à croire malgré votre silence que vous aurez pris ma demande en consideration, je dirai plus même, je dirai que je suis sur qu'elle a été accueillie favorablement puis qu'elle est juste . . ." (*Correspondence of the French Ministers with the United States Government*, part 1, 8).

To William Ellery

[*Philadelphia, September 10, 1794.* The description of this letter in the dealer's catalogue reads: "He discusses Ellery's suit against Pierce [1]—'confide in the Jury's doing their duty.' Comments on funds to be sent to Ellery for use in building fortifications." [2] *Letter not found.*]

LS, sold at Parke-Bernet Galleries, Inc., October 17, 1961, Lot 122.

1. Preserved Pierce. See Ellery to H, August 1–6, 1794.

2. For information concerning the fortifications, see Henry Knox to H, March 29, 1794; "Treasury Department Circular to the Collectors of the Customs," April 3–June 4, 1794.

To Richard Harrison [1]

Treasury Department
September 10th 1794

Sir

Inclosed I transmit herewith, an Account of Mr. Le Maigres [2] against the United States for the hire of his Vessell to carry Mr. Higginson, who was appointed by the President of the United States, Agent to go to the British West India Islands, on the subject of the American Vessells captured by the British Cruizers since the commencement of the War between France and England which Account you will be pleased to have adjusted with all possible dispatch.

The admission of the charge of forty Dollars noted at the foot of the account, must depend upon the question whether the United States are liable to make good expences of that Nature.

The only deduction to be made from the Account that I know of at present is the Sum of One hundred and seventeen Dollars credited by Mr. Le Maigre.[3]

I am with Consideration Sir Your most Obedt. Servt

A Hamilton

Richard Harrison Esqr
Auditor of the Treasury

[ENCLOSURE][4]

Alexander Hamilton Esqr in Behalf of the United States. Philadelphia [August 30, 1794]

To Peter Le Maigre Dr.

1794

August 28. For the Affreightment of the Brign. Molly John Tremells Mastr. from 16th. April last to this date inclusive, is 4 months & 12 days at Dollrs. 450 ℔ mo. (as ℔ Charter Party) } dollrs. 1980.—

Cr.

By Cash received ℔ Capt. Tremells from Mr. Higginson		117.—
Ballance due.	Dollrs.	1863.—

E. Excepted. Philadelphia 30, Augt. 1794 Pr Lemaigre Esq.

20 days detention of the Pilot at Fort Mifflin claiming 2 drs ℔ diem is Drs 40.—

LS, RG 217, Miscellaneous Treasury Accounts, 1790–1894, Account No. 5932, National Archives.

1. For background to this letter and information on Nathaniel C. Higginson's mission to the West Indies, see "Cabinet Meeting. Opinion on a Request for a Passport," April 2, 1794; H to George Washington, April 2, August 14, 1794; "Conversation with George Hammond, "April 15–16, 1794; H to Higginson, April 16, 1794; Edmund Randolph to H, September 5, 1794.

2. Peter Le Maigre.

3. On June 9, 1794, Tench Coxe wrote to Edmund Randolph and enclosed "an extract from the Note at the foot of Mr. Le Maigre's Charter party" (ALS, RG 59, Miscellaneous Letters, 1790–1799, National Archives). The extract reads: "Mr. Higginson, the public Agent of the united States, is authorized to pay from time to time to the Captain . . . of the above named brig Molly during her voyage such sums of money as he shall find necessary for her use, provided the said payment shall not exceed the sum due for her hire.
April 17th 1794 P Lemaigre."
"Ap 17th 1794 Directed Mr Higginson to make advances accordingly. A H." (Copy, RG 59, Miscellaneous Letters, 1790–1799, National Archives.)

4. DS, RG 217, Miscellaneous Treasury Accounts, 1790–1894, Account No. 5932, National Archives.

To Samuel Hodgdon[1]

Philadelphia Sepr
10. 1794

Sir

I request that you will immediately forward to Winchester in Virginia 75 pair Horsemen's pistols 150 ditto swords with Belts 200 valices, to Baltimore in Maryland, 50 pair of Horsemens pistols, one hundred ditto Swords with belts and 100 valices, together with Knapsacks canteens & Camp kettles sufficient for 1000 men.

Tents and the remainder of the camp equipage for the Maryland Militia must be forwarded to Frederick Town in that state. Whatever goes to Maryland must be addressed to the order of George Gale Esquire.[2] Not a moment should be lost in forwarding the remainder of the Camp Equipage destined for Virginia.

I rely too that all the needful ammunition of every sort will be forwarded without delay, that for Virginia to Winchester, that for Maryland to Williamsport that for Jersey & Pensylvania to Carlisle. It is the intention that one half the Artillery go to the Virginia & Maryland Militia who are to unite at Fort Cumberland—the other half to Carlisle.

The remainder of the horsemens pistols swords belts & valices which you have in store except what may be necessary for Lt Clough's detatchment are to be forwarded forthwith to Trenton.

With consideration & esteem I am Sir Your obedt ser

A Hamilton

Samuel Hodgsdon Esqr

Be so good as to send me a copy of this letter.

Mr. Charles E. Mather II, Mather & Co., Philadelphia.

1. For background to this letter, see "Minutes of a Meeting Concerning the Insurrection in Western Pennsylvania," August 24, 1794. See also H to Hodgdon, August 25, 1794; H to Henry Lee, second letter of August 25, 1794; H to Thomas Sim Lee, first letter of August 29, 1794.

2. Gale was supervisor of the revenue for Maryland. See H to Gale, August 27, 1794.

From Isaac Holmes

Collectors Office Charleston [South Carolina] 10th. Sepr 1794

Sir

The American Schooner named the Hawke Enroled and Licenced in this Office John Cook Master did on the 16 May last clear from this port for the port of St Marys in the United States during the period of the Embargo,[1] but instead of proceeding to her place of destination while at Sea She altered her Voyage and proceeded to a Foreign Port in the West Indies vizt Port au Paix. While there Capn Cook Sold the Vessel to Capt Alexander Bolchez a French Citizen who fitted the American schooner Hawke as a Privateer and arrived in this Port with a Legal French Commission. I considered this Conduct as a gross Violation of the Laws of the United States [2] and Seized the Vessel. The Trial commenced in the Court of Admiralty for the district and was argued for four days. A decree of Condemnation passed against the Hawke. The Claimants then appealed to the Fœderal District Court for the Ultimate decision of the Question whether the Vessel is liable to forfeiture for having departed to a foreign port without first delivering up her Enrolment and Licence to the Collector of the district. The Judge of the Court delivered up this Vessel to the Claimant Bolchez with her tackle furniture Apparel & Guns &ca upon receiving sufficient Security to the amount of the Value of the Vessel agreeably to 66 Sec: of the Collection Law [3] for the Ultimate decision. Upon the delivery of the Vessel armed as She came into the Port to the French Capt Bolchez he immediately applied to me to clear out his Vessel armed as she came in—to which I refused as I considered the Hawke to be still an American Bottom, untill the Court of appeals had establised or rejected her Condemnation and therefore to suffer her to depart with arms & a Commission would have been in my Judgment a National Commitment. However to prevent a mistake I wrote to the Fœderal Attorney [4] the enclosed Letter his answer you will See annexed. In consequence of that answer and the enclosed Order of Court I cleared out the Hawke much against my Judgment as I still hold She is an American Bottom untill her Case should be determined by the Court of appeals. I also wrote to the Governor [5] a Similar Letter. He acquiesced with the Attorney. I will remark here that the appeal is made by the Claimant with no other View than to procure time for the payment of the Value of the Forfeiture 12,000 dollars as there never could have been a Clearer forfeiture. I have thought proper to represent this Matter to you as this Vessel from her Construction is Capable of doing vast Injury and I cannot my Self see that she was entitled to a Clearance from this port while her Case was undetermined. The probability that the injuries & damage She may Commit may upon this ground be retorted to the United States has induced me to be particular on this Subject and as our Neutrality may be committed I have thought it best to give this statement requesting your Opinion.

With great Esteem I am Sir Your most Obt Sert

Isaac Holmes Col

Alexander Hamilton Esqr
Secretary of the Treasury

LS, Historical Society of Pennsylvania, Philadelphia.

1. On March 26, 1794, Congress in a joint resolution authorized the President to impose an embargo on all ships and vessels in United States ports for thirty days (1 *Stat.* 400). On April 18, 1794, the embargo was extended until May 25, 1794 (1 *Stat.* 401).

2. Holmes is referring to "An Act for enrolling and licensing ships or vessels to be employed in the coasting trade and fisheries, and for regulating the same" (1 *Stat.* 305–18 [February 18, 1793]). Section 8 of this act provided that a vessel be seized and forfeited for sailing to a foreign port without first giving up its enrollment and license and obtaining a register. Section 32 provided for forfeiture if ownership of the ship was transferred to a foreign citizen.

3. On July 4, 1794, Thomas Bee, United States judge for the District of South Carolina, in *United States* v *Schooner Hawke* declared: "In this case there is sufficient proof that the 8th and 32d clauses of the act of congress for licensing coasters have been infringed. I decree therefore that the schooner *Hawke*, with her tackle, furniture, and apparel, be condemned as forfeited to the *United States*" (Bee, *Reports of Cases Adjudged in the District Court of South Carolina*, 38). Bolchos (Bolchez) then petitioned the court on the basis of Section 67 of "An Act to provide more effectually for the collection of duties imposed by law on goods, wares and merchandise imported into the United States, and on the tonnage of ships or vessels" (1 *Stat.* 145–78 [August 4, 1790]). Holmes is incorrectly referring to Section 66 of this law. For the confusion over the numbering of the sections of the "Collection Law," see "Treasury Department Circular to the Collectors of the Customs," August 6, 1792.

Although Holmes's letter is dated September 10, 1794, the District Court did not act until September 15, when in *British Consul* v *Schooner Favourite and Alexander Bolchos* "A warrant of appraisement was accordingly issued, the other requisites of the act were complied with, and the vessel with everything belonging to her was transferred to the claimant accordingly. She then sailed from this port as French property, with the same equipment, crew, and commission, that she had obtained at Port-de-Paix" (Bee, *Reports of Cases Adjudged in the District Court of South Carolina*, 39).

4. Thomas Parker.
5. William Moultrie.

To Thomas Sim Lee

Duplicate

War Department
Sepr 10th. 1794

Sir

I have the honor of your Excellency's letter of the 4th Instant.

I am now instructed by the President to request that the whole quota of Maryland may be assembled and marched as speedily as may be towards their general rendezvous, Williamsport. It was my intention to forward to Frederick town the tents and other articles of Camp Equipage, in order that they might be there furnished to the Troops which came from below. But I will endeavour agreeably to your intimation to change this arrangement as to Knapsacks Canteens & Camp kettles. Swords & pistols for 100 horse will also be forwarded to Baltimore without delay.[1] It would rather involve too great a circuit to send the necessary articles to George Town but I will endeavour so to regulate the matter as to render it possible if demed indispensable.

The assembling a part of your Militia at Fort Cumberland will facilitate the general arrangement; for that is the place intended for a junction of the Militia of Virginia & Maryland.

The season is so far advanced that all possible dispatch is essential.

This final resolution has been taken by the President[2] in consequence of a very undecided state of things in the western Counties of this State when the last intelligence from thence came away. It appears that although the restoration of Order had gained powerful advocates & supporters; yet that there is a violent and numerous party which does not permit to count upon a submission to the laws without the intervention of force. Hence the advanced state of the

Season considered, it became indispensable to put the force which had been provisionally called for[3] in motion. I advise the appointment of a person in capacity of Quartermaster & Commissary of Military stores to the detachment with a competent Salary, I should think the pay & emoluments of a Major might suffice. But I do not make this observation as a restriction. I have been also honored with your letter of the 28th of August last, and shall desire the co-operation of the Officers of the Customs accordingly. The object of the Eighth section has [been] anticipated by an instruction to the Collector of Baltimore[4] in consequence of a representation from that place.[5]

With perfect respect I have the honor to be Sir Your most obedt servt

A Hamilton

His Excellency
Thomas S. L⟨ee⟩ Esqre

LS, Hall of Records of Maryland, Annapolis.

1. See H to Samuel Hodgdon, September 10, 1794.
2. See H to Thomas Mifflin, September 9, 1794.
3. See H to Thomas Sim Lee, first letter of August 29, 1794.
4. See H to Robert Purviance, first letter of August 22, 1794, note 2.
5. Letter not found. See H to Purviance, first letter of August 22, 1794.

To Thomas Mifflin

Treasury Department, Sept 10 1794.

Sir.

Having understood from you, that it was your intention, to appoint a person as Quarter Master to the detachment of Militia of this State, about to assemble, and march, and confiding that the person whom you may choose will be both capable and trustworthy, I propose, as a matter of simplicity and convenience, to commit to him the procuring of Waggons for the transportation of every thing connected with the detachment, except provisions, during the expedition, and also the procuring of forage and fuel for the detachment to the rendezvous at Carlisle. There some general ulterior arrangement will be made. I except provisions, because they are already embraced in another arrangement.[1]

Allow me therefore to request, that you will inform me who the person designated for this service is, and will direct him to furnish me without delay, with an estimate specifying particulars of the articles to be furnished, and their cost, in order to the requisite pecuniary supply.[2]

With perfect respect, I have the honor to be, your Excellency's Most obedient Servt. A. Hamilton

His Excellency
The Governor of Pennsylvania.

LS, MS Division, New York Public Library.

1. Elie Williams was the agent for provisions for the militia army. See H to Williams, September 12, 1794.

2. This letter is endorsed: "Referred to Mr Cl: Biddle to answer, as Qr. Mr. Genl."

Clement Biddle was marshal for the District of Pennsylvania from 1789 to 1793, when he resigned and was succeeded by David Lenox (*Executive Journal*, I, 29, 31, 144, 143).

To George Washington

Treasury Department, September 10, 1794. Encloses "a claim of Joseph Tatlow's against the United States for his services as an Express in April 1794 from New Castle to Philada." [1] Asks "whether it ought not to be discharged out of the fund of twenty thousand Dollars appropriated the last Session of Congress to defray the Contingent charges of Government." [2]

LC, George Washington Papers, Library of Congress.

1. Tatlow's bill, dated April 21, 1794, amounted to $12.11 for "The Hire of My Horse & Carriage from Newcastle to Philadelphia Carraing the Dispatches from Mr. [Thomas] Pinckney our Minnister At the Court of London Brought by the Delaware Capt. Thos. Truxton" (AD, RG 217, Miscellaneous Treasury Accounts, 1790–1894, Account No. 5917, National Archives). On the back of this bill Edmund Randolph wrote the following note, which is dated September 5, 1794: "The Letters by Capt. Truxton from Mr Pinckney were delivered to me. I do not know Mr. Tatlow and therefore I cannot say whether he did deliver them or not. But I cannot doubt it after the statement within. As to what the worth of such a service is, I am no judge" (ALS, RG 217, Miscellaneous Treasury Accounts, 1790–1894, Account No. 5917, National Archives).

2. "An Act making appropriations for certain purposes therein expressed" appropriated twenty thousand dollars "For defraying the contingent expenses of government . . . under the direction of the President of the United States" (1 *Stat.* 394–95 [June 9, 1794]).

On September 12, 1794, the President approved Tatlow's account (JPP, 309).

From Joseph Howell, Junior

W. D. Accountants Office
September 11th. 1794

Sir

I have to request in the absence of the Secretary of War, you will be pleased to direct the sum of five thousand dollars to be placed in the hands of the Treasurer, being for the use of the department of war, namely—

For the pay of the recruits	2000.
" the recruiting service	1500
" incidental expences	1500
Dollars	5000

I am Sir &c Joseph Howell

The Secretary of the Treasury

LC, RG 93, Letter Book, 1794, National Archives.

From John Jay

London 11 Septr. 1794

Dear Sir

I had last week the Pleasure of recieving from you a few Lines by Mr. Blaney.[1] You will recieve this Letter by the Hands of Mr. Morris.[2] He will also be the Bearer of my Dispatches to Mr. Randolph.[3] They will be voluminous, particular, and in many Respects interesting. It should not be forgotten that there is Irritation here, as well as in America, and that our *party* Processions, Toasts; Rejoicings &c &c. have not been well calculated to produce goodwill and good Humour. The government nevertheless destinguishes between national acts, and these party Effusions, and have entertained hitherto an opinion and Belief that the Presidt. and our Governmt. and nation in general, were really desirous of an amicable Settlement of Differences, and of laying a Foundation for Friendship as well as peace between the two Countries.

The Secretary's Letters by Mr. Munro, and his Speech on his Introduction to the Convention have appeared in the English papers.[4] Their Impression in this Country may easily be conjectured. I wish they had both been more guarded. The Language of the United States at Paris and at London, should correspond with their neutrality. These things are not favorable to my Mission.

A speedy Conclusion to the negociation is problematical, tho not highly improbable, If I should be able to conclude the Business on admissible Terms, I shall do it, and risque Consequences; rather than by the Delays of waiting for, and covering myself by opinions & Instructions hazard a Change in the Disposition of this Court—for it seems our Country, or rather some parts of it, will not forbear Asperities. I hear that Virga. is taking british property by Escheat;[5] and other things which in the present moment are unseasonable, are here reported.

As the proposed Articles are under Consideration—as they have already undergone some Alterations, and as I am not without Hopes of other and further Amendments, I really think they ought not to be published in their present crude State; especially as in the Course of a few weeks I expect to be able to communicate their *ultimate* Form. If *then*, they should not appear to me to be such as I ought to sign, I will transmit them, and wait for further Instructions.

I am Dear Sir Yours sincerely John Jay

Col. Hamilton

ALS, Hamilton Papers, Library of Congress; ADfS, Columbia University Libraries.

1. Letter not found. David Blaney not only delivered H's letter to Jay but he also had the distinction of delivering the text of the "Treaty of Amity, Commerce, and Navigation," or the Jay Treaty, which Blaney gave to Edmund Randolph on March 7, 1795 (Blaney to Randolph, March 11, 1795 [ALS, RG 59, Miscellaneous Letters, 1790–1799, National Archives]).

For Blaney's bill to "the US. for bringing the Treaty from London to Phila.," see the enclosure in Blaney to Timothy Pickering, March 11, 1797 (copy, RG 59, Miscellaneous Letters, 1790–1799, National Archives).

2. Robert Morris, Jr.

3. Jay's dispatches to Randolph are dated September 13, 14, 1794 (ALS, RG 59, Despatches from United States Ministers to Great Britain, 1791–1806, Vol. 1, April 19, 1794–June 1, 1795, National Archives).

4. On August 15, 1794, shortly after his arrival in Paris, James Monroe, the United States Minister Plenipotentiary to France, addressed the French National Assembly in a speech in which he enthusiastically endorsed United States friendship for France (LC, RG 59, Despatches from United States Ministers to France, 1789–1869, Vol. 6, August 15, 1794–October 21, 1796, National Archives). Monroe's address is printed in *ASP*, *Foreign Relations*, I, 673–74. At the same time Monroe delivered two letters from Randolph to the Committee

of Public Safety of the French Republic, dated June 10, 1794, both of which emphasized the friendly attitude of the United States toward France (copies, RG 59, Despatches from United States Ministers to France, 1789–1869, Vol. 6, August 15, 1794–October 21, 1796, National Archives). Randolph's letters are printed in *ASP, Foreign Relations,* I, 674.

5. As early as 1784, state laws obstructed the execution of Article 4 of the peace treaty of 1783, which provided "that Creditors on either Side shall meet with no lawful Impediment to the Recovery of the full Value in Sterling Money of all bona fide Debts heretofore contracted" (Miller, *Treaties,* II, 154). British creditors pressed for redress, and their protests increased when negotiations between the United States and Great Britain began in 1794. After Congress defeated the 1794 Non-Intercourse Bill, the grand jury of the United States Circuit Court for the District of Virginia, in the May session, presented as "a national Grivance" the payment of debts due to British creditors unless Britain made reparations for spoliations and fulfilled her 1783 treaty obligations by evacuating the northwest posts (1 Ms. Order Book 358, United States Circuit Court for the District of Virginia, Virginia State Library, Richmond).

To Edmund Randolph

[Philadelphia, September 11, 1794]

Dr. Sir,

I cannot entertain a doubt that Mr. Jaudenes request for a guard ought to be complied with.[1] The protection due to a foreign Minister is absolute and the courtesy of nations dictates that *military* means shall be used in cases where there may be doubt of the adequateness of the civil—as here where the menace of assassination may require an armed guard. Nor have I the least doubt that the standing forces can legally be applied to this purpose whatever may be said of the Militia. We have here an Officer and twelve Dragoon who may be used. But I take it for granted an escort of Volunteers from New York or New Jersey may without difficulty be had. I really think the United States would be disagreeably compromitted by a refusal.[2]

Yours with esteem A Hamilton

The Secy of State

LC, RG 59, Domestic Letters of the Department of State, Vol. 7, June 27–November 30, 1794, National Archives.

1. Josef de Jaudenes was one of the Spanish commissioners to the United States. On September 2, 1794, while in New York City and about to return to Philadelphia, he wrote to Randolph that he had reason to believe that certain Frenchmen were plotting to murder him. He asked that the President provide him and his family, as well as his house in Philadelphia, with some form of armed protection (LC, RG 59, Notes from the Spanish Legation in the United

States to the Department of State, 1790–1906, Vol. 2, August 22, 1794–October 15, 1798, National Archives). On September 3, 1794, Randolph replied to Jaudenes that his request would be referred to the President (LC, RG 59, Domestic Letters of the Department of State, Vol. 7, June 27–November 30, 1794, National Archives). On the following day Randolph wrote to Jaudenes: "The laws of the United States do not suffer the military force to be employed, as you wish. But the civil authority is the proper resort. The efficacy of the civil authority being manifested by the interposition of the Mayor of New York, so far as relates to your residence there, I beg leave to recommend to you still to apply to the Civil Officers" (LC, RG 59, Domestic Letters of the Department of State, Vol. 7, June 27–November 30, 1794, National Archives). On September 6, Jaudenes wrote in reply to Randolph that he was surprised at the President's refusal to grant his request and that he considered the President's refusal an affront to him, his monarch, and his country (LC, RG 59, Notes from the Spanish Legation in the United States to the Department of State, 1790–1906, Vol. 2, August 22, 1794–October 15, 1798, National Archives).

2. On September 11, 1794, Randolph sent H's letter to the President (LC, George Washington Papers, Library of Congress). He also sent to Washington the draft of a letter which he had prepared rejecting Jaudene's application. At the top of this proposed letter is written: "Letter proposed by E. Randolph to be written to Mr. Jaudenes—but the Presdt. preferred sending the *horse*" (LC, RG 59, Domestic Letters of the Department of State, Vol. 7, June 27–November 30, 1794, National Archives).

To Ephraim Blaine [1]

Philadelphia Sepr. 12. 1794

Sir

I am desirous of availing myself of your Agency for supplying with transportation forage straw & fuel the Pensylvania & New Jersey Militia destined to act against the insurgents in the Western Parts of Pensylvania. The number to be supplied may amount to 6300 infantry and 1000 horse.

You will have to take up the supply at Carlisle and continue it Westward—preparing as fast as it can be done three weeks supply of forage & having due regard to the *security* of the Deposits.

With regard to waggons you need do nothing more at present than ascertain where & how soon they can be had; as the Pensylvania Militia will come forward with Waggons for the entire expedition, and the Jersey Militia with waggons that will answer to transport them to Bedford, but not over the Mountains as I am told they are not fit for that service. You will observe that provision-waggons are to be procured by Mr. Eli Williams [2] the bearer of this letter.

The Jersey Militia will amount to 1600 infantry & 500 Cavalry.

With esteem I am Sir Your obed servant Alex Hamilton

P.S Your compensation would be a salary per Month equal to the pay & subsistence of a Lt Col. Commandant. Mr. Williams is instructed to deliver you 5000 Dollars to enter upon the service.[3]

Ephrain Blaine Esqr

ALS, Ephraim Blaine Papers, Library of Congress; copy, Connecticut Historical Society, Hartford.

1. This letter was enclosed in H to Elie Williams, September 12, 1794.

Blaine, who had succeeded Jeremiah Wadsworth as commissary general during the American Revolution, was a resident of Carlisle, Pennsylvania. In 1794 he was assistant quartermaster general of the militia army.

2. Elie Williams and Robert Elliot of Maryland were Army contractors for the western posts. Williams, a brother of Otho H. Williams, had been appointed agent for provisioning the militia army. See H to Elie Williams, September 12, 1794.

3. Williams paid Blaine five thousand dollars on September 22, 1794 (D, RG 217, Miscellaneous Treasury Accounts, 1790–1894, Account No. 9550, National Archives).

To Samuel Hodgdon

War Department
Sepr 12th: 1794

Sir

I request that some person in character of chief Armourer who may also have charge of the Artificers be provided to accompany the Militia Army. Let him also engage such wheelwrights and other mechanics as may not certainly be found among the troops, and let every correspondent arrangement be made.

One half the Intrenching tools intended for the expedition are to be forwarded without delay to Williamsport. The other half is destined for Carlisle.

With consideration & Esteem I am Sir Your Obedient Servt
A Hamilton

Samuel Hodgsdon Esqr

Typescript supplied by Lincoln Library, Shippensburg, Pennsylvania.

From Thomas Sim Lee

Annapolis September 12th 1794.

Sir.

I have had the honor to receive your letters of the 6th and the 10th of this month. I had already been informed of the turbulent disposition manifested in Baltimore County and at Hagerstown, as also of similar proceedings at Fort Cumberland, and had been deliberating whether the circumstances disclosed were of sufficient importan[c]e and authenticity to justify a public notice of them.[1] The earnest manner in which I find myself called upon in your letter of the 6th Instant to use all legal methods for suppressing this dangerous spirit in its origin has decided me to issue a Proclamation on the subject, to which, the President may be assured, I shall add every possible effort of authority and influence that may aid the object in view.

In Conformity with the President's directions intimated in your letter of the 10th Inst I shall without delay give orders for the march of our quota of Militia to Williams Port excepting a part which I shall push on immediately to Fort Cumberland, having reason to apprehend that the Militia of that Quarter which are all that I originally proposed to assemble there, are not to be depended on, but may require some others to keep them Steady.

I had on the first notice of suspicious appearances in that part of the State, directed Brigadier General Bayley[2] to establish a Guard (not less than that of a Captain) over the Magazine and Armoury at Frederick Town, and I have reason to believe that my orders have been Carefully obeyed; but in Consequence of information just received of some alarming indications in the neighbourhood of that place,[3] I shall immediately send instructions for doubling the Guard and shall urge the commanding officer to give the most vigilant attention to the Safety of these objects.

I have already at the request of the Field officers of Allegany County forwarded to them under the care of an escort from Frederick Town two hundred stand of arms and some ammunition, which being placed in proper hands will, I trust, enable them to keep the turbulent in line, untill the Troops arrive.

I have understood that, part of the Eastern Shore Militia are already arrived at Baltimore and the whole body will probably be ready in two or three days to proceed, I hope therefore that if the Camp Kettles &c should not have been sent forward before this reaches you, immediate orders will be given for their being dispatched.[4] The sending articles of this kind to George Town may be dispensed with.

I have appointed Mr John Usher Chaulton of Frederick Town Quarter Master and Commissary of Military Stores and shall fix his salary at the rate you propose unless upon enquiry it shall appear that this double employment ought to entitle him to something more.

I am &c Thomas S Lee

The Honorable
Alexander Hamilton Esq
Secretary of the Treasury.

Copy, RG 56, Letters 2d Comptroller, 2d Auditor, Executive of Maryland and Georgia, 1789–1833, Maryland, National Archives.

1. See H to Thomas Sim Lee, September 6, 1794.
2. Mountjoy Bayly of Frederick, Maryland.
3. See H to Thomas Sim Lee, September 6, 1794, note 4.
4. See H to Samuel Hodgdon, September 10, 1794.

From Thomas Sim Lee

Annapolis September 12th 1794

Sir.

The enclosed Copy of a Letter from Peter Engels the State's Armourer at Frederick Town, contains information[1] which tho' not of the most authentic kind, it is proper the President should be immediately apprized of.

In consequence of its receipt, I have thought it prudent for the security of the Public magazine to take the provisionary step which the enclosed Copy of my letter to Brigadier General Bayley[2] will explain.

The suggestion contained in Engel's letter that all the powder and lead has lately been bought up in the Neighbouring Towns is, I am told, confirmed by a private letter from a respectable Gentleman in Frederick to his friend in Baltimore.

I am &c Thomas S Lee

The Honorable
Alexander Hamilton Esqr
Secretary of the Treasury

Copy, RG 56, Letters 2d Comptroller, 2d Auditor, Executive of Maryland and Georgia, 1789–1833, Maryland, National Archives.

1. This is a reference to a possible attack against the magazine at Frederick, Maryland. See H to Thomas Sim Lee, September 6, 1794, note 4.
2. Mountjoy Bayly.

From James Moland

Bantry [*Ireland*] *September 12, 1794.* Recalls Hamilton's "very polite and disinterested behaviour" when Moland was last in America. Asks Hamilton's assistance as a lawyer in a case in which Moland is being unjustly sued for the recovery of a debt.

ALS, Hamilton Papers, Library of Congress.

To Robert Purviance[1]

Treasury Department September 12th 1794

Sir,

The Congress of the United States, having at their last Session passed an Act entitled "An Act declaring the consent of Congress to an Act of the State of Maryland passed the 28th of December 1793 for the appointment of Health Officer."[2] And the Governor of Maryland having requested of me by his letter of the 28th of last Month, to direct the Officers of the Revenue at Baltimore, to afford their assistance towards accomplishing the object contemplated by the Act of the State of Maryland—I have therefore to request that you and the other Officers of the Customs at Baltimore will be pleased to cooperate with such person as may be appointed by the Governor, for the purpose, in effectuating as far as you legally can the execution of the said Act.

I am with consideration Sir, Your most obedient Servant

A Hamilton

Robert Purviance Esquire
Collector of Baltimore

LS, Columbia University Libraries.

1. For background to this letter, see H to Purviance, first letter of August 22, 1794; Thomas Sim Lee to H, August 28, 1794; H to Lee, September 10, 1794.
2. 1 *Stat.* 393–94 (June 9, 1794).

To Elie Williams

Treasury department
September 12. 1794

Sir

I have directed a Warrant for fifteen thousand dollars [1] to issue in your favour in addition to the sum heretofore advanced.[2]

Of these 15000 I request 5000 may be paid to Ephraim Blaine Esquire at Carlisle in case he should agree to accept the Agency offered to him by the enclosed letter.[3] Should he decline it which I request you to ascertain from him, I will then thank you to make an arrangement for the purpose with some other competent character and to put the money in his hands. The receipt of the Agent for the money will discharge you as the services are meant to be distinct.[4]

As it is expected the Agent at Trenton [5] and the Contractors at Philadelphia Reading [6] and Lancaster [7] will supply almost all the provisions that may be wanted as far as Carlisle which will deduct so much from your estimate and as some of the other expences will be successive and gradual I conclude that thirty thousand dollars will suffice at present. A further sum can be forwarded in measure of the demand. And the goodness of the public Credit will enable you to supply any temporary deficiency without disadvantage. As to such articles indeed as can be promptly commanded it may be sufficient to assemble a supply for a fortnight only at and from Carlisle Westward. You will of course have regard to the security of the collections you shall make.

When I express a reliance on the Contractors at Reading and Lancaster it will be necessary for you in your Route Westward to ascertain with them the adequateness of the means they are taking and to supply any probable deficiency.

With consideration and esteem I am Sir Your obedt. Serv.

A. H

Eli Williams Esqr
Agent for supplies with provisions
The Militia Army

Copy, Connecticut Historical Society, Hartford.

1. On September 13, 1794, Warrant No. 4028 for fifteen thousand dollars was issued to Williams (D, RG 217, Miscellaneous Treasury Accounts, 1790–1894, Account No. 9550, National Archives).

2. On September 10, 1794, Warrant No. 4022 for twenty thousand dollars had been issued to Williams (D, RG 217, Miscellaneous Treasury Accounts, 1790–1894, Account No. 9550, National Archives).

3. H to Blaine, September 12, 1794.

4. See H to Blaine, September 12, 1794, note 3.

5. Abraham Hunt.

6. Jacob Bower.

7. Matthias Slough.

To the President, Directors, and Company of the Bank of the United States[1]

Treasury Department September 13th 1794

Gentlemen,

I have to request that you will be so obliging as to pay to Mr. Peter Le Barbier Duplessis[2] Attorney for Peter Le Maigre the sum of Eighteen hundred and Sixty Three dollars being so much certified by the Comptroller of the Treasury[3] to be due from the United States to the said Peter Le Maigre, for the hire of his Brig Molly to carry Mr. Higginson,[4] who was appointed by the President Agent to go to the British West India Islands, on the subject of the American Vessels captured by the British Cruisers since the commencement of the War between France & England.

This money will be reimbursed to the Bank, by a Warrant in the usual form as soon as an appropriation is made for that purpose.

I have the honor to be Very respectfully, Gentlemen, Your most Obedient Servant, A Hamilton

You will be pleased to let Mr. Duplessis sign the inclosed Receipt as Attorney for Peter Le Maigre.[5]

The President, Directors and Company
of the Bank of the United States.

LS, Hamilton Papers, Library of Congress.

1. For background to this letter, see H to George Washington, August 14, 1794; Edmund Randolph to H, September 5, 1794; H to Richard Harrison, September 10, 1794.

2. Duplessis is listed in the Philadelphia Directory for 1791 as a notary public and interpreter (Clement Biddle, *The Philadelphia Directory* [Philadelphia, 1791]).

3. Oliver Wolcott, Jr.

4. Nathaniel C. Higginson.
5. On October 24, 1794, Duplessis signed a receipt for Treasury Warrant No. 4077 for $1,863 (DS, RG 217, Miscellaneous Treasury Accounts, 1790–1894, Account No. 5932, National Archives).

From Thomas Sim Lee

Council Chamber [Annapolis]
September 13th 1794

Sir.

Since forwarding my letter of yesterday's date I have received intelligence of a most alarming nature from Brigadier General Bayly [1] Colo: Sprigg [2] and others relative to the Spirit of disorder now existing in Washington and Allegany Counties in this State, and actual riots and disturbances that have taken place in consequence.[3]

It is represented that combinations inimicable to the measures of Government are every day gaining accessions of strength—that the declarations, the conduct and the views of those involved in these combinations are of the most licentious and daring nature—that they have established a correspondence and connected themselves with the insurgents of Pennsylvania—that they have refused to submit to the draft prescribed by my orders under the late requisition of the President: [4] or in any manner to aid the object of the intended Expedition—that they have supported this refusal by a shew of Force and in some instances by the actual use of it—that they have erected Liberty Poles at various places and guarded them by armed bodies of men—that they have made declarations in favour of a Revolution—that they have refused to acknowledge the Militia officers appointed by the Constitutional Authority asserting the right of making such appointments in themselves and in some instances acting accordingly—that they are endeavouring to collect in force sufficient to attack and plunder the public armoury and Magazine at Frederick Town—and that in short every thing wears the aspect of confusion and danger.

I had already, as stated in my last,[5] provided (as far as former accounts had suggested the necessity) against the spirit above described, by ordering a Captain's Guard for the security of the Armoury and Magazine, by putting arms into the hands of the well-affected Militia in and about Frederick Town, and by ordering two hundred stand of arms &c into Allegany to be distributed by Major Lynn,[6] a Gentleman of merit, among such of the Militia in that County as could be safely relied on.

Under a persuasion that these measures were greatly inadequate to their object in the Situation of affairs as above represented and feeling the vast importance of protecting the public arms and military stores from the attempts of these lawless associations and of overawing in its infancy, by a display of strength and firmness this dangerous and turbulent spirit, I have ordered the immediate formation of a detachment of about seven hundred Militia (including Artillery and Horse) from Baltimore Town—the City of Annapolis, George Town and City of Washington and the Upper part of Montgomery County to be marched without delay to Frederic-Town as a Station to act as Circumstances may require.

I feel a confidence that this operation will be speedily completed, and that its effect will be to check (without violence or bloodshed which a smaller force would probably be unable to avoid) the views of these misguided men and to reduce them to quiet and obedience.

But if measures of a less decided complexion are resorted to I am really apprehensive that the consequences will be fatal and that submission will ultimately be produced with difficulty.

In order to enable me to carry the foregoing views into execution and to answer the demands which the march and subsistence of the Troops heretofore required would occassion, I have been compelled to request from Mr Gale [7] an advance of money to the amount of six hundred dollars (exclusive of a former advance of fifteen hundred dollars) to be deposited in our Treasury for the above purposes.

I hope the arrangements I have disclosed, which have appeared to me to result from the most pressing exigency, will meet with the approbation of the President; but if in any particular they are deemed exceptionable, you will be pleased to give me the earliest notice of it that so far as they are found to be improper they may be corrected.

I am &c. Thos S Lee

Alexander Hamilton Esq
Secretary of the Treasury.

Copy, RG 56, Letters 2d Comptroller, 2d Auditor, Executive of Maryland and Georgia, 1789–1833, Maryland, National Archives.

1. Mountjoy Bayly's letter to Lee is dated September 10, 1794, and reads in part as follows: "I have thought it necessary to Send with the Arms &c Ordered to Allegany County a Strong Escort Consisting of one Complete Company. This I conceive will not be thought over cautious when your Excellency takes into View the existing Circumstances, these Arms &c will have to pass through Washington County Where the people are generally unfriendly to the present Views of the Government. Under this Idea of things I conceive it would be imprudent to risque the Supplies which you have Ordered" (ALS, Hall of Records of Maryland, Annapolis).

2. Thomas Sprigg's letter to Lee is dated September 11, 1794, and describes the "confused state" of the people in Washington County. He stated that although a return of militia volunteers was scheduled for August 29, all but one company still had no volunteers on August 28 and that ". . . Several hundreds of persons assembled around with Guns Swords and Clubs, (most of them from the country) to the no Small terror of the inhabits., they brought with them a Nother Liberty pole wch. they errected at the Court house. They have kept up an Armed Guard by Night to prevent its being cut down . . ." (ALS, Hall of Records of Maryland, Annapolis).

3. The disorders in Washington and Allegany counties in Maryland are described in the following newspaper item: "Baltimore. September 16. On Sunday morning . . . brigadier general Samuel Smith received, by express, dispatches from the governor of Maryland, informing him of a most alarming insurrection of a lawless banditti, in the counties of Allegheney and Washington in this state, *in concert* with the insurgents of the western counties of Pennsylvania, and that they were busily and extensively preparing to move *in force* against the town of Frederick, for the purpose of securing to themselves the arms and other military stores of the state of Maryland . . ." (*The* [Philadelphia] *Independent Gazetteer,* September 20, 1794).

4. For the requisition by the President, see H to Thomas Sim Lee, September 10, 1794.

5. Lee to H, first letter of September 12, 1794.

6. John Lynn.

7. George Gale, supervisor of the revenue for the District of Maryland.

To Daniel Morgan[1]

War Department September 13th 1794

Sir,

I am instructed by the President to express to you his wish that every practicable exertion may be made to accelerate the assembling of the Militia at their appointed places of Rendevous, Winchester and the Vincinity of old Fort Pleasant Alias Moorefield. You are probably informed that a junction of the Virginia and Maryland Troops at *Fort Cumberland* has been contemplated.[2]

You are at liberty to hasten to that *Point* all such as may be ready, and which you Judge it adviseable should move that way, but if you think that those who are to assemble at Moorefield, had better proceed by a Route different from that of Fort Cumberland, they may continue at Moorefield till further instruction.

With consideration & esteem I am sir, Your obedient Servant

On behalf of the Secy at War [3]

PS. It will be well to have runners sent into the Insurgent Counties to ascertain what they are about the degree of unanimity & probable strength. Col Carrington [4] will furnish the means.

Major General Morgan

L[S], MS Division, New York Public Library; LS (marked "duplicate"), MS Division, New York Public Library.

1. Morgan was in command of the Virginia militia.

2. For the rendezvous of the militia, see "Minutes of a Meeting Concerning the Insurrection in Western Pennsylvania," August 24, 1794. See also H to Henry Lee, second letter of August 25, 1794.

3. This line and the postscript are in H's handwriting. For Henry Knox's absence from Philadelphia, see George Washington to H, August 12, 1794, note 1.

4. Edward Carrington, supervisor of the revenue for the District of Virginia.

From Tench Coxe

[*Philadelphia, September 14, 1794.* On March 11, 1795, Hamilton wrote to Joseph Anthony: [1] "I . . . send you the copy of a letter from Mr. Coxe of the 14th of September 1794." *Letter not found.*]

1. Anthony was a Philadelphia merchant.

To Samuel Hodgdon

Philadelphia Sep. 14, 1794

Sir

Mr. Abraham Hunt informs me that he can procure waggons as far as Reading but not further.[1] It is therefore adviseable for you immediately to send on a person to engage waggons to take the troops up at Reading. Governor Howel [2] with 500 horse will move from Trenton on Tuesday. The continental troops have already marched for Reading. The rest of the Jersey Militia will follow in all the ensuing week.

The person you send on will have nothing to do but to engage

Waggons. General Miller[3] goes off to Reading tomorrow to make arrangements for forage fuel & straw. Your Agent[4] must be directed to report to him & follow his directions. Pray let him depart this Evening as I should be mortified at a moments detention of the troops on the road for want of transportation.

I have mislaid the report you made me of the Artillery in Tour.[5] Send me this Evening or early in the morning a Copy & note how many of them you are *actually* prepared to send off.

With esteem Yr obed Ser A Hamilton

Typescript supplied by Mr. H. L. Phillips, Langhorne, Pennsylvania.

1. See H to Hunt, August 17, 27, 1794; H to Elie Williams, September 12, 1794.

2. Richard Howell, governor of New Jersey.

3. Brigadier General Henry Miller, commander of the First Brigade, Second Division, of the Pennsylvania militia. Miller was also supervisor of the revenue for the District of Pennsylvania. See H to Tench Coxe, June 28, 1794. Miller subsequently was acting quartermaster general of the militia army. See H to Miller, September 15, 1794.

4. Richard Parker, keeper of public stores at Carlisle, Pennsylvania.

5. Letter not found.

To Samuel Hodgdon

[*Philadelphia, September 15, 1794.* "For the Virginia and Maryland Militia Six six-pounders, three three-pounders and two howitzers. For the Pennsylvania Militia Six six-pounders, four three-pounders and three howitzers. For the Jersey Militia Three six-pounders, three three-pounders and one howitzer."[1] *Letter not found.*)

LS, sold by Stan V. Henkels, Jr., January 19, 1932, Lot 73.

1. Extract taken from dealer's catalogue.

To Thomas Sim Lee

War Department, September 15, 1794. ". . . It is the President's desire, that no time should be lost in uniting the whole of the militia of Maryland at Fort Cumberland. If the commanding officer[1] has not already taken the field, it is desirable that he should do it without delay, in order to combine, arrange and accelerate the ulterior movements."

LS, Hall of Records of Maryland, Annapolis.

1. Samuel Smith. See Thomas Sim Lee to H, September 4, 1794.

From Pierre Charles L'Enfant[1]

Philadelphia, September 15, 1794. "After all possible exertions on my part, to progress the fortification at and near Mud Island, and however attentive I have been in confining the extent of my operations to the limited sums assigned for, it is with the greatest concern I am to inform you that those means, by proving too small, have long since forced me to relent of the progress; they are at present so far exhausted, that, unless you can procure a sufficiency of supply to continue the work for two months longer, the whole must stop before any part is brought to that state of perfection necessary to be guarded against winter, and answer to some object of defence. . . ."

ASP, Military Affairs, I, 83.

1. L'Enfant had been a French volunteer in the Corps of Engineers during the American Revolution. He had been hired to plan the new Federal City on the banks of the Potomac, but because of a dispute with the commissioners of the Federal District he stopped working on this project in February, 1792. In July, 1792, the directors of the Society for Establishing Useful Manufactures hired L'Enfant to lay out the society's manufacturing center in Paterson, New Jersey. In April, 1794, he was appointed temporary engineer at Fort Mifflin on Mud Island in the Delaware River.

Henry Knox enclosed this letter in his report on fortifications to the House of Representatives on December 19, 1794 (*ASP, Military Affairs,* I, 71–107). For information on the fortifications, see Knox to H, March 29, 1794. See also Tench Coxe to H, June 20, July 5, 1794.

To Henry Miller

Philadelphia
Sepr. 15. 1794

Sir

I have it in contemplation to propose it to The President to appoint You to the capacity of Quarter Master General to the Militia Army destined to act against the Insurgents in the Western parts of Pensylvania; nor do I at present foresee that any obstacle will arise to the appointment. But as the President is not in Town a definitive arrangement must be deferred.

It is my wish, that you would proceed immediately to Reading to make an arrangement for supplying the New Jersey Militia and about two hundred troops of the UStates with forage straw & fuel and from Reading to Carlisle. The Jersey Militia consist of 1600 Infantry & 500 Horse.

Mr. Jacob Brower[1] is Contractor at Reading, and will, I expect, undertake the business as far as you judge eligible. But it will remain with you to ascertain the point & the dependence which can be placed upon it & to act as you see necessary & expedient.

A Mr. Parker[2] Agent for Mr. Hodgsdon[3] is gone forward to Reading to procure Waggons. He is to communicate with You & take your Directions.

In a word when at Reading you will please to see that an adequate arrangement be made for securing to the Militia & troops abovementioned transportation forage straw and fuel on the route above mentioned. You will of course appoint any Agents you find necessary & settle reasonable compensations for them.

I presume you have funds in your hands adequate to the object—if not on your signifying it the sum requisite shall immediately be furnished.

With great consideration & esteem I am Sir Your obed ser A

General Miller
Supervisor of Pensylvania

ADfS, Connecticut Historical Society, Hartford.

1. Jacob Bower.
2. Richard Parker, keeper of public stores at Carlisle, Pennsylvania.
3. Samuel Hodgdon.

To Samuel Smith[1]

[*War Department, September 15, 1794.* "You will ere this (I presume) have received from the Governor of Maryland[2] information and instructions respecting the assembling of all the Militia of that State destined to act against the Insurgents. The place of ultimate rendezvous is, Fort Cumberland. The whole are to assemble there as fast as they can be ready. I request that you will immediately open a correspondence with Governor Lee of Virginia,[3] who will be at Winchester, advising him of the situation and progress of the Militia under your command, and that you will pursue such instructions as you may receive from him in order to the intended cooperation between the Militia of Virginia and Maryland. With a view of this it may be adviseable for you to take without delay some interior position of which I shall be glad to be informed. It will be satisfactory, to hear frequently from you concerning your situation and prospects.[4] A careful mustering & Inspection in the first instance is of great importance, that every deficiency may be truly ascertained & supplied without waste. You are confided on to make all arrangements requisite to order & consequent economy." [5] *Letter not found.*]

LS, sold by Stan V. Henkels, Jr., February 23, 1915, Lot 186.

1. Smith was in command of the Maryland militia.
2. Thomas Sim Lee.
3. Henry Lee.
4. The remainder of this letter is in H's handwriting.
5. Text taken from dealer's catalogue.

To Nicholas Fish

[Philadelphia, September 16, 1794]

Dear Sir

Mr. Smith,[1] the bearer of this, a citizen who I believe has had a good zeal in the public cause, & is in great distress has applied to me for some public appointment. I know nothing that will suit him & that he will suit at present. I give him a line to you to satisfy him but with an anticipation that it is not likely you have any thing in your power. If you have I shall be glad he may be served.

Yrs. A Hamilton

Sep 16, 1794

ALS, Columbia University Libraries.

1. This may be a reference to William M. Smith, who in an undated letter thanked H for "Your kindness" in the past and asked him to "continue your kind Assistance" (ADf, Hamilton Papers, Library of Congress). Although Smith's letter is undated, it was apparently written between 1796 and 1800, for it is addressed to H at 26 Broadway, New York City, H's address during those years. In his letter Smith reminded H that they had served in the American Revolution together.

To Thomas Mifflin

[*War Department, September 16, 1794.* ". . . Disagreeable Symptoms have appeared in the two most Western Counties of Maryland. . . .[1] Everything is doing to press forward the Jersey Militia to Carlisle. . . . It is indeed of the highest moment, that the spreading of so mischievous a spirit should be checked. . . ."[2] *Letter not found.*]

ALS, sold at C. F. Libbie and Company, November 15, 1889, Item 344.

1. See H to Thomas Sim Lee, September 6, 1794; Thomas Sim Lee to H, first letter of September 12, September 13, 1794.

2. Extract taken from dealer's catalogue.

From Samuel Smith

[*Baltimore, September 16, 1794.* On September 19, 1794, Hamilton wrote to Smith: "I have had the pleasure of receiving your two letters of the 16th: instant."[1] *Neither letter has been found.*]

1. Smith referred to one of these letters when he wrote to William Pinkney, president of the Maryland Council, on September 21, 1794, as follows: ". . . In Consequence of a Letter I wrote to the Secretary of the Treasury 1000 pair of Shoes are sent forward from Philadelphia for the use of the Maryland Detachment together with Artillery & Its Apparatus . . ." (ALS, Hall of Records of Maryland, Annapolis).

From John Stephens[1]

[*New York, September 16, 1794.* On September 25, 1794, Stephens wrote to Hamilton: "I have not recieved an Answer to my letter of the 16th Inst." *Letter not found.*]

1. Stephens was an inspector of the customs in New York City.

From Tench Coxe

Treasury Department, Revenue Office, September 17, 1794. Requests "a warrant to be issued . . . for five hundred & five Dollars, on account of the Cape Fear & Tybee Light Houses."[1]

LC, RG 26, Lighthouse Letters, Vol. I, National Archives; LC, RG 75, Letters of Tench Coxe, Commissioner of the Revenue, Relating to the Procurement of Military, Naval, and Indian Supplies, National Archives.

1. See Coxe to H, February 18, March 5, May 20, August 19, 1794.

To Samuel Hodgdon

War Department
Sept 17th 1794

Sir

You will forward as speedily as may be to Winchester two Marquees, 1000 pair shoes, and two medicine chests; to Carlisle

1000 blankets, 1000 shoes, 200 rifles, 800 muskets with accoutrements proportioned, & Pistol & Musket flints—also two medicine chests. Doctor Brewster[1] will take charge of the medicine chests for Winchester. I am informed that one of the medicine chests contains a double quantity, let that be sent to Winchester.

Please to give orders to your Agent at Trenton[2] to issue the residue of the blankets in his possession to the Militia there. Col Mentges[3] informs me that 1000 have been delivered to the Troops. Send to Trenton 500 pair shoes for the Militia.

With esteem, I am Sir, Your Obedt. Servt A Hamilton

Samuel Hodgdon Esq.

Typescript furnished by the Historical Society of York County, York, Pennsylvania.

1. Francis G. Brewster of New Jersey was a surgeon's mate in the United States Army.

2. Abraham Hunt.

3. Colonel Francis Mentges of the Pennsylvania militia. See "Deposition of Francis Mentges," August 1, 1794.

From John Jay

London 17 Septr. 1794

Dear Sir

There is something very pleasant in the Reflection that while war discord and oppression triump in so many parts of Europe, their Domination does not extend to our Country. I sometimes flatter myself that Providence in Compassion to the afflicted in these countries, will continue to leave america in a proper state to be an azylum to them.

Among those who have suffered severely from these Evils, is Monsr. De Rochefoucauld Liancourt,[1] formerly President of the national assembly of France. His Rank and Character are known to you. He will be the Bearer of this Letter, and I am persuaded that his Expectations from it will be realized.

Yours Sincerely John Jay

The Honble Col. Hamilton

ALS, Hamilton Papers, Library of Congress.

1. François Alexandre Frédéric, Duc de La Rochefoucauld-Liancourt, was a French social reformer who had established a model farm at Liancourt and

founded a school of arts and crafts, which became known in 1788 as *Ecole des Enfants de la Patrie.* He was elected to the Estates-General in 1789 and became president on July 18. He fled to England and then to America after the royal palace was captured on August 10, 1792. He arrived at Philadelphia on November 26, 1794, and returned to Europe in 1797, arriving finally in Paris in 1799. He was the author of *Voyages dans les Etats-Unis d'Amérique, fait en 1795, 1796 et 1797* (8 Vols., Paris, 1799; Translated, 2 Vols., London, 1799).

To Rufus King[1]

Philadelphia Sepr. 17. 1794

When you recollect, that I have two departments on my shoulders[2] and when I tell you that I have been out of health in the bargain You will perhaps admit an excuse for my not answering sooner your letter some time since received.[3]

Mr. Jay has given nothing conclusive. His letters to the 26 of June[4] barely gave the idea that appearances were not unfavourable. His last letter,[5] I forget the date, but it came by the last arrival at New York, refers to letters[6] which were not received but which are supposed to have been confided to the Portuguese Minister.[7] This letter is couched in the same cautious terms—considers the scale as capable of turning either way, & advises not to relax in military preparation. The Ministry however have certainly continued to countenance shipments to this Country & very large ones were making. 'Tis a strange mysterious business. The change in Administration[8] has made some pause in the negotiation.

Nothing from the Western Country authorises an expectation of a pacific termination of that business. All the Militia are going forward as fast as they can be got forward. Virginia all below the Mountains is *zealous*, beyond neutral in conduct & divided in affection. Jersey is also zealous—so are the Eastern shore of Maryland & the Town of Baltimore—Thence to Frederick Town a pretty good temper prevails—beyond that a very insurgent spirit & some insurrection. In Philadelphia an excellent & productive zeal embracing all parties has been kindled. A good spirit will generally pervade the old Counties. But there is much bad leaven in the new Counties, this side of as well as beyond the Mountains—Cumberland Franklin Mifflin & even Northumberland.

Governor Lee[9] is at the head of the Virginia Militia & will command if the President does not go out. He is all zeal. Governor Howel[10] with equal zeal was to march from Trenton to day with the van of the Jersey Militia consisting of 500 horse. Mifflin[11] who at first shewed some untoward symptoms appears now to be exerting himself in earnest & with effect & goes at the head of his Militia.

The President will be governed by circumstances. If the thing puts on an appearance of magnitude he goes—if not, he stays. There is a pro & a Con in the case. If *permitted* I shall at any rate go.

Affecty yrs. A Hamilton

Rufus King Esq

ALS, Hamilton Papers, Library of Congress.

1. King was United States Senator from New York.
2. H was in charge of the War Department while Henry Knox was in Maine on private business. See George Washington to H, August 12, 1794, note 1.
3. Letter not found.
4. John Jay's letters to Edmund Randolph may be found in RG 59, Despatches from United States Ministers to Great Britain, 1791–1906, Vol. 1, April 19, 1794–June 1, 1795, National Archives. They are printed in *ASP, Foreign Relations*, I, 475–76.
5. Jay to Randolph, July 9, 1794. See Randolph to Jay, September 17, 20, 1794 (LC, RG 59, Diplomatic and Consular Instructions of the Department of State, 1791–1801, August 22, 1793–June 1, 1795, National Archives).
6. Jay to Randolph, July 6, 1794. See Randolph to Jay, September 17, 20, 1794 (LC, RG 59, Diplomatic and Consular Instructions of the Department of State, 1791–1801, August 22, 1793–June 1, 1795, National Archives).
7. Don João de Almeida de Melo e Gastro, 5th Conde das Galveias.
8. See Jay to H, July 18, 1794, note 4.
9. Henry Lee.
10. Richard Howell.
11. Thomas Mifflin, governor of Pennsylvania.

To Thomas Sim Lee

War department
September 17. 1794.[1]

Sir,

I had the honor of receiving by the post of yesterday two letters from your Excellency which having been sent to the President I cannot quote the dates.[2]

Nothing could be more proper than the measures you announce to have been taken in consequence of the insurrection in the Western parts of your State.[3] The movements of the Virginia Militia pursuant to the general arrangement will I trust second your measures. Governor H. Lee will I presume before this reaches you be at Alexandria. I mention this that you may avail yourself of the knowledge if any circumstances should render a correspondence with him useful.

The Jersey Militia are coming forward with great zeal and are hastening to Carlisle. An excellent spirit has sprung up in this City and will I doubt not diffuse itself. All accounts from Virginia are encouraging.

The disease however with which we have to contend appears more and more of a malignant nature not confined to the opposition to a particular law but proceeding from a general disorderly spirit. Much is evidently at stake. But the friends of good government have every thing to hope with proper exertion of energy.

I have sent on to Virginia what I deem a competent supply of Arms, but lest there should be a deficiency I have authorized an application to you for a loan having understood that you have more than sufficient for your own detachment in your magazine at Frederick. Should it be made I request it may be complied with in the full assurance that the arms furnished will be replaced by the United States. The only motive to this arrangement is dispatch as we are well provided for the occasion.

With perfect respect I have the honor to be Sir Your obedient servant A Hamilton

His Excellency
Thomas Sim Lee
Governor of Maryland

LS, Hall of Records of Maryland, Annapolis.

1. In Roger Thomas, ed., *Calendar of Maryland State Papers, No. 3: The Brown Books* (Annapolis, 1948), VI, 144, this letter is incorrectly dated September 4, 1794.

2. Lee to H, first letter of September 12, September 13, 1794.

3. See Lee to H, September 13, 1794.

From George Mathews [1]

[*Augusta*] *September 17, 1794.* "On application to Colo. Wylly [2] Commissioner of Loans of the United States, in this State, for the payment of Interest due on the Non-Subscribed part of the assumed

Debt of this State, he informed me that his instructions[3] did not authorise him to pay it. I must therefore request Sir, that you will be explicit with him on this subject, and that arrangements may be made so that the State may be enabled to receive the interest regularly."

Copy, RG 56, Letters 2d Comptroller, 2d Auditor, Executive of Maryland and Georgia, 1789–1833, Georgia, National Archives.

1. Mathews was governor of Georgia.

2. Richard Wylly.

3. See "Treasury Department Circular to the Commissioners of Loans," June 6, 1791.

To Thomas Mifflin

[*War Department, September 17, 1794.* "Gov. Howell[1] of New Jersey moves today with the van of the Militia of that State. If the Cavalry and artillery of this City could be hastened onward it would be particularly desirable."[2] *Letter not found.*]

ALS, sold at C. F. Libbie and Company, November 15, 1889, Item 345.

1. Richard Howell.

2. Extract taken from dealer's catalogue. For a summary of the contents of this letter, see H to Mifflin, second letter of September 17, 1794.

To Thomas Mifflin

War Department, Sept. 17, 1794.

Sir:

Major Stagg[1] has informed me that you wished an explanation in writing of the letter which I had the honor of writing to you this Morning,[2] on this point, to wit: whether the corps were to be *equipped* previous to their march or not?

I answer, that it is intended they should be provided previous to their march with a competent supply of essential articles. But that they ought not to be retarded on account of a partial deficiency of articles, the want of which might not be material, as these can be sent after them to Carlisle, where it is interesting there should be a good collection of force without delay, & where there will necessarily be some halt.

Your military experience must guide your discretion in drawing the line.

If anything more precise is desired from me, it will best be obtained by directing a return of deficient articles of each corps, & I will give an opinion on each case in detail.

With perfect respect, I have the honor to be your obed. hum. serv.,

A. Hamilton.

His Excellency Governor Mifflin.

Pennsylvania Archives, 2nd ser., IV, 311.

1. John Stagg, Jr., was chief clerk in the War Department.

2. H to Mifflin, first letter of September 17, 1794.

From Tench Coxe[1]

Treasury Department, Revenue Office, September 18, 1794. "I have to request that a warrant may Issue in my favor for one Thousd. Dollars to make a payment to Samuel Wheeler the maker of the two Lanterns for Baldhead & Tybee Light houses. As Mr. Wheeler is under marching orders in the 1st City Troop tomorrow morning all possible dispatch is requested."

DfS, RG 26, Lighthouse Letters, Vol. I, National Archives.

1. For background to this letter, see H to George Washington, April 25, 1793; Tobias Lear to H, April 27, 1793; Coxe to H, January 1, May 20, 1794.

From Joseph Howell, Junior[1]

War Department, Accountant's Office, September 18, 1794. "I have the honor to inclose you extracts of a letter dated 16th Ulto. from the Agent for the War Department in Georgia,[2] and of a letter from the Secretary of War to the Governor of that State,[3] respecting the pay of a Troop of Dragoons consisting of four Commissioned Officers and seventy nine Non-Commissioned Officers & privates amounting to 8,268 dolls ⟨&⟩ 86 Cents, for their service between December 93 and June 1794. If this claim is authorized be pleased to furnish the Treasurer with the amount."

LC, RG 93, Letter Book, 1794, National Archives.

1. For background to this letter, see Edmund Randolph to William Bradford, H, and Henry Knox, July 11, 1794; H to George Washington, July 13, 1794; Randolph to H, September 6, 1794.

2. Constant Freeman.

3. George Mathews.

To Thomas Sim Lee[1]

War department, Septr. 18. 1794

Sir,

The intelligence received from the western Counties of Pennsylvania, which comes down to the 13th: instant, and announces as far as it was then known the result of the Meetings of the people in the several townships and districts, to express their sense on the question of submission or resistance to the laws[2]—while it shews a great proportion of the inhabitants of those Counties disposed to pursue the path of duty, shews also that there is a large and violent party which can only be controuled by the application of Force. This being the result, it is become the more indispensable and urgent to press forward the forces destined to act against the insurgents with all possible activity and energy. The advanced season leaves no time to spare and it is extremely important to afford speedy protection to the well disposed and to prevent the preparation and accumulation of greater means of resistance and the extension of combinations to abet the insurrection. The President counts upon every exertion on your part which so serious and eventful an emergency demands.

With perfect respect, I have the honor to be Sir, Your obedient Servant
Alexander Hamilton

His Excellency Thomas S. Lee
Governor of Maryland.

LS, Hall of Records of Maryland, Annapolis.

1. On September 20, 1794, H sent the same letter to Thomas Mifflin.

2. H is referring to the excise laws. See "Deposition of Francis Mentges," August 1, 1794, note 1.

The United States commissioners appointed to confer with the representatives of the insurgents in western Pennsylvania did not formally present their views to George Washington until September 24, 1794 (*Pennsylvania Archives*, 2nd ser., IV, 348–59). As early as September 13, however, they realized that they had not been able to eliminate the possibility of violence. On that date, the judges in Westmoreland County concerned with the subscription to the oath submitting to the excise laws declared that ". . . in our opinion, as ill-disposed lawless persons could suddenly assemble and offer violence, it would not be safe in immediately establishing an office of inspection therein" (*Pennsylvania Archives*, 2nd ser., IV, 298, 536). According to the commissioners' report of September 24, Allegheny, Washington, and Fayette counties presented similarly discouraging results (*Pennsylvania Archives*, 2nd ser., IV, 356–57). In addition, the *Gazette of the United States* on September 22, 1794, carried the following account: "An express arrived in town this morning from the westward, and brought dispatches for the Secretary of State. They inform that Mr. [James] Ross will be in town in a few days to meet the other Commissioners; when, a particular account of the issue of their mission may be expected. Part of the returns from the different townships has been received, from which it appears that the terms required by the Commissioners have not been *generally* complied with. The general returns made by those who superintended the meetings, do not give the assurances required that the submission in any of the counties is such that an office of inspection may be safely opened therein; and one of them expressly states an opinion that such a measure would not be safe. . ." ([Philadelphia] *Gazette of the United States and Daily Evening Advertiser*, September 22, 1794). For the appointment of the United States commissioners and for their earlier activities, see H and Henry Knox to Washington, August 5, 1794; H to William Bradford, August 8, 1794; Bradford to H, August 23, 1794; H to Thomas Sim Lee, second letter of August 29, 1794. The commissioners' reports and their correspondence with Edmund Randolph may be found in Pennsylvania Miscellany, Whiskey Rebellion, Vol. I, Library of Congress.

To Thomas Mifflin

War department
September 18. 1794.

Sir

I beg leave to represent to your Excellency that among the Militia ordered out from this City for the Western expedition is a Mechanic of the name of Samuel Owner of Captain Guy's Company of Artillery.[1]

Mr. Joshua Humphreys the Constructor of one of the United States Frigates to be built here represents that this man has been hitherto employed in assisting him in preparing the models which he is now making to be sent to the Constructors in the respective States where the Ships of War are to be built agreeably to an Act of Congress [2] and that the absence of Mr Owner at this time would be a material injury to the public service as he is one of his principal workmen.

If it could be done with propriety, I would be glad your Excellency would please to order that he be permitted to remain behind and not to march with his Company. This indulgence is very material to the public service.[3]

I have the honor to be with perfect respect your obedt. Servant

A Hamilton

His Excellency
Governor Mifflin

LS, The Andre deCoppet Collection, Princeton University Library.

1. The company commanded by Captain William Guy was the 2nd Pennsylvania Regiment.

2. "An Act to provide a Naval Armament" (1 *Stat.* 350–51 [March 27, 1794]). For information on the naval armament, see Henry Knox to H, April 21, 1794.

3. This sentence is in H's handwriting.

To Thomas Mifflin

War department
September 18. 1794

Sir,

I have the honor to inform your Excellency that a detachment of the Troops of the United States under the command of Lieut. Daniel Bissell is to march from this City as an escort to a train of Artillery and Military Stores, intended for the Maryland and Virginia Militia called out against the Western Insurgents. This detachment will march through Lancaster and York Town and from thence to Williamsport in Maryland. I have to request that your Excellency would be pleased to give instructions to the commanding Officer of the Militia at York [1] to furnish a reinforcement from his Militia to the said escort if Lieutt. Bissell should think it necessary for the protection of his important charge.

I have the honor to be with great respect Your Excellencys obedient Servant A Hamilton

His Excellency
Governor Mifflin

LS, Delaware Historical Society, Wilmington.

1. Alexander Russell. See Mifflin to H, September 18, 1794.

From Thomas Mifflin

Philadelphia, September 18, 1794. "Agreeably to your request,[1] I have inclosed a letter of instructions to the Brigade Inspector of York County, for the purpose of furnishing any reinforcement, that Lieutenant Bissel may require on his march to Williamsport in Maryland." [2]

LC, Division of Public Records, Pennsylvania Historical and Museum Commission, Harrisburg; copy, Division of Public Records, Pennsylvania Historical and Museum Commission, Harrisburg.

1. See H to Mifflin, second letter of September 18, 1794.

2. An entry in the "Executive Minutes of Governor Thomas Mifflin" reads: "Lieutenant Daniel Bissel commanding a detachment of the Troops of the United States, escorting a Train of Artillery and Military Stores, intended for the Maryland and Virginia Militia about to pass through Lancaster and Yorktown, and thence to Williamsport in Maryland—the Governor Instructed the Brigade Inspector of York County to furnish such a reinforcement from the Militia of York County . . . as that Officer shall deem adequate to the emergency" (*Pennsylvania Archives*, 9th ser., II, 866). The letter book copy of Mifflin's letter to Alexander Russell, September 18, 1794, may be found in Division of Public Records, Pennsylvania Historical and Museum Commission, Harrisburg.

From William Pinkney

In Council [Annapolis]
September 18th 1794.

Sir,

In the absence of the Governor, we have received information from General Smith,[1] that the Spirit of insurrection in the Upper Counties of this State has arisen to so alarming a Heigth, as actually to prompt a part of the misguided Inhabitants to embody for the purpose of marching to Frederic Town, with the object no doubt, of obtaining possession of the State's armoury and Magazine.[2] The prompt and vigorous arrangements adopted by the Governor on the receipt of the intelligence, announced in his letter of the 13th Instt. will, it is hoped, not only prevent the execution of this daring and profligate design, but awe the persons concerned in it into future Submission.

You will perceive by the enclosed copys of General Smith's letter above alluded to, that a number of infantry and horse from Baltimore had probably arrived at Frederic Town some days ago, sufficient in conjunction with the Troops already stationed there, as to give timely and effectual opposition to the meditated attack.

It is certain too, that about three hundred infantry and thirty or forty horse from General Forrest's [3] Brigade, and a part of infantry and horse from General Davidson's [4] Brigade, had marched for the Same Station in time to reach it before the Insurgents could arrive there—and we have every reason to believe that the Troops required from General Crabb's [5] Brigade had also commenced their march in time.

The Governor has thought it advisable to proceed in person to Frederick for the purpose of being enabled with more certainty to ascertain the views of the Malcontents, and to direct the measures necessary for Counteracting their operations and restoring tranquility and obedience.

The Militia who have marched upon this expedition are Volunteers Composed of the most respectable of our Citizens, and are implicitly to be depended upon because actuated by Principle.

Their Zeal and their Attachment to Law and order, leave no room to doubt their success, and indeed it is reasonable to presume that when men like these are found to oppose themselves in arms to the efforts of this abandoned Combination, their frenzy will Cease to disturb the public quiet.

We have the honor &c Wm Pinkney President

The Honorable
Alexander Hamilton
Secretary Treasury

Copy, RG 56, Letter 2d Comptroller, 2d Auditor, Executive of Maryland and Georgia, 1789–1833, Maryland, National Archives.

1. Samuel Smith was in command of the Maryland militia.

2. See H to Thomas Sim Lee, September 6, 1794, note 3; Thomas Sim Lee to H, two letters of September 12, September 13, 1794.

Smith's letter to Pinkney is dated September 17, 1794, and reads in part as follows: ". . . I am Inform'd by Letter from Genl. [Mountjoy] Bayley & Doctr. [Philip] Thomas that Colo. [Thomas] Sprig with 20 Gentlemen from Hagars Town had that Moment Arrived & reported that the Insurgents of our state were Actually imbodying & would probably march yesterday or this Day for Frederick. Genl. Bayley says he hopes they will Come that a good Account may be given of them: he Calls his force 500 Men well Armed—the first 30 Horse from Balt. were met within a few Miles of Fredk. . ." (ALS, Hall of Records of Maryland, Annapolis).

For another account of the events described in Pinkney's letter to H, see *The Maryland Journal, and the Baltimore Advertiser*, September 19, 1794.

3. Uriah Forrest, a Federalist member of the House of Representatives from Maryland from 1793 to 1795, was a major general of the Maryland militia.

4. John Davidson of Annapolis.

5. Jeremiah Crabb.

To Robert Purviance

Treasury Department
September 18th 1794

Sir,

The Congress of the United States having by their Act of the 20th of March 1794[1] authorised the President to receive a Cession of the Lands, on which any of the fortifications directed to be made by the said Act may be erected, or where such Cessions shall not be made, to purchase such Lands on behalf of the United States—I am directed by the President [2] to request that you will take measures for ascertaining the value of the ground upon which the fortifications are now constructing at Whetstone point in your District and to enter into a conditional treaty with Mr. Alexander Furnival [3] the proprietor for the purchase thereof, referring the agreement here accompanied with a description of the Premisses for ratification.

I am with consideration Sir, Your most obedient Servant

A Hamilton

P.S. I will thank you to communicate the contents of this letter to Mr. Furnival.

Robert Purviance Esquire
Collector of Baltimore

LS, Columbia University Libraries.

1. "An Act to provide for the Defence of certain Ports and Harbors in the United States" (1 *Stat.* 345–46). See also Henry Knox to H, March 29, 1794.

2. On June 6, 1794, George Washington "Sent to the Secy of war a letter from Alexr Furnival, dated Baltimore 3d. June on the subject of the sale of ground at that place to erect fortifications on—desired the Secy. to pay proper attention to it" (JPP, 296–97).

3. Furnival, a Baltimore merchant, had been a lieutenant in Smith's Independent Company of Maryland Artillery during the American Revolution. He retired in 1779 as a captain.

From Angelica Church [1]

London, September 19, 1794.

My Dear Brother:

I have very particular and very good motives to ask your kindness for the Duke de Liancourt,[2] he loved liberty with good sence and moderation; and he meant so well towards his country as to introduce into France a better system of Agriculture and to soften the situation of the Lower class of people there. Virtue, has not found its reward, for in the many scenes of distress that has afflicted his unfortunate country, he like many more good men, has been obliged to leave his possessions and seek an Asylum in this country.

He goes to America, and goes there without a friend, unless my dear Brother, who is always so good, will extend to Monsieur de

Liancourt his care—besides many good qualities, this gentleman is the friend of the Marquis de LaFayette.

Adieu my dear friend, remember me to Beaumetz[3] and Monsieur de Talleyrand.[4] Angelica Church.

Hamilton, *Intimate Life*, 36.

1. Angelica Church was Elizabeth Hamilton's sister and the wife of John B. Church.

2. See John Jay to H, September 17, 1794, note 1.

3. Bon Albert Briois, Chevalier de Beaumetz. See H to George Washington, May 5, 1794, note 3.

4. Charles Maurice de Talleyrand-Perigord. See H to Washington, May 5, 1794; Washington to H, May 6, July 11, 1794; Washington to Lord Lansdowne, August 30, 1794.

From Alexander J. Dallas

Philadelphia, September 19, 1794. "The Governor directs me to inform you, that in compliance with the request, stated in your letter of the 18th. instant, he has given Orders for the discharge of Samuel Owner,[1] a workman employed in the service of the United States, but drafted for the Western expedition."

LC, Division of Public Records, Pennsylvania Historical and Museum Commission, Harrisburg; copy, Division of Public Records, Pennsylvania Historical and Museum Commission, Harrisburg.

1. On September 19, 1794, the following entry appears in the "Executive Minutes of Governor Thomas Mifflin": "In compliance with the request of the Secretary of the Treasury of the United States, the Governor gave orders to the Adjutant General [Josiah Harmar] for the discharge of Samuel Owner, a workman employed in the service of the United States but drafted for the Western Expedition, which was communicated to the Secretary" (*Pennsylvania Archives*, 9th ser., II, 867–68).

Mifflin's orders, which Dallas communicated to Harmar, read: "It has been represented to the Governor, by Mr. Hamilton, who acts for General Knox in the War Department, that Samuel Owner, of Captain Guy's Artillery, has been employed in an important work for the United States, and that it is very material to the public service, that he should not be included in the drafts for the western expedition. Under these circumstances, the Governor requests that you will confer with the commanding officer of the Corps, in which Samuel Owner serves, and signify his request and approbation that the man should be discharged" (*Pennsylvania Archives*, 2nd ser., IV, 329–30).

From Isaac Holmes

[*Charleston, South Carolina, September 19, 1794.* On October 3, 1794, Oliver Wolcott, Jr., answering "for the Secty of the Treasy," wrote to Holmes: "Your letter dated Sept. 19th has been rec'd." [1] *Letter not found.*]

1. Wolcott's letter to Holmes of October 3, 1794, reads as follows: "Your Letter dated Sept. 19th. has been rec'd and on consideration of the case stated it is deemed proper that copies of the Entries of prize vessels be granted on the application of the Agents Consuls or Vice Consuls of any of the belligerent nations, but nothing further is to be certified than that the copies are true" (ADf, Connecticut Historical Society, Hartford).

From Jeremiah Olney [1]

Custom House
District of Providence 19th Septr. 1794.

Sir.

I have been Honored with your Letter of the 9th. Instant in reply to mine of the 11th August last on the Subject of Arnold and Dexter's Suits against me, which were both Tried before the Superiour Court on the 17th Instant when Virdicts by Jury were rendered against me in the Case of Arnold for £ 13-5 / LM Damages with £ 8. 8. 6 Cost and in the Case of Dexter for £ 2-10/ Damages with £ 7. 12. 8. Cost. Since the Receipt of your Letter I have again Consulted Mr. Barnes [2] Relative to the Future management of those Suits and he is of opinion that the application we Contemplated to be made to the Genl. Assembly at their Session in Octr. next, for a re-hearing, will not prove so favourable as we had at first Expected as the Court during the Trial Manifested a disposition not very Friendly, having refused any Evidence to be offered, to the Jury, on my part, to Show that the Transfer from Arnold to Dexter was Collusive and made for the Sole purpose of Evading the Statute, in order therefore to a avoid a nother Trial, (which Seems not very flattering) before the State Court & to Save time. I have Deemed it most adviseable to Carry Said Suits by writ of Error before the Supreme Court of the United States where I doubt not of a Just and favourable Decision.

I have the Honor to be &c. Jereh. Olney Collr.

Alexander Hamilton Esqr.
Secretary of the Treasury.

ADfS, Rhode Island Historical Society, Providence.

1. For background to this letter, see Olney to H, November 7, 15, 28, December 10, 13, 27, 1792, March 14, 25, April 15, 25, September 23, October 7,

21, November 21, 1793, February 17, March 31, April 14, first letter of April 24, May 5, August 11, 1794; H to Olney, November 27, 1792, November 7, 1793, March 19, April 24, September 9, 1794.

2. David Leonard Barnes.

To Samuel Smith

War department, Sept: 19, 1794

Sir,

I have had the pleasure of receiving your two letters of the 16th: instant.[1] The circumstances they announce are upon the whole satisfactory. The zeal which has been called forth by the threatened attack upon the magazine at Frederick[2] is in the highest degree commendable and is an earnest of the ultimate reliance which may be placed on the principles of good Order in our Country. As circumstances unfold every where they become more and more encouraging.

One thousand pair Shoes have been ordered to Frederick Town to take your Orders.[3] More will follow.

I mentioned to you in a former letter[4] the detachment of a Lieutenant and forty men, Continentals, destined as an Escort of the Artillery for the Virginia and Maryland Militia. I have added a Cornet and sixteen Dragoons. Lieutenant Bissell commands.[5] You may if you please detain these as a part of your brigade though it was the original intention that they should join the companies from which they have been detached at Bedford.[6]

Copy, Samuel Smith Papers, Library of Congress.

1. Letters not found.

2. See H to Thomas Sim Lee, September 6, 1794, note 3; Lee to H, two letters of September 12, September 13, 1794; William Pinkney to H, September 18, 1794.

3. See Smith to H, September 16, 1794, note 1.

4. See H to Smith, September 15, 1794.

5. Daniel Bissel. See H to Thomas Mifflin, second letter of September 18, 1794; Mifflin to H, September 18, 1794.

6. The remainder of this letter has not been found.

To George Washington

Philadelphia Sept 19 1794.

Sir

Upon full reflection I entertain an opinion, that it is adviseable for me, on public ground, considering the connection between the immediate ostensible cause of the insurrection in the Western Country and my department, to go out upon the expedition against the insurgents. In a government like ours, it cannot but have a good effect for the person who is understood to be the adviser or proposer of a measure, which involves danger to his fellow citizens, to partake in that danger: While, not to do it, might have a bad effect. I therefore request your permission for the purpose.

My intention would be not to leave this till about the close of the month so as to reach one of the columns at its ultimate point of rendezvous. In the meantime I take it for granted General Knox will arrive,[1] and the arrangements which will be made will leave the Treasury department in a situation to suffer no embarrassment by my absence; which if it be thought necessary may terminate about or shortly after the meeting of Congress.[2]

With perfect respect, & the truest attachment, I have the honor to be, Sir, Yor: obt. Servt.

The President of the United States

Copy, Hamilton Papers, Library of Congress; LC, George Washington Papers, Library of Congress.

1. Henry Knox was in Maine. See Washington to H, August 12, 1794, note 1.

2. The second session of the Third Congress was due to meet on November 3, 1794.

From Alexander J. Dallas

[Philadelphia, September 20, 1794]

Sir.

The engagements of the Governor preventing his immediate attention to some of the details for the western expedition, permit me on his behalf to enquire whether it is understood to be within the Province of the State Executive to appoint a Surgeon General for the State of Pennsylvania. The object is of considerable importance; and I have requested Doctr. Dorsey,[1] to do me the favor to wait on you for an answer to this letter. The Militia-acts of the United States and of this state [2] leave the matter in some degree doubtful.

I take this opportunity to inform you, that upon the receipt of your letter of the 20th. instant,[3] I called on the Master Warden, with instructions to send off an Express to Fort Mifflin for the purpose of stopping and detaining any vessel of the description which you mention.[4] The answer of the officer commanding at the Fort [5] is enclosed for your perusal.

I am, Sir Your Most Obed: Serv: A: J: Dallas, Secretary.

Secretary's Office
20th Septr. 1794
To Alexander Hamilton, esquire.

LC, Division of Public Records, Pennsylvania Historical and Museum Commission, Harrisburg; copy, Division of Public Records, Pennsylvania Historical and Museum Commission, Harrisburg.

1. On September 22, 1794, Governor Thomas Mifflin appointed Nathan Dorsey surgeon general of the militia of Pennsylvania.

2. Section 3 of "An Act more effectually to provide for the National Defence by establishing an Uniform Militia throughout the United States" reads in part as follows: "That the said militia shall be officered by the respective states, as follows: . . . That there shall be a regimental staff, to consist of one adjutant and one quartermaster, to rank as lieutenants; one paymaster; one surgeon, and one surgeon's mate; one sergeant-major; one drum-major, and one fife major" (1 *Stat.* 272 [May 8, 1792]).

Section 6 of "An Act For the Regulation of the Militia of the Commonwealth of Pennsylvania," dated April 11, 1793, includes this same provision (*Pennsylvania Laws,* 1793, Sess., Ch. CLXXVI).

3. Letter not found, but H's letter of September 20, 1794, is described as follows in the "Executive Minutes of Governor Thomas Mifflin": "It being represented to the Governor, that a French privateer is fitting out of which the Captain is named Mulinary and the second in Command Palaugay the Master Warden [Nathaniel Falconer] was this day instructed to ascertain the situation of the vessel and to cause a good look out to be kept, and to stop and detain any vessel of the above description which has not a clearance from the Custom House" (*Pennsylvania Archives,* 9th ser., II, 869).

On September 20, 1794, Josef de Jaudenes, one of the Spanish commissioners to the United States, wrote to Edmund Randolph that the French were arming *Le Petit Republicain* on the Delaware and asked that the President issue orders to prevent the ship's departure (LS, RG 59, Notes from the Spanish Legation in the United States to the Department of State, 1790–1906, Vol. 2, August 22, 1794–October 15, 1798, National Archives).

4. Dallas to Nathaniel Falconer, September 20, 1794 (LC, Division of Public Records, Pennsylvania Historical and Museum Commission, Harrisburg).

5. John Rice.

To Thomas Mifflin

War Department, September 20, 1794. Sends same letter he sent to Thomas Sim Lee on September 18, 1794.

Pennsylvania Archives, 2nd ser., IV, 334.

From Meletiah Jordan[1]

Frenchman's Bay [*District of Maine*] *September 21, 1794.* "I embrace the first opportunity to communicate to you the particulars of a seizure lately made in this District. . . . The account from the person who appeared as Master is as follows. That the Schooner William of St. John's sailed from Martinique last July, that the day after their Departure the Master died, that the next day the Mate jumped or fell overboard they could not tell which, on the next a passenger who was a freighter died. . . . One Joseph Jamate who gave this account & brought the Vessel safe in 27 Days to the aforesaid harbour, says he cannot write; a young lad on board marked the Log but the account of the deaths in the Log does not correspond with a private minute kept by the same person. These circumstances with their having lain four days in the District without making any Report at the Custom House[2] with a great probability of some violence having been committed on board, and their being in sight of a British Fleet at Guadaloupe where they might have relief induced me to stop the Vessel till the Owners at St. Johns might have an opportunity of clearing up the matter; One of the Owners accordingly came here & brought a descriptive Certificate of the Vessel from the Custom House at St. Johns, which corresponded with the one on board. As I had reason on enquiry to think that they had not infringed the Revenue Laws by landing or otherwise disposing of any part of their Cargo, And that if the Vessel was stopt for the fine liable for laying longer than the time limited by Law, Yet that on Trial she would be returned their being no Officer on board—and the distress manifest. Considering these circumstances & fearful of accumulating a further expense to the Revenue; after taking the advice of Counsel on the subject I liberated the Vessel yesterday the 20 on the Owners paying the expense that had already accrued in siezing bringing up & securing the Vessel, the expense of the Master & hands &c. . . ."

Copy, RG 56, Letters to Collectors at Gloucester, Machias, and Frenchman's Bay, National Archives.

1. Jordan was collector of customs at Frenchman's Bay, District of Maine.

2. This is a reference to Section 16 of "An Act to provide more effectually for the collection of the duties imposed by law on goods, wares and merchan-

dise imported into the United States, and on the tonnage of ships or vessels," which reads in part as follows: "That within twenty-four hours after the arrival of any ship or vessel from any port or place, at any port of the United States established by law, at which an officer of the customs resides, or within any harbor, inlet or creek thereof, if the hours of business at the office of the chief officer of the customs at such port will permit, or as soon thereafter as the said hours will permit, the master or other person having the charge or command of such ship or vessel, shall repair to the said office, and shall make report to the said chief officer of the arrival of the said ship or vessel; and within forty-eight hours after such arrival, shall make a further report to the collector of the district in which such port may be, of the name, burthen and lading of such ship or vessel, whether in packages or stowed loose, and of the particular marks, numbers and contents of each package, and the place or places, person or persons to or for which or whom they are respectively consigned or destined, also of the place or places where she took in her lading, of what country built, from what foreign port or place she last sailed, who was master or commander of her during the voyage, who is at the time of such report master or commander of her, and (if a vessel of the United States) who are owners of her; unless the whole of such information required on the second report as aforesaid, shall have been given at the time of making the first report, in which case it shall not be necessary to make a further report. . ." (1 *Stat.* 158–59 [August 4, 1790]).

From Isaac Holmes

Charleston [*South Carolina*] *September 22, 1794.* "In my Letter to you under date 10th Currt. relatively to the Schooner Hawke, the value of the vessel was expressed thro mistake in the Copiest at 12000 dollars. If it is so, you will please read 1200 dollars. . . ."

ALS, Historical Society of Pennsylvania, Philadelphia.

To Rufus King

[Philadelphia, September 22, 1794]

I thank you My Dr. Sir for your letter of the .[1] A few days previously I wrote you pretty fully.[2] I hope my letter got to hand.

The inclosed paper gives you the substance of our European intelligence under the Philadelphia head.

The Returns from the Western Counties of this state are just come to hand. They shew a valuable division, ranging on the side of the laws the most influential men & a respectable body of others[3] —but leaving a great number still uncomplying and violent so as to afford no assurance of submission to the laws without the application of Force. It will give you pleasure to learn that there is every prospect of our being able to apply this effectually & of the issue being favourable to the authority of the laws. It will occasion a large bill of Costs, but what is that compared with the object?

Adiu Affecty Yrs A Hamilton

Sep 22d. 1794
Rufus King Esqr

ALS, New-York Historical Society, New York City.

1. Space left blank in MS. Letter not found.

2. H to King, September 17, 1794.

3. On September 17, 1794, Albert Gallatin wrote from Uniontown, Pennsylvania, to Governor Thomas Mifflin: "A very favorable & decisive change has taken place since, & has, indeed, been the result of the event of that day. The general disposition now seems to be to submit, & a great many are now signing the proposals of the Commissioners, not only in the neighboring Counties, but even in this, where we had not thought it necessary. We have, therefore, thought the moment was come for the people to act with more vigour and to show something more than mere passive obedience to the laws, & we have, in consequence, (by the Resolutions of this day, herein inclosed, & which, we hope, will be attended with salutary effects,) recommended associations for the purpose of preserving order and of supporting the civil authority, as whatever heat existed in this County, was chiefly owing to what had passed in the neighbouring Counties" (*Pennsylvania Archives*, 2nd ser., IV, 317).

The resolutions to which Gallatin was referring were adopted at a meeting in Uniontown on September 17, 1794, and are printed in *Pennsylvania Archives*, 2nd ser., IV, 319–20.

To William Moultrie

[*Philadelphia, September 22, 1794.* On this date George Washington "Approved drafts of Letters to the Governors of South Carolina & Georgia [1] submitted by the Secretary of the Treasury." [2] *Letter to Moultrie not found.*]

1. See H to George Mathews, September 25, 1794.

2. JPP, 309.

From Tench Coxe[1]

Treasury Department, Revenue Office, September 23, 1794. Requests a "Warrant to be Issued for the sum of two thousand Dollars, for the purpose of making a payment of that sum on a/count of a contract for Iron cannon ball & ballast or Kentledge, to L. Holingsworth & Son as agents for the Company of the sd. contractors, consisting of Richard Edwards, George Leonard, Levi Holingsworth and Paschal Holingsworth." [2]

LC, RG 75, Letters of Tench Coxe, Commissioner of the Revenue, Relating to the Procurement of Military, Naval, and Indian Supplies, National Archives.

1. For information concerning the naval armament in 1794, see Henry Knox to H, April 21, 1794.

2. The contract with Levi Hollingsworth and Son, a Philadelphia merchant firm, was dated July 9, 1794. See Coxe to Edwards, Leonard, and Levi and Paschal Hollingsworth, July 24, 1794 (LC, RG 75, Letters of Tench Coxe, Commissioner of the Revenue, Relating to the Procurement of Military, Naval, and Indian Supplies, National Archives).

To Alexander J. Dallas

[*War Department, September 23, 1794.* The catalogue description of this letter reads as follows: "on the appointment of a Surgeon in the Pennsylvania Militia." [1] *Letter not found.*]

ALS, sold at Anderson Galleries, June 3, 1914, Lot 109.

1. See Dallas to H, September 20, 1794.

To Samuel Hodgdon

War Department
Sep 23. 1794

Sir

You will furnish the Pensylvania Militia with the additional supply of arms & accoutrements which you mention have been called for.

You will forward to the Virginia Militia swords, pistols & other horsemens equipments [1] saddles excepted sufficient with those already sent to complete the detachment of horse called for.

I am uneasy at the delay which has attended the forwarding of the articles destined for that quarter. Let the Blankets & shoes be carried as far as three thousand of each—and let a due quantity of the smaller articles bowls & pails go forward. In short let a full supply of all necessary articles of Camp Equipage be completed as fast as possible. I hope the complement of arms heretofore mentioned has been expedited. If any further delay attends the sending on the articles destined for the South we shall be too late.

With consideration & esteem I am Sir Your obed servant

Alex Hamilton

P. I send you a return transmitted me by Governor Lee [2] of the articles at New London [3] that you may compare with your information.

Samuel Hodgsdon Esq [4]

ALS, The Sol Feinstone Collection, American Philosophical Society, Philadelphia.

1. See H to Hodgdon, September 10, 1794.

2. Governor Henry Lee of Virginia, commander in chief of the militia army assembled to march against the insurgents in western Pennsylvania.

3. See H to Henry Lee, August 25, 1794, note 9.

4. This letter is endorsed: "stores to be forwarded to Cumberland."

From Jared Ingersoll [1]

Carlisle [Pennsylvania] Sept. 23d 1794

Dear Sir.

I am endeavouring to collect the necessary information, respecting the Irregularities that have taken place in this town,[2] in order that I may secure the Offenders before I proceed to the Westward with the Militia.

I find that the military Stores said to have been expected from Col Hodgsdon [3] are not arrived, the Jersey & City Militia may probably be here to-morrow—I mean the Cavalry.

Apprehensive that some inconveni⟨ence⟩ might arise from a disappointment in this particular I have taken the liberty to suggest the circumstance that if any difficulty has occurred it may be obviated.

I just now saw a person who left Pittsburgh last Friday he says he saw no appearance of any Militia embodying, & does not think it likely that any opposition by force of Arms is contemplated, he did not however speak positively on this point nor do I know the degree of credit to which he is entitled.

I am With much respect Yr obed servt Jared Ingersoll

Be so good as to forward the enclosed Letter to Mrs Ingersoll.

Honle A. Hamilton Esqr.

ALS, RG 94, Hodgdon and Pickering Papers, National Archives.

1. Ingersoll was attorney general of Pennsylvania.

2. The "irregularities," which occurred in Carlisle on September 11, 1794, are described in the following newspaper account: "We are credibly informed, that the spirited exertions of the Chief Justice [Thomas McKean], and Judge [Jasper] Yeates, to suppress the seditious measures which some violent people were fomenting in Cumberland County, gave offence to their partizans, who, determined to be revenged on the Judges. . . . On the evening of the day that the Judges left Carlisle, about two hundred armed men marched into the borough, and being disappointed in their main object, they erected a Liberty-Pole near the Court-House, with some seditious inscriptions, and burnt the Chief-Justice in effigy. Another pole was erected near the door of one of the persons arrested, amidst the shouts of the mob, having '*Liberty and Equality*' inscribed on it. They fired many vollies during the night time, and dispersed about day-light. . ." (*The* [Philadelphia] *Independent Gazetteer*, September 17, 1794). See also "Letter to the Governor on the Feeling at Carlisle," September 15, 1794, which is printed in *Pennsylvania Archives*, 2nd ser., IV, 300–01.

Depositions of several witnesses to the events at Carlisle may be found in the Historical Society of Pennsylvania, Philadelphia.

3. Samuel Hodgdon. See H to Hodgdon, August 25, September 10, 1794.

From Thomas Sim Lee

Council Chamber [Annapolis]
September 23rd 1794.

Sir

I have the pleasure to inform you that the opposition to the Government in this State [1] is entirely crushed without the loss of one Life. The alacrity with which the Militia on the first notice marched from the different parts of the State, and the general spirit disclosed by the Citizens precluded all hope of success to the Insurgents and induced them to abandon their design on the arsenal without a trial of their strength.

Many have been taken by small detachments of Horse and delivered over to the Civil Authority; those thought most criminal are Confined in gaol, those less so, have been admitted to bail, and an order for disarming such as are suspected of being accomplices is now executing.[2]

As there is reason to believe that the Western Insurgents hold a correspondence with the disaffected of this State, the happy termination of the business here will be more important, and cannot fail of having an influence in restoring the peace and order of the government in that Quarter.[3]

I have thought it prudent to deliver a part of our arms to particular corps of our Militia, a surplus however will still remain and every assistance that can be given in furnishing the Virginia Troops will be rendered with pleasure. The Maryland Quota of Militia will be full, or nearly so, and are moving on to Cumberland.

I have the honor to be &c Tho: S Lee

The Honble
Alexander Hamilton
Secretary Treasury.

Copy, RG 56, Letters 2d Comptroller, 2d Auditor, Executive of Maryland and Georgia, 1789–1833, Maryland, National Archives.

1. See H to Thomas Sim Lee, September 6, 1794; Lee to H, first letter of September 12, September 13, 1794; William Pinkney to H, September 18, 1794; H to Samuel Smith, September 19, 1794.

2. Lee's information is based on the following letter which Mountjoy Bayly wrote to him on September 19, 1794: "In obedience to those orders, honoring me with the direction of the troops which your Excellency had commanded to rendezvouz at Frederick Town for the purpose of repressing that turbulent spirit which had violated peace & order and seemed to threaten Government itself in the Counties of Frederick Washington and Allegany. . . . For that purpose I marched about 300 Infantry together with 70 horse through Harmans Gap which opens into the County of Washington near the Pennsylvania line, a rout which led me through the midst of those people whose turbulency it was your object to punish and repress. This was done with an intention to apprehend the characters who had been most active in their opposition to Governmt and whose names had been previously furnished to me for that purpose. It was supposed too that the appearance of an Armiment would have a very good effect, and convince those who had lost sight of their duty that Government could send forward a force at any time when necessity required it sufficient to inforce obedience to the Laws. On my arrival into Washington I proceeded to carry into effect my arrangements by despatching the cavalry in quest of the Ringleaders. But upon the first display of the Horse, I found a party from Hagarstown had superceded the necessity of any exertion on my part, by having previously brought in those disorderly people to Justice. About the number of twenty have been apprehended, all of which have been admitted to Bail except eight, these have not yet undergone their examination but most of them perhaps all of them will be committed to close Jail, without bail, however this is but opinion. Martin Bear and John Thompson had been examined before my arrival, and although both of them had been considered as notorious offenders they were admitted to Bail and to my great surprize Cols. [Thomas] Sprigg & [Rezin] Davis were their Securities. It is however but proper to add that upon the examination of these two men their was no evidence of their guilt save the general report as I am informed by those who were present. . ." (ALS, Hall of Records of Maryland, Annapolis). A similar account of these events is in *The Maryland Journal, and the Baltimore Advertiser*, September 22, 1794.

3. See H to Thomas Sim Lee, September 6, 1794, note 3.

To the President and Directors of the Bank of the United States

Treasury Department
Sep 24. 1794

Gentlemen

The large extra demand upon the Treasury, which has been occasioned by the expedition going on against the Western Insurgents, obliges me to request of you to permit me by anticipation to draw upon you for the whole of the remainder of the last Million loan on the first of October ensuing.[1] You will recollect that 400,000 Dollars are on that day to be paid to you on account of a former loan.[2] This payment will be then made accordingly. I request a speedy answer.[3]

With great respect & esteem I have the honor to be Gentlemen
Your obed ser A Hamilton

The President & Directors
of The Bank of The UStates

ALS, Free Library of Philadelphia; copy, RG 217, Miscellaneous Treasury Accounts, 1790–1894, Account No. 6336, National Archives.

1. See H to the President and Directors of the Bank of the United States, August 21, 1794.

2. In accordance with proposals made by H in "Report Relative to the Additional Supplies for the Ensuing Year," March 16, 1792, Congress on May 2, 1792, adopted "An Act for raising a farther sum of money for the protection of the frontiers, and for other purposes therein mentioned" (1 *Stat.* 259–63). Among other things, this act authorized the President to borrow $523,500 at an interest rate of not more than five percent per annum (1 *Stat.* 262). Of this amount only $400,000 was actually borrowed ("Report on Foreign Loans. Supplementary Statement Showing the Sums Borrowed in the United States," January 10, 1793).

3. In a statement describing a meeting of the directors of the Bank of the United States on September 26, 1794, Thomas Willing, president of the bank, wrote: "Read a letter from the Secretary of the Treasury dated September 24th 1794 relative to advancing the sums agreed to be loaned on the 1st. of November & 1st of December next at an earlier period. Whereupon Resolved That the Bank will advance the sum of Four hundred thousand Dollars on the 1st day of October.

"Resolved That Mr. [Isaac] Wharton & Mr. [William] Bingham be a Committee to wait on the Secretary of the Treasury to inform him that the Direction had agreed to his proposition and to state to him the situation of the Bank." (DS, RG 217, Miscellaneous Treasury Accounts, 1790–1894, Account No. 6336, National Archives.)

From Clement Biddle

Philad Sept 24. 1794.

Sir

Having been much delayd in Waggons for sending on the Arms and Camp Equipage to the different places appointed for assembling the Militia of this State, but a small porportion of the necessary supplies have gone forward and I expect that the men are assembled in most of the Counties. This day several Waggons which I had sent for to the Counties for the purpose, have arrived in town and more are hourly expected, but on my application to Colo Hodgdon [1] to furnish the Arms and Camp Equipage, he sent me word that he could not issue any until he had first by your orders fully compleated the Supplies for Virginia.[2] I shall be much embarrassd if I should not receive the Stores and shall be prevented from setting off tomorrow as I intended for Reading and Harrisburgh, which makes me think it necessary to submit the matter to you and wait your orders thereon.

I have the Honor to be with the greatest respect Your obedient Servant

Clement Biddle
QMG Pennsy

Alexander Hamilton Esq

LS, Hamilton Papers, Library of Congress.

1. Samuel Hodgdon. See H to Hodgdon, August 25, September 10, 1794.
2. See H to Hodgdon, September 23, 1794.

To John Cochran [1]

Treasury Department, September 24, 1794. "I have directed the Treasurer . . . to remit to you, a draught for Ninety Thousand Dollars on account of the Interest payable . . . on the several species of stocks standing on your books." [2] *Letter not found.*]

LS, sold at Swann Galleries, March 8, 1945, Lot 18.

1. Cochran was commissioner of loans for New York.
2. Extract taken from dealer's catalogue.

On September 24, 1794, Warrant No. 4060 for ninety thousand dollars was issued to Cochran (D, RG 217, Miscellaneous Treasury Accounts, 1790–1894, Account No. 6392, National Archives).

From Tench Coxe[1]

Treasury Department, Revenue Office, September 24, 1794. "I have the honor to enclose proposals from Mr. John McCauley for the Copper work of the Tybee Lantern. . . . No 1 was his first proposal . . . which induced me to make a second endeavour to procure propositions. . . . Mr. McCauley reconsidering the matter, sent in No 2, which was lower than any other that was offered. The War in Europe and other circumstances, have greatly advanced the prices of Metal, & Workmanship is constantly rising here from the increase of the expences of living and the prodigious increase of the capital employed in manufactures & other domestic operations. I am satisfied it will be difficult to procure as low a proposal from any other person. I therefore transmit this for the decision of the President." [2]

LC, RG 26, Lighthouse Letters, Vol. I, National Archives; LC, RG 75, Letters of Tench Coxe, Commissioner of the Revenue, Relating to the Procurement of Military, Naval, and Indian Supplies, National Archives.

1. For background to this letter, see Coxe to H, August 19, September 17, 1794.

2. On May 12, 1794, McCauley sent a revised proposal to Coxe. On July 23, 1794, he submitted another revised proposal to Coxe. The President approved the second revised proposal on September 29, 1794 (copies, RG 26, Lighthouse Deeds and Contracts, National Archives).

To Thomas Sim Lee[1]

War department
September 24. 1794

Sir,

I have the honor to acknowledge the receipt of a letter of the 18. instant from the Executive Council of Maryland [2] and to congratulate you & them on the disappearance of the insurrection in Maryland.

The President has seen with great satisfaction the laudable vigour with which it was met by the Government, the excellent disposition manifested by the Citizens, and the speedy termination of the disturbance. Such an example cannot but have the best effect.

Though severity towards offenders is to be avoided as much as can consist with the safety of society; yet impunity in such cases is apt to produce too much promptitude in setting the laws at defiance. Repeated instances of such impunity in Pennsylvania are perhaps the principal cause of the misfortune which now afflicts itself and through it the United States. The disturbers of the peace familiarly appeal to the past experience of unpunished offences as an encouragement to the perpetration of new ones. This general reflection will no doubt be duly adverted to by the Judiciary and other authorities of Maryland.

With great respect and esteem I have the honor to be Sir Your most obed. Servant Alexander Hamilton

His Excellency Thomas Sim Lee
Governor of Maryland

LS, Columbia University Libraries.

1. For background to this letter, see H to Thomas Sim Lee, September 6, 1794; Lee to H, first letter of September 12, September 13, 23, 1794; William Pinkney to H, September 18, 1794; H to Samuel Smith, September 19, 1794.

2. For the letter from the Maryland Council, see Pinkney to H, September 18, 1794.

From Edmund Randolph

[*Philadelphia*] *September 24, 1794.* "The Secretary of State, not having time to have the inclosed from Mr. Jaudenes[1] translated, presents it to the Secretary of Treasury; as it relates to a privateer fitted out in the neighborhood under French colours, and being just ready to sail."

LC, RG 59, Domestic Letters of the Department of State, Vol. 7, June 27–November 30, 1794, National Archives.

1. For Josef de Jaudenes's letter to Randolph, see Alexander J. Dallas to H, September 20, 1794, note 3.

To George Washington[1]

[Philadelphia, September 24, 1794]

The Secry. of the Treasury presents his respects to The President. He finds it will be impracticable for him without injury to the public service to leave town on *Monday*, but he will do it the day after & overtake the President. However he begs leave to inform the President that from the information received, there is no prospect of a pretty *general* assembling of the Pennsylvania & N Jersey militia at Carlisle before the 6 or 7 of Octor., so that The President will have some time to spare & perhaps it may be useful for him to remain here as long as will comport with the object of his journey & his convenience in making it.[2]

24 Sept. 1794.

LC, George Washington Papers, Library of Congress.

1. For background to this letter, see H to Washington, September 19, 1794.

2. On September 30, 1794, Washington wrote in his diary: "I left the City of Philadelphia about half past ten oclock this forenoon accompanied by Colo. Hamilton (Secretary of the Treasury) and my private Secretary [Bartholomew Dandridge]" (*GW Diaries,* IV, 209).

From Tench Coxe

[*Philadelphia, September 25, 1794.* At the foot of a memorandum dated September 29, 1794, Coxe wrote: "The above is the original note of the Contracts [1] referred to in my Letter of the 25 Septbr. 94 to the Secy. of the Treasury." [2] *Letter not found.*]

1. Coxe wrote two letters to H on this date concerning contracts. The contracts which Coxe discussed in this letter to H concerned stakage on the North Carolina coast. For this memorandum, see H to George Washington, September 29, 1794, note 2.

2. Copy, RG 26, Lighthouse Deeds and Contracts, National Archives.

From Tench Coxe

Treasury Department
Revenue Office septr. 25. 1794

Sir

I had the Honor this day to transmit to you a Contract with Mr. John McCauley for the Copper work &c of the Tybee Lighthouse for the purpose of procuring the presidents decision thereon.[1] In addition to this there is a Former Contract with John McCauley for the Copper work of the Cape Fear Lighthouse not yet approved it was transmitted the 18th. of February.[2] The appointment of the

Keeper for Cape Fear Light house, a Report on which was transmitted on the 11th. of March, And the Contract for Building a house for the Keeper of Plumb Island Lighthouse, a report on which was transmitted to you on the 24 of May also remains to receive the Presidents approbation.

I have the honor to be with great Respect sir, Your most Obed Servant

Tench Coxe
Commissioner of the Revenue

The secretary of The Treasury

LS, Hamilton Papers, Library of Congress; LC, RG 26, Lighthouse Letters, Vol. I, National Archives.

1. See Coxe to H, August 19, September 17, 24, 1794.
2. See Coxe to H, March 5, May 20, September 17, 1794.

From George Gale

[*Baltimore, September 25, 1794.* On September 28, 1794, Hamilton wrote to Gale: "Your two letters of the 25th. are before me." *Neither letter has been found.*]

To Samuel Hodgdon

War Department
September 25. 1794

Sir

I request that you will furnish me on Saturday Evening at my house with a complete return of all the articles you will by that time have forwarded for the Militia army distinguishing how much to the Militia of each state and at the same time of all arms accoutrements cloathing and Camp Equipage fit for service which remain in store at and near Philadelphia. Substantial accuracy will suffice & it is essential I should then have the return. With consideration & esteem

I am Sir Your obed ser A Hamilton

Samuel Hodgsdon Esqr

ALS, Columbia University Libraries.

To Samuel Hodgdon

[Philadelphia, September 25, 1794]

Mr. Hamilton requests Mr. Hodgsdon to specify in the returns which he is desired to make on Saturday [1] the particular destinations of the different parcels which have been sent on.

Sep 25

AL, The Sol Feinstone Collection, American Philosophical Society, Philadelphia.

1. See H to Hodgdon, first letter of September 25, 1794.

To Samuel Hodgdon

[Philadelphia, September 25, 1794]

Mr. Hamilton requests Mr. Hodgsdon to be so obliging as to inform him whether he has in his power or eye any horse which would be proper as a riding horse for Mr. Hamilton—easy gated of some blood & capable of rendering service. Mr. Hamilton would mean to purchase him.

Thursday Morning

AL, The Indiana Historical Society Library, Indianapolis.

To George Mathews [1]

War department September 25th, 1794

Sir.

In the absence of the Secretary at War,[2] I have the honor to

LC, RG 107, War Office Letter Book, 1791–1794, National Archives; copy, RG 233, Messages from the President, Third Congress, National Archives.

1. For background to this letter, see Edmund Randolph to William Bradford, H, and Henry Knox, July 11, 1794; H to George Washington, July 13, 1794; Randolph to H, September 6, 1794; Joseph Howell, Jr., to H, September 18, 1794.

An entry in JPP for September 22, 1794, reads as follows: "Approved drafts of Letters to the Governors of South Carolina & Georgia submitted by the Secretary of the Treasury" (JPP, 309). H's letter to William Moultrie has not been found.

2. Knox was in Maine on private business. See Washington to H, August 12, 1794, note 1.

acknowledge the receipt of your letters to his department, of the 5th, 19th, and 30th of August [3] and to reply to such parts as are the most pressing, referring the others to the return of that Officer.

Among the Posts which have been established that at Doctor's Town creates a question in consequence of Lieut. Colonel Gaithers [4] information, that it is within the Indian Boundary.[5] This is a matter which ought to be unequivocally ascertained, and if found to be within the Indian line, or if it be even doubtful, whether that be the case, the Post must be immediately removed. It is deemed essential that no encroachment should take place. And your Excellency is relied upon for a strict and scrupulous adherence to this principle.

Under the circumstances which led to it the President has thought proper to authorize the adoption by the United States of the new troop ordered by you, into service, from the time of its commencement, and to continue until the first of November ensuing, when it is to be disbanded.[6] And you are at liberty, if the state of things shall render it in your judgment essential to substitute at that time a company of Infantry for the same service. Corps of Horse upon the terms on which that in question is engaged, are expensive in the extreme, and in a much greater proportion compared with Infantry, than any supposeable superiority of usefulness can justify. Indeed it would require a Treasury much better supplied than that of the United States to support the expence of a multiplication or extension of such Corps. Consequently that multiplication or extension would tend to defeat its own object—for our instruments of defence to be durable must be relative to our means of supporting them. And

3. Mathews's letter to Knox of August 5, 1794, has not been found. His two letters to Knox of August 19 and 30 are printed in *ASP, Indian Affairs*, I, 495, 497.

4. Lieutenant Colonel Henry Gaither was the commanding officer of the United States troops in Georgia.

5. This is a reference to an attempt by some citizens of Georgia to establish an independent government on territory belonging to the Creeks. See Randolph to Bradford, H, and Knox, July 11, 1794; H to Washington, July 13, 1794; Randolph to H, September 6, 1794.

6. On August 19, 1794, Mathews wrote to Knox: "Enclosed is a copy of my instructions to Captain [Jonas] Fauche, who commands the troop I informed you, in my letter of the 5th instant, I had called into service. It will be necessary, I conceive, for the captain to be reinforced with another troop, which I shall immediately order, and with which I am hopeful the objects of his command will be effected; should it prove otherwise, I shall lose no time in having recourse to a sufficient military force. . ." (*ASP, Indian Affairs*, I, 495).

when we find as in the instance of the insurrection now existing in the western parts of Pennsylvania, that those for whose immediate benefit the objects of military expenditure occur, are among the first to resist even to violence the necessary means of defraying them—it is easy to appreciate the perplexing dilemma, to which the Government is reduced between the *duty* and the *means* of affording protection; and the necessity consequently of oœconomy in the modes of effecting it.

Your Excellency is pleased to express your concern at being so repeatedly compelled to solicit protection for the State of Georgia.[7] This is not understood as implying any want of due disposition on the part of the Executive of this Government to afford all the protection which is within the compass of the means placed within its power—having regard to all the objects which along a very extended frontier, equally demand attention. It is not doubted that you render justice in this respect to the views of the Executive.

But the observation you have made in this particular, naturally leads to another, which calls for the most serious attention of the Governments of the States exposed to Indian depredations. It is this that there is a reciprocal duty in the case. The obligation upon the United States to afford adequate protection to the inhabitants of the frontiers, is no doubt of the highest and most sacred kind. But there is a duty no less strong upon those inhabitants to avoid giving occasion to hostilities, by an irregular and improper conduct and upon the local Governments sincerely and effectually to punish and repress instances of such conduct, and the spirit which produces them. If these inhabitants can with impunity thwart all the measures of the United States for restoring or preserving peace—if they can with impunity commit depredations, and outrages upon the Indians, and that in violation of the faith of the United States, pledged not only in their general treaties, but even in the special (and among all Nations peculiarly sacred) case of a safe conduct, as in the instance of the attack upon the Indians while encamped within our protection on the tenth of May last.[8]

7. No letter has been found in which such a request was made, but see Mathews to Knox, August 19, 30, 1794 (*ASP, Indian Affairs*, I, 495, 497).

8. For a description of this attack on the Indians, see *ASP, Indian Affairs,* I, 482–87.

Can it be surprising if such circumstances should abate the alacrity of the national Councils to encounter those heavy expences, which the protection of the frontiers occasions, and of the readiness of the Citizens of the United States, distant from the scenes of danger to acquiesce in the burdens they produce?

It is not meant by these remarks to diminish the force of the excuse, within due limits, which is drawn from the conduct of the Indians, towards the frontier inhabitants. It cannot be denied that frequent and great provocations to a spirit of animosity and revenge are given by them; but a candid and impartial survey of the events which have from time to time occurred, can leave no doubt that injuries and provocations have been too far mutual—that there is much to blame in the conduct of the frontier inhabitants, as well as in that of the Indians. And the result of a full examination must be, that unless means to restrain, by punishing the violences which those inhabitants are in the habit of perpetrating against the Indians, can be put in execution, all endeavours to preserve peace with them, must be for ever frustrated.

An example, worthy of imitation, in its spirit, has lately been given, by the Surrender to Governor Blount of some Indians who lately committed a murder upon one John Ish, an inhabitant of the southwestern Territory—and who have been tried and executed.[9] The record of such an example of justice and fair dealing,[10] will

9. On September 23, 1794, the [Philadelphia] *Gazette of the United States and Daily Evening Advertiser* reprinted an article from the *Knoxville Gazette* of August 4, 1794, which stated that on July 24, 1794, "a party of Creeks killed John Ish, at his plough, in his field, within 180 yards of his own block-house and scalped him. Ish lived eighteen miles below this place [Knoxville] . . . he has left a wife and eight children, the eldest not eleven years of age." On July 29 Governor William Blount of the Southwest Territory ordered "the trial of a Creek Indian apprehended on suspicion of being guilty of the Murder of John Ish a citizen of the United States" (Carter, *Territorial Papers*, IV, 461).

10. This is a reference to the fairness of the trial which the Indian (not Indians, as H states) received. According to the record of this trial, which was held August 1–2, 1794, "A bill being found by the Grand Jury, the Creek Indian, Abongpohigo . . . was brought before the court [of Oyer and Terminer]. . . . The prisoner was then charged on his indictment which being explained to him by the interpreter he confessed the fact. But the court being willing to afford the prisoner the benefit of a trial by jury, (permitted him to withdraw his plea) and plead not guilty: whereupon a traverse jury was empannelled and sworn in due form, the prisoner being first informed of his right of challenge. The prisoner having counsel assigned him; the Attorney General [Archibald Roane] proceeded upon the trial, and the jury, upon the fullest

give occasion to us to blush—if we can cite no instance of reciprocity amidst the numerous occasions which are given for the exercise of it.

These reflections, Your Excellency may be assured, are merely designed to present to consideration some very important truths; Truths, a due attention to which are of the most serious concern to those States which have an exposed frontier. To give full weight to their claims upon the exertions of the Union to afford the requisite protection, it is of great moment to satisfy the United States, that the necessity for them has not been created, or promoted by a culpable temper, not sufficiently restrained, among those to whom the protection is immediately to be extended.

The President learns with great pleasure, the measures your Excellency had begun and was about to pursue for the removal of the settlers under Genl: Clarke.[11] It is impossible to conceive a settlement more unjustifiable in its pretexts, or more dangerous in its principle, than that which he is attempting. It is not only a high handed usurpation of the rights of the General and State Governments, and a most unwarrantable encroachment upon those of the Indians, but proceeding upon the idea of a seperate and independent Govern-

---

testimony, brought into court a verdict, 'guilty of the murder of John Ish, as charged in the bill of indictment.' Whereupon the prisoner being asked, What he had to offer why sentence of the law should not be pronounced upon him? he replied he had not any thing. . . . The judge then proceeded to pronounce sentence of death in the usual form.

"In consequence of the above sentence, the Creek Indian, Abongpohigo, was executed this afternoon, at four o'clock." (*Dunlap and Claypoole's* [Philadelphia] *American Daily Advertiser,* August 26, 1794.)

11. On August 19, 1794, Mathews wrote to Knox: "On the 14th July I received a letter from Lieutenant Colonel Gaither, stating that Elijah Clarke, late a Major General in the militia of this State, with a party of men, had encamped on the southwest side of the Oconee. . . . On the 24th, General [Jared] Irwin sent a couple of officers to Clarke, with orders for him to move off immediately which he positively refused; and, on the 28th, I issued a proclamation, forbidding such unlawful proceedings. I also wrote to one of our judges to issue his warrant, and have Clarke apprehended. . ." (*ASP, Indian Affairs,* I, 495). Mathews's proclamation is printed in *Dunlap and Claypoole's American Daily Advertiser,* September 4, 1794. On August 30, 1794, Mathews sent to Knox a copy of Judge Richard Walton's charge to the grand jury of Richmond County, Georgia, on the attempt of Clark and his followers to establish settlements on Indian lands (*ASP, Indian Affairs,* I, 497–99). Randolph informed Washington on October 6, 1794, that Clark had "abandoned his expedition in Georgia, and, under the influence of General [James] Gunn and Mr. [Thomas Petters] Carnes, has come in, with all his followers" (AL, RG 59, Miscellaneous Letters, 1790–1799, National Archives).

ment, to be erected upon a *Military* basis, it is essentially hostile to our Republican systems of Government, and is pregnant with incalculable mischiefs. It deeply concerns the great interests of the Country that such an establishment should not be permitted to take root, and that the example should be checked by adequate punishment; in doing which, no time is to be lost, for such is the nature of the establishment, that it may be expected rapidly to attain to a formidable magnitude, involving great expence and trouble to subvert it.

The President therefore depends absolutely upon measures equally prompt and efficacious to put an end to it.

Mr. Habersham Agent for supplies [12] is instructed to co-operate and the Governor of South Carolina is requested [13] to afford upon your application the aid of the Militia of that State, if circumstances, as does not appear probable, should require it.

No agreement or arrangement which may be made, or pretended to be made between these settlers and the Indians, ought to be suffered to make any alteration in the plan of suppressing the settlement, for no such agreement or arrangement can possibly be legal, or considering the manner in which the settlement has been commenced can without affording a most pernicious example receive the future sanction of Government.

You desire instructions with regard to the Prisoners that may be made, in the event of the employment of force.[14] You will be pleased to cause them to be delivered over to the custody of the Judiciary, and in preference to that of the United States; as their laws define and prescribe particular punishments in such cases.[15]

12. John Habersham was collector of customs at Savannah. See Randolph to Bradford, H, and Knox, July 11, 1794, note 2.

13. H's letter to William Moultrie has not been found. See note 1.

14. The request was made in the letter which Mathews wrote to Knox on August 30, 1794 (*ASP, Indian Affairs*, I, 497).

15. "An Act to regulate Trade and Intercourse with the Indian Tribes" (1 *Stat.* 329–32 [March 1, 1793]). Section 5 of this act reads: "That if any such citizen or inhabitant shall make a settlement on lands belonging to any Indian tribe, or shall survey such lands, or designate their boundaries, by marking trees, or otherwise, for the purpose of settlement, he shall forfeit a sum not exceeding one thousand dollars, nor less than one hundred dollars, and suffer imprisonment not exceeding twelve months, in the discretion of the court, before whom the trial shall be: And it shall, moreover, be lawful for the President of the United States, to take such measures, as he may judge necessary, to remove from lands belonging to any Indian tribe, any citizens or inhabitants of the United States, who have made, or shall hereafter make, or attempt to make a settlement thereon."

[*Proclamation by George Washington*] [1]

[Philadelphia, September 25, 1794]

JCH Transcripts; *JCHW*, V, 31–33; *HCLW*, VI, 442–45; Hamilton, *History*, VI, 99.

1. Although this document has been attributed to H, no evidence has been found that it was written by H.

From John Stephens

New York, September 25, 1794. "As I have not recieved an Answer to my letter of the 16th Inst,[1] requesting of you to send me a Certificate which would enable me to Cancel my Mortgage which I suppose is owing to your Multiplicity of business, therefore to give you as Little trouble as possible, I have got a Certificate made out & sent . . . for the purpose of your signing it. . . ." [2]

ALS, Hamilton Papers, Library of Congress.

1. Letter not found.

2. In this transaction Stephens was the mortgagor of property in New York City, and H was representing the mortgagee. The "Certificate" enclosed by Stephens, known as a "satisfaction piece," indicated that Stevens, having fulfilled the terms of the mortgage, was released from further obligation.

To Anthony Wayne

[*Philadelphia, September 25, 1794.* On November 12, 1794, Wayne wrote to Henry Knox: "I have the honor . . . to acknowledge the receipt of a letter from Colo Alexr Hamilton of the 25th. of September enclosing an extract of a letter from Mr. Jay . . . dated the 12th of July 1794,[1] also a letter from Major Stagg, of the 4th Ultimo. . . ." [2] *Letter not found.*]

Knopf, *Wayne*, 361–62.

1. The extract from John Jay's letter to Edmund Randolph, dated July 12, 1794, reads as follows: "We [Jay and Lord Grenville] had an informal Conversation relative to [John Graves] Simcoe's hostile measure. We concurred in opinion that during the present negotiation, and until the conclusion of it, all things ought to remain and be preserved in Statu quo—that therefore both parties should continue to hold their Possessions, and that all encroachments on either Side should be done away—that all hostile measures (if any such should have taken place) shall cease, and that in case it should unfortunately have happened that prisoners or Property should have been taken, the Prisoners shall be released and the Property restored. And we have agreed that both Govern-

ments shall immediately give orders & instructions accordingly" (ALS, RG 59, Despatches from United States Ministers to Great Britain, Vol. 1, April 19, 1794–June 1, 1795, National Archives; copy, Historical Society of Pennsylvania, Philadelphia).

In April, 1794, Governor Simcoe had ordered three companies of Colonel Richard England's regiment into United States territory to establish a post on the Maumee River to protect Detroit from United States troops under Anthony Wayne (E. A. Cruikshank, ed., *The Correspondence of Lieut. Governor John Graves Simcoe, with Allied Documents Relating to His Administration of the Government of Upper Canada* (Toronto, 1924), II, 211–12).

On September 20, 1794, Randolph replied to Jay: "The President approves the agreement that, during the present negotiation, and until the conclusion of it, all things remain and be preserved in *statu quo*. The War department is instructed to issue correspondent orders, and the department of State to notify the governors in the neighborhood of those scenes, to which the agreement relates" (LC, RG 59, Diplomatic and Consular Instructions of the Department of State, 1791–1801, August 22, 1793–June 1, 1795, National Archives).

2. The letter of John Stagg, Jr., dated October 4, 1794, was to Isaac Craig. It reads in part as follows: ". . . I transmit enclosed in confidence an extract of a letter from Major General Wayne dated 14. August respecting a certain Robert Newman of Kentucky. This person arrived here last Week from Niagara and imposed himself on Colonel Hamilton as having been captured by the Indians, and been permitted by Governor Simcoe to return home by way of Philadelphia. Mr. [Samuel] Hodgdon was directed to, and actually did, advance him twenty dollars.

"He left this City on the 24 Ult. in the Harrisburg Stage intending to proceed on from thence to Carlisle and so forward to Pittsburg. I am particularly instructed by the President of the United States to request that you will take every measure in your power to apprehend this fellow and cause him to be immediately delivered to Colonel [Thomas] Butler and kept under a secure guard until the first opportunity offers to convey him in safety to Fort Washington from thence to be sent under a proper escort to the head quarters of Major General Wayne. It is very possible, if the matter is not made public, that he will call on you for some pecuniary assistance, as he had been in Colonel [James] O'Hara's employ." (LS, Isaac Craig Papers, Carnegie Library of Pittsburgh, Pennsylvania.)

From Tench Coxe

Treasury Department, Revenue Office, September 26, 1794. "I have the honor to request that a Warrant for 470 Dols. may be issued to Wm. Allibon Superintendent of the Delaware Light House establishment &c for the purpose of discharging the accounts which fall due on the 30th instant." [1]

LC, RG 26, Lighthouse Letters, Vol. I, National Archives.

1. On September 27, 1794, Warrant No. 4068 for this amount was issued to Allibone (D, RG 217, Miscellaneous Treasury Accounts, 1790–1894, Account No. 6194, National Archives). Allibone was superintendent of lighthouses, beacons, buoys, public piers, and stakage for Philadelphia, Cape Henlopen, and Delaware.

From Joseph Howell, Junior

War Department, Accountant's Office, September 26, 1794. "I have to request, in the absence of the Secty of War, that you will be pleased to place in the hands of the Treasurer Ten thousand dollars for the use of the Department of War. . . ."

LC, RG 93, Letter Book, 1794, National Archives.

From Wilhem and Jan Willink, Nicholaas and Jacob Van Staphorst, and Nicholas Hubbard

[Orig:] *London. Dupl. via New York pr. Ship Charlotte. Mallaby. Tripl. via N. York pr. Ship Jersey Gardner*

Duplicate Amsterdam 26th. September 1794

Sir!

Since our last respects of 1st. Instant, we have received your very esteemed favor of 7 July, inclosing the necessary Powers in good order, and your directions to us, to make a Loan on behalf of the United States, for Two Millions of Guilders, on the application of Mr. Humphreys for that object.

Our zeal is always devoted to the Interest of the United States, and does not stand in need of quickening, when it is possible to execute the orders you give us, of which the circumstances of the last Loan are an undeniable proof.[1] Seeing then how desirous You are to have money ready to consolidate the Treaty your Minister at the Court of Portugal is authorized to conclude with Algiers,[2] you cannot doubt our readiness to meet and fulfill your wishes on that head, in so far as circumstances will admit.

But Sir! the situation of this Country is such at present, that it is impossible at this moment, to foresee when the period will arrive that we may be able to negotiate another Loan for the United

LS, Connecticut Historical Society, Hartford; copy (extract), RG 46, Third Congress, 1793–1795, Messages Transmitting Reports of the Secretary of the Treasury, National Archives.

1. For a description of the January, 1794, Holland loan, see Willink, Van Staphorst, and Hubbard to H, December 27, 1793.
2. See George Washington to H, May 24, 1794, note 2.

States,[3] and the same cause will prevent the success of any temporary arrangement, to supply the money until the Loan can be compleated: Indeed such would in all times be extremely difficult, if not impracticable for sums to that Amount.

As the Avails for a Loan that has been undertaken, come in but by Instalments, permit us to suggest to you, that the only probable means of having monies here to make good the object you wish to provide for, is to direct us to open a Loan for the purpose whenever Circumstances will allow our doing it with success: This We allow is subjecting the United States to a certain Expence, for a matter that is entirely Contingent and may not at all occur, but at same time, It ought to be considered that the distance between our two Countries, and the nature of the Loan Business, renders the Assumption of risques of this sort sometimes inevitable, and that at all Events, the proceeds of such a Loan might be applied to the payments of the large Amounts of Interest and reimbursement of the Loans of the United States successively to be made in Amsterdam.

The payments next falling due here by the United States are

the 1 Janua.	f 120000.—	Interest a 4 pr. Ct.	on Loan	of	f	3000000—[4]
	" 150000.—	do. a 5 pr. do.	on	do	" "	3000000—[5]
" 1 February	" 80000.—	do. a 4 pr. do.	on	do	" "	2000000—[6]
	" 120000.—	Lotery	on	do	" "	do.[7]
	" 150000.—	Interest a 5 pr. Ct.	on	do	" "	3000000—[8]
" 1 March	" 125000.—	do. a do	on	do	" "	2500000—[9]
Holld. Curry.	f 745000.—					

which with contingent disposals on us, will probably absorb all the Cash in our hands, and leave You to provide for the reimbursement of

3. See Willink, Van Staphorst, and Hubbard to H, July 1, 1794, note 5.

4. For a description of the Holland loan of December, 1791, see William Short to H, December 23, 28, 1791.

5. For a description of the Holland loan of 1794, see Willink, Van Staphorst, and Hubbard to H, December 27, 1793.

6. For a description of the Holland loan of 1784, see H to Short, September 1, 1790, note 22.

7. The Holland loan of 1784 carried a premium or bonus to be distributed by lot among the subscribers to the loan.

8. For a description of the Holland loan of 1790, see Willink, Van Staphorst, and Hubbard to H, January 25, 1790; H to Willink, Van Staphorst, and Hubbard, November 29, 1790.

9. For a description of the Holland loan of March, 1791, see Short to H, February 17, 1791, note 2.

f 1000000.—Principal due the 1 June 1795
" 270000.—Interest due ditto

f 1270000.—That we are confident you will remit us for, so as to continue the regular discharge of the Engagements of the United States, It being highly uncertain, whether in the Intervals We shall be able to raise any further Loans on their Account: We therefore most seriously entreat You, not to rely upon such, to face the payments falling due here subsequent to next March.

Should any Events take place, to render probable the success of future Loans here, we shall not fail to give you the most early Intelligence thereof for your Government.

It may appear strange to you, that at a Crisis, when the Credit of all the Powers in Europe is greatly reduced, there should exist so little demand here and in England for the Bonds and Stocks of the United States; And we confess to you we cannot Account for it upon any reasonable grounds: The most prevailing motives however are, that many People conceive it prudent to hold their Coffers well filled in the actual Circumstances; that some uninformed entertain a general distrust of all public Funds; and that English Capitalists realize what they can, without considerable sacrifice, in hopes to replace it to great advantage in the new English Loan shortly expected to be opened: All which tending to render money very scarce, influence the price of American Bonds here, and of your Domestic Stocks in the Market of London, where they now sell at low prices.

We take the liberty to inclose you Abstract of a letter we received from our Correspondents at Copenhagen, under date of 6th. Instant,[10] which will clearly evince to you, that it is scarce possible at any rate, to purchase Salpetre [11] where the Agent of France can enter into competition: such being the case, in all the northern Ports, and your directions for that Article, of which the half has been executed, not being pressing, we have judged proper, to lodge orders for the remainder of the parcel to be purchased in Lisbon, whenever

10. See enclosure.

11. See H to Willink, Van Staphorst, and Hubbard, May 8, 1794, and Willink, Van Staphorst, and Hubbard to H, July 1, 15, August 1, 18, September 1, 1794.

any shall arrive there, and to be shipped to you from thence: It will afford us great pleasure to advise You its being effected, And we have good hopes it may be so, as that Market is not frequented by the Agents of France, nor we believe materially influenced by the rise in price of Salpetre in the northern parts of Europe.

We are ever with sincere Regard and esteem Sir! Your mo: ob: hb: Servants Wilhem & Jan Willink

N & J Van Staphorst & Hubbard

Alex: Hamilton Esqr. Secretary of the Treasury.

[ENCLOSURE]

From ——— to Wilhem and Jan Willink, Nicholaas and Jacob Van Staphorst, and Nicholas Hubbard[12]

Copenhagen, 6 September 1794.

The sale of 895,000. lb. Salpetre by our East India Company took place on Wednesday: We had orders from You to buy 100. to 110,000 lb. without limitation of price: Notwithstanding which We could but presume, whenever Orders are not given to be executed at any price, be it ever so high, that you relied upon our not going to prices extravagant beyond Conception, but on the Contrary, that We should be guided more or less by the prices of the Article as quoted from other places. On this ground We should have gone so far as f 70.—but this was nothing near the mark. Our prices have been from 30 RDr 1 p. to 51 RDr 1 p. rating at an average RDr 45. 3. 4. Thus gentlemen, the Saltpetre would have stood you in, Holld. Curry. f 122. 4.— free on board, but exclusive of freight and charges in America. Did you ever hear of any such prices for the Article?

The Calculation is,

Provision and Charges in Copenhagen	3 pr. ct.
Refraction	10 " "
Insurance	6 a 7 " "
	20 per Cent which added

12. Copy, Connecticut Historical Society, Hartford.

to the Avarage price of RDr 45. 3. 4. makes RDR 54. 4.— and at 112 pr. ct. Hd. Cy. f 122. 4.—. What an important Loss should We then not have occasioned you, had we acted up to the proverb, Follow orders altho' You do wrong.

Except for some small Commissions at the current prices, which other Houses (but not ours) have though fit to execute, the whole parcel was bought for French Account, and had we absolutely resolved to buy Your 100m to 110m the Average price would in all probability have risen to RDr 60. if not higher.

We impatiently expect every Day the arrival of the private ship Elseneur which has above 800m lb. on board: Should she reach port, And You judge, that We ought to have executed your order, We dare take upon ourselves to deliver You 100. lb at f 122.4 or RDr 45.3.4.

In a Boston price current of 23 May, Salpetre is quoted at 16 pence per lb which is not half the price that has been paid for it here. The mad prices to which that article is pushed in this place, can have no great influence upon other markets, from whence the French cannot export it. Granting to which Consideration its due weight and we doubt not Gentlemen, that you will fully approve our having assumed to protract the excution of your unlimited Order.

From Joseph Howell, Junior

W. D. Accountants Office
September 27th. 1794

Sir

In pursuance of your request as noted in my letter of Yesterday I have the honor to inform you that the sum required is contemplated to be expended for buildings, repairs and articles directed to be made and purchased by the President the sum of Dollars 5000
For the pay of the Army & for bounties to recruits 3000
″ Subsistence of Officers 1000
″ Incidental & Contingent expences 1000

Dollars 10000

The Treasurer [1] informs me that he has in his hands as Agent for the Department of War the sum of three hundred and ninety dollars & 69 Cts.

I am Sir &c Joseph Howell

The Secty of the Treasury

LC, RG 93, Letter Book, 1794, National Archives.
1. Samuel Meredith.

From Stephen Moylan

[*Philadelphia*] *September 27, 1794.* "The amount of Interest on the stock remaining on the books of this Office for the Quarter ending the 30th Septr. 1794 is 19.506.38 Cents 1 Mill dollars for which Sum you will please to issue a Warrant."

LC, RG 217, First Comptroller's Office, Pennsylvania Loan Office, Letter Book "A," National Archives; LC, RG 53, Pennsylvania State Loan Office, Letter Book, 1793–1795, Vol. "616-P," National Archives.

From George Washington

Philadelphia, September 27, 1794. "Pay to the Secretary of State, out of the fund appropriated to defray the Contingent Charges of Government,[1] the sum of Fifteen hundred Dollars, for the use of Colo. Innes." [2]

LC, George Washington Papers, Library of Congress.
1. "An Act making appropriations for certain purposes therein expressed" appropriated twenty thousand dollars for the contingent expenses of the Government under the direction of the President (1 *Stat.* 394–95 [June 9, 1794]).
2. James Innes, who had served as a lieutenant colonel in the 15th Virginia Regiment during the American Revolution, was attorney general of Virginia.
On May 15, 1794, the Senate resolved "That the President of the United States be and he hereby is requested to cause to be communicated to the Executive of the State of Kentucky, such part of the existing negotiation between the United States and Spain, relative to . . . [the free navigation of the Mississippi], as he may deem advisable and consistent with the course of negotiations" (*Annals of Congress,* IV, 100).
For the negotiations between the United States and Spain concerning free navigation on the Mississippi, see "Notes on Thomas Jefferson's Report of Instructions for the Commissioners to Spain," March 1–4, 1792; "Conversation with George Hammond," March 31, 1792, note 3, July 1–2, 1792.
On August 7, 1794, Edmund Randolph wrote to Washington: "You will be pleased to recollect, that the two houses of congress requested you, at the last

session, to communicate to the people of Kentucky certain information, relative to the negotiation concerning the Mississippi. The reason, which we have had for some time past, for expecting hourly decisive intelligence from Madrid, has been the cause of withholding the communication to this day. But it seems expedient to enter into the business some way or other. It is impossible in point of propriety, (as I conceive) to lay before the world copies of all the papers. But a substitute for this may be found in the following course—to depute some sensible and firm man to go to Kentucky; carrying with him the most accurate knowledge of the whole transaction, and such minutes and copies of those things, which upon examination it shall be thought adviseable to attend to. This person shall immediately proceed to Kentucky, where he shall explain to the legislature and executive of the state the circumstances of the affair: the governor is to be requested that if the legislature shall not assemble upon its own adjournment or by the constitution before a given day, they may be convened to receive the proposed communication. The deputy shall urge every consideration, proper to allay the prevailing ferment. . ." (ALS, RG 59, Miscellaneous Letters, 1790–1799, National Archives).

On August 8, 1794, Randolph wrote to Innes: "The President has determined to send a Commissioner immediately to Kentucky, to lay before that Government the State of the negotiation respecting the Mississippi. I wish you could make it convenient to go. The pay will be eight dollars per day and all expenses" (LC, RG 59, Domestic Letters of the Department of State, Vol. 7, June 27–November 30, 1794, National Archives). Innes accepted the appointment, but because of poor health he did not go to Kentucky until November, 1794. His instructions are dated November 11, 1794 (LC, RG 59, Domestic Letters of the Department of State, Vol. 7, June 27–November 30, 1794, National Archives).

On September 27, 1794, Randolph wrote to Washington and requested "a Warrant from the President's Contingent Fund for such a sum of money . . . for the use of Colo. Innes, as the President may judge proper" (copy, RG 59, Miscellaneous Letters, 1790–1799, National Archives).

To Wilhem and Jan Willink, Nicholaas and Jacob Van Staphorst, and Nicholas Hubbard

[*Philadelphia, September 27, 1794.* On January 5, 1795, Willink, Van Staphorst, and Hubbard wrote to Hamilton: "We have to acknowledge the Receipt of your esteemed favors of 27 September and 27 October, the latter signed by Oliver Wolcott Esqr." *Letter of September 27 not found.*]

To the President and Directors of the Bank of New York

[*Philadelphia, September 28, 1794.* On September 28, 1794, Hamilton wrote to Gulian Verplanck: [1] "Inclosed is a Letter for the President & directors of the Bank of New York." *Letter not found.*]

1. Verplanck was president of the Bank of New York.

To George Gale

Treasury Department
Septr. 28th. 1794

Sir

Your two letters of the 25th. are before me.[1]

It will be agreeable to me that you have made and forwarded to Fort Cumberland as many Jacketts and Trowsers as you will be able to get there by the 15th. of October; sending them forward as fast as they are ready. The Jacketts ought to be made of some of the Stuffs of which sailors Jacketts are usually made, and like them without Skirts, but of sufficient length of Body to protect well the Bowells. The Trowsers or rather overalls ought also to be of some strong coarse cheap Woolen Stuff. It will be well to know here early what you think you can accomplish in this particular.

Let them be sent forward addressed to the order of Genl Miller acting Quarter Master General.[2] Inform General Smith[3] of this order.

With great Consideration & esteem I am Sir Your Obt. Servt.

AH

P.S. Being about to leave Town for the Westward[4] you will address your future communications respecting the Military supplies to Tench Coxe Esqr.[5]

George Gale Esqr.

Copy, Connecticut Historical Society, Hartford.

1. Letters not found.
2. Henry Miller. See H to Miller, September 15, 1794.
3. Samuel Smith, commander of the Maryland militia.
4. See H to George Washington, September 24, 1794, note 2.
5. On September 30, 1794, Tench Coxe wrote to Samuel Hodgdon: "I received this day after the departure of the Secy of the Treasy. a letter desiring me to attend to the forwarding of supplies for the militia army. . ." (LC, RG 75, Letters of Tench Coxe, Commissioner of the Revenue, Relating to the Procurement of Military, Naval, and Indian Supplies, National Archives).

H's letter to Coxe has not been found.

To Gulian Verplanck

Philadelphia
Sep. 28. 1794

Dear Sir

Inclosed is a Letter for the President & directors of the Bank of New York.[1] I have it at heart for various reasons as a matter very interesting to the public service that the loan requested should be made—but I would not wish the Letter to be formally presented until it was certain there would be a compliance. For this reason I send it to you that you may sound the Directors before presenting it & present it or not as you find them disposed.

The rate of interest may perhaps appear exceptionable but it is of consequence to the Country & ultimately the interest of all monied institutions that the Government rate of Interest should be low. Beside this I shall postpone drawing for the money as long as possible which may render the loan in fact more profitable than is one to Individuals at six ℔ Cent.

I will thank you for a reply as soon as may be;[2] putting the *initials* of your name on the superscription of the Letter.

Yrs. with true esteem & regard A Hamilton

PS. You will of course open the inclosed. I say this because it is directed to The President *& Directors.*

G V Planck Esq

ALS, Hamilton Papers, Library of Congress.

1. Letter not found.

2. On October 8, 1794, Oliver Wolcott, Jr., wrote "for the Secretary of the Treasury" to Charles Wilkes, cashier of the Bank of New York: "I have had the pleasure to receive your Letter of the 6th Instant addressed to the Secretary of the Treasury, announcing that the President Directors and Company of the Bank of New York have generously complied with his proposals for a Loan of Two Hundred thousand Dollars for the public Service . . ." (LS, Hamilton Papers, Library of Congress).

Wilkes's letter to H of October 6, 1794, has not been found.

This loan was authorized by "An Act making further provision for the expenses attending the intercourse of the United States with foreign nations; and further to continue in force the act intituled 'An act providing the means of intercourse between the United States and foreign nations'" (1 *Stat.* 345 [March 20, 1794]).

The loan of two hundred thousand dollars from the Bank of New York was for four months at five percent interest (D, RG 217, Miscellaneous Treasury Accounts, 1790–1894, Account No. 7276, National Archives).

To Ephraim Blaine

Philadelphia
Sep. 29. 1794

Dr. Sir

The President whom I have the honor to accompany leaves this place tomorrow for Carlisle, where he will probably remain three or four days. He wishes you to provide for him some convenient rooms (say three) during his stay. It will be most agreeable for them to be at a private house on the *express condition* that they are to be paid for; for The President will not by any means be accommodated on any other terms. If they cannot be had on these terms at a private house let the best thing possible be done at a Tavern.[1]

Yours with esteem & regard A Hamilton

Ephraim Blaine Esqr

ALS, Hamilton Papers, Library of Congress.

1. George Washington and his staff remained in Carlisle, Pennsylvania, from October 4 to October 12, 1794. Blaine placed both his houses at the disposal of the President (Freeman, *Washington,* VII, 202, note 212).

To Philip A. and Alexander Hamilton, Junior

[Philadelphia, September 29, 1794]

Dear Children

We have been very sorry to hear that our dear Alexander has been unwell but thank God that he was better. We hope he will soon be quite well.

Your Mama will leave this place tomorrow or next day for Trenton to bring you herself to Town.

I expect to set out tomorrow for Carlisle. But you must not be uneasy about it. For by the accounts we have received there will be no fighting and of course no danger. It will only be an agreeable ride which will I hope do me good.

I give you both my best love & blessings as does your Mama. It will give me great pleasure when I come back to know that you have not neglected your studies & have been good boys during the vacation.

Yr. Affect. Father A Hamilton

Masters Philip and Alex Hamilton
Trenton

ALS, Hamilton Papers, Library of Congress.

1. Philip (born January 22, 1782) and Alexander (born May 16, 1786) studied under William Frazer, the Episcopal rector of St. Michael's Church in Trenton, New Jersey. See H to Philip A. Hamilton, December 5, 1791.

From Samuel Hodgdon

[*Philadelphia, September 29, 1794.* On September 30, 1794, Hamilton wrote to Hodgdon: "I perceive by your return of yesterday that there is still a considerable deficiency of some essential articles for the Militia." *Letter not found.*]

To Samuel Hodgdon

[*Philadelphia, September 29, 1794.* On September 30, 1794, Tench Coxe wrote to Hodgdon: "Permit me to ask your greatest attention & exertion to fulfill the requests of the Secy. of the Treasury in his letter to you of the 29 inst."[1] *Letter not found.*]

1. LC, RG 75, Letters of Tench Coxe, Commissioner of the Revenue, Relating to the Procurement of Military, Naval, and Indian Supplies, National Archives.

From Joseph Nourse

Treasury Department
Registers Office 29th septemr. 1794

Sir,

I have the honor to enclose a Certificate[1] of the sums issueable from the Treasury of the United states for the payment of Interest becoming due to the several creditors on the Books of the Treasury on the 30th September 1794 and to the Trustees for the redemption of the Public debt for Interest arising to the same period upon the stock standing in their names, and in the name of Samuel Meredith in trust for the United States.

	dollars
To the several Creditors	291,945.20
To the Trustees for the redemption of the public debt	19,291.76
Total sum issuable	311,237. 4

With the greatest respect I am Sir your most obedient humble servt.

The Honble. Alexander Hamilton Esquire
secretary of the Treasury.

Copy, RG 53, Register of the Treasury, Balances of Stocks of Domestic Debts, 1793–1799, Vol. "156-T," National Archives.

1. D, RG 53, Register of the Treasury, Balances of Stocks of Domestic Debts, 1793–1799, Vol. "156-T," National Archives.

To Samuel Smith

War Department September 29th 1794

Sir.

I have received your letter informing me of your determination to proceed to Frederick Town.[1]

It is the wish of the President, that you proceed with the Militia under your command with all reasonable expedition to Fort Cumberland there to form a junction with that of Virginia, which he is desirous should not be delayed.

Orders went yesterday to Mr. Gale[2] by express to provide and forward to Fort Cumberland as many Jackets and Overalls of the description of those you mention as he can get there by the 15th of October. Supplies of the same articles will go immediately from hence. In short every thing possible will be done for the Comfort and accomodating of the Troops.

With great consideration & esteem, I am Sir Your Obt. Servant

A Hamilton

PS. I have accepted your drafts for 20,000 and 17,000 Dollars for the 1st of November & the 1st of December, which I presume will enable your friends to do the needful. It is expected that the Pennsylvania and Jersey Militia will unite at Carlisle the 5th of October whence they will immediately go to Bedford.

General S Smith
Frederick Town

Copy, Connecticut Historical Society, Hartford.

1. Letter not found.

2. H to George Gale, September 28, 1794.

To George Washington

Treasy. Depart. Sep: 29. 1794

Sir,

I have the honor to transmit you two communications from the Commissioner of the Revenue dated the 24 & 25 [1] instant, and to submit my opinion, that it is adviseable to ratify all the contracts to which they refer except that last mentioned with Green Parker.[2]

With perfect respect &c A Hamilton.

LC, George Washington Papers, Library of Congress.

1. Tench Coxe's first letter to H of September 25, 1794, has not been found.

2. A copy of the following memorandum by Tench Coxe may be found in RG 26, Lighthouse Deeds and Contracts, National Archives:

"Amount of the Different Contracts made with Nathan Keais Superintendent of the Stakeage &c &c. North of the District of Wilmington in the State of North Carolina for the year ending the 31st December 1795 as follows.

Swashes, Royal Shoal, Wallaces channel, Teaches hole, upper roads, all the Shoals in Pamplico Sound that has heretofore been Staked, to John Wallace principal John Bragg Security for two hundred and forty four Dollars (225

Core Sound including old topsail inlet to the town of Beaufort, the same principal & security as above for sixty nine Dollars (69

Neuse River, John Bragg principal, security Robt Wallace for ninety two Dollars (92

Croeton Shoals. Albemarle sound and the Marshes to Robert Wallace principal & J Bragg Security for one hundred forty five Dollars (132

Pamplico River, Pringo river & all the Navigable creeks to the Town of Washington, to Green Parker principal & Wm McDaniel Security, for one hundred Dollars. (60

The above is the original note of the Contracts referred to in my Letter of the 25 Septbr. 94 to the Secy. of the Treasury. The sum in crotchets are the terms of the last year. Tench Coxe C:R

Treasy. Departmt. Septbr. 29. 1794.

Approved
except as to the Last

Go. Washington"

To Oliver Wolcott, Junior

Treasury Department
29th September 1794

Sir

Being about to leave the seat of Government for a few Weeks to accompany the Army on its march against the Western Insurgents of Pennsylvania, I commit to you during my absence the management of those matters which are reserved to my superintendance under the constitution and regulations of the Department, especially the receipts and expenditures of money, and I rely upon your deligence and zeal, that nothing will suffer during my absence.

With regard to remissions & mitigations of penalties and forfeitures it will be best to avoid acting in any case in which particular inconvenience will not arise from delay, as there is not time to explain the priniciples which have governed in the past, and the course of policy may without such explanation be innovated upon, so as to occasion something like inconsistency. But in urgent cases you will act, consulting the most recent precedents in similar cases.

To preserve the usual forms I have signed and left in my Office a large number of Blank Warrants, of the different kinds which issue.

Inclosed is a letter to the President and Directors of the Bank of New York.[1] If they agree to the loan you will conclude it. You will find in the Office a Power from the President for the purpose.

It will be regular in any contract which may be made to pursue the terms of the power as to parties.[2]

With great consideration & esteem I am Sir Your obedient Servant

A Hamilton
Secy of the Treasy

Oliver Wolcott Esqr.
Comptroller of the Treasury

LS, Connecticut Historical Society, Hartford; ADf, Connecticut Historical Society, Hartford; copy, RG 59, Miscellaneous Letters, 1790–1799, National Archives.

1. Letter not found, but see H to Gulian Verplanck, September 28, 1794.

2. At this point in the draft H wrote and crossed out the following sentence: "The contract may be concluded if not more than 6 per Cent interest is demanded."

To ———

[*Philadelphia, September 30, 1794.* The dealer's catalogue description of this letter reads: "Directing that Mrs. Hamilton shall have authority to draw checks against his private account." *Letter not found.*]

ALS, sold by Stan V. Henkels, Jr., March 22, 1910, Lot 96.

From Tench Coxe

Treasury Department, Revenue Office, September 30, 1794. Requests "a warrant to issue for the sum of one hundred Dollars in favor of . . . Joel Gibbs with whom a contract has been made for seven hundred & sixty eight Hats for the Artillerists, being on a/count of the above mentioned contract." [1]

LC, RG 75, Letters of Tench Coxe, Commissioner of the Revenue, Relating to the Procurement of Military, Naval, and Indian Supplies, National Archives.

1. On September 30, 1794, Warrant No. 4081 for one hundred dollars was issued to Gibbs (D, RG 217, Miscellaneous Treasury Accounts, 1790–1894, Account No. 6922, National Archives).

To Tench Coxe

[*Philadelphia, September 30, 1794.* On October 1, 1794, Coxe wrote to Hamilton: "I received . . . your letter of the 30~ Ulo. relative to the forwarding of the militia supplies." *Letter not found.*]

From William Ellery

Newport [*Rhode Island*] *September 30, 1794.* "I acknowledge the receipt of your letter of the 10th. of this month; [1] I shall do every thing in my power to secure a just issue in the case of Pierce.[2] It is not the practice in this State to strike juries. . . ."

LC, Newport Historical Society, Newport, Rhode Island.

1. Letter not found, but see dealer's catalogue description printed under this date.

2. Preserved Pierce. See Ellery to H, August 1–6, 1794.

To Samuel Hodgdon

War department
September 30. 1794

Sir,

It is with regret I perceive by your return of yesterday [1] that there is still a considerable deficiency of some essential articles for the Militia Army Knapsacks Canteens Musket Cartridges Blankets and shoes.

I am to request that you will press forward additional supplies of these articles as fast as possible to Fort Cumberland and Carlisle proportioned to the number of Militia to assemble at those places respectively. Your object is to equip every man called for with one Knapsack or Valice and Canteen, one pair of shoes and thirty rounds of Musket Cartridges for every foot Soldier.

With regard to Blankets a number equal to half the whole number of Men called for will it is presumed suffice.

I observe that the Virginia Militia are still deficient in Camp Kettles. It ought to be a primary object to make up that deficiency.

When you have completed thirty rounds ℔ man of Cartridges you will forward an additional supply for the whole army equal to thirty rounds more by way of Carlisle and Bedford. The ammunition for the field pieces is also very defective. These ought to be at least thirty rounds ℔ piece.

Mr. Francis[2] has been directed to make a further provision of the foregoing articles except ammunition and also to provide a number of woolen Jackets and Overalls which are also to be forwarded with all possible expedition proportionally to the before mentioned places. But after the 5. of October whatever is sent forward must take the route by Carlisle to Bedford. The supplies for the Southward therefore ought to be hastened on before that date. But no time should be lost in sending more ammunition to Carlisle.

You will also forward immediately one thousand of the Coats, two thousand of the Overalls and three thousand of the shirts you report to be on hand. Divide them between Fort Cumberland and Carlisle.

I should be glad to have to morrow morning by 9 oClock a return of whatever you may have forwarded since the return of yesterday.

It is relied upon that this instruction will be executed to the full extent. The Instructions you may receive from Tench Coxe Esqr with regard to supplies till the return of the Secretary at War are to be complied with.[3]

You will on the 5. of October forward by express to Carlisle a return of all the articles which you send on not included in the return you are requested to make to morrow and another by the post of Tuesday the 7. of October of every thing subsequently forwarded.

Nothing must be omitted to obtain with dispatch the means of transportation. All accounts prove that the Troops are a head of their supplies which is a very disagreeable circumstance.

With consideration and esteem I am Sir your obedt. Servant

Alexander Hamilton
Secy of the Treasy

Samuel Hodgdon Esqr

LS, The Andre deCoppet Collection, Princeton University Library.

1. Letter not found.
2. Tench Francis.
3. See H to George Gale, September 28, 1794, note 5.

From Thomas Sim Lee

Council Chamber [Annapolis, Maryland]
September 30th 1794.

Sir.

The enclosed copy of a Letter from Brigadier General Smith at Frederick Town will explain to you a variety of difficulties annexed to his situation which he seems to consider as sufficiently formidable to delay his march to the Ultimate place of rendezvous.[1]

My view in transmitting to you a copy of this Communication is simply to afford the General Government an opportunity of removing as far as possible such of the alledged difficulties as have been beyond my power.

The enclosed Copy of my answer [2] to his Letter will apprize you of the nature of my exertions for completing the Maryland Detachment and for effecting their accommodation and it will remain with the President to adopt such further arrangements with regard to the latter object as may be thought expedient for supplying what is yet deficient.

I can truly say I have used every possible effort to gratify the objection of the General Government, and that I shall not in future omit any opportunity of giving it my utmost support and assistance.

The marked Inadequacy of our Militia Law [3] has placed obsticles in my way which it has been impracticable wholly to surmount. I have endeavoured to meet this Inadequacy by every means that could be devised, but have not been able to succeed to the extent required. I have no doubt that General Smith upon receipt of my letter and the Medicine and Blankets from Baltimore, will take the earliest measures for getting in motion; and I feel a Confidence that the displeasure resulting from the disappointment of the expectations with which he received his Command will be but temporary.

I am &c Tho: S Lee

The Honble
Alexander Hamilton
Secretary Treasury.

Copy, RG 56, Letters 2d Comptroller, 2d Auditor, Executive of Maryland and Georgia, Maryland, National Archives.

1. The letter from Samuel Smith to Lee is dated September 27, 1794, and reads in part as follows: ". . . I find here a want of many things. No Quarter master who knows his Duty, No Waggon Master, No Forage Master, no Medicine and the Men Sickly. It can Scarcely be expected that We Shall march under those Circumstances. I was promised 2300 Men with a proper Number Say 200 of Horse. I Shall have about 1250 or at most 1500 without a Horseman except those from Harford Say 15 who are coming on by mistake" (ALS, Hall of Records of Maryland, Annapolis).

2. A copy of Lee's answer has not been found, but on October 3, 1794, Smith wrote to Lee acknowledging the receipt of Lee's letter of September 30, 1794 (ALS, Hall of Records of Maryland, Annapolis).

In response to Smith's letter of September 27, Lee wrote on September 30 to the contractors for the militia in Baltimore requesting that blankets be forwarded immediately to Frederick (ALS, Hall of Records of Maryland, Annapolis).

3. This is a reference to "An Act to regulate and discipline the militia of this state," passed December 28, 1793 (*Maryland Laws*, November, 1793, Sess., Ch. LIII).

From Richard Kidder Meade[1]

[Frederick County, Virginia, September 30, 1794]

My dear Hamilton

It is some considerable time since I gratified myself with a letter to you. This short one I do not hesitate now to write in order to afford an intimate acquaintance of mine the pleasure he has long wish'd of an introduction to the person of my friend. He is deeply attached to your politics & official character, to say no more, & I partake with him in the enjoyment he will derive in taking you by the hand. Mr. Lewis Burwell[2] is the bearer & I can venture to introduce him as a good man & a good Citizen, most firmly well affected to our Constitution. I know my friend the nature of your office & your zeal to fill it perfectly in all its parts leaves you but little time to attend to other matters, but the anxiety of Mr. Burwell to make even a small acquaintance with you induc'd me to trouble you with this letter, for which I will make no further apology. And now my Dear friend how do you do, how is my old acquaintance your better half & all your little offspring—you are often in my mind & my heart is with you, I only lament that I cannot see you all. If you have not leisure to grant Us a line, send me word by some chance acquaintance, your number of Children, their Sexes & how you all do. I have added a fifth to my number since I wrote to you,[3] a hearty male, & a very few months will furnish the half dozen, but I am not knowing enough in the business to foretel the kind. Present us in a friendly way to Mrs H., & I beg you my Dr Hamilton to believe that I am unalterably.

Yr truely Affece Friend R K Meade

Frederick Septr 30th 1794

ALS, Hamilton Papers, Library of Congress.

1. Meade and H had become friends when each served as an aide-de-camp to George Washington during the American Revolution. After the war Meade purchased and operated a thousand-acre farm in Frederick County, Virginia.

2. Burwell was a resident of Richmond, Virginia.

3. Letter not found.

To Oliver Wolcott, Junior

[*Philadelphia*] *September 30, 1794.* On October 2, 1794, Wolcott wrote to Hamilton: "I have recd. your letter of Sept. 30th." *Letter not found.*]

From Tench Coxe[1]

T. D. R. O. October 1st 1794

Sir

I received after your departure[2] your letter of the 30~ Ulo.[3] relative to the forwarding of the militia supplies. I called upon Mr. Stagg[4] on the subject & found he had set out after the President with Genl. Waynes[5] dispatches. I wrote first to Major

Hodgdon[6] requesting information, what he had expedited since his last information to you, & of what he should dispatch this day. To Mr. Frances I wrote in like manner,[7] requesting him to inform me what remained to be procured, of the Articles heretofore ordered for the militia from this Office, and what remained to be procured on the orders for the same service heretofore received by him otherwise than from this Office; which I understand to have been frequent. He called on me to day, and informed me, that he had procured every thing ordered in both ways, except the Articles in your letter to me, which was delivered to him on Sunday by one of the Gentlemen of your office. I have seen the rough draught of your letter to Mr. Hodgdon of the 29~ Ulo.[8] & have urged his expediting the objects therein mentioned. A letter from Colo. Fish of the 22d Ulo. assured me that 2000 blankets &c. would be forwarded by the middle of that week i.e. the 24th, or 25 Sepr. Similar assurances were given about the Shoes. Not one of either are received, nor a line of apology. I wrote to him urgently on the 24 & 29.[9]

Capt. Barry will sail for Georgia on Saturday in a Brig. that can carry 100 Tons of Live Oak or more.[10] Two Vessels from New York and New London will also bring wood if they can take it.

This business for the War Department does no service to the business of the Revenues & Light houses. It obstructs me from them in a degree that is not satisfactory to my self.

I have the honor to be with great respect Sir, yr mo: obedt Sert

T. Coxe C.R.

The Secy. of the Ty.

LC, RG 75, Letters of Tench Coxe, Commissioner of the Revenue Relating to the Procurement of Military, Naval, and Indian Supplies, National Archives.

1. For background to this letter, see H to Coxe, April 4, 1794; Henry Knox to H, March 29, April 21, 1794.

2. On September 30, 1794, H left Philadelphia with George Washington to go to western Pennsylvania. See H to Washington, September 24, 1794, note 2.

3. Letter not found.

4. John Stagg, Jr., chief clerk in the War Department.

5. Major General Anthony Wayne.

6. Coxe to Samuel Hodgdon, September 30, 1794 (LC, RG 75, Letters of Tench Coxe, Commissioner of the Revenue, Relating to the Procurement of Military, Naval, and Indian Supplies, National Archives).

7. Coxe to Tench Francis, September 30, 1794 (LC, RG 75, Letters of Tench Coxe, Commissioner of the Revenue, Relating to the Procurement of Military, Naval, and Indian Supplies, National Archives).

8. Letter not found.

9. Coxe to Nicholas Fish, September 24, 29, 1794 (LC, RG 75, Letters of Tench Coxe, Commissioner of the Revenue, Relating to the Procurement of Military, Naval, and Indian Supplies, National Archives).

10. John Barry was born in Ireland and came to the United States in the seventeen-sixties. He settled in Philadelphia and became a shipmaster and shipowner. On June 4, 1794, Barry was appointed one of the "captains of the ships to be procured in pursuance of the act to provide 'a naval armament'" (*Executive Journal*, I, 161).

From Tench Coxe

Treasury Department, Revenue Office, October 1, 1794. Requests "that a warrant be issued in the name of Tench Francis Esqr. Agent for military purchases for twenty five Thousand Dollars."

LC, RG 75, Letters of Tench Coxe, Commissioner of the Revenue, Relating to the Procurement of Military, Naval, and Indian Supplies, National Archives).

From Meletiah Jordan

Frenchman's Bay [*District of Maine*] *October 1, 1794.* "Your letter of 23d June [1] requesting to know the issue of the suit instituted against the Schooner Polly & Cargo [2] I received but yesterday Sir. I am sorry to inform you that the issue has proved unfavorable to the States. The trial was in Sept. but the particular proceedings of the Court I have not yet been able to obtain but expect them hourly when I will immediately forward them to your Office.[3] The Libel against the Grindstones [4] through some inattention of the Marshall [5] or Attorney [6] is not yet published though I expect it will [be] time enough for the December term at Portland.[7] I will beg leave to inform you that this District is particularly deficient in proper Officers to attend to the accounts of the Revenue whether that or my ignorance of the existing authority or their unwillingness to aid may be the reason. . . . You will pardon my prolixity on this subject but the extent & detached situation of the District is very commodious for Smugglers and every precaution in my power is used though they are sometimes useless. . . ."

Copy, RG 56, Letters to Collectors at Gloucester, Machias, and Frenchman's Bay, National Archives.

1. Letter not found.

2. For information on the schooner *Polly,* see Jordan to H, May 7, July 1, 1794.

3. On September 5, 1794, the United States District Court for the District of Maine in the case of *Meletiah Jordan* v *Schooner Polly* "Decreed . . . that the

said Schooner Polly with her tackle, apparel, & the Goods, Wares & Merchandise found on board thereof, be forthwith restored to the respective Claimants" (D, Records of the United States District Court for the District of Maine, Federal Records Center, Boston).

4. See Jordan to H, May 7, 1794.

5. Henry Dearborn.

6. Daniel Davis was acting United States attorney for the District of Maine in the September and December, 1794, terms of the court, replacing William Lithgow, Jr., who was ill.

7. On December 3, 1794, the United States District Court for the District of Maine in *Meletiah Jordan* v *11 Grindstones* ruled "no Claimant appearing *declared* forfeited" (D, Records of the United States District Court for the District of Maine, Federal Records Center, Boston).

From Joseph Nourse

Treasury Department
Registers Office 2d. October 1794

Sir,

I would beg leave to intimate that upon an adjustment of the several dividend accounts of the registered debt, the sum of Nineteen thousand and twenty nine dollars 57/100 remained to be issued from the Treasury for payment of interest and arrearages of Interest to the 1st October 1794; but as only a part of the Arrearages will be called for in the course of the present Quarter; I wou'd recommend that a Warrant for five thousand dollars be issued in favour of John Kean Esqr Cashier of the Bank of the United states, he to be held accountable for the expenditure being with great respect, sir,

Your most obedient & most humble servant JN

Honble Alexr Hamilton Esqr.
Secretary of the Treasury

	dollars
arrearages of Interest due on the several Quarterly dividends on the 30th Septr 1794	18.598.96
Quarter Yearly dividend from 1st. July 1794 to 30th September following	3.141.44
Total payable 1st October 1794 Dolls	21.740.40
deduct balance cash in the hands of the Cashier of the Bank of the United states on the 1st October 1794	2.710.83
Leaves the amot as within stated	19.029.57

Copy, RG 53, Register of the Treasury, Estimates and Statements for 1794, Vol. "136-T," National Archives.

From Oliver Wolcott, Junior

[Philadelphia] Oct. 2d. 1794

I have recd. your Letter of Sept. 30th.[1] & have lost no time in causing Notes to be prepared for the remittances directed to be made to Genl. Miller[2] & Mr. Williams,[3] which will go forward to morrow by Colo. Presley Nevil[4] to whom a reasonable compensation has been promised.

I expect to be able to forward ninety thousand Dollars by the same conveyance to Fort Cumberland for the pay of the army.

I judge it proper to transmit Copies of papers relating to a heavy requisition from Elliot & Williams[5] on acot. of their Contract for the Army. I understand that this is exclusive of about 40000 Dollars for which Mr. Smiths[6] bills are registered in your Office. If you have it in your power I must request you to advise & instruct me on this subject.

Genl. Knox is expected this Evening.[7]

I have the honor to be with perfect respect Sir &c

The Hon A H

ADf, Connecticut Historical Society, Hartford.

1. Letter not found.

2. Henry Miller, acting quartermaster general for the militia army. See H to Miller, September 15, 1794.

3. Elie Williams had been appointed agent for provisioning the militia army. See H to Williams, September 12, 1794. On October 1, 1794, Warrant No. 4101 for twenty-five thousand dollars was issued to Williams (D, RG 217, Miscellaneous Treasury Accounts, 1790–1894, Account No. 9550, National Archives).

4. See "Deposition of Francis Mentges," August 1, 1794, note 2.

5. In addition to his appointment as an agent for the militia army, Williams was a partner with Robert Elliot in Maryland as contractors for the army on the western frontier. On October 1, 1794, Warrant No. 4132 for ten thousand dollars was issued to Elliot and Williams (D, RG 217, Miscellaneous Treasury Accounts, 1790–1894, Account No. 9483, National Archives).

6. Samuel Smith, commander of the Maryland militia.

7. Henry Knox had left Philadelphia in August to go to Maine on private business. See George Washington to H, August 12, 1794, note 1.

From Tench Coxe[1]

T. D. R. O. October 4 1794

Sir

You will receive by this express a copy of a letter to me from Mr. Gale.[2]

A letter has been sent from your Office, from Col. Carrington to you[3] a copy is enclosed. Major Hodgdon whom I have seen, assured me 5 or 6000 blankets have gone forward; the last this day. Ten bales containing as he supposed 1600 more have arrived from N. York, & are in good time, as he could not get more off than have this day gone. He says that Invoices of all parcels were sent with them. The Arms had gone before this letter was received from Mr. Carrington. Mr. Hodgdon informs me that he sends you daily an account of what he forwards.

I have not received any information from Mr. Stagg[4] relative to the Objects of your letter of the 30th.[5] I made this day another unsuccessful call to see him. He was absent on business. The Clerk with whom I left the request for the tellers, said he had informed him of my request.

The Money for Mr. Gale (3000 Dolls.) had been applied for by the exhibition of his letter at your Office.

I have cautioned Mr. Gale to take care that the disease at Baltimore be not communicated to the Militia by the clothing from there.[6]

It appears to me expedient that the agency or Commissareate for 1795[7] should be considered if not filled while the President is to the westward. Several of Gen. Wilkins's[8] friends wish the situation for him. Mr. Ross[9] particularly. I have the honor to be

Sir your mo. obedt. Servt. T. Coxe C. R:

The Secty. of the Treasy.

LC, RG 75, Letters of Tench Coxe, Commissioner of the Revenue, Relating to the Procurement of Military, Naval, and Indian Supplies, National Archives.

1. For background to this letter, see H to Coxe, April 4, 1794.

2. George Gale was supervisor of the revenue for Maryland. On October 4, 1794, Coxe wrote to Gale: "I have desired the remittance of 7 or 8000 Dollars be made to you by mondays post, as desired in your letter of the 2d. instant . . ."

(LC, RG 75, Letters of Tench Coxe, Commissioner of the Revenue, Relating to the Procurement of Military, Naval, and Indian Supplies, National Archives).

3. Edward Carrington's letter to H has not been found. Carrington was supervisor of the revenue for Virginia. On October 4, 1794, Coxe wrote to Samuel Hodgdon, commissary of Army stores: "I have just seen a letter to the Secy of the Treasy. From Col: Carrington in which he urges the speedy transmission of the Blankets, and also requests a particular a/count of each parcel sent. . ." (LC, RG 75, Letters of Tench Coxe, Commissioner of the Revenue, Relating to the Procurement of Military, Naval, and Indian Supplies, National Archives).

4. John Stagg, Jr., chief clerk in the War Department.

5. Letter not found, but see Coxe to H, October 1, 1794.

6. See Coxe to Gale, October 4, 1794 (LC, RG 75, Letters of Tench Coxe, Commissioner of the Revenue, Relating to the Procurement of Military, Naval, and Indian Supplies, National Archives). Coxe is referring to the outbreak of yellow fever in Baltimore.

7. Coxe is referring to the appointment of a commissary for Army supplies in the western territory.

8. Brigadier General John Wilkins, Jr.

9. Presumably James Ross, one of the Federal commissioners appointed by George Washington to confer with representatives of the insurgents in western Pennsylvania. See H and Henry Knox to Washington, August 5, 1794, note 3.

To Henry Lee

Carlisle [1] [Pennsylvania] Oct 4 [1794]

My Dear Lee

There is something about our friend Smith [2] that perplexes and distresses me. I cannot suppose any thing wrong yet it is certain that he has done nothing but paint black from the beginning.[3] However the force of Maryland may be suffered to melt away it is a consolation that a sufficient force will be had elsewhere. Smith is mistaken when he supposes Pensylvania will do nothing. She has now on the ground 1500 men & there is every probability of another 1500 by the 10th instant. Jersey has here also 500 horse & 500 infantry & another Regiment of infantry will be here by the 10th. In my opinion this force alone would be fully adequate to the object though I hold with you the principle sacred that nothing is to be risked, & therefore felicitate you & myself on the prospect of a more adequate force. In the humour Friend Smith seems to be in it may be adviseable to facilitate to him a return to Maryland. Adieu A Hamilton

Govr. Lee

ALS, The Hamilton Library and Historical Association of Cumberland County, Carlisle, Pennsylvania.

1. George Washington and H had left Philadelphia on September 30, 1794, and arrived in Carlisle on October 4.

2. Samuel Smith, commander of the Maryland militia.

3. For Smith's complaints, see Thomas Sim Lee to H, September 30, 1794, note 1. In addition, as early as August 26, 1794, Edmund Randolph had written to Washington: "I have received a letter from Colo S. Smith of Baltimore, which I will lay before you in the morning. He considers the militia-law of Maryland, as insufficient for the purpose of drawing forth the quota, required from that state; and expresses himself with great strength against shedding blood, if it can be in any manner avoided" (ALS, RG 59, Miscellaneous Letters, 1790–1799, National Archives; LC, RG 59, Domestic Letters of the Department of State, Vol. 7, June 26–November 30, 1794, National Archives).

From Nicholaas Van Staphorst[1]

Amsterdam 4 October 1794.

Sir!

The difference of opinion between the several Gentlemen constituting the joint Correspondents of the United States of America, for the Department of Finance, about the Doctrine of Liberty and Equality, and every other Matter relating to the French Revolution, is the cause of your not receiving from us such compleat communications and advice of the situation of things, as might otherwise be necessary.

I venture to give you a private account of my thoughts on that subject, in hopes of it's proving in some manner useful to you as Secretary of the Treasury. And I am the more induced to it, on account of some merits, I think I can claim from the United States, above my Copartners, (except my Brother, who being banished from this Country these seven years past, is prevented from taking an active part in the business)[2] by the very warm Interest I took during the American War, in the fortunate issue of that grand Insurrection for the Cause of liberty, and by having been accessary to it, According to the Circumstances, We then were in, at a period

LS, Connecticut Historical Society, Hartford.

1. Nicholaas Van Staphorst was a member of the banking firm of Willink, Van Staphorst, and Hubbard, the bankers of the United States in Amsterdam.

2. Jacob Van Staphorst had been forced to leave Holland because of his support of the 1787 revolution against the Stadtholder, William V. See William Short to H, December 2, 1790, note 14.

when, Mr. Hubbard[3] was not yet in Holland, and when the Contest was still a matter of perfect indifference to Messrs. Willinks.[4]

That sacred flame of Liberty, is still glowing in my bosom, and has received additional purity from the important examples set forth by the French Revolution, as well in regard to the cause and magnitude of the Evil, which is common to all the European Nations, as with respect to the infaillible means of redress, from the Adhibition of those forces, every people is possessed of. From these motives I am as eager a partizan to the rights of man, and the principles of liberty and equality, brought to light and put into practice by the People of France, as I have been to American Freedom. And I omitted none of those exertions, the fatal Circumstances, We hitherto laboured under, would allow me to use, with the assistance of some Friends, who agreed with me in this point, to make those principles known among our Countrymen, and to render the same acceptable to them. In which our efforts have not been fruitless.[5]

3. Nicholas Hubbard, an Englishman, had served as a clerk with Willink and Van Staphorst before becoming a member of the firm.

4. Wilhem and Jan Willink.

5. See Willink, Van Staphorst, and Hubbard to H, July 1, 1794. When it appeared likely in the fall of 1794 that the French armies would take Amsterdam in the absence of concerted opposition by the Allies, the Stadtholder was faced with two choices: to open the dykes and flood the city or to permit the soldiers of the Allies to prepare a defense of Amsterdam. On October 14, 1794, spokesmen of the Patriotic Party, which had been quiescent since the abortive revolution of 1787 but which had recently revived, presented a petition to the Stadtholder requesting that the dykes not be opened and that foreign soldiers not be admitted to the city. Since the Patriotic Party was widely considered to be pro-French, the Stadtholder moved quickly against the leaders, one of whom was Nicholaas Van Staphorst. Nicholas Hubbard described the results in a letter to William Short: "It is with great chagrin that I have to Inform you that the Persons who lately presented a request to the Magistracy of this City, having been summoned to answer for their Conduct, Six or Seven of them appeared and have been committed to Prison. My partner Mr. Nics. Van Staphorst had good Information of the Fate that awaited his Colleagues in this Business, and therefore has left the Country. Thus the management of the House devolves solely upon me. How long it may last so is very uncertain as a sentence of Banishment will issue against him. . ." (Hubbard to Short, November 7, 1794 [ALS, Short Family Papers, Library of Congress]). The attempts of the Stadtholder to defend the city proved fruitless, and on January 20, 1795, French troops entered Amsterdam (see John Quincy Adams to Edmund Randolph, January 19–20, 1795 [LC, Adams Family Papers, deposited in the Massachusetts Historical Society, Boston]). Even before the return of the French, the Patriotic Party had become too powerful for the Stadtholder to enforce his decrees of banishment, and on January 7, 1795, Hubbard informed Short that Nicholaas Van Staphorst had returned to Amsterdam and that Jacob Van Staphorst was expected shortly from Paris (ALS, Short Family Papers, Library of Congress).

This labour has given me more insight in politics, and enables me to impart to you better information, or at least with more intimate Conviction and upon good grounds, of the actual Situation of our Country and of what you may expect from us in your Character.

The French are upon our frontiers, and even in the territory of the generality on the left Bank of the Mase.[6]

The Dutch army is so far reduced, that they would not be able to draw five thousand Men into the field, besides the garrisons, of the frontier places not yet conquered, and those of the interior Cities, where they cannot oppose the Enemy, and are solely employed in supporting the Authority of our Aristocratic Government.

The English Army under the Duke of York, is indeed not quite ruined, and if well employed, might still hinder the French very much in crossing the Rivers. But it is so deficient in point of Courage and Discipline, as to spoil and plunder those it was sent to protect. There is no doubt but it will set to flight at the first serious attempt the French may make upon it.

Of the dear purchased Sixty two thousand Prussian troops, who were chiefly intended to defend this Country, not a single man came in it.

The Austrian Army at the Mase has been of late so completely beaten, as to be in full retreat towards the Rhine, and wishes most ardently to enjoy some repose on the other side of that River.

Such Sir, is our present situation abroad. At home, a general discontent prevails, and the people are prepared for an insurrection: which I dare say, will break out as soon as the French will have crossed the Rivers in any point.

As this may be shortly looked for, you may likewise expect to hear by the first accounts from hence, that the Revolution will have been effected: that We will thereby be very narrowly connected with France; that their Friends will have become our Friends, and their Enemies our Enemies. I am sanguine, the Revolution itself may be compleated without great Struggle, or the shedding of much blood. But the consequences it will have on the situation of this Country, and it's inhabitants, will be most important, especially in point of the means of subsistance and the fortunes of the rich people.

6. Maas or Meuse River, which flows into the North Sea.

We are to meet the public finances in the most shocking condition, and loaded with enormous Debts. For this We shall have to make provision, and to circumscribe our expenditure in proportion to the revenue. The revenue system itself must be established on a different principle. The plain citizen, the industrious tradesman, the husbandman, and in general the lower class of Citizens must be releaved from the burthensome taxes, and on the contrary the wealthy and rich must be more charged in proportion to their income. This will of course occasion a considerable reduction in the surplus they annually invested in New Loans.

It is not quite unprobable that some Powers, as Austria and Russia, seeing they are to expect no more assistance from the Dutch, will pay no further interest, and be unable to redeem the Capital.

Freedom will I hope be attended here with the same consequences as in America, it will prove an incitement to Industry and Activity, and offer an opening for employing Funds to advantages, that are now invested in Foreign Loans.

These are considerations that make me apprehend that in the period now to come, hardly any foreign negotiation will be practicable.

It is true, that if any thing in that Line will be possible, it will be for America. But in my opinion it would be imprudent to calculate upon it, at least for the next year. Of consequence I fear that it will be impossible to do any thing towards the execution of your late Order for the Treaty with Algiers.[7] On the contrary I think You may be under the necessity of making provision for the whole amount of Interest and reimbursmt. falling due in 1795, over and above the Balance that will remain due to the United States. I will be happy if in this respect, things turn out the reverse from what I think they will. But I conceived it my duty rather to give you this circumstantial communication, and considering the possibility of a different issue. If I was allowed to give you an advice, it would be to direct Mr Adams[8] or any body else, at all times to watch the favorable opportunities, and to avail the United States thereof; for such sums of Money as their service may require, with such stipulations of Interest and Charges as you think proper.

7. See H to Willink, Van Staphorst, and Hubbard, July 7, 1794.
8. John Quincy Adams, United States Minister Resident at The Hague.

For want of a similar precaution, it may happen that some propitious moment may slip by unimproved, through the delay of writing to and from America.

When the Revolution I expect to take place shortly, will have happened, my further addressing you in private will be needless. I shall then no more fear to suppeditate such Ideas as will from time, to time appear to me, proper to be inserted in our Letters to You.

I have only to add, that I dare boldly assure You, that no manner of danger attends the moneys belonging to the United States in the hands of Messrs Willinks and my house by what will happen: and further that I remain with great esteem

Sir! Your most obedient servant Nics: van Staphorst.

Alexr. Hamilton Esqr, Secreta. of the Treasury U.S.

From Alexander J. Dallas [1]

[Carlisle, Pennsylvania, October 6, 1794]

Sir

I have the honor to transmit, for the perusal of the President, the original papers received by Mr Laing,[2] from the County of Fayette, and a copy of the answer, which was sent by the Governors directions.[3]

Carlysle
6 Octr: 94
To Alexr Hamilton Esq

ADf, Division of Public Records, Pennsylvania Historical and Museum Commission, Harrisburg; LC, Division of Public Records, Pennsylvania Historical and Museum Commission, Harrisburg.

1. For background to this letter, see H and Henry Knox to George Washington, August 5, 1794, note 3; William Bradford to H, August 23, 1794; "Minutes of a Meeting Concerning the Insurrection in Western Pennsylvania," August 24, 1794.

2. James Lang of Fayette County, Pennsylvania, was one of the committee of conference appointed on August 14, 1794, by the insurgents in western Pennsylvania to confer with the commissioners of the United States. Like the other members of the committee, he supported submission to the excise laws.

3. The papers enclosed in this letter are described as follows in the "Executive Minutes of Governor Thomas Mifflin" for October 6, 1794: "The original papers received by Mr. James Lang from the County of Fayette, containing

the submission of some of the People of that County to the laws of the United States; with a copy of the answer thereto which was sent by the Governor's direction—were this day transmitted to Alexander Hamilton esquire, for the perusal of the President of the United States" (*Pennsylvania Archives,* 9th ser., II, 882).

For a copy of the submission of the people of Fayette County, which included the "Resolves at Uniontown," see Albert Gallatin to Mifflin, September 17, 1794 (*Pennsylvania Archives,* 2nd ser., IV, 316–20). See also "Declarations of David Bradford and Others," September 13, 1794 (*Pennsylvania Archives,* 2nd ser., IV, 297–99). For Mifflin's answer to Lang, see Dallas to Gallatin, September 26, 1794 (*Pennsylvania Archives,* 2nd ser., IV, 368–69).

To Edmund Randolph

[*Carlisle, Pennsylvania, October 6, 1794.* On October 8, 1794, Randolph wrote to William Rawle: "The Secretary of State . . . has the honor to communicate . . . the following Extract of a letter of the 6th instant [1] this moment received from the Secretary of the Treasury. . . ." [2] *Letter not found.*]

LC, RG 59, Domestic Letters of the Department of State, Vol. 7, June 27–November 30, 1794, National Archives.

1. The extract reads as follows: "It is material that the District attorney [William Rawle] should come forward immediately; and further information shews that it is necessary the District Judge [Richard Peters] should also repair without delay to the army. You will make the requisite communications to those Gentlemen urging their departure" (LC, RG 59, Domestic Letters of the Department of State, Vol. 7, June 27–November 30, 1794, National Archives).

2. On October 8, 1794, Randolph wrote to George Washington: "I have the honor to acknowledge Colo Hamilton's letter of the 6th instant, written by your direction.

"Judge Peters and Mr. Rawle intend to proceed to-morrow. They will carry with them copies of all the subscriptions. Some of the names indeed are so badly written, that mistakes are inevitable. If therefore any individuals, whose names do not appear, or may be inaccurately transcribed, should claim the benefit, it may be perhaps right to indulge competent proof from some other source." (LC, RG 59, Domestic Letters of the Department of State, Vol. 7, June 27–November 30, 1794, National Archives.)

A "subscription paper" was a pledge made by volunteers to join in support of the militia to effect submission to the excise laws.

From Charles Wilkes [1]

[*New York, October 6, 1794.* On October 8, 1794, Oliver Wolcott, Jr., wrote to Wilkes: "I have had the pleasure to receive your Letter of the 6th Instant addressed to the Secretary of the Treasury. . . ." [2] *Letter not found.*]

1. Wilkes was cashier of the Bank of New York.
For background to this letter, see H to Gulian Verplanck, September 28, 1794.
2. LS, Hamilton Papers, Library of Congress.

From Tench Coxe

Treasury Department, Revenue Office, October 7, 1794. Requests "that a remittance of three thousand Dollars may be made to . . . Mr. Terence Reiley on a/count of the contract for clothing made with him." [1]

LC, RG 75, Letters of Tench Coxe, Commissioner of the Revenue, Relating to the Procurement of Military, Naval, and Indian Supplies, National Archives.
1. On October 9, 1794, Warrant No. 4141 for three thousand dollars was issued to Reilay (D, RG 217, Miscellaneous Treasury Accounts, 1790–1894, Account No. 7030, National Archives). Reilay was a New York City hatter.

To Samuel Hodgdon

Carlisle [Pennsylvania] October 7. 1794

Sir

It is with distress I find that the troops are every where a head of their supplies. Not a shoe, blanket or ounce of ammunition destined for this place is yet arrived—except what Mr. Wright [1] conductor for the Pensylvania division brought on with him. I begin to fear infidelity in some of your conductors of Waggons. For Heaven sake send forward a man that can be depended upon on each route to hasten them on. My expectations have been egregiously disappointed.

With consideration & esteem I am sir Your obed ser

A Hamilton

Samuel Hodgsdon Esq

ALS, Broadcast Music, Inc., New York City.
1. John Wright. See John Scull to Isaac Craig, July 1, 1792 (Neville B. Craig, *The History of Pittsburgh with a Brief Notice of Its Facilities of Communication and Other Advantages for Commercial and Manufacturing Purposes* [Pittsburgh, 1917], 201–02).

To Samuel Hodgdon

Carlisle [Pennsylvania] October 7. 1794

Sir

I wrote you this Morning by post, mentioning the tardiness of the waggons with Stores. I just learn that one or two are arrived which were part of the brigade with ⟨–⟩ of which the part destined for Fort Cumberland had previously past. The rifles have also arrived from Lancaster & are gone on.

The bearer tells me there is no chain of expresses established to this place but that he came the whole way from Philadelphia. The President wishes the plan may be changed & expresses established at convenient distances to this place from which they will be continued to Bedford. You will inform me of the station. With consideration & esteem

yr Obed ser A Hamilton

S Hodgsdon Esq

ALS, The State Historical Society of Wisconsin, Madison.

From Joseph Whipple[1]

Portsmouth [*New Hampshire*] *October 7, 1794.* "I enclose you a Statement of Payments on Account of the Fortifications[2] for the harbour of Portsmouth (to the 4th. instant), amounting to Dolls 2229 24/100 dollars. The estimated amount of the expence of compleating the Work directed . . . is 348 dollars. . . ."

LC, RG 36, Collector of Customs at Portsmouth, Letters Sent, 1793–1794, Vol. 5, National Archives; copy, RG 56, Letters from the Collector at Portsmouth, National Archives.

1. Whipple was collector of customs at Portsmouth, New Hampshire.

2. For information concerning the fortifications, see Henry Knox to H, March 29, 1794; "Treasury Department Circular to the Collectors of Customs," April 3–June 4, 1794.

To Oliver Wolcott, Junior

[*Carlisle, Pennsylvania, October 7, 1794.* On October 11, 1794, Wolcott wrote to Hamilton: "I have recd. your favour dated 7: & 8: inst." *Letter of October 7 not found.*]

From Tench Coxe[1]

T: D: R: O: October 8th 1794

Sir,

I have the honor to enclose to you the eight following contracts. Vizt.

1. Mathew Spillard for the supply of Rations at Philada. fm. 1st April 1794[2]
2. John Tinsley for 5000 Cartridge Boxes[3]
3. Samuel Hughes of Maryland for Cannon.[4]
5. James Byers of Massachusts. for ten Brass Howitz.[5]
6. Paul Revere of Ditto for ten Ditto.[6]
7. John J. Feach & Co. of N. Jersey for Cannon Ball & Iron ballast[7]
8. Copy of an Agreemt. of commutation with G & J: Gilberts to furnish Artillery Coats dated July 28th 1794[8]
9. Contract with Joel Gibbs of N. Jersey for 768 Artillery Hats[9]

And to be with great respect Sir your mo. Obt. Servant

T. Coxe C: R:

The Secy. of the Treasy.

LC, RG 75, Letters of Tench Coxe, Commissioner of the Revenue, Relating to the Procurement of Military, Naval, and Indian Supplies, National Archives.

1. For background to this letter, see Henry Knox to H, March 29, April 21, 1794; Coxe to H, April 4, 1794.
2. See Coxe to H, May 8, July 24, 1794.
3. See Coxe to H, June 27, July 19, 1794.
4. See Coxe to H, third letter of June 30, 1794, note 2.
5. Byers was a resident of Springfield, Massachusetts. His contract with Coxe for casting "ten brass Eight Inch Howitzers" is dated July 23, 1794 (D, RG 217, Miscellaneous Treasury Accounts, 1790–1894, Account No. 7380, National Archives). A draft of the contract between Coxe and Byers may be found in RG 58, Records of the Bureau of Internal Revenue, General Records, 1791–1803, National Archives.
6. See Coxe to H, August 6, 1794.
7. See Coxe to H, August 1, 1794.
8. See Coxe to H, July 21, 1794.
9. See Coxe to H, September 30, 1794.

From Tench Coxe

Treasury Department, Revenue Office, October 8, 1794. Requests "a remittance to John S. Dexter Esqr. Supervisor of Rd. Island, for the purpose of making a payment of eight thousand Dollars to

Brown & Francis & others owners of the Furnace Hope,[1] on account of a contract for supplying cannon for the Frigates and Fortifications."

LC, RG 75, Letters of Tench Coxe, Commissioner of the Revenue, Relating to the Procurement of Military, Naval, and Indian Supplies, National Archives.

1. See Coxe to H, June 27, second letter of August 9, 1794.

From Henry Knox

Philadelphia 8 Oct 1794

My dear Sir

Your exertions in my department during my absence will never be obliterated.[1] I regret my long stay. If things shall be so serious as to require the President to go forward, I hope I may be indulged in joining him. I have not seen Mr. Jays dispatches.

I am yours affectionately H Knox

Colo Hamilton

ALS, Massachusetts Historical Society, Boston.

1. Knox had left Philadelphia for Maine in August because of adverse news regarding his financial affairs and landholdings in Maine. See George Washington to H, August 12, 1794, note 1.

To Henry Knox

Carlisle [Pennsylvania] October 8, 1794

My Dear General

Hodgsdon[1] is a worthy man but between us incompetent to a great operation. It is impossible in my judgment that transportation should be so difficult to procure as he makes it. The troops are every where a head of their supplies.

Before I left Town I directed some Cloathing to be forwarded.[2] Not an iota of them has arrived or that I can find had been sent so late as the 6th & some of the Militia must remain from nakedness. He seems to me to content himself with waiting for the waggons that come to look for him without sending in quest of them. If Pensylvania Waggons were scarce Jersey ones might have been had to bring on the supplies destined for this place. For Gods sake My Dear Sir see to the affair. Let some cloathing come forward—

I mean coats or Jackets & Overalls & some shirts. They are in store & there can be no good excuse for the delay. One half the blankets directed may be retained, For there is not so great a want of this article as was expected.

Adieu God bless you A Hamilton

P. The waggons go now at the rate only of 15 Miles a day. I have some destined from this place go at the rate of 20 by promising an extra compensation proportioned to their celerity.[3]

General Knox

ALS, Blumhaven Library and Gallery, Philadelphia.

1. Samuel Hodgdon. See H. to Hodgdon, October 7, 1794.

2. See H to Hodgdon, September 30, 1794.

3. H addressed this letter as follows: "The Secretary at War if not arrived to be opened by O Wolcott Esq." See Wolcott to H, October 2, 1794, note 7.

To Oliver Wolcott, Junior

[*Carlisle, Pennsylvania, October 8, 1794.* On October 11, 1794, Wolcott wrote to Hamilton: "I have recd. your favour dated 7: & 8: inst." *Letter of October 8 not found.*]

To Ephraim Blaine[1]

Carlisle [Pennsylvania] October 9. 1794

Sir

You have herewith a letter of credit upon Mr. Dallas for three or four thousand Dollars.[2] Of these you will advance to the Governor of New Jersey two thousand Dollars for which you will take his receipt.[3] The residue will be for your use, except what may be necessary to pay for about Twenty dozen pair of Stockings which Mr. Gamble[4] has been directed to procure & for which he will give orders upon you.

With consideration & esteem I am Sir Your obedt Servant

A Hamilton

Col. E Blaine

ALS, Ephraim Blaine Papers, Library of Congress; ADf, Connecticut Historical Society, Hartford.

1. For background to this letter, see H to Blaine, September 12, 1794.

2. See H to Alexander J. Dallas, October 9, 1794.

3. Blaine's account with the United States for his services during the Whiskey Insurrection, which contains this transaction with Richard Howell, may be found in RG 217, Miscellaneous Treasury Accounts, 1790–1894, Account No. 11475, National Archives.

4. James Gamble of Pennsylvania had been deputy commissioner of military stores during the American Revolution. On June 2, 1794, he had been appointed a captain in the United States corps of artillerists and engineers.

To Alexander J. Dallas

Carlisle [*Pennsylvania*] *October 9, 1794.* "I request that you will advance to Col Blaine[1] the sum which you mentioned to me. If it can without inconvenience be extended to four thousand the accommodation will be the greater." [2]

ADf, Connecticut Historical Society, Hartford.

1. See H to Ephraim Blaine, October 9, 1794.

2. On the back of this letter H wrote: "These letters explain the nature of an advance by Mr. Dallas as Pay Master of the Pensylvania Militia & which will constitute a charge against the UStates in favour of Pensa. & against the parties who received the money in favour of the U.S." "These letters" is a reference to the letter to Dallas printed above and H to Ephraim Blaine, October 9, 1794.

To Ephraim Blaine

Carlisle [Pennsylvania] October 10. 1794

Sir

Inclosed is an account which has been presented to me in order that provision might be made for the payment the whole amounts to seventeen pounds 13 Shillings & 6 pence. It is represented as relating altogether to sick persons of the New Jersey line. I have desired the surgeon[1] to refer the persons to you. When they apply you will desire them to present their accounts which you will please to pay. But you will have the items of the accounts examined & if there are any for any other object than the board & subsistence of sick soldiers you will please to note them & forward me an abstract of such items. You will please to understand that you are in no case to exceed the sum stated in the inclosed list.

With consideration & esteem I am Sir Your obed serv

A Hamilton

Col E Blaine

ALS, Ephraim Blaine Papers, Library of Congress.

1. Robert Welford, who was a physician in Fredericksburg, Virginia, served as surgeon general during the Whiskey Insurrection.

From Tench Coxe

Treasury Department, Revenue Office, October 10, 1794. "The Advertiset. for the military supply of Clothing for 1795 was predicated upon that from yr. office for 1794, there being at the time no regular requisition from you for the purchase. It is observed now, that no blankets were included in the advert. from this office. The contract being about to be closed it is wished to know what has been the mode by wh. the Blankets for 1794 were supplied. . . ."

LC, RG 75, Letters of Tench Coxe, Commissioner of the Revenue, Relating to the Procurement of Military, Naval, and Indian Supplies, National Archives.

To Elizabeth Hamilton

Carlisle [Pennsylvania] Oct 10 1794

My Loved Eliza

Tomorrow we leave this for Fort Cumberland. We are very strong & the Insurgents are all submissive so that you may be perfectly tranquil. My health thank God is excellent. But I have heared from you only once.[1] You must continue to write to this place sending your letters to General Knox to forward to me. God bless you & my dear Children.

Yr. ever affect A H

Mrs. Hamilton

ALS, Mr. George T. Bowdoin, New York City.

1. Letter not found.

To Jared Ingersoll

Carlisle [Pennsylvania] October 10th. 1794

Sir

The President directs me in reply to your letter of this day[1] to observe that nothing can be more proper than that the party by whom the homicide[2] was done should be placed under the disposition of the civil Magistrate. It is only desireable that this course may be so conducted as to satisfy reasonably all the considerations which are connected with the case. It is understood that Judge Yates of the Supreme Court of Pensylvania is now on the spot;[3] and it is not doubted that he will treat the subject according to its true merits and the real nature of the circumstances.[4]

The proper step will be taken to cause the party to be surrendered to that Magistrate.

With great consideration & esteem I am Sir Your obed servant

Alex Hamilton

Jared Ingersoll Esquire
Atty. General of Pensylvania

ALS, Charles Robert Autograph Collection of the Haverford College Library, Haverford, Pennsylvania.

1. No letter from Ingersoll to either George Washington or H has been found.

2. This is a reference to one of two homicides by members of the forces marching against the insurgents in western Pennsylvania. William Findley describes these homicides as follows: "Two men had been killed, one on the great road near Lebanon, and the other at a house in the neighborhood of Carlisle. The one in the road was killed by the Jersey troops. He provoked an officer by foolish and insulting language, and on laying hold on one of the bayonets of the guard, who were ordered to arrest him, he was run through the body. He was evidently drunk or deranged. Surely so many men in arms could easily have secured one unarmed fool, without killing him. The other was killed by a light horseman from Philadelphia, who went into the country to seize some persons who had asisted at erecting liberty poles in Carlisle. The young man, who was killed, was not only innocent, but very unwell. The party left him under guard of one of their number, until they would search the barn for others. The sick boy declaring his innocence, and that he was not able to stand, attempted to go into the house without leave; the light horseman ordered him to stop, on the peril of being shot, and if he could not stand to sit or lay down, and in the mean time cocked his pistol. When the boy was in the posture of laying himself down, and the light horseman about to uncock his pistol, it went off and shot the boy mortally. I state this case, as I had it from the best authority, and as taken from the examination of the light horseman" (Findley, *History of the Insurrection*, 143–44).

The first of these homicides was described somewhat differently by a volunteer in the New Jersey militia, who wrote as follows from Carlisle on October 4, 1794: ". . . One man at a little Dutch village, called Myer's-Town, between Lebanon and Reading, behaved so imprudently, in a tavern where some of our officers had stopped, as to huzza for the Whiskey Boys, and utter many other indecent and seditious expressions. Our officers desired him to go about his business; but he still persisted, till he was ordered to be taken under guard—he swore that he would not leave the room till he had drank his liquor—the guard insisted; and one of them seized him and attempted to bring him forward, but the fellow instantly caught hold of the soldier's bayonet and used every effort to wrest it from him. A contest ensued, in which our soldier stabbed him in such a manner that he expired in the course of half an hour . . ." ([Philadelphia] *Dunlap and Claypoole's American Daily Advertiser*, October 17, 1794).

Depositions of several witnesses to this homicide, sworn to before Judge Jasper Yeates of the Supreme Court of Pennsylvania, may be found in the Historical Society of Pennsylvania, Philadelphia.

The second of these homicides is described as follows by a soldier, writing from the "Camp, near Carlisle" on September 30, 1794: ". . . Nothing material has occurred, except that yesterday a detachment of twenty horse (of which I was one) under adjutant Jacob Cox, was dispatched with a constable at their head, to take several of those who are here called Whiskey Boys—Two were, but some others, having notice of our approach, escaped. One of the dragoons' pistols went off by accident, and shot a man in the groin, of which he since died: he was brother to one of the persons we were in pursuit of, and during a parley at a farmhouse the accident happened. . ." ([Philadelphia] *Gazette of the United States and Daily Evening Advertiser*, October 4, 1794).

3. Yeates was in Carlisle ". . . for the purpose of enquiring into the two homicides which have lately happened. This was done at the desire of the President, who it is said, expressed his determined resolution, that the army, while called out to support the laws should not, with impunity, do any injury to individuals" ([Philadelphia] *General Advertiser*, October 27, 1794).

4. The results fell somewhat short of H's anticipation, for an unnamed correspondent wrote: "I understand that on a strict and full investigation one of the cases appears to be the result of mere accident and that the other homicide was perfectly justifiable, being occasioned in a struggle between the deceased and one of the Jersey militia, who was opposed and assaulted by him in the regular execution of his duty. Judge Yeates, however, thought proper to take recognizances in small sums for the appearance of both persons at court, where they will, no doubt, be regularly discharged . . ." ([Philadelphia] *General Advertiser*, October 27, 1794).

To Thomas Mifflin

Carlisle [Pennsylvania] October 10. 1794.

Sir,

The President thinks he ought not to leave this place without a formal expression of the very poignant regret he has felt at the unfortunate accidents which happened in two instances [1] previous to his arrival at this place, having occasioned the death of two persons, and of his extreme solicitude that all possible pains may be taken to avoid in future not only accidents of a similar kind but all unauthorised acts of injury to the persons or property of the inhabitants of the Country through which the army may march.[2] It is a very precious & important idea, that those who are called out in support & defence of the Laws, should not give occasion, or even pretext to impute to them infractions of the laws. They cannot render a more important service to the cause of Government & order, than by a conduct scrupulously regardful of the rights of their fellow Citizens and exemplary for decorum, regularity & moderation. The vindication of the just authority of the laws, by effectual yet legal means, will not be neglected; but all good Citizens must unite in the wish that none other may be employed.

The President is not unaware of the circumstances of justification or excuse which have attended the accidents to which an allusion has been had. They afford him indeed much consolation. Yet as it is always important to cultivate the confidence & affections of the Citizens at large, & as it is frequently very difficult to cause circumstances which justify or excuse to be properly & generally understood, it is desirable that there should be an increased vigilance and caution to avoid any thing that may require explanation.

These observations & sentiments I have the honor to communicate by the special direction of the President.

It has also been mentioned to him that among various false reports in circulation, contrived no doubt to check the zeal of the Militia for the service they are to perform, it is given out that the real ultimate intention is to employ them against the British posts or against the Savages; he therefore desires me to authorise & instruct you to declare in his name to the troops, that no such intention has been or is entertained—that the sole object of their march was & is the suppression of the insurrection which exists in the western Counties in this State, & that their continuance in service will not be protracted a moment longer than is essential to this object.

In consideration of the difficulty of supplying with exactness certain small articles which enter into the composition of the ration, owing to the extent of the demand & the shortness of the time to provide, I have the President's permission to inform you that whenever the state of supply will admit of it, there will be added to each ration of beef issued a quarter of a pound.

With great respect & esteem I have the honor to be Sir Your Obedt. Servt. Alexander Hamilton

His Excely.
Governor Mifflin

LS, The Philip H. and A. S. W. Rosenbach Foundation, Phialdelphia; ADf, Connecticut Historical Society, Hartford.

1. This is a reference to two homicides committed by members of the forces

marching against the insurgents in western Pennsylvania. See H to Jared Ingersoll, October 10, 1794, note 2.

2. See H to Ingersoll, October 10, 1794, note 3.

To Ephraim Blaine

Carlisle [Pennsylvania] October 11 1794

Sir

There are in the store at this place under the care of Capt Gamble [1] or Mr. Parker [2] sundry Quarter Master's articles as Campkettles Knapsacks Canteens &c. which you will please to take under your direction and leaving a small supply here for accidental calls (the most of the troops being now up) You will cause the Residue to be forwarded to Bedford *without delay*. The same must be done with any of the like articles which may hereafter arrive. They will probably come addressed to Mr. Parker who is directed to report to You or Your Agent—But for fear of neglect it will be well for daily inquiries to be made of Mr. Parker.

I am with great esteem Sir Your obed ser A Hamilton

I hope for all possible dispatch in hastening forward the supply.

Col E Blaine

ALS, Hamilton Papers, Library of Congress.

1. James Gamble. See H to Blaine, October 9, 1794.

2. Richard Parker, keeper of public stores at Carlisle, was an agent for Samuel Hodgdon. See H to Hodgdon, September 14, 1794, and H to Henry Miller, September 15, 1794.

George Washington to Edmund Randolph

[*Carlisle, Pennsylvania, October 11, 1794.* On October 14, 1794, Randolph wrote to Washington: "At eight o'clock last night I was honored by Colo. Hamilton's public letter [1] of the 11th instant." [2] *Letter not found.*]

1. Although Randolph refers to "Colo. Hamilton's public letter," in actuality the letter in question was written by H for Washington. On October 11, 1794, Washington wrote a private letter to Randolph, which reads in part as follows: ". . . I had scarcely dispatched my letter to you yesterday, when the Commissioners of deputies (Findley and Redick) from the Insurgent Counties arrived. My Public letter, written by Colo. Hamilton will inform you of the result. I

believe they are scared" (ALS, letterpress copy, George Washington Papers, Library of Congress).

William Findley, who had emigrated from Ireland to America before the American Revolution, had served in the Pennsylvania legislature during the Confederation period. A "Constitutionalist" in state politics and an Antifederalist in national politics, he followed the political views most prevalent in western Pennsylvania. He had been an outspoken opponent of the excise laws. From 1791 to 1799 he was a member of Congress. In 1796 Findley wrote a history of the Whiskey Insurrection. See H to Washington, August 5, 1794, note 1.

David Redick, like Findley an emigrant from Ireland, was prominent in Pennsylvania state politics during the Confederation period. In 1791 he was appointed prothonotary of Washington County, and in 1792 he became clerk of the courts. On October 2, 1794, Findley and Redick were appointed at the second Parkinson's Ferry meeting to present to Washington and Thomas Mifflin resolutions declaring the general willingness of the people to submit to the laws of the United States (*Pennsylvania Archives,* 2nd ser., IV, 389).

Washington wrote about the meeting with Findley and Redick in his diary for October 9, 1794, as follows: ". . . William Findley and David Redick deputed by the Committee of safety (as it is dissignated) which met on the 2d of this month at Parkinson Ferry arrived in Camp with the Resolutions of the said Committee;—and to give information of the State of things in the four Western Counties of Pennsylvania to wit Washington, Fayette Wesd and Allegany in order to see if it would prevent the March of the Army into them.

"At 10 oclock I had a meeting with these persons in presence of Govr. [Richard] Howell (of New Jersey) the Secretary of the Treasury, Colo. Hamilton, and Mr. [Bartholomew] Dandridge: Govr. [Thomas] Mifflin was invited to be present, but excused himself on acct. of business.

"I told the Deputies that by one of the Resolutions it would appear that they were empowered to give information of the disposition and of the existing state of matters in the four Counties abovemend: that I was ready to hear and would listen patiently, and with candour to what they had to say.

"Mr. Findley began . . . viz—That the People in the parts where he was best acquainted, had seen there folly, and he believed were disposed to submit to the Laws; that he thought, but could not undertake to be responsible, for the reestablishment of the public Offices for the collection of the Taxes of distilled spirits and Stills—intimating however, that it might be best for *the present,* and until the peoples minds were a little more tranquilized, to hold the Office of Inspection at Pitsburgh under the protection—or at least under the influence of the Garrison;—That he thought the Distillers would either enter their stills or would put them down; That the Civilian authority was beginning to recover its tone; and enumerated some instances of it;—That the ignorance and general want of information among the people far exceeded any thing he had any conception of; That it was not merely the excise law their opposition was aimed at, but to all law, and Government;—and to the Officers of Government;—and that the situation in which he had been, and the life he had led for sometime, was such, that rather than go through it again, he would prefer quitting this scene altogether.

"Mr Redicks information was similar to the above. . . . He added, that for a long time after the riots commenced, and until lately, the distrust of one another was such, that even friends were affraid to communicate their sentiments to each other;—That by whispers this was brought about; and growing bolder as they became more communicative they found their strength, and that there was a general disposition not only to acquiesce under, but to support the Laws —and he gave some instances also of Magistrates enforcing them.

"He said the People of those Counties believed that the opposition to the Excise law—or at least that their dereliction to it, in every other part of the U. States was similar to their own, and that no Troops could be got to march against them for the purpose of coercion;—that every acct. until very lately, of Troops marching against them was disbelieved; and supposed to be fabricated tales of governmental men;—That now they had got alarmed;—That many were disposing of their property at an under rate, in order to leave the Country; and added (I think) that they wd. go to Detroit.—That no person of any consequence, except one, but what had availed themselves of the proffered amnesty; that those who were still in the opposition, and obnoxious to the laws, were men of little or no property, and cared but little where they resided;—That he did not believe there was the least intention in them to oppose the Army;—and that there was not three rounds of ammunition for them in all the Western Country.—He (and I think Mr. Findley also) was apprehensive that the resentments of the Army might be productive of treatment to some of those people that might be attended with disagreeable consequences; and on that account seemed to deprecate the March of it; declaring however, that it was their wish, if the people did not give proofs of unequivocal submission, that it might not stop short of its object.

"After hearing what both had to say, I briefly told them—That it had been the earnest wish of government. to bring the people of those counties to a sense of their duty, by mild, and lenient means;—That for the purpose of representing to their sober reflection the fatal consequences of such conduct Commissioners had been sent amongst them that they might be warned in time of what must follow, if they persevered in their opposition to the laws; but that coercion wou'd not be resorted to except in the dernier resort:—but, that the season of the year made it indispensible that preparation for it should keep pace with the propositions that had been made;—That it was unnecessary for me to enumerate the transactions of those people (as they related to the proceedings of government) forasmuch as they knew them as well as I did;—That the measure which they were now witness to the adoption of was not less painful than expensive—was inconvenient and distressing in every point of view;—but as I considered the support of the Laws as an object of the first magnitude, and the greatest part of the expence had already been incurred, that nothing short of the most unequivocal *proofs* of absolute submission should retard the March of the Army into the Western counties, in order to convince them that the government could, and would enforce obedience to the laws not suffering them to be insulted with impunity. . . .

". . . I assured them that every possible care should be taken to keep the Troops from offering them any insult or damage, and that those who always had been subordinate to the Laws and such as had availed themselves of the amnesty, should not be injured in their persons or property; and that the treatment of the rest would depend upon their own conduct. That the Army, unless opposed, did not mean to act as executioners, or bring offenders to a military Tribunal; but merely to aid the civil Magistrates, with whom offences would lye. . . ." (*GW Diaries*, IV, 212–16.)

2. ALS, RG 59, Miscellaneous Letters, 1790–1799, National Archives.

In his letter to Washington on October 14, 1794, Randolph also wrote: "I shall communicate without reserve the substance of it; as it is important, that the attempts to prove the nonexistence of the necessity for the further march of military force should be counteracted. The statement in that letter leaves no doubt on my mind that the execution of the laws would be at least problematical were military apprehension to be wholly withdrawn."

From Oliver Wolcott, Junior

Pha. Octr. 11. 1794.

Sir

I have recd. your favour dated the 7: & 8: inst: [1] & shall carefully attend to all your directions.

I find that owing to some neglect, your letter to the Bank of New York was not recd.[2] A duplicate which I transmitted produced a cordial & prompt compliance; [3] this accounts for a delay, which at one time I feared was owing to a reluctance to advance the sum requested.

It was not intended by me to intimate that Col: Nevil would act as Pay Master; [4] he was engaged to take charge of the remittances to Mr. Williams [5] & Genl Miller [6] & promised a compensation merely for that service.

The warrants for 90 M Drs for the pay of Genl Wayne's army,[7] have been issued & the notes made out. The Secretary of War will forward them to the army.

I have issued 50 M Drs. for the pay of the militia army, which will also be sent forward as soon as possible. The Cashier of the Bank [8] being indisposed, & a sum in *small notes* sufficient for the payment not being obtainable I fear some little delay. I have however advised the War dept. to attempt an exchange of the large notes of the Bank of the U:S: for small notes of the other banks this being the best thing that can be done under present circumstances & preferable to a remittance in specie.

I did not know that Mr. Gale [9] was in want of money or it would have been furnished. He has however lately recd. 40 M Drs. & I presume has suffered no inconvenience.

I have issued 10000 Drs. to Whelen & Miller [10] on a presing application from Elie Williams for the transport service dated the 1: instant.

It was not possible for me to judge whether the 25 M Drs. directed to be issued by you had been counted on, when Mr. Williams wrote. It may prevent mistakes & too great an expenditure if you adopt measures for combining the estimates for the provision dept. & Transport service into one view & requesting them to be addressed to you in person while you remain with the army.

I think that I may assure you that the means of the Treasury are adequate to any emergency that can be foreseen at present.

I am with perfect respect sir Yr. obt sert. O W Jn.

Hon: Alex Hamilton Esqr
at Head Quarters of the Army

Copy, Connecticut Historical Society, Hartford.

1. Letters not found.

2. H to Gulian Verplanck, September 28, 1794. See also H to Wolcott, September 29, 1794.

3. On October 6, 1794, the Bank of New York agreed to a loan of two hundred thousand dollars at five percent interest (Domett, *History of the Bank of New York*, 50). See also H to Verplanck, September 28, 1794, note 3.

4. Presley Neville. See Wolcott to H, October 2, 1794.

5. Elie Williams.

6. Henry Miller.

7. Under the command of Major General Anthony Wayne the Army had defeated the Indians at the Battle of Fallen Timbers on August 20, 1794.

8. John Kean, cashier of the Bank of the United States.

9. George Gale was supervisor of the revenue for the District of Maryland.

10. The firm of Israel Whelen and Joseph I. Miller.

From Tench Coxe[1]

Treasury Department, Revenue Office, October 13, 1794. Requests "that the sum of five thousd. dolls. be transmitted to Jacob Sheafe Esqr. Naval Agent at Portsmouth N. Hamp. the same being retained to this time on a/count of the late change of the Naval agency at that place." [2]

LC, RG 75, Letters of Tench Coxe, Commissioner of the Revenue, Relating to the Procurement of Military, Naval, and Indian Supplies, National Archives.

1. For background to this letter, see Henry Knox to H, April 21, June 25, third letter of July 9, 1794.

2. Sheafe became naval agent at Portsmouth after John Langdon had declined the appointment. See Knox to H, third letter of July 9, 1794.

On October 14, 1794, Warrant No. 4154 for five thousand dollars was issued to Sheafe (D, RG 217, Miscellaneous Treasury Accounts, 1790–1894, Account No. 6866, National Archives).

From Tench Coxe[1]

Treasury Department, Revenue Office, October 13, 1794. "I have the honor to request that a Wart. may be issued, to Jas. Seagrove Esqr.[2] for the balance of Money granted by Congress for the purpose of Fortifying the harbor of St. Mary's. Mr. Seagrove has already recd. one Thousd. Dolls. as I learn from him. . . ." [3]

LC, RG 75, Letters of Tench Coxe, Commissioner of the Revenue, Relating to the Procurement of Military, Naval, and Indian Supplies, National Archives.

1. For information concerning the fortifications, see Henry Knox to H, March 29, 1794.

2. James Seagrove was collector of customs at St. Mary's, Georgia, and inspector of the port at St. Mary's. He was also Indian agent to the Creeks.

3. On June 20, 1794, Warrant No. 3809 for one thousand dollars had been issued to Seagrove. On October 22, 1794, Warrant No. 4181 for $173.84 was issued to him (D, RG 217, Miscellaneous Treasury Accounts, 1790–1894, Account No. 8350, National Archives).

From John Fitzgerald[1]

[*Alexandria, Virginia, October 13, 1794.* On October 28, 1794, Oliver Wolcott, Jr., wrote to Fitzgerald: "Your letter of the 13th instant to the Secy of the Treasury has been rec'd in this office."[2] *Letter not found.*]

1. Fitzgerald was collector of customs at Alexandria, Virginia.

2. Wolcott's letter to Fitzgerald continues as follows: "It is deemed to be a clear principle that no person can become a 'Citizen of the United States' except in one of the modes prescribed by the act intitled 'An Act to establish a uniform rule of Naturalization'—consequently the gentleman whose case is stated by you cannot be regarded as legally qualified to become interested in Vessells of the U. States.

"The form of the Oath to which you refer was calculated to embrace the various modes by which the rights of Citizenship might be acquired, *previously* to the passing of the Act of Congress above recited, & not to sanction the opinion which it seems by your Letter some persons have maintained." (ADf, Connecticut Historical Society, Hartford.)

"An Act to establish an uniform Rule of Naturalization" provided "That any alien, being a free white person, who shall have resided within the limits and under the jurisdiction of the United States for the term of two years, may be admitted to become a citizen thereof, on application to any common law court of record, in any one of the states wherein he shall have resided for the term of one year at least, and making proof to the satisfaction of such court, that he is a person of good character, and taking the oath or affirmation prescribed by law, to support the constitution of the United States. . ." (1 *Stat.* 103–04 [March 26, 1790]).

Section 4 of "An Act concerning the registering and recording of ships or vessels" (1 *Stat.* 287–99 [December 31, 1792]) stated: "That in order to the registry of any ship or vessel, an oath or affirmation shall be taken and subscribed by the owner, or by one of the owners, . . . declaring . . . that he, she, or they, as the case may be . . . is or are citizens of the United States; and where an owner resides in a foreign country, in the capacity of a consul of the United States, or as an agent for, and a partner in, a house or co-partnership, consisting of citizens of the United States, and actually carrying on trade within the United States, that such is the case, and that there is no subject or citizen of any foreign prince or state . . . interested in such ship or vessel. . . ."

From Elizabeth Hamilton

[*Philadelphia, October 14, 1794.* On October 20, 1794, Hamilton wrote to his wife: "I thank you my beloved for your letter of the 14th." *Letter not found.*]

From Oliver Wolcott, Junior

Philadelphia, October 14, 1794. "Letters were yesterday recd. from our Bankers at Amsterdam dated July 1st. & 15th. and August 1st. & 18th. . . .[1] Mr. Willing[2] advised me some time since not to reduce the price of Excha. on Amsterdam—the bills however were not sold the last time I inquired. I shall make a further inquiry on the subject. I cannot be certain from an Examination of the statement made by Mr. Myer,[3] in your Office, that funds are retained for all the demands arising in Amsterdam. It may therefore be safest for you to inform me, whether I understand you right—*that all the sums recd. after June 1, 1794* may be drawn for."

ADf, Connecticut Historical Society, Hartford.

1. Willink, Van Staphorst, and Hubbard to H, July 1, 15, August 1, 18, 1794.
2. Thomas Willing was president of the Bank of the United States.
3. John Meyer was a clerk in the Treasury Department.

From Tench Coxe[1]

Treasury Department, Revenue Office, October 15, 1794. "It is the opinion of the Secy at War that provisions in advance amounting to 37,000 Drs must be forthwith laid in by the contractors for 1795. I have the honor to request an advance to them (Messrs. Scott & Ernest)[2] to that amount. . . . I have the honor to enclose a letter from the Secy. of War wh. having relation to advances of Provisions & consequently to advances of money it is proper that you should possess it."

LC, RG 75, Letters of Tench Coxe, Commissioner of the Revenue, Relating to the Procurement of Military, Naval, and Indian Supplies, National Archives.

1. For background to this letter, see H to Coxe, April 4, 1794.
2. Alexander Scott and Matthew Ernest were the contractors for provisions for the Army for 1794. Their contract is dated October 10, 1794 (copy, Isaac

Craig Papers, Carnegie Library of Pittsburgh, Pennsylvania). Their account with the United States may be found in RG 217, Miscellaneous Treasury Accounts, 1790–1894, Account No. 9812, National Archives.

From Tench Coxe[1]

Treasury Department, Revenue Office, October 15, 1794. The clothing contractors for the Service of 1795 [2] have requested of me to procure them an advance of 15 or 20,000 Dols. . . . I wish part of that sum to be advanced to them as may be convenient. The articles they are to supply will amount to about 120,000 Drs. in all."

LC, RG 75, Letters of Tench Coxe, Commissioner of the Revenue, Relating to the Procurement of Military, Naval, and Indian Supplies, National Archives.

1. For background to this letter, see H to Coxe, April 4, 1794.

2. Coxe's contract with Thomas Billington and Guy Bryan, merchant tailors in Philadelphia, for clothing for the Army for 1795 is dated October 15, 1794 (D, RG 217, Miscellaneous Treasury Accounts, 1790–1894, Account No. 7529, National Archives).

From Tench Coxe[1]

Treasury Department, Revenue Office, October 15, 1794. "It appears extremely probable that the supply of Whiskey for 1795 may require some share of your attention at Pittsburg.[2] Mr. Carrington [3] was authorized to procure the whole in consequence of the disorders which prevailed in the western parts of Pennsylvania. . . .[4] 75,000 rations are required this day by the Secy. at War to be deposited in advance at Fort Washington for the service of 1795 of which I have given Mr Carrington notice.[5] Messrs. Scott & Ernest are also required to furnish at the post 111.000 rations, & at Pittsburg 3600 rations for wh they have asked the amot: of 37,000 Drs. For this I have made application at your office.[6] Very great importations of bale goods are received & expected from G Britain; so that the clothing contractors [7] are much pleased, and do not expect to import much if any goods. . . ." [8]

LC, RG 75, Letters of Tench Coxe, Commissioner of the Revenue, Relating to the Procurement of Military, Naval, and Indian Supplies, National Archives.

1. Coxe was in charge of procuring military supplies. See H to Coxe, April 4, 1794.

2. H had left Philadelphia with George Washington on September 30, 1794, for western Pennsylvania. See H to Washington, September 24, 1794, note 2.

3. Edward Carrington, supervisor of the revenue for the District of Virginia.

4. For information concerning the Whiskey Insurrection, see "Deposition of Francis Mentges," August 1, 1794; H to Washington, August 5, 1794.

5. Coxe to Carrington, October 15, 1794 (LC, RG 75, Letters of Tench Coxe, Commissioner of the Revenue, Relating to the Procurement of Military, Naval, and Indian Supplies, National Archives).

6. See Coxe to H, first letter of October 15, 1794.

7. Thomas Billington and Guy Bryan. See Coxe to H, second letter of October 15, 1794.

8. On October 10, 1794, Billington and Bryan had informed Coxe that because of "the Uncertainty of a sufficient supply, of goods in the present market necessary for the Clothing," it would be necessary to import clothing for the Army (ALS, RG 59, Miscellaneous Letters, 1790–1799, National Archives).

To Thomas Mifflin

Fort Cumberland [Pennsylvania]
October 17. 1794

Sir

The President directs me to acknowlege the receipt of your letter of the 16th—enclosing one from Governor Howel.[1]

The Quarter-Master[2] & Commissary General[3] will leave this place early in the Morning for Bedford to endeavour to remedy any defects which may exist.

You observe that Col Blaine[4] has not been with the Column. I am sure I understood from him & I think I did from Col Biddle[5] that the latter had agreed to take charge of the column in his place to Bedford. As to Mr. Postlethwaite[6] I know not what can explain his absence.

The embarrassments which are experienced demonstrate the necessity of reducing the number of baggage waggons (which is so great as to defeat the operation) in order that the surplus ones may be applied to the objects of supply.

With great respect & esteem I have the honor to be Sir Your obed ser A Hamilton

PS Impress must be used where purchases are inadequate.

His Excelly Governor Mifflin

ALS, Charles Roberts Autograph Collection of the Haverford College Library, Haverford, Pennsylvania.

1. In his letter to George Washington of October 16, 1794, Mifflin wrote: ". . . The enclosed letter from Governor Howell, and my own experience, will not permit me any longer to be silent, upon the very great inattention which has been paid to the supplies of the Right Column of the army under my command, as well as in the Commissary as in the Quarter Master's department. . . .

the defects and disappointments to which I allude can only be imputed to a want of exertion in the proper Officers, and this is the more evident as neither Col. [Ephraim] Blaine, the Quarter Master Genl:, nor Mr [Samuel] Postlethwaite, the Commissary (both appointed by you) have hitherto attended the army, or sent any deputies who will assume any responsibility or appear to be competent to the duties of their departments" (LS, RG 59, Miscellaneous Letters, 1790–1799, National Archives).

The letter from Governor Richard Howell of New Jersey to Mifflin, dated October 15, 1794, reads in part as follows: "I think it my Duty to inform your Excellency that such Difficulties occur in my Route, as should be guarded against on your approach. . . . There are not waggons forward to Call in Necessaries, & I very much doubt any thing being procured in quantity at or near the next post, therefore empty waggons should be sent on, if you have not supernumerary Waggons with you, & if you have, they should advance immediately to draw in your Supplies" (ALS, RG 59, Miscellaneous Letters, 1790–1799, National Archives).

2. Henry Miller, acting quartermaster general of the militia army.

3. Samuel Hodgdon.

4. Ephraim Blaine. For Blaine's role in supplying the troops, see H to Blaine, September 12, 1794.

5. Clement Biddle was quartermaster general of Pennsylvania during the insurrection.

6. Samuel Postlethwaite was commissary of the militia army. During the American Revolution Postlethwaite had been in charge of guarding the stores at Carlisle, Pennsylvania, and had served as assistant deputy quartermaster from 1777 to 1782.

From Oliver Wolcott, Junior

Phila. Oct. 17th. 1794

Sir

I judge it proper to keep you apprised of every thing material which occurs in the department and therefore enclose you copies of two letters from the Secretary at war on which Mr. Coxe has requested that 37,000 dollars may be advanced to the Contractor for rations [1] and 15,000 or 20,000 dollars to the Contractor for cloathing [2] for the year 1795. As there is no special appropriation, it will be necessary to request informal advances of the Bank,[3] if the urgency of the demand shall require something to be done, before I can receive your opinion and advice.

I am embarrassed in determining what rate of exchange ought to be established for governing the sales of bills of exchange on Amsterdam. On inquiry of Mr. Simpson [4] I find, that by the last advices the current exchange between London and Amsterdam was 40 schgs 9 grts. ℔ £ Sterling. This estimating the par of exchange at 34 schs. 3 grts. would make the exchange against Amsterdam nearly 16 ℔ cent.

The exchange between London and Philadelphia is at this time at about 182½ and will probably fall, and this will operate against the sale of our bills on amsterdam as there will be few or no purchasers except with a view to remittances to London.

The events of the war are such that there is little prospect of a fall of exchange between Amsterdam & London or of a demand for remittances to Amsterdam from this Country. You are apprised of all the reasons which render it adviseable to command the funds here, and can judge how far it may be necessary to reduce the price to accomplish this object.

I shall receive the opinion of Mr. Willing [5] this day on this subject, and with his advice, I shall consent to sales at 40 cents and 5 mills ℔ guilder. If sales cannot be made at this rate, I shall wait for your special direction.

I am O:W:

Hon A. H. Esq

LS, Connecticut Historical Society, Hartford.

1. Alexander Scott and Matthew Ernest. See Tench Coxe to H, first and third letters of October 15, 1794.

2. Thomas Billington and Guy Bryan. See Coxe to H, second letter of October 15, 1794.

3. For a description of "informal advances," see "Report on Rules and Modes of Proceeding with Regard to the Collection, Keeping, and Disbursement of Public Moneys, and Accounting for the Same," March 4, 1794. See also note 20 to that report.

4. George Simpson, a teller in the Bank of the United States, in 1795 became cashier of the bank.

5. Thomas Willing, president of the Bank of the United States.

From Tench Coxe [1]

Treasury Department, Revenue Office, October 18, 1794. "I have the honor to inclose to you a letter from the Superv. of Maryland [2] on account of the pay of Genl. Smith's [3] Detachment. . . . I have sent a copy to the Secy. at War [4] and also because the agency of this office for the War Departmt. having been interfered with by some operations of other agents not made known to me, I am without the necessary knowledge of what has been done in order to determine now what ought to be done. I wish to be immediately informed of any thing wh. it may be useful or necessary for me to do. . . ."

LC, RG 75, Letters of Tench Coxe, Commissioner of the Revenue, Relating to the Procurement of Military, Naval, and Indian Supplies, National Archives.

1. For background to this letter, see H to Coxe, April 4, 1794.

2. George Gale was supervisor of the revenue for the District of Maryland.

3. Brigadier General Samuel Smith of the Maryland line.

4. On October 18, 1794, Coxe wrote to Henry Knox: "Mr. Coxe has the honor to inclose a copy of a letter . . . from Maryland. . . . The pay of the Troops . . . will of course meet all necessary attention from the War Department, the application concerning them to the Treasy. being obviously irregular.

"In regard to the reception of the Troops on their return, the secy. at War will be pleased to give it such share of his instructions as he may see proper; it will be attended to by Mr. Coxe also for which purpose, he is endeavouring to acquire a knowledge of what has been done in that respect in the course to the Rendezvous & from thence Westward. . . ." (LC, RG 75, Letters of Tench Coxe, Commissioner of the Revenue, Relating to the Procurement of Military, Naval, and Indian Supplies, National Archives.)

From Amos Marsh[1]

Bennington [*Vermont*] *October 18, 1794.* "Noah Smith Esquire has signified to me, that he has resigned the Office of Supervisor of this District.[2] Cephus Smith, Junr. Esquire of Rutland, wishes to obtain the appointment to that Office. He is a Gentleman of Education Integrity and ability. I can therefore recommend him as a person well qualified to discharge all the duties of a Supervisor. He is a reputable practitioner of Law, and is Thirty Three Years of Age." [3]

Copy, RG 58, General Records, 1791–1803, National Archives.

1. Marsh was United States attorney for the District of Vermont.

2. Noah Smith had been appointed supervisor of the revenue for the District of Vermont on March 4, 1791 (*Executive Journal*, I, 81, 82).

3. On November 24, 1794, the Senate approved the nomination of Nathaniel Brush as supervisor of the revenue for the District of Vermont (*Executive Journal*, I, 163, 164).

To Elizabeth Hamilton

Bedford [Pennsylvania] Oct 20 [1794]

I thank you my beloved for your letter of the 14th.[1] I am very sorry that some of my sweet angels have been again sick. You do not mention my precious John.[2] I hope he continues well.

The day after tomorrow I march with the army. Be assured that there is not the least appearance of opposition from the Insurgents &

that I shall take the greatest care of myself & I hope by the Middle of November to return. Have patience my love & think of me constantly as I do of you with the utmost tenderness.

Kisses & blessings without number to You & my Children

A Hamilton

Mrs. Hamilton

ALS, American Academy of Arts and Letters, on deposit in the Library of Congress.

1. Letter not found.

2. John Church Hamilton, H's fourth son.

From William Hill[1]

[*Wilmington, North Carolina, October 20, 1794.* On December 15, 1794, Oliver Wolcott, Jr., wrote to Hill: "Your favour of Oct. 20th. addressed to the Secretary of the Treasury, has been rec'd."[2] *Letter not found.*]

1. Hill was United States attorney for the District of North Carolina.

2. Wolcott's letter to Hill reads as follows: "Your favour of Oct. 20th. addressed to the Secretary of the Treasury, has been rec'd & I have the honour on his behalf to acknowledge it as an acceptable mark of your attention to the interests of the public. The subject will be brought under the view of Congress for further provision" (ADf, Connecticut Historical Society, Hartford).

To Henry Lee[1]

Bedford [Pennsylvania] 20th October 1794.[2]

Sir,

I have it in special instruction from the President of the United States,[3] now at this place, to convey to you on his behalf, the follow-

Copy, RG 46, Third Congress, 1793–1795, Messages from the President, Message of 19 November 1794, National Archives; ADf, Pickering Papers, Massachusetts Historical Society, Boston.

1. George Washington transmitted this letter to Congress in his message on November 19, 1794 (*Annals of Congress,* IV, 793).

The draft in the Massachusetts Historical Society is entitled "Minutes for Instructions to The Commanding General of the Militia on the march against the Western Insurgents—& to the Atty of the District & to the Supervisor of the Revenue for Pensylvania." No letters to William Rawle or to Henry Miller have been found.

Major differences between the draft and the copy have been noted.

2. In Hamilton, *History,* 106–17, this letter is dated October 30, 1794.

3. On October 20, 1794, Washington wrote in his diary: "Matters being thus arranged I wrote a farewell address to the Army through the Commander in Chief—Govr. Lee—to be published in orders—and having prepared his Instruc-

ing instructions for the general direction of your conduct in the command of the Militia army, with which you are charged.[4]

The objects for which the militia have been called forth are

1. To suppress the combinations [5] which exist in some of the western counties in Pennsylvania in opposition to the laws laying duties upon spirits distilled within the United States and upon Stills.

2. To cause the laws to be executed.

These objects are to be effected in two ways—

1. By military force.

2. By judiciary process, and other civil proceedings.

The objects of the military force are twofold.

1. To overcome any armed opposition which may exist.

2. To countenance and support the civil officers in the means of executing the laws.

With a view to the first of these two objects, you will proceed as speedily as may be, with the army under your command, into the insurgent counties to attack, and as far as shall be in your power subdue, all persons whom you may find in arms, in opposition to the laws above mentioned.[6] You will march your army in two columns, from the places where they are now assembled, by the most convenient routes, having regard to the nature of the roads, the convenience of supply, and the facility of co-operation and union; and bearing in mind, that you ought to act, till the contrary shall be fully develloped, on the general principle of having to contend with the whole force of the Counties of Fayette, Westmoreland, Washington and Alleghany, and of that part of Bedford which lies westward of the town of Bedford; and that you are to put as little as possible to hazard. The approximation, therefore, of your columns, is to be sought, and the subdivision of them, so as to place the parts

tions . . . I prepared for my return to Philadelphia. . ." (*GW Diaries*, IV, 222). For Washington's farewell address to the Army, see Washington to Henry Lee, October 20, 1794 (LC, George Washington Papers, Library of Congress), which Lee incorporated in his orders of October 21, 1794 (Baldwin, "Orders Issued by General Henry Lee," 90–94). Washington's instructions to Lee are in the letter H wrote to Lee on October 20, 1794, printed above.

4. This paragraph is not in the draft.

5. The remainder of this sentence is not in the draft. For the excise laws, see H to Washington, August 2, 1794, note 2.

6. In the draft H added the following words to this sentence: "with a caution to proceed in such manner as will leave as little as possible to hazard or casualty." The remainder of the paragraph does not appear in the draft.

out of mutual supporting distance, to be avoided as far as local circumstances will permit. Parkinson's Ferry appears to be a proper point, towards which to direct the march of the column for the purpose of ulterior measures.

When arrived within the insurgent Country, if an armed opposition appear, it may be proper to publish a proclamation, inviting all good citizens, friends of the Constitution and laws, to join the standard of the United States. If no armed opposition exist, it may still be proper to publish a proclamation, exhorting to a peaceable and dutiful demeanour, and giving assurances of performing, with good faith and liberality, whatsoever may have been promised by the Commissioners [7] to those who have complied with the conditions prescribed by them, and who have not forfeited their title by subsequent misconduct.

Of those persons in arms, if any, whom you may make prisoners; leaders, including all persons in command, are to be delivered up to the civil magistrate: the rest to be disarmed, admonished and sent home (except such as may have been particularly violent and also influential) causing their own recognizances for their good behaviour to be taken, in the cases in which it may be deemed expedient.

With a view to the second point, namely, "the countenance and support of the civil officers, in the means of executing the laws," you will make such dispositions as shall appear proper to countenance and protect, and, if necessary and required by them, to support and aid the civil officers in the execution of their respective duties; for bringing offenders and delinquents to justice; for seizing the stills of delinquent distillers, as far as the same shall be deemed eligible by the supervisor of the Revenue, or chief-officer of Inspection; and also for conveying to places of safe custody, such persons as may be apprehended and not admitted to bail.

The objects of judiciary process and other civil proceedings, will be,

7. This is a reference to the United States commissioners (Jasper Yeates, James Ross, and William Bradford) appointed by Washington to confer with representatives of the Pennsylvania insurgents. See H and Henry Knox to Washington, August 5, 1794, note 3. For the correspondence between the Federal commissioners and the insurgents, see *Pennsylvania Archives*, 2nd ser., IV, 182–237.

1. To bring offenders to Justice.

2. To enforce penalties on delinquent distillers by suit.

3. To enforce the penalty of forfeiture on the same persons by seizure of their stills and spirits.

The better to effect these purposes, the Judge of the District, Richard Peters Esquire, and the Attorney of the district, William Rawle Esquire, accompany the army.[8]

You are aware that the Judge cannot be controuled in his functions. But I count on his disposition to cooperate in such a general plan as shall appear to you consistent with the policy of the case. But your method of giving a direction to legal proceedings, according to your general plan, will be by instruction to the District Attorney.[9]

He ought particularly to be instructed, (with due regard to time and circumstance)—1st to procure to be arrested, all influential actors in riots and unlawful assemblies, relating to the insurrection, and combinations to resist the laws; or having for object to abet that insurrection, and those combinations; and who shall not have complied with the terms offered by the Commisioners;[10] or manifested their repentance in some other way, which you may deem satisfactory. 2dly. To cause process to issue for enforcing penalties on delinquent distillers.[11] 3d. To cause *offenders*, who may be arrested, to be conveyed to goals where there will be no danger of rescue: those for misdemeanors to the goals of York and Lancaster; those for capital offences to the goal of Philadelphia, as more secure than the others. 4th. To prosecute indictable offences in the Courts

8. This paragraph in the draft reads: "For these purposes, it is desireable that the Attorney of the district should accompany the army and that he should be instructed."

9. This paragraph does not appear in the draft.

10. At conferences between the United States commissioners and a committee of conference of the insurgents on August 28 and 29, 1794, the Federal commissioners offered amnesty to those who agreed to submit to the laws of the United States.

11. At this point in the draft the following paragraph appears: "As a guide to him it is desireable he should take with him as full information as can be obtained of offending individuals & the papers (or a competent abstract of them) which have been reported by the Com~ respecting the transactions of the 11th of September."

On September 11, 1794, citizens in the western counties in Pennsylvania voted on the question of submission to the excise laws. For the results of the voting, see *Pennsylvania Archives*, 2nd ser., IV, 297–99

of the United States—those for penalties on delinquents, under the laws beforementioned, in the courts of Pennsylvania.

As a guide in the case, the District Attorney has with him a list of the persons who have availed themselves of the offers of the Commissioners on the day appointed.

The seizure of Stills is the province of the Supervisor and other officers of Inspection. It is difficult to chalk out the precise line concerning it. There are opposite considerations which will require to be nicely balanced, and which must be judged of by those officers on the spot. It may be found useful to confine the seizures to stills of the most leading and refactory distillers. It may be adviseable to extend them far in the most refractory County.[12]

When the insurrection is subdued, and the requisite means have been put in execution to secure obedience to the laws, so as to render it proper for the army to retire (an event which you will accelerate as much as shall be consistent with the object) you will endeavour to make an arrangement for detaching such a force as you deem adequate; to be stationed within the disaffected Country, in such manner as best to afford protection to well-disposed Citizens, and to the officers of the revenue, and to repress by their presence, the spirit of riot & opposition to the laws.

But before you withdraw the army, you will promise on behalf of the President a general pardon to all such as shall not have been arrested, with such exceptions as you shall deem proper. The promise must be so guarded as not to affect pecuniary claims under the revenue laws.[13] In this measure, it is adviseable there should be a cooperation with the Governor of Pennsylvania.[14]

On the return of the army, you will adopt some convenient and certain arrangement for restoring to the public magazines the arms, accoutrements, military stores, tents & other articles of camp equipage, and entrenching tools which have been furnished & shall not have been consumed or lost.

You are to exert yourself by all possible means to preserve dis-

12. At this point in the draft the following sentences appear: "Strict Discipline to be enjoined and particular case to protect the persons families & property of good citizens. The like protection to be extended to the families & property of all."

13. This sentence is not in the draft.

14. The draft ends at this point.

cipline among the troops, particularly a scrupulous regard to the rights of persons and property and a respect for the authority of the civil magistrate; taking especial care to inculcate and cause to be observed this principle, that the duties of the army are confined to the attacking and subduing of armed opponents of the laws, and to the supporting and aiding of the civil officers in the execution of their functions.

It has been settled that the Governor of Pennsylvania will be second, the Governor of New Jersey third in command; and that the troops of the several States in line, on the march and upon detachment, are to be posted according to the rule which prevailed in the army during the late war—namely—in moving towards the seaboard, the most Southern troops will take the right—in moving westward, the most Northern will take the right.

These general instructions, however, are to be considered as liable to such alterations and deviations in the detail as from local and other causes may be found necessary the better to effect the main object upon the general principles which have been indicated.

With great respect I have the honor to be Sir, Your Obedt. Servt. Alex. Hamilton

From Ephraim Blaine [1]

Bedford [Pennsylvania] 21st. Octr. 1794

Sir

As they army are to March in two Collums, and the Quarter Master Genl [2] takes the Immediate charge of the right wing I conclude my Services will be no longer Necessary, and the Quarter Master Genl can have the Assistance of the Quartermaster General of the State [3] with his Deputies who are Numerous and I presume if well managed will be Sufficient therefore I beg leave to inform you that I shall have nothing further to do with this business after this day and too-morrow. I shall use every Exertion to lay in Sufficient Supplies at the first Encampment from this place, also take charge of the Magazines of Forrage at Ryans [4] upon the Penna. road to Carlisle which I presume will be the route the right Collum of they army will retun. There is three thousand Bushls. of Oats purchased by One of my Deputies in the Glades[5] which will be Colected at the most Convenient places where the troops are to Encamp.

Was I disposed to serve as a Deputy in any of Staff department of the army, no One Sooner than Genl. Miller—but I think my Exertions and Knowledge of the County Merrited more, I [am] at Ryans thirteen Miles west of Bedford upon the Penna. Road to Carlisle.

ADf, Ephraim Blaine Papers, Library of Congress.

1. For background to this letter, see H to Blaine, September 12, 1794.
2. Henry Miller, acting quartermaster general of the militia army.
3. Clement Biddle, quartermaster general of Pennsylvania during the insurrection.
4. Timothy Ryan owned more than eight hundred acres of land in the township of Bedford in Bedford County, Pennsylvania (*Pennsylvania Archives*, 3d ser., XXII [Harrisburg, 1897], 275).
5. The Glades was an open space in the woods about seven miles northeast of York, Pennsylvania, on the public road to the Susquehanna River.

From Tench Coxe

Treasury Department, Revenue Office, October 21, 1794. "Messrs. Thos. Billington & Guy Bryan, having contracted for the general clothing for 1795[1] the Blankets excepted,[2] they have requested an advance of 15 or 20,000 Dols. . . ."[3]

LC, RG 75, Letters of Tench Coxe, Commissioner of the Revenue, Relating to the Procurement of Military, Naval, and Indian Supplies, National Archives.

1. See Coxe to H, second letter of October 15, 1794.
2. See Coxe to H, October 10, 1794.
3. See Oliver Wolcott, Jr., to H, October 17, 1794.

From Tench Coxe

Treasury Department, Revenue Office, October 21, 1794. "By desire of T. Francis[1] Esqr. agent I have the honor to request that a warrant may be issued in his name for twenty five thousd. Dollars for the public service."

LC, RG 75, Letters of Tench Coxe, Commissioner of the Revenue, Relating to the Procurement of Military, Naval, and Indian Supplies, National Archives.

1. Tench Francis.

From Thomas Pinckney

[*London, October 21, 1794.* On January 21, 1795, Hamilton wrote to Pinckney: "Your letter of the 21st of October by duplicates . . . has recently come to hand." *Letter not found.*]

From George Washington

Hartley's[1] Tuesday Even⟨ing⟩
21st. October 1794

Dear Sir,

From Colo. Mentges'[2] information, there are detachments of Militia a considerable distance in the rear; compose⟨d⟩ in part, of those whose march was designe⟨d⟩ to be arrested. He adds, many of them are illy clad. This being the case, it appears to me, that an expence, without an equivalent advantage, would result from bringing them forward; and that the cloaths which they must draw to fit them for service woul⟨d⟩ actually be thrown away.

Under this view of the matter, and a full persuation that the Army which is alr⟨ea⟩dy advanced, is *more* than competent to an⟨y⟩ opposition that can be given by the Insurgen⟨ts⟩ I request that you would advise with Governors Mifflin & Howell[3] (after receiving the f⟨ul⟩lest information from Mentges) and cause all, which in your opinions cannot be up in time, all who are inadequately cloathed in the rear—and in a word, all who do not, upon mature consideration of circumstances appear to be essential to return, that the Country may not be unnecessarily burthened with the cloathing, pay and rations of them.

Open all letters of a public natu⟨re⟩ which may come to the army addressed to ⟨me⟩—and such as are in the Military line a⟨nd⟩ relating to the business you are upon, ⟨turn⟩ over to the Commanding General.[4]

I am &ca. &ca. Go: W⟨ashington⟩

Colo. Ham⟨ilton⟩

ALS, Hamilton Papers, Library of Congress.

1. Thomas Hartley's house in York County, Pennsylvania. Washington had left H and the militia force at Bedford, Pennsylvania, on the morning of October 21 to return to Philadelphia.

2. Colonel Francis Mentges of the Pennsylvania militia.

3. Governor Thomas Mifflin of Pennsylvania and Governor Richard Howell of New Jersey.

4. Henry Lee, governor of Virginia.

From Tench Coxe[1]

T: D: R O October 22d. 1794

Sir

Having contracted for a number of vessels for the timber for the Frigates in the middle & Southern States,[2] and having written to authorize the procuring a proportionate quantity for Boston and Portsmouth N:H: [3] I am mortified & somewhat embarrassed by the receipt of a letter of which a copy is enclosed from Mr. Morgan.[4] He sailed from Philada. on the 14~ of June. The agents messr. Habersham [5] & Clay [6] have notified the contracts to have been made as of the 2d Septbr. since wh. I have not a line from them or Mr. Morgan till this day. No copies of the contracts have come, nor any information to guide me. On the reasonable presumption that the New England men would be there by the 5th or 10th of October, and that Mr. Habersham & Mr. Morgan's authority to employ 100 hands would ensure 1500, or 2000 tons of wood by the middle of November, I had proceeded in procuring vessels rather faster than is now well. But upon the joint opinion of the Secy. at War & myself, Capt. Barry's [7] presence will be very useful, he has been gone about 15 days. Mr. Humphreys,[8] the captains who were here, and the Naval agents [9] have been unsuccessful in procuring a proper person in aid of Mr. Morgan to go thither. I just give you this state of the business, & shall send somebody else on in one of the vessels that is about to depart. Mr. Seagrove [10] will depart shortly for Georga. where I shall authorize him to use his exertions for the Shipment of the wood as long as it will be proper for him to remain there. T: Coxe C. R.

The Secy of the Treasy.
by Express

LC, RG 75, Letters of Tench Coxe, Commissioner of the Revenue, Relating to the Procurement of Military, Naval, and Indian Supplies, National Archives.

1. This letter concerns the naval armament for 1794. See Henry Knox to H, April 21, 1794.

2. For information on the timber cutting in the South, see Coxe to H, June 4, 1794.

3. Coxe to Henry Jackson and Jacob Sheafe, October 21, 1794 (LC, RG 75, Letters of Tench Coxe, Commissioner of the Revenue, Relating to the Procurement of Military, Naval, and Indian Supplies, National Archives). Jackson was naval agent at Boston, and Sheafe held the same position at Portsmouth, New Hampshire. See Knox to H, third letter of July 9, 1794.

4. John T. Morgan.

5. John Habersham, collector of customs at Savannah.

6. Joseph Clay was a merchant in Savannah.

7. John Barry, captain in the United States Navy.

8. Joshua Humphreys. See Knox to H, May 12, 1794.

9. See Knox to H, June 25, third letter of July 9, 1794.

10. James Seagrove. See Coxe to H, October 13, 1794.

To Angelica Church

Bedford Pensylvania
October 23. 1794
205 Miles Westward of
Philadelphia

I am thus far my dear Angelica on my way to attack and subdue the wicked insurgents of the West. But you are not to promise yourself that I shall have any trophies to lay at your feet. A large army has cooled the courage of those madmen & the only question seems now to be how to guard best aganst the return of the phrenzy.

You must not take my being here for a proof that I continue a quixot. In popular governments 'tis useful that those who propose measures should partake in whatever dangers they may involve. Twas very important there should be no mistake in the management of the affair—and I *might* contribute to prevent one. I wish to have every thing well settled for Mr. Church & you, that when you come, you may tread on safe ground. Assure him that the insurrection will do us a great deal of good and add to the solidity of every thing in this country. Say the same to Mr Jay [1] to whom I have not time to write & to Mr Pinkney.[2]

God bless You Dear Sister & make you as happy as I wish you. Love to Mr. Church. A Hamilton

Mrs. A Church

ALS, Judge Peter B. Olney, Deep River, Connecticut.

1. John Jay, Envoy Extraordinary to Great Britain.

2. Thomas Pinckney, United States Minister Plenipotentiary to Great Britain.

To George Washington

Bedford [Pennsylvania] October 23. 1794

Sir

Col Mentges [1] delivered me your letter from Hartley's.[2] Upon interrogating him, I do not find that there are more than two detachments of Militia on the way—one of New Jersey which by his account is likely to be pretty far advanced of Carlisle—the other of Pensylvania from Allen Town, about fifty or sixty, more in arrear. Mentges is not very perspicuous which may have led you to a different apprehension. I found Governor Howel [3] anxious that the Jersey Detachment which is so near at hand should be permitted to come up, so as to make it difficult to *urge* their return. That from Pensylvania will I hope be arrested. If the Jersey Men should not arrive tomorrow it may be adviseable to halt them at Bedford, till the column gets through the mountains & then if pacific appearances continue send them back.

The advanced corps moved this morning. The main body will move tomorrow.

Nothing new has occurred. With the truest respect & attachment I have the honor to be Sir Your obed servant A Hamilton

P S No doubt the measures taken ⟨re⟩specting *Clarkes* [4] encroachment on the Indians ⟨–⟩ issue will be noticed ⟨to⟩ Congress.[5] Together with other events it will serve to give great credit to the Govert.

The President of the UStates

ADf, Hamilton Papers, Library of Congress.

1. Francis Mentges.
2. Washington to H, October 21, 1794.
3. Richard Howell, governor of New Jersey.
4. Elijah Clark, major general in the Georgia militia. For information on Clark's expedition, see H to George Mathews, September 25, 1794.
5. On November 20, 1794, Washington forwarded to Congress papers relating to the Whiskey Insurrection, Anthony Wayne's campaign against the Indians, and the Georgia-Creek frontier (*Annals of Congress*, IV, 793). The letters about Clark's "encroachment on the Indians" included Constant Freeman to Henry Knox, September 29, October 12, 1794 (*ASP, Indian Affairs*, I, 500–01), and a letter from James Seagrove to Knox, dated October 30, 1794 (ALS, George Washington Papers, Library of Congress), which Knox transmitted to Washington on November 3, 1794 (LS, George Washington Papers, Library of Congress).

From Tench Coxe[1]

Treasury Department, Revenue Office, October 24, 1794. "I had the honor to request of you on the 8 October a remittance of 8000 to Col. J. S. Dexter, for Brown & Francis of Providence & wrote them it would be made. They inform me, that only 5400 Drs. have been received. This little difference has arisen from that being the sum first talked of. . . . I should be very glad if it should prove convenient to remit for them 4600 Drs. making in all 10,000 Dols. I have also to request a paymt of 250 Drs. to Joel Gibbs for Artillerists hats delivered by him." [2]

LC, RG 75, Letters of Tench Coxe, Commissioner of the Revenue, Relating to the Procurement of Military, Naval, and Indian Supplies, National Archives.

1. For background to this letter, see H to Coxe, April 4, June 27, August 9, second letter of October 8, 1794.

2. On October 24, 1794, Warrant No. 4192 for two hundred and fifty dollars was issued to Gibbs (D, RG 217, Miscellaneous Treasury Accounts, 1790–1894, Account No. 6922, National Archives). See Coxe to H, September 30, October 8, 1794.

To George Washington

Berlin [Pennsylvania] 3d days March
October 25. 1794
7 oClock in the
Evening

Sir

We arrived here this afternoon. A very heavy rain has rendered the march extremely arduous and distressing; but we find here much better shelter than was foreseen. Our baggage & stores are just beginning to arrive. The Jersey line & Brigade of Cavalry took the right hand road about five miles back.

Tomorrow we shall continue our march & I hope that we shall conform to the general arrangement though we must shorten tomorrows march & lengthen that of the day following.

The troops have shewn all the patience that could have been expected. In short I perceive nothing amiss.

Bradford[1] & Fulton[2] it is said are gone off. By tracing time, it is not probable they were at all influenced by the arrest of *Husbands & Philson.*[3]

With the highest respect & truest attachment I have the honor to be Sir Your obed ser A Hamilton

The President of The UStates

ALS, George Washington Papers, Library of Congress; copy, Hamilton Papers, Library of Congress.

1. David Bradford, an emigrant from Maryland, was a deputy of the attorney general of Pennsylvania from 1783 to 1794 and a member of the Pennsylvania legislature in 1792. He was the most militant of the leaders of the insurrection and was never offered amnesty. For an account of Bradford's escape down the Ohio River, see Francis D'Hebecourt to Henry Lee, November 10, 1794 (*Pennsylvania Archives*, 2nd ser., IV, 450–51). D'Hebecourt was a captain of militia at the French settlement of Gallipolis.

2. Alexander Fulton. According to William Findley, "Fulton was from Maryland," and in the early seventeen nineties "he was not only a federalist, but an open advocate of the excise law. . . ." By 1794, however, he was a leader of the opposition to the excise (Findley, *History of the Insurrection*, 96).

3. Herman Husband (Husbands) and Robert Philson of Bedford County, Pennsylvania, were two of four men who were arrested and sent to Philadelphia while the army was at Bedford. Husband, a backwoods preacher in North Carolina before he moved to western Pennsylvania, had played a leading part in opposition to the excise laws. Philson operated a store in the village of Berlin in Bedford County.

In his diary for October 20, 1794, Washington wrote: "I found also, which appeared to me to be an unlucky measure—that . . . [Judge Richard Peters] had issued his warrants against, and a party of light horse actually siez'd, one Herman Husbands and one Filson as Insurgents—or abetters of the Insurrection. I call it unlucky because my intention was to have suspended all proceedings of a civil nature until the Army had united its columns in the Center of the Insurgent Counties and then to have ciezed at one and the same all the leaders and principals of the Insurrection—and because it is to be feared that the proceeding above mentioned will have given the alarm and those who are most obnoxious to punishment will flee from the Country" (*GW Diaries*, IV, 223).

From George Washington

Susquehanna Wrights Ferry[1] [Pennsylvania] 26th Oct 1794.

Dear Sir,

I little advanced of this, yesterday afternoon, I met an Express with the letters herewith enclosed for you, with others for the Army; with which I have directed him to proceed.

Thus far I have proceeded without accident to Man, horse or Carriage, altho' the latter has had wherewith to try its goodness;

especially in ascending the North Mountain from Skinners [2] by a wrong road; that is by the old road which (never was good) and is rendered next to impassable by neglect.

I heard great complaints of Gurneys Corps [3] (& some of the Artillery) along the road to Strasburgh. There I parted from their Rout. In some places, I was told they did not leave a plate, a spoon, a glass or a knife; and this owing, in a great measure I was informed, to their being left without Officers. At *most* if not *all* the encampments, I found the fences in a manner burnt up. I pray you to mention this to Govr. Mifflin (and indeed to the Qr. Mr. General) [4] with a request (to the former) that the most pointed orders may be given, and every precaution used, to prevent the like on the return of the Army. If the Officers, from impatience to get home, should leave their respective commands; in a word, if they do not march with, and keep the Soldiers in their ranks and from stragling or loitering behind, the borderers on that road will sustain inconceivable damage from the disorderly Troops; whose names will be execrated for, and the service disgrac⟨ed⟩ by, such conduct.

There were some letters put into the hands of Govr. Lee [5] which it would be well for you to repossess yourself of. Among these were two to Messrs. Lynn [6] Mr Ross' [7] to you [8] and Messrs. Findley's and Redicks' [9] to me. Occasion may require the⟨m.⟩

I rode yesterday afternoon thro' the rain from York Town to this place, and got twice in the height of it, hung, (and delayed by that means) on the rocks in the middle of the Susquehanna, but I did not feel half as much for my own situation as I did on acct. of the Troops on the Mountains, and of the effect the rain might have on the Roads through the glades.[10]

I do not intend further than Lancaster today. But on Tuesday, if no accident happens I expect to be landed in the City of Philadelphia. My best wishes attend you, and all with you.

Yours sincerely Go: Washington

P.S. I hope you will be enabled by *Hook*, or by *Crook*, to send B——[11] and H——[12] together with a certain Mr. Guthrie,[13] to Philadelphia for their winter Quarters.

ALS, Hamilton Papers, Library of Congress.

1. Wright's Ferry was one of the first ferries on the Susquehanna River and for many years the most important one on the lower part of the river. It was

named for John Wright, a Quaker who came from Chester County, Pennsylvania, and settled on the east bank of the river, where Columbia now stands (John Gibson, ed., *History of York County, Pennsylvania, from the Earliest Period to the Present Time, Divided into General, Special, Township and Borough Histories, with a Biographical Department Appended* [Chicago, 1886], 595).

2. The place known as Skinner's was situated approximately three miles west of Strasburg at the foot of North Mountain in Franklin County, Pennsylvania. It was named for John Skinner, who in 1786 under contract from the Pennsylvania General Assembly built a road which was part of the new public road from Strasburg to Burnt Cabins. In 1789 Skinner was one of three commissioners appointed to review and mark out the road from Bedford to Pittsburgh (M. K. Burgner, "The Early Traveled Highways about Upper Strasburg," *Kittochtinny Historical Society. Papers Read before the Society. May, 1922 to March 1st, 1929* [n.p., 1929], X, 412–13; E. H. Blackburn and W. H. Welfley, *History of Bedford and Somerset Counties, Pennsylvania, with Genealogical and Personal History. . .* [New York, 1906], II, 192).

3. Colonel Francis Gurney was commander of the New Jersey brigade of infantry. On October 27, 1794, Governor Richard Howell of New Jersey issued the following division orders: "The troops of New Jersey are scandalized by the petty pilferings of a few who dishonor their fathers and their state, and every individual suffers for the faults of a few. All are hereby instructed to suppress the ignominious practice." Regimental orders of the same date read as follows: ". . . the officers commanding companies should be made accountable for the damage done by their companies to the inhabitants, and the officers commanding platoons are strictly ordered to keep their platoons properly dressed on their march, and that no man leave their ranks without leave of his officer" ("Journal by Major William Gould," 183–84).

4. Clement Biddle.

5. Governor Henry Lee of Virginia, commander in chief of the militia army.

6. John Lynn had been deputy inspector of the excise in Washington County, Pennsylvania. In 1791 he had been forced by opponents of the excise to resign.

7. James Ross was a Federalist politician and lawyer from Washington, Pennsylvania. On August 6, 1794, Washington had appointed him one of the United States commissioners to confer with representatives of the insurgents. See H and Henry Knox to Washington, August 5, 1794, note 3.

8. Letter not found.

9. William Findley and David Redick. See Washington to Edmund Randolph, October 11, 1794.

10. See Ephraim Blaine to H, October 21, 1794, note 5.

11. David Bradford. See H to Washington, October 25, 1794, note 1.

12. Herman Husband. See H to Washington, October 25, 1794, note 3.

13. James Guthrie was an opponent of the excise laws.

To George Washington

Berlin [Pennsylvania] October 26, 1794

Sir

The very late arrival of the waggons the injury to a number of them & the dispersed situation of the troops render it impracticable to leave this place today as was inten[d]ed. But the baggage

& stores go forward & tomorrow the troops must move. I apprehend no material derangement of the general plan. An express has been dispatched to Governor Lee [1] advising him of the state of things here.

Nothing from the Western Country.

With the greatest respect & attachment I have the honor to be Sir Your obed ser A Hamilton

The President of the UStates

ALS, George Washington Papers, Library of Congress; copy, Hamilton Papers, Library of Congress.

1. Henry Lee was in command of the militia army.

From Tench Coxe

Treasury Department, Revenue Office, October 27, 1794. "I have the honor to request that you will take order upon the subject of a remittance for the expenditures by Mr. Gorham. . . ." [1]

LC, RG 75, Letters of Tench Coxe, Commissioner of the Revenue, Relating to the Procurement of Military Naval, and Indian Supplies, National Archives.

1. Nathaniel Gorham was supervisor of the revenue for the District of Massachusetts. On October 30, 1794, Warrant No. 4201 for eighteen hundred dollars was issued to Gorham (D, RG 217, Miscellaneous Treasury Accounts, 1790–1894, Account No. 7701, National Archives).

To George Washington

Jones Mill [1] [Pennsylvania]
October 29. 1794

Sir

The Light Corps with the Jersey Infantry and Brigade of Cavalry are at Indian Creek in Legonien Valley, where they continue, 'till this division get up, which will be this Evening, as the march will commence in an hour. This division had, I believe, the worst road, and was besides encumbered with all the spare Stores, which has thrown it a day's march behind the other. But by a letter received yesterday from Governor Lee [2] it appears that the right wing is fully in measure with the left. All is essentially well with both wings & the troops continue to shew as much good humour as could possibly have been expected.

The Meeting at Parkinsons Ferry ended *we are told* in a new appointment of Commissioners to deprecate the advance of the army and in new expressions of pacific intentions.[3] But there is nothing which can occasion a question about the propriety of the army's proceeding to its ultim⟨ate⟩ destination. No appearances whatever of opposition occur.

You desired that a table of the routes of the left Wing might be sent you. None was left with an officer of this wing.

With the truest respect & attachment I have the honor to be Sir Your obed servt A Hamilton

P.S. It is hoped that the original papers have been forwarded, as the list furnished from the Secretary of States Office would be a deceptive guide.[4] Memoranda of the Atty General brought by the express, will greatly aid—perhaps sufficiently. But the originals would be best.

The President of the UStates.

ALS, George Washington Papers, Library of Congress; copy, Hamilton Papers, Library of Congress.

1. William Jones was the owner of this mill, which had been built in 1779. It was situated on Indian Creek in the southern part of the township of Donegal, Westmoreland County, Pennsylvania (Albert, *History of the County of Westmoreland*, 173, 582).

2. Henry Lee's letter to H has not been found.

3. The meeting at Parkinson's Ferry was held on October 24, 1794. The resolutions of the meeting are printed in *Pennsylvania Archives*, 2nd ser., IV, 423–24. William Findley, David Redick, Ephraim Douglass, and Thomas Morton were appointed to deliver the resolutions of the meeting to the President.

4. This is presumably a reference to the lists of those citizens of western Pennsylvania who had sworn to uphold the excise laws. See H to Henry Lee, October 20, 1794, note 10.

On November 4, 1794, Edmund Randolph wrote to George Washington: "I ought to have added . . . that the lists, for which Colo. Hamilton has written, were copied at the desire of Mr. [Richard] Peters and Mr. [William] Rawle, and after a consultation with Mr. [William] Bradford, it being supposed that the *originals* were proper for our archives" (ALS, RG 59, Miscellaneous Letters, 1790–1799, National Archives).

From Nathaniel Appleton

Boston, October 30, 1794. Requests payment of "Three hundred & seventy five Dollars for a quarters Salary due" to him "as Commissioner of the United States Loan Office in the State of Massachusetts to 30th September 1794."[1]

ALS, RG 217, Miscellaneous Treasury Accounts, 1790–1894, Account No. 6118, National Archives.

1. Warrant No. 4232 was issued to Appleton for this amount on December 2, 1794 (D, RG 217, Miscellaneous Treasury Accounts, 1790–1894, Account No. 6118, National Archives).

From Tench Coxe[1]

Treasury Department, Revenue Office, October 30, 1794. ". . . Messrs. Billington & Bryan[2] the contractors for the Army clothing for 1795 have requested an advance of ten or fifteen thousd. Dolls. . . . The Contractors for the provisions for the Western Army for 1795[3] are desirous to receive the sum of 12.000 Drs. . . . as soon as possible. . . ."

LC, RG 75, Letters of Tench Coxe, Commissioner of the Revenue, Relating to the Procurement of Military, Naval, and Indian Supplies, National Archives.

1. For background to this letter, see H to Coxe, April 4, 1794.

2. Thomas Billington and Guy Bryan. See Coxe to H, second letter of October 15, 1794; Oliver Wolcott, Jr., to H, October 17, 1794.

3. Alexander Scott and Matthew Ernest. See Coxe to H, first and third letters of October 15, 1794; Wolcott to H, October 17, 1794.

To Rufus King

Jones Mill [Pennsylvania] October 30. 1794

Dr. Sr

Our light corps, the Jersey infantry & a brigade of cavalry are about 8½ Miles in front, beyond all the Mountains. This division which has been delayed by a somewhat worse route & the incumbrance of the public stores will be at the same place this Evening. The left wing is at a corresponding point. All is essentially well—No appearance of opposition. It is of great consequence that a law should if possible be expedited through Congress for raising 500 infantry & 100 horse to be stationed in the disaffected country.[1] Without this the expence incurred will be essentially fruitless.

A law regulating a process of outlawry is also urgent;[2] for the best objects of punishment will fly & they ought to be compelled by outlawry to abandon their property houses & the UStates. This business must not be skinned over. The political putrefaction of Pensylvania is greater than I had any idea of. Without vigour every where our tranquillity is likely to be of very short duration & the next storm will be infinitely worse than the present one.[3]

Yrs. with true esteem & regard A Hamilton

R King Esqr

ALS, New-York Historical Society, New York City.

1. On November 29, 1794, George Washington approved "An Act to authorize the President to call out and station a corps of Militia, in the four western Counties of Pennsylvania, for a limited time" (1 *Stat.* 403).

2. On December 10, 1794, "A motion was made [in the Senate] that a committee be appointed to consider the expediency of passing an act of outlawry. . ." (*Annals of Congress*, IV, 799).

3. H addressed this letter as follows: "Rufus King Esquire. In his absence to be opened by Oliver Elsworth Esq or George Cabot." Ellsworth was a United States Senator from Connecticut and Cabot was a United States Senator from Massachusetts.

From Tench Coxe

Treasury Department, Revenue Office, October 31, 1794. Encloses "the contracts of Mess. Scott & Ernest[1] for the supplies of Rations therein expressed for the year 1795. . . ."

LC, RG 75, Letters of Tench Coxe, Commissioner of the Revenue, Relating to the Procurement of Military, Naval, and Indian Supplies, National Archives.

1. Alexander Scott and Matthew Ernest. See Coxe to H, first and third letters of October 15, October 30, 1794; Oliver Wolcott, Jr., to H, October 17, 1794.

From George Washington

Philadelphia 31. Octr 1794

Dear Sir

By pushing through the rain (which fell more or less on Saturday, Sunday and Monday) I arrived in this City before noon on Tuesday; without encountering any accident on the road, or any thing so unpleasant as the badness of the ways, after the rain had softened the earth and made them susceptible to deep impression, of the Wheels.

How you passed through the Glades[1] after the various accounts we had received of them, in such wet weather, I am at a loss to conjecture; but am extremely anxious to know; as I also am to learn the operations of the army, and the state & condition of it, since.

Nothing important, or new has been lately received from our Ministers abroad; and although accounts from London to the first of September, & from Ireland of still later date have been inserted in the Gazettes, they are not precise enough to be detailed in a letter. In general however, the French continue to be successful by land, and it might be added by Sea also, for they are capturing a great number of British Merchantmen. Nor does the fate of Robespierre [2] seem to have given more than a momentary stagnation to their affairs. The armies rejoice at it, and the people are congratulating one another on the occasion.

Mr. Monroe is arrived in France and has had his reception in the midst of the Convention,[3] at Paris, but no letter has been received from him.

Few members have yet come to town.[4] Tomorrow I presume will bring many. The papers say Mr. Trumbull [5] is elected to the Senate, in the room of Mr. Mitchell [6] who has resigned; but who has, or will, supply his place in the other house is not mentioned.[7]

Husbands [8] and the other prisoners [9] were safely lodged in this city on Wednesday afternoon. Press the Governors &ca. to be pointed in ordering the Officers under their respective commands, to march back with their respective Corps; and to see that the Inhabitants meet with no disgraceful insults, or injuries from them. The Secretary of War will, I expect, say something respecting the deposit of the Arms & public stores in *proper* places—to him therefore I shall refer.

Mrs. Hamilton & your family were very well yesterday afternoon. Your letter of the 23d. has been recd.

I am always and affectly Yours Go: Washington

Colo. Hamilton

ALS, Hamilton Papers, Library of Congress; ALS, letterpress copy, RG 59, Miscellaneous Letters, 1790–1799, National Archives; LC, George Washington Papers, Library of Congress.

1. See Ephraim Blaine to H, October 21, 1794, note 5.

2. Maximilien François Marie Isidore de Robespierre was executed on July 28, 1794.

3. James Monroe, United States Minister Plenipotentiary to France. See John Jay to H, September 11, 1794, note 4.

4. The second session of the Third Congress met in Philadelphia on November 3, 1794.

5. Jonathan Trumbull was a member of the House of Representatives from Connecticut from March, 1789, to March 3, 1795. He was United States Senator from Connecticut from March 4, 1795, to June 10, 1796.

6. Stephen Mix Mitchell was elected to the Senate from Connecticut as a Federalist to fill the vacancy caused by the death of Roger Sherman. Mitchell served in the Senate from December 2, 1793, to March 3, 1795. He did not seek renomination in 1794.

7. At the opening session of the Fourth Congress in December, 1795, the seats of former Connecticut Representatives Jonathan Trumbull, Amasa Learned, and Jeremiah Wadsworth were filled by Chauncey Goodrich, Roger Griswold, and Nathaniel Smith.

8. Herman Husband. See H to Washington, October 25, 1794, note 3; Washington to H, October 26, 1794, note 12.

9. Robert Philson, George Lucas, and George Wisecaver (Wisegarver) (Findley, *History of the Insurrection*, 212–13; Brackenridge, *Insurrection*, 330).

On October 21, 1794, Lucas wrote to Richard Peters, United States judge for the District of Pennsylvania: ". . . we are Detaind till Mr Husbands and Mr Filson Come in Now I hope You will Call Upon Mr Wisecaver & Lucas and Give Us a hearing As your Honour Detained Us till these Men would Come in we have Injured no Man we hope your Honour will Call Upon us and Give Us a Hearing" (ALS, Historical Society of Pennsylvania, Philadelphia).

Wisecaver's undated address to Peters reads in part as follows: "The Humble Address of George Wisecaver To the Honourable Court Seting fourth that the Sd. George Wisecaver Never was Against the Law and within this Eighteen Months Purchased two Stills and Never has Recd No Benefit out of the Same being Calld. from home told his wife if the Excise Officer Came About to Enter the Stills the Sd. Wisecaver Wife went into Bedford and told Henry Wood Esqr to Enter the Stills that was Neglected and the Excise Man Never Came About Nor Sent No person to Act for him which Can be proven by three Men that Mr [John] Webbster Never Came Nor Sent and I being Unaquainted with the Law and the Excise Man living Above thirty Miles from any hous I did Not think it my Duty to wait on him as Mr Webster got the Commission he was the fitest man to look after the Buisness then if I had Refuesed to Enter my Stills Mr Webbster had Tiome to inform on me. . ." (ADS, Historical Society of Pennsylvania, Philadelphia).

To George Washington

Camp 1½ Miles beyond
Cherrys Mill[1] [Pennsylvania] October 31
1794

Sir

The New Jersey Infantry and Brigade of Cavalry are at this place. The Pensylvania Infantry will be here this Evening. The light Corps is advanced about two Miles. No official account, since that heretofore communicated has come from the left wing. But a person who came from Union-Town yesterday informs, the *Morgan*[2] with the advance was there—the main body about twenty miles behind. I propose in about an hour to set out for Union Town.

All announces trepidation & submission. The new commissioners have been with Governor Mifflin charged with new declarations by townships, batalions of Militia & of a disposition to obey the laws.[3] The impression is certainly for the present strong but it will be stronger & more permanent by what is to follow. It does not appear that any great numbers have fled.

With truest respect & attachment I have the honor to be Sir Your obed servant A Hamilton

The President of The UStates.

ALS, George Washington Papers, Library of Congress; copy, Hamilton Papers, Library of Congress.

1. Cherry's Mill was named for Thomas Cherry, an early settler in Washington County, Pennsylvania. The mill was situated on Jacob's Creek and was near Cherry's Fort, which Cherry built in 1774, and his farm (Earl R. Forrest, *History of Washington County, Pennsylvania* [Chicago, 1926], 49, 118; Boyd Crumrine, *A History of Washington County, Pennsylvania* [Philadelphia, 1882], 854–55).

2. Major General Daniel Morgan was in command of the Virginia militia.

3. This is a reference to the delegates appointed from the four western counties of Pennsylvania to confer with Washington. See H to Washington, October 29, 1794, note 3. As the President had left for Philadelphia, the committee met with Governor Thomas Mifflin of Pennsylvania and H. On November 1, 1794, the committee met with Henry Lee, commanding general of the militia army (*Pennsylvania Archives,* 2nd ser., IV, 435–39).

From Tench Coxe[1]

Treasury Department, Revenue Office, November 1, 1794. "Mr. James Byers applies for four hundd. Doll. on a/count of his contract for casting ten brass Howitzers dated the 23rd day of July 94. . . ."[2]

LC, RG 75, Letters of Tench Coxe, Commissioner of the Revenue, Relating to the Procurement of Military, Naval, and Indian Supplies, National Archives.

1. Byers was a resident of Springfield, Massachusetts. For background to this letter, see Coxe to H, October 8, 1794, note 5.

2. On November 1, 1794, Warrant No. 4211 for four hundred dollars was issued to Byers (D, RG 217, Miscellaneous Treasury Accounts, 1790–1894, Account No. 7380, National Archives).

To George Washington

Cherrys Mill [Pennsylvania] Nov. 3d. 1794

Sir

I have returned to this place from Union Town. A letter from Governor Lee which goes with this probably informs you of the plan of future operations[1]—but lest it should not I shall briefly state it. The right wing is to take a position with its left towards Budds ferry[2] & its right toward Greensburgh. The left wing is to be posted between the Yocghagani[3] & Monongalia[4] with its left towards the latter & its right towards the former. Morgan with his command including the whole of the light corps & perhaps a part of the Brigade of Cavalry will go into Washington County.[5] It is not unlikely that in the course of the business a part of the troops will take a circuit by Pittsburgh—for the more places they can appear in without loss of time the better.

In adopting this plan the circumstance of much delay in crossing & recrossing water has weighed powerfully & the quiescent state of the Country renders the plan intirely safe. Boats however will be collected on both waters to facilitate mutual communication & support.

I received the letter you was so good as to write me on the road with those that accompanied it.[6]

The rainy weather continues with short intervals of clear. The left wing has suffered from sickness but the right has been & continues remarkably healthy. The troops also continue to behave well. A Court Martial[7] sits today to try one or two riotous fellows & one or two Marauders. The appointment of it has checked the licentious corps.

With the truest respect & attachment I have the honor to be Sir Your obed serv A Hamilton

PS Not many fugitives from Justice as yet.

The President of the UStates

ALS, George Washington Papers, Library of Congress; copy, Hamilton Papers, Library of Congress.

1. Henry Lee's letter has not been found, but his orders, dated November 2, 1794, read as follows: "The Army will resume its march on the morning of the 4th int at the hour of Eight when a signal gun will be fired.

"They will advance in two Columns. composed of the respective Wings, the right column will take the route by Lodges to Budds ferry, under the Command of his Excellency Governor [Thomas] Mifflin, who will please to take the most Convenient situation in the vicinity of that place, for the accomodation of the troops, & wait further Orders.

"The light column will proceed on the route to Petersons on the east side of Parkinsons ferry, under the orders of Majr Genl [Daniel] Morgan they will march by their left. . . ." (Baldwin, "Orders Issued by General Henry Lee," 99–100.) These orders, in a slightly different version, are also printed in *Pennsylvania Archives,* 2nd ser., IV, 439.

See also H to Henry Lee, October 20, 1794, and Lee's general orders of October 21, 1794, printed in Baldwin, "Orders Issued by General Henry Lee," 90–91.

2. Budd's Ferry was owned by Joseph and Joshua Budd, who had migrated from Somerset County, New Jersey, before the American Revolution and settled in Rostraver township, Westmoreland County, Pennsylvania. The ferry was situated south of West Newton on the Youghiogheny River (Albert, *History of the County of Westmoreland*, 564).

3. Youghiogheny River.

4. Monongahela River.

5. Daniel Morgan was in command of the Virginia militia.

6. Washington to H, October 26, 1794.

7. H is presumably referring to the following court-martial: "At a General Court Martial, whereof Brig. Gen. [Joseph] Bloomfield is President, Nicholas Fitzpatrick, Sergeant in Col. [Joseph] Copperthwaite's regiment of Pennsylvania militia, was brought before the Court charged with mutiny, to which charge he pleaded not guilty. The Court, after hearing the evidence for and against the prisoner, and his defence, found him guilty of a breach of the third and fifth articles for the better government of the troops; and sentenced him that he receive one hundred lashes and that he be dismissed the service. George Snyder, a corporal in Col. Copperthwaite's regiment of Pennsylvania militia, was also brought before the said Court and charged with mutiny, to which charge he pleaded not guilty; the Court, after hearing the evidence for and against the prisoner, and his defence, found him guilty of a breach of the third and fifth articles of the second section of the rules and articles for the better government of the troops, and sentenced him to receive one hundred lashes, and that he be dismissed the service. The commander of the right column approves the sentences, and directs they may be carried into execution under the direction of the Colonel or commanding officer of the regiment to-morrow morning at troop beating" ("Journal by Major William Gould," 186).

William Bradford and Alexander Hamilton to Edmund Randolph

Philada. Nov 4. [–December 9] 1794 [1]

Sir

The case of Mr. Green [2] upon which you request my opinion appears to be, in substance, as follows.

Mr Green being a subject of his britannic Majesty, emigrated to America after the treaty of peace in 1783, and by his residence & taking the requisite oaths became a citizen of the United States. He afterwards entered into a contract with certain British Merchants established at Ostend: and on a failure on their part, brought an action against them in the Court of King's Bench in England. On the trial of the cause the Judge directed the plaintiff to be non-suited, being of opinion that such a contract, was unlawful between british subjects & holding the plaintiff to be such. Mr Green, conceiving himself to be aggrieved, solicits the interposition of the government to cause justice to be done to him.

I apprehend, sir, that these facts do not authorise any complaint from the United States, or formal demand on the Executive Authority of Great Britain. It seems to have grown into a rule "that a nation ought not to interfere in the Causes of its Citizens brought before foreign Tribunals excepting in the Case of a refusal of Justice, palpable & evident injustice or a manifest violation of rules and forms." [3] In the case stated the opinion of the Judge is founded on the standing & ancient Laws of Great Britain, which can be altered only by the Legislative power of the nation. The decision could not be otherwise: and when a suitor applies to foreign tribunals for justice he must of necessity submit to the rules by which these tribunals are governed. How far the difficulties which may arise from the British Government strictly enforcing the principle, "that a natural born subject cannot divest himself of his allegiance," [4] may deserve the attention of government in case any negociations for a treaty of Commerce should be commenced, is another question, upon which it is not proper I should offer any opinion.

In addition, it may be observed, that it is upon a *definitive* sentence alone, that a complaint of injustice can regularly be founded. The opinion of a judge at Nisi prius—a nonsuit voluntarily submitted to by the plntf & no motion for a new trial made—cannot with propriety be made the subject of discussion. If such a plaintiff be not satisfied with the justice of the opinion it is his duty to put the cause in such a situation that its merits may be examined, in the court of the last resort.

There are other reasons which oppose themselves to Mr Green's request: but having had the honor of confering with you on this subject a few days ago I forbear enlarging upon it at present.

I have the honor to be with great Esteem sir Your most Obed. Serv. Wm Bradford.

I agree in opinion with the Attorney General that the case stated is not a proper one for a complaint by this Government or a formal demand on that of Great Britain.[5] Alexander Hamilton

The Secretary of State

LS, in the handwriting of William Bradford, RG 59, Letters and Opinions of the Attorney General, National Archives.

1. Bradford wrote this letter on November 4. As indicated in note 5 below, H did not concur with Bradford's opinion until December 9, 1794.

2. For information on William Green's case, see H to William Seton, July 17, 25, 1792; Seton to H, July 23, 1792; Green to H, July 24, 26, 1792.

On July 30, 1794, Randolph wrote to Green: "When I mentioned to the Attorney General of the United States my anxiety to obtain his opinion in your case, he informed me, that you wished him to withhold it, until you should again converse with him. The matter will therefore rest in this shape. . ." (LC, RG 59, Domestic Letters of the Department of State, Vol. 7, June 27–November 30, 1794, National Archives). On November 1, 1794, Green wrote to Randolph "to press to your consideration the circumstance of my particular situation, by which a dereliction of my Rights as a Citizen, and an acquiescance in foreign Sequestration, must operate in the manner of a Judgment of our Courts upon my property, and person at home. I have nothing to expect from the complaisance of the British Government.

"When you take the decision of the President of the United States on my case, I trust you will press this great point with energy, being . . . anxious for the speediest communication of the issue." (ALS, RG 59, Miscellaneous Letters, 1790–1799, National Archives.)

3. This is taken from Vattel, who wrote: "The prince ought not then to interfere in the causes of his subjects in foreign countries, and to grant them his protection, excepting in the cases of a refusal of justice, palpable and evident injustice, a manifest violation of rules and forms. . ." (Emeric de Vattel, *Law of Nations; or Principles of the Law of Nature: Applied to the Conduct and Affairs of Nations and Sovereigns* [London, 1759–1760], II, 148).

4. This is based on the following decision in the case of Æneas Macdonald in 1746–1747: "It is not in the power of any private subject to shake off his allegiance, and to *transfer it to a foreign prince*. Nor is it in the power of any foreign prince by naturalizing or employing a subject of *Great Britain*, to dissolve the bond of allegiance between that subject and the crown" (Sir Michael Foster, *A Report of Some Proceedings on the Commission for the Trial of the Rebels in the Year 1746, in the County of Surry; and of Other Crown Cases: To Which Are Added Discourses Upon a Few Branches of the Crown Law. By Sir Michael Foster, Knt. Sometime One of the Judges of the Court of King's Bench, and Recorder of the City of Bristol. The Second Edition, Corrected. With Additional Notes and References by his Nephew, Michael Dodson, Esq; of the Middle Temple* [Dublin: James Moore, College-Green, 1791]).

5. This sentence is in H's handwriting.

On December 11, 1794, Randolph wrote to Green: "The importance of your Case induced me to submit to the Secretaries of the Treasury and of War the Opinion, which the Attorney General of the United States, had given concerning it. The day before yesterday they signified their concurrence, and my own judgment going to the same conclusion, I have the honor of inclosing you a copy of it.

"To shew you, however, that I am duly impressed with the hardship of your situation, I have determined to write to Mr. [John] Jay and Mr. [Thomas] Pinckney the subjoined letter, and I beg you to be persuaded that if I do not come up to all, that you wish, it is because our Government ought not to be committed upon doubtful grounds." (LC, RG 59, Domestic Letters of the Department of State, Vol. 8, December 6, 1794–October 12, 1795, National Archives.)

On the same day Randolph wrote to Jay: ". . . it is the wish of our Government, that the heavy calamity which is caused to Mr. Green by the rigor of positive law, should receive every possible relief, consistent with the protection, which we can and ought to give to him. Morality and justice are on his side. I have therefore to request you to take his subject into consideration, and to find an occasion for bringing it into the view of the British Ministry in such a manner as may best promise success; but without committing our Government by a formal demand. . ." (LC, RG 59, Diplomatic and Consular Instructions of the Department of State, 1791–1801, Vol. 2, August 22, 1793–June 1, 1795, National Archives).

From George Washington

Philadelphia 5th. Novr. 1794

Dear Sir,

Since my last to you,[1] I have received your several letters of the 25th. 26th. and 29th. of last month, & am glad to hear that the Troops continued to be in good health & spirits, notwithstanding the bad weather & the Roads; and that further indications of submission were likely to be manifested by the Insurgents.

I have not received the rout of either column of the army—nor a copy of the order establishing them, issued on the day of my departure from Bedford.[2]

Upon enquiry, I find that it was copies *only* of Papers, that had been sent from the Secretary of State's Office, the originals being adjudge Necessary for the Archives.[3]

For want of a quorum in the Senate, Congress have not yet proceeded on business;[4] and it is questionable, it seems, whether it will make a house to day, five members being wanting for this purpose, yesterday afternoon.

Bache (as I expected) has opened his batteries upon your motives for remaining with the Army.[5] As the papers (I presume) are sent to you, I shall not repeat them. Although there are some late arrivals, the Gazettes have not, as yet, announced any thing new.

Mrs. Hamilton & your family were well yesterday. Mrs. Schuyler[6] and Son (John) and daughter, are there, but talk of going away to day, or to morrow.

I am Your Affect. Go: Washington

ALS, Hamilton Papers, Library of Congress.

1. Washington to H, October 31, 1794.

2. Henry Lee's general orders for October 21, 1794, read in part as follows: ". . . the Army will move in two columns, the right wing composed of the new

Jersey and Pennsylvania lines forming the right column, under the immediate Command of his excellency Governor [Thomas] Mifflin, The left wing composed of the Maryland & Virginia lines forming the left column, with the Commander in Chief. . ." (Baldwin, "Orders Issued by General Henry Lee," 90–91). See also H to Washington, October 29, November 3, 1794.

3. See H to Washington, October 29, 1794, note 4.

4. The second session of the Third Congress was scheduled to meet on November 3, 1794.

5. Benjamin Franklin Bache, the grandson of Benjamin Franklin, was publisher and editor of the [Philadelphia] *General Advertiser.* On November 8, 1794, the paper's name was changed to the *Aurora. General Advertiser,* and it subsequently was usually known as the *Aurora.*

On the day Washington wrote to H, the following appeared in the *General Advertiser:* "Those who consult the secret springs of the human mind will readily account for the Secretary of the Treasury's presence with the army. The excise as the child of his own heart, tho' a bastard in the soil that gave it birth, has called forth the feelings of the father, when the avenging sword was to be drawn for the punishment of its opposers. The Secretary by his presence with the army will, thro' the means of his talents and influence, to forward the views of his faction, assist in placing the principle which led to the almost unanimous exertions against the opposers of the law, in a false light, a favourite end with the faction at the present moment. It is their wish to make the friends of constitutional law be considered as friends to the introduction into our soil of all the poisonous exotics of the old world: But the discriminating sense of the people of this country will baffle the attempt and while they will hold up their hand against all illegal opposition to the measures of government will also ever raise their voice against all the *instrumentality* systems of the Secretary."

On the following day Bache wrote: "The public appear to have some curiosity to learn the object of the Treasury Secretary's presence with the army, and his meddling interference in a department totally irrelative to his official duties. It is truly inconceivable how the Secretary's presence at the seat of government can be spared, especially at the opening of an important session of Congress. By some it is whispered that he is with the army without invitation, and by many it is shrewdly suspected his conduct is a first step towards a deep laid scheme,—not for the promotion of his country's prosperity,—but the advancement of his private interests and the gratification of an ambition, laudable in itself, if pursued by proper means."

6. Mrs. Philip Schuyler, H's mother-in-law.

To Tench Coxe

Rostrave [1] Camp [Pennsylvania] Novr. 8. 1794

Sir

As the Army will shortly be on the return from this Country, it is necessary to make an arrangement for the Supply. Mr Eli Williams [2] will provide for the Virginia troops to Winchester, The Maryland troops to Williampsort, The Pensylvania Troops to Lancaster, The New Jersey troops to Trenton. The Quartermaster General [3] will do the Same in his department. A provision remains to be made to furnish & Convey the troops from those points to their respective homes.

You will engage *Carrington*[4] to take the Virginia troops at Winchester, Gale[5] to take up those of Maryland at Williamsport Hunt[6] of Trenton to take up those of New Jersey at that place & whomsoever you please to take up those of Pensylvania at Lancaster.[7]

You will confer with the secretary of War & take in Concert the needful Steps. Mr. Woolcott[8] will furnish the Money. No time is to be lost.

With Consideration I am Your obedient Servt Alex. Hamilton

Tench Coxe Esqr
Commissioner of the Revenue

Copy, Connecticut Historical Society, Hartford.

1. The township of Rostraver in the southwestern part of Westmoreland County, Pennsylvania.

2. See H to Elie Williams, September 12, 1794; Oliver Wolcott, Jr., to H, October 2, 1794.

3. Henry Miller was acting quartermaster general of the militia army. See H to Miller, September 15, 1794.

4. Edward Carrington, supervisor of the revenue for the District of Virginia.

5. George Gale, supervisor of the revenue for the District of Maryland.

6. Abraham Hunt was the War Department agent at Trenton, New Jersey, for supplying the militia army. See H to Williams, September 12, 1794.

7. On November 24, 1794, Coxe wrote to Jacob Bower of Reading: ". . . I have recd. from the Secy of the Treasy. a letter of the 8 inst. relative to the return of the Pnnsylva. Division of the Militia Army. That Division will be returned from the westward to Lancaster under the care of Elie Williams & Henry Miller Esqrs in regard to Rations, forage, transportation and all other Articles of commissary & Quarter master's supplies & aids. At that place (Lancasr.) Mr [Matthias] Slough will take them & provide for them, till they shall reach the place where you provided for them going up; there, you will be pleased to take them under your charge for all the objects of Supply, transportation, & aid in the line of those Officers, and you will procure them to be fully & regularly supplied and accommodated therewith 'till their departure from Reading, & to their next station of supply, in their way to their homes. . ." (LC, RG 75, Letters of Tench Coxe, Commissioner of the Revenue, Relating to the Procurement of Military, Naval, and Indian Supplies, National Archives). On November 21, 1794, Coxe had sent the same letter to Gale, Hunt, Carrington, and Slough (LC, RG 75, Letters of Tench Coxe, Commissioner of the Revenue, Relating to the Procurement of Military, Naval, and Indian Supplies, National Archives).

8. Oliver Wolcott, Jr.

To James O'Hara [1]

Camp, Rostrave Township,[2] November 8, 1794

Sir:

Information has been received that Mr. Elliott, one of the Contractors, has been lately killed by the Savages; [3] and Mr. Williams,[4] his partner, has represented that this, without the aid of your department, may embarrass the measures for furnishing and forwarding the supplies required by the Commander-in-Chief.[5] As it is all-important that these supplies should be duly furnished and conveyed to the respective posts, I must request and advise that you will co-operate in the article of transportation as far as may be necessary. For this purpose you will understand yourself with the Agents of the Contractors, ascertain what they can or cannot do, and endeavor to supply what may be deficient. In doing this you will, of course, keep and furnish such a record and statement of the aid you give as will enable the United States to make the proper charges against the Contractors, who are bound by their contract to transport as well as to procure and issue the provisions. It is understood that in the course of the Campaign similar aids have been, from time to time, given by your department. Of these, also, the Treasury ought to have as accurate a view as is practicable; otherwise the public will have to pay doubly for transportation—first in the price of the rations to the contractors, and secondly, in the expense of that which you furnish in aid of them.

With consideration, etc., I am your obt. servant,

Alexander Hamilton.

Mary Carson Darlington, ed., *Fort Pitt and Letters from the Frontier* (Pittsburgh, 1892), 280–81.

1. O'Hara was quartermaster general of the United States Army.

2. See H to Tench Coxe, November 8, 1794, note 1.

3. On October 6, 1794, Robert Elliot was killed by the Indians near Fort Hamilton in the Territory Northwest of the Ohio River (*ASP, Indian Affairs,* I, 525).

4. Elie Williams. See H to Williams, September 12, 1794; Oliver Wolcott, Jr., to H, October 2, 1794.

5. Major General Anthony Wayne. On October 17, 1794, Wayne wrote to Henry Knox: ". . . From the return of Provision, & duplicates of letters to the Contractors, & to the Q M General you will see the continued difficulties I am compeled to labour under with respect to supplies;

"The unfortunate death of Mr Robert Elliot, . . . added to the deranged state of that Department has made it my duty to order the Q M General to supply every defect on the part of the Contractors & at their expence in behalf of the United States to be settled at the treasury at a future day." (Knopf, *Wayne*, 359.)

To George Washington

Head Quarters Rostraver Township [1] [Pennsylvania]
November 8. 1794

Sir

Morgan [2] with the whole of the light troops has crossed into Washington County. Dispositions of different corps are making to strike at once in the most disaffected scenes.

It appears evident that to wait for preliminary investigations to apprehend the guilty upon process would defeat the object & produce delay beyond the patience of the troops or the time allowed by the season for operation. With the advice of the district Atty [3] the Commander in Chief [4] has concluded to take hold of all who are worth the trouble in a more summary way, that is by the military arm & then to deliver them over to the disposition of the Judiciary. In the mean time all possible means are using to obtain evidence & accomplices will be turned against the others.

This step is directed by that principle of common law that every man may of right apprehend a Traitor.

I hope good objects will be found notwithstanding many have gone off. It is proved that Brackenridge did not subscribe 'till after the day & that he has been the worst of all scroundrels.[5] The only question is how far the candour of the Government, owing to the use made of him by the Commissioners, might be compromitted? [6]

The Commander in Chief is taking measures with a good propect of success to engage a competent corps to be stationed in the Country—a Regiment of Infantry & four troops of horse. The plan is to engage them for 9 Months,[7] but a suit of Cloathing must be allowed.

Being not very well I am obliged to be brief.

With the truest respect & attachment I have the honor to be, Sir Your obed ser A Hamilton

The President of the UStates

ALS, The Andre deCoppet Collection, Princeton University Library; copy, Hamilton Papers, Library of Congress.

1. See H to Tench Coxe, November 8, 1794, note 1.

2. Major General Daniel Morgan was in command of the Virginia militia.

3. William Rawle.

4. Henry Lee was in command of the militia army.

5. The role of Hugh H. Brackenridge in the Whiskey Insurrection was equivocal. See "Deposition of Francis Mentges," August 1, 1794, note 4.

H is at this point referring specifically to the fact that Brackenridge did not subscribe to the oath prescribed by the Federal commissioners until September 12, 1794, which was one day after the deadline. On September 11 Brackenridge was not in Pittsburgh, and when he returned the hours prescribed for signing the oath had passed.

On October 26, 1794, Brackenridge wrote the following letter, which was addressed to "Citizens of the Army advancing to the Western Country":

"Serious intimations are given me, that I am considered by you, as greatly criminal in the late insurrection in this country; and that, though I might have shielded myself from the law, by taking advantage of the terms of the amnesty proposed by the commissioners, and sa[n]ctioned by the Proclamation of the President, yet that I shall not escape the resentment of individuals. It would seem to me totally improbable, that American soldiers would sully the glory of voluntary rising, by a single intemperate act. Nevertheless, as it would wound me . . . to be treated with indignity, by words, or looks, short of violence, I beg leave to suggest to you, that it is a maxim of reason, that a man 'shall be presumed innocent, until the contrary is proved,' and I give you a strong presumption of my innocence, viz. that though having the opportunity of relinquishing the country, I stand firm, and will surrender myself to the closest examination of the Judges, and put myself entirely on the merit or demerit of my conduct, through the whole of the unfortunate crisis" (*The* [Philadelphia] *Pennsylvania Gazette*, November 12, 1794).

6. The extent of Brackenridge's cooperation with the Federal commissioners appointed by the President to meet with the insurgents can be traced in Brackenridge, *Incidents*, I, 100–20; II, 11–44.

7. Henry Lee's plan of voluntary enlistment for nine months' service in the Army is described in his general orders of November 9, 1794 (Baldwin, "Orders Issued by General Henry Lee," 103–04). Lee's orders read in part as follows: "The flight of many of the ring leaders and promoters of the disturbances in this Country with other causes, renders it necessary that a Military force be stationed here during the winter, which must be ready to act before the Army returns, to effect this object in the best and most expeditious manner, the Commander in chief Proposes to raise by voluntary enlistment for the period of nine Months unless sooner discharged, One Regiment of Infantry Consisting of Ten Companies, one of which to be a Rifle Company, four troops of Cavalry . . . & one Company of Artillery."

From Alexander Mackenzie[1]

Montreal Novr. 9th. 1794.

Sir

Agreeable to your request I will give you Some few remarks on my last expedition.[2]

Having had no particular directions from the Company of course no promise on my part of undertaking such a jaunt. I left the Grand portage about the usual time for Arabasca,[3] but previously had obtained permission to remain the summer inland with no other view than of employing that time in discovery. The Cause of my not consulting the Company was the ill usage I had received upon my return from my former Expedition.[4] Upon my arrival as well as that of all the Canoes at Arabasca I left Mr. R. McKenzie[5] in charge of the principal post and went to winter at the Last of our settlements in the peace river or Unjegah Latitude 56°. 9″ north Longitude 117°. 43″ West from Greenwich.[6]

In the spring after I sent off all the property from Arabasca I on the 9th. May 1793 took my departure in a North Canoe, accompanied by A. Mc.Kay,[7] Six Canadians, and two young Indians up the peace river against a very strong current, in our route we were rather unfortunate in not meeting with Inhabitants till we had nearly got to the Mountains & come near the source of the river, and then we saw but three men with their families; they were well furnished with spears, daggers, bar Iron &ca. I prevailed with one of those men to come & guide us to the heighth of Land which he did; wishing to bring him further he deserted from us. The heighth of Land is only Seven hundred paces across; pass two small lakes & two small carrying places; from there we continued our route down a small river much embarrassed with wood rocks &ca, we broke our canoe lost all our Balls; we at last got into a large river[8] & this in half a days time led us into a more considerable body of water;[9] It was not before the third day from hence we met with Natives who were not very amicable at our first appearance; however, Peace being established, they gave us an account of the Country and informed us they got what european articles they had from the West by Land and that they did not know where this River emptied into the sea. I got some of them to conduct me to the next tribe; here I was convinced that the distance by the river which is very rapid, was great, and that I could not be able to perform it in the course of the season had I been better provided than I was; therefore I returned up the river according to the Indians directions to take the Route by which they procure their Goods, here I left my Canoe and the greatest part of what we had in her; Latitude 53°.

North Longitude 122°. 43 West travelled fifteen days to get to the sea coast,[10] there being many Islands I borrowed a Canoe from the Natives, wen⟨t⟩ about twenty leagues out amongst the Islands where ⟨I⟩ found the Latitude to be 52°. 23″ Longitude 128, 15, the 22 July 1793. I returned by the way I went, and was ba⟨ck⟩ at our settlement the 24th. Augt. I am Sir

Yrs. Alex M,Kenzie

ALS, Hamilton Papers, Library of Congress.

1. Alexander Mackenzie, a native of Scotland, was employed as an explorer by the North West Company.

2. An account of this expedition may be found in the second part of *Voyages from Montreal, on the River St. Laurence, Through the Continent of North America, to the Frozen and Pacific Oceans, in the Years 1789 and 1793; With a Preliminary Account of the Rise, Progress, and Present State of the Fur Trade of that Country: With Original Notes by Bougainville, and Volney, Members of the French Senate; Illustrated with Maps:* By Alexander Mackenzie Esq. (2 Vols., London: Printed for Cadell and Davies, Strand; Cobbett and Morgan, Pall-Mall; and W. Creech, Edinburgh, by R. Noble, Old Bailey, 1802).

3. Lake Athabaska.

4. In 1789 Mackenzie had set out from Fort Chipewyan on Lake Athabaska and at the northwestern end of the Great Slave Lake found the Mackenzie River, which he followed to its outlet in the Arctic Ocean. His partners in the North West Company made little of his discovery, for they hoped that he would instead find a route to the Pacific.

5. Roderick Mackenzie, Alexander Mackenzie's cousin, was permanently based at Fort Chipewyan.

6. Mackenzie is referring to Fork Fort near the junction of the Peace and Smoky rivers, which had been settled by men from the North West Company in the spring of 1792. Mackenzie arrived there on November 1, 1792 (*Voyages,* II, 12). In *Voyages,* II, 37, he gives the position of Fork Fort as latitude 56°9′ and longitude 117°35′15″.

7. Alexander McKay had been in the service of the North West Company since 1791 or earlier. He later became a prominent Canadian fur trader.

8. McGregor River.

9. Fraser River (*Voyages,* II, 116).

10. Mackenzie arrived at the Pacific on July 20, 1793, by way of the Bella Coola River (*Voyages,* II, 236).

To Henry Miller

Camp. Rostraver [1] [Pennsylvania] Novr 10th 1794

sir

It appears to me adviseable that a seizure of the Stills of delinquent distillers should be made generally within the Township of Elizabeth in Alleghany County & within the Township lying immediately on the Monongalia River on the West Side thereof from [2] to the Virginia Line. In order to this it will be necessary to employ not only the Collectors of the Revenue heretofore appointed to act within the Counties for which they have been appointed, but also an additional number to be appointed for the purpose & to accompany the parties which will be sent to protect the operation. The Business on the West side of the Monongalia [3] is committed to Genl Mathews [4] who will afford all requisite aid & that in Elizabeth Township is under the Direction of [5] who will do the Same. You will take up the Waggons of the Army to Convey the Stills seized to proper points on the Monongalia, thence to be Sent to Fort Pitt. The officers who are to command the military parties may be Constituted officers of Inspection for the occasion. You will designate those who are to Superintend the Execution of this business in the different Scenes.

with great Consideration I am Your obt. Servt A. Hamilton

Henry Miller Esqr
supervisor

Copy, Connecticut Historical Society, Hartford.

1. See H to Tench Coxe, November 8, 1794, note 1.

2. Space left blank in MS.

3. Monongahela River.

4. Brigadier General Thomas Matthews of the 9th Virginia Brigade (*Calendar of Virginia State Papers*, VII, 223).

5. Space left blank in MS.

From William S. Smith [1]

[*November 10, 1794.* On November 12, 1794, Oliver Wolcott, Jr., wrote to Smith: "Your letter of the 10th. instant covering a Contract dated the 10th. day of Oct. 1794 has in the absence of the Secretary of the Treasury been read by me." [2] *Letter not found.*]

1. Smith, John Adams's son-in-law, had been supervisor of the revenue for the District of New York from 1791 to 1793. When this letter was written, he was heavily involved in land speculation in western New York. For Smith's speculative activities, see Benjamin Walker to H, September 15, 1793, note 1.

2. ADf, Connecticut Historical Society, Hartford.

The contract in question has not been found, but in the remainder of his letter to Smith Wolcott wrote: "I cannot engage that any application to the Treasury Department on a subject which really or ostensibly concerns the Interest & rights of the United States shall be considered as confidential. If the papers are recd. they will be filed in the Secretarys office, by one of the principal Clerks, with an intimation that they are to be preserved with reasonable care at your risque, & that the contents are not to be unnecessarily or officiously promulgated.

"If these conditions are not satisfactory to you, the papers shall be interned for a few days. They shall however remain in my own possession, to afford you an opportunity to decide.

"It is however necessary for me to apprise you that the Treasury Department is not to be so viewed as in any respect implicated or concerned in any consequences resulting from this transaction, & that all authority not derived from the Government of the United States, to stipulate for the performance of a Contract by them, or for payments from their Treasury, is expressly disclaimed."

To George Washington

Rostraver Township [1] [Pennsylvania]
November 11. 1794

Sir

I have the honor of your note of the 5 instant.

Tomorrow the measures for apprehending persons & seizing stills will be carried into effect. I hope there will be found characters fit for examples & who can be made so. Col Hamilton Sheriff [2] is now at our quarters come to make a voluntary surrender of himself. It is not yet certain how much can be proved against him; but otherwise he is a very fit subject.

I observe what Mr. Bache is about.[3] But I am the more indifferent to it as the experience has proved to me (however it may be in ways which I could not *allege* in my justification) that my presence in this quarter was in several respects not useless. And it is long since I have learnt to hold popular opinion of no value. I hope to derive from the esteem of the discerning and in internal consciousness of zealous endeavours for the public good the reward of those endeavours.

I propose, if no urgent reason to the contrary occurs, to leave this country for Philadelphia about the 15th instant and I shall lose no time in reaching it. Mean while I trust the business of my department will suffer no injury from my absence.

Before I go I will try to see that a good arrangement is made with regard to arms stores &c.

With true respect & affectionate attachment I have the honor to be Sir Your obedt ser Alex Hamilton

P.S Poor *Lenox*[4] has been on the torture so long & has lately received such unpleasant accounts that we have all advised him to return to Philadelphia.

The substitutes devised will guarrd against injury to the service. Intelligence having been received of some of the insurgents having embodied about Beaver Creek[5] a plan is laid provisionally for giving them a stroke—the execution of which will be speedily attempted if nothing to the contrary occurs.

The President of the UStates

ALS, George Washington Papers, Library of Congress.

1. See H to Coxe, November 8, 1794, note 1.

2. John Hamilton, the sheriff of Washington County, surrendered to Judge Richard Peters, who denied Hamilton an immediate examination. Insurgents who refused to incriminate him were threatened with forfeiture of their amnesty.

3. Benjamin Franklin Bache. See Washington to H, November 5, 1794, note 5.

4. David Lenox, marshal for the District of Pennsylvania. For an account of his "torture," see Lenox to H, September 8, 1794.

5. Beaver Creek is in the southwestern part of Allegheny County, Pennsylvania.

From Henry Lee

[*Nailer's Farm,*[1] *Pennsylvania, November 13, 1794.* On November 13, 1794, Hamilton wrote to Lee: "I have received your Letter of this day." *Letter not found.*]

1. On November 12 and November 13, 1794, Lee issued orders from his headquarters at Nailer's farm (Baldwin, "Orders Issued by General Henry Lee," 106–17). The farm was the residence of William Nailer of Washington County.

To Henry Lee

Town of Washington [Pennsylvania] November 13 1794

Sir

If it has not been already done, I beg leave to recommend, that the routes of the troops under your command back to their respective homes and the place of discharge be immediately fixed and notified to the heads of the respective Staff Departments; in order that the requisite provision of every kind may be timely made. I will also thank you for a correspondent communication to me that the proper dispositions may be made in the War & Treasury Departments.

The Secretary at War has requested me to take with you an arrangement for the surrender & conveyance to proper Deposits of the arms, accoutrements, ammunition, Tents, Valices, Knapsacks, camp Kettles Canteens axes entenching tools and unissued articles of Cloathing. All such of these articles with the army as are not wanted for the troops while in the field or for their accommodation on their return may conveniently be deposited at Pittsburgh in the care of Major Craig [1] Assistant Qr. Master at that place.

It is also recommended that such of them as the troops take back with them may be sent to the following deposits respectively, those in possession of the Virginia line to New London in that state to be delivered to Mr. Holt Agent for Military Stores [2]—those in possession of the Maryland line to Frederick Town in that State to be delivered to the Inspector of the Revenue of that survey [3]—those in possession of the Pensylvania line to Lancaster & Philadelphia as the one or the other may be the most convenient to be delivered at Lancaster to the order of General Hand [4] at Philadelphia to Samuel Hodgson [5] Esquire—those in possession of the New Jersey line to Trenton in that state to be delivered to Mr. Hunt [6] Agent of Military Stores.[7]

I understand a number of arms (rifles) were left at Fort Cumberland. These it will be proper to return to the Magazine at Lancaster.

It is necessary that each delivery should be receipted for upon duplicate inventories of the articles delivered one of which to remain with the officer who makes the delivery the other to be forwarded to the Secretary at War who ought to be informed of the person of each line to whom the execution of this business is entrusted.

The earlier the troops are divested of the articles not necessary to their personal accommodation after they are out of the Insurgent Country the greater will be the security against embezzlement or waste.

It may deserve consideration whether all the artillery which will not be wanted for the garrisons established & to be established in this country ought not to be sent back some little time previous to the return of the troops to avoid embarrassing their march back as much as posisble. This however I take the liberty to suggest to your consideration as a mere point of convenience relative to dispatch & the comfort of the men. I would add however as more important that it would scarcely appear adviseable to leave any considerable number of Artillery in so disaffected a Country.

With the greatest respect & esteem I am Sir Your obed ser

His Excellency
Governor Lee Commander in Chief &c

PS.[8] Since writen the foregoing, I have received your Letter of this day.[9] I shall endeavour to put on train here your plan of inlistment.[10] The Judge[11] says he cannot at this moment determine when he ought to leave this place; but if any strong reasons urge to accelerate the movements from this place to Pitts Burg upon a hint it will be done because the examinations can be continued there. Let the Washington County people be sent here, those of Allegany to Pittsburgh. It may be well to make the experiment of bringing on McDonald and Mitchell[12] by a pardon if it can be done within a few days in order to benefit by their testimony previous to the general assurance of amnesty.[13]

ADf, Connecticut Historical Society, Hartford.

1. Isaac Craig. See "Deposition of Francis Mentges," August 1, 1794, note 2.
2. Thomas Holt was storekeeper of the Ordnance Department at New London, Virginia.
3. Philip Thomas was inspector of the revenue for Survey No. 2 in Maryland.
4. Major General Edward Hand, inspector of the revenue for Survey No. 3 in Pennsylvania.
5. Samuel Hodgdon.
6. Abraham Hunt. See H to Elie Williams, September 12, 1794.
7. In accordance with H's recommendation, Lee issued these orders on November 17, 1794. The orders are printed in *Pennsylvania Archives*, 2nd ser., IV, 455.
8. The postscript to this letter is not in H's handwriting.
9. Letter not found.
10. See H to George Washington, November 8, 1794, note 7.
11. Richard Peters, United States judge for the District of Pennsylvania, accompanied the Army in order to arraign the insurgents captured by the Army.
12. John Mitchell was present at the attack on John Neville's house on July 17, 1794, and robbed the United States mail on July 26, 1794. See H to Washington, August 5, 1794. John McDonald was secretary of the Mingo Creek Democratic Society.
13. On the back of this letter H wrote: "Copy to be sent to the Secy at

War" and also "John Robins on the head of Mingo can give evidence of Hami⟨lton's⟩ conduct." John Robins was a resident of Washington County, Pennsylvania. For information on John Hamilton and the Mingo Creek meeting, see "Deposition of Francis Mentges," August 1, 1794, note 5, and H and Henry Knox to Washington, August 5, 1794.

From Jeremiah Olney [1]

Custom House
District of Providence 13th Novr. 1794.

Sir

At the Circuit Court held in this Town on the 7th Instant, the Grand Jury found bills of Indictment against Metcalf Bowler and Zebedee Hunt Junr., Masters of the Brigantine Mariah and Schooner Nancy, for departing from the Harbour of Newport on a Forreign Voyage, in Violation of the Embargo Act passed the 26th of March last.[2] Capt. Hunt being arraigned, pled Guilty to the Charge. The Court fined him the *moderate* Sum of Forty Dollars and Cost of prossecution. Capt. Bowler being absent his Trial was put of untill June Term next.[3]

I have the Honor to be very respectfully Sir Your Most Obed. Hum. Serv. Jereh. Olney Collr.

Alexander Hamilton Esqr.

ALS, Rhode Island Historical Society, Providence; copy, RG 56, Letters from the Collector at Providence, National Archives.

1. For background to this letter, see William Ellery to H, April 8, 14, 1794; Olney to H, March 31, April 3, 1794; H to Olney, April 23, May 1, 1794.

2. This is a reference to a joint resolution of Congress, approved on March 26, 1794, "That an embargo be laid on all ships and vessels in the ports of the United States . . . for the term of thirty days" (1 *Stat.* 400).

3. A copy of the court proceedings, dated November 7, 1794, may be found in RG 59, Miscellaneous Letters, 1790–1799, National Archives.

From Arthur St. Clair [1]

Pittsburgh Novr. 14th. 1794

Sir

The Post which has been established at Le bœuf [2] by the State of Pennsylvania seems to be at present a place of some importance, and is in a critical situation. The time for which the Garrison is engaged is on the point of expiring, but the Governor has power by a late

Law to continue them, and I suppose will continue them.[3] The present commanding Officer is a prudent Man, and a good Officer. He, however, as I am informed, will not remain,[4] and the command will devolve upon a Person of the name of Miller,[5] from Washington County, who is strongly in the Interest of the Insurgents; and a part of the Garrison, from that County also, have been exceedingly disorderly and disposed to Mutiny.[6] Pardon me for taking the Liberty to suggest that it might be well [if] a Party of the standing Troops[7] were sent there, for there is a considerable quantity of Military Stores of every kind, and some Pieces of artillery deposited in that Place. The concurrence of Governor Mifflin will no doubt be necessary, and that, I suppose, would not be withheld.

With every sentiment of Respect and Regard I have the honor to be Sir Your very humble Servant A. St. Clair

ALS, Hamilton Papers, Library of Congress.

1. St. Clair was governor of the Territory Northwest of the River Ohio.

2. The French had built Fort Le Boeuf in Allegheny County on French Creek in the spring of 1753. It stood on the present site of Waterford, Erie County, Pennsylvania.

3. St. Clair is referring to "An Act to authorize the Governor to suspend the laying out a town at Presqu' Isle, and for other purposes therein mentioned," passed on September 23, 1794 (*Pennsylvania Laws*, September, 1794, Sess., Ch. CCLXVII). Section II of this act reads: "And whereas the Governor, agreeably to the power vested in him, by the third Section of the act, entituled 'An Act for more effectually securing the trade, peace and safety of the port of Philadelphia, and defending the Western Frontiers of the commonwealth,' passed the twenty-eighth day of February, one thousand seven hundred and ninety-four, did draft from the companies raised by virtue of the aforesaid act, a certain number of men for the protection of the Commissioners appointed to lay out a town at Presqu' Isle; and as the laying out said town has been hitherto suspended, and by this act the Governor is authorized to continue the suspension: And whereas the party so drafted as aforesaid, have made considerable fortifications at Le Bœuf, and that place being now considered as a post of great importance to this state, and may, perhaps, facilitate the operations of the general government; and as the time for which the troops were enlisted will expire before the meeting of the next legislature [December 2, 1794]: *Be it therefore enacted by the authority aforesaid*, That the Governor may, and he is hereby authorized, to enlist any number of men, not exceeding one hundred and thirty, to serve six months after the expiration of the present enlistment, unless sooner discharged. . . ."

For the settling of Presque Isle, see "Cabinet Meeting. Opinion on Drafting of Militia by Governor Thomas Mifflin," May 24, 1794.

On November 17, 1794, Mifflin wrote from Pittsburgh to Ebenezer Denny, captain of the Presque Isle detachment of the Pennsylvania militia, as follows: "I have made the . . . arrangement for the formation of the said Corps, which I have continued under your command. . . . I have employed Richard Clement of the militia, to recruit at this place where he may procure men from the militia now on service" (LC, Division of Public Records, Pennsylvania Historical and Museum Commission, Harrisburg).

4. On November 17, 1794, Mifflin gave permission to Denny to visit Pittsburgh and Philadelphia (LC, Division of Public Records, Pennsylvania Historical and Museum Commission, Harrisburg).

5. Captain William Miller. For Miller's activities during the Whiskey Insurrection, see H to George Washington, August 5, 1794, note 76. On November 17, 1794, Mifflin informed Denny that Captain Thomas Buchanan had been appointed to succeed Miller because of doubts concerning Miller's political principles (LC, Division of Public Records, Pennsylvania Historical and Museum Commission, Harrisburg).

6. Denny described the disorderly activities of the garrison at Le Boeuf in a letter to Josiah Harmar, September 3, 1794: ". . . There are several of the artillery men the most ungovernable villians that ever crossed the mountains. Five fellows, a few nights ago, broke open a small store house, which the contractor occupied outside the fort, & stole a quantity of Brandy. Early next morning the thing was detected, & some men who appeared to be drunk I ordered in confinement. An artillery man, who was not then suspected of being concerned, spoke out & said it was damned wrong the men should be confined, close in my hearing. I ordered him to be secured. The fellow sprung to his gun, and swore he would shoot the first man that would attempt to lay hands on him, & called to his comrades to turn out. As I advanced, the rascal took aim & snapped his piece. Fortunately, in the hurry, he had not taken up his own musket, for we found afterwards that she was charged . . ." (*Pennsylvania Archives*, 2nd ser., VI, 771).

7. See "An Act to authorize the President to call out and station a corps of Militia, in the four western Counties of Pennsylvania, for a limited time" (1 *Stat.* 403 [November 29, 1794]).

To George Washington

Town of Washington [Pennsylvania] November 15. 1794.

Sir

I had the honor of writing to you three Days since by Mr. Vaughan.[1] Nothing material has since occurred; except that a number of persons have been apprehended. Twenty of them are in confinement at this place—others have not yet arrived. Several of those in confinement are fit subjects for examples and it is probable from the evidence already collected & what is expected that enough for that purpose will be proved. The most conspicuous of these for character or crime are understood to be The Reverend John Corbly,[2] Col. Crawford,[3] Col John Hamilton,[4] Thomas Sedgwick, David Lock, John Munn,[5] John Laughery.[6] The evidence has not yet fixed the situation of Col. Hamilton.

A warrant has been sent after Col. Gaddis[7] of Fayette another very fit subject but from the lapse of time I fear he has escaped.

The bad spirit is evidently not subdued. Information is just received that within the last three Days a *Pole* has been erected about 16½ miles from this place on the road to Muddy Creek.[8] measures are taking on the Subject.

But it is more and more apparent that for some considerable time to come a military force in this Country is indispensable. I presume the temporary one[9] meditated will be accomplished.

Tomorrow I leave this place for Pittsburgh. If nothing extraordinary happens I shall leave that place for Philadelphia on the 19th. By that time every thing will have taken it's shape.

With true respect & affect. attachment I have the honor to be Sir Your obed. Servant. Alex Hamilton

The President of
the U. States

[ENCLOSURE][10]

List of persons in confinement at the Town of Washington

Col John Hamilton
Col William Crauford
Major John Powers[11]
The Reverend John Corbly
Thomas Sedgwick
James Kerr[12]
John Laughery
David Lock
John Munn
William Porter[13]
John Flannigin[14]
John Crawford (son of Col Crawford)
John Gaston[15]
John Husy[16]
John McGill[17]
Robert Martin[18]
Nathaniel Martin[19]
David McComb[20]
James Robinson[21]
William Johnson[22]

Copy, Hamilton Papers, Library of Congress.

1. John Vaughan was a Philadelphia merchant. H may be referring to the letter that he (H) wrote to Washington on November 11, 1794.
2. Corbly was a Baptist clergyman of Washington County.
3. William Crawford of Washington County.
4. Hamilton was sheriff of Washington County.
5. Sedgwick, Lock, and Munn were residents of Washington County.
6. Laugherty was one of the leaders of the opposition to the excise laws in Ohio County, Virginia.
7. Thomas Gaddis.
8. Muddy Creek is located in the northeast section of Washington County.

9. This is a reference to the military arrangement announced by Henry Lee on November 9, 1794. See H to Washington, November 8, 1794, note 7.

10. AD, George Washington Papers, Library of Congress.

11. Powers, a resident of Westmoreland County, was a delegate to the meeting between the insurgents and the commissioners of the United States and Pennsylvania on August 21–23, 1794. See William Bradford to H, August 23, 1794, note 3.

12. James Kerr of Washington County was granted bail on January 13, 1795.

13. H is referring to Captain Robert Porter, an officer during the American Revolution, who refused to sign the amnesty. On May 18, 1795, he was acquitted in the Circuit Court of the United States for the Pennsylvania District (Wharton, *State Trials*, 174–75, and Brackenridge, *Insurrection*, 331). Porter kept an account of the Whiskey Insurrection, which is published in part in Brackenridge, *Insurrection*, 328–32.

14. John Flanagan had been a delegate from Cline's district to a meeting of Washington County insurgents on August 23, 1791. For the resolutions of the meeting, see H to Washington, August 5, 1794, note 6.

15. John Gaston, a client of Hugh H. Brackenridge, had received the following note from "Tom the Tinker": "You will please to have this [notice] printed in the Pittsburgh paper, this week, or you may abide by the consequence" (Brackenridge, *Incidents*, II, 9). Gaston took the notice to John Scull, printer of *The Pittsburgh Gazette*, and the item appeared in the issue of September 13, 1794. For "Tom the Tinker," see H to Washington, November 17, 1794.

16. Husy was a resident of Washington County.

17. McGill was a resident of Cannonsburg, Washington County.

18. Martin was a resident of Washington County.

19. Nathaniel Martin came from Washington County.

20. H is probably referring to Thomas McComb, one of the insurgents who attacked Robert Johnson in September, 1791. See H to Washington, August 5, 1794, note 18.

21. Robinson had been a delegate to a Pittsburgh meeting of the insurgents on August 21–22, 1792. See H to Tench Coxe, September, 1792, note 5.

22. Johnson was a resident of Westmoreland County.

From Thomas Jones[1]

[*Hampton, Virginia, November 16, 1794.* On December 20, 1794, Oliver Wolcott, Jr., wrote to Jones and referred to "your letter of Nov. 16th. to the Secy of the Treasury."[2] *Letter not found.*]

1. Jones was collector of customs of the District of Hampton, Virginia, and inspector of the revenue for the port of Hampton.

2. Wolcott's letter to Jones reads: "The doubt suggested in your letter of Nov. 16th. to the Secy of the Treasury is presumed to be founded on the 5th. Section of the supplementary Collection Law passed on the 2d. of March 1793. Though the prohibition against ow[n]ing Ships or Vessels is expressed in general terms, yet it is not deemed to be within the spirit & intent of the provision to inhibit Officers of the Customs from owning Boats solely employed in transporting Passengers & Baggage over Ferries.

"The opinion of this Department cannot however justify you, in case the construction now given, should be adjudged erroneous by the Judiciary." (ADf, Connecticut Historical Society, Hartford.)

Section 5 of "An Act supplementary to the act, entitled 'An act to provide more effectually for the collection of the Duties imposed by law on Goods, Wares and Merchandise, imported into the United States, and on the Tonnage of Ships or Vessels'" [1 *Stat.* 336–38] reads in part as follows: "That . . . no officer of the customs . . . shall own, in whole or in part, any ship or vessel, or act as agent, attorney or consignee for the owner or owners of any ship or vessel, or of any cargo or lading on board the same: Nor shall any officer of the customs . . . import or be concerned directly or indirectly in the importation of any goods, wares or merchandise into the United States, on penalty that every person so offending and being thereof convicted, shall forfeit the sum of five hundred dollars."

From Tench Coxe

Treasury Department, Revenue Office, November 17, 1794. "The Contractors (Messrs Scott & Ernest) [1] are desirous of receiving now . . . the additional advance of 12,000 Dols. which was to have been made on the 15th day of Decmr. next. . . ."

LC, RG 75, Letters of Tench Coxe, Commissioner of the Revenue, Relating to the Procurement of Military, Naval, and Indian Supplies, National Archives.

1. Alexander Scott and Matthew Ernest. See Coxe to H, first and third letters of October 15, October 30, 31, 1794; Oliver Wolcott, Jr., to H, October 17, 1794.

From Tench Coxe [1]

Treasury Department, Revenue Office, November 17, 1794. Requests that "a further advance of money may be made to Henry Jackson Esqr. Naval agent at Boston In a sum not exceeding five thousand Dollars." [2]

LC, RG 75, Letters of Tench Coxe, Commissioner of the Revenue, Relating to the Procurement of Military, Naval, and Indian Supplies, National Archives.

1. For information concerning the naval armament, see Henry Knox to H, April 21, 1794.

2. See Knox to H, June 25, third letter of July 9, 1794; Coxe to H, August 2, 1794.

From Henry Knox

Philadelphia 17 Novr 1794

My dear sir

By the arrangement of the New Contract,[1] a Commissary will be required. I know not of any person in whose integrity I would have more confidence than Major I Craig[2] of Fort Pitt provided he would repair to Fort Washington. Will you consider of this point, and if you approve, will you offer it to him?[3] No time can be lost upon this subject.

Mr Jay will satisfactorily arrange all the points of dispute between Great Britain & the US. How happy are we! His communications are to the 14th Sept.[4]

Yours affectionly

Colo Hamilton

ADf, Massachusetts Historical Society, Boston.

1. This is a reference to a contract for provisioning the Army in 1795 which Tench Coxe, commissioner of the revenue, and Alexander Scott and Matthew Ernest signed on October 10, 1794 (copy, Isaac Craig Papers, Carnegie Library of Pittsburgh, Pennsylvania). The contract provided that "the Quarter Master General will have to transport the provision to the posts advanced from Fort Washington and also from Pittsburgh" (Knox to Anthony Wayne, December 5, 1794 [Knopf, *Wayne*, 367]).

2. Isaac Craig was deputy quartermaster general of the United States Army and storekeeper at Pittsburgh. See "Deposition of Francis Mentges," August 1, 1794, note 2.

3. On November 9, 1794, Knox wrote to Craig to offer him the position of commissary, which Craig refused (Knox to Craig, November 9, December 18, 1794 [LC, Isaac Craig Papers, Carnegie Library of Pittsburgh, Pennsylvania]). In a letter to Craig on December 27, 1794, Knox stated: "I hope nothing will prevent Major [Abraham] Kirkpatrick executing the duties of Commissary according to your intimation. His instructions will not be ready until next post, when he will I hope be fully prepared to descend instantly upon the receipt of them" (LS, Isaac Craig Papers, Carnegie Library of Pittsburgh, Pennsylvania). See also "Deposition of Francis Mentges," August 2, 1794, note 2.

4. John Jay's dispatches may be found in RG 59, Despatches from United States Ministers to Great Britain, 1791–1906, Vol. 1, April 19, 1794–June 1, 1795, National Archives. They are printed in *ASP, Foreign Relations*, I, 475–96.

To Henry Miller

Pittsburgh November 17th 1794

Sir

It has already been settled that an Office of Inspection is to be opened in each of the counties of this Survey. It remains to settle what is to be done with regard to unpaid arrears. As it has so happened that Offices have not been regularly opened in some of the Counties which would involve legal difficulties in the collection of arrears, and as that collection if extended to the arrears for the whole time, would occasion a burthen greater than could probably be borne without real distress; it appears to me adviseable to require the payment of the duty in arrear only for the year which ended the first of July last.

In the adjustment of this arrear the rate of duty per annum according to the capacity of the still appears to be at this time the only legal & practicable rule with regard to those who did not enter their stills & avail themselves of some other of the options allowed by law.[1]

It has been much insisted upon, that this part of the Country could not without oppression pay the duty in cash. The supply of the Western Army enables us to accommodate in this particular, an option may therefore be either to pay in cash or in Whiskey. The whiskey to be delivered by the party paying at the place where the Office of Inspection for the County is kept, unless where it is most convenient both to the party & to the Public that it be delivered at some other place to be agreed upon between the Inspector of the Revenue for the survey[2] and the Agent for procuring Whiskey for the Army, who is Prestly Neville Esqr.[3] The whiskey received in payment is to be delivered to the said Prestley Neville, whose receipt for it will be accepted at the Treasury as a remittance for the amount. Mr. Neville will receive it at the place of delivery and provide for its transportation to where it is wanted.

The price at which whiskey is to be received, is three Shillings & Six pence Pennsylvania currency per gallon.

With consideration & Esteem I am &c. Alexander Hamilton

The Supervisor of the Revenue

Copy, Historical Society of Pennsylvania, Philadelphia; copy, Connecticut Historical Society, Hartford; copy, RG 58, "Special Cases," Whiskey Rebellion, 1792–1796, National Archives.

1. "An Act concerning the Duties on Spirits distilled within the United States" provided "that it shall be at the option of the proprietor or possessor of any such still, instead of the said yearly duty, either to pay seven cents for every gallon of spirits by him or her distilled, or to pay at the rate of ten cents per gallon of the capacity for each and every month of the employment of any such still . . ." (1 *Stat.* 268 [May 8, 1792]).

2. John Neville was inspector of the revenue for Survey No. 4 in Pennsylvania.

3. See H to Presley Neville, November 18, 1794.

To William Rawle[1]

[Pittsburgh, Nov 17–19, 1794]

Persons to be excepted from the Amnesty[2]

1 All those actually in arrest at the time of issuing the proclamation

2 David Bradford[3]
Edward Cook[4]
Daniel Hamilton[5]
Benjamin Parkinson[6]
John Holcroft[7]
Richard Holcroft
Mc.Kinley[8] } of Ohio County
Southerland[9] }
Alexander Fulton[10]
John Mitchel
William Bradford[11]
Thomas Spiers[12]

The Proclamation ought to conform to the idea of the Commissioners[13]—that is to refer the amnesty to the first of July next then to take effect in favour of all those not excepted who shall demean themselves obediently to the laws till then.[14]

Mr. Rawle will furnish such other names for exceptions out of the fugitives as the atrocity of their characters & offences may indicate.

Gallatin[15] & Brackenridge[16] ought *not* to be excepted out of the amnesty.

☞ Mr. Hamilton requests Mr. Rawle to forward to Judge Addison[17] the forms for subscription papers[18] copied by Mr. De Haven[19] & believed to be with him.

AD, Historical Society of Pennsylvania, Philadelphia.

1. On October 3, 1794, Edmund Randolph had written to Rawle: "The President finding that the pardon offered to those who have been guilty of treason or other indictable offences against the United States committed in the fourth survey of Pennsylvania, before the 22d day of August last, has been only partially accepted, and that so strong a spirit of resistance still exists in that Country as to render it necessary to march the Militia thither, in order to

suppress the combinations & to aid the execution of the laws, has thought it proper to direct that measures should, at the same time, be taken to bring to justice such of the offenders as have been influential in exciting the insurrection or particularly active and violent in supporting it. But as the President is desirous of preserving the utmost good faith towards those who have bona fide accepted the terms offered by the Commissioners, care must be taken to except all such persons from prosecution, unless by their subsequent conduct they have forfeited their right to a pardon. Such also, as have in any manner which shall be deemed sufficiently satisfactory and sincere, by the General commanding the Troops, evidenced their repentance, may be excepted.

"Considering the conduct of this business as a matter of delicacy and importance he has thought proper, to commit the superintendance of it to you: and you are hereby accordingly authorized to repair to the Western Counties of Pennsylvania and to take such legal and proper measures, as may in your judgment be necessary to cause the said Offenders or those who have aided them (in the said survey or elsewhere in this district) to be arrested, secured and brought to trial." (LC, RG 59, Domestic Letters of the Department of State, Vol. 7, June 27–November 30, 1794, National Archives.)

2. The list compiled by H in this letter was for Rawle's use in determining those to whom Henry Lee's proclamation of pardon on November 29, 1794, should not apply. Lee's proclamation is printed in *Pennsylvania Archives*, 2nd ser., IV, 479–80.

3. For information on the activities of David Bradford, see George Clymer to H, October 10, 1792; H to George Washington, September 2, October 25, 1794; Washington to H, October 26, 1794.

4. For information on Edward Cook, see H to Washington, August 5, September 2, 1794.

5. Daniel Hamilton was involved in the attacks on Robert Johnson, Robert Wilson, and Roseberry. See H to Washington, August 5, 1794, note 27.

6. Benjamin Parkinson was a leading member of the Mingo Creek Democratic Society.

7. For Holcroft, see H to Washington, November 17, 1794, note 1.

8. William McKinley.

9. William Sutherland. See H to Henry Lee, August 25, 1794, note 11.

10. See H to Washington, October 25, 1794.

11. John Mitchell and William Bradford were accused of the mail robbery of July 26, 1794. Fulton took the mail packet to a tavern in Cannonsburg, Washington County, where John Cannon and Thomas Speer, two local leaders, were present when the mail was opened. See also "Conference Concerning the Insurrection in Western Pennsylvania," August 2, 1794, note 8.

12. See note 11.

13. On August 8, 1794, George Washington had appointed three commissioners to deal with the insurrectionists in western Pennsylvania. See H and Henry Knox to Washington, August 5, 1794, note 3. During the latter part of August the Federal commissioners held conferences with a committee appointed by the disaffected citizens of western Pennsylvania. The "idea" to which H is referring was among the concessions made by the United States commissioners and is described as follows: "If there shall be a general and sincere acquiescense in the Execution of the said acts, until the said tenth day of July next, a general pardon and oblivion of all such offenses shall be granted; excepting therefrom, nevertheless, every person who shall, in the mean time, willfully obstruct, or attempt to obstruct the Execution of any of the laws of the United States, or be in any wise aiding or abetting therein" (*Pennsylvania Archives*, 2nd ser., IV, 192). See also William Bradford to H, August 23, 1794.

14. Lee's proclamation of November 29, 1794, reads: "By virtue of the powers and authority in me vested by the President of the United States, and in obedience to his benign intentions, therewith communicated, I do, by this my proclamation, declare and make known to all concerned that a full, free, and entire pardon, (excepting and providing as hereafter mentioned) is hereby granted to all persons residing within the counties of Washington, Alleghany, Westmoreland, and Fayette, in the state of Pennsylvania, and in the county of Ohio, in the state of Virginia, guilty of treason, or misprison of treason against the United States, or otherwise directly or indirectly engaged in the wicked and unhappy tumults and disturbances lately existing in those counties; excepting nevertheless from the benefit and effect of this pardon all persons charged with the commission of offences against the United States, and now actually in custody, or held by recognizance to appear and answer for such offences at any judicial court or courts excepting also all persons avoiding fair trial by abandonment of their homes; and excepting moreover the following persons, the attrocity of whose conduct renders it proper to mark them by name for the purpose of subjecting them, with all possible certainty, to the regular course of judicial proceedings, and whom all officers, civil and military, are required to endeavour to apprehend and have brought to justice, to wit.

Benjamin Parkinson,	Arthur Gardner,
John Holcroft,	Daniel Hamilton,
Tho. Lapsley,	William Miller,
Edward Cook,	Edward Wright,
Richard Holcroft,	David Bradford,
John Mitchell,	Alexander Fulton,
Thomas Spiers,	William Bradford,
Geo. Parker,	Wm. Hanna,
Edward Magner, jun.	Thomas Hughes,
David Lock,	Ebenezer Gallaher,
Peter Lyle,	John Shields,
William Hay,	William M'Elhenny,
Tho. Patton,	Stephenson Jack,
Patrick Jack, and	Andrew Hiland, of the state of Pennsylvania, and
William Sutherland,	Robert Stephenson,
Wm. M'Kinley,	John Moore, and

John M'Cormick, of Ohio County, in the state of Virginia.

"Provided, That no person who shall hereafter wilfully obstuct, or attempt to obstruct the execution of any of the laws of the United States, or be in any wise aiding or abetting therein, shall be entitled to any benefit or advantage of the pardon herein before granted: And provided also, That nothing herein contained, shall extend, or be construed to extend to the remission of mitigation of any forfeiture of any penalty incurred by reason of infractions of, or obstructions to, the laws of the United States for collecting a revenue upon distilled spirits and stills. . . ." (*The* [New York] *Daily Advertiser,* December 6, 1794.)

15. For Albert Gallatin's activities during the Whiskey Insurrection, see Henry Adams, ed., *The Writings of Albert Gallatin* (Philadelphia, 1879), III, 1–67.

16. Hugh H. Brackenridge. See "Deposition of Francis Mentges," August 1, 1794, note 4; H to Washington, November 8, 1794, note 5.

17. Alexander Addison was presiding judge of the County Court of the western district of Pennsylvania.

18. A "subscription paper" was a pledge made by volunteers to join in sup-

port of the militia to effect submission to the excise laws. See H to Edmund Randolph, October 6, 1794, note 2.

19. This may be a reference to Moses De Haven, a major in the Montgomery County, Pennsylvania, militia in 1794.

To George Washington

Pittsburgh November 17. 1794

Sir

I wrote to you two days since by express from Washington. The judiciary corps with myself arrived here last Evening. The list of prisoners has been very considerably increased, probably to the amount of 150 but it is not yet so digested as to be forwarded. Governor Lee just informs me that he has received a letter from Marietta advising him of the apprehending of John Holcroff the reputed *Tom the Tinker*[1] & one Wright[2] a notorious offender.

Subsequent intelligence shews that there is no regular assemblage of the fugitives where it is supposed—there are only small vagrant parties in that quarter affording no point of Attack.[3]

Every thing is urging on for the return of the troops. The engagement of a corps to remain here goes on, it is said, well.

With perfect respect & true attachment I have the honor to be Sir Yr. Obed ser A Hamilton

The President of the UStates

ALS, George Washington Papers, Library of Congress; copy, Hamilton Papers, Library of Congress.

1. "Tom the Tinker" was the signature on broadsides and letters to the press in western Pennsylvania in 1794 that gave advice to those who were opposed to the excise laws. The name "Tom the Tinker" was first used by John Holcroft during the attack on William Cochran (see H to Washington, August 5, 1794, note 67). According to H. H. Brackenridge, "His [Cochran's] still was cut to pieces; and this was humorously called, mending his still; and the members, of course, must be tinkers, and the name, collectively, became Tom the Tinker" (Brackenridge, *Incidents,* I, 79). Holcroft later denied that he knew the identity of "Tom the Tinker" (Brackenridge, *Incidents,* III, 148). Both the technique and the style of "Tom the Tinker" are illustrated by the following item in *The Pittsburgh Gazette:*

"Mr. [John] Scull [editor of *The Pittsburgh Gazette*],

"I am under the necessity of requesting you to put the following in your next paper—It was found posted on a tree near my distillery.

John Reed,

"July 23, 1794.

"ADVERTISEMENT

"In taking a survey of the troops under my direction in the late expedition against the insolent exciseman John Nevill, I find there were a great number of delinquents; even among those who carry on distilling; it will therefore be observed that, I Tom the Tinker, will not suffer any certain class or set of men to be excluded the service of this my district, when notified to attend on any expedition carried on in order to obstruct the execution of the excise law, and obtain a repeal thereof.

"And I do declare on my solemn word, that if such delinquents do not come forth on the next alarm, with equipments, and give their assistance as much as in them lies, in opposing the execution and obtaining a repeal of the excise law, he or they will be deemed as enemies, and stand opposed to virtuous principles of republican liberty, and shall receive punishment according to the nature of the offence.

"And whereas a certain John Reed, now resident in Washington, and being at his place near Pittsburgh, called Reedsburgh, and having a set of stills employed at said Reedsburgh, entered on the excise docket, contrary to the will and good pleasure of his fellow citizens, and came not forth to assist in the suppression of the execution of said law by aiding and assisting in the late expedition, have, by delinquency manifested his approbation to the execution of the aforesaid law, is hereby charged forthwith to cause the contents of this paper, without adding or diminishing, to be published in the Pittsburgh Gazette, the ensuing week, under no less penalty than the consumption of his distillery.

"Given under my hand the 19th day of July,
one thousand seven hundred and ninety four.
Tom the Tinker

"P.S. To prevent a great deal of trouble, it will be necessary to repeal the excise law and lay a direct tax on all located and patented land in the United States." (*The Pittsburgh Gazette*, July 26, 1794.)

See also another letter from "Tom the Tinker" in *The Pittsburgh Gazette*, September 13, 1794. This letter begins: "You will please have this printed in the Pittsburgh paper this week, or you may abide by the consequence," and concludes: "traitors take care for my hammer is up and my ladel is hot. I cannot travel the country for nothing." See also H to Washington, November 15, 1794, note 15.

2. Edward Wright had participated in the attack on John Neville's house. See H to Washington, August 5, 1794. See also *Pennsylvania Archives*, 2nd ser., IV, 501.

3. See H to Washington, November 11, 1794, note 5, and November 15, 1794.

Examination of Hugh Henry Brackenridge

[Pittsburgh, November 18–19, 1794]

Early next morning, a subpena was read to me, from judge Peters,[1] commanding me before him, at his chamber, to give testimony, touching all such matters as should be enquired of me. I considered this as, in fact, an examination touching myself; and that,

Brackenridge, *Incidents*, II, 75–78.

1. Richard Peters was United States judge for the District of Pennsylvania.

on the opinion formed from this, was to depend my being or not being arrested.

I attended the judge, and was referred by him to secretary Hamilton, for examination. I was received by Hamilton, with that countenance, which a man will have, when he sees a person, with regard to whom his humanity and sense of justice struggles;—he would have him saved, but is afraid he must be hanged;—was willing to treat me with civility, but was embarrassed with a sense, that, in a short time, I must probably stand in the predicament of a culprit, and be in irons. He began, by asking me some general questions, with regard to any system or plan, within my knowledge, of overthrowing the government. I had known of nothing of the kind. After a number of general questions, to which I had to answer in the negative, I proposed putting an end to that, by giving him a narrative of every thing I did know. It was agreed; and he began to write. I gave him the outlines of the narrative I have given in this publication, until I came to that particular, where, after the burning Neville's house,[2] I represented the people calling upon Bradford and Marshall[3] to come forward, and support what was done, under the pain of being treated as Neville himself had been. At this the secretary laid down his pen, and addressed himself to me; Mr. Brackenridge, said he, I observe one leading trait in your account, a disposition to excuse the principal actors; and before we go further, I must be candid, and inform you of the delicate situation in which you stand; *you are not within the amnesty*; *you have not signed upon the day*;[4] a thing we did not know until we came upon this ground, I mean into the western country; and though the government may not be disposed to proceed rigorously, yet it has you in its power; and it will depend upon the candour of your account, what your fate will be. My

2. For the burning of John Neville's house, see "Deposition of Francis Mentges," August 1, 1794, note 2.

3. David Bradford and James Marshall of Washington County. See "Conference Concerning the Insurrection in Western Pennsylvania," August 2, 1794, note 8, and H to George Washington, October 25, 1794, note 1.

4. H is referring to the "elections" held on September 11, 1794, to determine if the citizens of the four western counties of Pennsylvania were prepared to submit to the excise laws. Brackenridge arrived in Pittsburgh late in the day and did not sign the submission papers until September 12, 1794 (Brackenridge, *Incidents*, II, 14–20). As a result, Brackenridge was excluded from the amnesty. See H to William Rawle, November 17–19, 1794, note 8.

answer was, *I am not within the amnesty*, and am sensible to the extent of the power of the government; but were the narrative to begin again, I would not change a single word. I went on. Having passed through the circumstances of the marshal and Neville [5] being privy to my giving my opinion to Black and Hamilton, [6] on the effect of the writs of subpœna against delinquent distillers, and Neville requesting me to go to the Mingo meeting-house, my examination was adjourned; Mr. Hamilton being called upon to dinner; and I was desired to attend in the afternoon.

I came home; but declined dining with general Lee [7] that day, though pressed by several messages. I could not bear to shew myself with that company, in the doubtful predicament in which I stood.

At three o'clock I returned to my examination; Mr. Hamilton entering the room where I waited for him, appeared to have been reflecting, and said, "Mr. Brackenridge your conduct has been horribly misrepresented." I saw that he never before heard the least of my being solicited by Neville the younger, [8] to go to the meeting at Mingo Creek, but having just dined in company with Neville, at the house of major Craig,[9] where I was then examined, he had asked Neville, and he had acknowledged it. This is conjecture.

I went on to give an account of the Mingo Creek meeting.[10] The secretary appeared not satisfied. "Mr. Brackenridge," said he, "you must know we have testimony extremely unfavourable to you, of speeches made at this meeting; in particular your ridiculing of the executive." I saw that some fool had misunderstood, and had been giving account of what I had deduced from the lenity of the President, in the case of the Presqu'isle establishment,[11] and my intro-

5. David Lenox and Presley Neville. See Lenox to H, September 8, 1794.

6. John Black and David Hamilton.

7. Governor Henry Lee of Virginia, the commander in chief of the militia army, had established headquarters in Brackenridge's house, which was one of the largest in Pittsburgh.

8. Presley Neville. See "Deposition of Francis Mentges," August 1, 1794, note 2.

9. Isaac Craig. See "Deposition of Francis Mentges," August 1, 1794, note 2.

10. For information on the Mingo Creek meeting, see "Deposition of Francis Mentges," August 1, 1794, note 5; H to George Washington, August 5, 1794, note 84.

11. For the settling of Presque Isle, see "Cabinet Meeting. Opinion on Drafting of Militia by Governor Thomas Mifflin," May 24, 1794, and Arthur St. Clair to H, November 14, 1794, note 3.

ducing general Knox and the Seneca Indian, Obeal, or Cornplanter, making speeches.[12] I was extremely hurt to think, that, after I had been called upon, in the manner I was to go forward on that occasion, I should be at the mercy of the accounts of persons who did not understand me, and obliged to answer the pleasantry I had found necessary to use, to carry off their minds, for a time, from the object they were upon, until I saw them better disposed to hear what I had farther to say. My answer was, "Five persons were chosen to go with me[13] to that meeting; for the express purpose of bearing testimony of what I should say; let these be called upon. Is it reasonable I should be at the mercy of the misconceptions, or a voluntary misrepresentation of weak or prejudiced individuals?" He was silent. I went on giving an account of the town meeting of Pittsburgh.[14] I stated it, as moved by me, that we should march and affect to join the people at Braddock's fields. I saw the secretary pause at this, and sink into a deep reflection. It staggered him. Was it any more, said I, than what Richard the second did, when a mob of 100,000 men assembled on Blackheath? the young prince adressed them, put himself at their head, and said, What do you want, gentleman? I will lead you on.[15]

12. Brackenridge's speech at the Mingo Creek meeting reads as follows: ". . . the evidences which the executive had already given, of a disposition to avoid war; even to a degree that was blamed, or perhaps, blameable; in the case of the spoilations on our commerce, by the British, and in the case of the Indian tribes. Here I introduced the countermand of the Presqu,ile establishment, at the interference of the executive of the United States, in consequence of threats from Cornplanter, a Seneca Indian; and, in order to put them in good humour, and at the same time lead to the point I had in view, the practicability of obtaining an amnesty, I indulged a good deal of pleasantry at the expence of the executive, on the subject of Indian treaties: I introduced general [Henry] Knox on the one side, and Cornplanter on the other; and made them make speeches. Now, said I [Brackenridge], if Indians can have treaties, why cannot we have one two?" (Brackenridge, *Incidents*, I, 34).

13. The five men from Pittsburgh who accompanied Brackenridge were George Robinson, the chief burgess; Joseph Tannehill, the first assistant burgess; William H. Beaumont, a Pittsburgh regulator; Peter Audrain and Colonel William Semple, merchants. Affidavits from each of these men on Brackenridge's conduct at the Mingo Creek meeting may be found in Brackenridge, *Insurrection*, 68–74.

14. For the meeting at Pittsburgh, see H to Washington, August 12, 1794, note 2.

15. Brackenridge has confused two incidents in the English Peasants' Revolt of 1381. Provoked by the imposition of a shilling poll tax, groups of peasants from East Anglia and Kent, the two main sources of the rising, converged on London in June. The Kentish men, led by Wat Tyler, arrived at Blackheath,

My narrative now continued. After some time the secretary observed, "My breast begins to ach, we will stop to night; we will resume it tomorrow morning at 9 o'clock." I withdrew, but was struck with his last expression. I was at a loss to know whether his breast ached for my sake, or from the writing; but disposed to construe every thing unfavourable, I supposed it was for my sake, and that he saw I must be arrested.

Next morning general Lee made an apology to Mrs. Brackenridge, that for the sake of retirement, and to be in a less central part of the town, he was about to withdraw to other quarters, with some part of his family. I considered this as owing to the delicacy of his feelings, that he wished to be out of the way, and not a witness of the circumstance of one with whom he had been acquainted in juvenile years, sinking into a melancholy situation just under his eye. I had taken it for granted that he had received a hint from Mr. Hamilton, of what was to take place.

Waiting on the secretary, at 9 o'clock, my examination recommenced. In the course of the narrative, his countenance began to brighten, and having finished the history, there was an end. "Mr. Brackenridge," said he, "in the course of yesterday I had uneasy feelings, I was concerned for you as for a man of talents; my impressions were unfavourable; you may have observed it. I now think it my duty to inform you, that not a single one remains. Had we listened to some people, I do not know what we might have done. There is a side to your account; your conduct has been horribly misrepresented, owing to misconception. I will announce you in this

---

outside London, on June 12 and demanded through royal messengers to speak to the king, Richard II, who was then a boy of fourteen. Richard set out, intending to land from the Thames at Greenwich, but was dissuaded by the rebels' numbers from doing so. There followed an attack on London by the Kentish men, who opened prisons, burned buildings, and executed a number of lawyers and other enemies. On June 14, however, Richard confronted a group of insurgents at Mile End in east London, agreed to their demands, and received demonstrations of loyalty. Meanwhile, more militant rebels broke into the Tower of London, where they attacked members of the royal household and killed, among others, the then chancellor and archbishop of Canterbury, Simon Sudbury. The following day, Richard met another group, among them Wat Tyler, at Smithfield. More demands were made; the king agreed to them; but this time Tyler offered opposition, and two of the king's party cut him down. Most of the chroniclers agree in their accounts that, at this point, Richard turned to the crowd and said: "I am your leader; follow me."

point of view to governor Lee, who represents the executive. You are in no personal danger. You will not be troubled even by a simple inquisition by the judge; what may be due to yourself with the public, is another question."

In so delicate a case, where life had been fought by insidious men; and where, what I felt with more sensibility, my hopes of estimation in the world, were likely to be blasted, at least for a time, it may easily be supposed, that no word escaped me, or will ever be forgotten.

My sensibility had been greatly wounded, when I waited on judge Peters with the narrative to sign it, as directed by Mr. Hamilton. It was with difficulty, I could write my name. I cursed the circumstance of having to write it five times, to the five different sheets of paper, of which my narrative consisted. I returned to my house with different feelings from those I had for a long time before.

To Presley Neville[1]

Pitts Burgh November 18. 1794

Sir,

I hereby appoint you Agent for procuring supplies in the Western Country for the use of the army with a Compensation of two hundred and fifty dollars per annum in lieu of Commission. The purchase of Whiskey is the first object which will engage your attention concerning which you will receive directions from the Commissioners of the Revenue.[2]

Permission will be given to the distillers to pay in Whiskey to be deliver'd at certain places. The Officers of inspection are instructed to deliver what they may receive to you. You will cause what is so delivered to be transported to the proper points for the use of the army. I mean to Pittsburgh and such other places in this country at which troops may be stationed in order to their support. And the residue to be forwarded down the Ohio for the Army under General Wayne.[3] The forwarding from Pittsburgh to the Western army will belong to the Quarter Master General.[4]

With great esteem, I am &c

⟨Presley Nevi⟩lle Esq.

Copy, Connecticut Historical Society, Hartford.

1. For background to this letter, see H to Henry Miller, November 17, 1794.

2. On December 17, 1794, Tench Coxe wrote to Presley Neville: "I have understood from the Secretary of the Treasury that he had communicated with you in writing upon the subject of the military supply for 1795 of distilled Spirits. A sight of that communication and an opportunity to confer with you concerning it will be agreeable at any moment, that may be convenient to you" (LC, RG 58, Letters of Commissioner of Revenue, 1794–1795, National Archives). Coxe sent Neville more specific instructions on December 19, 1794: "As I have not yet rec'd. a copy of the letter to you from the Secy. of the Treasy it is not in my power to give more than general Instructions upon the subject of purchase of Whiskey.

"You will be pleased to proceed in the purchase of Whiskey for the military supply of 1795 *with all possible dispatch.* No purchase to be made but of spirits ascertained to be lawfully distilled. The price to be kept at 3/3 or 3/6 if practicable, but not to exceed 3/9 or 50 cents without a previous communication, yt. purchases may be extended to ten thousd. drs. including all costs & charges on the spirits delivd at Pittsburgh. Monies will be paid to you here on demand, or upon yr. bills as mentioned in your conference on Thursday last." (LC, RG 75, Letters of Tench Coxe, Commissioner of the Revenue, Relating to the Procurement of Military, Naval, and Indian Supplies, National Archives.) Coxe modified these instructions in the following letter to Neville, dated January 13, 1795: "It appears upon reflection, that it will be inexpedient to give more for Whiskey in actual purchases for Cash, than the price (3/6) limited by the Secretary, as that at which the distillers might deliver whiskey to the officers of the Revenue, for their duties. I make this remark, because in a former letter the ultimatum of 50 cents was mentioned if necessary. It did not appear probable to you that more than 3/6 would be requisite" (LC, RG 58, Letters of Commissioner of Revenue, 1794–1795, National Archives).

3. Anthony Wayne.

4. James O'Hara. See H to O'Hara, November 8, 1794.

Report of the Commissioners of the Sinking Fund

[Philadelphia, November 18, 1794
Communicated on November 19, 1794][1]

The vice President of the United States and President of the Senate, the Chief Justice, the Secretary of State, the Secretary of the Treasury and the Attorney General respectfully report to Congress as follows:

That pursuant to the act entitled "An Act, making provision for the reduction of the Public Debt"[2] and in conformity to resolutions agreed upon by them and severally approved by the President of the United States, they have since their report dated the sixteenth of december 1793,[3] caused purchases of the said debt to be made through the agency of Samuel Meredith,[4] to the amount of One hundred and thirty nine thousand and seventy-seven dollars and eight eight cents, for which there have been paid in Specie One hundred thousand and sixty one dollars and seventy six cents.

That pursuant to the act entitled "an act supplementary to the act making provision for the debt of the United States" [5] and in conformity to resolutions agreed upon by them and severally approved by the President of the United States, they have also caused purchases of the said debt to be made subsequent to their said report of the sixteenth day of december 1793, to the amount of One hundred and six thousand seven hundred and fifty dollars and thirty seven cents, for which there have been paid eighty five thousand eight hundred and thirty two dollars and ninety one cents in specie.

That the documents accompanying this report marked B, C, D & E,[6] shew the aforesaid purchases generally and in detail, including the places where, the times when, the prices at which and the persons of whom, the purchases were made.

That the documents marked A,[7] shew the proceedings of the accounting Officers of the Treasury in respect to the settlement of an account for the expenditure of fifty thousand dollars in purchases, which were stated in our former report,[8] at the date of which the said settlement had not been completed.

That the purchases now and heretofore reported amount together to two millions two hundred and sixty five thousand and twenty two dollars & fifty seven cents in Stock, for which there have been paid in Specie, one million five hundred and eighty one thousand three hundred and twenty three dollars and sixty seven cents, as will be more particularly seen by the document marked F.[9]

On behalf of the Board John Adams

Philadelphia Novemr. 18th: 1794.

D, signed by John Adams, RG 46, Third Congress, 1793–1795, Reports of the Commissioners of the Sinking Fund, National Archives.

1. *Annals of Congress*, IV, 792–93, 891.
2. 1 *Stat.* 186–87 (August 12, 1790).
3. "Report of the Commissioners of the Sinking Fund," December 16, 1793.
4. Meredith was treasurer of the United States.
5. 1 *Stat.* 281–83 (May 8, 1792).
6. These documents may be found in RG 46, Third Congress, 1793–1795, Reports of the Commissioners of the Sinking Fund, National Archives. They are printed in *ASP, Finance*, I, 304–15.
7. These documents may be found in RG 46, Third Congress, 1793–1795,

Reports of the Commissioners of the Sinking Fund, National Archives. They are printed in *ASP, Finance*, I, 302–04.

8. See note 3.

9. This document may be found in RG 46, Third Congress, 1793–1795, Reports of the Commissioners of the Sinking Fund, National Archives. It is printed in *ASP, Finance*, I, 316.

From Tench Coxe[1]

Treasury Department, Revenue Office, November 19, 1794. "It appears by the enclosed receipt that Mr. Joel Gibbs has dld. . . . 132 Hats for wh he is to be paid at the rate of 102 cents ℔ hat. I have the honor to request that a Wart. for 134 Drs 64/100 may be issued in his favor. . . ."[2]

LC, RG 75, Letters of Tench Coxe, Commissioner of the Revenue, Relating to the Procurements of Military, Naval, and Indian Supplies, National Archives.

1. For background to this letter, see Coxe to H, September 30, October 8, 24, 1794.

2. On November 20, 1794, Warrant No. 4261 for $134.64 was issued to Gibbs (D, RG 217, Miscellaneous Treasury Accounts, 1790–1894, Account No. 6922, National Archives).

From John Jay

London 19. Nov. 1794

My dear Sir

My Task is done—whether Finis *coronat* opus, the President Senate and Public will decide. This Letter goes by the Packet, and the Treaty with it.[1] Some parts of it require Elucidation to common Readers. I have not Time for comments. Lord Grenville is anxious to dismiss the Packet.[2] If this Treaty fails, I dispair of another. If satisfactory, care should be taken that public opinion be not misled respecting it—for this Reason the sooner it is ratified and published, the better. I really think the good Disposition of this Country should be cherished. I came here in the moment of Exultation and Triumph on account of Lord Howe's Victory.[3] From that Day to this I have experienced no change in Sentiments or conduct relative to the negociation. I must tho' not without Reluctance conclude—not being fit for a winters voyage I shall stay here 'till Spring—indeed I shall want Repairs before I am quite fit for any voyage. God bless you.

Yours John Jay

ALS, Hamilton Papers, Library of Congress; ADfS, Windsor Castle, England.

1. John Jay and Lord Grenville, the British Secretary of State for Foreign Affairs, signed the "Treaty of Amity, Commerce, and Navigation" on November 19, 1794. On the same day Jay wrote to Edmund Randolph describing the treaty and enclosing a copy of it (LS (marked duplicate), RG 59, Despatches from United States Ministers to Great Britain, 1791–1906, Vol. 1, April 19, 1794–June 1, 1795, National Archives), which was thrown into the sea to escape interception when the packet carrying it was captured by the French (Miller, *Treaties*, II, 267). Jay sent a second copy of the treaty to Randolph on November 21, 1794 (ALS, RG 59, Despatches from United States Ministers to Great Britain, 1791–1906, Vol. 1, April 19, 1794–June 1, 1795, National Archives), which Randolph received in Philadelphia on March 7, 1795 (*Executive Journal*, I, 178). For the treaty, see Miller, *Treaties*, II, 245–67.

In the Hamilton Papers, Library of Congress, are two extracts in Jay's handwriting from his letters to Randolph of October 29 and November 19, 1794. Both extracts concern the time allowed for the British to evacuate the posts in the Northwest. Both letters are printed in full in *ASP, Foreign Relations*, I, 500, 503–04.

2. In the draft at this point Jay wrote: "I therefore write in Haste."

3. This is a reference to the victory of the First of June (1794) by the British channel fleet, commanded by Lord Howe, over a French fleet. The battle has no place name, for it was fought more than four hundred miles from land.

To George Washington

Pittsburgh November 19. 1794
7 o Clock in the Morng

Sir

I wrote you the day before yesterday by express. Nothing material remains to be said. The army is generally in motion homeward; the Virginia line by way of Morgan Town to Winchester &c. The Maryland by way of Union Town to Williamsport &c. The Pensylvania & New Jersey by the old Pensylvania route to Bedford. The Judiciary is industrious in prosecuting the examinations of prisoners among whom there is a sufficient number of proper ones for examples & with sufficient evidence.[1] Col Gaddis[2] has been brought in.

With perfect respect & true attachment I have the honor Yr obed st

A Hamilton

P In five Minutes I set out for Philadelphia.

The President

ALS, George Washington Papers, Library of Congress; copy, Hamilton Papers, Library of Congress.

1. See H to William Rawle, November 17–19, 1794.

2. Thomas Gaddis. See H to Washington, November 15, 1794.

From John Randall[1]

[*Annapolis, November 22, 1794.* On November 27, 1794, Hamilton wrote to Randall: "Agreeably to the request contained in your letter of the 22d instant." *Letter not found.*]

1. Randall was collector of customs at Annapolis.

From Edward Carrington

[*Richmond, November 23, 1794.* On December 2, 1794, Hamilton wrote to Carrington: "Your letter of the 23rd of November is this moment received." *Letter not found.*]

From Henry Knox

[Philadelphia] Monday 24 Nov 1794. 1/2 past three oClock P.M.

My dear Hamilton

Among other reasons for wishing your return is Mrs Hamiltons earnest desire.

It seems that she has had, or has been in danger of a miscarriage, which has much alarmed her. But Doctor Khun[1] by whom she is attened with Doctor Stephens,[2] Assures that she is in no danger. However as she is extremely desirous of your presence in order to tranquilize her this note is transmited by the Presidents request.

I am my dear Sir Your affectionate friend HK

ALS, Massachusetts Historical Society, Boston.

1. Adam Kuhn was professor of the theory and practice of physics at the University of Pennsylvania.

2. Edward Stevens. See H to John Langdon, September 6, 1794.

From Tench Coxe[1]

T: D: R: O: Novembr. 25th 1794

Sir

The state of information in the War & Treasury Departments has rendered it necessary to employ Col: Francis Nicholls to Superintend generally the supply & accommodation of the Pennsylva. division of the Militia Army from Lancasr. to their homes.[2] He will depart on this service immediately, & as he may have occasion to make some disbursements of Cash, I have to request that you will advance to him the sum of two Thousand Dollars.[3]

I have the Honor to be &ca. T. Coxe C: R:

The Secy. of the Treasy.

LC, RG 75, Letters of Tench Coxe, Commissioner of the Revenue, Relating to the Procurement of Military, Naval, and Indian Supplies, National Archives.

1. For background to this letter, see H to Coxe, November 8, 1794.

2. See H to George Washington, June 14, 1794.

On November 25, 1794, Coxe wrote to Nichols: "In consequence of a letter received from the Secy. of the Treasury, I find it is desired that arrangements shall be made by me to have the *Pennsyla.* Division of the Militia Army supplied, at & from Lancasr. to their homes . . . with all the articles of commissaries & Quar master's supplies and aids. . . . You will therefore be pleased immediately to commence . . . a Tour, which will carry you through the whole of the Routes wh the . . . Penna. division of the Militia will take after their arrival at Lancaster. . . . The objects of supply & aid, are rations, fuel, straw, Waggons & other commissary & quarter masters stores . . ." (LC, RG 75, Letters of Tench Coxe, Commissioner of the Revenue, Relating to the Procurement of Military, Naval, and Indian Supplies, National Archives).

3. On November 25, 1794, Warrant No. 4266 for two thousand dollars was issued to Nichols (D, RG 217, Miscellaneous Treasury Accounts, 1790–1894, Account No. 6329, National Archives).

From Tench Coxe

Treasury Department, Revenue Office, November 27, 1794. Requests "that a remittance of seven or eight thousand Dolls. may be made to Geo: Gale Esqr. Supervr. of Maryland for the purpose of supplying with provisions &c. the Maryld Division of the Militia Army returning from the Westward."[1]

LC, RG 75, Letters of Tench Coxe, Commissioner of the Revenue, Relating to the Procurement of Military, Naval, and Indian Supplies, National Archives.

1. See H to Coxe, November 8, 1794.

From Tench Coxe[1]

Treasury Department, Revenue Office, November 27, 1794. "Mr. Mathew Spillard the contractor for furnishing Rations at the posts of Philada. represents that his accounts have been settled the 30 of Septemr. Last. That he has continued furnishing the rations since that period & wishes to have an advance of three hundred Dollars. . . ." [2]

LC, RG 75, Letters of Tench Coxe, Commissioner of the Revenue, Relating to the Procurement of Military, Naval, and Indian Supplies, National Archives.

1. For background to this letter, see Coxe to H, May 8, July 24, October 8, 1794.

2. On November 28, 1794, Warrant No. 4287 for three hundred dollars was issued to Spillard (D, RG 217, Miscellaneous Treasury Accounts, 1790–1894, Account No. 6325, National Archives).

To William Ellery

[*Philadelphia, November 27, 1794.* On December 14, 1794, Ellery wrote to Hamilton: "I acknowledge the receipt of your two letters of the 27th. of the last month." *Letters not found.*]

To Thomas FitzSimons [1]

[Philadelphia, November 27, 1794]

Dr. Sir,

Seeing the Debates on the subject of Democratic Societies I called at your house to state some facts.[2]

It is true that the *opposition* to the Excise laws began from causes foreign to Democratic societies, but it is well ascertained by proof in the course of Judiciary investigations that the *insurrection* immediately is to be essentially attributed to one of those Societies sometimes called the Mingo Creek Society [3]—sometimes the *Democratic* Society. An early & active member of it commanded the first attack on Neville's House.[4] Another active member of that society, McFarlane,[5] the second attack. Benjamin Parkinson, the President, & several other members of it seem to have directed the second attack as a *Committee*.[6]

This may be asserted as founded upon good proof and information recently received, though it would not be consistent with decorum to name me. Make what use you please of this, & communicate it to other friends.

Yrs truly

A Hamilton

Philad
November 27. 1794.
Thos. Fitzsimmons Esq.

JCH Transcripts; ALS, sold by Charles F. Heartman, January 12, 1929, Lot 200, Item 68.

1. FitzSimons, a merchant of Philadelphia, was a Federalist member of the House of Representatives from 1789 to 1795.

2. In his sixth annual address to Congress on November 19, 1794, George Washington described the disturbances in western Pennsylvania and the measures that had been taken to suppress the insurrection there. In speaking of the opposition to the excise law in Pennsylvania, he said: ". . . The very forbearance to press prosecutions was misinterpreted into a fear of urging the execution of the laws; and associations of men began to denounce threats against the officers employed. From a belief, that by a more formal concert, their operation might be defeated, certain self-created societies assumed the tone of condemnation" (*GW*, XXXIV, 29). The President's reference to the Democratic societies provoked a partisan debate in the House, which was set off by FitzSimons's motion that "we cannot withhold our reprobation of the self-created societies, which have risen up in some parts of the Union . . . and which, by deceiving and inflaming the ignorant and the weak, may naturally be supposed to have stimulated and urged the insurrection" (*Annals of Congress*, IV, 899).

3. The Mingo Creek Society in Washington County, Pennsylvania, was established on February 28, 1794.

4. John Neville, inspector of the revenue for Survey No. 4 in Pennsylvania. See "Deposition of Francis Mentges," August 1, 1794, note 2.

5. James McFarlane. See "Deposition of Francis Mentges," August 1, 1794, note 3.

6. For information on the attacks on John Neville by those citizens of western Pennsylvania who opposed the excise laws, see H to Washington, August 5, 1794; H to William Rawle, November 17–19, 1794.

To Benjamin Lincoln

Treasury Department November 27th 1794

Sir,

I have found it necessary, in order to provide for the punctual payment of the *Allowances to fishing Vessels*, which will become due on the 31st of the ensuing month [1] to authorise the Collectors of the several Districts in Massachusetts to draw on you, when the funds in their hands shall be inadequate to discharge the demands upon them.[2]

The Collectors who may have occasion to resort to this resource have been instructed to transmit their Signatures to you, and to furnish Weekly returns therein, accurately describing the drafts which they may issue which are to be according to the form hereto annexed.[3]

As a Check upon the Collectors, I request you to furnish me Weekly with a Schedule of the bills which shall be presented for payment—and none which shall not be presented prior to the first day of March next are to be paid, until they shall have been previously notified to me, & the payment specially authorised.

To enable you to face these payments in case the funds accruing in your Office should prove inadequate, you may draw upon the Office of Discount and Deposit in Boston for a sum not exceeding Forty Thousand Dollars—a credit to that amount having been opened with the said Office in your favor, to be replaced by you, out of duties on Import and Tonnage, as they shall accrue in your Office.

It will be necessary to an orderly Settlement of the Accounts at the Treasury, that you Keep a separate account of the transaction with the Office of Discount and Deposit.

I am with great consideration Sir, Your Obedient Servant

A Hamilton

Benjamin Lincoln Esquire
Collector,
Boston

LS, RG 36, Boston Collector, Letters from the Treasury, 1790–1817, Vol. 4, National Archives; copy, RG 56, Letters to Collectors at Small Ports, "Set G," National Archives; copy, RG 56, Letters to the Collector at Boston, National Archives.

1. H is referring to Section 1 of "An Act concerning certain Fisheries of the United States, and for the regulation and government of the Fishermen employed therein" (1 *Stat.* 229–32 [February 16, 1792]). For this section, see H to Benjamin Lincoln, December 5, 1793.

2. See "Treasury Department Circular to the Collectors of the Customs in Massachusetts," November 29, 1794.

3. See "Treasury Department Circular to the Collectors of the Customs in Massachusetts," November 29, 1794, note 3.

To Jeremiah Olney

Treasury Department November 27th 1794

Sir

I have to request, that you will retain Sufficient funds in your hands to discharge the Allowances to fishing Vessels, which will become due in your District on the 31st of the ensuing Month.[1] You will therefore pay these allowances agreeably to the instructions heretofore given for that purpose.[2]

I request however, that you will immediately furnish me with an estimate of the sum, which will be required, in order that I may regulate future draughts of the Treasurer accordingly.

I am with consideration Sir Your most Obedient Servant

A Hamilton

Jeremiah Olney Esquire
Collector of Providence

LS, Rhode Island Historical Society, Providence; copy, RG 56, Letters to the Collector at Providence, National Archives; copy, RG 56, Letters to Collectors at Small Ports, "Set G," National Archives.

1. H is referring to Section 1 of "An Act concerning certain Fisheries of the United States, and for the regulation and government of the Fishermen employed therein" (1 *Stat.* 229–32 [February 16, 1792]). For this section, see H to Benjamin Lincoln, December 5, 1793.

2. See "Treasury Department Circular to the Collectors of the Customs," October 25, 1792.

To John Randall

Treasury Department
November 27th 1794

Sir

Agreeably to the request contained in your letter of the 22d instant [1] I have directed the Treasurer of the United States to remit to your draught on the office of Discount & Deposit at Baltimore for seven hundred and fifty dollars—which sum when added to the funds already placed in your hands forms the whole of the monies allotted for the Fortification [2] to be erected at Annapolis, excepting two hundred and fifty dollars reserved for the purchase of the land.[3]

If it should be the opinion of the Engineer that a further sum will be required to complete the works it would be adviseable to transmit an estimate thereof immediately to this Office to enable Congress to determine whether any and what fu[r]ther provision is necessary to be made in this case.

I am with consideration Sir Your Obedient Servant

A Hamilton

John Randall Esqr
Collector
Annapolis

Copy, RG 56, Letters to and from the Collectors at Bridgetown and Annapolis, National Archives; copy, RG 56, Letters to Collectors at Small Ports, "Set G," National Archives.

1. Letter not found.

2. For information concerning the fortification of ports and harbors, see Henry Knox to H, March 29, 1794.

3. "An Act supplementary to 'An act to provide for the Defence of certain Ports and Harbors in the United States'" (1 *Stat.* 367 [May 9, 1794]) provided "That the port and harbor of the city of Annapolis be fortified, in such manner, and at such time or times, as the President of the United States may direct." The act also authorized the President to "receive from the State of Maryland, a cession of lands on which the said fortification, and its necessary buildings, may be erected."

From John Lamb[1]

New York 29. November 1794

Sir

I acknowledge the receipt of your favour of the 22d. instant respecting the articles, seized on board the French Ship the Favorite; and agreeably to your directions, have ordered them to be restored.[2]

At the time the seizure was made the Favorite, having been totally dismantled, her crew sent on board other ships of war, and her sails, rigging, and other materials, having been sold at public auction, she was considered as a Hulk, otherwise the event would not have taken place.

With respect to the charge, That the officers of the Customs had pulled down the national flag on board of the abovementioned vessel, and hoisted another in its place; it is groundless; as will appear by the papers transmitted to the Secretary of State by Mr. Harrison, the District Attorney.

I am with great respect Sir &c. John Lamb.

Copy, RG 46, Fourth Congress, 1795–1797, Message of President re relations with France, National Archives.

1. Lamb was collector of customs at New York.

2. On September 23, 1794, Jean Antoine Joseph Fauchet, the French Minister to the United States, wrote to Edmund Randolph: "Une nouvelle violation et de la souveraineté de la République Française et des traités que vous avez contractés avec elle, vient d'avoir lieu à New-York. Des hommes, de la douane je suppose, se sont transportés à bord de la Favorite vaisseau de guerre Français, et se sont permis d'enlever des effets appartenans à la République: un des exécuteurs de cet ordre, outrageant pour la Nation que je représente, a osé menacer d'un coup de sabre l'officier chargé de hisser notre pavillon pour la fête du 21 Septembre. Ses menaces se sont terminées par hisser celui de la douane. Celui-là a été respecté par les Français, mais le nôtre a été insulté d'une manière sanglante. Je demande justice contre les auteurs de cette infraction aux loix des nations. C'est à un Gouvernement libre que je m'adresse; je l'obtiendrai . . ." (*Correspondence of the French Ministers with the United States Govern-*

ment, part 1, 25–26). A translation of this letter is printed in *ASP, Foreign Relations,* I, 598–99.

Randolph on September 25, 1794, requested Richard Harison, the United States attorney for the District of New York, to investigate Fauchet's charges (LC, RG 59, Domestic Letters of the Department of State, Vol. 7, June 27–November 30, 1794, National Archives). Harison replied to Randolph on October 17 as follows: "Upon the whole It appears that the officers of the Customs made the seizure . . . by express orders from the Collector given under an Idea that the Ship Favorite was used for promoting a species of Commerce forbidden by Law. . . . But from the Evidence it is apparent That there has been no Intentional Disrespect manifested . . . towards the Flag minister or Citizens of the French Republic" (LS, RG 59, Miscellaneous Letters, 1790–1799, National Archives). On November 17, 1794, Randolph wrote to Fauchet: ". . . [The President] has thought proper to instruct me to inform you, that on the faith, which he always reposes in your assertions, he takes these points for granted: that the Favourite is a public vessel of war, bearing the Commission of the French Republic: and that no contravention of the act prohibiting the exportation of military Stores, was meditated, in the application of those, which were found on board.

"The President highly disapproves that a public vessel of war belonging to a foreign nation, should be searched by Officers of the Customs, upon a suspicion of illicit commerce. The propriety of representing such a suspicion to the Consul of that nation, or the commander of the vessel will not be controverted, this being a course respectful and customary. A general instruction will therefore be given to pursue this course; with the view, that, if it should be ineffectual, the government of the United States may adopt those measures, which the necessity of the case, and their rights may require.

"A particular instruction founded on the same principles will be also forwarded to the Collector of New York; with this addition, to discontinue the prosecution against the property, and restore what may be within his power or command. . . .

"An insult to the French flag will not be tolerated by the President, whensoever he can prevent or punish it. But the depositions, do not place this subject in so clear a light, as to prove its existence, or designate the culpable person. It is the President's purpose therefore to cause the Officers of the Customs to be admonished to respect your flag, and if this be not satisfactory, and you are still persuaded, that an insult has been committed, I shall be ready to concur in any arrangement, which may be convenient, for the full examination of such other witnesses as may be produced." (LC, RG 59, Domestic Letters of the Department of State, Vol. 7, June 27–November 30, 1794, National Archives; copy, Connecticut Historical Society, Hartford.) This letter is printed in *ASP, Foreign Relations,* I, 599.

On November 21, 1794, Randolph sent to Oliver Wolcott, Jr., his letter of November 17 to Fauchet and requested Wolcott "to send from the department of the treasury, the general and particular instructions, therein mentioned . . ." (ALS, Connecticut Historical Society, Hartford; LC, RG 59, Domestic Letters of the Department of State, Vol. 7, June 26–November 30, 1794, National Archives). Wolcott, who was in charge of the Treasury Department during H's absence with the militia army in western Pennsylvania, wrote to Lamb on November 22, 1794: ". . . in consequence of the Letter of the Secretary of State, you are instructed to discontinue the prosecution and to restore the property which may be in your power or command.

"You are also informed that *public* Vessels of War belonging to foreign nations are not to be searched by the Officers of the Customs upon a suspicion of illicit Commerce—instead of this course, where just causes of suspicions arise, it will be proper to represent the same, to the Consul of the Nation or the Commander of the Vessell. If this mode should however prove ineffectual a representation to the proper Department of Government ought instantly to be made. . . .

"You will be pleased to cause the flags of all nations to be treated with respect, as far as may be in your power; all insults or neglects which may be misconstrued are to be avoided. . . ." (ADf, Connecticut Historical Society, Hartford; copy, Connecticut Historical Society.) H endorsed the draft of Wolcott's letter to Lamb: "The rule with regard to not searching appears to me right—but the officers should be cautioned to increase their vigilance in other ways over such vessels. AH. A circular to the effect should go. AH."

On February 7, 1795, Randolph sent Fauchet a copy of Lamb's letter to H (LC, RG 59, Domestic Letters of the Department of State, Vol. 8, December 6, 1794–October 12, 1795, National Archives).

Treasury Department Circular to the Collectors of the Customs in Massachusetts[1]

Treasury Department, Nov. 29th 1794.

Sir,

I have to request, that you will retain in your hands a sufficient sum of the monies arising from the duties on Imports and Tonnage for the purpose of discharging the Allowances to Fishing Vessels which will become due in your District on the 31st of December ensuing, and which are to be paid agreeably to the instructions heretofore given for that purpose.[2] If the funds accruing in your office should fall short of the amount required, you will pay the deficiency by drafts, according to the inclosed form[3] on Benjamin Lincoln Esquire Collector of Boston, in which case it will be necessary, that you transmit your Signature to the said Collector, and furnish him with Weekly statements, accurately describing therein the drafts issued. Copies of these Statements are also to be regularly forwarded to this Office.

With consideration, I am Sir, Your Obedient Servant,

A Hamilton.

LS, to Samuel Gerry, Harvard College Library; LC, to Benjamin Lincoln, RG 56, Circulars of the Office of the Secretary, "Set T," National Archives; LS, sold at Goodspeed's Book Shop, Boston, Catalogue 255, Item 401.

1. For background to this letter, see H to Benjamin Lincoln, November 27, 1794.

2. "Treasury Department Circular to the Collectors of the Customs," October 25, 1792.

3. The form which was enclosed reads as follows:

"District of Collectors Office.

Exchange Dollars —— After ten days, and within Sixty days after date pay to ——, or order, —— being for the Allowances due to the Owner and Crew of the —— employed during the last Season in the Bank and other Cod-Fisheries; with or without further advice" (LC, RG 56, Circulars of the Office of the Secretary, "Set T," National Archives).

From Tench Coxe

Treasury Department
Revenue-office Novemr. 30th. 1794

Sir

It appears from Inspection of the report of the committee of the Representatives upon the ways and means that they estimated the new Revenues of 1794 [1] to produce as follows.

1st The revenue on carriages [2]	150,000
2dly On Stamps, which was not laid by law [3] 100,000 Dollars.	—
3dly On Sales by auction [4]	100,000
4thly on Tobacco and Snuff—the last of which only was laid by law [5] 100,000 Dollars	—
5thly on loaf and lump Sugars [6]	50,000
6thly on licences to foreign spirits and wines [7]	100,000

The above Revenues not being concocted at the Treasury, I have not the details of the Estimates, nor are any returns yet received, by which their respective produce can be more certainly stated. It is reasonable to suppose that the licences under the 6th head having been confined to the Venders of foreign Spirits by an alteration of the plan of the Committee,[8] the expected Revenue may not be collected.

The returns of the Spirits distilled from foreign materials for during the year ending the 30th June 1794, amg. only to	Dolls 174,347
The returns to be received may amount to	35,653
	210,000
In 1792 entire the gross Revenue on Spirits from foreign materials was	354,000
In 1793 entire the gross revenue on Spirits from foreign materials was *about*	240,000

The fluctuations in the ownership, and agriculture of the Sugar Colonies, and of the intercourse with them, place the supplies of the materials for the manufacture of this spirit upon a footing admitting only of conjecture.

As much duty on Domestic Spirits however, as 400,000 Dolls may accrue in 1795 if the laws can be effectually executed. It is to be observed that the high price of grain has diminished the distillery therefrom, in some of the States, and that fruit is an uncertain Material.

It may be remarked upon the whole that as the country is not only increasing in consumers, but in expensive consumers, and in ability to purchase, the duties on wines, and foreign and domestic distilled Spirits are not likely to fall off materially.

With great respect, Sir, Your most obedient Servant

Tench Coxe
Commissr. of the Revenue

The Secretary
of the Treasury

LC, RG 58, Letters of Commissioner of Revenue, 1794–1795, National Archives.

1. The House of Representatives first considered this committee's report on January 9–10, 1794. See *Annals of Congress*, IV, 168–69. Various features of the report were debated in the House for the remainder of the session.

2. Duties on carriages were imposed by "An Act laying duties upon Carriages for the conveyance of Persons" (1 *Stat.* 373–75 [June 5, 1794]).

3. On May 27, 1794, a bill "laying duties on stamped vellum, parchment, and paper" was defeated in the House of Representatives (*Annals of Congress*, IV, 725–26).

4. This tax was imposed by "An Act laying duties on property sold at Auction" (1 *Stat.* 397–400 [June 9, 1794]).

5. On May 17, 1794, "a bill laying certain duties upon manufactured tobacco and refined sugar" was introduced in the House of Representatives (*Journal of the House*, II, 167). The House agreed to strike out the tax on tobacco on May 23, 1794 (*Annals of Congress*, IV, 716). "An Act laying certain duties upon Snuff and Refined Sugar" became law on June 5, 1794 (1 *Stat.* 384–90).

6. See note 5.

7. See "An Act laying duties on licenses for selling Wines and foreign distilled spirituous liquors by retail" (1 *Stat.* 376–78 [June 5, 1794]).

8. The bill was presented to the House of Representatives on May 28, 1794, as "a bill laying duties on licences for selling wines, and distilled spirituous liquors by retail" (*Journal of the House*, II, 183). After the bill passed the House on May 31, 1794, the members resolved that the title should be changed to "An act laying duties on licenses for selling wines and foreign distilled spirituous liquors, by retail" (*Journal of the House*, II, 190).

To John Quincy Adams

(Duplicate) Treasury Department
December 1st 1794

Sir

The United States have funds of some consequence in the hands of our Commissioners at Amsterdam,[1] over and above what may be required for approaching payments. The Situation of Holland according to the last advices,[2] leaves me not without disquietude on this account; for bidding the negotiation of bills upon that Country without great sacrifice. I have therefore directed the Treasurer to draw upon those Commissioners in favour of Thomas Pinckney Esquire our Minister at London [3] for a considerable part of the Surplus in their hands of which I request you to apprise them—not having time to write to them by this opportunity.

But besides the amount of the bill in favour of Mr. Pinckney, the United States will have a sum not unimportant in the hands of the Commissioners. I beg your attention to this & that in case of extremity you will concert with them the best means of securing it. Two modes occur as most obvious—one to remit to Mr. Pinckney in London—the other to invest in the funds of the United States.

I feel great consolation in your being on the Spot to aid our Commissioners in taking care of the Interests of our Country. On their integrity and prudence I have also the greatest reliance.

With respectful consideration & true esteem I have the honor to be Sir, Your very Obedient Servant Alexander Hamilton

John Adams Junr. Esquire
Minister at the Hague

LS (duplicate), Adams Family Papers, deposited in the Massachusetts Historical Society, Boston.

1. Willink, Van Staphorst, and Hubbard.

2. For the effect of the international situation on the money market in Holland, see Willink, Van Staphorst, and Hubbard to H, September 26, 1794; Nicholaas Van Staphorst to H, October 4, 1794.

3. On November 21, 1794, George Washington nominated "Thomas Pinckney to be Envoy Extraordinary of the United States to His Catholic Majesty, for the purpose of negotiating of and concerning the navigation of the river Mississippi . . . and of and concerning the general commerce between the said

United States and the kingdoms and dominions of his . . . Catholic Majesty." The Senate approved the nomination on November 22, 1794 (*Executive Journal*, I, 163–64). On November 28, 1794, Edmund Randolph sent to Pinckney his instructions and commission (LC, RG 59, Diplomatic and Consular Instructions of the Department of State, 1791–1801, Vol. 2, August 22, 1793–June 1, 1795, National Archives).

On December 2, 1794, Samuel Meredith, the treasurer of the United States, wrote to Willink, Van Staphorst, and Hubbard: "Ten days after Sight, pay this my third of Exchange . . . to the Honorable Thomas Pinckney Minister from the United States to the Court of Great Britain or Order, Three hundred and Three thousand One hundred and fifteen Current Guilders Value received; which place to the Account of the United States of America" (ALS, RG 59, Miscellaneous Letters, 1790–1799, National Archives).

To William Buchanan and Samuel Smith[1]

Treasury Department, December 1, 1794. "A Bill from you for Ten thousand Dollars in favour of Philips & Cramond[2] has been presented and will be paid to morrow. But though intirely disposed to give effectual support to Messrs. Elliot & Williams[3] and every facility to your House in their Agency for those Gentlemen[4]—I cannot countenance the practice of drawing upon the Treasury without previous communication and permission. I am obliged therefore to apprise you that future Bills without such communication & permission must be refused, and I rely consequently that none will be drawn. . . ."

Copy, Connecticut Historical Society, Hartford.

1. Smith and Buchanan were Baltimore merchants. Smith had been commander of the Maryland militia during the Whiskey Insurrection.

2. William Crammond and Henry Philips were Philadelphia merchants who were associated with George and Robert Philips, merchants of Manchester, England. See Robert Morris to Crammond, March 14, 1795; Morris to George and Robert Philips, March 16, October 10, 1795; Morris to William Temple Franklin, May 14, 1795 (LC, Robert Morris Papers, Library of Congress).

3. Robert Elliot and Elie Williams, contractors for supplying the Army on the western frontier.

4. Smith supplied Elliot and Williams with dry goods for the Indian trade.

To Edward Carrington

[*Philadelphia, December 1, 1794.* On December 12, 1794, Carrington wrote to Hamilton: "I have been favored with yours of the 1st. Instant." *Letter not found.*]

From Tench Coxe

Treasury Department, Revenue Office, December 1, 1794. Requests "that a Warrant may be issued for two thousand Dollars in the name of Levi Holingsworth & Son, as Agents for Richd. Edwards, George Leonard, Levi Holingsworth & Paschall Holingsworth, on a/count of the contract for furnishing Kentledge & Iron Cannon ball." [1]

LC, RG 75, Letters of Tench Coxe, Commissioner of the Revenue, Relating to the Procurement of Military, Naval, and Indian Supplies, National Archives.

1. See Coxe to H, September 23, 1794.

To Frederick A. C. Muhlenberg

Philadelphia December 1st 1794

Sir

I beg leave through you to make known to the House of Representatives—That I have signified to The President of the UStates my intention to resign my office of Secretary of the Treasury on the last day of January next.[1] I make this communication in order that an opportunity may be given previous to that Event, to institute any further proceeding which may be contemplated, if any there be, in consequence of the inquiry during the last session into the State of this Department.[2]

With perfect respect I have the honor to be Sir Your most Obedt & hum ser

The Honorable The Speaker of the House of Representatives

ADf, Hamilton Papers, Library of Congress; copy, RG 233, Reports of the Secretary of the Treasury, 1784–1795, Vol. IV, National Archives.

1. See H to George Washington, December 1, 1794.

2. H is referring to the select committee appointed by the House of Representatives to examine the Treasury Department. See the introductory note to H to Muhlenberg, December 16, 1793.

To the President and Directors of the Bank of New York[1]

[*Treasury Department, December 1, 1794.* Henry W. Domett states that on this date Hamilton wrote to the president and directors of the Bank of New York asking that the bank lend one hundred thousand dollars to the United States.[2] *Letter not found.*[3]]

1. Gulian Verplanck was president of the Bank of New York.
2. Domett, *History of the Bank of New York*, 50.
3. Although this letter has not been found, see the similar letters which H wrote to the president and directors of the Bank of North America and of the Bank of Pennsylvania on December 1, 1794.

To the President and Directors of the Bank of North America[1]

Treasury Department, December 1, 1794. This letter is the same as that which Hamilton wrote to the president and directors of the Bank of Pennsylvania on December 1, 1794.

Copy, Historical Society of Pennsylvania, Philadelphia.

1. John Nixon was president of the Bank of North America.

To the President and Directors of the Bank of Pennsylvania[1]

Treasury Department December 1st 1794

Gentlemen

A plan for the Redemption of the debt of the United States on more comprehensive principles than have been hitherto adopted, may be expected to be shortly under the consideration of the House of Representatives.[2] The practicability of such a plan may be materially connected with the answer that shall be given to the following Inquiry.

Would it be convenient to the Bank of Pennsylvania to make an *annual* loan of one hundred thousand Dollars for the term of five Years; that is to say a Loan of one hundred thousand Dollars for the term of one Year to be reimbursed and renewed annually for five Successive Years. The Interest to be five per Cent per Annum?

It will be readily understood that the Loan at no one time could exceed one hundred thousand Dollars.

In proposing the question under the shape of an annual Loan rather than of one to continue for the whole term of five Years, I am influenced by the opinion that Banks ought cautiously to go into the business of permanent Loans or Loans of any considerable duration.

It will be seen that I do not propose a Contract, but only ask an *opinion* of the present Directors how far it may comport with the ability, convenience and policy of Your Institution, to come in aid of the Government in the way suggested. It would not be expected that the loan for one year should be accompanied by an *engagement* to renew it another; for this would be equivalent to a stipulation for the whole term. A view of what would be probably convenient is all that is desired.

The object is one which affecting strongly the interest and wishes of the Community, cannot but make a correspondent impression on the dispositions of Your Board. A similar inquiry has been extended to other Banks.[3]

I request a Speedy reply.

With great consideration & esteem I have the honor to be Gentlemen Your Obedient Servant Alexander Hamilton
Secy of the Treasy

The President & Directors of
the Bank of Pennsylvania.

LS, MS Division, New York Public Library.

1. John Barclay was president of the Bank of Pennsylvania.

2. On November 21, 1794, the House of Representatives "resolved itself into a Committee of the Whole House" and adopted five resolutions. The second of these resolutions reads: "*Resolved,* That it is the opinion of this committee that further provision ought to be made by law for the redemption of the public debt." The House also "*Ordered,* That a committee be appointed to prepare and report a plan. pursuant to the second resolution, and that Mr. William Smith, Mr. [Fisher] Ames, Mr. [Thomas] Fitzsimons, Mr. [Gabriel] Duvall, and Mr. [John] Nicholas, be the said committee" (*Journal of the House*, II, 238). On December 15, 1794, "Mr. William Smith, from the committee appointed to prepare and report a plan for the redemption of the public debt, made a report" (*Journal of the House*, II, 266). The Smith committee's report is printed in *ASP, Finance*, I, 317–19.

H also reported subsequently on the same subject. See "Report on a Plan for the Further Support of Public Credit," January 16, 1795.

3. See H to the President and Directors of the Bank of New York, December 1, 1794; H to the President and Directors of the Bank of North America, December 1, 1794.

To Thomas Pinckney

Treasury Department December 1st 1794

Sir,

I have directed the Treasurer to remit you a bill on our Commissioners at Amsterdam drawn in your favour for the sum of 303,115 Guilders.[1] This step has been adopted in consequence of the precarious Situation of Holland which renders the Sale of bills on Amsterdam impracticable.[2]

You will please to take the means which shall appear to you most eligible to transfer the amount of the bill from Amsterdam to London, causing the money to be placed liable to your order in the Bank of London, or in some other situation which shall appear to you not less secure. If subsequent intelligence shall render it safe the Treasurer will draw upon you for the proceeds of the bill which he is directed to remit.

Among the modes of transferring the money from Amsterdam to London you will no doubt consider whether the shipping it in specie in the name and on account of the United States in a bottom of the United States and properly insured, may not be most adviseable. This will depend on circumstances which can only be judged of on the Spot—rate of exchange, rate of insurance &c. In case of Capture by a French armed Vessel in such a Situation there would be ground of claim for retribution by way of set off upon the French Government.

Besides the amount of the above mentioned bill there will be funds in the hands of our Commissioners more than sufficient for any approaching payments. Our Minister at the Hague[3] is instructed if necessary to provide for the safety of these also by causing them to be remitted to You.

I will make no apology for the trouble I give you on this occasion knowing your zeal for the public service & counting on your obliging dispositions.

With great respect & esteem I have the honor to be Sir, Your very Obedient Servant Alexander Hamilton

Thomas Pinckney Esquire
Minister Plenipotentiary
London

LS, Pinckney Family Papers, Library of Congress; LS (marked duplicate), Pinckney Family Papers, Library of Congress.

1. See H to John Quincy Adams, December 1, 1794, note 3.

2. On December 3, 1794, Edmund Randolph wrote to Pinckney: "I have the honor of informing you that the President has put your mission upon the same footing as to pecuniary considerations with that of Mr. Jay. I had therefore collected Bills to the amount of Eighteen thousand Dollars to be remitted to Amsterdam, as a fund for your expences. . . . But the probable situation of Amsterdam, according to the report of yesterday, has determined me to cancel those Bills, and get others on London, which I shall dispatch by the next vessel" (LC, RG 59, Diplomatic and Consular Instructions of the Department of State, 1791–1801, Vol. 2, August 22, 1793–June 1, 1795, National Archives).

3. John Quincy Adams.

To Edmund Randolph[1]

[Philadelphia, December 1–12, 1794][2]

Remarks on Lord Grenvilles project of a Commercial Treaty made at the request of E Randolph Esquire Secty of States

A[3] Inasmuch as the light house duties, which are *excepted*, constitute an additional charge on Vessels of the UStates beyond those of G. Britain in British Ports, this article, which puts British vessels in our ports exactly upon the same footing with ours wants reciprocity.[4] But the most important consideration will be, that as the distinctions which now exist between foreign and our own vessels are really of importance to our Trade, our Merchants will see them relinquished with reluctance unless there be some clear equivalent.[5] If the stipulation extends to duties on *goods* brought in British Bottoms, the conclusion is so much the stronger.[6]

B[7] This article in its operation wants reciprocity. The British system[8] contains *now* numerous prohibitions, ours none. To fix this state of things is to renounce an important right to and place ourselves on an unequal footing. It gives a claim to some equivalent.

C[9] It may be supposed that the Equivalent in both cases is to be found in this article. It would be so (excepting one circumstance that will be presently mentioned) if the duration of the privileges granted was coextensive with that of the other parts of the Treaty.[10] But the short term of the privileges here proposed to be granted renders them of *inconsiderable* value. The Proviso too prohibits vessels of the UStates from carrying "*West India*" productions from the British Islands or the UStates to any other part of the World. If this prohibition is to be taken in a *literal* sense and to extend to the West

India possessions of other countries than GBritain, it would be to renounce a valuable branch of Trade now enjoyed and probably more than would be gained.[11]

D [12] The giving a duration of twelve years to the Treaty as it respects the Trade with Europe and of only two years as it respects the West Indies will be very unacceptable.[13] It will be the more so as the Project does not even secure the *Status Quo* with the European Dominions of Great Britain that is it does not *secure* the particular privileges and exemptions which we now enjoy by Proclamation compared with other foreign Nations.[14] AH

Mr. Hamilton communicates these remarks in personal confidence to Mr. Randolph with this request that no *copy* of them may be taken & that this paper may be returned after it serves the purpose for which the remarks were requested.

ADS, Hamilton Papers, Library of Congress.

1. On September 13, 1794, John Jay sent to Randolph copies of two "Drafts or Projects" of treaties which Lord Grenville, the British Secretary of State for Foreign Affairs, had submitted to Jay on August 30, 1794 (LC, RG 59, Despatches from United States Ministers to Great Britain, 1792–1870, Vol. 1, June 23, 1794–March 5, 1795, National Archives; copy, New-York Historical Society, New York City). Randolph received Jay's letter on November 11, 1794 (Randolph to Jay, November 12, 1794 [LC, RG 59, Diplomatic and Consular Instructions of the Department of State, Vol. 2, August 22, 1793–June 1, 1795, National Archives]). The first draft deals with all points in dispute between the United States and Great Britain; the second is concerned with commercial regulations between the two nations. In response to Randolph's request for comments on Grenville's proposed commercial treaty, H prepared the "Remarks" printed above. Randolph incorporated H's "Remarks" in the instructions which he sent to Jay on December 15, 1794 (LC, RG 59, Diplomatic and Consular Instructions of the Department of State, 1791–1801, Vol. 2, August 22, 1793–June 1, 1795, National Archives).

2. In *JCHW*, V, 29, this document is dated "1794."

3. This section of H's "Remarks" refers to Article 3 of Grenville's proposed commercial treaty. Article 3 reads: "The Vessels of the Two contracting parties respectively coming to the Dominions or Territories aforesaid, shall enjoy the same liberty in respect of the Entry & Discharge of their lawfull Cargoes, and all other regulations which respect the general convenience and advantage of Commerce as now are, or shall at any time be enjoyed by any other Foreign Nation, which shall be the most favored in that respect, and no distinction shall exist of Tonnage or other Duties, (such Light House Duties excepted, as are levied for the Profit of Individuals or of Corporations,) by which the Vessels of the one party shall pay in the Ports of the other, any higher or other Duties, than shall be paid in similar Circumstances, by the Vessels of the Foreign nation the most favored in that respect, or by the Vessels of the Party into whose Ports they shall come" (copy, RG 59, Despatches from the United States Ministers to Great Britain, 1792–1870, Vol. 1, June 23, 1794–March 5, 1795, National Archives).

4. Opposite this paragraph H wrote: "Note I observe the light house duties of the particular kind are afterwards relinquished." H is referring to changes which had been made in the proposed commercial treaty in the course of conversations and letters between Grenville and Jay. In his "Observations" on the treaty, dated September 7, 1794, Grenville changed the last sentence in Article 3 to read as follows: ". . . by which the Vessels of the One Party shall pay in the Ports of the other, any higher or other duties than shall be paid in similar circumstances by the Vessels of the Foreign Nation the most favored in that respect, or any higher or other duties than shall be paid in similar cases by the Vessels of the Party itself into whose Ports they shall come" (copy, RG 59, Despatches from United States Ministers to Great Britain, 1792–1870, Vol. 1, June 23, 1794–March 5, 1795, National Archives).

5. In distinguishing between United States and foreign commerce, British commercial policy provided that ". . . the commerce of the United States, with respect to certain articles above enumerated and described . . . [be granted] the same preference as is granted to the commerce of the islands and plantations in America, remaining under your Majesty's dominion" (*Report of the Lords of the Committee of Privy Council, Appointed for all Matters relating to Trade and Foreign Plantations, on the Commerce and Navigation between his Majesty's Dominions, and the Territories belonging to the United States of America* [London, 1791], in Nathaniel Atchenson, ed., *Collection of Interesting and Important Reports and Papers on the Navigation and Trade of Great Britain, Ireland, and the British Colonies in the West Indies and America, with Tables of Tonnage and of Exports and Imports, &c, &c. &c.* [Printed by Order of "The Society of Ship-Owners of Great Britain." And Sold by J. Stockdale, Piccadilly: J. Butterworth, Fleet-Street: and J. and J. Richardson, Cornhill, 1807], 53). The same report also notes that the United States was exempt from the British duty on aliens, which other foreign nations were required to pay (*Report of the Lords of the Committee of Privy Council* . . ., 54).

6. For these duties, see "An Act to provide more effectually for the collection of the duties imposed by law on goods, wares and merchandise imported into the United States, and on the tonnage of ships or vessels" (1 *Stat.* 145–78 [August 4, 1790]).

7. This section of H's "Remarks" refers to Article 5 of Grenville's proposed commercial treaty. Article 5 reads: "No new Prohibition shall be laid in any of the Territories or Dominions aforesaid, by one of the contracting Parties, on the importation of any Article being the Growth Produce or Manufacture of the Territories or Dominions of the other, nor shall Article being of the growth produce or Manufacture, of any other Country be prohibited to be imported into the Dominions of one of the contracting Parties by the Vessels of the other, except such Articles only as are now so prohibited" (copy, RG 59, Despatches from United States Ministers to Great Britain, 1792–1870, Vol. 1, June 23, 1794–March 5, 1795, National Archives).

8. For the rules of the "British system," see "An Act for regulating the Trade between the Subjects of his Majesty's Colonies and Plantations in *North America*, and in the West India Islands, and the Countries belonging to the United States of *America;* and between his Majesty's said Subjects and the Foreign Islands in the *West Indies*" (28 Geo. III, C. 6 [1788]).

9. This section of H's "Remarks" refers to Article 6 of Lord Grenville's proposed commercial treaty. Article 6 reads: ". . . His Majesty consents that it shall and may be lawfull, during the Time hereinafter limited, for the Citizens of the United States of America, to carry to any of his Majesty's Islands and Ports in the West Indies, from the United States, in their own Vessels, not being above the burthen of Seventy Tons, any goods or merchandise being of the growth or produce of the said States, which it is or

may be lawfull, to carry to the said Islands and Ports from the said States in British Vessels, and that the said American Vessels and their Cargoes shall pay there no other or higher Duties than shall be payable by British Vessels in similar circumstances: And that it shall be lawfull to the said American Citizens to purchase, load and carry away in their said Vessels to the United States, from the said Islands and Ports, all such Articles being of the growth and Produce of the said Islands, as may by Law be carried from them to the said States in British Vessels; and subject only to the same duties and Charges on Exportation, to which British Vessels are or shall be subject in similar circumstances; Provided always, that they carry and land the same in the United States only, it being expressly agreed and declared that, during the continuance of this Article, The United States will prohibit the carrying any West India productions or manufactures in American Vessels, either from his Majesty's Islands or from the United States, to any part of the World except the United States,—reasonable Sea Stores excepted, and excepting also Rum made in the United States from West India Molasses" (copy, RG 59, Despatches from United States Ministers to Great Britain, 1792–1870, Vol. 1, June 23, 1794–March 5, 1795, National Archives).

10. Although Article 7 specified that the treaty was to be effective for twelve years after the end of the European war, Article 6 was to be in force for only two years after the war ended (copy, RG 59, Despatches from United States Ministers to Great Britain, 1792–1870, Vol. 1, June 23, 1794–March 5, 1795, National Archives).

11. In 1784, France opened the French West Indies to foreign ships, which were allowed to bring enumerated goods into specified ports and to take back rum and molasses (*Recueil Général des Anciennes Lois Françaises, Depuis L'An 420 Jusqu'à La Révolution de 1789, par MM. Jourdan, Docteur en droit, Avocat à la Cour royale de Paris; Isambert, Avocat aux Conseils du Roi et à la Cour de Cassation; Decrusy, ancien Avocat à la Cour royale de Paris* [Paris, 1827], XXVII, 459–64).

12. See note 10.

13. See note 10.

14. See note 5.

From Ebenezer Stevens[1]

New York 1 December 1794

Dear Sir,

I will thank You to direct John Lamb[2] Esqr to make me a further advance on account of the United States for fortifying the Harbour of New York. I have vouchers for the whole amount of the appropriation made by Congress and will forward them to the proper office agreeable to Your written instructions to Mr Lamb under date of the 13. of April last.[3] I wish to be informed whether the Chief Engineer[4] and his assistants Salaries are to come out of the above appropriation or not.

I am Very truly Yours Ebenezer Stevens

Copy, New-York Historical Society, New York City.

1. Stevens was "Agent for erecting the Fortifications at New York" (DS, RG 217, Miscellaneous Treasury Accounts, 1790–1894, Account No. 6749, National Archives). For information concerning the fortifications, see Henry Knox to H, March 29, 1794.

2. Lamb was collector of customs for New York City.

3. "Treasury Department Circular to the Collectors of the Customs," April 3–June 4, 1794.

Stevens's accounts with the United States for the fortification of New York may be found in RG 217, Miscellaneous Treasury Accounts, 1790–1894, Account Nos. 6749, 7058, 7061, National Archives.

4. Charles Vincent.

To George Washington

Philadelphia December 1. 1794

Sir

I have the honor to inform you that I have fixed upon the last of January next as the day for the resignation of my office of Secretary of the Treasury.[1] I make the communication now, that there may be time to mature such an arrangement as shall appear to you proper to meet the vacancy when it occurs.[2]

With perfect respect & the truest attachment I have the honor to be Sir Your very obedient servt

The President of The UStates

ADf, Hamilton Papers, Library of Congress; LC, George Washington Papers, Library of Congress.

1. See H to Washington, June 21, 1793, May 27, 1794; Washington to H, May 29, 1794.

2. On the back of the draft H wrote: "Remember to order Chariot & Chair & pay the duty." See "An Act laying duties upon Carriages for the conveyance of Persons" (1 *Stat.* 373–76 [June 5, 1794]).

From Jonathan Williams[1]

Philadelphia Decr 1. 1794.

Sir.

The Expence of provision and Forage for the Detachment that escorted you from Pittsburgh to Bedford, say six Horsemen, 100 miles, was Twenty two Dollars. I presume that this will be a sufficient Document for the Reimbursement.

I am with great Respect Sir Your obedient Servant

Jona Williams
Occasional Qur Mastr.

The Honble
A. Hamilton Esqr.

[ENCLOSURE]

Memorandum.

[Philadelphia, December 1, 1794]

Recd from Colel Hamilton seventy Dollars	$70.
Expence of the Escort from Pittsburgh to Bedford	22
	48
Colel Hamilton's proportion of the Expence from Bedford to the place of Separation on the Lancaster Road	8
	40

Returned to Colel Hamilton.
Forty Dollars

Philadelphia Dec 1. 1794.
Jona. Williams
Occasional Quartermaster to the Escort

ALS, Hamilton Papers, Library of Congress.

1. Williams, a native of Boston and a great-nephew of Benjamin Franklin, had been prize agent and commercial agent at Nantes during the American Revolution. After the adoption of the Constitution he returned to the United States, settled in Philadelphia, and speculated in stocks and land. On September 11, 1794, he had written to Governor Thomas Mifflin of Pennsylvania: "Not being called upon in a Line of militia Duty, & being impressed with the Importance of the present Crisis, I cannot hesitate in making an offer of my personal services in any way you may think proper to command . . ." (*Pennsylvania Archives*, 2nd ser., IV, 284).

Bank Draft

[Philadelphia, December 2, 1794]

Cashier of the Bank of The UStates Dollars 50—

Pay to E Hamilton or bearer Fifty Dollars.

A Hamilton

Philadelphia. December 2d. 1794

ADS, The Huntington Library, San Marino, California.

To Edward Carrington[1]

Treasury Department
December 2nd. 1794

Sir

Your letter of the 23rd of November is this moment received.[2]

Governor Lee[3] while in the Western Country informed me, after the Steps had been taken, that he had been under a necessity in two instances to facilitate the return of detachments of sick men, of calling upon Mr. Smith[4] to advance Moneys to Them. The inconveniences of the Measure could not but strike at first view, yet the motives were Laudible, and in collateral aspects the measure expedient. But it was too late to disapprove or remedy, My answer would of course accord with the state of things.

Unapprised of the means in yours or Mr. Smiths Command or the extent of this extra demand I am wholly at a loss how to meet it with accuracy. But as I ought to suppose it cannot exceed two thousand Dollars, I have instructed the Treasurer[5] to send you Blank Drafts for that sum to be placed on yourself as Supervisor on the Collector of Alexandria[6] or the Cashier of the Bank of the United States[7] as occasion may require.

For the rest I must entreat you to do the Best which circumstances admit, in order that no body may be compromotted & the public interest may not finally suffer.

With Great consideration & Esteem I am sir Your Obedient Servant.

Edward Carrington Esqr.
Agent for Military Supplies

Copy, Connecticut Historical Society, Hartford.

1. During the Whiskey Insurrection Carrington, who was supervisor of the revenue for Virginia, had been agent for supplying the Virginia militia.

2. Letter not found.

3. Henry Lee, commander in chief of the militia army in western Pennsylvania, had completed his term as governor of Virginia on November 30, 1794.

4. Edward Smith, inspector of the revenue for Survey No. 5 in Virginia, had been assistant agent for supplying the Virginia militia.

5. Samuel Meredith.

6. John Fitzgerald.

7. John Kean.

To George Washington

Treasury Dept. Decemb. 2d. 1794.

The Secretary of the Treasury has the honor respectfully to make the following representation to The President of the United States, in order that he may determine on the expediency of laying the subject of it before Congress. The procuring of military supplies generally, is with great propriety, vested by law in the Department of the Treasury.[1] That Department from situation, may be expected to feel a more habitual solicitude for œconomy than any other; and to possess more means of information respecting the best modes of obtaining supplies. It is however, important that the particular arrangement should be such as to enable the Department to execute the trust in the best manner. This branch of the public business forms a very considerable one of the public expenditure. Including supplies for the Navy it is so extensive as, to be well executed, would occupy the whole time & attention of one person, possessing the requisite qualifications. This, with the growth of the country, must be every year more & more the case. It cannot therefore be conducted in detail by the head of the Department, or by any existing officer of it now charged with other duties, without being less well executed than it ought to be, or interfering with other essential duties, or without a portion of both these inconveniences, to the material detriment of the public service. Experience has already verified the position.[2]

It must then of necessity either be confided to a special Agent employed by the head of the department, or to a new officer of the Department to be constituted by law & to act under the direction

& superintendance of that head. The last mode is preferable to the first for obvious reasons.

Wherever an object of public business is likely to be permanent, it is more fit that it should be transacted by an officer of the Government regularly constituted, than by the agent of a Department specially intrusted. The officer can be placed by law under more effectual checks. In the present case, that idea is particularly important. The person entrusted ought to be prohibited under penalties from all dealing on his own account in the objects of supply. The duration & emoluments of a mere agency being precarious, a well qualified man disposed to make the necessary sacrifices of other pursuits & to devote himself exclusively to the business could with much greater difficulty, if at all, be found.

The compensation to such an officer ought it is conceived to weigh nothing as an objection. Independent of the equivalent expense arising from the necessity of employing & compensating an Agent, it is morally certain that the close, constant & undivided attention of a person charged exclusively with this object, & in condition, for that reason, to make the minute as well as extensive enquiries & investigations which are often requisite, would produce savings to the United States with which the salary of the officer could bear no comparison. It is equally evident that it would contribute greatly to punctuality, dispatch & efficiency in procuring the supplies.[3]

Respectfully submitted. Alexander Hamilton
Secy of the Treasy

LC, George Washington Papers, Library of Congress; copy, RG 46, Third Congress, 1793–1795, Messages transmitting reports from the Secretary of the Treasury, National Archives.

1. Section 5 of "An Act making alterations in the Treasury and War Departments" reads: "That all purchases and contracts for supplying the army with provisions, clothing, supplies in the quartermaster's department, military stores, Indian goods, and all other supplies or articles for the use of the department of war, be made by or under the direction of the treasury department" (1 *Stat.* 280 [May 8, 1792]).

2. See, for example, Tench Coxe to H, December 4, 1794.

3. On December 11, 1794, Washington transmitted to the Senate and House of Representatives "a representation made to me by the Secretary of the Treasury, on the subject of constituting an officer to be specially charged with the business of procuring certain public supplies" (*Annals of Congress*, IV, 973).

On February 23, 1795, Congress passed "An Act to establish the Office of Purveyor of Public Supplies," which incorporated the recommendations H made in this letter.

To George Washington

[Philadelphia] December 2, 1794. "The Secretary of the Treasury has the honor to send the President some additional communications from the Supervisor of Ohio District.[1] The State of that scene[2] renders the arrangement with regard to District Attorney delicate & important."

LC, George Washington Papers, Library of Congress.

1. On August 23, 1794, when the Senate was not in session, Washington had signed a commission appointing Thomas Marshall, inspector of the revenue for Survey No. 7 in the District of Virginia, as supervisor of the revenue for the District of Ohio and inspector of the revenue for Survey No. 1 in the District of Ohio. On December 10, 1794, Washington nominated Marshall for these positions, and on December 12, 1794, the Senate confirmed the nomination (*Executive Journal*, I, 164–65). Washington signed Marshall's commission on December 18, 1794 (JPP, 313).

2. This is a reference to reports that certain residents in the Ohio region of the Territory Northwest of the River Ohio were aiding the insurgents in western Pennsylvania and in particular that they had assisted David Bradford, one of the leaders of the Whiskey Insurrection, to escape capture by the authorities. On November 5, 1794, Winthrop Sargent, secretary of the territory, wrote to the justices of the peace of Hamilton County. After reminding them of the President's proclamation of September 25, 1794, warning "all persons whomsoever and wheresoever not to aid abet or comfort the Insurgents of the Western Counties of Pennsylvania," Sargent wrote: "I have reason to believe that there are in the Town of Cincinnati at this Time a number of men in the Service of the Army provision Contractors who have presumed in Contempt of the said proclamation to protect or rescue from Authority by Force of Arms a man who has been principally instrumental and active in promoting the Insurrections in the Counties aforesaid—and that they have aided him to make his escape from the United States" (Carter, *Territorial Papers*, III, 427).

On the same day that Sargent wrote this letter, "Christopher Cunningham and Daniel Duffey, citizens of Cincinnati, were arrested under the aforementioned proclamation, for aiding the escape of Mr. Bradford, an insurgent, into Kentucky" (William Henry Smith, ed., *The St. Clair Papers: The Life and Public Service of Arthur St. Clair* [Cincinnati, 1882], II, 336).

For an account of Bradford's escape, see Francis D'Hebecourt to Henry Lee, November 10, 1794 (*Pennsylvania Archives*, 2nd ser., IV, 450–51).

To George Washington

Treasury Department December 2, 1794. "The Secretary of the Treasury has the honor to transmit to The President of the UStates, triplicates of a statement of Expenditures upon the funds heretofore appropriated for defraying the contingent charges of Government[1] up to the 30 of September last."

LC, George Washington Papers, Library of Congress.

1. "An Act making appropriations for certain purposes therein expressed" appropriated twenty thousand dollars to defray the contingent expenses of government (1 *Stat.* 394–95 [June 9, 1794]).

From Tench Coxe[1]

Treasury Department, Revenue Office, December 3, 1794. "In consequence of a second experiment to provide for the stakage of Pamplico and Matchapungo Rivers, and the Navigable Creeks to the Town of Washington . . . Green Parker has reduced his terms from 100 to 79 Dollars. . . . I beg the favor of your obtaining the pleasure of the President upon the proposal."[2]

LC, RG 26, Lighthouse Deeds and Contracts, National Archives; LC, RG 26, Lighthouse Letters, Vol. I, National Archives.

1. For background to this letter, see H to George Washington, September 29, 1794.

2. The following statement appears at the bottom of this letter: "The Secretary of the Treasury Philada. Decbr. 8th 1794. The reduced terms as mentioned within are approved. Go. Washington."

From Tench Coxe[1]

Treasury Department
Revenue-Office, Decemr 4th 1794.

Sir,

I have the honor to remind you of the conviction I communicated to you before your departure to the Westward,[2] that the duties of the Treasury Department under the 5th Sectn of the act of May 8th 1792[3] as transferred to this office were actually incompatible with the due execution of the proper and other business of the Commissioner of the Revenue. I entertain a confirmed and increased conviction of the truth of that Idea, which you observed had occurred to your own observation. The importance of both Divisions of the public business, your intended resignation,[4] my wish to have every thing in order before that Event shall take place, and other considerations, induce me to request an early arrangement for the execution of the Duties of the Treasury under the 5th Section of the Act making alterations in the Treasury and war Department, otherwise than by this Office.

I have the honor to be with great Respect, Sir, Your most obedient Servant,

Tench Coxe
Commissr. of the Revenue

The Secretary
of the Treasury

LC, RG 58, Letters of Commissioner of Revenue, 1794–1795, National Archives.

1. For background to this letter, see H to Coxe, April 4, 1794.

2. No letter from Coxe to H of this date on the subject of this letter has been found, but see H to George Washington, December 2, 1794.

H had left Philadelphia with Washington for western Pennsylvania on September 30, 1794. See H to Washington, September 24, 1794, note 2.

3. "An Act making alterations in the Treasury and War Departments" (1 *Stat.* 278–81). See H to Washington, December 2, 1794, note 1.

4. See H to Washington, December 1, 1794; H to Frederick A. C. Muhlenberg, December 1, 1794.

From John Quincy Adams

The Hague December 5. 1794.

Sir.

The Bankers of the United States at Amsterdam, have written to you upon the present state of affairs in this Country, which would in their opinion render the negotiation for eight hundred thousand Dollars, for which they have been commissioned altogether impracticable,[1] even if they had received from Coll. Humphreys the intimation for which they are instructed to wait.[2]

Under these circumstances therefore, I find myself deprived not only of the happiness of contributing to the success, but even of the satisfaction of making all the exertions in my power for the attainment of an object so near to the wishes of the President and so important to the interests of the United States. As the contingency upon which the loan was at any rate to be attempted has not happened, it would have been perfectly unnecessary to dispute the opinion of the Commissioners. As the management of this business has been committed to them entirely, it would have been improper. As their means of information upon this point are so much superior to mine it would have been indecorous. I have therefore only observed to them that the object to which the money was intended to be applied, was of extreme urgency and importance. And that I hoped they would take advantage of the first favourable moment that should offer to make their dispositions so as to be prepared for the receipt of the order from Lisbon.

The zeal and fidelity with which these Gentlemen have served the United States from the time they were first interested in their affairs has been so thoroughly tried and proved, that it will certainly not be deficient upon the present occasion. Their personal interest will also concur with their public duty to animate their activity, if they see a possible chance of succeeding. So that when they tell me that the negotiation of the proposed loan would be *impracticable*, I cannot doubt but that the fact is really so; and that with the whole latitude of power given them as to the terms, they will not venture to undertake it.

It is with much pleasure however that I learn from them, and from many other quarters, that in point of credit here the United States stand upon a higher footing than any other power That their obligations at 4 per cent with premium are ten per cent above par; & their 5 per cents at par: while those of the Emperor and of Russia are vibrating from 75 to 90, and some others bear no price at all.

By the capture of Antwerp,[3] a difficulty has occurred upon which the Gentlemen at Amsterdam have no doubt already written you.[4] The annual interest upon the loan made there of 3 millions of florins, is by the tenor of the obligations made payable at the compting house of Mr. De Wolff,[5] and the bankers here have annually remitted the money to Antwerp for the purpose. As the circulation of Assignats is compulsive the Brabanters, holders of the American obligations are apprehensive of receiving their interest in that currency, and our bankers have not transmitted the money for the interest that becomes due for the last year. It may be added that many of these creditors are now emigrants, and may possibly have other apprehensions, for the fate of the principal as well as of the interest. One of them called upon me at Amsterdam, last week, to enquire whether I could give him any relief. I told him that I had neither instructions nor power relating to that loan, but would readily transmit any representation he wished to make, and I did not doubt but the United States would do their creditors full justice. He said an expedient had already been adopted by the Court of Denmark, upon the same occasion which had been satisfactory to their creditors in their Brabant Loans, and which if equally adopted by the United States would very much accomodate him and many others in the same predicament. It was to declare that the holders of their obligations, might receive their interest at Copenhagen instead of Antwerp, and that they might exchange the obligations themselves for others bearing the same interest.

The communication between Antwerp and this Country is interrupted, and I do not know whether Mr: de Wolff has paid the interest due upon the loan, this year. The money for the purpose has certainly not been remitted from hence. I hope that before the revolution of another year some settled order of things will take place, which will render any measures on the part of the United States in favour of their Netherland creditors unnecessary. I suspect that the impossibility of obtaining the two million Guilders here, must arise altogether from the dread of confiscation or requisition to which they imagine their obligations may be liable.

I have the honour to be, with the highest Sentiments of Respect, Sir, your very humble & obedient Servant. John Q. Adams.

Alexander Hamilton Esqr
Secretary of the Treasury.

ALS, Hamilton Papers, Library of Congress; LC, Adams Family Papers, deposited in the Massachusetts Historical Society, Boston.

1. Willink, Van Staphorst, and Hubbard to H, September 26, 1794.

2. For the role of David Humphreys, United States Minister to Portugal, in the attempt to liberate American prisoners in Algiers, see H to Willink, Van Staphorst, and Hubbard, July 7, 1794; H to John Quincy Adams, August 8, 1794. For the proposed loan, see George Washington to H, May 24, 1794, note 2, first letter of May 29, June 7, July 9, 1794; Henry Knox to H, April 21, 1794, note 1; H to Washington, second letter of May 27, June 4, 10, 1794; Edmund Randolph to H, June 24, 28, July 1, 15, 1794.

3. Antwerp had been captured by the French on July 27, 1794.

4. Willink, Van Staphorst, and Hubbard to H, December 6, 1794.

5. Charles John Michael De Wolf was the agent who had assisted in negotiating the Antwerp loan of 1791. For a description of this loan, see William Short to H, November 8, 1791, note 4, and November 12, 1791.

To John Quincy Adams[1]

Treasury Department December 5th 1794

Sir

Since writing to you on the first instant, of which the foregoing is a Copy, it has become necessary to inform you, that in consequence of the Presidents having directed Mr. Pinckney to repair immediately to the Court of Madrid, there is a possibility, that he may set out upon his Mission, before the bill drawn upon our Commissioners in Amsterdam reaches London. If this should prove to be the Case, I will then thank you to take upon yourself the negociation of the business, by placing in the Bank of England or in some other situation not less secure and at the disposal of Mr. Pinckney, a sum equal to the amount of the bill in question, say Three hundred and three thousand One hundred and fifteen current guilders with respect to the remainder of the Funds belonging to the United States, in the hands of our Commissioners, I shall refer you to the instructions contained in my letter to you of the first instant.

I am with great respect Sir Your most obedient servant

Alexander Hamilton

John Q Adams Esquire
Minister Resident at
the Hague

LS, Adams Family Papers, deposited in the Massachusetts Historical Society, Boston.

1. For background to this letter, see H to Adams, December 1, 1794; H to Thomas Pinckney, December 1, 1794.

From Tench Coxe[1]

T: D: R: O: Decbr. 5 1794

Sir,

In pursuance of the order of the Senate of the 18th day of February 1793[2] An enquiry into the expediency of erecting a Light House upon watch Hill in the state of Rhode Island was duly instituted.[3] It appears that a Light house of the first class or of very considerable expence is not desired, nor necessary to Navigation in that quarter. That a light on Watch Hill would not be extensively useful to vessels in the Foreign trade; That however, from the frequent passing & repassing of coasting vessels, a light House of the smallest class or a lighted Beacon would be really useful. That watch hill point, being considerably elevated above the sound at High Water, a light House or Beacon of sufficient height could be erected at a moderate expence.[4] That the Land around it, tho broken, is fertile, & that five families reside within half a mile; wherefore the expence of maintenance would be moderate.

I have the honor &c. T: Coxe C R

The Secy. of the Treasury

LC, RG 26, Lighthouse Letters, Vol. 1, National Archives; copy, RG 46, Third Congress, 1793–1795, Reports from the Secretary of the Treasury, National Archives.

1. A copy of this letter was enclosed in H's "Report on the Expediency of Erecting a Lighthouse on Watch Hill in Rhode Island," January 23, 1795.

2. On February 18, 1793, the Senate received "The memorial of a number of the inhabitants of the States of Connecticut and Rhode Island . . . praying that a light-house may be erected, at the expense of the United States, on Watch Hill, in the State of Rhode Island." The memorial was referred to H on the same day (*Annals of Congress*, III, 650). A copy of the memorial, dated January 29, 1793, may be found in RG 46, Third Congress, 1793–1795, Reports from the Secretary of the Treasury, National Archives.

3. Coxe to Jeremiah Olney, William Ellery, and Jedediah Huntington, May 22, 1794 (LC, RG 26, Lighthouse Letters, Vol. I, National Archives).

4. Coxe's "Estimate of a lighted Beacon, or small Light-House for Watch Hill 50 feet high including the Lantern frame" may be found in RG 46, Third Congress, 1793–1795, Reports from the Secretary of the Treasury, National Archives.

To George Washington

Treasury Department, December 5, 1794. "The Secretary of The Treasury has the honor to submit to the President a letter from the Commissioner of The Revenue of the 3d. instant. . . .[1] The present offer appears admissible. If the President thinks so—his approbation noted on the letter of the Commissioner of the revenue,[2] will put the business in execution."

LC, George Washington Papers, Library of Congress.

1. Tench Coxe to H, December 3, 1794.

2. For Washington's approval, see Coxe to H, December 3, 1794, note 2.

To Tench Coxe

[*Philadelphia*] *December 6, 1794.* "Mr. Hamilton requests Mr. Coxe to state to him how far the supplies procured & expected to be procured from measures already taken are adequate to the requisitions from the War Department for Gun Powder including Salt Petre as the Ingredient." [1]

LC, RG 58, Records of the Bureau of Internal Revenue, "Special Cases," Army, 1793–1865, National Archives.

1. Coxe endorsed this letter: "and. 8th December 8th 1794." Coxe, however, was mistaken, for his reply to H is dated December 9, 1794.

From Wilhem and Jan Willink, Nicholaas and Jacob Van Staphorst, and Nicholas Hubbard

Quadruplicate Amsterdam 6th. December 1794

Sir!

We had the pleasure to address You the 23d. September,[1] and are Since deprived of your esteemed favors.

Mr. Humphreys having applied to us, to know what Sums He might rely upon our furnishing him, in case of success in the Negotiation He is charged with; [2] We answered him the 28th November, and inclose you Copy [3] thereof for your Government, premising to you, that we only forwarded him the first part of our Letter to you of 23 September [4] treating solely upon the Loan in question.

Mr. Pinckney transmitted us an order for Bunting &c: for Six Frigates,[5] which He afterwards recalled because He had expended on other objects the Funds destined to pay for it, unless we could purchase same on Credit: This is not practicable here: but rather than the united States should suffer a Disappointment in anything depending upon us, we have offered him to Ship the order and wait remittances from you for its payment: We therefore only wait to learn from him the Number of yards of Bunting wanted to direct it to be made got ready, and shipped in all Celerity. The Amount we are directed to have covered by Insurance:

The Portuguese Government having monopolized all the Salpetre in Lisbon,[6] we are obliged to renounce the execution of the remainder of your order for that Article unless you shall renew it

LS, Connecticut Historical Society, Hartford.

1. Willink, Van Staphorst, and Hubbard are presumably referring to their letter to H of September 26, 1794.

2. For information on the attempt of the United States to secure a loan of eight hundred thousand dollars to be used by David Humphreys to negotiate a treaty with Algiers, see George Washington to H, May 24, 1794, note 2, first letter of May 29, June 7, July 9, 1794; H to Washington, second letter of May 27, June 4, 10, July 8, 1794; H to Willink, Van Staphorst, and Hubbard. July 7, 1794; H to John Quincy Adams, August 8, 1794; and Adams to H, December 5, 1794.

3. See enclosure.

4. This letter is dated September 26, 1794.

5. See H to Thomas Pinckney, June 25, 1794.

6. See H to Willink, Van Staphorst, and Hubbard, May 8, 1794, and Willink, Van Staphorst, and Hubbard to H, July 1, 8, 15, August 1, 18, September 1, 26, 1794.

with express directions to fulfill it at any price it may be procured for. Our regret at this Circumstance is much diminished by the Treaty concluded between Mr. Jay[7] and the British Ministry rendering improbable ye want of it speedily.

Upon this Accomodation honorable and advantageous to the united States in the highest degree, permit us to present you our most sincere and hearty Congratulations: happy would it be for suffering humanity, was it the harbinger of a general pacification.

Several Persons who emigrated from Antwerp, at the Entrance of the French Armies into Brabant,[8] have applied to us, to know if we would pay the Interest that fell due this Month on the Loan negotiated by Mr. DeWolff at Antwerp,[9] for Account of the united States, To which we naturally answered in the Negative, until we should receive orders from you to discharge it. We however promised to write you on the Subject, and to recommend the case of the Emigrant Brabanter's, owners of the Bonds of the united States to your Consideration: They flatter themselves that the same Loyalty, which induced your Government in the Discharge of its Debt to France, to disdain availing itself of the advantages it might have reaped, by paying it off in Assignats, will operate to its directing us to discharge their Demands here at the medium Course of Exchange that existed between Holland and their Country, previous to its Invasion by the French, and the consequent circulation of Assignats. These people derive strength to their hope, by the example of the Court of Denmark, which instead of profiting of the Actual Circumstances, to pay at a very cheap rate the Interests upon its Loans at Antwerp, has consented to open an office at Copenhagen, where the Bearers of its Bonds will have the choice to convert them into Annuities by that Kingdom, of which the Interest to be paid either in Amsterdam or Copenhagen, at the option of the Creditors, and thus are the Holders secure from all depreciation of Specie upon the Amount of their Interests due by Denmark.

The like faculty was granted to the Holders of Danish Bonds Negotiated in Holland, probably under the presumption our Country would share the same Fate as Brabant.

7. See John Jay to H, November 19, 1794.

8. Antwerp had been captured by the French on July 27, 1794.

9. For a description of the Antwerp loan, see William Short to H, November 8, 1791, note 4, and November 12, 1791.

We have deemed it our duty, to say thus much on the subject, but without pretending to influence your Decision, which We refer entirely to your own Superior judgment.

There has lately been a little more Stir in American Bonds, owing to the Treaty signed between Mr. Jay, and the British Government; but the hopes of an approaching peace declining, and some movements on our Frontiers indicating that the Campaign is not yet at an End, our Money Lenders are again seized with a Timor, that relaxes the purchases of Bonds.

A new Stamp Tax has been laid, and is to operate from the 1 proximo, whereby the original Bond or Instrument of all future Loans negotiated here, must be registered and subjected to a Stamp of one quarter per Cent on the principal of said Loan, and a Tax of One fifth part of the price of the Stamp: So that the Stamp duty upon the principal Bond of a Loan of one Million will amount to f 3000. Besides which each subdivided Bond of f 1000. must be printed upon a Stamp of 8 Stuyvers, and each Coupon or receipt of Interest upon a Stamp of 4½ Sts. The whole forming a very heavy duty.

The drafts of the Treasury of the United States upon us No. 1061 a 1067 and No. 1081 dated 16 & 17 October, have appeared, and met the usual honor at presentation.

We are with great esteem and respect Sir! Your mo: ob: hb: Servt

Wilhem & Jan Willink
N & J. Van Staphorst & Hubbard[10]

Ex: on London 5 Dec.
3/d Sight 39/10
2/m. date 39/6
Bank money 89½ pct.
Bond U.S. 5 pc. 99½ pct.
Do. 4 do. 88½ pct.

Alex. Hamilton Esqr.

10. This letter arrived in the United States after H had resigned as Secretary of the Treasury. For the reply to this letter, see Oliver Wolcott, Jr., to Willink, Van Staphorst, and Hubbard, April 13, 1795 (ADf, Connecticut Historical Society, Hartford).

[ENCLOSURE]

Wilhem and Jan Willink, Nicholaas and Jacob Van Staphorst, and Nicholas Hubbard to David Humphreys [11]

[Amsterdam, November 28, 1794]

In reply to your very esteemed favor of 20 Septbr:, which reached us only last Post, we beg your reference to the inclosed Copy of a Letter we addressed to the Secretary of the Treasury of the United States under date of 23 of said Month, as containing all the information in our Power to give on the subject of your Enquiry.

Should the present Rumours of Peace, produce that desireable effect, we flatter ourselves, we might soon be able to procure a new Loan for the United States: We hope our representations to the Secretary of the Treasury, will operate to obtain from him the Permission, to avail ourselves of the first favorable opportunity to launch such a Loan upon the Market, so as to have the Monies ready at your call, otherwise we are only authorized to present it after receipt of advice from you, that it will be wanted for the purposes, committed to your Management; And then supposing it to succeed, the Monies will enter but by Monthly Instalments probably one Sixth Part in each Month, for your Government.

We are &c:

11. Copy, Connecticut Historical Society, Hartford.

To Angelica Church

Philadelphia, December 8, 1794.

You say I am a politician, and good for nothing. What will you say when you learn that after January next, I shall cease to be a politician at all? [1] So is the fact. I have formally and definitely announced my intention to resign at that period,[2] and have ordered a house to be taken for me at New York.

My dear Eliza has been lately very ill.[3] Thank God, she is now quite recovered, except that she continues somewhat weak. My absence on a certain expedition was the cause (with army to suppress the whisky insurrection in Pennsylvania). You will see, notwithstanding your disparagement of me, I am still of consequence to her.

Liancourt[4] has arrived, and has delivered your letter.[5] I pay him the attentions due to his misfortunes and his merits. I wish I was a Croesus; I might then afford solid consolations to these children of adversity, and how delightful it would be to do so. *But now,* sympathy, kind words, and *occasionally a dinner, are all I can contribute.*

Don't let Mr. Church be alarmed at my retreat—all is well with the public. Our insurrection is most happily terminated. Government has gained by it reputation and strength, and our finances are in a most flourishing condition. *Having contributed to place those of the Nation on a good footing, I go to take a little care of my own; which need my care not a little.*

Love to Mr. Church. Betsy will add a line or two. Adieu.

James A. Hamilton, *Reminiscences of James A. Hamilton* (New York, 1869), 14.

1. See H to George Washington, December 1, 1794.
2. H to Frederick A. C. Muhlenberg, December 1, 1794.
3. See Henry Knox to H, November 24, 1794.
4. See John Jay to H, September 17, 1794.
5. Angelica Church to H, September 19, 1794.

From Tench Coxe[1]

Treasury Department, Revenue Office, December 8, 1794. States that "contracts for the large Anchors can not be made in the U: S: upon terms more favorable than 12½ & 13 cents, to be deliver'd in time, and that an importation of them from England can be made at 10 cents . . .[2] the anchors wanted . . . being about 20 in number."

LC, RG 75, Letters of Tench Coxe, Commissioner of the Revenue, Relating to the Procurement of Military, Naval, and Indian Supplies, National Archives.

1. For information concerning the naval armament, see Henry Knox to H, April 21, 1794.
2. See H to Thomas Pinckney, June 25, 1794; Coxe to H, June 25, first letter of July 5, 1794.

To George Gale

[*Philadelphia, December 8, 1794.* On December 20, 1794, Hamilton wrote to Gale and referred to "my letter of the 8th. Instant." *Letter not found.*]

From Timothy Hurst[1]

New York, December 8, 1794. "Some months ago I requested[2] the favor of your Assistance . . . in a Chancery suit I was unfortunately involved in with the Executor of the late Doctr Brownjohn[3] provided you returned to this City & engaged in your former profession & seeing lately your Intentions of quitting your present Department[4] I have now to request your Assistance in my Chancery Suit. You will particularly oblige me by your answer. . . ."[5]

ALS, Hamilton Papers, Library of Congress.

1. Hurst was a New York City druggist.
2. Letter not found.
3. Samuel Brownjohn of Jamaica, Queens County, New York.
4. See H to Frederick A. C. Muhlenberg, December 1, 1794; H to George Washington, December 1, 1794.
5. H endorsed this letter: "Deferred till I go to Town. A H." After returning to New York, H accepted this case. See the entry for June 1, 1795, in H's Cash Book, 1795–1804 (AD, Hamilton Papers, Library of Congress). See also the "Memoranda of Retainers" in H's Law Register, 1795–1804 (D, partially in H's handwriting, New York Law Institute, New York City).

From Tench Coxe

Treasury Department, Revenue Office, December 9, 1794. "Mr. Coxe has the honor to enclose to the Secretary of the Treasy. several petitions adverse to the building of a Light House on Seguin Island. It is authorized by law to be built on that Island and appropriation of money has been made, but no contract has been effected."[1]

LC, RG 26, Lighthouse Letters, Vol. I, National Archives.

1. "An Act for erecting a Lighthouse on the Island of Sequin in the district of Maine, and for erecting a beacon and placing three buoys at the entrance of Saint Mary's river, in the state of Georgia" had appropriated "a sum not exceeding five thousand dollars" for building a lighthouse on Seguin Island (1 *Stat.* 368–69 [May 19, 1794]). On June 3, 1794, Coxe wrote to Benjamin Lincoln, collector of customs at Boston, requesting that Lincoln go to Seguin Island and "fix upon the most eligible spot for the actual site" of the lighthouse after conferring with "the collectors of the Customs, Merchants, & others" (LC, RG 26, Lighthouse Letters, Vol. I, National Archives). On August 6, 1794, Lincoln sent Coxe a letter containing the information on the lighthouse which Coxe had requested as well as letters from residents of Maine objecting to the lighthouse on Seguin Island (LC, Massachusetts Historical Society, Boston).

From Tench Coxe[1]

Treasury Department, Revenue Office, December 9, 1794. "I have the honor to enclose a copy of a letter from Mr. Francis[2] relative to the purchase of ingredients for gun powder, or gun powder itself: to this I have to add, that the only parcel of Salt Petre known to have been Imported elsewhere than in Philada. was procured by me at Providence R. I: being about 22 Tons.[3] You were apprized of the unsuccessful efforts made by me to procure a contract to Import. . . .[4] The contract with Messrs. Willing & Francis[5] which has been pending some days, has not been completed. . . . No powder could be got under the prices offered by Whelen & Miller. . . .[6] I understand some Salt Petre ordered by you from Europe has been received. . . ."[7]

LC, RG 75, Letters of Tench Coxe, Commissioner of the Revenue, Relating to the Procurement of Military, Naval, and Indian Supplies, National Archives.

1. This letter is in reply to H to Coxe, December 6, 1794.

For background to this letter, see Henry Knox to H, March 29, April 21, 1794.

2. Tench Francis.
3. See Coxe to H, June 20, 1794.
4. Coxe to H, July 8, 1794.
5. The Philadelphia mercantile firm of Thomas Willing, Thomas Mayne Willing, and Thomas Willing Francis.
6. Israel Whelen and Joseph I. Miller.
7. See H to Willink, Van Staphorst, and Hubbard, May 8, 1794; Willink, Van Staphorst, and Hubbard to H, July 15, 1794, note 4, August 8, September 1, 1794.

To Tench Coxe

Treasury Department Decemr 9.
1794

Sir

It is now a considerable time since provision was made by law for additional compensation to the Officers of Inspection;[1] so that I become desirous that the proper statements in order to a revision and readjustment of the compensations of those Officers should be laid before the President without further delay.

I take it for granted you must before this have received those communications from the Supervisors,[2] upon the desire and expectation of which the business was originally suspended, and that every thing is now mature for the completion of the arrangement.

with consideration I am Sir Your obedient Servant

A Hamilton

Tench Coxe Esquire
Commissioner of the Revenue

LS, RG 58, General Records, 1791–1803, National Archives.

1. H is referring to Section 13 of "An Act making further provision for securing and collecting the Duties on foreign and domestic distilled Spirits, Stills, Wines and Teas" (1 *Stat.* 380 [June 5, 1794]). For this section, see Coxe to H, July 15, 1794, note 4.

2. See Coxe to H, July 15, 1794, note 5.

From Bartholomew Dandridge

[Philadelphia, December 9, 1794]

Br. Dandridge respectfully informs the Secretary of the Treasury that the President does not object to granting Mr Bowen's request [1] if it can be done without injury to the public service.

B. Dandridge will thank the Secretary to cause a Warrant to be transmitted to him for two thousand dollars on account of The President's compensation.[2]

Decem. 9. 1794.

LC, George Washington Papers, Library of Congress.

1. Jabez Bowen was commissioner for loans for Rhode Island.

"Mr Bowen's request" concerned the distribution of the funds which Congress had provided for the relief of refugees from the Santo Domingan revolution by "An Act providing for the relief of such of the inhabitants of Santo Domingo, resident within the United States, as may be found in want of support" (6 *Stat.* 13 [February 12, 1794]). The act appropriated fifteen thousand dollars, which was to be distributed by the President among the refugees in the various states. See Edmond Charles Genet to H, July 19, 1793; George Washington to H, March 4, 1794.

Bowen and Edmund Randolph had corresponded about the relief money for the refugees since March, 1794 (Randolph to Bowen, April 30, 1794 [LC, RG 59, Domestic Letters of the Department of State, Vol. 6, January 2–June 26, 1794, National Archives]). Rhode Island had received one thousand dollars from the Federal Government, but on April 30, 1794, Randolph wrote to Bowen: ". . . The money, which I remitted to you was for the relief of those inhabitants of St. Domingo, who come within the description of the law, granting it. If the liberality of your State has already satisfied their wants, it will not be legal to reimburse your Treasury out of that money, or to spend it at all . . ." (LC, RG 59, Domestic Letters of the Department of State, Vol. 6,

January 2–June 26, 1794, National Archives). On May 12, 1794, Bowen informed Randolph that the towns of Newport, Providence, and Bristol having found the burden of aiding the refugees too great, had petitioned the Rhode Island General Assembly for assistance (ALS, RG 59, Miscellanoeus Letters, 1790–1799, National Archives). On May 20, 1794, Randolph replied to Bowen that ". . . to render the affair free from complexity, . . . It is agreed that the following arrangement, which you are hereby authorized to make, will probably be satisfactory, to wit, that you may pay to the Treasurer of your State so much of the money sent by me to you, as will reimburse the advances, which have been made by the State, since the passing of the act of Congress, or shall be hereafter made" (LC, RG 59, Domestic Letters of the Department of State, Vol. 6, January 2–June 26, 1794, National Archives).

On May 31, 1794, Randolph informed the President that out of the sum of fifteen thousand dollars appropriated by Congress for the Santo Domingan refugees, six hundred dollars remained "to be disposed of, as the President shall choose" (ALS, Miscellaneous Letters, 1790–1799, National Archives).

On October 1, 1794, Oliver Wolcott, Jr., wrote to Henry Sherburne of Newport: ". . . The reimbursement of the balance expended beyond the funds which were remitted, may justly be expected from the French Republic, when the motives & object of the advance is considered, and you may rest assured that the claim of the State will be presented with that of the United States, for the consideration of the French Government" (ADf, Connecticut Historical Society, Hartford). On February 24, 1795, Randolph sent a copy of a letter, dated February 1, 1795, which he had received from Bowen, to James Monroe, United States Minister Plenipotentiary to France, for Monroe to use in negotiating with the French government (LC, RG 59, Diplomatic and Consular Instructions of the Department of State, 1791–1801, Vol. 2, August 22, 1793–June 1, 1795, National Archives).

On April 23, 1795, Bowen again wrote to Randolph requesting additional Federal funds and stating that Rhode Island had "paid 1956 Doll 74 cts after deducting the 1800 Dollars I paid the General Treasurer by your Orders" (ALS, RG 59, Miscellaneous Letters, 1790–1799, National Archives).

The problem was finally resolved when Randolph wrote to Bowen on May 20, 1795: "I have the pleasure to inform you, that the President approves, that the remaining six hundred dollars, which belong to the St. Domingo fund shall be appropriated, as your letter of the 23d. ultimo requests . . ." (LC, RG 59, Domestic Letters of the Department of State, Vol. 8, December 6, 1794–October 12, 1795, National Archives). Bowen's receipt for this sum, dated June 1, 1795, may be found in RG 59, Miscellaneous Letters, 1790–1799, National Archives.

2. George Washington's salary was twenty-five thousand dollars per year. See "Report on Estimates for the Year 1794," December 21, 1793.

To the President and Directors of the Bank of New York[1]

[*Philadelphia, December 9, 1794.*] "It gives me pleasure to have this fresh opportunity of bearing testimony to the liberal and patriotic zeal for the service of the United States which the Bank of New York has on every occasion evinced."

Domett, *History of the Bank of New York*, 51.

1. This letter is an acknowledgment of the acceptance by the president and directors of the Bank of New York of H's proposal that the Bank of New York agree to lend one hundred thousand dollars to the United States. See H to the President and Directors of the Bank of New York, December 1, 1794.

To Thomas Pinckney [1]

[*Treasury Department, December 9, 1794.* ". . . Be assured that in this and in every thing which concerns you whatever and however my lot may be cast, I must feel, according to the dictates of a genuine esteem and true attachment." [2] *Letter not found.*]

ALS, sold at Parke-Bernet Galleries, Inc., November 30, 1943, Lot 143.

1. Extract taken from manuscript dealer's catalogue. The catalogue description reads: "Regarding shipment of copper for frigates & extending sympathy for domestic misfortune."

For information about the copper for the frigates, see H to Pinckney, June 25, 1794. The "domestic misfortune" was the death in London of Elizabeth Motte Pinckney, Pinckney's wife (*The* [Charleston, South Carolina] *City Gazette & Daily Advertiser*, October 23, 1794).

From Robert Purviance

Baltimore, December 9, 1794. "Your letter of the 18th Sepr. directing me to take measures for ascertaining the value of the ground upon which the fortifications are now constructing at whetstone point was immediately communicated to Mr. Alexander Furnival and a day appointed to meet at the Fort, when, I was very much surprized to find that I could not procure from mr: F the necessary information respecting the Lines and extent of his ground. . . . From the very best information I can procure, the property that mr. Furnival holds there, comes higher . . . than any estimate I have had of it's present Value, notwithstanding mr. Furnivals lowest value is a demand of Four Thousand Dollars. I have repeatedly waited on him in order that he might probably reconsider the matter. . . ."

ADf, RG 53, "Old Correspondence," Baltimore Collector, National Archives.

Edmund Randolph to William Bradford, Alexander Hamilton, and Henry Knox

Philadelphia December 9th. 1794

The Secretary of State begs the favor of the opinion of the Secretaries of the Treasury and of War, and of the Attorney General upon the inclosed Letter of Mr. Hammond, of the 9th. ultimo.[1] The point on which your advice will be particularly interesting is, whether the government of the United States is bound to urge the payment requested?

LC, RG 59, Domestic Letters of the Department of State, Vol. 7, June 27–November 30, 1794, National Archives.

1. Although George Hammond's letter of November 9, 1794, has not been found, it concerned the capture in 1793 of the "British Brig William Tell, taken by a french armed vesel, within a mile of . . . [the United States] shores . . . and brought into New York" (Thomas Jefferson to Edmond Charles Genet, September 9, 1793 [LC, RG 59, Domestic Letters of the Department of State, Vol. 5, February 4, 1792–December 31, 1793, National Archives]). The British, who demanded the payment of damages, maintained that "all Losses and Damages which may have been sustained by His Majesty's Subjects by reason of the Capture of their Vessels and Merchandize, taken within the limits and jurisdictions of the States, and brought into their Ports, or taken by Vessels originally armed in Ports of the said States, . . . shall be compensated by the United States" (Lord Grenville to Hammond, March 7, 1794 [LC, PRO: F.O. (Great Britain), 5/5]). See also Article 7 of the Jay Treaty in Miller, *Treaties*, II, 252–53. In response to Hammond's request for the payment of damages in his letter of November 9, Randolph replied on December 29, 1794: "I do myself the honor of informing you, that after mature consideration of your letter of the 9th ultimo, the President of the United States does not consider our Government as responsible to effect, beyond the ordinary course of judiciary process, the payment of the Damages in question; but he will use his endeavours by a representation to the French Republic thro' our Minister there to procure such payment" (LC, RG 59, Domestic Letters of the Department of State, Vol. 8, December 6, 1794–October 12, 1795, National Archives). On December 30, 1794, Randolph wrote to James Monroe, United States Minister Plenipotentiary to France: "I do myself the honor of inclosing to you two Records, one in the case of the Brigantine Catharine belonging to . . . Citizens of the United States, the other in the case of the William Tell, belonging to a British Subject. You will perceive that they have both been unjustly seized by the French Ship of War L'Ambuscade, and that damages have been assessed accordingly. But there is no redress, unless the French Republic becomes responsible for the acts of its own public Cruizers. You will therefore be pleased to make such representations upon this subject as the nature of the affair will admit, and as existing circumstances may render proper. At the same time you will observe from the enclosed Letter which I wrote to Mr. Hammond, what the sense of our Government is, with respect to the compensation urged by him

in his letter of the 9th. ultimo for the owners of the William Tell . . ." (LC, RG 59, Diplomatic and Consular Instructions of the Department of State, 1791–1801, Vol. 2, August 22, 1793–June 1, 1795, National Archives).

From Tench Coxe

Treasury Department, Revenue Office, December 10, 1794. ". . . in consequence of your verbal authorizations, I have commenced proceedings in the Military business of the Treasury,[1] in places other than Pennsylva. thro the Agency of Mr. Francis.[2] This will diminish the avocations from my proper Office business, which have retarded it, but does not remove the necessity for an early relief from the avocations which yet result from the War business." [3]

LC, RG 75, Letters of Tench Coxe, Commissioner of the Revenue, Relating to the Procurement of Military, Naval, and Indian Supplies, National Archives.

1. See H to Coxe, April 4, 1794.
2. Tench Francis was agent for purchasing War Department supplies.
3. See H to George Washington, December 2, 1794; Coxe to H, December 4, 1794.

From Nathan Keais [1]

[*Washington, North Carolina, December 10, 1794.* On January 31, 1795, Oliver Wolcott, Jr., wrote to Keais: "The Secretary of the Treasury has referred your letter of Decr. 10 to this office to which I reply." [2] *Letter not found.*]

1. Keais was collector of customs at Washington, North Carolina, and inspector of the port of Washington.
2. ADf, Connecticut Historical Society, Hartford.

The remainder of Wolcott's letter indicates that Keais's letter to H concerned a problem of collecting duties under Section 38 of "An Act to provide more effectually for the collection of the duties imposed by law on goods, wares and merchandise imported into the United States, and on the tonnage of ships or vessels" (1 *Stat.* 145–78 [August 4, 1790]).

From John Barclay [1]

[*Philadelphia, December 11, 1794.* On December 17, 1794, Hamilton wrote to Barclay: "I have been favoured with your letter of the 11th instant." *Letter not found.*]

1. Barclay's letter of December 11 was a reply to H to the President and Directors of the Bank of Pennsylvania, December 1, 1794. That Barclay replied in the affirmative to H's request in his letter of December 1 is indicated by the contents of H to Barclay, December 17, 1794.

From Tench Coxe[1]

Treasury Department, Revenue Office, December 11, 1794. Requests that "a Warrt. may issue in favor of Messrs. Gurney & Smith Naval Agents[2] for the sum of five thousd. one hundred Dollars as a further paymt. on a/count. . . ."[3]

LC, RG 75, Letters of Tench Coxe, Commissioner of the Revenue, Relating to the Procurement of Military, Naval, and Indian Supplies, National Archives.

1. For information concerning the naval armament, see Henry Knox to H, April 21, 1794.

2. Francis Gurney and Daniel Smith were the naval agents in Philadelphia in charge of building frigates. See Knox to H, third letter of July 9, 1794.

3. On December 15, 1794, Warrant No. 4322 for $5,100 was issued to Gurney and Smith (D, RG 217, Miscellaneous Treasury Accounts, 1790–1894, Account No. 7403, National Archives).

From Tench Coxe[1]

Treasury Department, Revenue Office, December 11, 1794. Requests "that a duplicate Warrant may issue in favor of Joel Gibbs for the sum of two hundred & eight Dollars & eight cents, in paymt. for Artillery Hats delivered by him agreeably to contract. . . ."[2]

LC, RG 75, Letters of Tench Coxe, Commissioner of the Revenue, Relating to the Procurement of Military, Naval, and Indian Supplies, National Archives.

1. For background to this letter, see Coxe to H, September 30, October 8, 24, November 19, 1794.

2. On January 4, 1795, Warrant No. 4426 for $208.08 was issued to Gibbs (D, RG 217, Miscellaneous Treasury Accounts, 1790–1894, Account No. 6922, National Archives).

From Jacob Mark and Company[1]

[New York, December 11, 1794]

Sir,

The Directors of the Mine commonly called Schuylers Copper Mine[2] take the liberty of informing the Secretary of the Treasury that they have raised sufficient bar to enter into Contract for the delivery of 50 Tons Refined Copper by the last of May next.

If you have not already orderd the Quantity which is required for the Mint we beg to be favoured with the preference of your Commands. Your answer will oblige us.[3]

Your sincere friends & Obedient Humble sers. Jacob Marks Co.

LS, RG 59, Miscellaneous Letters, 1790–1799, National Archives.

1. Jacob Mark was a New York City merchant. The firm was variously known as Jacob Mark and Company, Jacob Marks Company, and Jacob and Philip Mark (see "Report on Bank Deposits, Surplus Revenue, and Loans," January 16, 1793). The name was also on occasion spelled Marck (see *Executive Journal*, I, 158, and John Murray to H, May 3, 1793).

2. The Schuyler mine was located in the vicinity of what is now Belleville, New Jersey, on land purchased by Arent Schuyler early in the eighteenth century. Before the American Revolution it was operated by John Schuyler, one of Arent's sons. In 1793, Philip A. Schuyler of Bergen County, New Jersey, Jacob Mark, and Nicholas J. Roosevelt of New York formed the New Jersey Copper Mine Association in the hope of reviving the mine. See William Nelson, "Josiah Hornblower, and the First Steam-Engine in America, with Some Notices of the Schuyler Copper Mines at Second River, N.J.," *Proceedings of the New Jersey Historical Society*, 2nd ser., VII (1882–1883), 177; Collamer M. Abott, "Colonial Copper Mines," *The William and Mary Quarterly*, XXVII (April, 1970), 299–302; Elizabeth Marting, "Arent Schuyler and His Copper Mine," *Proceedings of the New Jersey Historical Society*, Vol. 65, No. 2 (April, 1947), 126–40.

3. H endorsed this letter as follows: 'The Secretary of State will enable me to answer the within. The copper from that mine has always had the reputation of being particularly good. AH."

After receiving the above note from H, Edmund Randolph on December 15, 1794, sent it to David Rittenhouse, director of the Mint, and asked for "his opinion upon the subject of contracting with them for the fifty tons of Copper, which they say will be ready by the last of may next" (LC, RG 59, Domestic Letters of the Department of State, Vol. 8, December 6, 1794–October 12, 1795, National Archives).

From Edward Carrington

Richmond Decr. 12. 1794

My dear Sir,

I have been favored with yours of the 1st Instant.[1] All accounts from the scene of the late insurrection agree that the measures which have been pursued have been as successful in their issue, as they were wise in their commencement. I have also the satisfaction of finding that our returned Troops pretty generally agree, that a less force

ALS, Hamilton Papers, Library of Congress.

1. Letter not found.

than was called forth would have been opposed, and that a small army could have effected nothing but the establishment of a civil War. This operates as strong evidence against our good democrats, who had been loud against the Executive for unnecessarily interrupting the quiet of our Citizens, and incurring an unjust expence. The propriety of a force being left in the Country [2] is also supported by the same authority, to the no small discontentment of those immaculate Guardians of our liberties, who were charging upon the president an avidity in seizing an opportunity for an advance to the establishment of a standing Army. In truth our Militia have come home better Citizens than they went out, in as much as that they have seen this fallacious spirit of liberty, stripped of its Hypocricy, and exhibited in its own Garb. I have no doubt that their returning amongst their Neighbours, thus undeceived, will be productive of good consequences. Our Virginians were, before this excursion, much better Citizens than certain circumstances had led those of other States to suppose them, and the ready obedience paid to the late call [3] must have, in some degree, counteracted the opinions entertained concerning them. You will recollect that after the Insurgency broke out, & before the call was put to the test, I ventured to communicate to you a temper as belonging to our people different from the Contraband politics of our Representatives.[4] I predicted the alacrity with which the people would turn out to Support their Govt. & its Laws, and endeavored to account for the real existence of such a contradiction in the conduct of the people, when called on to act for themselves, and when acting, or said to be acting, by their Representatives. The event has verified the prediction; nor can I attempt to solve the enigma otherwise than I then did. We have vicious & virtuous men of abilities—the vicious are bold in their charges upon government & its administration—the virtuous are ⟨essentially⟩ backward. The people naturally give their suffrages to those who

2. This is a reference to the temporary military arrangement which Henry Lee had announced on November 9, 1794 (see H to George Washington, November 8, 1794, note 7). On November 29, 1794, Congress passed "An Act to authorize the President to call out and station a corps of Militia, in the four western Counties of Pennsylvania, for a limited time" (1 *Stat.* 403).

3. For the calling up of the militia to march against the insurgents in western Pennsylvania, see H to Lee, second letter of August 25, 1794

4. Carrington to H, August 25, 1794.

discover the greatest Solicitude to obtain them & who shew the greatest confidence in their Claims to be trusted. In truth my dr sir, I have fallen out with both, for he from whom an active injury is received, is little less a Freind than he that stands by and quietly sees the injuries done.

Your observations upon the deplorable increase of a disorganizing spirit, in the quarter from whence it has before been felt in Congress, are I apprehend too well founded; nor have you a consolation in the event of our late election here to fill the senatorial seats.[5] There is indeed something extremely unaccountable in all this—it would seem that the events of last Summer & fall were calculated to have changed, even the sentiments of the former actors on the Stage of our political farce, much more might a Change of Conduct have been expected from a conviction that their constituents had received impressions no longer to tolerate their opinions. Speak with the people of Virginia, in parties, or individually, & far the greater number appear to disapprove of the violent measures espoused by their representatives in both Houses last session[6]—yet all their elections, in whatever form made, turn on Men the most distinguished for their violence of enmity to the Govt. & its administration. All this I feel & lament exceedingly, I however have a consolation, which I do not think a mistaken one—that the people of Virga. will always revolt against the wickedness or follies of their leaders, whenever they are brought near enough to the precipice to see plainly their danger.

You do not feel more sensibly than I do the critical situation in which we stand; nor are you more thoroughly convinced that the southern politics have a tendency, a limited one I hope, to a severment which cannot be taken into prospect by any Man who feels

5. The Virginia election of 1794 was a victory for the Republicans. Samuel Griffin and Richard Bland Lee, Republicans who had become Federalists, were not re-elected to the House of Representatives, and Henry Tazewell and Stevens T. Mason were elected to the Senate to fill the seats left vacant by their fellow Republicans, John Taylor and James Monroe.

6. Carrington is referring to the debate on the House resolution to continue the embargo against Great Britain in April, 1794 (*Annals of Congress*, IV, 84, 575–94, 597–98). Richard Bland Lee had proposed an amendment "for excepting foreign bottoms from the operation of the Embargo," but the motion was lost (*Annals of Congress*, IV, 597). Republicans had no desire to conciliate Britain and supported the embargo in its original form. The resolution as finally agreed to is printed in *Annals of Congress*, IV, 598.

the pride of a free American, but with chagrine & humility; the transition would be nothing less than from the exalted Nation of the freest, happiest, & wisest people the sun ever Shone upon, to that of the most vile, the most wretched & the most foolish that ever stamped the human character. Being an united people, we dictate our own laws, and say to all the rest of the world what shall be their conduct towards us—divide us, and we instantly become little puppets to be played off on each other, as shall be convenient to foreign Nations, & even foreign individuals—it would seem that the succcss of Genets projects, should have stamped this lesson deeply on the mind of every American, who was not involved in his vices.

I most heartily re-echo your opinion that good men should come forward & Set their faces against the ills which awaite us—and trust it will 'ere long be the case in Virga. Let our Eastern bretheren, whose good sence & solid republicanism, I daily more & more admire, continue their zeal in supporting the true Interests of the commonwealth—they will prevail—an enthusiastic folly Cannot be of long duration.

On the subject of your resignation—you appear to have taken your final determination. I wish your Successor may be as successful in the effects of his measures, and that he may be as fortunate in repelling the attacks of faction. The papers have announced a precaution[7] which I should certainly have taken the liberty to recommend to you. Your notification to the House of Representatives[8] is a necessary caveat against future Slander, for had you remained 'til the last day of the session, and then resigned without such a precaution, a retreat from enquiry would have been charged upon you.

I anticipate with pleasure, your appearance in the Character of a Representative, & beg you to be assured that you will retain in any Station you may occupy the public confidence & private friendship of

My Dr Sir your affectionate Fellow Citizen Ed Carrington

Alexr. Hamilton Esq

7. H's "precaution" is a reference to his determination that the House of Representatives have ample time to investigate the Treasury Department before he resigned. See H to Frederick A. C. Muhlenberg, December 1, 1794.

8. H to Muhlenberg, December 1, 1794.

From Jeremiah Olney

Providence, December 12, 1794. Acknowledges receipt of Hamilton's "Letter of the 27th of November, relative to the payment of Allowances to fishing Vessels." States that "there is not one, belonging to this District, entitled to any."

ADfS, Rhode Island Historical Society, Providence.

From Ephraim Blaine[1]

Carlisle [*Pennsylvania*] *December 13, 1794.* "I arived here on last Monday with the Jersey troops and Started them from this place upon their March home on thursday principally in good health and Spirrits—and hope they will arive safe at Trenton about the 22nd or 23d. I have not had one Shillings in money Since I left Greens burgh therefore have left all my Accounts from that to this place and here unsettled untill I Obtain reliefe from you—therefore beg and Entreat you to send me Eight thousand Dollars to enable Me to settle those Accounts. . . .[2] The sum which I aske will barely enable me to prepare my Accounts for a final settlement[3] therefore request I may not meet with any disappointment whatever. . . ."

ADfS, Ephraim Blaine Papers, Library of Congress.

1. Blaine, who was an assistant quartermaster general of the militia army sent to western Pennsylvania, had agreed to remain on duty until provision had been made for transportating the troops home.

2. A warrant for this amount was issued to Blaine on December 31, 1794 (RG 217, Miscellaneous Treasury Accounts, 1790–1894, Account No. 11475, National Archives).

3. Blaine's account was settled at the Treasury on December 31, 1800 (RG 217, Miscellaneous Treasury Accounts, 1790–1894, Account No. 11475, National Archives).

From Tench Coxe

Treasury Department, Revenue Office, December 13, 1794. "It being possible that Inconvenience may arise from the want of information concerning the purchases of Whiskey in Pennsylvania, for the military supply of 1795, I have to request a copy of the instructions therein given by you to Col. P. Nevil in the month of November. . . ."[1]

LC, RG 75, Letters of Tench Coxe, Commissioner of the Revenue, Relating to the Procurement of Military, Naval, and Indian Supplies, National Archives.

1. H to Presley Neville, November 18, 1794.

From Tench Coxe

Treasury Department, Revenue Office, December 13, 1794. "It is necessary that a keeper of the Lighted Beacon near Sherburn in Nantucket be appointed. Tristam Coffin is mentioned as a person the collector [1] has engaged, from whence may be inferred that he approves of the said Coffin as a qualified person. . . ."

LC, RG 26, Lighthouse Letters, Vol. I, National Archives.

1. Stephen Hussey had been appointed collector of customs at Nantucket and Sherburne, Massachusetts, on August 3, 1789 (*Executive Journal*, I, 13).

From Tench Coxe [1]

Treasury Department
Revenue-office, Decemr 13th. 1794

Sir,

I have this day received your letter concerning the additional compensations to the officers of the Revenue.[2] The increase of the Emoluments by the extension of the rate of commissions and by the allowance of fees for documents are the prevailing ones in the letters of the Supervisors. You will remember that I requested the arrangement of this business prior to the Presidents departure for mount Vernon in the last summer,[3] and you thought the state of the business before him would inevitably exclude it, 'till his return. Since that the attention of the President and of yourself to the urgent Business of the Insurrection with the absences [4] incidental thereto have left no opportunity for this object. Before the receipt of your letter this day I had given you all the information I possess with my opinions, and I requested your determination of the principles upon which an arrangement should be made.

I have the honor to be, Your most Obedt Servant

Tench Cox
Commissr. of the Revenue

The Secretary
of the Treasury

LC, RG 58, Letters of Commissioner of Revenue, 1794–1795, National Archives.

1. For background to this letter, see Coxe to H, July 15, 1794, notes 4 and 5.

2. H to Coxe, December 9, 1794.

3. George Washington went to Mount Vernon on June 24 and returned to Philadelphia on July 7, 1794.

4. Washington and H had left Philadelphia for western Pennsylvania on September 30, 1794.

From Tench Coxe[1]

Treasury Department, Revenue Office, December 13, 1794. "I beg the favor of your procuring the Presidents determination upon the subject of the Keeper of the Light House at Cape Fear North Carolina and of the Compensation to be allowed him. . . ."

LC, RG 26, Lighthouse Letters, Vol. I, National Archives.

1. For background to this letter, see Coxe to H, March 11, September 25, 1794.

From William Ellery

[*Newport, Rhode Island*] *December 14, 1794.* "I acknowledge the Receipt of your two letters of the 27th of the last month[1] & I shall retain sufft. funds in my hands to discharge the allowances to fishing vessels[2] which I estimate at about twelve hundred dolls. . . . Permit me to mention that advice has not been received of your decision in the case of the Fair American Benjamin Lee master,[3] and of the Sloop Joanna, Daniel Anthony master."[4]

LC, Newport Historical Society, Newport, Rhode Island.

1. Neither of these letters has been found.

2. For information on the allowances to fishing vessels, see H to Benjamin Lincoln, November 27, 1794.

3. See Ellery to H, June 16, 1794.

4. See Ellery to H, April 21, July 21, 1794.

From Médéric Louis Elie Moreau de St. Méry[1]

philadelphia 15th. Xbr 1794.

Sir

The Kind Reception I have been honoured with by your Excellency, Seems authorize me to hope that my Enterprize will not be intirely indifferent for your Goodness. Nobody feels more deeply than me the grief of Seing your Excellency Leaving a Department where his ability & his fondness of his country was so eminently perceived. But for the true Citizen the means of Serving his native land, may be meet with at every Step or at every Instant.

I am with Respect, Sir, of your Excellency the most obedient & very humble servant Moreau de st méry

J'ose attendre La complaisance de Votre Excellence qu'elle Suppléera à ce que mon Anglois incorrect ne lui exprimera pas bien par rapport à mon respectueux devouement et à mon regret en pensant qu'elle quitte une place qui m'auroit permis de lui faire ma Cour quelque fois.

ALS, Hamilton Papers, Library of Congress.

1. Moreau de St. Méry was a native of Martinique who resided in Santo Domingo until the outbreak of the French Revolution. One of the leaders of the anti-monarchist movement in France after 1789, he migrated to the United States in 1793. After living in Norfolk and New York City, he moved in October, 1794, to Philadelphia, where he conducted a printing and bookselling business. He was the author of *Loix et Constitutions des Colonies Françoises de l'Amérique sous le Vent* (Paris, 1784–1790).

From Jeremiah Olney[1]

Custom House
District of Providence 16th Decer. 1794

Sir

I have the Honor to Transmit (under cover of your care) for the Clerk of the Supreme Court of the United States, the writs of Error and Citations with copies of the proceedings (before the State court) in the Suits of Welcome Arnold and Edward Dexter, against me, relative to the Brigantine Neptune. I respectfully request Sir, after examining those papers, you will please to cause them to be lodged with the Clerk aforesaid, and that you will Seasonably, acquaint me whether it will be expedient for me, personally, to attend the Tryal in Feby. next at Philadelphia and whether it will be important for me to engage (as counsil to assist the Attorney General of the United States) David Leonard Barnes Esqr. who has had the chief management of those Suits since the Death of the late District Attorney.[2] As my attendance at Philadelphia, or that of Counsil from hence would be a considerable Expense to the public, I have deemed it my indispensable Duty (as I have heretofore) not to take a Single step relative to the Subject in question, but such as you may think Proper to Direct which shall be particularly and promptly executed. The enclosed assignments of Error are with Deference, Submitted by Mr. Barnes, and which will be Subject to the revision of the Attorney Genl. of the United States.

I am very respectfully Sir Your Most Obedt. Hum. Serv.

Jereh. Olney Collr.

Alexander Hamilton Esqr.
Secretary of the Treasury.

ADfS, Rhode Island Historical Society, Providence.

1. For background to this letter, see Olney to H, November 7, 15, 28, December 10, 13, 27, 1792, March 14, 25, April 15, 25, September 23, October 7, 21, November 21, 1793, February 17, March 31, April 14, first letter of April 24, May 5, August 11, September 19, 1794; H to Olney, November 27, 1792, November 7, 1793, March 19, April 24, September 9, 19, 1794.

2. Shortly after the death in September, 1793, of William Channing, who had been United States attorney for the District of Rhode Island, Olney wrote to H: "I have taken the Liberty to recommend to the President, David Leonard Barnes Esqr. of this Town attorney at Law as a gentleman well qualified to fill the Office of District Attorney" (Olney to H, October 7, 1793). The President, however, did not take Olney's advice, for on January 24, 1794, he nominated Ray Greene for the position (*Executive Journal*, I, 147). Greene held this position until 1797, when he was succeeded by Barnes (*Executive Journal*, I, 252).

To John Barclay

Treasury Department
December 17. 1794

Sir

I have been favoured with your letter of the 11th instant.[1] More than was consistent with the constitutional powers of the Bank could not have been expected or desired. In manifesting a readiness to do all that is lawful, a proof is afforded that the Bank of Pensylvania will not be behind any other institution of this kind in a proper zeal for the service of the UStates. I beg through you to make my acknowlegements to the Board & that You & they will be persuaded of my respect & esteem.

I have the honor to be Sir Your most Obedt servant

Alex Hamilton

John Barclay Esq
President of The Bank of Pensylvania

ALS, Historical Society of Pennsylvania, Philadelphia.

1. Letter not found, but see H to the President and Directors of the Bank of Pennsylvania, December 1, 1794, to which Barclay was replying in his letter of December 11.

From Tench Coxe

Treasury Department, Revenue Office, December 17, 1794. "I shall be glad of your opinion whether I shall direct the purchase of canvas[1] (other than which is to be home made) at such prices as considering certainty, may be as advantageous as contracts resting on future importation."

LC, RG 75, Letters of Tench Coxe, Commissioner of the Revenue, Relating to the Procurement of Military, Naval, and Indian Supplies, National Archives.

1. For information concerning the naval armament for which this purchase was to be made, see Henry Knox to H, April 21, 1794.

From Henry Knox

[*Philadelphia, December 17, 1794.* On December 17, 1794, Hamilton wrote to Knox: "In reply to your letter of this date." *Letter not found.*]

To Henry Knox[1]

Treasury department
Decr 17. 1794

Sir,

In reply to your letter of this date[2] I have the honor to inform you, that no general Instructions have gone from this department to the Collectors relative to the purchase of the Lands on which Fortifications might be erected,[3] from an expectation, that the information necessary for the Government of the Treasury would come in course through the Channel designated in your letter to me of the 24th of July last.

The enclosed memorandum exhibits a view of all the cases in which Cessions and Purchases have been made or measures taken to effect the Object thereof.[4] The Treaty for the purchase of the Land on which the fortifications are erecting at Baltimore is suspended for the present on account of a very material difference in Opinion with respect to the value of it.[5]

I am Sir, respectfully, Your most obedient Servant,

A Hamilton.

Copy, RG 233, Reports of the Secretary of War, Third Congress, National Archives.

1. This letter was enclosed in a report of the Secretary of War to the House of Representatives dated December 19, 1794 (*ASP, Military Affairs*, I, 71–107).

2. Letter not found.

3. The purchase of lands for fortifications was provided for by "An Act to provide for the Defence of certain Ports and Harbors in the United States" (1 *Stat.* 345–46 [March 20, 1794]). See Knox to H, March 29, 1794.

4. Copy, RG 233, Reports of the Secretary of War, Third Congress, National Archives. This memorandum is printed in *ASP, Military Affairs*, I, 106–07.

5. See H to Robert Purviance, September 18, 1794, and Purviance to H, December 9, 1794.

From Joseph Whipple

Portsmouth [New Hampshire] December 18, 1794. ". . . The estimated allowances to Fishing Vessels payable in this district on the 31st. day of December instant is Sixteen hundred & twenty nine dollars." [1]

LC, RG 36, Collector of Customs at Portsmouth, Letters Sent, 1794–1796, Vol. 6, National Archives.

1. See "Treasury Department Circular to the Collectors of the Customs," October 25, 1792.

To Edward Carrington

[*Philadelphia, December 19, 1794.* On December 26, 1794, Carrington wrote to Hamilton: "I have been favored with yours of the 19th. Instant." *Letter not found.*]

To Henry Lee

[*Philadelphia, December 19, 1794.* On December 31, 1794, Lee wrote to Hamilton and referred to "your favor of the 19th. Decr." *Letter not found.*]

To George Washington

Treasury Department, December 19, 1794. Sends "a letter from the Commissioner of the Revenue of the 13 instant,[1] on the subject of the Keeper of the Lighthouse . . . near Sherburn in Nantucket." States that "it is advisable to appoint the person therein mentioned." [2]

LC, George Washington Papers, Library of Congress.

1. Tench Coxe to H, December 13, 1794.

2. On December 23, 1794, Coxe wrote to Stephen Hussey, collector of customs at Nantucket and Sherburne, Massachusetts: ". . . The President of the United States, has been pleased to approve of Mr. Tristram Coffin, as Keeper of the lighted Beacon near Sherburn in Nantucket" (LC, RG 26, Lighthouse Letters, Vol. I, National Archives).

From Tench Coxe

Treasury Department,
Revenue-office, Decemr 20th 1794

Sir,

The contractor, Mr. G. Hieskell,[1] at Fredericksburg, Virginia, has applied for the sum of 300. Dollars on Account, having as he alleges furnished supplies to that amount. W: Wiatt [2] Esquire the Postmaster was the person, who contracted with him, from circumstances heretofore communicated.[3] You will be pleased to direct such remittance as you may find proper.

I have the honor to be, Sir your obedient Servant

Tench Coxe
Commissr. of the revenue

The Secretary
of the Treasury

LC, RG 58, Letters of Commissioner of Revenue, 1794–1795, National Archives.

1. Godlove Hieskell.

2. William Wiatt.

3. Coxe to H, July 30, August 5, 1794.

From Tench Coxe

Treasury Department,
Revenue-office, Decemr. 20th 1794

Sir,

I believe it will be found on Inspection that the northwestern Territory does not extend easterly further than the western Bank of the River Ohio. Consequently the officers of Inspection in the 2d. Survey of the district of Ohio (St. Clairs Governt.) [1] cannot make seizures upon that River. This may be remedied by extending the said 2d. Survey by an act of the President, so as to include the Ohio.[2] It will be well also, that the officers in Virginia and Kentucky have a similar power to act on the River, and it may be a matter of some difficulty to adjust it so as to include the River in both Districts.

The revenue laws of the Union contemplate *federal* and *state* courts—are the courts of the two territories, absolutely and strictly of either quality? There is no Marshall of the United States in either Territory, and the Inspector I observe is the Sheriff in St. Clairs Government.[3]

I communicate these Ideas for consideration.

I have the honor to be, Sir Your most obedient Servant,

Tench Coxe
Commissr. of the revenue

The Secretary
of the Treasury

LC, RG 58, Letters of Commissioner of Revenue, 1794–1795, National Archives.

1. Arthur St. Clair was governor of the Territory Northwest of the River Ohio.

2. Provision for the extension of the excise laws of the United States to "the territories northwest and south of the river Ohio" was made in Section 1 of "An Act making further provision for securing and collecting the Duties on foreign and domestic distilled Spirits, Stills, Wines and Teas" (1 *Stat.* 378–81 [June 5, 1794]). This section reads: "That in order to facilitate and secure the collection of the revenue on distilled spirits, and stills, in such states as have been, or hereafter may be erected, and in the territories northwest, and south of the river Ohio, the President of the United States shall be, and he is hereby authorized and empowered to form and erect such new districts and surveys, and to make such alterations in, and additions to the several districts, and in and to the several surveys thereof, as from time to time appear, in his judgment, expedient and necessary; and that it shall also be lawful for the President, by and with the advice and consent of the Senate, to appoint such and so many

supervisors, inspectors of surveys, and inspectors of ports, therein and therefor, as may be found necessary, and to assign to them, compensations proportionate to those heretofore, or which may hereafter be allowed, to the officers of the revenue. *Provided*, That if the appointment of such supervisors and inspectors cannot be made, during the present session of Congress, the President may, and he is hereby empowered to make such appointments, during the recess of the Senate, by granting commissions, which will expire at the end of their next session."

3. Coxe is referring to Ebenezer Sproat, inspector of the revenue for Survey No. 2 in the District of Ohio and sheriff of Washington County, which was in the same district.

To Tench Coxe

[*Philadelphia, December 20, 1794.* On December 22, 1794, Coxe wrote to Hamilton and referred to "your letter of the 20th. instant." *Letter not found.*]

To George Gale

Treasury Department December 20th. 1794

Sir

I have directed the Treasurer of the United States to remit to you draughts on John Muir, Collector of Vienna Maryland to the amount of four thousand dollars. As this gentleman however has not been altogether regular in his transactions, I am not willing that the Credit of the United States should be hazarded by a negociation of the bills. I have therefore to request that you will employ some carefull person to go to Vienna with them and receive the Money.[1] If you should obtain payment, you will apply three thousand dollars thereof towards repaying the Loan which I informed you in my letter of the 8th Instant[2] I had directed the office of Discount & Deposit to make to you—the remainder may be appropriated to the use of the Militia Army. If however the bills should not be paid you will then keep them in your hands untill you hear further from me on the subject. Inclosed is a letter for the Collector.[3]

I am with great consideration Sir Your most Obedient Servant

A Hamilton

George Gale Esquire
Supervisor for the
District of Maryland

LS, William Andrews Clark Memorial Library, University of California, Los Angeles; copy, RG 217, Miscellaneous Treasury Accounts, 1790–1894, Account No. 8440, National Archives.

1. In January, 1795, Gale paid $60.13 to William Frazier "for going express from Baltimore to Vienna with drafts of the Treasurer on John Muir Collector of the last mentioned port, pursuant to directions from the Secretary of the Treasury dated Decemr. 20th 1794" (D, RG 217, Miscellaneous Treasury Accounts, 1790–1894, Account No. 8440, National Archives).

2. Letter not found.

3. Letter to Muir not found.

To Philip Schuyler[1]

[*Philadelphia, December 20, 1794.* On January 5, 1795, Schuyler acknowledged receipt of Hamilton's "favor of the 20th Ult." *Letter not found.*]

1. Schuyler was H's father-in-law.

From Tench Coxe[1]

Treasury Department
Revenue Office December 22d: 1794

Sir,

I have had the honor to receive this day the order of the House of Representatives relative to the measures that have been adopted concerning the naval armament,[2] in your letter of the 20th. instant.[3]

LC, RG 233, Reports of the Secretary of War, Third Congress, National Archives; LC, RG 75, Letters of Tench Coxe, Commissioner of the Revenue, Relating to the Procurement of Military, Naval, and Indian Supplies, National Archives.

1. On December 23, 1794, H sent this letter to Henry Knox. Knox enclosed Coxe's letter in his report to the House of Representatives of December 29, 1794 (*ASP, Naval Affairs,* I, 6–17).

For information concerning the naval armament in 1794, see Knox to H, April 21, 1794.

2. On December 16, 1794, the House of Representatives "*Resolved,* That the President of the United States be requested to cause a report to be laid before the House of the measures that have been adopted, pursuant to the act of the twenty-seventh of March last, for building ships; of the progress hitherto made; the compensations allowed to persons employed in the different branches of the business; together with an estimate of the expense for completing the same" (*Journal of the House,* II, 267).

The House resolution refers to "An Act to provide a Naval Armament" (1 *Stat.* 350–51 [March 27, 1794]).

On December 18, 1794, Coxe wrote to Knox: "Mr Coxe has the honor to inform the Secy at War, that he suggested to the Secy of the Treasy the Elec-

It was on the 4th. day of April that a participation with you in the Treasury business for the War Department was committed to this office.[4]

After the requisite examination into the objects to be procured, advertisements were issued on the 16th. of April for the Live Oak & Cedar timber required by the Secretary at War; as also on the same day for Cannon ball, twenty four pound Cannon, & Kentledge or Iron ballast.[5] On the 7th. of May, advertisements were issued for the yellow & pitch pine & white oak materials, & for the locust treenails; & measures were taken for examining into the terms on which the Cordage could be procured.[6]

Many other enquiries were likewise made, but no contracts or purchases were or could be completed before the 9th of June, the legislature not having granted until that time, the money requisite for the naval armament.[7] On that day (the first moment when it was legal) an agreement was made with John T. Morgan a master shipwright of Boston to go to Charleston for the purpose of procuring in concert with persons in that place & in Savannah the live oak,

---

tion of *Mr Co's passing a letter to him, & its being communicated to the Secy of the Treasy.*, or its going directly from this Office to the War department.

"The *former* being elected, a letter communicating to the Secy. the order of the House relative to the Naval armament is rendered necessary." (LC, RG 75, Letters of Tench Coxe, Commissioner of the Revenue, Relating to the Procurement of Military, Naval, and Indian Supplies, National Archives.)

3. Letter not found.

4. Letter not found.

5. On April 17, 1794, Coxe wrote to newspaper publishers in New York, Baltimore, Richmond, Savannah, and Charleston asking them to place an advertisement in their newspapers for these materials (LC, RG 75, Letters of Tench Coxe, Commissioner of the Revenue, Relating to the Procurement of Military, Naval, and Indian Supplies, National Archives). For this advertisement, see [Philadelphia] *Gazette of the United States & Evening Advertiser*, April 17, 1794.

6. See Coxe to John Hunter, May 3, 1794 (LC, RG 75, Letters of Tench Coxe, Commissioner of the Revenue, Relating to the Procurement of Military, Naval, and Indian Supplies, National Archives). Hunter was a member of the House of Representatives from South Carolina. See also *Gazette of the United States & Evening Advertiser*, May 7, 1794.

7. Section 1 of "An Act making appropriations for certain purposes therein expressed" (1 *Stat.* 394–95 [June 9, 1794]) provided "That there be appropriated for the several purposes herein after specified the respective sums following, to wit: To defray the expenses which shall be incurred, pursuant to the act, intitled 'An act to provide a naval armament,' six hundred and eighty-eight thousand eight hundred and eight-eight dollars, and eighty-two cents. . . ."

red cedar & pitch pine materials.[8] His business was to search for the timber, to superintend the cutting & forming it by the moulds for the frigates, & to procure it to be shipped for the six several ports at which the frigates were to be built, it was further agreed, with consent of the Secretary of War, that he should be employed to build a Frigate at Charleston, if one should be built there.[9] By the concurrence of both Departments, he was to be allowed pay at the rate of two thousand dollars ℔ annum in full of all claims of services & expences in the Carolina's & Georgia, or while building. Like this all the principal contracts were made, as you will remember in concert with you after the necessary conferences from time to time.

Daniel Stephens Esqr Supervisor of the Revenue & Isaac Holmes Esqr. Collector of the Customs, both of Charleston were appointed, by you to make the contracts for the timber in North & South Carolina & John Habersham Esqr Collector of the customs & Joseph Clay Esqr both of Savannah in Georgia were appointed to make the contracts for the timber in Georgia & to give all possible aid towards the advancement of the business to Mr. Morgan.[10] No allowance for their agency has been yet made.

On the 16th of June, a letter was written to Jedediah Huntington Esqr. Collector of the customs at New London,[11] to procure 60 Axemen & 30 Ship Carpenters in the Ports of Connecticut, Rhode Island & the Western Coast of Massachusetts, & provisions & other supplies were sent from New London, New York & Philadelphia as œconomy & the nature of the articles appeared to require.

The time necessary for the collection of these persons and their apprehensions from the Climate & season occasioned their departure from New London to be delayed until the 23d day of September.

The agreements for the Live oak were made on the 2nd. day of September at Savannah at the rate of Six pence, money of Georgia ℔ foot, to be cut by the United States, but hauled to Water, navigable for Vessels of Eleven feet draught, by the Contractors.

8. See Coxe to H, June 4, 1794.

9. See Knox to H, June 25, 1794.

10. See Coxe to H, June 4, 1794.

11. LC, RG 75, Letters of Tench Coxe, Commissioner of the Revenue, Relating to the Procurement of Military, Naval, and Indian Supplies, National Archives.

On the 7th day of July, instructions were given to Mr. Habersham & Mr: Clay to hire such additional wood cutters & other hands as the public service might require & admit,[12] it being deemed more expedient, that the business should be effected in a short time by a certain number, than that it should be effected in a term of twice the length by half the force of hands.

On the 25th day of June I furnished you with an estimate of the composition-metal, sheathing-copper, bolts & nails, bunting & Iron kitchens, for the Six frigates, all which were ordered from Europe; and a note of the anchors, which last were postponed for further inquiry, whether they could not be manufactured in the United States. The articles ordered are daily expected to arrive.

On the 30th of June some further measures to procure Anchors, by a circular application were taken,[13] & proposals to make those of the smaller sizes at 8 Cents ℔ lb were received & accepted:[14] as also proposals to furnish those of the larger sizes, which tho' accepted by the United States,[15] were not confirmed by the Proposer, from unexpected circumstances.

Immediately after the appointment of the Naval Agents at the Six ports by the Secretary at War,[16] it was determined from considerations of œconomy to employ the same Agents in the Treasury business. Instructions were sent to them in consequence, on the 5th: & 7th:[17] days of July to procure all the White oak, yellow pine & treenails it being found, that they could be more easily, &

12. See Coxe to H, July 5, 1794, note 6.

13. "Treasury Department Circular," June 30, 1794 (LC, RG 75, Letters of Tench Coxe, Commissioner of the Revenue, Relating to the Procurement of Military, Naval, and Indian Supplies, National Archives).

14. Coxe to Nathaniel Cushing, September 25, 1794; Coxe to Hodijah Baylies, September 25, 1794 (LC, RG 75, Letters of Tench Coxe, Commissioner of the Revenue, Relating to the Procurement of Military, Naval, and Indian Supplies, National Archives). Cushing was a resident of Pembroke, Massachusetts. Baylies was collector of customs at Dighton, Massachusetts.

15. Coxe was negotiating with Elijah Phelps of Norfolk, Connecticut, and Solomon Townsend of the Stirling Works, Orange County, New York, for large anchors. See Coxe to Phelps, September 25, 1794; Coxe to John Blagge, November 18, 27, December 24, 1794 (LC, RG 75, Letters of Tench Coxe, Commissioner of the Revenue, Relating to the Procurement of Military, Naval, and Indian Supplies, National Archives).

16. See Knox to H, June 25, third letter of July 9, 1794.

17. Coxe to the Naval Agents, July 5, 7, 1794 (LC, RG 75, Letters of Tench Coxe, Commissioner of the Revenue, Relating to the Procurement of Military, Naval, and Indian Supplies, National Archives).

œconomically procured by those Agents & in most instances from the country in their vicinity.

On the 15th day of July other instructions were sent to them to procure the articles usually supplied or made by the Mastmakers, blockmakers, coopers, & boat builders; also to pay further attention to the procuring of Cordage & to make measures for the procuring of Sail Cloth, made in the United States.[18]

On the 9th day of July a Contract was executed with Messrs. Levi Hollingsworth, Son & Company of Jersey & Pennsylvania for 92 tons of Cannon ball at 37⅓ dollars, & 198 tons of Kentledge, at 28⅔ dollars,[19] & some time after the Contract was further extended to about 340 Tons.[20]

On the 28th of July a contract was made with Messrs. J.J. Faesch & Compy. of New Jersey for 98 tons of Cannon ball & 256 tons of Kentledge at the same prices; [21] and authority was since given to Henry Jackson Esqr. Naval agent at Boston to purchase 150 tons of Foreign Kentledge which had lain some time in the hands of a Citizen of Boston & which was sold at the reduced price of 25 dollars, because of that circumstance.[22]

On the 28th day of June, a contract was made with the Cecil Iron Company (Samuel Hughes Esqr & others of Maryland) for three sixth parts of the twenty four pound Cannon.[23]

On the 8th of August a contract was made with the owners of the furnace Hope (Messrs. Brown Francis & Co. of Providence) [24] for two sixth parts of the same. The prices were 106⅔ dollars & the difference of expence for boring from the solid. The first contract was made in concert with the Secretary at War & yourself; and 2nd: in concert with you. The two parties were then willing

18. LC, RG 75, Letters of Tench Coxe, Commissioner of the Revenue, Relating to the Procurement of Military, Naval, and Indian Supplies, National Archives.

19. See Coxe to H, September 23, December 1, 1794.

20. Coxe to Levi Hollingsworth and Son, October 18, 1794 (LC, RG 75, Letters of Tench Coxe, Commissioner of the Revenue, Relating to the Procurement of Military, Naval, and Indian Supplies, National Archives).

21. See Coxe to H, August 1, October 1, 1794.

22. See Coxe to Jackson, August 26, 1794 (LC, RG 75, Letters of Tench Coxe, Commissioner of the Revenue, Relating to the Procurement of Military, Naval, and Indian Supplies, National Archives).

23. See Coxe to H, June 27, 30, October 8, 1794.

24. See Coxe to H, June 27, August 9, October 8, 24, 1794.

to have agreed for the remaining sixth part, but it was postponed to give to the Iron masters, in different quarters, an opportunity to contract. Since that, Contracts for the remaining sixth have been offered to the two parties abovementioned[25] who are to give answers as soon as they shall have proved some of those Cannon for which they have already contracted.

Vessels amounting to about 2600 Tons have been dispatched or ordered to transport the timber from Georgia to the Six several ports, & they carried to the Southward, Axemen, Carpenters, provisions, Oxen, forage & implements.

Captain John Barry was dispatched to Georgia, in one of the Public Vesels, on the 5th of October to examine into the state of the business & to give expedition to the procuring & transportation of the timber.[26] He had no allowance, but the amount of his expences. About the time of his return Mr Asa Copeland was sent thither to assist permanently in the Superintendance of one division of the Wood Cutters, & to expedite the transportation to the water side, & the shipment & stowage of the timber[27] as Mr: Habersham & Mr: Clay are too remote to be of any use in that part of the business. His compensation is 3⅓ Dollars ℔ day.

Oxen with grain & hay for them, & setts of timber wheels have been necessarily sent to Georgia for the purpose of transporting the timber, as the Contractors were deficient in means of that kind & on account of the live oak timber for one frigate, which was procured under circumstances that rendered it necessary to provide for its transportation.

On the 30th of August 100 tons of Kentledge was engaged of

25. Coxe to Brown and Francis, October 9, 1794; Coxe to Samuel Hughes and Company, October 9, 1794 (LC, RG 75, Letters of Tench Coxe, Commissioner of the Revenue, Relating to the Procurement of Military, Naval, and Indian Supplies, National Archives).

26. See Coxe to Barry, October 5, 1794 (LC, RG 75, Letters of Tench Coxe, Commissioner of the Revenue, Relating to the Procurement of Military, Naval, and Indian Supplies, National Archives).

27. On October 23, 1794, Coxe wrote to Knox: ". . . in pursuance of the Idea entertained by you and my self in a late conference, I have engaged Mr. Asa Copeland a trader in this town, To go to Georgia for the purpose of assisting Mr. J. T Morgan in expediting the hauling &c. of Timber & dispatching the Vessels . . ." (LC, RG 75, Letters of Tench Coxe, Commissioner of the Revenue, Relating to the Procurement of Military, Naval, and Indian Supplies, National Archives).

Messrs Gardner & Olden of Philadelphia, at the price of 28⅔ Dollars.[28]

A second party of Carpenters have been engaged on the Delaware, 20 in number by Tench Francis[29] Esqr & are now about to sail for Georgia.

The Naval Agents have been authorized to contract for Blacksmiths work, including the bar iron, when it may have or shall become necessary: also for composition bolts so far as the same may be requisite before the arrival of those ordered from Europe.[30]

It is understood that agreements have been made by those Agents for the white oak timber, & other articles in pursuance of several instructions already mentioned.

It remains only to notice the Contract made in the month of September with the Boston Company for sail Cloth,[31] sufficient for one entire suit of Sails for each frigate. The price which I understand to have been settled is from 13 to 15 dollars ℔ bolt of 39 yards.

Besides the foregoing measures, which have been thus far matured, others are in that train of investigation, which the time necessary for the collection of the timber admits, in most instances & which is peculiarly desirable, in a new undertaking, of so great moment & expence.

I cannot transmit to you this communication without suggesting the inconveniences & injuries to the United States particularly from

28. This contract between H for the United States and John Gardiner, Jr., and Ephraim Olden may be found in RG 217, Miscellaneous Treasury Accounts, 1790–1894, Account No. 7907, National Archives.

29. Francis was agent for purchasing supplies for the War Department.

30. See Coxe to the Naval Agents, July 15, 1794 (LC, RG 75, Letters of Tench Coxe, Commissioner of the Revenue, Relating to the Procurement of Military, Naval, and Indian Supplies, National Archives).

31. On December 29, 1794, Coxe wrote to Samuel Breck, a resident of Philadelphia and agent for the Proprietors of the Boston Sail Cloth Manufactory: "Mr. Coxe presents his compliments to Mr. Breck & requests the favor of a call at the Treasury when convenient. The Secy of The Treasy has acceded to the prices at which the canvas was first offered . . ." (LC, RG 75, Letters of Tench Coxe, Commissioner of the Revenue, Relating to the Procurement of Military, Naval, and Indian Supplies, National Archives). On January 1, 1795, H signed a contract with Samuel Breck. See "Articles of Agreement Between H and Samuel Breck," January 1, 1795. The account between the "Proprietors of the Sail Cloth Manufactory at Boston" and the United States may be found in RG 217, Miscellaneous Treasury Accounts, 1790–1894, Account No. 7567, National Archives.

external Quarters, which may arise from giving publicity to all its details.

I have the honor to be Sir, Your most obedt. servant

Tench Coxe

Commissioner of the Revenue

The Secretary
of the Treasury.

Conversation with George Hammond[1]

[Philadelphia, December 23, 1794–January 5, 1795][2]

Although I have had no reason to suspect, that this government has ever deviated from the resolution, which I have formerly attributed to it, of declining to enter into any political connexion with Sweden and Denmark,[3] I have nevertheless, since the receipt of your Lordship's last instructions,[4] renewed my enquiries upon the subject, in an incidental conversation with Mr. Hamilton, from whom I have had the satisfaction of learning that, since his last communication to me respecting it, the propriety of this connexion has been discussed by the American ministers,[5] who concur in opinion that, in no political situation of this country, would such a measure be expedient; as it would involve it in engagements with powers, with which it can have no common interest, and from which, in the moment of difficulty or danger it would derive no benefit or assistance. Exclusively of these obvious considerations, which dictates this policy, this country is generally in too unsettled a state, to admit of its entangling itself in connexions, which might eventually have a tendency to add a participation in the disputes of Europe to the internal causes of agitation. I could not with propriety attempt to discover from Mr. Hamilton whether the attention of this government had been directed to this object, in consequence, of the communications of Mr. D'Engerstroem[6] to Mr. Pinckney (as mentioned in your Lordship's No. 12) or of any more recent or formal overtures on the part of Sweden. I might have been inclined to conjecture that some proposition on this point had been made by the Court of Denmark, through the medium of General Walterstorff[7] (the Governor of Santa Cruz) who has been some months in this country; had I not collected from various quarters, and positively from Mr. Hamilton, that General Walterstorff is charged with no public mission whatsoever, and that his visit to this city is merely of a private nature. In any case the result has been such as I have stated.[8]

PRO: F.O., Series 5, Vol. 8; PRO: F.O. (Great Britain), 5/8.

1. This "conversation" has been taken from Hammond to Lord Grenville, January 5, 1795, Dispatch No. 1.

2. Hammond states that he had talked with H "since the receipt of your Lordship's last instructions." As Hammond received these instructions on December 23, 1794, he presumably held this conversation between that date and January 5, 1795.

3. See "Conversation with George Hammond," July 1–10, 1794.

4. Hammond is referring to Grenville's instructions of October 2, 1794. After expressing satisfaction with Hammond's statement, based partly on a conversation with H, that the United States would not form an alliance with Sweden or Denmark, Grenville stated: "It will however be necessary that you should still attend to this subject, and that you should renew it from time to time in conversation with those whom you may have reason to think well disposed; as there is strong ground to believe that the Project is not wholly dropped by Sweden" (PRO: F.O. [Great Britain], 5/5).

5. See "Conversation with George Hammond," July 1–10, 1794, note 5.

6. Lars D'Engestrom, the Swedish Minister to Great Britain. See "Conversation with George Hammond," July 1–10, 1794, note 1.

7. Ernst Frederich von Walterstorff, governor of the Danish West Indies. See H to John Langdon, September 6, 1794, note 3.

8. In the remainder of this letter Hammond refers to H's resignation as Secretary of the Treasury and states: "However I may lament this circumstance, which deprives me of the advantages I derived, from the confidential and friendly intercourse, that I have uniformly had with him, when the most influential member of this administration, I cannot but concur in opinion with his friends, that a proper regard to his own character has rendered this step necessary."

From Tench Coxe

Treasury Department, Revenue Office, December 23, 1794. In answer to "enquiries . . . made by a committee of the house of Representatives relative to the clerks in the public offices," [1] lists the clerks in his office, their duties, and their compensations.

LC, RG 58, Letters of Commissioner of Revenue, 1794–1795, National Archives.

1. On December 17, 1794, the House of Representatives appointed a select committee composed of Thomas FitzSimons of Pennsylvania, John S. Sherburne of New Hampshire, John Watts of New York, William Lyman of Massachusetts, and Anthony New of Virginia" to inquire into the establishment of Clerks in the several Departments, and to report a plan for ascertaining the number necessary to be permanently employed in each, and their compensations" (*Journal of the House*, II, 269). This committee's report, which was submitted to the House on February 6, 1795, consisted of several lists with the

proposed number of clerks for each department and the proposed salary for each clerk (LC, RG 233, Records of the United States House of Representatives, "Transcribed Copies of Reports and Papers of Various Select Commitees," National Archives). No evidence has been found that the House acted on this report.

From Tench Coxe

Treasury Department, Revenue Office, December 23, 1794. "I have the honor of sending to you, herewith, two commissions for officers, designated as 'Supervisors of the *United States* for the District of Pennsylvania &ca.' [1] It appears to me, that a question may arise, with respect to the validity of Official Acts performed by those Supervisors, by reason of the Stile of the designation of their offices, respectively, in their commissions: I therefore beg leave to suggest the propriety of stiling them Supervisors of the *Revenue*, for the District of Pennsylvania and Ohio, respectively."

LC, RG 58, Letters of Commissioner of Revenue, 1794–1795, National Archives.

1. On December 18, 1794, George Washington had signed commissions for Henry Miller as supervisor of the revenue for the District of Pennsylvania and Thomas Marshall as supervisor of the revenue for the District of Ohio (JPP, 313).

To Henry Knox [1]

Treasury Department, December 23, 1794. "I send you a letter this moment received from the Commissioner of the Revenue, dated yesterday [2] which contains the answer to your letter founded upon the order of the House of Representatives relative to the measures which have been adopted concerning the naval armament."

Copy, RG 233, Reports of the Secretary of War, Third Congress, National Archives.

1. Knox enclosed this letter in his report to the House of Representatives on December 29, 1794 (*ASP, Naval Affairs*, I, 6–17).
2. Tench Coxe to H, December 22, 1794.

To Robert Purviance [1]

Treasury Department December 23d 1794.

Sir

Messrs. Zacharie Coopman & Co. of Baltimore have represented to me, that you have said, that unless the principal of their Bonds lately put in Suit should be speedily discharged, you will discontinue the granting to them the customary credit on the duties arising from importations. It being my wish however to allow them a further indulgence, I have to request that you will continue to conform to the instruction contained in my letter to your predecessor in Office of the 20th of June last[2] untill you hear from me again on the subject. A copy of the letter alluded to is transmitted herewith.

I am with consideration Sir Your most Obedient Servant

A Hamilton

Robert Purviance Esquire
Collector of Baltimore

LS, Columbia University Libraries.

1. For background to this letter, see Otho H. Williams to H, February 27, March 20, 1794; H to Williams, June 20, 1794.

2. H to Williams, June 20, 1794.

From Edmund Randolph[1]

Department of State, December 23d 1794

Sir

The Director of the Mint being of opinion, that it may be advantageous to contract for the fifty tons of Copper, offered by the Schuyler Copper Mine Company to be delivered by the last of May next, I must request you to obtain information whether the contract can be punctually fulfilled. In that case, I shall get the favor of you to enter into *an engagement* in behalf of the United States, at a price not exceeding that of imported Copper; provided there be funds, which the Mint can command.

I have the honor to be, Sir, with great respect and esteem Your most obedient servant Edm: Randolph.

LC, RG 59, Domestic Letters of the Department of State, Vol. 8, December 6, 1794–October 12, 1795, National Archives.

1. For background to this letter, see Jacob Mark and Company to H, December 11, 1794.

To George Washington

Treasy. Dept. Decembr. 23d. 1794.

Sir,

The present state & prospects of the Treasury render it necessary, without delay, to exercise the power vested in the President by the act passed the 18 instant, intitled "an act authorizing a Loan of two millions of Dollars." [1]

To enable him to determine this a probable view of receipts & expenditures distributed quarter yearly is herewith presented, and the form of a power [2] as usual to The Secretary of the Treasury to make the Loan, is submitted.

With perfect respect &c.

Alexander Hamilton
Secy. of the Treasy.

[ENCLOSURE] [3]

View of Probable state of the Treasury

Jany. 1.	Cash in Command of the Treasury	600.000.
	Deficiency	1.265.000.
		1.865.000.
April 1.	Receipts from Imports & tonnage	
	℔ returns received, nearly	900.000.
	℔ Estimate on cases not returned	500.000.
	℔ Estimate on account of internal duties	150.000.
	Deficiency	2.315.000.
		3.865.000.
July 1.	Receipts from Imports & tonnage	
	pr. return nearly.	600.000.
	pr. Estimate (as above)	300.000.
	pr. Estimate on accot. of internal duties	150.000.
	Deficiency	2.665.000.
		3.715.000.
Octo. 1.	Receipts as last quarter	1.050.000
	Deficiency	3.015.000
		4.065.000.
Jany. 1.	Receipts pr. Estimate	1.800.000.
	Deficiency	2.265.000
		4.065.000

in the Year—1795.

Jan: 1.	Interest nearly	740.000.
	Support of Government	125.000.
	Military & naval Departmt. & miscellany	400.000.
	Instalment of temporary Loans	600.000.
		1.865.000.
April 1.	Deficiency	1.265.000.
	Interest	775.000.
	Support of Government	125.000.
	Military & naval Departmt. & miscellany	500.000
	Installments of temporary Loans which fell due since January 1st	1.200.000.
		3.865.000.
	Deficiency brot. down	2.315.000.
July 1.	Interest	775.000.
	Support of Government	125.000.
	Military & naval Departmt. & miscellany	500.000
		3.715.000.
Octor. 1.	Deficiency brought Down	2.665.000.
	Interest &ca as last quarter	1.400.000.
		4.065.000.
1795.	Deficiency brought down	2.665.000.
Jany. 1.	Interest &ca. as last Quarter	1.400.000.
		4.065.000.

LC, George Washington Papers, Library of Congress.

1. 1 *Stat.* 404 (December 18, 1794).
2. See Washington to H, December 24, 1794.
3. LC, George Washington Papers, Library of Congress.

To George Washington[1]

Treasury Department Dec. 23d. '94.

Sir,

I have the honor of transmitting to you an account between the Collector of New York, and the United States, which has been adjusted at the Treasury, and a balance of Dolls. 1533. 89/100. stated to be due to the said Collector.[2]

As all claims of a similar nature with the foregoing have been hitherto paid out of the Fund destined to defray the Contingent Charges of Government, I have deemed adviseable to ask your permission, to discharge the said sum of Dolls. 1533 89/100 out of the twenty thousand dollars appropriated for these purposes, at the last session of Congress.[3]

With the most perfect respect &c. A Hamilton

LC, George Washington Papers, Library of Congress.

1. For background to this letter, see Thomas Jefferson to H, December 12, 1793; H to John Lamb, December 16, 1793.

2. Lamb's account with the United States may be found in RG 217, Miscellaneous Treasury Accounts, 1790–1894, Account No. 6074, National Archives.

3. "An Act making appropriations for certain purposes therein expressed" (1 *Stat.* 394–95 [June 9, 1794]).

To Tench Coxe

[*Philadelphia, December 24, 1794.* On December 25–27, 1794, Coxe wrote to Hamilton: "I have Just received your letter of the 24th istant." *Letter not found.*]

From Stephen Moylan

[*Philadelphia*] *December 24, 1794.* "The Amount of interest on Stock remaining on the books of this office for the quarter ending the 31st Instant is 18963. dollars 44. Cents 8 Mills for which sum you will please to issue a Warrant."

LC, RG 217, First Comptroller's Office, Pennsylvania Loan Office, Letter Book "A," National Archives; LC, RG 53, Pennsylvania State Loan Office, Letter Book, 1793–1795, Vol. "616-P," National Archives.

From George Washington[1]

[Philadelphia, December 24, 1794]

For carrying into execution the provisions of the Act of the 18 day of this present month, whereby the President of the Ud. States is authorised & empowered to borrow a certain sum of money on the credit of the United States.[2]

I do hereby authorize you the said Secretary of the Treasury, in the name and on the credit of the said United States, to borrow of the Bank of the United States, or of any other body or bodies politic, person or persons whomsoever, a sum not exceeding Two Millions of Dollars, at an interest not exceeding five per centem per annum, and to enter into such agreements for the reimbursement thereof as shall be needful & proper, hereby promising to ratify whatever you shall lawfully do in the premises.

In testimony whereof I have hereunto subscribed my hand at the City of Philadelphia the 24 day of december in the year 1794.

Go. Washington

LC, George Washington Papers, Library of Congress; copy, Historical Society of Pennsylvania, Philadelphia.

1. For background to this letter, see H to Washington, first letter of December 23, 1794.

2. "An Act authorizing a Loan of two million of Dollars" (1 *Stat.* 404 [December 18, 1794]).

From Tench Coxe[1]

T: D: R: O: December 25th [–27] 1794

Sir

I have Just received your letter of the 24th instant[2] with the papers from the President of the U: S:[3] and the letter of the Secretary at War contained in the same enclosure.

LC, RG 75, Letters of Tench Coxe, Commissioner of the Revenue, Relating to the Procurement of Military, Naval, and Indian Supplies, National Archives.

1. For background to this letter, see Henry Knox to H, April 21, 1794.

2. Letter not found.

3. On November 30, 1794, Pierce Butler, United States Senator from South Carolina, wrote to George Washington: "I feel it a duty incumbent on me, to inform You, that there is a defect in the Arrangement made for getting Timber in this State, to build the Frigates with. I do not observe anything wrong in the Overlooker, Mr. [John T.] Morgan, but there is a deficiency some where; And unless it is timely Corrected, the Ships might as well, were it possible, be Built of Bars of Silver as of Live Oak" (ALS, RG 59, Miscellaneous Letters, 1790–1799, National Archives).

On January 7, 1795, Washington replied to Butler: "The Letter with which you were pleased to favor me, dated the 20th. Novr. came duly to hand: a copy of which, immediately upon the rect. thereof, I transmitted to the Secy of War (in whose Department the building of the Frigates is) with directions

It is proper for me to remind You that the arrangement which was made for procuring the timber for the Frigates,[4] was the result of our United Judgments founded upon enquiry & consideration, that the appointments of the Superintendent[5] then here, & of the Agents in Georgia[6] were made by you. The principles of the measures taken by me in pursuance thereof, were always adjusted with you, as also the details of all important proceedings upon those principles, And as often as convenient or practicable: the whole course of the business at the Seat of Government, in the other states, & particularly in Georgia. It is also proper for me to observe that my suggestions were very generally coincident with your final views, And that my ultimate opinions accorded, I believe I may say universally with your ultimate opinions in regard to the arrangement for procuring the Timber from the Southern States and to the proceedings adopted to that end.

It may not be improper to state likewise that the Secy. at War from the coincidence of the duties of the Departments in this business,[7] had as he observes a gnowledge of the arrangement, and that during your absence[8] I deemed it in every view proper, not only to keep him well informed of the course of the business but to resort to him upon all points or occurrences of delicacy or difficulty. I constantly extended my enquiries & consultations to the commanders of the ships[9] who were at the seat of Government and to the Naval constructor there.[10]

It may be correctly said then, that the arrangements for procuring

---

to cause an enquiry into the abuses of which you made a general complaint, & report the result to me.

"It would have been satisfactory, & might have contributed essentially to expedite this enquiry if you had been so obliging as to have pointed your information to the particular instances of abuse." (ALS, RG 59, Miscellaneous Letters, 1790–1799, National Archives; LC, George Washington Papers, Library of Congress.)

Washington's letter to Knox is dated December 23, 1794 (LC, George Washington Papers, Library of Congress).

4. See Coxe to H, June 4, October 22, December 22, 1794.

5. John T. Morgan. See Coxe to H, June 4, 1794.

6. John Habersham and Joseph Clay. See Coxe to H, June 4, 1794.

7. See H to Coxe, April 4, 1794.

8. Coxe is referring to H's trip to western Pennsylvania during the Whiskey Insurrection. See H to Washington, September 24, 1794, note 2.

9. Thomas Truxton, John Barry, and Richard Dale.

10. Joshua Humphreys. See Coxe to H, May 12, 1794.

the Timber for the Frigates from Georgia and the proceedings thereon, have been the result of the combined Judgment of the proper Officers of the Treasury, and of the proper Officers in or connected with the war Department.

In the case of a new, very expensive, and highly important operation of the Government, wherein a suggestion of great evil, very strong indeed in its terms, and indefinite as to its objects must have created an anxiety of some duration, I conceive that it is not inexpedient to give this preliminary view of the conduct of the Departments.

To avoid repetitions, I do my self the honor to refer the President for many details; to my letter to you of the 22d. instant, which is already before him, in the report of the Secy. at War.[11]

The appointment of John T. Morgan to the two services of *Superintendent for procuring the Timber* & *Naval constructor* was made by you and the Secy. at War, Upon the knowledge and recommendation of several Gentlemen of Massachusetts.

No 1 is a note concerning the business prior to the execution of the Contract.

No 2 contains the instructions from this Office.[12]

No 3 is the contract with him.[13]

No 4 is a letter introducing Mr. Morgan to certain Officers of the general government in Charleston and Savannah,[14] by two of whom in the usual course of the Ty. business payments of money for the War Departmt. would be made.[15] It was supposed that their commercial & local knowledge would be convenient to Mr Morgan & servicable to the U. States. It will be perceived, that the Agents to contract were not decided upon when No 4 was written. The hope then was, that a person able to contract with advantage, would

11. See Coxe to H, December 22, 1794, note 1.

12. Coxe to Morgan, June 12, 1794 (LC, RG 75, Letters of Tench Coxe, Commissioner of the Revenue, Relating to the Procurement of Military, Naval, and Indian Supplies, National Archives).

13. The contract is dated June 9, 1794. See Coxe to H, June 4, 1794.

14. Daniel Stevens, Isaac Holmes, John Habersham, and Joseph Clay. See Coxe to H, June 4, 30, 1794.

15. See "Treasury Department Circular to the Collectors of the Customs," April 3–June 4, 1794. Holmes was collector of customs at Charleston, South Carolina, and Habersham was collector at Savannah, Georgia. See also Coxe to H, June 30, 1794.

have been procured here. You will remember that this hope was not fulfilled. In consequence, Messr. Stevens & Holmes; for the Carolina's & Messr. Habersham & Clay for Georgia were appointed. This was done from the uncertainty whether Mr Morgan would be equal to that part of the business. Mr. Clay who was added for the greater prudence is a judicious & experienced Man and was paymaster to the Southern Army in the late war; Enquiries at the moment were made about him.

The purchase of live Oak was effected at 6d Sterg. ℔ cubic foot & the sellers were to cart it to a Landing at 11 feet water. Considering the heavy expence & difficulty of hauling such large & weighty ⟨objects⟩ the price of timber in general, & the impression which has been made upon the live oak forests on the Sea Isld. & shores in general; there appears no reason to consider that price as meriting the observations in Mr. Butlers[16] representation. It is important & perfectly true, that it has been found impossible to this day, to procure a qualified master builder to go to Georgia upon the same terms as Mr Morgan, or indeed upon any terms: The attempt having been made by the Treasy & War Departs. the Captain[17] and the Philada. constructor,[18] in order that Mr. Morgan might have been transferred to the public yard at Norfolk for the purpose of proceeding with the Frigate to be built there.[19] Hence may be fairly inferred the necessity of having given as great a compensation as that allowed him.

The Axemen & carpenters which were in Georgia when the representation to the President is dated were procured from that part of the U: S: in which the nature of the population & the state of the Ship building warranted an exception that persons of each description of the right sort would be procured with promptness & upon reasonable terms. A further inducement resulted from the opportunity of employing an agent (J. Huntington Esqr.)[20] of correctness & discretion, and zeal for the public Interests & Service. The terms proved to be reasonable. But it has been elledged by

16. Pierce Butler. See note 3.
17. John Barry.
18. Joshua Humphreys.
19. See Knox to H, June 25, 1794.
20. Jedediah Huntington, collector of customs at New London, Connecticut. See Coxe to H, June 4, 1794.

Mr Morgan, Captain Barry, & a Mr. Leake[21] that a much smaller proportion of them (from 3 to 6 in 21) were carpenters, than was stated by General Huntington, & that the remainder were very exceptionable as axemen. In consequence of this, & because of the sickness and shortness of the number required by Mr Morgan, nineteen Carpenters with two head men, have been dispatched at his request from Philada. having been procured as you will remember from Philada. by Mr. Francis.[22] Some few have been engaged in Georgia as there is reason to believe.[23]

It is alledged that the axes were bad. These were procured of workmen of the most established repute in Philada. by Mr. Francis who has really had much experience in matters of that nature. I have requested him to procure some from Boston, to satisfy Mr. Morgan.

It does not yet appear that any demurrage has accrued on any vessel by reason of delay on this or any other account. There is an abundance of foreign axes at Savannah some of which no doubt may serve upon an Extremity, and there are Smiths likewise who have been employed by the Agents to make & mend. More axes have been also sent fm. hence.

It is to be observed that the people of Philada. are used to make axes for live Oak as there is a good deal of that species of timber cut by the Philada. coasting traders for that market, & as a very large proportion of the Philada. Ships have been built since the War, and indeed before it, of that kind of Timber. Axes, however, & all steeled implements & tools are only to be relied on after trial; because it is impossible by any other means to ascertain the temper of the metal.

Some complaint was made in Savannah of the quality of the salt provisions which were shipped by N. Fish Esqr.[24] for cash from N. York, that place combining the supplies of N. Jersey, N. York & Connecticut Pork, and of N England & No: River Beef, was in my Judgment proper for the purchase. The season of the year, not long before killing time, was the most unfavorable; good meats are

21. Richard Leake, a resident of St. Simon's Island, Georgia.

22. Tench Francis.

23. See Coxe to H, October 22, 1794.

24. Nicholas Fish, supervisor of the revenue for New York. See Coxe to H, second letter of June 30, 1794.

often injured in the summer by a little want of care about the Pickle, by the consumption of the Fat by the Salt, and the consequent hardening of the lean parts. No complaint however has been transmitted from the Camp against the quality of the Provisions, altho' much of them had been used when the last letter came away. The provisions shipped were considered as adequate to the supply of 100 men for six months. It is therefore a matter of surprize that a letter of the [25] instant requiring more (without stating any quantity) has been received from Mr. Morgan. The provisions were under the care of Messrs. Habersham & Clay at Savannah, and under the care of Mr. Morgan at the place of cutting the Wood. It would be possible, that a waste of these might constitute some part of the ground of the representation of Mr Butler, but that the provisions were in course to be ⟨given⟩ under the care of Mr. Morgan whom he approves. I made Mr. Morgan responsible by contract for the care of the provisions & fidelity therein.[26] If any improvement can be made in Georgia in point of œconomy, or dispatch which involves œconomy it is to be regretted on that score as well as from the general considerations wh. have occurred in our conferences, that Capt. Barry did not remain there so long as to see accomplished the haling of the Timber to the landing. So far as his mission was to be considered as a measure of the Treasy. his execution of the duty assigned to him may be deemed by the Departmt. imperfect. He informed me on his return that no contracts for the Live Oak were made in consequence of wh. I wrote to messr. Habersham & Clay.[27] These Gentlemen informed me that the execution of the contract had been delayed, because the sellers of the wood objected to the hauling of the Timber; tho' it was sold under that condition. They urged the unexpected size of it: and finally Messr. Habersham & Clay appear to have changed the condition of haling, without authority from Governmt. to an allowance therefor of two pence Georgia money ℘ Cubic foot. This sum is considered as

25. Space left blank in MS.

26. See Coxe to Morgan, June 12, 1794 (LC, RG 75, Letters of Tench Coxe, Commissioner of the Revenue, Relating to the Procurement of Military, Naval, and Indian Supplies, National Archives).

27. Coxe to Habersham and Clay, November 24, 1794 (LC, RG 75, Letters of Tench Coxe, Commissioner of the Revenue, Relating to the Procurement of Military, Naval, and Indian Supplies, National Archives).

inadequate, it was feared the contractors would refuse to sign without the alteration. Capt Barry thinks very unfavorably of Messr. Habersham & Clays conduct and has handed a letter of Mr. Leake one of the Sellers who refused to execute the contract, in wh. that gentleman throws great blame upon the Government for the People sent by Gl. Huntington and for the quality of the axes. He suggests considerations against the continuance of Messr. Habersham & Clay in the Agency on a/count of their distance and offers his own Service in that capacity wh. as a contractor, & with an open question concerning the Hauling, it appeared inexpedient to accept. Mr. Asa Copeland[28] who had been sent from hence before Mr. Leak's letter was exhibited is expected to be very useful. He has been accustomed to the Coasting trade and to the procuring of ship Timber, and was recommended as a fit assistant to Mr Morgan by the Naval constructor, (Mr. Josa. Humphreys) of Philada. It will be observed that he was engaged by anticipation before any difficulties were represented to have occurred & has been gone about two months.

The true design of the appointment of Messrs. Clay & Habershm. was the better to secure judicious & fair contracts. Mr. Habersham was to pay the necessary monies. He of course was desired to receive, the Vessels People, Stores, Implements &ca. from the Northward, wh. might go to Savannah, & to send them forward, with others procured at Savannah to the place of cutting. These Agents were never expected to be with the wood cutters. Mr. Morgan as a builder & equal to the construction of a Frigate, was in course deemed adequate to the Superintendence of that whole business. Supplies, tools, & Teams, were sent to him with more than 80 People, & authority to hire others. It was convenient to him that Genl. Huntington had sent Leaders with the Division of the axemen & Carpenters, especially as he had been sick. Mr. Copeland was sent, before such an aid was asked. Mr. Rice, a Philada. bred carpenter resident at Savannah, & engaged by the Agents there, has since arrived to his assistance; and Mr Leake represents that he has given great personal attendance himself. Mr. Morgan however has had much ill health.

The extent to which the authority to engage hands in Georgia

28. See Coxe to H, December 22, 1794, note 27.

is used, is, the employment of some black Labourers, supposed from the Letters to be about twenty, & a few Carpenters whose numbers are unknown.

Vessels have been taken up, or ordered at Philada. Portsmouth N: Hr: & Boston.[29] The first was chartered by the Naval agents in Phila.[30] to take Capt Barry, & to transport oxen, & timber wheels, with Hay &c. Those timber wheels were required for Mr Butlers Wood,[31] the rest being deliverable by the contractors. The sending of them was however, induced by suggestions, that Teams were not possessed by the Planters on the ⟨Coast.⟩ Of these oxen 18 in number, fourteen died there. Three yoke were immediately bought by Mr. Habersham. Twenty Oxen more have been Since Sent, with Hay &ca. for which another vessel was taken up by the Treasy. Several other vessels have also been taken up by the Treasy. & one more by the Naval agents of Philadelphia, & several ordered in New England, to secure the transportation before winter of a quantity of the principal Timbers to the six ship-yards. We had no advice either of the place to which the vessels should go, the time when they would be wanted, the draught or construction of wh. they should be, nor the number desired. On advising with the Secy. at War, during your absence it was determined for the reasons stated to run the risk of about [32] Tons. The freights of the two Vessels taken up by the Naval agents at Philada. were as low as the current freights, those of the Treasy. were considerably lower. Half the applicants refused our terms; yet all the Charters were very expensive. This is accounted for by the fact, that Seamens Wages which used to be, 8, 9, & 10, Dollars, are now 26 to 28 & all other things are excessively advanced.

The desire of forwarding the Armament; the press of the season, the Urgency of the agents, Captains, & constructor the Transportation of necessary supplies & the conveyance of necessary persons, impelled to these charters. The freights elsewhere, were not known.

29. Coxe to Henry Jackson and Jacob Sheafe, October 21, 1794 (LC, RG 75, Letters of Tench Coxe, Commissioner of the Revenue, Relating to the Procurement of Military, Naval, and Indian Supplies, National Archives).

30. Francis Gurney and Daniel Smith.

31. On November 14, 1794, Knox wrote to Coxe and referred to "The Honorable Mr Butler having made an offer of Live Oak for the building of the Ships" (LC, RG 45, Letters Sent Concerning Naval Matters, National Archives).

32. Space left blank in MS.

One favorable experiment has been made in Portsmouth, one was ordered at the same time from Boston,[33] The result of that order is not yet communicated. The instructions to charter in New England have been extended; & it has been some time determined to rely upon them as much as possible, if they should prove favorable.

The Revenue Cutter has been employed to transports between Savannah & St Simons, where the wood is cutting at this time; but from her absence when the Carpenters & axe men arrived from New London, the vessel that carried them from thence to Savannah was engaged to take the men to St Simons at a very high freight. Mr Habersham informs that it could not be avoided.

It is understood from Capt. Barry, that there is not perfect harmony between the agents at Savannah & Mr Morgan; and the Agents represent that there is a disposition in Mr Morgan to proceed in cutting at St. Simons. They wished the cutting, also to go on at Ossabaw. Contracts have been made for wood at both places. A letter is just received from which it appears that the Agents understand Mr. Morgan to have been cutting wood at St Simons on Lands, with the owners of which they have no sort of agreement. Mr Morgan's reply to these statements will be forthwith obtained; but in the mean time, as the vessels have been ordered to St Simons it will be inexpedient at this moment, to break in upon the operations there.

To increase by every possible means the chances of advantage to the US. I gave Mr Morgan a letter to Chrisr. Hillary Esqr. Collecr. at Frederica on St Simons Island,[34] but I have no letter from him, nor do I find him mentioned in any of the letters to this Office. No letter has yet been received from Asa Copeland,[35] whom I instructed to transmit me a weekly letter without fail. Time and opportunity perhaps, have not admitted of his letter reaching me. I requested Mr. Seagrove[36] before his departure, to express in conversation with Mr. Habersham whom he knows The extreme sollicitude of the Government about expedition & œconomy, in the pro-

33. See note 29.

34. Coxe to Christopher Hillary, October 4, 1794 (LC, RG 75, Letters of Tench Coxe, Commissioner of the Revenue, Relating to the Procurement of Military, Naval, and Indian Supplies, National Archives).

35. See Coxe to H, December 22, 1794, note 27.

36. James Seagrove. See Coxe to H, October 13, 22, 1794.

curing of the timber for the Naval armament, and the necessity of previous or timely information upon all points. He is fully possessed of all the Ideas wh. prevailed here, and I have considerable expectations of the impulse he will give to any movements in Georgia which may require it. In my instructions to Mr: Copeland I suggested to him that he would find Mr Butler & Mr Seagrove there and disposed to give him advice and to assist him thro' difficulties wh. might occur.

This auxiliary Idea occured to my mind as one which might tend to obviate impediments, which might arise to persons who were strange to all other persons around or near them.

It will be perceived that several things in the execution of the arrangements do not appear to have been as they were to be desired; and the occurrence & consequently the prevention of them has been sometimes anticipated and the correction of others has been effected or commenced. I do not recollect any matter which could have been done by the Treasury upon more favorable terms. Nor do I know any thing at this time wh. can increase the expectation of œconomy & dispatch except the employment of a person in that character proposed for Col. Jos. Cowperthwaite,[37] the determination on wh. I strongly recommend. He might have liberty to return Mr Rice to Savannah & Mr Copeland to Philada. if he should not find the public service really to require them, and he would be a substitute for the agents at Savannah in the greater part of the business.

I am, Sir, &ca T: Coxe C. R.

The Secy. of the Treasy.

P.S. In addition to papers No 1 to first No 4. there are eight others from second No 4 to 11 which will exhibit the manner in which the business has been done; there are many more of the like degree of particularity, which can be exhibited on requisition.

37. Joseph Copperthwaite was a resident of Philadelphia. On January 5, 1795, Coxe wrote to Habersham: ". . . Col: Cowperthwaite is a man, personally entitled to respect here. He has been since the Revolution the High Sherrif of the City & Co. of Philada. for several years and he now commands one of the Battalions of the Philadelphia Militia" (LC, RG 75, Letters of Tench Coxe, Commissioner of the Revenue, Relating to the Procurement of Military, Naval, and Indian Affairs, National Archives).

To Tench Coxe

[*Philadelphia, December 25, 1794.* On December 26, 1794, Coxe wrote to Hamilton: "I have received your letter of the 25th. inst: relative to anchors." *Letter not found.*]

To the President and Directors of the Bank of the United States[1]

Treasury Department
December 26. 1794

Gentlemen

Inclosed are the copies of two Acts one of Congress authorising The President to borrow two millions of Dollars[2] another of the President authorising me to carry that act into effect.[3] The extensive payments becoming due to the Bank of the UStates added to the large demands for the current service oblige me to ask of the Bank the loan of the whole sum. The expence of suppressing the late insurrection has created a necessity for larger anticipations than usual and for a longer term of reimbursement.

I therefore hope that it will be found convenient to the Bank to make the loan to the above extent payable in the following installments (to wit) one Million of Dollars on the first of January next, One Million of Dollars on the first of April next, each installment to be reimbursed in one year after it is advanced.

With great respect & esteem I have the honor to be Gentlemen Your obedient servant Alex Hamilton

The President & Directors of The
Bank of The UStates

ALS, Historical Society of Pennsylvania, Philadelphia.

1. Thomas Willing was president of the Bank of the United States.
2. "An Act authorizing a Loan of two million of Dollars" (1 *Stat.* 404 [December 18, 1794]).
3. See George Washington to H, December 24, 1794.

To the President and Directors of the Bank of the United States

[*Philadelphia, December 26, 1794.* The dealer's catalogue description of this letter reads as follows: "Asking for an extension of a loan to Treasury." [1] *Letter not found.*]

AL, sold at Anderson Galleries, February 3, 1909, Lot 170.

1. See H to Joseph Ball, December 28, 1794.

From Edward Carrington

Richmond Decr. 26th. 1794

Dr. Sir,

I have been favored with yours of the 19th. Instant [1] covering your private letter of the same date to Governor Lee.[2] I hear he has left Winchester,[3] & will probably be here tomorrow or next day, and have thought it best to keep his letter until his arrival. The explanations contained in this letter to him, are such as I had anticipated, as you might have perceived from mine to you of the 11th.[4]

Had there been no difficulties to encounter from a want of appropriated Funds, it would have been impossible, upon an arrangement taken at Camp on the 23d. Nov. & was still to be communicated at Philada., for you to have sent the money to the places designated, in time for the arrival of the several detachments; [5] nor

ALS, Hamilton Papers, Library of Congress.

1. Letter not found.

2. Letter to Henry Lee not found. Lee, who had completed his term as governor of Virginia on November 30, 1794, had been commanding general of the militia army called out to suppress the insurrection in western Pennsylvania.

3. Lee had been at Winchester, Virginia, because that was the place at which the Virginia militia was discharged.

4. Carrington is mistaken; his letter to H is dated December 12, 1794.

5. On November 17, 1794, Lee had issued orders describing the routes which the various state militia were to take on their return home. The places in the respective states from which the troops were to be discharged also were designated. Lee's general orders are printed in Baldwin, "Orders Issued by General Henry Lee," 108–10. See also H to Lee, November 13, 1794; H to George Washington, November 19, 1794.

does it appear to me, that such an arrangement should have been made, without a previous knowledge of the readiness of Government to meet it, as it was well known that the service was an unforeseen one, for which the existing Revenues had not been assigned; nor yet am I of opinion, that dissatisfaction would have been the consequence of an explained communication to the Troops, that balances of pay must remain unpaid for some short time after their return home. As reasonable & patriotic Citizens, they ought not to have been dissatisfied, because such treatment would have been consistent with every practicable application of unascertained Sums at a distance from the Treasury, even had appropriated Funds been there: much much should it be considered such in a case which, being unforseen, had not been provided for by the Legislature. Indeed, I think it extremely unpolitic, to impress upon the minds of the people, ideas, that the degree of punctuality which has, in this instance, been attempted, is the only ground on which Government can expect their services when necessary for its support. Good Men may be treated like petulant Children, and by that means, be made equally unreasonable & perverse; on the other hand, both good & bad Men may, by firm & plain lessons of reason, be taught to accommodate their demands upon Government to the due course of an honest administration. It has been said that this degree of punctuality is necessary from the impossibility of getting the balances into the hands of the disposed individuals, and that Speculators would, for trifles, purchase up the Claims; it, however, appears to me that every evil suggested could easily have been provided against; and, if the Troops have been duly Mustered, they very probably are provided against. Every soldier who remained, to the last of his Service, under the head of his original Officer, whether discharged at the end of the Service, or imtermediately, is locally known; if, by any means, he has appeared under the head of another Officer, his locality was, or should have been, noted in the subsequent Musters, particularly on the final one. Under these precautions the balances of pay might be sent to the respective Brigadiers in the Country, who should be relied on to provide for the payment thereof to the individuals entitled, by the persons whom they might appoint, and be responsible for; the actual recTs. of the individuals to be rendered in the settlement of the Accounts, and the genuineness of the Receipts to be proven by the oaths of the payers of the monies. An arrangement of this kind discards every idea of Assignees recovering payment, & presents a certain and sufficiently rapid course for the passage of unpaid balances to the identical persons entitled thereto. Moderate commissions might be allowed to the Brigadiers & their agents on these special occasions, which would be amply compensated by the relief Govt. would receive under convenient postponements of such demands, & the satisfaction to the claimants when payments are necessarily deferred. It appears to me that the Brigadiers of Militia may be made very happy instruments in both the commencement & ending of every tour of Militia duty, & it would be well to introduce practices of making them such. The Brigade districts embrace, each, an extent of space & numbers, convenient for individual Communications; and the Brigadiers are naturally presented as convenient & safe Agents, both for the public, & the respective individuals concerned. In all the arrangements which have been entrusted to me in relation to the late expedition, I have endeavored to call into practice the services of the Brigadiers, when they could possibly be embraced; and they have been found to contribute greatly to facilitate the service, and to accomodate individuals.

Your observations upon the experience and unweildy arrangements of some of the lines, arising from an overproportion of Officers, & a multiplied Staff, *I trust & believe*, had not reference to the Virginia line. I think the Staff was put on as Moderate a Scale as was practicable, and early measures were taken to consolidate the thin Corps, and dismiss the Supernumerary Officers. Genl Morgan,[6] as well as Darke[7] & Mattews,[8] under whom the Virga. line was formed, were good enough to act very confidentially with me and enclosed you will receive copies of communications between me & Genl Morgan, leading to early reductions of officers & Waggons, two of the most devouring sources of expence, & the most produc-

6. Major General Daniel Morgan was in command of the Virginia militia.

7. William Darke had been a lieutenant colonel of the 4th Virginia Regiment in the Continental Army during the American Revolution and in the Kentucky militia during Arthur St. Clair's expedition against the Indians in 1791.

8. Brigadier General Thomas Matthews.

tive of impediment, that can possibly hang upon an Army. I have every reason to hope, from the sums furnished to Colo. Byrd,[9] who has supplied transportation forage fuel & Straw to the Virga. line throughout the expedition, including forage fuel & straw to that of Maryland from, & back to, Fort Cumberland, that the moderation of our Staff arrangement will be apparent: I have the satisfaction to hear from all concerned that his supplies have been timely & ample.

Whether the Inspections & Musters of the Troops have been well attended to in the Virga. line, will appear by a view of the Returns. The inclosed letter from me to Major Pryor[10] of the 12th. of October, will shew you that the various objects of his appointment were fully presented to him, and, from my knowledge of his Capacity & usual diligence, I am in hopes the purposes of his appointment have been well effected.

I have not felt that the observations and information which I now communicate were necessary to remove from your mind impressions to the disadvantage of the arrangements of the Virga. li⟨ne⟩ but it will not be unsatisfactory to you to receive them.

I am with the greatest regard & Esteem Dr sir Your Most Obt st Ed Carrington

Alexander Hamilton Esq
Secretary of the Ty.

9. Colonel Otway Byrd, quartermaster general of the Virginia line.
10. Colonel John Prior, inspector and mustermaster of the Virginia line.

From Tench Coxe[1]

Treasury Department, Revenue Office, December 26, 1794. "I have received your letter of the 25th. inst: relative to anchors.[2] You will find my letter of the 25th June, the highest supposed prices &c. of the anchors, and in mine of the 8th. inst. you will find the particular anchors yet wanted. . . ."

LC, RG 75, Letters of Tench Coxe, Commissioner of the Revenue, Relating to the Procurement of Military, Naval, and Indian Supplies, National Archives.

1. For background to this letter, see Henry Knox to H, April 21, 1794.
2. Letter not found.

From Tench Coxe

Treasury Department, Revenue Office, December 26, 1794. "It is with extreme concern that I enclose to you a letter of a very improper tenor indeed, from Messr. Nicholas Hoffman & Co.[1] at New York, to Tench Francis[2] Esqr. dated on the 22d instant, and this day received by me from the hands of Mr. Francis. . . ."

LC, RG 75, Letters of Tench Coxe, Commissioner of the Revenue, Relating to the Procurement of Military, Naval, and Indian Supplies, National Archives.

1. Coxe, who was responsible for procuring military, naval, and Indian supplies, had hired Nicholas Hoffman and Company to obtain goods for the Indians. See Coxe to H, June 23, 1794.

2. Francis was the agent for purchasing War Department supplies.

From Tench Coxe

Treasury Department, Revenue Office, December 26, 1794. "Enclosed is a copy of a letter from T: Francis Esqr: of this date, concerning advances for Fort Mifflin &ca.[1] You will be pleased to cause such order to be taken on it as the necessity of the case shall appear to require." [2]

LC, RG 75, Letters of Tench Coxe, Commissioner of the Revenue, Relating to the Procurement of Military, Naval, and Indian Supplies, National Archives.

1. The letter from Francis reads as follows: "My Money in Bank is entirely expended—in ⟨fact⟩ I have over drawn considerably. Be pleased to direct ⟨a⟩ Warrant for 25,000 dollrs. to be issued in my name. The Monies put into my hands to carry on the works at Fort Mifflin, is all expended. The Secretary of the Treasury Verbally directed me to go as far as 1,000 dolrs. beyond the sums I have received for Fort Mifflin, provided it was found necessary to secure the Wharf that was sunk on the Bar opposite the Fort; part of this sum is spent and perhaps the whole may be wanted. I wish to have the 1,000 dolrs." (copy, RG 58, Records of the Bureau of Internal Revenue, General Records, 1791–1803, National Archives).

2. H endorsed Francis's letter as follows: "Applications of this kind ought to be accompanied with a summary of past expenditures & a general indication of the purposes for which the money is wanted. And it will be regular that the Com~ of the Revenue express his opinion. I have no data whatever to guide me except as to the 1000 Dollars Fort Mifflin. A H" (ALS, RG 58, Records of the Bureau of Internal Revenue, General Records, 1791–1803, National Archives).

From Tench Coxe

Treasury Department, Revenue Office, December 26, 1794. "A considerable impediment to the arrangement of compensations[1] adjusted on Thursday night has just occurred. The 13th Section of the law of the 5th June[2] has been inadvertently caused to refer to the 30th day of June 1795 ('next') by the postponement of the consummation of the Act from the preceding month until the commencement of the month of June 1794."

LC, RG 58, Letters of Commissioner of Revenue, 1794–1795, National Archives.

1. For background to this letter, see Coxe to H, July 15, 1794, notes 4 and 5, December 13, 1794; H to Coxe, December 9, 1794.

2. Coxe is referring to "An Act making further provision for securing and collecting the Duties on foreign and domestic distilled Spirits, Stills, Wines and Teas" (1 *Stat.* 378–81). For Section 13 of this act, see Coxe to H, July 15, 1794, note 4.

From Tench Coxe

Treasury Department, Revenue Office, December 26, 1794. "The Superintendent of the Virginia Lt. House (col William Lyndsay) has reported the Death of the late keeper Captain Goffigan.[1] He has placed in that Station Mr. Henry James a native of the place, an old Seafaring Man, whom he thinks every way calculated for a keeper. No other person offers for the service. . . ."[2]

LC, RG 26, Lighthouse Letters, Vol. I, National Archives.

1. Laban Geoffigan. See H to George Washington, May 2, 1793; Tobias Lear to H, May 3, 1793.

2. On December 15, 1794, Coxe informed Lindsay that "the appointment of a keeper will in the course of business be brought forward. In the mean time it will be agreeable that Mr. Henry James perform the business under your direction . . ." (LC, RG 26, Lighthouse Letters, Vol. I, National Archives). On January 3, 1795, Coxe wrote to Lindsay: "I have this day received from the Secretary of the Treasury a note of the confirmation by the President of the Appointment of Mr. Henry James as keeper of the Light House on Cape Henry . . ." (LC, RG 26, Lighthouse Letters, Vol. I, National Archives).

H's "note" of Washington's confirmation has not been found.

From Tench Coxe

[Philadelphia, December 26, 1794]

Mr. Coxe presents his compliments to Mr. Hamilton, with the inclosed, just received from a Committee of the Snuff manufacturers.

December 26th 1794

[ENCLOSURE][1]

The Manufacturers of Snuff in Philadelphia Remonstrate[2]

Against the manner in which the Excise or Duty is laid and to be collected on Snuff—eight Cents per pound this is on an average fifty ℔ Cent.[3] This is an encouragement for a defraud of the Revenue as the Excise is an encouragement so to do.

Also give Bond in the Sum of Five thousand Dollars and must keep an account from day to day of the quantity manufactured.[4] This is impossible for the following Reasons—

First There is is no person can be at his Mill from fifteen to thirty

LC, RG 58, Letters of Commissioner of Revenue, 1794–1795, National Archives.

1. D, Hamilton Papers, Library of Congress.

2. The snuff manufacturers were remonstrating against "An Act laying certain duties upon Snuff and Refined Sugar" (1 *Stat.* 384–90 [June 5, 1794]). For an earlier remonstrance against the tax on snuff, see Samuel Hodgdon to H, May 9, 1794.

3. Section 1 of "An Act laying certain duties upon Snuff and Refined Sugar" reads as follows: "That from and after the thirtieth day of September next, there be levied, collected and paid, upon all snuff, which, after that day, shall be manufactured for sale, within the United States, at any manufactory, for every pound of snuff, eight cents" (1 *Stat.* 384–85).

4. Section 4 of this act reads as follows: "That every manufacturer of snuff, who shall be such previous to, and on the thirtieth day of September next, shall, on the said day; and every manufacturer of snuff who shall be, and become such, after the said day, shall, twenty days, at the least, previous to commencing the business or trade of manufacturing snuff for sale, make true and exact entry and report in writing, at the office of inspection, which shall be nearest to the house or building where he or she shall carry on, or intend to carry on, the business or trade aforesaid, of every house or building where such business or trade shall be by him or her carried on, or intended so to be, and of every mill, specifying the number of mortars to each, which he or she shall have or keep therein, for the performing of any process, operation, matter or thing in or about the manufacturing of snuff, and shall also give bond in the sum of five thousand dollars, with condition, that he or she shall, and will,

miles and attend at a Market where he must dispose of his goods.
Secondly There is no person can take all the Snuff out of his mortars or Mills without taking them down which may be done in one hour and then will take one to two days to put them up and get them in order as there is from one to six pounds will lay at the bottom of the Mortars and there is no miller can boult all his snuff the same day it is ground.

Thirdly There is no person would wish to swear to his journeyman or miller's account unless he was present at the weighing of the same, and he labors under the difficulty of being embarrased by the said man if any difference should arise between the parties he there goes and informs which leaves a censure and trouble of a defraud and every person that is under an Excise System is so suspected.

Fourthly An honest man has no chance with one that is dishonest for the honest man will swear to the truth and the dishonest man delights in perjury and fifty per cent is full encouragement as we will deliver Snuff from one to two Shillings ℔ lb.

But if we are to be excised for God's sake lay it on the mortars of the two evils let us take the least—for then the poor man will have a chance for a living for the following reasons—

---

from day to day, enter in a book, or on a paper to be kept for that purpose, all snuff, which he or she shall manufacture, or cause to be manufactured, and of the quantities, from day to day, by him or her sent out, or caused to be sent out of the house or building, where the same shall have been manufactured; and shall and will, on the first day of January, April, July and October, in each year, render a just and true account of all the snuff which he or she shall have manufactured or made, and sent out, or caused or procured to be manufactured or made and sent out, first from the time of his or her entry and report aforesaid, until the day which shall first ensue, of the days abovementioned for the rendering of such account, and thenceforth, successively, from the time when such account ought to have been, and up to which it shall have been last rendered, until the day next thereafter, of the days abovementioned for the rendering of such account; producing therewith the original book or paper whereon the entries, from the day to day to be made, as aforesaid, have been made, and shall, at the time of rendering each account, pay or secure the duties, which, by this act ought to be paid upon the snuff, in the said account mentioned and stated: And if any such manufacturer shall omit to make any such entry or report, or to give any such bond, as is herein before directed, he or she shall forfeit and lose every mill, together with the mortars and other utensils thereto belonging, which he or she shall have or keep for the performing of any process, matter or thing, in or about the manufacturing of snuff, and shall also forfeit and pay the sum of five hundred dollars, to be recovered with costs of suit" (1 *Stat.* 385).

First That he can come forward and give bond and security or deposit the money and can enter his mortars by the year half year or quarter. Then there is no fraud no Excise Officers to take our business from us and take a part of the revenue to support them—we wish to support Government with our lives and property. Secondly Then we all become Excise officers one over another as it is common to undersell each other. Then there would be no danger of the Revenue being defrauded—no trouble for the Excise Officer but to receive his money. These and many other difficulties we labor under.

No manufacturer of Snuff can work his mill above half the Year as his goods must go under certain preparations. Mortars often out of repair differences of the Seasons violent heat or violent cold will not admit us to work.

There is no man can comply with the present System of the Law without he is fond of perjury and God keep us from it.

There is one circumstance which I have been informed of and believe to be true as it came from good authority—that a person of Some other State ground Snuff for forty shillings per hundred entered his Mill to grind is own at eight cents per pound. This has a suspicious appearance of perjury. But for God's Sake make the System direct that we may go to our business that is perishing on hand and our Interest is daily suffering.

In respect to the exportation of the article of Snuff it might as well be a total prohibition as there are few persons ever exports more than from one to ten Barrels which few Masters of Vessels would give Bond for the freight of that amount—as there is little snuff exported only to English Islands where certificates could not be obtained.[5]

5. Section 15 of this act provided that a drawback on the duties paid on snuff should be made on all snuff exported. Section 16 provided that in order to qualify for the drawback, ". . . the exporter or exporters shall make oath or affirmation, that the said snuff . . . are truly intended to be exported to the place, whereof notice shall have been given, and are not intended to be relanded within the United States . . . and shall also give bond to the collector, with two sureties one of whom shall be the master, or other person having the command or charge of the ship or vessel in which the said snuff . . . shall be intended to be exported . . ." (1 *Stat.* 388). Section 19 provided that this bond should be discharged upon delivery of a certificate signed by designated persons at the place at which the snuff was delivered "testifying the delivery of the said snuff . . . at the said place" (1 *Stat.* 389).

We beg your serious attention to the above difficulties as there is seventeen snuff Mills in the United States fifteen of which have been standing since the thirtieth of September the others being obliged to Enter to finish what was likely to perish.

These objections are facts which can be proved by the majority of that Branch which is in this State at present.

This law appears to be a Copy from the British Statute [6] and the difference is they work by Hand Mills and Horse mills and here we work on an improved scale by water which is a great difference in the Implements and the reason is the difference of populousness of that country to this.[7]

6. This is a reference to "An Act for repealing the Duties on Tobacco and Snuff; and for granting new Duties in lieu thereof" (29 Geo. III, C. 68 [1789]) and "An Act to explain and amend an Act, made in the last Session of Parliament, intituled, *An Act for repealing the Duties on Tobacco and Snuff, and for granting new Duties in lieu thereof*" (30 Geo. III, C. 40 [1790]).

7. By "An Act to alter and amend the act intituled 'An act laying certain duties upon Snuff and refined Sugar'" (1 *Stat.* 426–30 [March 3, 1795]) Congress repealed the features of "An Act laying certain duties upon Snuff and Refined Sugar" about which the snuff manufacturers were remonstrating.

Report on an Account of Receipts and Expenditures of the United States for the Year 1793

Treasury Department, December 26th. 1794.
[Communicated on December 29, 1794] [1]

[To the Speaker of the House of Representatives]

Sir,

I have the honor to transmit a letter of this date, from the Comptroller of the Treasury,[2] together with the Statements mentioned in

An Account of the Receipts and Expenditures of the United States, for the Year 1793. Stated in Pursuance of the Standing Order of the House of Representatives of the United States, Passed on the Thirtieth Day of December, One Thousand Seven Hundred and Ninety-One. Published for the House of Representatives (Philadelphia: Printed by John Fenno, No. 119, Ches[t]nut Street, 1794). A copy of the covering letter for this report may be found in RG 233, Reports of the Secretary of the Treasury, 1784–1795, Vol. IV, National Archives.

1. *Journal of the House*, II, 276.

2. Oliver Wolcott, Jr., to H, December 26, 1794.

it, which it has been impracticable to transmit Earlier in the Session, And to be, with perfect respect,

Sir, Your obedient Servant, Alex: Hamilton.

The Honorable
The Speaker of the House of Representatives.

STATEMENT OF MONIES DRAWN FROM THE APPROPRIATION MADE BY THE ACT OF AUGUST 12TH, 1790,[3] OF THE SURPLUS OF DUTIES TO THE END OF THE YEAR 1790, FOR THE REDUCTION OF THE PUBLIC DEBT.

MONIES DRAWN.

From the said surplus being 1,374,656 dollars and 40 cents, the following sums have been drawn by warrants on the Treasurer, *viz.*

1790, December 15,	No. 776,	in favour of	Samuel Meredith,
1791, January 26,	856,		ditto,
February 5,	869,		Benjamin Lincoln,
	870,		William Heth,
September 30,	1265,		Samuel Meredith,
	1266,		William Seton,
1792, March 31,	1605,		Samuel Meredith,
June 30,	1864,		ditto,
	1867,		William Seton,
December 29	2328,		Samuel Meredith,

EXPENDITURE IN PURCHASES.

Auditor's report.

By whom purchased.	Date.		No.	When purchased or redeemed.
	1790.			
Samuel Meredith,	Dec.	20.	810.	to Dec. 6, 1790,
	1791.			
Ditto,	Jan.	31,	961.	from Dec. 7, 1790, to Jan. 11, 1791,
Ditto,	Feb.	12,	989.	Jan. 12, 1791, to Feb. 1,
William Heth,	Sept.	20,	1,575.	Feb. 24, to Ap. 2, for expenses attending his purchases,
Samuel Meredith,	Oct.	12,	1,659.	from Aug. 17, 1791, to Sep. 19, 1791 for interest on stock purchased.
	1792.			
Benj. Lincoln,	Feb.	10,	1,991.	part of purchases from Feb. 22, 1791, to March 3, 1791,
William Seton,		11,	1,993.	from Aug 19, 1791, to Sep. 12, 1791
Samuel Meredith,	June	18,	2,575.	Mar. 21, 1792, to Ap. 25, 1792
William Seton,		30,	2,617.	April 2, to Ap. 17,
	1793.			
Samuel Meredith,	Jan.	25,	3,558.	Dec. 15, to Dec. 22, for interest on stock purchased,

Balance on Dec. 31, 1793, being money remaining in the hands of William Heth, of the sum advanced to him for making purchases, accounted for in the year 1794,

3. "An Act making Provision for the Reduction of the Public Debt" (1 *Stat.* 186–87).

Dolls. Cts.
200,000.
50,000.
50,000.
50,000.
149,984.23
200,000.
28,915.52
62,673.90
151,098.89
15,098.11
957,770.65

Six per cent. stock.		Three per cent. stock.		Deferred stock.		Amount of the several species of stocks.	Amount of monies expended.
Original.	Assumed.	Original	Assumed.	Original	Assumed.		
Dolls. Cts.	Dolls. Cts.	Dols. Cts.	Dolls. Cts.	Dolls. Cts.	Dolls. Cts.	Dolls. Cts.	Dolls. Cts.
56,308.50		61,306.33		61,072.47		278,687.30	150,239.24
37,781.68		15,402.51		26,477.13		79,661.32	51,449.32
42,198.91		14,798.63		11,779.18		68,776.72	48,550.68
32,192.07		27,466.46		14,714.77		74,373.30	49,934.09
							4.15
5,627.94		94,487.67		138,605.87		238,721.48	148,984.71
							760.28
37,010.27		28,716.84		2,712.36		68,439.47	50,000.
		67,439.96		255,257.68		322,697.64	200,000.
6,500.	19,466.07	24,597.69	10,165.28	42,064.03	30,634.02	133,427.09	91,589.42
	86,790.65	14,282.31	42,409.22	36,108.05	12,361.30	191,951.53	151,098.89
8,812.14	6,259.27					15,071.41	15,063.84
							34.27
26,431.51	112,515.99	348,498.40	52,574.50	588,791.54	42,995.32	1,471,807.26	957,708.89
							61.76
							957,770.65

STATEMENT OF THE APPLICATION OF MONIES DRAWN FROM THE APPROPRIATION OF TWO MILLIONS OF DOLLARS, AUTHORISED TO BE BORROWED BY THE ACT OF CONGRESS PASSED ON THE 12TH OF AUGUST, 1790, FOR THE REDUCTION OF THE PUBLIC DEBT.

MONIES DRAWN.

The following sums have been drawn from the said appropriation by warrants on the Treasurer, *viz.*

1793, February 4,	No. 2454, in favour of	Jonathan Burrall,
19,	2482,	Samuel Meredith,
Septemb. 2,	3085,	Ditto,

EXPENDITURE IN PURCHASES.

By whom purchased.	Auditor's report Date. 1793.		No.	When purchased or redeemed.
Jonathan Burrall,	Jan.	25,	3,566.	from Dec. 21, 1792, to Dec. 22, 1792,
Samuel Meredith,	Feb.	9,	3,626.	part of purchases, Jan. 17, 1793, to Feb. 1, 1793 for interest on stock purchased,
Ditto,		18,	3,653.	from Feb. 7, 1793, to Feb. 11, 1793,
Ditto,	Mar.	6,	3,729.	21, 23,
Ditto,	Dec.	20,	4,712.	Sept. 5, Dec. 16,

Dollars. Cts.
50,000.
234,901.89
50,000.
334,901.89

Six per cent. stock		Three per cent. stock		Deferred stock.		Amount of the several species of stocks.	Amount of monies expended.
)riginal.	Assumed.	Original.	Assumed.	Original	Assumed		
olls. Cts.	Dolls. Cts.	Dolls. Cts	Dolls. Cts.	Dolls. Cts.	Dolls. Cts.	Dolls. Cts.	Dolls. Cts.
23,060.83	26,939.17					50,000.	50,000.
97,499.65	19,983.16		2,968.80	18,379.07	7,495.58	146,326.26	134,750.19
							151.70
34,028.39	5,000.			15,784.19	6,781.60	61,594.18	50,779.02
24,313.84	7,397.44			24,102.50	10,464.88	66,278.66	49,220.98
34,955.05	7,993.75			11,246.33	5,522.06	59,717.19	50,000.
13,857.76	67,313.52		2,968.80	69,512.09	30,264.12	383,916.29	334,901.89

STATEMENT OF THE APPLICATION OF MONIES DRAWN FROM THE APPROPRIATION MADE BY THE ACT OF THE 8TH OF MAY, 1792,[4] FOR REDUCING THE PUBLIC DEBT, ARISING FROM INTEREST ON THE SUMS OF SAID DEBT PURCHASED, REDEEMED AND PAID INTO THE TREASURY OF THE UNITED STATES.

MONIES DRAWN.

1791.
March. Interest received and expended in purchases by Benjamin Lincoln,
31. Interest due this day,
June 30. ditto,
Sept. ditto,
Dec. 31. ditto,
1792.
Mar. ditto,
June 30. ditto,
Sept. ditto,
Dec. 31. ditto,
1793.
March. ditto,
ditto, received from William Heth, arising on stock purchased by him,
ditto, Benjamin Lincoln,
ditto ditto,

June 30. ditto, due this day
ditto, received from Samuel Emery, due on part of the commutation of Simeon Thayer,
ditto, John Hopkins, due on part of ditto of Willis Wilson,
Septemb. ditto, due this day,
Dec. 31. ditto,

EXPENDITURE IN PURCHASES.

Auditor's report.

By whom purchased.	Date.	No.	When purchased or redeemed,
	1792.		
Benj. Lincoln,	Feb. 10,	1,991.	part of purchases from Feb. 22, 1791, to March 3, 1791,
Samuel Meredith,	Nov. 13,	3,309.	from Oct. 29, 1792, to Oct. 31, 1792,
	1793.		
Ditto,	Feb. 9,	3,626.	part of purchases from Jan. 17, 1793, to Feb. 1, 1793,
Ditto,	May 11,	4,067.	from April 18, to May 2,
Ditto,	Dec. 4,	4,623.	from July 31, to August 1.
			for interest on stock purchased,

Balance on Dec. 31, 1793, accounted for in purchases, in the year 1794,

4. "An Act supplementary to the act making provision for the Debt of the United States" (1 *Stat.* 281–83).

	Dollars.Cts.
	5.51
	4,230.63
	5,013.02
	8,635.18
	6,989.01
	7,037.64
	9,564.69
	9,436.08
	9,649.70
	25,445.76
	658.83
154.49	
which had been stated in his name, and returned to the Treasury among unclaimed dividends, 368.56	
	523.05
	15,298.59
	327.29
	3.24
	15,575.22
	16,074.11
	134,467.55

Six per cent. stock.		Three per cent. stock.		Deferred stock.		Amount of the several species of stocks.	Amount of monies expended.
Original. Dolls.Cts.	Assumed. Dolls.Cts.	Original. Dolls.Cts.	Assumed. Dolls.Cts.	Original. Dolls.Cts.	Assumed. Dolls.Cts.	Dolls.Cts.	Dolls.Cts.
4.07		3.16		30		7.53	5.51
				28,046.15	10,668.36	38,714.51	25,969.96
1,504.42		23,577.15	19,628.28	1,556.35	10,289.11	56,555.31	34,585.99
9,507.81	600.15	523.39	16,953.69	10,447.97	5,695.69	43,728.70	26,627.64
2,547.68	3,728.68	7,840.93	831.80	6,594.96	2,920.67	24,464.72	15,576.74
							52.38
13,563.98	4,328.83	31,944.63	37,413.77	46,645.73	29,573.83	163,470.77	102,818.22
							31,649.33
							134,467.55

STATEMENT OF THE REVENUE ARISING FROM THE POSTAGE OF LETTERS, &C. FROM THE 1ST OF OCTOBER, 1789, TO 30TH JUNE, 1791.

		EXPENSES	
Postmaster General,	Gross amount of postage.	For transportation of the mails.	For compensation to the postmaster general, his assistants and clerks including inciden tal expenses.
Samuel Osgood.	71,295.93	43,363.21	6,721.01

STATEMENT OF THE REVENUE ARISING FROM THE POSTAGE OF LETTERS, &C. FROM 1ST JULY, 1791, TO 31ST DECEMBER, 1792.

			EXPENSES	
Postmaster General,	Net amount on the 30th June, 1791, brought forward.	Gross amount of postage.	For transportation of the mails.	For compensations to the postmaster general, his assistants and clerks, including incidental expenses.
Timothy Pickering.	4,182.27	92,988.40	44,129.56	7,698.08

STATEMENT OF THE REVENUE ARISING FROM THE POSTAGE OF LETTERS, &C. IN THE YEAR 1793.

			EXPENSES	
Postmaster General,	Net amount on the last day of Decemb. 1792, brought forward.	Gross amount of postage.	For transportation of the mails.	For compensations to the postmaster general, his assistants and clerks, including incidental expenses.
Timothy Pickering.	20,584.07	103,883.19	43,252.78	5,160.40

Note—In printing the preceding statements of duties on stills, and spirits distilled in th United States, a number of fractional parts, of gallons and cents, were omitted.

'or compensations to the deputy postmasters, including incidental expenses.	For ship letters.	Total amount.	Net amount of postage in the hands of the postmaster general, and the deputy postmasters, on the 30th June, 1791.
16,241.88	787.56	67,113.66	4,182.27

'or compensations to the deputy postmasters, including incidental expenses.	For ship letters.	Total amount.	Net amount of postage in the hands of the postmaster general and the deputy postmasters, on 31 Dec. 1792.
22,561.10	2,197.86	76,586.60	20,584.07

'or compensations to the deputy postmasters, including incidental expenses.	For ship letters.	Total amount.	Net amount of postage.	Payments made into the Treasury	Balance due by the postmaster general and the deputy postmasters, on the 31st Decemb. 1793.
22,729.65	3,018.20	74,161.03	50,306.23	11,020.51	39,285.72

A SUMMARY STATEMENT OF MONIES RECEIVED INTO THE TREASURY OF THE UNITED STATES, IN THE YEAR 1793.

FOR DUTIES ON MERCHANDISE AND TONNAGE.

From the Collectors of the Customs, agreeably to the preceding statement of the said duties.		
On warrants passed to the credit of the respective collectors in the year 1792, which are included in the treasurer's accounts for the year 1793,	44,905.96	
On warrants included in the treasurer's accounts for the year 1793, which are passed to the credit of the respective collectors in the year 1794,	170,032.48	
On warrants included in both the accounts of the treasurer, and of the respective collectors for the year 1793,	4,040,368.12	
		4,255,306.5

FOR DUTIES ON STILLS, AND SPIRITS DISTILLED IN THE UNITED STATES.

From the supervisors of the revenue, agreeably to the preceding statements of the said duties.		
On warrants passed to the credit of the respective supervisors in the year 1792, which are included in the treasurer's accounts for the year 1793,	5,979,92	
On warrants included in both the accounts of the treasurer, and of the respective supervisors in the year 1793,	260,715.18	
On warrants included in the treasurer's accounts for the year 1793, which were paid by supervisors whose accounts are not finally adjusted,	71,010.60	
		337,705.7

FOR REVENUE ARISING FROM THE POSTAGE OF LETTERS, &C.

From Timothy Pickering postmaster-general, agreeably to the preceding statement of the said revenue,		11,020.5

FOR DIVIDENDS ON THE CAPITAL STOCK IN THE BANK OF THE UNITED STATES.

From the President, Directors and Company of the said Bank, for the excess of two half yearly dividends on the said capital stock from July 1st, 1792, to June 30th, 1793, over and above the interest payable during said period, on the loan of two millions of dollars,[5]		500.

5. This sum had been borrowed under the terms of Section 11 of "An Act to incorporate the subscribers to the Bank of the United States" (1 *Stat.* 196 [February 25, 1791]), which provided "That it shall be lawful for the President of the United States, at any time or times, within eighteen months after the first day of April next, to cause a subscription to be made to the stock of the said corporation, . . . on behalf of the United States, to an amount not exceeding two millions of dollars; to be paid out of the monies which shall be borrowed by virtue of either of the acts, the one entitled 'An act making provision for

FOR FEES ON LETTERS PATENT.

om Samuel Meredith, the amount of monies received by him from sundry persons, for letters patent issued from the office of the secretary of state,		660.

FOR BALANCES OF ACCOUNTS WHICH ORIGINATED UNDER THE LATE GOVERNMENT.

om Richard Harrison, attorney for the district of New-York, on account of Margaret Livingston's bond given for a bill of exchange purchased of her by the late secret committee, and which was protested.	7,325.18	
om Morgan Lewis, late deputy quarter master general for the state of New-York, for a balance found due by him,	1,123.40	
		8,448.58

FOR CENTS AND HALF CENTS, COINED AT THE MINT OF THE UNITED STATES.

om Tristram Dalton, treasurer of the said mint,		1,281.79

FOR THE PROCEEDS OF BILLS OF EXCHANGE DRAWN ON ACCOUNT OF FOREIGN LOANS.

om the President, Directors and Company of the Bank of N. America,	177,998.80	
om the President, Directors and Company of the Bank of the U. States,	752,738.51	
om the President and Directors of the Office of Discount and Deposit of the Bank of the United States, at New York,	195,898.96	
om the President and Directors of the Office of Discount and Deposit of the Bank of the United States, at Baltimore,	20,635.74	
om Thomas Jefferson, secretary of state,	50,000.	
		1,197,272.01

FOR THE PROCEEDS OF DOMESTIC LOANS.

om the President, Directors and Company of the Bank of the United States, on account of a loan of 800,000 dollars, made in pursuance of the act entitled, "An act making appropriations for the support of government for the year 1793," [6]		600,000.
nount carried to a general account of receipts and expenditures in page 65,[7]		6,450,195.15

---

e debt of the United States;' and the other entitled 'An act making provision r the reduction of the public debt;' borrowing of the bank an equal sum, to applied to the purposes, for which the said monies shall have been procured; imbursable in ten years, by equal annual instalments; or at any time sooner, in any greater proportions, that the government may think fit."

6. 1 *Stat.* 325–29 (February 28, 1793).

7. This page number refers to the pagination of the original document. For is material, see page 553 of this volume.

PAYMENTS FOR THE SUPPORT OF THE CIVIL LIST.

TO THE PRESIDENT OF THE UNITED STATES, ON ACCOUNT OF HIS COMPENSATION.

1793.	January	4.	Warrant No.	2364	1500.	
		15.	do.	2398	1000.	
	March	9.	do.	2548	4000.	
		22.	do.	2606	1000.	
		30.	do.	2617	1000.	
	April	11.	do.	2686	1000.	
		24.	do.	2720	1000.	
	May	10.	do.	2765	2000.	
	June	3.	do.	2829	1000.	
		12.	do.	2858	1000.	
	July	15.	do.	2963	2000.	
		25.	do.	2984	1000.	
	August	17.	do.	3060	2000.	
	September	5.	do.	3105	1000.	
	November	27.	do.	3153	1000.	
		30.	do.	3171	2000.	
	December	11.	do.	3236	1000.	
		17.	do.	3241	1000.	
		27.	do.	3278	2000.	
						27,500.

TO THE VICE-PRESIDENT OF THE UNITED STATES, ON ACCOUNT OF HIS COMPENSATION.

March	1.	Warrant No.	2504	1250		
June	5.	do.	2831	1250		
September	5.	do.	3104	1250		
December	11.	do.	3235	1250		
					5,000.	
						32,500

JUDICIARY DEPARTMENT.

For compensations to the Judges, the Attorney General, the Marshals, including Jurors, Witnesses and certain contingent expenses, the district Attornies, the Clerks of the several Courts, and for the expense of keeping prisoners, committed under the authority of the United States.

To John Jay, Chief Justice of the United States.

1793	January	31.	Warrant No.	2434	1000.	
	April	4.	do.	2650	1000.	
	July	5.	do.	2948	1000.	
	November	28.	do.	3160	1000.	
						4,000.

To John Blair, one of the Associate Judges of the Supreme Court.

January	4.	Warrant No.	2368	875.	
April	5.	do.	2667	875.	
July	3.	do.	2939	875.	
December	3.	do.	3209	875.	
					3,500.

To James Wilson, one of the Associate Judges of the Supreme Court.

January	5.	Warrant No.	2373	875.	
April	5.	do.	2667	875.	
July	12.	do.	2960	875.	
December	3.	do.	3212	875.	
					3,500.

To Thomas Johnson, one of the Associate Judges of the Supreme Court.

January	15.	Warrant No.	2400	875.

To William Cushing, one of the Associate Judges of the Supreme Court.

January	28.	Warrant No.	2429	875.	
April	5.	do.	2667	877.	
July	3.	do.	2939	875.	
November	27.	do.	3142	875.	
					3,500.

To James Iredell, one of the Associate Judges of the Supreme Court.

January	4.	Warrant No.	2365	875.	
April	4.	do.	2660	875.	
July	5.	do.	2947	875.	
November	27.	do.	3142	875.	
					3,500.

To William Paterson, one of the Associate Judges of the Supreme Court.

July	27.	Warrant No.	2991	1147.22	
November	27.	do.	3142	875.	
					2,022.22

District of Maine.

	February	9. To David Sewall, Judge, warrant No.		2465	250.	
	July	5. do.	do.	2944	250.	
		11. do.	do.	2958	250.	
	November	29. do.	do.	3167	250.	
						1,000
1792.	November	27. To Henry Dearborn, marshal, warrant No.		2263	104.92	
		29. do.	do.	2266	307.60	
						412.52
1793.	December	28. To John Hobby, marshal,	do.	3281		160.

District of New-Hampshire.

January	8. To John Sullivan, Judge war. No.		2387	250.	
April	4. do.	do.	2663	250.	
July	2. do.	do.	2924	250.	
December	3. do.	do.	3214	250.	
					1,000
	26. Nathaniel Rogers, marshal, do		3273		200

District of Massachusetss.

May	4. To John Brooks, marshal, war. No.		2755	1253.94	
December	31. do.	do.	3305	300.	
					1,553.94

District of Rhode-Island

January	4. To Henry Merchant, Judge, war. No.		2369	200.	
April	5. do.	do.	2671	200.	
July	5. do.	do.	2944	200.	
November	29. do.	do.	3167	200.	
					800.
May	13. To William Peck, marshal,	do.	2770	679.28	
December	26. do	do.	3274	300.	
					979.28

District of Connecticut.

Jan.	3. To Richard Law, Judge, warrant, No.		2360	250.	
April	5. do.	do.	2671	250.	
July	5. do.	do.	2944	250.	
Novem.	29. do.	do.	3167	250.	
					1,000.
June	5. Philip B. Bradley, marshal,	do.	2833		414.90

District of Vermont.

Jan.	11. To Nathaniel Chipman, Judge,	war No.	2390	200.	
April	18. do.	do.	2707	200.	
July	27. do.	do.	2987	200.	
	31. do.	do.	3004	58.69	
					658.69
Jan.	19. Lewis R. Morris, marshal,	do.	2414	130.75	
March	30. do.	do.	2618	69.44	
June	10. do.	do.	2846	156.39	
	22. do.	do.	2875	142.70	
					499.28

District of New-York.

1792. Decem.	18. To Matthew Clarkson, late marshal,	warrant No.	2312	364.85	
1793. May	28. Aquilla Giles, marshal,	do.	2817	517.45	
					882.30

District of New-Jersey

Jan.	23. To Robert Morris, Judge,	warrant, No.	2419	250.	
April	8. do.	do.	2674	250.	
July	17. do.	do.	2968	250.	
Novem.	28. do.	do.	3164	250.	
					1,000.
March	5. Thomas Lowrey,	do.	2527		221.25

District of Pennsylvania.

Jan.	14. To Richard Peters, Judge,	warrant No.	2395	400.	
April	5. do	do.	2666	400.	
July	5. do.	do.	2944	400.	
Novem.	29. do.	do.	3167	400.	
					1,600.
1792. Decem.	27. Clement Biddle, marshal,	do.	2324	101.57	
1793. June	10. do.	do.	2849	439.98	
					541.55

District of Delaware.

Jan.	7. To Gunning Bedford, Judge	war. No.	2380	400.	
April	25. do.	do.	2721	200.	
					600.
March	16. Allen McLean, marshal,	do.	2583	469.90	
Decem.	31. do.	do.	3295	80.	
					549.90

District of Maryland.

	Jan.	4. To William Paca, Judge, warrant, No.		2367	375.	
	April	25. do.	do.	2738	375.	
	July	8. do.	do.	2952	375.	
	Nov.	27. do.	do.	3145	375.	
						1,500.
	July	1. Nathaniel Ramsay, marshal,	do.	2905		1,078.64

District of Virginia.

	Jan.	8. To Cyrus Griffin, Judge, warrant, No.		2386	450.	
	April	4. do.	do.	2664	450.	
	July	2. do.	do.	2927	450.	
	Decem.	3. do.	do.	3215	450.	
						1,800.
	Jan.	7. Edward Carrington, late marshal,	do.	2381		79.95
		19. David M. Randolph, marshal,	do.	2413	667.29	
	Aug.	7. do.	do.	3025	948.98	
		17. do.	do.	3058	40.60	
						1,656.87

District of Kentuckey.

	Jan.	16. To Harry Innes, Judge warrant, No.		2402	250.	
	May	16. do.	do.	2783	250.	
	July	3. do.	do.	2938	250.	
	Nov.	29. do.	do.	3167	250.	
						1,000.
	May	16. Samuel McDowell, marshal,	do.	2779		127.40

District of North-Carolina.

	Jan.	4. To John Sitgreaves, Judge,	warrant, No.	2370	375.	
	April	4. do.	do.	2658	375.	
	July	3. do.	do.	2933	375.	
	Nov.	27. do.	do.	3149	375.	
						1,500
1792.	Decem.	22. John Skinner, marshal,	do.	2318	52.22	
		do.	do.	2319	113.17	
1793.	Jan.	26. do.	do.	2425	548.06	
	May	3. do.	do.	2752	161.42	
		16. do.	do.	2782	206.29	
	Aug.	5. do.	do.	3018	2,584.09	
		20. do.	do.	3064	116.	
						3,781.25

District of South-Carolina.

Jan.	3.	To Thomas Bee, Judge, warrant, No.	2362	450.		
April	5.	do. do.	2671	450.		
July	16.	do. do.	2965	450.		
Nov.	29.	do. do.	3167	450.		
					1,800	
May	2.	Isaac Huger, marshal, do.	2748	163.24		
Aug.	10.	do. do.	3029	119.66		
	16.	do. do.	3054	118.23		
					401.13	
Jan,	29,	Thomas Hall, Clerk, do.	2432		83.57	

District of Georgia.

Jan.	23.	To Nathaniel Pendleton, Judge, war. No.	2420	375.		
April	4.	do. do.	2661	375.		
July	27.	do. do.	2989	375.		
Nov.	28.	do. do.	3162	375.		
					1,500.	
Feb.	21.	Robert Forsyth, marshal, do.	2488		740.90	

Edmund Randolph, Attorney General of the United States.

Jan.	5.	Warrant No.	2374	375.		
March	6.	do.	2529	100.		
	8.	do.	2541	100.		
April	5.	do.	2668	475.		
July	3.	do.	2937	475.		
Decem.	3.	do.	3213	475.		
					2,000	
						54,020.54

LEGISLATIVE DEPARTMENT.

For Compensation to the Senators and Members of the House of Representatives their Officers and Clerks, and for the contingent expences of both Houses.

Continuation of the Second Session of the Second Congress.

To Samuel A. Otis to enable him to pay the compensations due to the Senators.

1792. Decem.	31.	Warrant No.	2336	1,200.
1793. March	8.	do	2539	17,604.
				18,804.

Amount of monies advanced to Mr. Otis in the year 1792, the expenditure of which was not accounted for in the last statement	6,502.20
Amount received by him to the eighth day of March, 1793.	18,804.
	25,306.20
For which he has accounted by payments to the following Senators, viz.	
To Stephen R. Bradley;	918.
Richard Basset,	651.
John Brown,	1200.
Aaron Burr,	483.
Pierce Butler,	1,204.80
George Cabot,	939.
Philemon Dickinson,	732.
John Edwards,	1,218.
Oliver Ellsworth,	858.60
William Few,	1,288.80
Theodore Foster,	910.20
James Gunn,	814.20
Benjamin Hawkins,	955.80
Ralph Izard,	1,210.80
Rufus King,	777.
John Henry,	799.80
John Langdon,	969.
Samuel Livermore,	6.
James Monroe,	893.40
Robert Morris,	714.
Richard Potts,	264.
George Read,	740.40
Moses Robinson,	891.
John Rutherfurd,	732.
Samuel Johnston,	949.20
Roger Sherman	831.
Caleb Strong,	879.
Joseph Stanton, jun.	876.60
John Taylor,	639.60
Paine Wingate,	960.
	25,306.20

First Session of the Third Congress.

To Samuel A. Otis, to enable him to pay the compensations due to the Senators.

1793. Dec.	5.	Warrant No. 3218	*3,000.

* The expenditure of this sum will appear in the next statement.

To the Reverend William White, Chaplain to the Senate.

March	14. Warrant No. 2567			164.38

To Samuel A. Otis, Secretary to the Senate.

Jan.	5. Warrant No.	2376	375.	
	8. do.	2384	B222.50	
March	4. do.	2518	B536.50	
	9. do.	2545	B441.	
April	2. do.	2636	375.	
	5. do.	2670	B135.	
July	2. do.	2926	375.	
Dec.	3. do.	3208	B651.	
				3,111.

To Robert Heysham, principal Clerk to the Secretary of the Senate.

March	5. Warrant No.	2519	381.	
Aug.	24. do.	3069	273.	
				654.

To James Mathers, Doorkeeper to the Senate.

March	1. Warrant No.	2506	125.	
April	3. do.	2643	125.	
July	2. do.	2925	125.	
Nov.	28. do.	3159	125.	
				500.

To Cornelius Maxwell, Assistant Doorkeeper to the Senate.

March	1. Warrant No.	2508	112.50	
	13. do.	2557	112.50	
April	3. do.	2644	112.50	
July	2. do.	2923	112.50	
Nov.	27. do.	3150	112.50	
				562.50

To Samuel A. Otis, on account of the contingent expenses of the Senate.

March	8. Warrant No. 2538			2,000.
				28,795.88

B The daily compensations of his Clerks are included in these Warrants.

Continuation of the Second Session of the Second Congress.

To Jonathan Trumbull, Speaker of the House of Representatives, to enable him to pay the compensations due to the Members and Officers of said House.

March 4.	Warrant No. 2517			36,076.21
	Amount of monies advanced to Mr. Trumbull in the year 1792, the expenditure of which was not accounted for in the last statement		24,000.	
	Amount paid to him on the 4th of March 1793.		36,076.21	
			60,076.21	
	For which he has accounted by the following payments, viz.			
	To Nicholas Gilman, one of the Members of the House of Representatives of the United States.		960.	
	To Samuel Livermore,	do.	978.	
	Jeremiah Smith	do.	969.	
	Fisher Ames	do.	930.	
	Shearjashub Bourne	do.	975.	
	Eldridge Gerry	do.	930.	
	Benjamin Goodhue	do.	942.	
	George Leonard	do.	930.	
	Theodore Sedgwick	do.	816.	
	George Thatcher	do.	990.	
	Artemas Ward	do.	906.	
	Benjamin Bourne	do.	904.20	
	James Hillhouse	do.	804.	
	Amasa Learned	do.	858.	
	Jonathan Sturges	do.	810.	
	Jeremiah Wadworth	do.	738.	
	Nathaniel Niles	do.	960.	
	Israel Smith	do.	930.	
	Egbert Benson	do.	816.	
	James Gordon	do.	885.	
	John Lawrence	do.	771.	
	Corn. C. Schoonmaker	do.	813.	
	Peter Silvester	do.	834.	
	Thomas Tredwell	do.	798.	
	Elias Boudinot	do.	762.	
	Abraham Clark	do.	762.	
	Jonathan Dayton	do.	762.	
	Aaron Kitchell	do.	762.	
	William Findley,	do.	867.	
	Thomas Fitzsimons	do.	714.	
	Andrew Gregg	do.	600.	

Thomas Hartley	do.	696.
Daniel Heister	do.	735.60
Israel Jacobs	do.	711.
John W. Kittera	do.	687.
Fred. A. Muhlenberg	do.	714.
Philip Key	do.	834.
John F. Mercer	do.	558.
William V. Murray	do.	792.
William Hindman,	do.	270.
Samuel Sterrett	do.	414.
William B. Giles	do.	894.
Samuel Griffin	do.	911.40
Richard Bland Lee	do.	804.
James Madison	do.	864.
Andrew Moore	do.	913.80
John Page	do.	911.40
Josiah Parker	do.	942.
Abraham Venable	do.	930.
Alexander White	do.	834.
Christopher Greenup	do.	1,170.
Alexander D. Orr	do.	1,218.
John Baptist Ashe	do.	936.
William Barry Grove	do.	990.
Nathaniel Macon	do.	942.
John Steel	do.	1074.
Hugh Williamson	do.	979.20
Robert Barnwell	do.	1203.
Daniel Huger	do.	1156.80
William Smith	do.	1204.80
Thomas Sumpter	do.	1182.
Thomas Tudor Tucker	do.	1204.80
Abraham Baldwin	do.	1290.
John Milledge	do.	1126.20
Francis Willis	do.	1290.
Jonathan Trumbull, Speaker of the House of Representatives.		1578.
		59,437.20
The Rev. A. Green, Chaplain,		163.01
J. Wheaton, Serjeant at Arms,		476.
		60,076.21

First Session of the Third Congress.

To Frederick A. Muhlenberg, Speaker of the House of Representatives, to enable him to pay the Compensations due to the Members and Officers of said House.

1793. Dec. 5. Warrant No. 3222 C 20,000.

C The expenditure of this sum will be shewn in the next statement.

To Daniel Huger one of the Members of the House of Representatives.

	14.	Warrant No.	3238		348.

To John Beckley, Clerk of the House Representatives, and the Clerks in His Office.

Jan.	5.	Warrant No.	2379	375.	
March	1.	do.	2505	696.	
	13.	do.	2558	276.	
	19.	do.	2594	400.	
April	9.	do.	2679	1127.	
July	2.	do.	2916	830.	
Nov.	28.	do.	3161	835.	
					4,539.

To Gifford Dally, Doorkeeper to the House of Representatives.

March	1.	Warrant No.	2509	125.	
April	1.	do.	2631	125.	
July	2.	do.	2917	125.	
Nov.	28.	do.	3158	125.	
					500

To Thomas Claxton, Assistant Doorkeeper to the House of Representatives.

March	1.	Warrant No.	2507	112.50	
April	3.	do.	2645	112.50	
July	3.	do.	2930	112.50	
Nov.	27.	do.	3151	112.50	
					450

To John Beckley, on account of the Contingent Expenses of the House of Representatives.

March	5.	Warrant No.	2521	3000.			
	9.	do.	2546	220.13			
	19.	do.	2595	1150.			
June	13.	do.	2860	1200.			
Dec.	28.	do.	3282	1202.			
					6,772.13		
						68,685.34	
							97,481.

TREASURY DEPARTMENT

For the Salaries of the Officers the Clerks and Messengers, and for the contingent expences of the Department.

To Alexander Hamilton, Secretary of the Treasury, his Clerks and Messenger.

Jan.	1.	Warrant No.	2347	2087.50	
Feb.	27.	do.	2498	16.	
April	1.	do.	2628	2087.50	
July	1.	do.	2908	1962.50	
Nov.	25.	do.	3139	1861.69	
					8,015.19

To Oliver Wolcott, Jun. Comptroller of the Treasury, his Clerks and Messenger.

Jan.	2.	Warrant No.	2351	1865.47	
March	6.	do.	2528	100.	
April	1.	do.	2629	1965.83	
July	1.	do.	2906	2141.34	
Nov.	25.	do.	3140	2300.	
					8,372.64

To Richard Harrison, Auditor of the Treasury, his Clerks and Messenger.

Jan.	1.	Warrant No.	2348	2,507.50	
March	6.	do.	2531	100.	
April	1.	do.	2630	2,607.50	
May	24.	do.	2802	74.18	
July	1.	do.	2907	2,645.68	
Nov.	25.	do.	3138	2,507.50	
					10,442.36

To Samuel Meredith, Treasurer of the United States, his Clerks and Messenger.

Jan.	5.	Warrant No.	2378	775.	
March	6.	do.	2530	100.	
	8.	do.	2542	100.	
	30.	do.	2619	267.85	
April	3.	do.	2648	1,025.	
July	5.	do.	2941	1,025.	
Dec.	3.	do.	3210	1,025.50	
					4,317.85

To Tench Coxe, Commissioner of the Revenue, his Clerks and Messenger.

March	13.	Warrant No.	2555	891.84	
		do.	2556	965.47	
April	2.	do.	2640	1,182.60	
July	1.	do.	2911	1,525.	
Nov.	27.	do.	3148	1,525.	
					6,089.91

To Joseph Nourse, Register of the Treasury, his Clerks and Messengers.

Jan.	3.	Warrant No.	2356	4,605.15	
March	6.	do.	2532	125.	
April	3.	do.	2642	4,361.81	
	17.	do.	2702	108.06	
June	19.	do.	2872	100.	
July	1.	do.	2909	4,120.26	
Nov.	28.	do.	3165	3,694.67	
					17,114.95,

To David Henley and Isaac Sherman, Clerks employed to count bills of credit of the old and new emissions and indents of Interest.

Jan.	3.	Warrant No.	2358	125.	
	4.	do.	2363	125.	
April	3.	do.	2646	125.	
	3.	do.	2647	125.	
July	3.	do.	2935	83.79	
Aug.	31.	do.	3083	81.52	
					665.31

For the Contingent Expenses of the Treasury Department.

March	14.	To Joseph Nourse, Register,	war. No.	2565	2,400.	
		do.	do.	2566	1,000.	
	15	do.	do.	2573	80.	
	30.	Samuel Meredith, Treasurer,	do.	2623	229.88	
April	2.	Henry Kuhl	do.	2637	166.67	
May	9.	Joseph Nourse, Register,	do.	2764	1,200.	
	17.	do.	do.	2789	1,200.	
June	29.	Samuel Meredith, Treasurer,	do.	2903	46.97	
July	19.	Joseph Nourse, Register,	do.	2974	1,200.	
Sept.	5.	do.	do.	3106	1,200.	
		do.	do.	3109	100.	
Dec.	5.	do.	do.	3219	1,089.99	
		do.	do.	3220	350.	
	31.	Samuel Meredith Treasurer,	do.	3309	173.15	
						10,436.66

65,454.8

DEPARTMENT OF STATE

To Thomas Jefferson, Secretary of State, his Clerks and Messenger.

Jan.	2.	Warrant No.	2352	1,496.67		
April	2.	do.	2638	1,541.67		
July	1.	do.	2913	1,465.11		
Nov.	27.	do.	3144	1,575.		
					6,078.45	

For the Contingent Expenses of his Office.

Mar.	21.	Warrant No.	2602	1,200.		
April	25.	do.	2727	651.67		
					1,851.67	
						7,930.12

DEPARTMENT OF WAR

To Henry Knox, Secretary at War, his Clerks and Messenger.

1793. Jan.	1.	Warrant No.	2349	1,605.15		
March	4.	do.	2524	50.		
April	1.	do.	2633	1,762.22		
July	1.	do.	2915	1,695.18		
Nov.	27.	do.	3147	1,546.47		
					6,659.02	

To Joseph Howell, Accountant to the Department of War for his own and Clerks salaries and the contingent expenses of his Office.

Jan.	8.	Warrant No.	2383	625.		
March	7.	do.	2533	572.10		
	9.	do.	2544	494.72		
April	2.	do.	2635	1,050.		
July	2.	do.	2918	1,050.		
Nov.	27.	do.	3143	1,020.11		
					4,811.93	
						11,470.95

To William Irvine, John Kean and W. Langdon, Commissioners for adjusting the accounts between the United States and the Individual States, their Clerks and Messenger.

Jan.	3.	Warrant No.	2357	3,149.72	
April	3.	do.	2649	3,075.	
July	2.	do.	2920	2,901.92	
					9,126.64

For the Contingent Expenses of their Office.

March	7. Warrant No.	2534	150.		
Aug.	8. do.	3026	50.63		
				200.63	
					9,3

DEPARTMENT OF THE MINT.

To Tristram Dalton, Treasurer of the Mint for the use of that Establishment.

1793. June	4. Warrant No.	2832	5,000	
July	3. do.	2928	1,275.	
Dec.	20. do.	3251	4,094.88	
	do.	3252	7,003.40	
	30. do.	3288	1,275.	
				18,64

GOVERNMENT OF THE WESTERN TERRITORIES.

District North-West of the River Ohio.

For the compensations of the Governor, the Judges and the Secretary of the North western Territory.

Jan.	5. To Arthur St. Clair, Gov. war. No.	2377	500.		
April	4. do. do.	2662	500.		
July	5. do. do.	2944	500.		
Nov.	27. do. do.	3146	500.		
				2,000.	
Jan.	9. George Turner one of the Judges,	2388	200.		
April	4. do. do.	2651	200.		
July	8. do. do.	2951	200.		
				600.	
Feb.	2. Rufus Putnam, one of the Judges,	2453	400.		
April	11. do. do.	2685	200.		
				600.	
Jan.	8. John Cleves Symmes, one of the Judges, do.	2841	1000.		
Aug.	1. do. do.	3008	200.		
				1,200.	
Jan.	22. Winthrop Sargent, Sec'ry, do.	2418		62.50	
				4,462.50	

District South of the River Ohio.

For the compensations of the Governor, the Judges, the Secretary and the contingent expenses of the Government.

Jan.	2.	To William Blount, Governor,	war. No.	2353	500.		
April	4.	do.	do.	2653	500.		
July	2.	do.	do.	2922	500.		
Nov.	29.	do.	do.	3169	500.		
						2,000.	
Jan.	3.	John McNairy, one of the Judges,		2359	200.		
April	4.	do.	do.	2654	200.		
July	3.	do.	do.	2931	200.		
						600.	
Jan.	5.	Joseph Anderson, one of the Judges,		2375	200.		
April	4.	do.	do.	2665	200.		
July	5.	do.	do.	2940	200.		
Nov.	25.	do.	do.	3133	200.		
						800.	
Jan.	11.	David Campbell, one of the Judges,		2391	200.		
May	1.	do.	do.	2743	200.		
July	3.	do.	do.	2932	200.		
Nov.	29.	do.	do.	3168	200.		
						800.	
Jan.	2.	Daniel Smith, Secretary,	do.	2354	187.50		
April	4.	do.	do.	2655	187.50		
July	20.	do.	do.	2975	187.50		
						562.50	
June	10.	do. for the contingent expenses of the Offices of the Government.	do.	2845	198.83		
	12.	do.	do.	2855	74.25		
						273.08	
							9,498.08

TO THE COMMISSIONERS OF LOANS, FOR THEIR OWN AND CLERK'S SALARIES, AND FOR THE AUTHORIZED CONTINGENT EXPENSES OF THEIR SEVERAL OFFICES.

Jan.	4.	To William Gardner, New-Hampshire,	2372	650.	
March	18.	do.	2591	475.47	
April	9.	do.	2681	162.50	
July	5.	do.	2945	162.50	
Nov.	28.	do.	3155	162.50	
					1,612.97
Jan.	23.	Nathaniel Appleton, Massachusetts, No.	2422	375.	
April	17.	do.	2703	3427.38	
	19.	do.	2710	375.	
May	29.	do.	2818	1631.40	
July	17.	do.	2970	375.	
					6,193.78

Jan.	28.	Jabez Bowen, Rhode-Island	2428	150.	
March	21.	do.	2605	779.54	
April	6.	do.	2673	203.04	
	9.	do.	2681	150.	
May	17.	do.	2791	175.72	
July	5.	do.	2945	150.	
Nov.	28.	do.	3155	150.	
					1,758.30
Jan.	4.	William Imlay, Connecticut,	2372	250.	
March	18.	do.	2586	2234.67	
April	9.	do.	2681	250.	
June	15.	do.	2865	225.26	
July	5.	do.	2945	250.	
Nov.	28.	do.	3155	250.	
					3,459.93
Jan.	2.	John Cochran, New-York	2350	375.	
March	13.	do.	2563	1719.70	
		do.	2564	5718.38	
April	4.	do.	2657	375.	
	10.	do.	2684	1043.84	
July	2.	do.	2921	375.	
Nov.	27.	do.	3141	375.	
					9,981.92
Jan.	4.	James Ewing, New-Jersey,	2372	175.	
March	14.	do.	2572	459.28	
April	9.	do.	2681	175.	
	22.	do.	2718	60.60	
July	5.	do.	2945	175.	
Nov.	28.	do.	3155	175.	
					1,219.88
Jan.	4.	Thomas Smith, Pennsylvania,	2372	375.	
March	15.	do.	2578	642.17	
		do.	2579	462.50	
		do.	2580	925.	
		do.	2581	258.55	
April	4.	do.	2652	308.34	
		do.	2659	375.	
July	5.	do.	2945	375.	
		do.	2946	223.10	
Nov.	28.	do.	3155	375.	
					4,319.66
Jan.	4.	James Tilton, Delaware,	2372	150.	
March	18.	do.	2589	206.13	
April	9.	do.	2681	150.	
May	6.	do.	2756	55.72	
		do.	2757	50.	
July	5.	do.	2945	150.	
Nov.	28.	do.	3155	150.	
					911.85

May	20.	Thomas Harwood, late Commissioner for Maryland	War. 2792	1519.93		
		do.	2793	1013.70		
		do.	2794	1250.		
		do.	2795	1000.		
					4,783.63	
	1.	Benjamin Harwood, Commissioner for Maryland	2741	163.33		
		do.	2742	250.		
July	10.	do.	2953	250.		
					663.33	
Jan.	4.	John Hopkins, Virginia,	2372	375.		
March	18.	do.	2587	928.64		
		do.	2588	1961.69		
April	9.	do.	2681	375.		
May	16.	do.	2781	425.96		
July	5.	do.	2945	375.		
Nov.	28.	do.	3155	375.		
					4,816.29	
Jan.	2.	William Skinner, N. Carolina,	2353	250.		
March	18.	do.	2590	281.48		
April	9.	do.	2681	250.		
May	13.	do.	2819	364.70		
July	5.	do.	2945	250.		
Nov.	28.	do.	3155	250.		
					1,646.18	
Jan.	4.	John Neufville, South Carolina,	2372	250.		
April	9.	do.	2681	250.		
July	5.	do.	2945	250.		
	15.	do.	2961	2552.27		
		do.	2962	639.52		
Nov.	28.	do.	3155	250.		
					4,191.79	
Jan.	4.	Richard Wylly, Georgia,	2372	175.		
April	9.	do.	2681	175.		
July	5.	do.	2945	175.		
	27.	do.	2990	320.73		
Nov.	28.	do.	3155	175.		
					1,020.73	
						46,580.24

PENSIONS ANNUITIES AND GRANTS, PAID TO THE FOLLOWING PERSONS PURSUANT TO SUNDRY ACTS OF CONGRESS.

To Baron De Steuben, per act of June 4, 1790.[8]

Jan.	4.	Warrant No.	2366	625.	
April	5.	do.	2672	625.	
July	16	do.	2966	625.	
Nov.	28.	do.	3157	625.	
					2,500.

8. "An Act for finally adjusting and satisfying the claims of Frederick William de Steuben" (*6 Stat.* 2).

To Joseph Brussels, per act of September 15, 1783.[9]

Jan.	15.	Warrant No.	2401	30.	
Aug.	14.	do.	3038	20.	
					50.

To Dominique, L'Eglize, per act of August 8, 1782.[10]

Jan.	18.	Warrant No.	2411	30.	
April	10.	do.	2682	30.	
July	10.	do.	2954	30.	
Nov.	28.	do.	3163	30.	
					120.

To John Jordan, per act of September 15, 1783.[11]

Feb.	12.	Warrant No.	2467	10.	
April	2.	do.	2634	10.	
July	2.	do.	2919	10.	
Nov.	30.	do.	3172	10.	
					40.

To David Williams, per act of November, 3, 1780,[12]

March	15.	Warrant No.	2577	200.	
May	17.	do.	2787	50.	
					250.

To James McKenzie, per act of September 15, 1783.[13]

April	9.	Warrant No.	2675	20.	
Nov.	27.	do.	3152	20.	
					40.

To Elizabeth Bergen, per act of August 24, 1781.[14]

April	11.	Warrant No.	2688	13.33	
	29.	do.	2737	13.33	
July	17.	do.	2969	13.33	
Dec.	3.	do.	3211	13.33	
					53.32

To John Warren, Guardian to the younger children of the late Major General Joseph Warren, per act of the first of July 1780.[15]

May	3.	Warrant No.	2754	318.75

9. *JCC*, XXV, 569.
10. *JCC*, XXII, 456–57.
11. *JCC*, XXV, 569.
12. *JCC*, XVII, 1009–10.
13. *JCC*, XXV, 569.
14. *JCC*, XXI, 908.
15. *JCC*, XVII, 581.

To John Paulding, per act of November 30, 1780.[16]

May	17. Warrant No. 2786	100.		
Nov.	30. do. 3173	100.		
			200.	

To Lewis Joseph De Beaulieu, per act of the fifth of August, 1782.[17]

June	11. Warrant No. 2854		213.04

To Isaac Van Wart, per act of November 3, 1780.[18]

June	25. Warrant No. 2882		200.

To Lieutenant Colonel De Touzard, per act of the 27th of October, 1778.[19]

July	6. Warrant No. 2950		360.

To Joseph Traversie, per act of August 8, 1792.[20]

	10. Warrant No. 2955	60.	
Dec.	10. do. 3228	30.	
			90.

To Richard Gridley, per acts of the 17th of November, 1775, and the 26th of February, 1781.[21]

July	10. Warrant No. 2956		444.40

To the Widow and Orphan Children of the late Colonel John Harden, per act of the 27th of February 1793.[22]

Dec.	10. Warrant No. 3227		450.	
				5,329.51
				358,241.08

16. *JCC*, XVIII, 1009–10.
17. *JCC*, XXII, 428–29.
18. *JCC*, XVIII, 1009–10.
19. *JCC*, VII, 1068.
20. *JCC*, XXII, 457.
21. *JCC*, III, 358–59; *JCC*, XIX, 197.
22. "An Act making provision for the persons therein mentioned" (6 *Stat.* 12).

PAYMENTS ON ACCOUNT OF THE WAR DEPARTMENT

To Samuel Meredith, on account of the pay of the Army, the subsistence and forage of Officers, the bounties to Soldiers, the expenses of the Recruiting service, and the incidental and contingent expenses of the Department of War.

1793. Jan.	14.	Warrant No.	2393	1400.
		do.	2394	2600.
	19.	do.	2415	1000.
	26.	do.	2426	55,317.
		do.	2427	2000.
March	5.	do.	2525	7500.
		do.	2526	2000.
	19.	do.	2596	3000.
		do.	2597	2000.
	21	do.	2603	16,000.
April	9.	do.	2677	1000.
	13.	do.	2690	3000.
		do.	2691	1000.
	18.	do.	2706	2000.
		do.	2707	2500.
May	1.	do.	2744	2000.
		do.	2745	1000.
	9.	do.	2762	22,688.
		do.	2763	2000.
	13.	do.	2771	2000.
		do.	2772	1000.
	17.	do.	2788	17,000.
	22.	do.	2798	1832.
	25.	do.	2808	1800.
		do.	2809	1200.
June	3.	do.	2827	6000.
	6.	do.	2837	3000.
	10.	do.	2850	21,413.59
	12.	do.	2856	1189.41
	13.	do.	2862	2130.
	22.	do.	2874	1966.
	24.	do.	2879	2000.
		do.	2880	1500.
July	5.	do.	2942	1400.
		do.	2943	600.
	19.	do.	2971	3556.
		do.	2972	19,283.
		do.	2973	2000.
	22.	do.	2977	12,028.98
	29.	do.	2994	756.52
	30.	do.	3001	1000.
		do.	3002	1000.
Aug.	7.	do.	3024	10,000.
	12.	do.	3036	3015.82
	14.	do.	3041	2000.
	26.	do.	3071	45,408.57
		do.	3072	3478.21
	28.	do.	3078	4367.54

Sept.	2.	do.	3084	8 103.40	
Nov.	5.	do.	3111	100,000.	
	20.	do.	3114	10,000.	
	22.	do.	3118	10,400.	
		do.	3119	1000.	
		do.	3120	4000.	
		do.	3121	2000.	
Dec.	20.	do.	3249	3500.	
	20.	do.	3250	3500.	
	26.	do.	3269	3000.	
					449,434.04

To Robert Elliott and Elie Williams, Contractors for supplying the Army.

1792	Dec.	31.	Warrant No.	2332	20,000.	
1793	March	2.	do.	2512	20,000.	
		13.	do.	2559	20,000.	
	April	1.	do.	2626	20,000.	
	June	1.	do.	2824	10,000.	
	July	1.	do.	2904	10,000.	
	Aug.	1.	do.	3007	10,000.	
		30.	do.	3082	10,000.	
	Nov.	20.	do.	3112	20,000.	
		22.	do.	3126	10,000.	
			do.	3127	20,000.	
		29.	do.	3170	20,000.	
						190.000.

To James O'Hara, Quarter-Master General for the Army, for the use of his Department.

Jan.	17.	Warrant No.	2409	1600.	
Feb.	8.	do.	2462	3300.	
	19.	do.	2484	1800.	
		do.	2485	2000.	
March	5.	do.	2522	18,000.	
April	16.	do.	2698	40,000.	
	17.	do.	2704	8500.	
	30.	do.	2738	5000.	
May	14.	do.	2774	3000.	
	23.	do.	2801	1000.	
	31.	do.	2821	1104.	
June	13.	do.	2861	18,696.	
Aug.	5.	do.	3020	3000.	
	12.	do.	3035	5000.	
	28.	do.	3077	1000.	
Nov.	20.	do.	3113	5000.	
		do.	3115	10,000.	
	22.	do.	3124	4000.	
		do.	3125	6045.	
		do.	3128	5000.	
Dec.	5.	do.	3221	12,000.	
	26.	do.	3268	5000.	
					160,045.

To Tench Francis, Agent for procuring certain supplies.

Feb.	1.	Warrant No.	2439	2000.	
March	20.	do.	2600	3000.	
April	17.	do.	2701	5000.	
May	2.	do.	2750	5000.	
	14.	do.	2775	4000.	
	23.	do.	2800	10,000.	
June	11.	do.	2851	10,000.	
July	24.	do.	2982	10,000.	
Aug.	21.	do.	3067	10,000.	
Dec.	28.	do.	3283	15,000.	
					74,000.

To William Young and George Dannacker Contractors for supplying the Army with Clothing.

March	7.	Warrant No.	2535	12,000.	
	8.	do.	2543	39,500.	
	9.	do.	2547	3000.	
	20.	do.	2598	6000.	
April	3.	do.	2641	5000.	
	17.	do.	2700	1000.	
	25.	do.	2726	5000.	
May	10.	do.	2769	5000.	
	23.	do.	2799	4000.	
June	7.	do.	2840	5000.	
July	3.	do.	2934	5000.	
Aug.	16.	do.	3053	5000.	
Nov.	22.	do.	3123	5000.	
Dec.	16.	do.	3239	5113.19	
					105,613.19

To the following Contractors and Agents for supplies of different kinds furnished for the use of the Army.

Clement Biddle, for supplies furnished in Philadelphia.

1792. Dec.	27.	Warrant No.	2325	362.57	
1793. Jan.	18.	do.	2412	927.92	
					1,290.49

John Nicholson, for Rifle Guns delivered into the public Store in Philadelphia.

1792. Dec.	31.	Warrant No.	2329	156.	
1793. Jan.	31.	do.	2435	120.	
					276.

Thomas Billington and Charles Young for Clothing supplied in Philadelphia.

Jan.	14.	Warrant No. 2397	2000.	
Feb.	14.	do. 2477	3619.84	
				5,619.84

Abraham Hunt, for supplies furnished at Trenton in the State of New-Jersey.

Jan.	15.	Warrant No. 2399	296.50	
March	28.	do. 2611	300.	
June	27.	do. 2886	600.	
Aug.	1.	do. 3010	296.79	
				1,493.29

Melancton Smith, for supplies furnished in the state of New-York.

Jan.	23.	Warrant No. 2421	140.12	
Feb.	9.	do. 2464	792.67	
April	29.	do. 2736	227.45	
June	22.	do. 2876	216.26	
Aug.	29.	do. 3080	168.25	
Dec.	6.	do. 3223	177.03	
				1,721.78

Jackson and Smith, for Medicines furnished for the use of the Army.

Jan.	24.	Warrant No. 2424	108.42	
Aug.	19.	do. 3062	34.16	
				142.58

Rufus Putnam, for expenditures and supplies furnished in the Indian Department.

Feb.	12.	Warrant No. 2469	1,029.80	
March	16.	do. 2585	165.27	
				1,195.07

Matthias Slough, for supplies furnished at Lancaster, in Pennsylvania.

Feb.	21.	Warrant No. 2489	586.06	
March	13.	do. 2560	400.	
Aug.	20.	do. 3063	205.57	
Nov.	28.	do. 3156	413.64	
				1,605.27

John Bray, for supplies furnished at New-Brunswick, in New-Jersey.

Feb.	27. Warrant No.	2499	274.18	
March	13. do.	2561	250.	
May	25. do.	2805	600.	
	do.	2806	350.72	
Aug.	29. do.	3081	400.	
				1,874.90

Chauncey Whittelsey, for supplies furnished at Middletown, in Connecticut.

Feb.	28. Warrant No.	2500	361.96	
June	28. do.	2895	200.	
Aug.	2. do.	3013	200.	
Dec.	14. do.	3237	200.	
	31. do.	3306	200.	
				1,161.96

Jacob Millart, for supplies furnished at Richmond, in Virginia.

March	14. Warrant No.	2571	255.36	
June	28. do.	2892	600.	
Aug.	2. do.	3012	383.33	
Dec.	23. do.	3259	166.66	
				1,405.35

Matthew Spillard, for supplies furnished in Philadelphia.

March	15. Warrant No.	2574	530.24	
April	9. do.	2678	246.25	
June	10. do.	2848	397.95	
Aug.	14. do.	3037	297.38	
Nov.	22. do.	3122	300.	
				1,771.82

Richmond Pearson, for supplies furnished at Salisbury, in North-Carolina.

March	19. Warrant No.	2592	596.60	
May	15. do.	2778	60.50	
				657.10

Stephen Bruce, for supplies furnished at Boston.

April	9. Warrant No.	2680	200.59	
June	1. do.	2825	250.	
				450.59

Doctor J. K. Read, for medicine and attending the recruits at Richmond, Virginia.

Date		Warrant		Amount	Total
June	28.	Warrant No.	2889	90.	
Aug.	1.	do.	3009	90.	
					180.

James Glenholm, for supplies furnished at Winchester, in Virginia.

Date		Warrant		Amount	Total
1793. June	28.	Warrant No.	2890	133.	
Aug.	3.	do.	3015	68.	
Dec.	23.	do.	3260	170.	
		do.	3261	60.	
		do.	3262	145.	
		do.	3263	80.	
		do.	3264	120.	
					776.

John Robinson, for supplies furnished at Montgomery Court-House, in Virginia.

Date		Warrant		Amount	Total
June	28.	Warrant No.	2891	1100.	
Dec.	23.	do.	3258	600.	
					1,700.

Nathaniel Rochester, for supplies furnished at Hagers-Town, in Maryland.

Date		Warrant		Amount	Total
June	28.	Warrant No.	2893	450.	
Aug.	3.	do.	3014	450.	
Dec.	23.	do.	3256	250.	
		do.	3257	300.	
					1,450.

Benajah Smith, for supplies furnished in the state of Georgia.

Date		Warrant		Amount	Total
July	29.	Warrant No.	2996	11,055.95	
		do.	2997	3261.	
		do.	2998	1650.	
Aug.	10.	do.	3033	3528.26	
					19,495.21

William Minor, for supplies furnished in the state of Georgia.

Date		Warrant		Amount	Total
July	29.	Warrant No.	2999	500.	
Aug.	10.	do.	3030	554.04	
		do.	3031	32,259.84	
		do.	3032	500.	
					33,813.88

John Habersham, for supplies furnished in the state of Georgia.

Aug.	9. Warrant No. 3027		739.77	
Dec.	16. do. 3240		11,000.	
				11,739.77

Jacob Bower, for supplies furnished at Reading, in Pennsylvania.

Aug.	21. Warrant No. 3066		300.	
Dec.	19. do. 3244		267.93	
	do. 3245		100.	
				667.93

1792. Dec.	10. Archibald Woods, for supplies furnished in the state of Virginia, Warrant No.	2293	148.72
	31. Captain Joseph Savage, for supplies furnished in the state of Georgia,	2334	247.59
1793. Jan.	7. John Deniston, for supplies furnished in the state of Pennsylvania	2382	982.40
	8. Patrick Campbell, for supplies furnished at Pittsburgh,	2385	1639.20
	11. William Cooke, for supplies furnished at Northumberland,	2392	324.85
	17. Goldthwait and Baldwin, for medicines furnished for the use of the General Hospital,	2410	256.94
Feb.	23. Aaron Robinson, for supplies furnished in the state of Vermont,	2493	131.
	25. Thomas Johnson, jun. for supplies furnished at Richmond, in Virginia,	2494	202.06
March	1. John Stewart, for supplies furnished at Lewisburg, in Virginia,	2503	34.30
	14. Burrell Brown, for supplies furnished at Charlotte court-house, in Virginia,	2569	165.
	Andrew Hannah, for supplies furnished at the said court-house	2570	172.42
	23. Henry Van Der Burg, for supplies furnished at Post Vincennes,	2607	1000.
April	15. Captain Howell Lewis, for supplies furnished at Charlotte court-house, in Virginia	2694	136.10
	19. Francis Vigo, for supplies furnished at Post Vincent,	2711	353.
	20. Matthews and Bodwell, for repairing a block-house at Galliopolis,	2715	87.87
May	16. Ebenezer Stott and Co. for freight of two boxes of clothing,	2784	10.78
	22. Daniel Tillinghast, for supplies furnished at Providence, in Rhode-Island,	2797	366.51
	27. Doctor Moses Scott, for medicines furnished at New-Brunswick, in New-Jersey.	2810	279.60
	Captain R. H. Greaton, for so much paid for medical assistance rendered to himself and recruits at Boston,	2811	30.

	28. Abraham Morrow, for rifle-guns delivered into the public store in Philadelphia,	2815	312.
	30. John Duncan, for expences attending pack-horses, the payment whereof was guaranteed by General St. Clair on behalf of the public, and for which Theodosius Fowler is charged on account of his contract of the twenty-eighth of October 1790,	2820	255.03
June	3. William Smith, for supplies furnished at Springfield, in Massachusetts,	2828	1270.96
	12. Strong and Porter, for supplies furnished at Bennington, in Vermont,	2857	539.64
	28. David Poe, for supplies furnished and to be furnished at Baltimore,	2894	500.
July	23. I. and C. Wilkins, & Co. for distilled spirits purchased for the use of the army,	2981	1000.
	24. Nathaniel Waters, for inspecting hats for the use of the army,	2983	40.
	26. Leonard Marbury, for supplies furnished in the state of Georgia,	2985	4259.39
	29. Speirs McLeod and Co. for supplies furnished in the said state of Georgia,	2995	10,027.01
Aug.	14. Thomas Edgar, for supplies furnished in the state of Virginia,	3039	23.10
	25. John Sullivan, for supplies furnished at New-York,	3065	97.35
	24. Peter Cooper, for inspecting the clothing furnished by Young and Dannacker, for the troops of the United States.	3070	106.21
	27. John Miller, for inspecting clothing furnished for the use of the army,	3075	160.
Dec.	20. Israel Chapin, for supplies furnished and expences incurred by him for the five nations of Indians,	3247	999.76

To William Blount, Governor of the Territory South of the Ohio, for the use of the Department of War within the said Territory.

May	16.	Warrant No.	2780	5000.	
June	6.	do.	2836	10,000.	
	20.	do.	2873	6000.	
	31.	do.	3005	1211.59	
Aug.	5.	do.	3019	1582.92	
					23,794.51

To James King, for supplies furnished in the Territory south of the Ohio.

May	31.	Warrant No.	2822	7408.38	
Aug.	14.	do.	3040	3334.80	
Nov.	27.	do.	3154	2166.37	
					12,909.55

TO THE FOLLOWING AGENTS FOR PAYING PENSIONS DUE TO MILITARY INVALIDS.

State of New-Hampshire.

Feb.	1.	William Gardner,	War. No.	2440	2010	
Dec.	10.	do.	do.	3231	1885.	
						3895.

State of Massachusetts.

Feb.	1.	Nathaniel Appleton,	war. No.	2442	6600.	
Aug.	14.	do.	do.	3042	5780.	
						12,380.

State of Rhode-Island.

Feb.	1.	Jabez Bowen,	war. No.	2441	1492.	
Aug.	14.	do.	do.	3043	1560.	
						3,052.

State of Connecticut.

Feb.	1.	William Imlay,	war. No.	2444	4148.	
	7.	Jedediah Huntington,	do.	2460	2.83	
Dec.	10.	William Imlay,	do.	3229	3550.	
						7,700.83

State of Vermont.

Feb.	1.	Noah Smith,	war. No.	2443		250.

State of New-York.

Feb.	1.	John Cochran,	war. No.	2445	7986.	
Aug.	14.	do.	do.	3045	7985.	
						15,971.

State of New-Jersey.

Jan.	31.	James Ewing,	war. No.	2436	2047.	
Aug.	14.	do.	do.	3047	1990.	
						4,037.

State of Pennsylvania.

Feb.	26.	Thomas Smith,	war. No.	2495	8261.82	
Aug.	22.	do.	do.	3068	8580.	
						16,841.82

State of Delaware.

Jan.	31. James Tilton,	War. No. 2437	918.			
Aug.	14. do.	do. 3046	942.			
				1,860.		

State of Maryland.

Feb.	1. Benjamin Harwood, war. No. 2448		2104.			
Aug.	14. do.	do. 3044	2150.			
				4,254.		

State of Virginia.

Feb.	1. John Hopkins,	War. No. 2446	3000.			
Dec.	10. do.	do. 3230	4000.			
				7,000.		

State of North-Carolina.

1792. Feb.	6. William Skinner,	war. No. 1521	443.			
1793. Feb.	1. do.	do. 2447	443.			
April	20. The State of N. Carolina,	2714	522.16			
Dec.	31. William Skinner,	do. 3292	504.			
				1,912.16		

State of Georgia.

Feb.	1. Richard Wylly,	War. No. 2449	509.			
Dec.	26. do.	do. 3271	425.			
				934.		
					80,087.81	
						1,212,531.72

FOR DEFRAYING THE EXPENCES OF TREATIES OF PEACE WITH THE INDIAN TRIBES.

To Benjamin Lincoln, Beverly Randolph and Timothy Pickering, Commissioners for treating with the Indians Northwest of the Ohio.

March	20. Warrant No. 2601	2500.		
April	25. do. 2725	20,000.		
	26. do. 2784	1500.		
			24,000.	
	13. To William Hull, for his services going as Agent to Upper Canada for the purpose of making arrangements for the supply of the Indians at said Treaty, Warrant No. 2693		1,088.	
				25,088.

TOWARDS DISCHARGING DOMESTIC LOANS.

Payments on account of the Principal.

To the President Directors and Company of the Bank of the United States.

July	20.	Warrant No. 2976, being for the first instalment due on the Loan of 2,000,000. of dollars made in pursuance of the act for incorporating the Subscribers to the said Bank,[23] paid out of the proceeds of Foreign Loans.	200,000.		
Dec.	24.	Warrant No. 3266, on account of the Loan of 800,000 dollars made in pursuance of the Act entitled, "An act making appropriations for the support of government for the year 1793." [24]	200,000.		
	31.	Warrant No. 3291, on account of the said Loan of 800,000 dollars	200,000.		
				400,000.	

To the President Directors and Company of the Bank of North-America.

	21.	Warrant No. 3255, for the amount of a Loan made to the United States without interest, for the use of the department of war.		156,595.56	
					756,59

Payments on account of the Interest.

To the President Directors and Company of the Bank of the United States.

Aug.	26.	Warrant No. 3074, for interest to the first of January, 1793, on the Loan of 400,000 dollars made in pursuance of the Act entitled, "An act for raising a farther sum of money for the protection of the Frontiers, and for other purposes therein mentioned." [25]		8,753.41	
		Warrant No. 3073, for interest from the first day of January 1793, to the 30th of June following, on the said Loan of 400,000 dollars		10,000.	
					18,75
					775,34

23. See note 5.
24. 1 *Stat.* 325–29 (February 28, 1793).
25. 1 *Stat.* 259–63 (May 2, 1792).

TOWARDS DEFRAYING THE EXPENSES INCURRED IN RELATION TO THE INTERCOURSE BETWEEN THE UNITED STATES AND FOREIGN NATIONS.

To Thomas Jefferson, Secretary of State.

March	28, Warrant No. 2612		39,500.	
July	31. do.	3006	50,000.	
				89,500.

TOWARDS DISCHARGING CERTAIN DEBTS CONTRACTED BY ABRAHAM SKINNER, LATE COMMISSARY OF PRISONERS.

June	28. To John Kelty, a Cornet of Dragoons in the late Army, Warrant No. 2888	46.42

TOWARDS DISCHARGING CERTAIN DEBTS CONTRACTED BY COLONEL TIMOTHY PICKERING, LATE QUARTER MASTER-GENERAL.

1793. Jan.	22. To Isaac Bronson, Warrant No.		2417	32.86	
Feb.	20. Thomas Wicks,	do.	2487	135.	
March	2. William Ellison,	do.	2511	100.60	
	William Edmunston,	do.	2513	42.37	
	8. Israel Honeywell,	do.	2540	22.94	
	11. George I. Deniston,	do.	2551	282.66	
	Jonathan Capron,	do.	2552	254.65	
	Joseph Cheeseman,	do.	2553	474.43	
	15. David Hobby,	do.	2575	13.13	
April	2. Richard Norwood,	do.	2639	432.99	
	18. John Palmer,	do.	2705	550.70	
July	22. Joseph Lewis, Attorney for George D. Brinkerhoff and Alletta Bogart, Administrators of the Estate of Theunis Bogart, deceased.		2979	333.23	
					2,675.56

INTEREST ON THE DOMESTIC DEBT.

For discharging the Interest which became due on the different species of Stock standing on the books of the several Commissioners of Loans, and the funded and unfunded registered debt on the books of the Treasury.

To William Gardner, Commissioner for New-Hampshire.

Jan.	29. Warrant No.	2430	5000.	
June	4. do.	2830	5500.	
	18. do.	2871	2200.	
July	26. do.	2986	4450.	
Dec.	10. do.	3234	5050.	
				22,200.

To Nathaniel Appleton, Commissioner for Massachusetts.

Month	Day		No.	Amount	Total
Feb.	26.	Warrant No.	2497	11,000.	
Dec.	27.	do,	3277	55,000.	
					66,000.

To Jabez Bowen, Commissioner for Rhode-Island.

Month	Day		No.	Amount	Total
1793. March	30.	Warrant No.	2624	4500.	
Dec.	31.	do.	3293	1000.	
		do.	3294	6000.	
		do.	3308	5500.	
					17,000.

To William Imlay, Commissioner for Connecticut.

Month	Day		No.	Amount	Total
Jan.	29.	Warrant No.	2431	7450.	
March	30.	do.	2620	6550.	
		do.	2622	900.	
April	25.	do.	2733	4700.	
June	17.	do.	2867	1350.	
		do.	2885	12000.	
	29.	do.	2900	2300.	
Aug.	17.	do.	3059	700.	
Dec.	10.	do.	3233	7900.	
	24.	do.	3265	12000.	
	26.	do.	3270	3000.	
	31.	do.	3297	1000.	
		do.	3298	6100.	
					65,950.

To John Cochran, Commissioner for New-York.

Month	Day		No.	Amount	Total
March	25.	Warrant No.	2609	90,000.	
June	24.	do.	2877	90,000.	
Nov.	23.	do.	3129	86,000.	
Dec.	20.	do.	3253	88,665.87	
					354,665.87

To James Ewing, Commissioner for New-Jersey.

Month	Day		No.	Amount	Total
March	25.	Warrant No.	2608	6000.	
June	24.	do.	2878	3900.	
	29.	do.	2901	2100.	
Nov.	25.	do.	3136	5000.	
Dec.	20.	do.	3254	4000.	
					21,000.

To the Commissioners for Pennsylvania.

March	28.	Thomas Smith, Warrant No. 2615	24,812.70	
June	27.	do. do. 2887	26,000.	
Nov.	25.	do. do. 3134	22,067.88	
			72,880.58	
Dec.	28.	Stephen Moylan, do.	21,568.58	
				94,449.16

To Benjamin Harwood, Commissioner for Maryland.

March	30.	Warrant No. 2621	12,000.	
Dec.	31.	do. 3301	8000.	
		do. 3302	20,000.	
		do. 3303	3000.	
		do. 3307	15,000.	
				58,000.

To John Hopkins, Commissioner for Virginia.

Jan.	29.	Warrant No. 2433	2000.	
Feb.	22.	do. 2491	4750.	
		do. 2492	3900.	
April	25.	do. 2732	9700.	
May	21.	do. 2796	5000.	
	24.	do. 2804	300.	
July	27.	do. 2988	12900.	
Aug.	5.	do. 3017	8000.	
Dec.	10.	do. 3232	6800.	
	27.	do. 3280	9300.	
	31.	do. 3299	6000.	
		do. 3300	3000.	
				71,650.

To William Skinner, Commissioner for North-Carolina.

April	25.	Warrant No. 2730	1000.	
		do. 2731	1700.	
Dec.	31.	do. 3311	650.	
				3,350.

To John Neufville, Commissioner for South-Carolina.

March	30.	Warrant No. 2625	13000.	
June	29.	do. 2899	6800.	
		do. 2902	8200.	
Dec.	31.	do. 3304	15000.	
				43,000.

To Richard Wylly, Commissioner for Georgia.

June	5.	Warrant No. 2834	1550.		
Dec.	27.	do. 3275	1000.		
		do. 3276	900.		
				3,450.	
					820,71

INTEREST PAYABLE AT THE TREASURY.

On the Funded Debt.

1793 March	28.	To John Kean, Cashier of the Bank of the United States, war. No. 2613			278,943.76		
June	29.	do.	do. 2896		281,816.88		
Nov.	25.	do.	do. 3135		277,052.01		
Dec.	30.	do.	do. 3286		279,765.18		
					1,117,577.83		
March	28.	To Samuel Meredith, Agent for the Trustees for the redemption of the Public Debt, being the Interest on Stock purchased and transferred in trust for the United States, war.	2614	25,445.76			
June	29.	do.	2897	15,298.59			
Dec.	5.	do.	3217	15,575.22			
	30.	do.	3287	16,074.11			
					72,393.68		
						1,189,971.51	

On the Unfunded Registered Debt.

1792. Dec.	31.	To John Kean, Cashier of the Bank of the United States, war. No. 2337		8000.	
1793. April	5.	do.	do. 2669	7,500.	
July	1.	do.	do. 2910	6,000.	
Dec.	5.	do.	do. 3216	24,000.	
					45,500.

For Discharging Unclaimed Dividends.

Jan.	16.	To John Kean, Cashier of the Bank of the United States, war. No. 2404		932.60
		do.	do. 2405	258.61
		do.	do. 2406	151.20
		do.	do. 2407	27.35
		do.	do. 2408	21.40
	19.	do.	do. 2416	2.22
	31.	do.	do. 2438	252.14

Feb.	2.	do.	do.	2452	1,998.06		
	4.	do.	do.	2455	645.85		
	6.	do.	do.	2456	367.37		
		do.	do.	2457	225.49		
		do.	do.	2458	554.93		
		do.	do.	2459	10.06		
	7.	do.	do.	2461	67.50		
	8.	do.	do.	2463	806.21		
	12.	do.	do.	2468	195.12		
		do.	do.	2470	222.30		
		do.	do.	2471	16.69		
		do.	do.	2472	132.88		
		do.	do.	2473	544.27		
		do.	do.	2474	36.67		
		do.	do.	2475	24.		
	14.	do.	do.	2478	131.41		
		do.	do.	2479	3.27		
	16.	do.	do.	2481	598.02		
	21.	do.	do.	2490	21.40		
April	15.	do.	do.	2696	378.48		
	20.	do.	do.	2712	690.25		
		do.	do.	2713	1,301.61		
	25.	do.	do.	2722	313.58		
		do.	do.	2723	409.11		
	26.	do.	do.	2735	62.81		
May	3.	do.	do.	2753	3,161.66		
	8.	do.	do.	2761	1,807.86		
June	8.	do.	do.	2843	19.64		
July	17.	do.	do.	2967	18.99		
	22.	do.	do.	2978	290.76		
		do.	do.	2980	29.56		
	31.	do.	do.	3003	516.28		
Aug.	6.	do.	do.	3021	953.59		
		do.	do.	3022	171.90		
		do.	do.	3023	401.05		
	14.	do.	do.	3048	666.19		
	15.	do.	do.	3049	102.07		
		do.	do.	3050	29.97		
		do.	do.	3051	3,346.84		
						22,919.22	
							1,258,390.73
							2,079,105.76

FOR THE SUPPORT OF LIGHT HOUSES, BEACONS, BUOYS, &C.
AND THE IMPROVEMENT OF NAVIGATION.

Light House in New-Hampshire.

1793. Aug. 2. To Joseph Whipple, Superintendant thereof,
War. No. 3011 320.37

Light House in Rhode-Island.

May	24.	To William Ellery, Superintendant thereof,	War. No.	2803	293.08	
June	6.	do.	do.	2838	218.40	
	8.	do.	do.	2842	41.60	
						55.

Light House near New-London.

July	29.	To Jedediah Huntington, Superintendant thereof,	War. No.	2992		44

Light House at Sandy-Hook.

Jan.	24.	To Thomas Randall, Superintendant thereof,	Warrant No.	2423	160.	
April	25.	do.	do.	2729	560.83	
July	29.	do.	do.	2993	180.56	
Dec.	10.	do.	do.	3226	269.67	
						1,171

Light House at Cape Henlopen, and Beacons &c. in the Bay and River Delaware.

Jan.	3.	To William Allibone, Superintendant thereof,	War. No.	2361	415.	
March	28.	do.	do.	2616	427.	
June	29.	do.	do.	2898	770.	
Nov.	30.	do.	do.	3205	400.	
						2,012

Light House at Cape Henry, and Beacons, &c. at the entrance of Chesapeak Bay.

1792. Dec.	31.	To John McCauley	War. No.	2330	15.13	
		Matthew Van Dusen,	do.	2335	305.78	
1793. March	2.	Thomas Newton, jun.	do.	2516	48.	
April	1.	Joseph Anthony & Son,	do.	2632	440.75	
	12.	Tench Cox, commissioner of the revenue,		2689	690.	
	30.	Thomas Newton, jun.	do.	2739	633.67	
July	12.	do.	do.	2959	84.24	
Aug.	3.	William Lindsay,	do.	3016	74.11	
						2,291

Navigation of certain Channels and Rivers in the State of North-Carolina.

Aug.	12.	To Nathan Keais, Superintendant thereof,	War. No.	3034		708

Light House Beacons. &c. in the State of South-Carolina.

June	10.	To Edward Blake, Superintendant thereof,	war.	2847	600.	
Aug.	15.	do.	do.	3052	263.45	
Dec.	31.	do.	do.	3310	674.04	
						1,537.49

Light House in the State of Georgia.

March	12.	To John Habersham, Superintendant thereof,	War. No.	2554	1849.71	
Aug.	9.	do.	do.	3028	173.38	
						2,023.09
March	19.	To Tench Coxe, Commissioner of the Revenue for the purpose of defraying certain expences incurred for the Light House Establishment,	War. No.	2593	300.	
June	26.	do.	do.	2884	200.	
July	16.	do.	do.	2964	500.	
						1,000.
						12,061.68

FOR DEFRAYING THE CONTINGENT CHARGES OF GOVERNMENT.

Feb.	26.	To Lewis R. Morris, Marshal for the District of Vermont, for so much paid by him for a Seal for the said District, War. No. 2496	8.
May	31.	James Seagrove, for his expences whilst on public business by order of the President of the United States to the Spanish government of East Florida, War. No. 2823	140.
			148.

REDUCTION OF THE PUBLIC DEBT.

For Purchases made of the Domestic Debt.

Feb.	19.	To Samuel Meredith, Agent for the Trustees for the redemption of the Public Debt,	War. No.	2482	234,901.89	
Sept.	2.	do.	do.	3085	50,000.	
Feb.	4.	Jonathan Burrall, Agent for the said Trustees,	War. No.	2454	50,000.	
						334,901.89

Payments on account of the French Debt.

To Antoine R. C. M. De La Forest, Consul-General of France.

1792. Dec.	31.	Warrant No.	2331	10,000.	
1793. Jan.	14.	do.	2396	8,000.	
	16.	do.	2403	36,000.	
Feb.	2.	do.	2450	10,000.	
		do.	2451	8,072.26	
	11.	do.	2466	5,000.	
	19.	do.	2483	6,670.12	
	20.	do.	2486	6,000.	
March	1.	do.	2501	10,000.	
		do.	2502	17,500.	
	15.	do.	2576	24,500.	
April	1.	do.	2627	6,700.	
	15.	do.	2695	5,100.	
	25.	do.	2724	34,200.	
May	1.	do.	2746	16,900.	
	14.	do.	2776	6,000.	
					210,642.38

To John De Ternant, Minister Plenipotentiary of France.

March	5.	Warrant No.	2523	10,000.	
	16.	do.	2582	5,000.	
April	4.	do.	2656	80,000.	
	15.	do.	2697	33,459.	
	18.	do.	2708	40,624.33	
May	1.	do.	2740	9,980.28	
	2.	do.	2747	3,630.	
		do.	2749	33,459.	
	6.	do.	2758	1,757.50	
	15.	do.	2777	20,000.	
	16.	do.	2785	33,459.	
June	1.	do.	2826	33,459.	
	17.	do.	2868	33,459.	
July	1.	do.	2914	33,459.	
					371,746.11

To Charles Edmund Genet, Minister Plenipotentiary of the Republic of France.

May	27.	Warrant No.	2812	9,851.25
		do.	2813	2,064.
	28.	do.	2814	30,000.
		do.	2816	20,000.
June	7.	do.	2839	34,250.
	10.	do.	2844	25,000.
	13.	do.	2859	6,000.
June	14.	do.	2863	22,514.83
	17.	do.	2866	2,000.
		do.	2869	22,000.

		do.	2870	45,620.
July	1.	do.	2912	30,007.07
	30.	do.	3000	46,013.79
Aug.	17.	do.	3056	2,539.44
		do.	3057	431.68
Sept.	3.	do.	3086	745.96
		do.	3087	13,000.
		do.	3088	12,500.
		do.	3089	6,190.72
		do.	3090	2,500.
		do.	3091	30,000.
		do.	3094	40,000.
		do.	3103	30,000.
Nov.	30.	do.	3175	10,000.
		do.	3176	1,000.
		do.	3177	4,000.
		do.	3178	10,000.
		do.	3179	5,000.
		do.	3180	3,242.19
		do.	3181	3,000.
		do.	3182	26,000.
		do.	3183	4,000.
		do.	3184	1,200.
		do.	3185	8,000.
		do.	3186	448.16
		do.	3187	1,948.75
		do.	3188	213.82
		do.	3189	448.16
		do.	3190	659.36
		do.	3191	5,365.02
		do.	3192	3,975.52
		do.	3193	4,000.
		do.	3194	6,000.
		do.	3195	544.50
		do.	3196	1,588.12
		do.	3197	1,941.65
		do.	3198	942.34
		do.	3199	30,000.
		do.	3200	1,144.50
		do.	3201	20,000.
		do.	3202	40,000.
		do.	3203	15,000.
		do.	3204	14,000.
Dec.	2.	do.	3206	2,000.
	19.	do.	3246	2,620.64
	26.	do.	3272	448.16

661,959.63

For discharging Bills of Exchange drawn by the Administration of Saint Domingo upon the late Consul General of the Republice of France.

Sept.	3.	To John Vaughan,	War.	3092	3254.12
		George C. Schroppel,	do.	3093	6877.87
		Philips Crammond and Co.	do.	3095	10711.99½

		Mr. Varinot,	do.	3096	283.94		
		Philip Nicklin and Co.	do.	3097	18015.90½		
		Nottnagel Montmollin & Co.	do.	3098	945.33		
		Robert Ralston,	do.	3099	1770.		
		John Vaughan,	do.	3100	5803.76½		
		E. Dutilh and Wachmuth,	do.	3101	15676.18		
		Stephen Girard,	do.	3102	3566.91		
	5.	Joseph Latil,	do.	3107	14557.45½		
		John Bringhurst,	do.	3108	800.		
Nov.	23.	Joseph Anthony,	do.	3130	481.72		
		do.	do.	3131	197.45		
		do.	do.	3132	5412.49		
	25.	do.	do.	3137	1963.		
	28.	do.	do.	3166	481.15		
	30.	Mr. Bournonville,	do.	3174	798.99		
Dec.	2.	John Kean,	do.	3207	885.		
	17.	James Yard,	do.	3242	554.66		
	20.	John Vaughan,	do.	3248	495.27		
						93,533.20	
							1,337,881.

Payments on account of the Debt due to certain Foreign Officers.[26]

Jan.	4.	To Jonathan B. Smith, Assignee of Captains John Sharp and Philippe Shubing, war.	2371	3207.12
	10.	Major Rochfontaine,	2389	5868.56
Feb.	15.	Joseph Anthony and Son Attornies for Catharine Green, for the amount of a Certificate issued for pay due to Baron de Glaubeck,	2480	909.59
March	7.	John Kean Attorney for Major L'Enfant	2536	2369.89
		Major L'Enfant	2537	4363.57
May	7.	Robert Morris, Attorney for Captain Augustine Briffault,	2759	3484.07
	10.	Ditto for the amount of Certificates issued to Captain John Baptiste Verdier	2767	2674.85
	25.	William and James Cramond Attornies for Captain de Beaulieu,	2807	785.27
June	11.	Captain de Beaulieu,	2852	1240.
		William and James Cramond Attornies for Captain de Beaulieu,	5853	188.46
Aug.	17.	Theophilus Cazenove, Attorney for Le Roy and Bayard, Attornies to Lieutenant Colonel Ferdinand I. S. de Brahm,	3055	6520.78

26. For a description of this debt, see William Short to H, August 3, 1790, note 5. Section 5 of "An Act supplementary to an act making provision for the Debt of the United States" (1 *Stat.* 282 [May 8, 1792]) authorized the President "to cause to be discharged the principal and interest of the said debt, out of any of the monies which have been or shall be obtained on loan. . . ." For the negotiations on the payment of these officers, see H to Short, August 16, September 13, 1792; H to George Washington, August 27, 1792; Washington to H, August 31, 1792; H to Gouverneur Morris, September 13, 1792.

Nov. 22.	Le Roy and Bayard Attornies for Major Chevalier James de Segond,	3116	5630.05	
	Ditto Attornies for Cornet Peter Benigne Raffanau,	3117	1758.26	
				39,000.47

Payments on account of the Dutch Debt.

To the following persons for Bills of exchange purchased and remitted to Messrs. W. and J. Willink, N. and J. Van Staphorst and Hubbard of Amsterdam, on account of certain sums which became due, in the year 1793, on the Dutch Loans.

March 16.	To Robert Morris,	Warrant No.	2584	50,000.	
27.	Joseph Anthony,	do.	2610	27,240.	
April 13.	Jonathan Burrall, Cashier of the Office of Discount and Deposite at New-York,	do.	2692	29,229.30	
May 3.	Thomas M. Willing,	do.	2751	23,000.	
7.	John Kean, Cashier of the Bank of the United States.	do.	2760	32,200.	
Dec. 30.	The President Directors and Company of the Bank of the United States,	do.	3285	42,000.	
					203,669.30
	Paid out of the monies arising from Foreign Loans				1,915,452.98

STATEMENT OF THE INTEREST FUND TO THE END OF THE YEAR 1793, VIZ.

The Interest to the first day of January 1793, on the Stock purchased and redeemed, which was included in the aggregate amount of dividends paid at the Treasury to that period, amounted to	60,555.95
The dividends of Interest Paid at the Treasury in the year 1793, on the said stock purchased and redeemed, amounted to	72,393.68
The Interest paid at the Loan Office in Massachusetts, on Stock purchased by Benjamin Lincoln, Agent to the Trustees for the redemption of the Public Debt, amounted to	528.56
The Interest paid at the Loan Office in Virginia, on Stock purchased by William Heth, Agent to the Trustees aforesaid, amounted to	658.83
The Interest received by Samuel Meredith Agent to the said Trustees, on the Commutation of Simeon Thayer, amounted to	327.29
The Interest received by the said Samuel Meredith on the commutation of Willis Wilson, amounted to	3.24
	134,467.55

Payments made by the Trustees for the redemption of the Public Debt, for Stock purchased out of the Interest Fund to the last day of December, 1793, the particulars whereof are contained in their reports to Congress.

1791. From February 22, to March 3,	5.51	
1792. From October 29, to October 31,	25,969.96	
1793. From January 17, to February 1,	34,585.99	
From April 18, to May 2,	26,627.64	
From July 31, to August 1,	15,629.12	
		102,818.22
Balance unexpended on the last day of December 1793, which being invested in the purchase of Stock in the month of January 1794, will be included in the next annual Statement,		31,649.33
		134,467.55

FOR COMPENSATION TO THE MARSHALS OF THE UNITED STATES AND THEIR ASSISTANTS FOR TAKING THE ENUMERATION OF THE INHABITANTS WITHIN THEIR RESPECTIVE DISTRICTS.

1792. Dec.	29.	To William Moore Assistant to the Marshal for the District of Kentucky, War. 2327		73.54
1793. May	10.	Elliston and John Perot, Assignees of John Gray and James Craig, Assistants to the Marshal for the District of South Carolina, Warrant 2768	641.75	
June	5.	Jacob Milligan, Assistant to the Marshal for the said District of South Carolina, Warrant 2835	166.59	
				808.34
				881.88

FOR SATISFYING MISCELLANEOUS CLAIMS.

1792. June	4.	To Stephen Keyes, for procuring Surveys of the North west part of Lake Champlain in October 1791, for the purpose of ascertaining a proper position for a Custom House, War. No. 1819	44.55
1793. March	2.	Samuel Baird, for laying off the town of Vincennes and returning a plan of the same into the Office of the Secretary of the Western Territory, Warrant 2510	60.
		Robert Fenner late Agent for settling the accounts of the North Carolina line, for commission on sundry payments made by him to the Officers of the said line, Warrant 2514	169.05

	5. John Steele late one of the Commissioners appointed to negociate a Treaty with the southern Tribes of Indians, for a balance due to him as Commissioner aforesaid, Warrant 2520		206.75
March	9. To Joseph Nourse, Assignee to the following persons, for compensations due to them for bringing lists of the votes given by the Electors of the President and Vice-President of the United States, Warrant No. 2549 viz.		
	Ezra Bartlett, for the votes of New-Hampshire	105.75	
	John S. Tyler, Massachusetts,	87.	
	Lot Hall, Vermont	90.25	
	Daniel Updike, Rhode-Island	80.	
	Enoch Parsons Connecticut	52.25	
	Robert Williams, New-York	44.50	
	Stephen Stephenson, Pennsylvania,	26.	
	Gunning Bedford, Delaware,	19.	
	E. Vallette, Maryland,	35.	
	Samuel Pettus, Virginia,	69.50	
	Notley Coun, Kentucky	234.25	
	Stephen White, North-Carolina	134.	
	Thomas Fitzpatrick, South-Carolina	168.25	
	Anderson Watkins, Georgia,	195.75	
			1,341.50
Mar.	13. To Dunlap and Claypoole, for printing done in the year 1787 for the Convention which framed the Constitution, Warrant 2562		420.
	14. William Irvine, for his expenses from the first of December 1792 to the 26th of February 1793 in going to and returning from Charleston South-Carolina, by direction of the Comptroller of the Treasury, on business relating to the Loan Office, War. 2678		218.33
April	9. Miers Fisher and Joshua Gilpin Attornies for the Trustees of the Public Grammar School of Wilmington in the State of Delaware, for Damages done to the said school; pursuant to an act of Congress of the 13th of April 1792,[27] War. 2676		2,553.64
	10. James Burnside, for his expenses going from Philadelphia to Trenton, relating to a suit commenced by the United States against Thomas Fennimore Warrant 2683		11.70

27. "An Act to compensate the corporation of trustees of the public grammar school and academy of Wilmington, in the state of Delaware, for the occupation of, and damages done to, the said, school, during the late war" (6 *Stat.* 8).

	11.	Timothy Pickering, for so much paid by him to Samuel Bradshaw, for going express from Philadelphia to Kentucky, with a letter from the Secretary of State to the Judge of the District Court Warrant 2687	150.
	16.	Alexander McComb, Agent for Udney Hay Attorney for Return Jonathan Meigs and Job Green, legal Representatives of Christopher Green, deceased, pursuant to a resolve of Congress of the 28th September, 1785, and An Act of the 14th January 1793[28] Warrant 2699	401.96
	22.	William Simmons Attorney for Henry Remsen late chief Clerk to the Secretary of State, for the expenses of said Remsen incurred by the removal of Congress from New-York to Philadelphia Warrant 2716	25.
		Samuel Emery, for so much paid by him to two persons for their expenses from Boston to Philadelphia to attend as evidence in a suit instituted by the United States, Warrant 2717	174.
May	10.	John Fenno, for the paper and printing five hundred copies of sundry communications, made by the Secretary of the Treasury to the House of Representatives of the United States, during the second session of the second Congress, War. 2766	295.66
	14.	George Taylor junior, for thirteen Seal Presses purchased by him for the use of the Western Territories, Warrant 2773	303.54
May	7.	To Francis Bailey, for fifteen Seals made by him for the use of the Supervisors of the Revenue in the year 1791, Warrant 2790	160.
June	25	Aaron Rowley, Attorney for Elijah Bostwick for so much granted to the said Bostwick by an Act of Congress passed the second of March 1793,[29] Warrant 2881	145.42
		William Bradford late Attorney General of the State of Pennsylvania, for his Counsel and Attorney's fees on sundry suits commenced by him, on behalf of the United States, against sundry persons in the years 1784, 1787 and 1788, Warrant 2883	151.40

28. *JCC*, XXIX, 776; "An Act to provide for the allowance of interest on the sum ordered to be paid by the resolve of Congress, of the twenty-eighth of September, one thousand seven hundred and eighty-five, as an indemnity to the persons therein named" (6 *Stat.* 11).

29. "An Act for the relief of Elijah Bostwick" (6 *Stat.* 12).

July	10. Thomas Williams for his expenses on a journey from Richmond in Virginia to Hillsborough in North-Carolina in the year 1791, for the purpose of giving testimony on the part of the United States against a person charged with counterfeiting Public Securities, Warrant 2957		77.50
Dec.	24. Benjamin Philips, for his services as a messenger employed by Edward Church Consul from the United States at the Port of Lisbon, for the purpose of carrying dispatches to the Secretary of State. Warrant 3267		72.76
1792. Nov.	23. George Thatcher Attorney for John Burbank late Master at Arms on board the ship Bon Homme Richard, for the said Burbanks proportion of prizes captured by the squadron under the command of John Paul Jones in the northern seas, Warrant 2252	83.12	
1793. April	24. Abraham Bradley late Marine on board the Frigate Alliance for his share of the said prizes. War. 2719	36.25	
July	3. John Anniball late a seaman on board the Frigate Alliance, for his proportion of the said prizes, Warrant 2929	37.36	
	John Chaffee Administrator to the Estate of Henry Wrightington late a seaman on board the Frigate Alliance, deceased, for the said Wrightington's share of the said prizes, Warrant 2936	37.36	
			194.09
March	2. To Ashbel Steele, for five sets of Bills of Exchange drawn by Francis Hopkinson Treasurer of Loans on the late Commissioners of the United States at Paris, for interest due on Loan Office Certificates Warrant 2515	126.	
	11. John Lawrence, for two sets of Bills of Exchange drawn by the said Francis Hopkinson on the said Commissioners for interest due on Loan Office Certificates, Warrant 2550	30.	
			156.
	21. John Lamb Assignee to Christopher Colles, for one hundred and twenty-nine hydrometers with cases, furnished by the said Colles in October 1792 for the use of the United States, War. 2604	1,456.40	
June	15. Martin Fisher, for forty Thermometers furnished by him for the Officers of the Customs and Inspectors of the Revenue, Warrant 2864	106.67	
			1,563.07
			8,895.92

STATEMENT OF MONIES TRANSFERRED TO THE UNITED STATES, AND OF THE PROCEEDS OF FOREIGN LOANS APPLIED TO DISCHARGE THE FOREIGN DEBT AND OTHER PURPOSES DURING THE YEARS 1791, 1792, and 1793, *VIZ.*

		Guilders.	*Rate of exch.*	*Dols. Cts.*	*Dols. Cts.*
Amount of bills of exchange drawn by the Treasurer on the Commissioners in Amstedam, *Guilders*	5,649,621.2.8				
Deduct bills repurchased of the Bank of the United States, and cancelled,	495,000. .				
		5,154,621.2.8	sold for		2,104,566.24
Amount applied in Europe and at the Treasury for the interest on the foreign debt, in the years 1791, 1792 and 1793, and which being a charge upon the domestic revenue, is credited as though the same had been drawn to the United States, viz.					
FRENCH DEBT					
Interest for the year 1791, *Livres*		1,622,291.13.4	at $18\frac{15}{100}$ *Cts.*	294,445.93	
Ditto, 1792,		1,284,361.2.2		233,111.54	
Ditto, 1793,		912,486.2.2		165,616.23	
DUTCH DEBT					
Interest for the year 1791, *Guilders*	549,783.6.				
Commission on interest paid,	5469.19.				
Expences for advertising payment of interest, &c.	283.1.				
Postage of letters	144.1.8				
		555,680.7.8.	at 40 *Cents.*	222,272.16	

Interest for the year 1792, *guild.*	996.142.10.				
Commission on interest paid,	9,944.9.2				
Expences for advertising payment of interest, &c.	292.1.				
Postage of letters,	201.2.				
		1,006,580.2.2	at do.	402,632.02	
Interest for the year 1793, *guild.*	1,213,673.8.				
Commission on interest paid,	12,153.11.7				
Postage of letters	70.16.8				
		1,225,897.15.15	at do.	490,359.13	

ANTWERP DEBT.

Interest for the year 1792, *guilds.*	83,968.15.				
Commission on negociating drafts on the Commissioners in Amsterdam,	66.15.				
Postage of letters,	3.5.				
		84,038.15.	at do.	33,615.50	
Interest for the year 1793, *guilds.*	92,250. .				
Commission on negociating drafts on the Commissioners in Amsterdam,	64.13.				
		92,314.13.	at 40 *Cents.*	36,925.86	

SPANISH DEBT

Interest from the 1st of January, 1791, to the 21st of August, 1793, when the balance of the debt was remitted from Amsterdam,				17,651.12	
					1,896,629.49
					4,001,195.73

EXPENDITURE.

Amount expended in purchases of the domestic debt of the United States, pursuant to the fourth section of the Act of August, 12, 1790, entitled "An Act making provision for the reduction of the public debt,"[30] *viz.*		
By Jonathan Burrall, per warrant, No. 2454, dated February 4, 1793,	50,000.	
By Samuel Meredith, 2482, dated Feb. 19, 1793,	234,901.89	
By ditto, 3085, dated Sept. 2, 1793,	50,000.	
		334,901.89
Amount appropriated for paying the principal and interest of the debt due to foreign officers, by the fifth section of the Act, entitled "An Act supplementary to the Act making provision for the debt of the United States," passed on the 8th day of May 1792.[31]		
Principal,	186,988.23	
Interest,	44,987.58	
		231,975.81
Payment of the first instalment due on the 31st of December, 1792, on a loan made of the Bank of the United States, in pursuance of an Act for the purpose passed on the 2d of March, 1793,[32]		200,000.
Payment on account of the French debt, in the year 1792, on warrants particularised in page 52, of the printed statement for said year,[33]	435,263.83	
in the year 1793, on warrants particularised in the statement herewith, for said year,	1,337,881.32	
		1,773,145.15

Payment for bills of exchange purchased and remitted to the Commissioners at Amsterdam, on account of the Dutch debt, viz. Sterling £34,436:15:6 credited in their accounts for the year 1793, at 406,565.4.

30. 1 *Stat.* 186–87.

31. 1 *Stat.* 281–83.

32. "An Act providing for the payment of the First Instalment due on a Loan made of the Bank of the United States" (1 *Stat.* 338).

33. This is a reference to the original pagination of H's "Report on an Account of the Receipts and Expenditures of the United States for the Year 1792," December 18, 1793. For this material, see *Hamilton Papers,* XV, 534–35.

Guilders 30,000. do. do.	30,000. .				
Ditto 100,000. do. for the year 1794,	100,000. .				
Guilders	536,565.4.				
which bills cost, per warrants particularised in the statement herewith, for the year 1793,		203.669.30			
			2,743.692.15		
Balance remaining on the 31st of December, 1793, to be applied to replace the foreign fund,			1,257,503.58		
			4,001,195.73		

A GENERAL STATEMENT OF CERTAIN APPROPRIATIONS MADE BY LAW FOR THE SERVICE OF THE YEAR 1793, INCLUDING THE BALANCES OF FORMER APPROPRIATIONS UNEXPENDED ON THE LAST DAY OF DECEMBER, 1792; EXHIBITING ALSO, THE EXPENDITURES OF THE UNITED

Date	Dates, and Titles of the Acts of Appropriations,	For discharging Warrants issued by the late Board of Treasury.	For the Support of the Civil List.
	Balances of former appropriations unexpended on the last day of December, 1792	32,176.73	209,247.11
1790, July 1. and 1793, Feb. 9.	An act providing the means of intercourse between the United States and Foreign Nations,[34]	......	......
1790, Aug. 4.	An act making provision for the Debt of the United States,[35]	......	......
12.	An act making provision for the reduction of the Public Debt,[36]	......	......
1791, Mar. 3.	An act for raising and adding another regiment to the Military Establishment of the United States, and for making farther provision for the protection of the frontiers,[37]	......	......
1792, May 2.	An act for raising a further sum of money for the protection of the frontiers, and for other purposes therein mentioned,[38]	......	......
8.	An act supplementary to the act making provision for the Debt of the United States,[39]	......	......
1793, Feb. 28.	An act making appropriations for the support of Government for the year 1793,[40]	......	409,951.29
Mar. 2.	An act making an appropriation to defray the expense of a treaty with the Indians north west of the Ohio,[41]	......	......
	An act providing for the payment of the first installment due on a loan made of the Bank of the United States,[42]	......	......
	An act making certain appropriations therein mentioned,[43]	......	30,709.66
	Amount of the appropriations and unexpended balances before recited,	32,176.73	649,908.06
	Amount of the expenditures for the year 1793,	......	358,241.08
	Balances unexpended to be transferred to the statement for the year 1794,	32,176.73	291,666.98

STATES FOR THE YEAR 1793, ON WARRANTS ISSUED BY THE SECRETARY OF THE TREASURY, AND THE UNEXPENDED BALANCES OF THE SAID APPROPRIATIONS, WHICH ARE TO BE ACCOUNTED FOR IN THE NEXT ANNUAL STATEMENT.

For the Support of the Army, &c.	For paying Pensions due to military Invalids.	For defraying the Expenses of Treaties of Peace with the Indian Tribes.	Towards discharging Domestic Loans.		For maintaining Intercourse between the United States and Foreign Nations.	For effecting a Recognition of the Treaty of the United States with the new Emperor of Morocco.	For the Building, Equipment and Support of Revenue Cutters.	Towards discharging certain Debts contracted by Abraham Skinner, late Commissary of Prisoners.	Towards discharging certain Debts contracted by Colonel Timothy Pickering, late Quarter Master General.
			For the Principal.	For the Interest.					
318,539.90	82,849.89	13,000.	......	2,401.88	89,500.	7,000.	34,704.48	209.62	35,939.74
......	......	......	......	......	40,000.	......	......	.....	......
......	......	......	......	......	......	......	......	.....	......
......	......	......	......	......	......	......	......	.....	......
......	......	......	156,595.56	......	......	......	......	.....	......
......	......	......	400,000.	18,753.41	......	......	......	.....	......
......	......	......	......	......	......	......	......	.....	......
,067,807.07	82,245.32	......	600,000.	......	......	......	3,000.	.....	......
......	......	100,000.	......	......	......	......	......	.....	......
......	......	......	200,000.	......	......	......	......	.....	......
569.45	......	......	......	......	......	......	......	.....	......
,386,916.42	165,095.21	113,000.	1,356,595.56	21,155.29	129.500.	7,000.	37,704.48	209.62	35,939.74
,132,443.91	80,087.81	25,088.	756,595.56	18,753.41	89,500.	......	......	46.42	2,675.56
254,472.51	85,007.40	87,912.	600,000.	2,401.88	40,000.	7,000.	37,704.48	163.20	33,264.18

Dates, and Titles of the Acts of Appropriations,	For Interest payable on the Domestic Debt in the Year 1793.	For the Support of Light Houses, Beacons, Buoys, and public Piers.
Balances of former appropriations unexpended on the last day of December, 1792	31,532.12	25,643.86
1790, July 1. and 1793, Feb. 9. An act providing the means of intercourse between the United States and Foreign Nations,[34]	......	......
1790, Aug. 4. An act making provision for the Debt of the United States,[35]	A. 2,250,167.33	......
12. An act making provision for the reduction of the Public Debt,[36]	......	......
1791, Mar. 3. An act for raising and adding another regiment to the Military Establishment of the United States, and for making farther provision for the protection of the frontiers,[37]	......	......
1792, May 2. An act for raising a further sum of money for the protection of the frontiers, and for other purposes therein mentioned,[38]	......	......
8. An act supplementary to the act making provision for the Debt of the United States,[39]	......	......
1793, Feb. 28. An act making appropriations for the support of Government for the year 1793,[40]	......	20,000.
Mar. 2. An act making an appropriation to defray the expense of a treaty with the Indians north west of the Ohio,[41]	......	......
An act providing for the payment of the first instalment due on a loan made of the Bank of the United States,[42]	......	......
An act making certain appropriations therein mentioned,[43]	......	22,955.66
Amount of the appropriations and unexpended balances before recited,	2,281,699.45	68,599.52
Amount of the expenditures for the year 1793,	2,079,105.76	12,061.68
Balances unexpended to be transferred to the statement for the year 1794,	202,593.69	56,537.84

	TOWARDS THE REDUCTION OF THE							
	DOMESTIC DEBT.		FOREIGN DEBT.					
For defraying the Contingent Charges of Government.	Out of the Surplus of the Revenue on 31st Dec, 1790, and the Proceeds of foreign Loans.	Out of the Interest Fund.	Due to the French.	Due to the Dutch.	Debt due to certain foreign Officers.	For defraying the Expenses of the Enumeration of the Inhabitants of the United States.	For satisfying miscellaneous Claims.	Total Amount.
02.50	416,885.75	60,555.95	290,736.17	......	213,621.02	2,822.98	13,468.	1,889,137.70
....	......	......	......	......	......	......	......	40,000.
....	......	......	1,047,145.15	203,669.30	......	......	......	3,500,981.78
....	334,901.89	......	......	......	......	......	......	334,901.89
....	......	......	......	......	......	......	......	156,595.56
....	......	......	......	......	......	......	......	418,753,41
....	......	73,911.60	......	......	......	......	......	73,911.60
....	......	......	......	......	......	......	7,839.10	2,190,842.78 B.
....	......	......	......	......	......	......	......	100,000.
....	......	......	......	......	......	......	......	200,000.
....	......	......	......	......	......	......	2.319.	56,553.77 C.
302.50	751,787.64	134,467.55	1,377,881.32	203,669.30	213,621.02	2,822.98	23,626.10	8,961,678.49
148.	334,901.89	102,818.22	1,377,881.32	203,669.30	39,000.47	881.88	8,895.92	6,582,796.19
154.50	416,885.75	31,649.33	......	......	174,620.55	1,941.10	14,730.18	2,378,882.30

[Balance carried forward]			2,378,882.30
To which is added, the balance of the foreign funds transferred to the United States, including the appropriation for interest on the foreign debt for the years 1791, 1792 and 1793, per statement,			1,257,503.58
Total of unsatisfied appropriations at the close of the year 1793, agreeably to the statements made at the Treasury,			3,636,385.88
The expenditures in the year 1793, were made out of the following funds.			
Out of the proceeds of foreign loans, viz.			
for the first instalment due on a loan of two millions of dollars obtained from the Bank of the United States,	200,000		
for the reduction of the domestic debt.	334,901.89		
for the reduction of the French debt,	1,337,881.32		
for the reduction of the Dutch debt,	203,669.30		
for the reduction of the debt due to foreign officers,	39,000.47		
		2,115,452.98	
Out of the proceeds of domestic revenues and loans,		4,364,524.99	
Out of the - interest fund, applicable to the reduction of the domestic debt,		102,818.22	
Total of expenditures in the year 1793, as above stated,			6,582,796.19
The unsatisfied appropriations above stated are payable out of the following funds, viz.			
The surplus of duties on the last day of December, 1790, applicable to the reduction of the domestic debt,		416,885.75	
The interest fund not expended in the year 1793, ditto,		31,649.33	
The proceeds of foreign loans, for the balance of the debt due to foreign officers,		174,620.55	
The domestic revenues, since the year 1790, applicable to the reimbursement of the balance of foreign funds transferred to the U. States, and the payment of domestic appropriations,		3,013,230.25	
Total of unsatisfied appropriations including the surpluses on certain appropriations, which will be accounted for in the next statement,			3,636,385.88

34. 1 *Stat.* 128–29; 1 *Stat.* 299–300.

35. "An Act making provision for the (payment of the) Debt of the United States" (1 *Stat.* 138–44).

36. 1 *Stat.* 186–87.

37. 1 *Stat.* 222–24.

38. 1 *Stat.* 259–63.

39. 1 *Stat.* 281–83.

40. 1 *Stat.* 325–29.

41. 1 *Stat.* 333.

42. 1 *Stat.* 338.

43. 1 *Stat.* 339–40.

A.—The amount of interest payable on the domestic debt in the year 1793, agreeably to the divident accounts settled at the Treasury.

B.—The specific sums appropriated by this act, amount to		1,589,044.72
To which the following sums are added,		
The Amount of monies received in the year 1793, on account of the loan of 800,000 dollars made of the Bank of the United States,	600.000	
The net amount of fines, penalties and forfeitures in the year 1792 and 1793,	1,798.06	
		601,798.06
		2,190,842.78

C.—The amount appropriated by this act, is	59,107.41
From which is deducted the sum allowed to compensate the Corporation of Trustees of the public grammar school and academy of Wilmington in the State of Delaware, it being included in the statement of appropriations for the year 1792,	2,553.64
	56,553.77

Dr. GENERAL ACCOUNT OF THE RECEIPTS AND EXPENDITURES OF THE PUBLIC MONIES IN THE YEAR 1793. Cr.

To amount of Expenditures in the year 1793, as stated in page 63 [44]	6,582,796.19		By balance in the Treasury on the last day of December 1792,	783,444.51
From which deduct the expenditures of the Trustees for the redemption of the public debt, out of the Interest Fund	102,818.22		Amount of Receipts in the Year 1793, as stated in page 13 [45]	6,450,195.15
		6,479.977.97		
Balance in the Treasury on the last day of December 1793		753,661.69		
	Dollars	7,233,639.66	Dollars	7,233,639.66

Comptroller's Office,
November 25th, 1794.
Examined by
Oliv. Wolcott, Junior, *Comptroller.*

Treasury Department,
Register's Office,
November 25th, 1794.
Stated from the Records of the Treasury
Joseph Nourse, *Register*

44. This page number refers to the pagination of the original document. For this material, see page 552 of this volume.

45. This page number refers to the pagination of the original document. For this material, see page 497 of this volume.

Appendix, Containing Statements Shewing the Operation of the Funds for Reducing the Domestic Debt, to the Close of the Year 1793. Also, Statements of the Foreign and Domestic Debts of the United States, and of the Expenditure of the Proceeds of Foreign Loans, to the Same Period.

A STATEMENT OF THE DOMESTIC DEBT OF THE UNITED STATES AS DUE ON THE 31st OF DECEMBER 1793, INCLUDING THE SUMS PASSED TO THE CREDIT OF THE TRUSTEES OF THE SINKING FUND AND EXCLUDING THE BALANCES OF UNSATISFIED APPROPRIATIONS PAYABLE AT THE TREASURY.

			Dollars. Cents.
FUNDED DOMESTIC DEBT.			
Six per Cent. stock		18,169,213.15	
Deferred six per Cent. stock		9,084,608.46	
Three per Cent. stock		12,432,649.64	
			39,686,471.25
FUNDED ASSUMED DEBT.			
Six per Cent stock		8,120,824.11	
Deferred six per Cent. stock		4,060,411.78	
Three per Cent. stock		6,090,551.57	
			18,271,787.46
REGISTERED DEBT.			
Principal of registered debt remaining on the books of the Treasury	481,903.28		
Estimated amount of interest on the above sum from various periods to the 31st December 1790; which becomes three per Cent. stock on being subscribed to the Loan	118,150.59		
		600,053.87	
Amount of Certificates issued to non-subscribing creditors, which remain to their credit on the books of the Commissioners of Loans, in the following states, viz.			
New Jersey			
Principal	178.83		
Interest to December 31st 1790	84.40		
		263.23	
Pennsylvania			
Principal	59.95		
Interest to December 31st 1790	10.68		
		70.63	
Maryland			
Principal	4,262.32		
Interest to December 31st 1790	1,992.37		
		6,254.69	
			606,642.42

Balances due to Creditor States pursuant to the final report of the Commissioners appointed to execute the acts for the settlement of the accounts between the United States and the Individual states,[46] exclusive of interest thereon since December 31st 1789, viz.		
To the state of New Hampshire	75,055.	
Massachusetts	1,248,801.	
Rhode Island	299,611.	
Connecticut	619,121.	
New Jersey	49,030.	
South Carolina	1,205,978.	
Georgia	19,988.	
		3,517,584.
Domestic Debt receivable on loan, but which not being registered is not entitled to a dividend; consisting of loan office and final settlement certificates, arrearages of interest to the 31st of December 1790, indents of interest and bills of old emissions also of unliquidated claims upon the government for services and supplies during the late war, arrearages of military pensions to March 4th 1789, and credits on the books of the Treasury, for which certificates remain to be issued—estimated upon the principles of the report of the Secretary of the Treasury dated January 9th 1790.[47]		2,120,972.27
Estimated amount of the Domestic Debt of the United States on the 31st of December 1793, including the sums passed to the credit of the Trustees of the Sinking Fund, and exclusive of sums received on certain domestic loans which are repayable out of the established revenues and which are included in the statement of unsatisfied appropriations,		64,203,457.40

46. See Tobias Lear to H, August 19, 1793, note 1.

47. "Report Relative to a Provision for the Support of Public Credit," January 9, 1790.

FOREIGN DEBT OF THE UNITED STATES ON THE 31st OF DECEMBER, 1793, AGREEABLY TO STATEMENTS MADE AT THE TREASURY, INCLUDING SUMS WHICH HAD BEEN RECEIVED FOR THE PROCEEDS OF LOANS, AND WHICH REMAINED UNEXPENDED, AND THE BALANCE OF FOREIGN FUNDS TRANSFERRED TO THE UNITED STATES, WHICH ARE COMPRISED IN THE STATEMENT OF UNSATISFIED APPROPRIATIONS PAYABLE AT THE TREASURY.

DEBT DUE TO FRANCE CONTRACTED BY THE LATE GOVERNMENT.		*Livres. s.d.*	*Rate of exch.*	*Foreign Debt on Dec. 31, 1793 Dollars. Cents.*
Loan of eighteen millions of livres, bearing an interest of five per cent. per annum, from the 3d of September, 1783, and repayable in twelve equal annual payments; the first of which became due on the 3d of September, 1787,[48]		18,000,000		
Loan of ten millions of livres, bearing interest at four per cent. per annum, from the 5th of November, 1781, and repayable in ten equal annual payments; the first of which became due on the first of November, 1787,[49]		10,000,000		
Loan of six millions of livres, bearing interest at five per cent. per annum, from the first day of January, 1784, and repayable in six equal annual payments; the first of which will become due on the first of January, 1797,[50]		6,000,000		
Balance of an account for supplies furnished,		134,065.7.6		
		34,134,065.7.6		
Interest which fell due before and in the year 1790, on the several loans above recited,	12,000,000.			

48. For a description of the French loan of eighteen million livres, see H to William Short, September 1, 1790, note 17.

49. For a description of the loan of ten million livres borrowed by France for the United States in Holland, see Willink, Van Staphorst, and Hubbard to H, January 25, 1790, note 3.

50. For a description of the French loan of six million livres, see Short to H, November 30, 1789, note 3.

From which is deducted the amount of payments made by grand banker at Paris,	1,600,000.			
		10,400,000.		
Interest on the balance of the above-mentioned account for supplies furnished,		48,598.13.11		
Interest which fell due on the several loans in the years 1791, 1792 and 1793,		3,819,138.17.8		
		48,401,802.19.1		
On account of which debt the following sums had been paid on the 31st day of Dec. 1793.				
By Wilhem and Jan Willink, Nicholas and Jacob van Staphorst and Hubbard of Amsterdam, *Guilders.*	8,105,043.8	19,452,104.3.2		
By C.J.M. de Wolf, of Antwerp, *ditto.*	1,975,375.13	4,740,901.1.12		
By the department of war, for arms, ammunition, &c. delivered in the year 1791, *Dollars.*	8,962.	49,377.8.2		
By the treasury of the United States, in the years 1792 and 1793, *ditto.*	1,773,145.15	9,769,394.14.9		
		34,011,777.17.3		
Balance due to France on the 31st of December, 1793, agreeably to the statement made at the Treasury; payable at different future periods ascertained by contracts dated July 16th, 1782, and February 25th, 1783,		14,390,025.1.10	at 18 15/100 cts.	2,611,789.55
		48,401,802.19.1		

		Guilders.	Rate of exch.	Foreign Debt on Dec. 31, 1793. Dollars. Cents.
DEBT CONTRACTED IN HOLLAND, VIZ. BY THE LATE GOVERNMENT.				
Loan of five millions of guilders, per five contracts, dated June 11, 1782, at five per cent. per annum,[51]	5,000,000			
Loan of two millions of guilders, per contract dated March 9, 1784, at four per cent. per ann.[52]	2,000,000			
Loan of one million of guilders, per contract dated June 1, 1787, at five per cent. per ann.[53]	1,000,000			
Loan of one million of guilders, per contract dated March 13, 1788, at five per cent. per annum,[54]	1,000,000			
Premiums to the lenders and gratifications on the loan of two millions,[55] 837,500				
From which deduct this amount paid out of funds obtained by the late government, 180,000				
	657,500			
		9,657,500.		

51. For a description of the 1782 Holland loan of five million guilders, see Willink, Van Staphorst, and Hubbard to H, January 25, 1790, note 15.

52. For a description of the 1784 Holland loan of two million guilders, see H to Short, September 1, 1790, note 22.

53. For a description of the 1787 Holland loan of one million guilders, see H to Short, September 1, 1790, note 24.

BY THE PRESENT GOVERNMENT.

Loan of three millions of guilders, per contract dated February 1, 1790, at five per cent. per ann.[56]		3,000,000
Loan of two and a half millions of guilders, per contract dated March 2, 1791, at five per cent. per annum,[57]		2,500,000
Loan of six millions of guilders, per contract dated December 14, 1791, at five per cent. per annum,[58]		6,000,000
Loan of three millions of guilders, per contract dated December 24, 1791, at four per cent. per annum,[59]		3,000,000
Loan of three millions of guilders, per contract dated August 9, 1792, at four per cent. per annum,[60]	3,000,000	
Deduct this sum not received	50,000	
		2,950,000

54. For a description of the 1788 Holland loan of one million guilders, see H to Short, September 1, 1790, note 25.

55. See note 52.

56. For a description of the 1790 Holland loan of three million guilders, see Willink, Van Staphorst, and Hubbard to H, January 25, 1790, and H to Willink, Van Staphorst, and Hubbard, November 29, 1970, note 1.

57. For a description of the 1791 Holland loan of two and one-half million guilders, see Short to H, August 31, 1791.

58. For a description of the 1791 Holland loan for six million guilders, see Short to H, August 31, 1791.

59. For a description of the December, 1791, Holland loan of three million guilders, see Short to H, December 23, 28, 1791.

60. For a description of the 1792 Holland loan of three million guilders, see Short to H, June 28, 1792, note 17.

Loan of one million of guilders, at five per cent. per annum, being a reloan of the instalment due on June 1, 1793,[61] on the loan of five millions, per contracts dated June 11, 1782,	1,000,000			
		18,450,000.		
		28,107,500.		
On account of which debt, there had been paid on the 31st of Dec. 1793, by Wilhem and Jan Willink, Nicholas and Jacob van Staphorst and Hubbard, of Amsterdam.				
For premiums which fell due in the years 1791 and 1793, on the loan of two millions obtained by the contract dated March 9, 1794,[62]	190,000			
Instalment which fell due on the 1st of June, 1793, on the loan of five millions of guilders obtained by the contracts dated June 11, 1782,	1,000,000			
		1,190,000.		
Balance due for monies received on contracts made in Holland previous to Dec. 31, 1793,		26,917,500.	at 40 *Cents.*	10,767,000.
		28,107,500.		

DEBT CONTRACTED IN ANTWERP BY THE PRESENT GOVERNMENT, VIZ.

Loan of three millions of guilders, per contract dated November 30,

61. For a description of the 1793 Holland loan, see Willink, Van Staphorst, and Hubbard to H, May 1, 1793.

62. This is an error. It should read "1784."

1791, at four and a half per cent. per annum, amount received (950,000 guilders having been suppressed)[63]	2,050,000.		
Remaining due on the 31st of December, 1793,	2,050,000.	at 40 *Cents.*	820,000.

DEBT CONTRACTED IN SPAIN BY THE LATE GOVERNMENT.

		Dolls. Cts.	
Amount due to the Government of Spain on the 21st of March, 1782,[64] bearing interest at five per cent. per annum, as stated by the late Commissioner for settling foreign accounts,		174,011.	
Interest which fell due before and in the year 1790,		76,371.50	
Interest from January 21, 1791, to August 21, 1793, when said debt is considered as having been finally discharged, agreeably to an account received from Holland,		17,651.12	
		268,033.62	
Which debt is considered as discharged by remittances made to the Government of Spain, by Wilhem and Jan Willink, Nicholas and Jacob van Staphorst and Hubbard, of Amsterdam, Guilders	615,307.11.3	268,033.62	
Amount of the foreign debt of the United States on the 31st of December, 1793, agreeably to statements made at the Treasury, including sums which had been received for the proceeds of loans and which remained unexpended, and the balances of foreign funds transferred to the United States, which are comprised in the statement of unsatisfied appropriations payable at the Treasury,			14,198,789.55

STATEMENT EXHIBITING THE RECEIPT OF MONIES ON LOANS EFFECTED IN EUROPE ON ACCOUNT OF THE UNITED STATES UNDER THE PRESENT GOVERNMENT, AND OF THE EXPENDITURE THEREOF, TO THE 31st DECEMBER, 1793.

SUMS RECEIVED, VIZ.

Received by W. & J. Willink, N. & J. van Staphorst & Hubbard, at Amsterdam. balance remaining unexpended of the proceeds of loans under the late government, agreeably to a statement of their accounts at the Treasury,	331,188.5.13

63. For a description of the 1791 Antwerp loan, see Short to H, November 8, 1791, note 4, and November 12, 1791.

64. For a description of the United States debt to Spain, see H to Short, September 1, 1790, note 12; Joseph Nourse to H, October 9, 1792; Short to H, February 25, 1793, note 13.

remittance by the Secretary of the Treasury, in the year 1790, out of the funds of the present government,		100,000.	
on a loan of 3,000,000 guilders, per contract dated Feb. 1, 1790,	3,000,000.		
do. of 2,500,000 Mar. 2, 1791,	2,500,000.		
do. of 6,000,000 Dec. 14, 1791,	6,000,000.		
do. of 3,000,000 Dec. 24, 1791,	3,000,000.		
do. of 3,000,000 Aug. 9, 1792,	2,950,000.		
do. of 1,000,000 being a reloan of the first instalment due on the first of June, 1793, on the loan of 5,000,000 guilders, per contracts dated June 11, 1782,	1,000,000.		
		18,450,000.	
remittances by the Secretary of the Treasury in the year 1793, out of proceeds of foreign loans transferred to the United States, which remittances cost 203,669 30/100 dollars, and produced		536,565.4	
			19,417,753.9.13
Received by C. J. M. de Wolf, at Antwerp,			
on a loan of 3,000,000 guilders, per contract dated November 30th, 1791,		2,050,000.	
for bills drawn on W. & J. Willink, N. & J. van Staphorst & Hubbard, of Amsterdam, to enable him to pay the interest due on December, 1792, guilders 88,941.9. which produced,		91,913.15.	
for bills drawn on Amsterdam, to enable him to pay the interest due on December, 1st, 1793, 86,514.1.8. the product of which at Antwerp is not ascertained,		86,514.1.8	
			2,228,427.16.8
		Guilders,	21,646,181.6.9

SUMS EXPENDED, VIZ.

Expended by W. & J. Willink, N. & J. van Staphorst & Hubbard, at Amsterdam.	
on account of the debt due from the United States to France,	8,105,043.8.
on account of the debt due from the United States to Spain,	615,307.11.8
for an advance to Governeur Morris, on account of the interest on the debt due to certain foreign officers,[65]	105,000.
for an advance to Major General La Fayette, on account of his pay and emoluments,	10,000.
for the payment of bills of exchange drawn by the Treasurer of the United States,	5,154,621.2.8

65. See note 26.

for the instalment due on the first of June, 1793, on the loan of five millions under the late government,	1,000,000.	
for premiums drawn by lottery, in 1791 and 1793, by the lenders of two millions, ditto,	190,000.	
Expended for interest which fell due in the year 1790, on the Dutch debt, commission on payment and expenses of postage,	348,818.10.	
for charges of effecting the loans under the present government, commission on payment of premiums drawn by lottery, brokerage on remittances to France and Spain, and on remittances from the United States,	831,871.7.	
for bills drawn by C. J. M. de Wolf, in 1792 and 1793, for interest due on the Antwerp loan,	175,455.10.8	
for interest which fell due in the years 1791, 1792 and 1793, on the Dutch debt, commission on payment, expenses of postage and of advertising in said years the payment of interest,	2,788,158.5.9	
		19,324,275.15.1
Expended by C. J. M. de Wolf, at Antwerp, on account of the debt due from the United States to France,	1,975,375.13.	
for the payment of the charges of effecting the loan at Antwerp, and brokerage on payments to France,	82,499.7.	
for interest which fell due in the years 1792 and 1793, on the loan at Antwerp, commission on the negociation of bills drawn on the commissioners in Amsterdam, and expenses of postage in 1791 and 1792,	176,353.8.	
		2,234,228.8.
		21,558,504.3.1
Balance remaining unexpended on December 31st, 1793, of loans obtained before that period, agreeably to accounts stated at the Treasury, viz.		
In the hands of W. & J. Willink, N. & J. van Staphorst & Hubbard,	93,477.14.12	
From which is deducted balance stated to be due to C. J. M. de Wolf,	5,800.11.4	
		87,677.3.8
	Guilders,	21,646,181.6.9

From John Wendell[1]

Portsmouth [New Hampshire] Decr. 26th 1794

Respected Sir

It is with great Reluctance that I address myself again to you on the Subject of Monsr Dumons Memorial which I presented several Congresses & which was committed to you for yr. Consultation & Report.[2] I am conscious that I have tresspesed upon your Important Station when so many Matters of public Exigencies call for yr most attentive Exertions but I have submitted with patience & Subserviency to more important Avocations Until I find that you had determined to retire[3] & injoy an Otium cum Dignitate and that the injurious Calumnies of intriguing Men had induced you to quit the public Exercise of yr Department longer than the last of next Month. Your previous Annunciation of this Event and yr oblique Challenge to your Enemies to come forward with every Proof of Insinuating Aspersions,[4] has done you Honour And your Services will immortalize yr. Name with Posterity, but I fear the public Revenue will receive such a Stabb as may occasion a deep Wound not easily to be healed, as one Individual of the Community give me Leave to wish you Happiness & the Injoyment of Health during a good Old Age.

With Respect to Mr Dumons Affair There is with the Papers a considerable Sum of Continental Money—of the very first Impression which I hope will be taken Care of as my Friend Mr Gerry[5] put it in on purpose to prove the Facts. I know it is a discouraging Time to seek Retribution or Compensation, but I wish your Report if even to reject the Memorial if you could Annex a Clause that it might be revived under some other Form.[6] If it shd be productive ⟨–⟩ of Embarrasments to Congress by granting the Prayer of the Petition, yet fiat Justitia, ruat Cœlum is an Established Maxim of Equity. I salute you with the Compliments of the Season and with Sentiments of Respect and Esteem I am

Sir Your most Obedt Hb Servt John Wendell

Honble A Hamilton Esqre.
Philadelphia

ALS, Hamilton Papers, Library of Congress.

1. Wendell was a merchant in Portsmouth, New Hampshire.

2. On December 21, 1791, the House of Representatives received "A petition of Jean Baptist Dumon, son and heir of Jean Baptist Dumon, deceased, late of Canada, merchant, praying to be reimbursed certain advances made by the deceased, for the support of the American Army, and also for losses and injuries sustained, both in his person and property, by adhering to the American cause, during the late war" (*Journal of the House*, I, 479). See H to Wendell, August 30, 1792.

3. See H to George Washington, December 1, 1794, and H to Frederick A. C. Muhlenberg, December 1, 1794.

4. See H to Muhlenberg, December 1, 1794.

5. Elbridge Gerry had been a member of the House of Representatives from Massachusetts from March 4, 1789, to March 3, 1793.

6. On January 12, 1795, the House resolved that Dumon's petition could not be granted (*Journal of the House*, II, 411). Dumon presented his petition again on December 16, 1796, and was again refused on January 11, 1797 (*Journal of the House*, II, 620, 644). Wendell introduced the petition on February 1, 1798, and requested that the House reconsider its decision. The petition was laid on the table, and no record has been found of any further action by the House (*Journal of the House*, III, 157).

From Oliver Wolcott, Junior[1]

TD

C. Off 26th Decemr. 1794

Sir

I have the honour to transmit a Statement of the Rects. & Expenditures of The United States for the year 1793 which has been prepared pursuant to the Order of the House of Representatives passed on the 30th. of Dece. 1791.[2]

To this Statement an Appendix has been added, exhibiting the operation of the Fund for reducing the Domestic Debt, to the close of the year 1793, also statements of the Foreign & Domestic Debts & of the Expenditure of Foreign Loans obtained under the present Government, to the same period.

Five hundred Copies of this work being the number heretofore directed by the house of Representatives,[3] have been printed and will be delivered to the Clerk of the House.

I am &c

The Hon
A.H.

ADf, Connecticut Historical Society, Hartford; copy, RG 233, Reports of the Secretary of the Treasury, 1784–1795, Vol. IV, National Archives.

1. A copy of this letter was enclosed in H's "Report on Receipts and Expenditures for the Year 1793," December 26, 1794.

2. The order reads as follows: "*Resolved,* That it shall be the duty of the Secretary of the Treasury to lay before the House of Representatives, on the fourth Monday of October in each year, if Congress shall be then in session, or if not then in session, within the first week of the session next following the said fourth Monday of October, an accurate statement and account of the receipts and expenditures of all public moneys, down to the last day inclusively of the month of December immediately preceding the said fourth Monday of October, distinguishing the amount of the receipts in each State or District, and from each officer therein; in which statements shall also be distinguished the expenditures which fall under each head of appropriation, and shall be shown the sums, if any, which remain unexpended, and to be accounted for in the next statement, of each and every of such appropriations" (*Journal of the House,* I, 484).

3. On December 19, 1793, the House of Representatives had ordered: "That five hundred copies of the said account of receipts and expenditures [for 1792] be printed under the direction of the Treasury Department, for the use of the members of both Houses" (*Journal of the House,* II, 17).

From Tench Coxe[1]

T: D: R: O: Decbr. 27. 1794

Sir

I enclose to you, a letter to me from Tench Francis Esqr. this moment received, as the explanation of his application of yesterday for Cash. *You will observe he now requires 35,000 Dols.*

You will perceive that it would be necessary to my expressing an opinion, 1st That a statement of the business between the Treasy. & the Agent has been furnished with your letter of the 4th of April[2] committing to me with certain reservations & restrictions the business of the Treasury for the War Department. 2dly That all the orders for expenditure by Mr. Francis should have been made through this Office or at least made known to it. This, from the press of business it is presumed, has not been the case. These circumstances and the 3d paragraph of your letter reserving the money matters to yourself, have occasioned me not to give an opinion upon Mr. Francis's applications for Cash, but only to transmit them to your Office.

I am Sir &ca T: Coxe C. R.

The Secy. of the Treasy.

LC, RG 75, Letters of Tench Coxe, Commissioner of the Revenue, Relating to the Procurement of Military, Naval, and Indian Supplies, National Archives.

1. For background to this letter, see Coxe to H, second letter of December 26, 1794.

2. Letter not found.

To Robert Purviance[1]

Treasury Department December 27th 1794

Sir,

The President of the United States having been pleased to pardon and remit to Munnikhuysen & Sadler, Owners of the Schooner Martha the Offence and Penalty incurred by them by the Captain's permitting certain goods to be laden on board the said Schooner in the Island of St. Domingo, contrary to the intent and meaning of an Embargo Bond given by them to your predecessor in Office[2]—I have to request that in pursuance of the said Pardon duly filed in this Office, You will proceed to cancel the Embargo Bond given by the Parties as aforesaid. A Duplicate of my remission in the case of the Taffia & Molasses imported in the Schooner Martha has been already transmitted to the District Judge.[3]

I am with consideration Sir Your most obedient servant

A Hamilton

Robert Purviance Esquire

LS, Columbia University Libraries.

1. For background to this letter, see H to Purviance, August 18, 1794.

2. Otho H. Williams.

3. H's remission of the penalties and forfeitures, dated December 18, 1794, reads in part as follows: "Whereas a Statement of facts with the Petition of Munnikhuysen and Sadler Owners of the Schooner Martha of Baltimore thereunto annexed touching a certain penalties and forfeitures incurred under the Statutes of the United States . . . was on the twelfth day of September last transmitted to me . . . by direction of the Judge of the United States for the District of Maryland [William Paca] . . . Now therefore know ye that I the said Secretary of the Treasury . . . have decided to remit and by these presents do remit to the said Munnikhuysen & Sadler all the right claim & demand of the United States . . . to the said penalties and forfeitures. . ." (DS, RG 59, Miscellaneous Letters of the Department of State, 1790–1799, National Archives; copy, Columbia University Libraries).

Four days after H's remission of penalties and forfeitures in this case, William Bradford wrote: "I am of the opinion that the penalty incurred by the petitioners may be remitted & the offence pardoned by the President of the United States" (ADS, RG 59, Miscellaneous Letters of the Department of State, 1790–1799, National Archives).

To Joseph Ball[1]

Treasury Department
Decr. 28. 1794

The Secretary of the Treasury presents his Compliments to Mr. Ball Chairman of a Committee of the Bank of The UStates. He would propose that the three hundred thousand Dollars remaining unpaid of the 400000 loan[2] should be paid in three equal installments on the first of November December and January. The point of credits for bills deposited is reserved for further consideration but will be arranged before Mr. Hamilton leaves the Office.[3]

AL, Yale University Library.

1. Ball, in addition to being a director of the Bank of the United States, was a Philadelphia merchant.

2. For information on the four hundred thousand dollar loan, see H to the President and Directors of the Bank of the United States, September 24, 1794, note 2.

3. See H to George Washington, December 1, 1794; H to Frederick A. C. Muhlenberg, December 1, 1794.

A note at the bottom of this letter in an unidentified handwriting reads: "acceded to by the board."

From Tench Coxe

[Philadelphia] Sunday Morning Decr. 28th. 1794

Sir

I finished yesterday my letter relative to the Arrangements for procuring the timber from Geora. having commenced the same on Christmas day in Consequence of the receipt of your letter of that date.[1] This last communication (which it will require two days to copy) and that made under the date of the 22d. inst. concerning the naval armament[2] in consequence of the order of the House of Representatives[3] together with the other business for the war department have entirely engrossed my time for the last ten days.

It is in my Judgment indespensibly necessary, that the business committed by law to this office[4] & the light House Business should receive my particular attention during the month prior to your resignation.[5] Your calls from the Seat of Government which occured in August[6] October & November[7] & ⟨your occupation in⟩[8] the interval between those calls in attention to the Western Insurrection have naturally increased the general reasons for this desire on my part. To these are to be added the weighty considerations enforcing that desire, which result from my great occupation since the 4th. of April by the Business of the War Department,[9] and from the disorders in the Business of the Revenue produced by insurrection opposition and the imperfections of the laws, and arrangements. The Resignation of the Secy. at War[10] affords many reasons for my wishing to make ⟨a⟩ complete arrangement of all that has been done in 1794, before he shall depart from the Seat of Government. If he should conceive that any thing remains to be done which considering the limitations of my power and your participation in the Business I ought to have effected, it will be my wish to have time & opportunity to perform it before he shall return home, and you shall retire from your public station.

I have therefore from a reflected sense of duty to request that the Business of the Treasury for the War department so far as it has lain with me may be considered as not in my hands after the 31st. of Decemr. instant. This I presume will not appear unreasonable taking the foregoing ideas into view & when it is remembered that it was transferred to me on the 4th. of April upon an hour's Notice & conference in the afternoon of that day[11] and that it was agreed in a conversation between us three Months ago that it should be transfered from my office.[12]

On due reflexion I have not deemed it adviseable for me to engage Mr. Francis in a general agency for all the States[13] without a written Authorization from you, tho with your oral permission. The circumstances which occasion you to wish not ⟨to⟩ appear to do it, and some others drawn from his relationship to me, influence my views of the subject.

I have the honor to be Sir Yr. obedt. st. T. C——

Secy. of Try.

ADfS, Tench Coxe Papers, Historical Society of Pennsylvania, Philadelphia; LC, RG 58, Letters of Commissioner of Revenue, 1794–1795, National Archives.

1. H's letter of December 25 has not been found. Presumably Coxe is referring to a letter from H dated December 24, 1794, which has not been found. See Coxe to H, December 25–27, 1794.

2. For information on the naval armament, see Henry Knox to H, April 21, 1794.

3. For the order of the House of Representatives, see Coxe to H, December 22, 1794, note 2.

4. Coxe is referring to "An Act making alterations in the Treasury and War Departments" (1 *Stat.* 279–81 [May 8, 1792]). See H to Coxe, April 4, 1794.

5. See H to George Washington, December 1, 1794.

6. Coxe is mistaken, for H was absent from Philadelphia not in August, but for part of July, 1794. See H to Washington, July 11, 23, 1794; Washington to H, July 11, 1794; H to Elizabeth Hamilton, July 31, 1794.

7. On September 30 H left Philadelphia with Washington for western Pennsylvania. See H to Washington, September 24, 1794, note 2.

8. Material within broken brackets has been taken from the letter book copy in the National Archives.

9. This is a reference to the work in the Treasury Department in carrying out the naval armament and the fortifications of ports. See Knox to H, March 29, April 21, 1794.

10. On December 28, 1794, Knox wrote to Washington that he would resign as Secretary of War on December 31, 1794 (LS, George Washington Papers, Library of Congress).

11. See H to Coxe, April 3, 4, 1794.

12. See also Coxe to H, December 4, 1794.

13. Tench Francis. See Coxe to H, December 10, 1794.

To Tench Coxe

[*Philadelphia, December 28, 1794.* On December 30, 1794, Coxe wrote to Hamilton and referred to "your letter of the 28th inst." *Letter not found.*]

To William Rawle

Treasury Department
December 28. 1794

Sir

Mr. Delaney has obtained information as to the fitting out of some privateers[1] from this & a neighbouring port which I have desired him to communicate to you without delay. The most delicate considerations render it essential that whatever is now practicable should be done. Pray give the matter the most particular attention.[2]

With consideration & esteem I am Sir Your obed serv

A Hamilton

William Rawle Esq
Atty of the District of Pennsylvania

ALS, Historical Society of Pennsylvania, Philadelphia.

1. Sharp Delany was collector of customs at Philadelphia. The information which had been obtained concerned three privateers. See H to Delaney, January 20, 1795. One privateer is described as follows in a circular letter from Timothy Pickering to the governors of the states, dated January 6, 1795: "A ship called Les . . . [Jumeaux], (or the Twins) Captain Ruault, armed and equipped in the port of Philadelphia as a cruizer, contrary to our neutrality and the law of the United States in such cases provided, has lately escaped from the river Delaware. It appears by the report of the officers employed to seize her, that she sailed from Bombay Hook the 2d instant.

"The proof is positive that the ship has been unlawfully fitted out as above mentioned. A description of her and her equipments, so far as known is enclosed. As the necessity of concealment prevented her completing her equipments in such manner as to commence an immediate cruize, it is probable that in order to complete them she will put into some port in the Chesapeake or other port in the United States.

"It is therefore the request of the President of the United States that you will cause the requisite measures to be taken for seizing the above mentioned ship, with her tackle, furniture, and stores, and also for apprehending the Captain. . . ." (Pickering to Robert Brooke [*Calendar of Virginia State Papers*, VII, 417–18]; Pickering to John Hoskins Stone [Roger Thomas, ed., *Calendar of Maryland State Papers, No. 3: The Brown Books* (Annapolis, 1948), VI, 150].)

On May 11, 1795, John Etienne Guinet and John Baptist Le Maitre were found guilty on charges of "furnishing, fitting-out and arming a certain ship or vessel called Les Jumeaux. . ." (Wharton, *State Trials*, 93–101). The name of *Les Jumeaux* was changed to *Le Cassius,* and the dispute with the French government over the detention of the ship and the conviction of Guinet and Le Maitre continued until December, 1796 (*ASP, Foreign Relations*, I, 629–39).

The second privateer was presumably the *General Greene*, which Walter Stewart, surveyor of the District of Pennsylvania, referred to in a letter to Delany on December 18, 1794. Stewart's letter reads as follows: "I think it proper to inform you that the General Green Schooner Capt. Hodge, laying at the Three stores in Kensington has undergone a thorough repair & although she had no ports when she arrived, is now pierced for five guns on each side" (copy, Division of Public Records, Pennsylvania Historical and Museum Commission, Harrisburg).

2. Rawle endorsed this letter: "ansd." Letter not found, but see Rawle to H, December 29, 1794.

From Tench Coxe

Treasury Department, Revenue Office, December 29, 1794. "I beg the favor of a payment as usual on account, to the Superintendent of the Delaware Light House,[1] & the establishments for the Shipping to the amount of three hundred & eighty five Dollars.[2] It is to enable him to discharge, the accounts which will become due on or before the 31st instant."

LC, RG 26, Lighthouse Letters, Vol. I, National Archives.

1. William Allibone was superintendent of lighthouses, beacons, buoys, and public piers for Philadelphia, Cape Henlopen, and Delaware Bay.

2. A warrant for this sum was issued to Allibone on December 31, 1794 (RG 217, Miscellaneous Treasury Accounts, 1790–1894, Account No. 6467, National Archives).

From Tench Coxe[1]

Treasury Department, Revenue Office, December 29, 1794. "I enclose copy of a letter from Wm Pennock Esqr. Naval Agent at Norfolk Virginia with an estimate of money wanted to the amount of 7450 Drs exclusive of the freight of Timber from Georgia. . . ."

LC, RG 75, Letters of Tench Coxe, Commissioner of the Revenue, Relating to the Procurement of Military, Naval, and Indian Supplies, National Archives.

1. This letter concerns the naval armament. See Henry Knox to H, April 21, 1794.

To Tench Coxe

Treasury Department, December 29, 1794. "In answer to your letter of the 26 instant, I remark, that it is not clear the words 'the thirtieth day of June next' may not be understood as equivalent to the '*next thirtieth* day of June'[1] which last would conform to the known intent of the Legislature. At least this is a point to be referred to the President. It will naturally come up when the new arrangement of compensations is presented to his consideration."

ALS, RG 58, General Records, 1791–1803, National Archives.

1. H is referring to Section 13 of "An Act making further provision for securing and collecting the Duties on foreign and domestic Spirits, Stills, Wines and Teas" (1 *Stat.* 380 [June 5, 1794]). For this section, see Coxe to H, July 15, 1794, note 4.

To Tench Coxe

Treasury Depart December 29. 1794

Sir

I have received your two letters of the 13th & 28 instant.

I think my conduct must have proved to you that it has not been my intention to impute to you blame for any delays or deficiencies, which may have existed or which may exist in the execution of those portions of the business of the Department which are confided to you. I have resolved them into the natural effects of an extensive and diversified scene of occupation—not, as I conceived, beyond the practicability of such a discharge of the trusts reposed in you as would essentially fulfil the objects of the public service, with exertion and an exclusive attention to them—but of magnitude and difficulty sufficient to render partial defects and omissions probable and if they happened intitled to be exempt from censure. In conformity with this impression, I have meant to treat all such as have fallen under my observation.

But while I have foreborne to draw conclusions on the subject to your prejudice I cannot be expected to be willing to acquiesce in a transfer of the responsibility for any delays or deficiencies which may have occurred from you to me—more than facts will really warrant. I am not sure that any such transfer is aimed at by any of the suggestions contained in your letter, but there are some of them which seem to me capable of bearing the construction and I have concluded not by my silence to give sanction to it.

You appeal to me for your having proposed an arrangement of the business of compensations to the officers of Inspection before the President's departure for Mount Vernon in the last summer; and you observe that since that period the attention of the President & myself to the urgent busi⟨nes⟩s[1] of the insurrection, with the absences incidental ther⟨eto,⟩ left no opportunity for the object.

I have some though an imperfect recollection of your having made the proposal you state—but my memory, if I may trust it, also informs me that upon conferring together, besides ⟨the⟩ obstacles which the state of the business before the President at the time may have presented, we were both of opinion, that it would conduce to a proper arrangement to obtain beforehand the ideas which the experience of the Supervisors might furnish on the subject, and indeed that this information ought to precede the arrangement; and that accordingly you undertook to write them a circular letter for the purpose. So that the state of the Presidents business immediately preceding his departure was but a *circumstance* in the postponement.

It is true also that the affair of the Insurrection occupied much of the time and atten⟨tion⟩ both of the President and myself; but I am not conscious that I ever declined going into the arrangement of the compensations on this account and I feel persuaded that if you had matured and prepared the materials, I should have made time and opportunity to cooperate with you in their application. Nor do I doubt that the President would have bestowed the necessary attention on his part. The only effect then of this situation (of which I am at present sensible) is that it withdrew my attention from an *active* or *anticipating* pursuit of the object. I must add too that since my return from the Westward I first spoke of the subject to you and had occasion to repeat it verbally before you presented to me for consideration the requisite materials—and my impression was that your avocations, especially with regard to the revenue laws & the navy business,[2] ha⟨d⟩ prevented you even to so late a period from maturing your own ideas on the matter

In your letter of the 28th you again allude, as among the causes of some derangement or extreme present pressure of your business, to my absences from the seat of government in August October and November and to my occupation in the interval of those calls in attention to the Western Insurrection.

My absence in August (You must mean July) lasted about a fortnight. As to my absences In October and November you were informed that Mr. Woolcott[3] was to act in my stead during those absences. As to military and naval supplies you had the greatest part of the time the Secretary at War to advise with. With a representative of me on the spot, with no particular restrictions on the freedom of your conduct, I do not readily ⟨per⟩ceive that these absences ought to have been material interruptions of the business in your charge.

I make these observations with reluctance & merely to avoid the appearance of admitting by silence what may be hereafter liable to misconstruction. I assure you sincerely that I do not mean to imply the least blame upon you or to intimate that there has been any exceptionable deficiency on your part. On the point of leaving the department, as I am,[4] it is more than ordinarily my wish to avoid any thing like official collision.

As you urge it, I consent that your charge ⟨of the busine⟩ss of military ⟨supplies⟩ cease after ⟨the⟩ end of this month. I ⟨reque⟩st that ⟨you will commit⟩ to the agency of Mr. ⟨Francis⟩[5] what regards ⟨the⟩ frigates—continuing for a time ⟨to⟩ assist him with information which the past course of the business may ren⟨der⟩ indispensable. I also will communicate with you on the subject. ⟨The⟩ residue of this business of military supplies, I will myself resume the management of while I stay in office. You will make known this change of the arrangement to all the subordinate Agents.

With consideration I am Sir Your obedt servant Alex Hamilton

⟨Tench⟩ Coxe Esquire

ALS, RG 58, Records of the Bureau of Internal Revenue, General Records, 1791–1803, National Archives; copy, Connecticut Historical Society, Hartford.

1. The material within broken brackets has been taken from the copy in the Connecticut Historical Society.

2. H is referring to the naval armament in 1794. See Henry Knox to H, April 21, 1794. See also H to Coxe, April 4, 1794.

3. See H to Oliver Wolcott, Jr., September 29, 1794.

4. See H to George Washington, December 1, 1794; H to Frederick A. C. Muhlenberg, December 1, 1794.

5. Tench Francis. See Coxe to H, May 14, 1794, note 1.

To Thomas Pinckney

Treasury Department
December 29th. 1794

Sir

The Treasurer [1] has been directed to remit to you a Bill on our commissioners [2] at Amsterdam for 303,115 Florins.[3]

It appears upon more particular examination that it would not leave in the hands of the Commissioners a sufficient sum for payment of interest to the first of March inclusively, which was the intention.

I request therefore that you will so arrange the matter as that there be left in their hands a sum adequate to the above object. If before this gets to hand the whole amount of the Bill should have been drawn to England, you will authorise the commissioners, to redraw for as much as they may require for the object.

With great respect & Esteem I am Sir Your Obedient Servt
Alexander Hamilton

Thomas Pinkney Esquire
Minister Plenipotentiary
In his absence The Chargé des affaires [4]
of the United States
London

LS (marked triplicate), Thomas Pinckney Papers, Library of Congress.

1. Samuel Meredith.
2. Willink, Van Staphorst, and Hubbard.
3. See H to John Quincy Adams, December 1, 1794.
4. William Allen Deas.

From William Rawle

[*Philadelphia, December 29, 1794.* On January 2, 1795, Edmund Randolph wrote to George Hammond[1] "respecting the privateer Gemeaux"[2] and enclosing a "Copy of a letter from Mr. Rawle, Dist. Atty. of Pennsyla. to the Secretary of the Treasury dated 29th Decemr. 1794." *Letter not found.*]

1. LC, RG 59, Domestic Letters of the Department of State, Vol. 8, December 6, 1794–October 12, 1795, National Archives.
2. See H to Rawle, December 28, 1794, note 1.

To Wilhem and Jan Willink, Nicholaas and Jacob Van Staphorst, and Nicholas Hubbard

[*Philadelphia, December 29, 1794.* On June 10, 1795, Willink, Van Staphorst, and Hubbard wrote to Oliver Wolcott, Jr., Secretary of the Treasury, and referred to letters "from your Predecessor of 29 December and 25 January."[1] *Letter of December 29, 1794, not found.*]

1. LS, Connecticut Historical Society, Hartford.

From Tench Coxe[1]

T: D: R. O: Decbr. 30th 1794

(private)

Sir

I trust that the first reason suggested, in your letter of the 28th inst.[2] is that which has occasioned the letter it returned to me. It appeared indispensable that you should see it, as Mr. Francis found himself impelled to shew it to me, & requested advice.

Messr. N: H: & Co.[3] have had two or three Agencies for the purchase of Objects of no great size, which have been terminated. They were similar to those they had executed in your time, and in pursuance of the information you communicated that they had been so employed. There is no evidence of any thing improper in those matters. I believe there is no public trust in their hands at this moment under the Treasury or indeed within my knowledge.

I am, Sir, &ca T: Coxe C: R:

The Secy. of the Treasy.

LC, RG 75, Letters of Tench Coxe, Commissioner of the Revenue, Relating to the Procurement of Military, Naval, and Indian Supplies, National Archives.

1. For background to this letter, see Coxe to H, second letter of December 26, 1794.

2. Letter not found.

3. Nicholas Hoffman and Company of New York City. See Coxe to H, June 23, 1794.

From Tench Coxe[1]

Treasury Department
Revenue-office, Decemr 30th 1794

Sir,

I shall apply myself to the draughting the plan of Revenue for the President as fast as possible. In the mean time such is the press of Business that to prepare it in a form, which may not eventually be adopted, will be to be regreted.

I therefore request the favor of your obtaining the sense of the President upon the point.

As the Revenue or Excise has been a topic of public feeling, as the legislature is in Session, and as I in draughting the bill meant the words to apply to the month of June which should next ensue and moreover as the verbage used in the laws wherein a day is designated is uniformly variant from this, and clear, I submit an opinion of the inexpediency of risquing the construction which refers "*next*" to the day and not to the month.

With great respect, I am, Sir Your most obedient servant,

Tench Coxe
Commissr. of the revenue

The Secretary of the Treasury

LC, RG 58, Letters of Commissioner of Revenue, 1794–1795, National Archives.

1. For background to this letter, see Coxe to H, July 15, 1794, note 4, December 13, 26, 1794; H to Coxe, December 9, 29, 1794.

To Thomas Pinckney[1]

Treasury Department December 30th 1794

Sir.

It has been determined to import from Europe as expeditiously as may be, Twenty Anchors for the use of the Six Frigates for which provision was made in the last Session of Congress.[2]

I have been induced therefore to take the liberty of asking your care of the business and to request that you will without delay cause the number of Anchors required to be procured and shipped agreeably to the Memmorandum transmitted to you herewith. If direct conveyances should not immediately offer for the several Ports in the United States designated in the Memmorandum, I would then advise the shipping of them in four divisions—Those for instance intended for Norfolk might go to Baltimore Those for Portsmouth to Boston, and so *Vice Versa.* There being a material difference however in the size of the Anchors, it will be necessary in order to avoid confusion, that there be not only Seperate bills of loading for each parcel but that the names of the respective places to which they are destined should be marked thereon.

The proceeds of the Treasurer's draught for Three Hundred and three thousand One Hundred and fifteen Guilders on our Commissioners in Amsterdam[3] remitted to you on the first instant[4] will form the fund out of which you are to pay for the Anchors—but least from the progress of military events in the Netherlands[5] you might not have been able to negotiate the bill, or that any delay should arise in the business—it would then be most adviseable to purchase the Anchors immediately on the credit of the United States and either draw upon the Treasury for the amount or engage Remittance to be made from it.[6]

I shall only add that it will be necessary to insure the amount of the Invoice, so as not to subject the United States to any loss—and that in the Shipment, a preference ought to be given to American Bottoms, unless reasons to the contrary should occur on the spot of which an estimate cannot before hand be formed here.

With the most perfect respect and truest esteem, I have the Honor to be Sir Your most Obedient Servant

Alexander Hamilton

Thomas Pinckney Esquire
Minister Plenipotentiary
at the Court of London

Typescript furnished by the South Carolina Historical Society, Charleston, and taken from the original owned by Mr. Beverly Middleton, Charleston.

1. For background to this letter, see Tench Coxe to H, June 25, first letter of July 5, December 8, first letter of December 26, 1794; H to Pinckney, June 25, July 12, 1794.

2. The construction of the frigates was authorized by "An Act to provide a Naval Armament" (1 *Stat.* 350–51 [March 27, 1794]). For information on the naval armament, see Henry Knox to H, April 21, 1794, note 1.

3. Willink, Van Staphorst, and Hubbard.

4. See H to John Quincy Adams, December 1, 1794, note 3; H to Pinckney, December 1, 1794.

5. See Nicholaas Van Staphorst to H, October 4, 1794, note 5.

6. Pinckney's account with the United States for the purchase of articles for the naval armament may be found in RG 217, Miscellaneous Treasury Accounts, 1790–1894, Account No. 10234, National Archives.

From Edmund Randolph

Philadelphia, December 30th. 1794.

Dear Sir

I am sorry to trouble you so often upon the same subject but Mr. Fauchet so constantly presses me and urges the right to arm merchant vessels for the mere purpose of defending them and their cargoes,[1] that I must take the liberty of reminding you of your promise to send me not only the Instructions which have been given from the Treasury department to the Collectors in relation to this subject,[2] but also the Draft of another letter which you were preparing upon the same point.[3]

With great regard, I am, Dear Sir, &c: Edm: Randolph

LC, RG 59, Domestic Letters of the Department of State, Vol. 8, December 6, 1794–October 12, 1795, National Archives.

1. On December 9, 1794, Randolph wrote to Jean Antoine Joseph Fauchet, the French Minister to the United States: "It was necessary for me to consult the Secretary of the Treasury upon the subject of your letter of the 12th. ultimo, before I could answer it. He yesterday assured me, that he would submit to my perusal a letter, which would contain the information desired. . ."

(LC, RG 59, Domestic Letters of the Department of State, Vol. 8, December 6, 1794–October 12, 1795, National Archives). Although Fauchet's letter of November 12, 1794, has not been found, the arming of French merchant vessels is discussed in the following letter which Fauchet wrote to Randolph on September 18, 1794: "Un Français apprend à Charleston la reprise de la Gaudeloupe. Son premier mouvement le porte à aller au secours de ses frères nouvellement arrivés; il achète une goëlette qu'il charge de provisions, son intention étant de profiter des papiers Américains du bâtiment acquis. On lui observe avec justice, que d'après les loix des Etats Unis, la translation du bâtiment dans des mains étrangères nécessite la restitution des papiers; il est donc obligé conformément aux loix Françaises, de prendre au Consulat un certificat d'acquisition pour lui servir jusqu'à son arrivée dans le premier port Français. Pour la défense de sa propriéte il met à son bord 13 cans qu'il possédait avant l'acquisition du bâtiment; il en prévient le Gouverneur de la Caroline du Sud, qui le voyant armé simplement pour sa défense et non point pour la course, ne fait aucune objection. Il part; un accident l'obligè à entrer à Norfolk; à peine arrivé on veut l'arrêter. Je vous laisse à juger de l'indignation d'un homme qui dévorant l'espace qui le séparait de ses concitoyens mourants de faim, se voit traité comme un criminel chez une Nation alliée. Il calcule chaque instant de retard qu'on lui fait éprouver, comme autant d'assissinats contre des Français menacés d'une famine prochaine. Pour mettre le comble à cette conduite inhospitalière on s'adresse au Consul de la République pour faire arrêter ce Capitaine, sans lui donner les motifs du procès qu'on intente contre lui; de manière enfin qu'on veut faire jouer au Consul le role de constable. . ." (*Correspondence of the French Ministers with the United States Government*, part 1, 20–21).

2. See "Treasury Department Circular to the Collectors of the Customs," August 4, 22, 1793; H to Isaac Holmes, September 4, 1794, note 10. See also "War Department Circular to the Governors of the States," August 18, 1794.

3. H's draft has not been found, but see H to Randolph, January 2, 1795.

From Tench Coxe

T: D: R: O: Decr. 31st 1794

Mr Coxe presents his complts. to the Secy. of the Treasy. & requests that he will be pleased to take the necessary measures for the reception of the whiskey (to be purchased for 1795) at the deposite posts of Fort Washington & Pittsburg, and wherever besides the public service may be deemed to require it to be received. A Letter this day received from Kentuckey expresses a wish that this may be particularly attended to.

LC, RG 75, Letters of Tench Coxe, Commissioner of the Revenue, Relating to the Procurement of Military, Naval, and Indian Supplies, National Archives.

From Henry Lee

Shirley near Richmond
31st. Decr. 1794.

dear sir

Forced to meander on my ride home to close as far as I could the various matters which I considered under my care I never got to Richmond until the 29th. when Col. Carrington gave to me your favor of the 19th Decr.[1]

I am sure you understand too well my conviction of your constant efforts to give comfort to the late army with me, to suppose that I could for a moment impute to want of exertion in you any disappointment to which they may have been submitted.

I will not therefore recur to that part of your letr. which explains the causes of incomplete remittance, for sure I am every possible assistance in every way has been afforded by you.[2] But I will rather try to make you as happy as you ought to be, by telling you that the money sent to Winchester answered an excellent purpose as it allayed all the discontents which Genl. Matthews[3] letr. to me, announced.

From that place I wrote to the S of W for the ballance & sent forward to the P. M. Gen[4] his deputy[5] who will I presume return charged with means & instructions unless Mr Smith may have pursued your orders of drawing bills for the money wanting.[6] In this case the D. P. master ought to return.

Mr Smith had reced. no instructions to that effect, before I left Winchester.

I hear that you certainly leave govt. in all next month.[7] I lament the event but heartily wish that it may be productive of every advantage to your family you expect, & that the affectionate gratitude of our country to whose good you have so constantly & eminently contributed may surround you in your retirement.

From me reckon always on the most affec: respect & regard. farewell

Henry Lee

ALS, Hamilton Papers, Library of Congress.

1. Letter not found, but see Edward Carrington to H, December 26, 1794.

2. For information on the problem of paying the militia army, see Carrington to H, December 26, 1794.

3. Brigadier General Thomas Matthews of the Virginia militia.

4. Edward Carrington.

5. Edward Smith, inspector of the revenue for Survey No. 5 in Virginia.

6. See H to Carrington, December 2, 1794.

7. See H to George Washington, December 1, 1794; H to Frederick A. C. Muhlenberg, December 1, 1794.

Measures in the War Department Which It May Be Expedient to Adopt

[Philadelphia, December, 1794] [1]

I To organize anew the Militia on a plan something like the following

To be divided into five clases

1 Class consisting of all unmarried men from 18 to 25 except apprentices under 21 to Merchants Mechanics and Manufacturers and students under the same age in universities colleges & academies and of Divinity Law and Medecine.

2 Class consisting of all unmarried men from 25 to 40.

3 Class consisting of all married men from 18 to 25 excepted in the first class

4 Class consisting of all married men from 25 to 40.

5 Class consisting of all men above 40 and not exceeding 50.

Each Class to be formed into corps of Infantry Artillery Cavalry combined into legions to consist of four Regiments of Infantry one Regiment of horse & a batalion of Artillery. All who choose to enter into the Cavalry & provide themselves with horses arms & accoutrements to be at liberty to do it. Each class to be called out in succession as numbered, in whole or in part, liable to serve for a year. None of a higher number to be called out until all of any preceding lower number have been called out and served their tour.

In case of domestic insurrection no man *able* to serve shall be excused on any condition.

In case of foreign war any man may be excused paying $^{50}/_{100}$ Dollars.

No militia (except those inhabiting frontier Counties) shall be obliged to serve against Indians, nor those inhabiting frontier Counties for more than [2] in one year.

Any man who shall refuse to serve his tour when required to be imprisoned during the term of service or compelled to labour at some public work, at the option of the Government.

Cases of exempts to be defined in the laws.

The respective classes to be liable to be called out for Inspection & exercise as follows:

1st Class days in a year
2 Class days in a year
3 Class days in a year
4 Class days in a year
5 Class one day in a year

The Militia, *when in service*, to be subject to the same rules of Discipline and Government as the army of the UStates.

II A Regiment to be raised consisting of commissioned officers and persons engaged as serjeants and with the pay of such; that is to say in their own corps they shall serve by rotation as serjeants corporals & privates but out of their regiment they shall only be employed as serjeants. All new Regiments which may be raised shall have their serjeants from this corps which shall have a fixed station & be carefully instructed in all the parts of Camp field & garrison service. It may be considered whether this idea may not be extended to artillery & cavalry. This corps to constitute the bones of an army in case of need.

III. To establish a *provisional* or auxiliary army composed of four Regiments of Infantry 1 Regiment of Cavalry & 1 batalion of Artillery formed into a legion of two brigades each brigade commanded by a Brigadier & the Legion by a Major General.

This Legion to be raised by voluntary inlistment, according to a certain distribution, in the following parts of the UStates—in the part of Pensylvania & Virginia lying West of the Alleghany, the N Western & S Western Governments, Kentucke South Carolina & Georgia.

The considerations of inlistment to be a suit of Cloaths of the value of ten Dollars per annum & when in the field the same pay and allowance as other troops of the UStates. To be engaged for a term of years, but except in case of Domestic Insurrection or Foreign Invasion not to be obliged to serve in the field more than months in one year.

One brigade to be raised in the Western parts of Pensylvania & Virginia the N Western Territory & the State of Kentucke. The brigadier to be immediately charged with all the Military Affairs of the UStates in that scene. The other Brigade to be raised in the other part of the Country above described with the same immediate charge to its Brigadier of the military affairs of the UStates in that scene. The Major General to have the general Direction.

IV The following miscellaneous objects to be aimed at

I The establishment of a system of trade with the Indians under the Agents of Govert.—a plan in detail for this purpose.

II The establishing it as a principle that every man in arms to attack or resist Indians except in some County under the *actual* jurisdiction of the laws shall be *ipso facto* liable to the rules for the Government of the army.

III The establishment of manufactories under public authority of Cannon Muskets & other arms Powder & Ball all articles of Cloathing except hats & shoes.

☞ The organization of the army to be revised, it is presumed to be susceptible of one more perfect.

ADf, Henry Knox Papers, Massachusetts Historical Society, Boston; copy, Hamilton Papers, Library of Congress.

1. In *JCHW*, V, 191–93, and *HCLW*, VII, 55–58, this document is printed as an enclosure to H to James McHenry, January 16, 1799.

2. This and subsequent spaces in the document left blank in MS.

From Edmund Randolph

Private

Saturday Morning [Philadelphia, December, 1794]

Dear sir

When I renewed the note for your friendly favor,[1] just before your departure for the Westward,[2] I did not take up the former one. If you have it, I will thank you for it, when it is convenient to you to send it. But I cannot close this subject, without assuring you of the sense, which I have ever entertained, of this, your disinterested kindness, and which, I can truly say, has never been forgotten by me in any transaction, which has occurred.

For the happiness of yourself and family in every future destination, I offer with absolute sincerity my ⟨war⟩mest wishes.

I am dear sir with great regard & respect Yr. mo. ob. serv.

Edm: Randolph

Colo. Hamilton

ALS, Hamilton Papers, Library of Congress.

1. This is a reference to a note for a loan from H. On the cover of this letter H wrote: "Secty of State his *Note* of Loan." See also Randolph to H, April 3, June 4, 1793; William Bell to H, June 2, 1793.

2. This is a reference to H's trip to western Pennsylvania during the Whiskey Insurrection. H left Philadelphia on September 30, 1794, and returned in late November, 1794.

The Cause of France

[Philadelphia, 1794]

The cause of France! We are every day told, that this is a cause, which ought to engage our warmest affections our best wishes, and there are not a few who think that we ought to hazard upon it our dearest interests. If we ask what is the cause of France, the ready answer is that it is *the cause of Liberty*. It is the cause of a nation nobly struggling for the rights of man, against a combination of despots and Tyrants labouring to destroy them—of a nation on whose fate our own is suspended.[1]

Let us dare to look this question in the face. The world has been scourged with many fanatical sects in religion—who inflamed by a sincere but mistaken zeal have perpetuated under the idea of serving God the most atrocious crimes. If we were to call the cause of such men the cause of religion, would not every one agree, that it was an abuse of terms?

The best apology to be made for the terrible scenes (of which every new arrival shocks us with the dreadful detail) is the supposition, that the ruling party in France is actuated by a zeal similar in its nature (though different in its object) to that which influences religious fanatics. Can this political phrenzy be dignified with the honorable appellation of the cause of Liberty with any greater propriety than the other kind of phrenzy would be denominated the cause of religion?

But even this comparison is too favourable to the ruling party in France. Judging from their acts, we are authorised to pronounce the cause in which they are engaged, not the cause of Liberty, but the cause of Vice Atheism and Anarchy.

ADf, Hamilton Papers, Library of Congress.

1. This paragraph should be compared with the tenth paragraph of "Pacificus No. VI," July 17, 1793.

The French Revolution

[Philadelphia, 1794]

In the early periods of the French Revolution, a warm zeal for its success was in this Country *a sentiment truly universal*. The love of Liberty is here the ruling passion *of the Citizens of the UStates* pervading every class animating every bosom. As long therefore as the Revolution of France bore the marks of being the cause of liberty it united all hearts concentered all opinions. But this unanimity of approbation has been for a considerable time decreasing. The excesses which have constantly multiplied, with greater and greater aggravations have successively though slowly detached reflecting men from their partiality for an object which has appeared less and less to merit their regard. Their reluctance to abandon it has however been proportioned to the ardor and fondness with which they embraced it. They were willing to overlook many faults—to apologise for some enormities—to hope that better justifications existed than were seen—to look forward to more calm and greater moderation, after the first shocks of the political earthquake had subsided. But instead of this, they have been witnesses to one volcano succeeding another, the last still more dreadful than the former, spreading ruin and devastation far and wide—subverting the foundations of right security and property, of order, morality and religion—sparing neither sex nor age, confounding innocence with guilt, involving the old and the young, the sage and the madman, the long tried friend of virtue and his country and the upstart pretender to purity and patriotism—the bold projector of new treasons with the obscure in indiscriminate and profuse destruction. They have found themselves driven to the painful alternative of renouncing an object dear to their wishes or of becoming by the continuance of their affection for it accomplices with Vice Anarchy Depotism and Impiety.

But though an afflicting experience has materially lessened the number of the admirers of the French Revolution among us and has served to chill the ardor of many more, who profess still to retain their attachment to it, from what they suppose to be its ultimate tendency; yet the effect of Experience has been thus far much less than could reasonably have been expected. The predilection for it still continues extensive and ardent. And what is extraordinary it continues to comprehend men who are able to form a just estimate of the information which destroys its title to their favour.

It is not among the least perplexing phœnomina of the present times, that a people like that of the UStates—exemplary for humanity and moderation surpassed by no other in the love of order and a knowlege of the true principles of liberty, distinguished for purity of morals and a just reverence for Religion should so long perservere in partiality for a state of things the most cruel sanguinary and violent that ever stained the annuals of mankind, a state of things which annihilates the foundations of social order and true liberty, confounds all moral distinctions and *substitutes to* the mild & beneficent religion of the Gospel a gloomy persecuting and desolating atheism. To the eye of a wise man, this partiality is the most inauspicious circumstance, that has appeared in the affairs of this country. It leads involuntarily and irresistibly to apprehensions concerning the soundness of our principles and the stability of our welfare. It is natural to fear that the transition may not be difficult from the approbation of bad things to the imitation of them; a fear which can only be mitigated by a careful estimate of the extraneous causes that have served to mislead the public judgment.

But though we may find in these causes a solution of the fact calculated to abate our solicitude for the consequences; yet we can not consider the public happiness as out of the reach of danger so long as our principles continue to be exposed to the debauching influence of admiration for an example which, it will not be too strong to say, presents the caricature of human depravity. And the pride of national character at least can find no alleviation for the wound which must be inflicted by so ill-judged so unfortunate a partiality.

If there be any thing solid in virtue—the time must come when it will have been a disgrace to have advocated the Revolution of France in its late stages.

This is a language to which the ears of the people of this country have not been accustommed. Every thing has hitherto conspired to confirm the pernicious fascination by which they are enchained. There has been a positive and a negative conspiracy against the truth which has served to shut out its enlightening ray. Those who always float with the popular gale perceiving the prepossession of the people have administered to it by all the acts in their power—endeavouring to recommend themselves by an exaggerated zeal for a favourite object. Others through timidity caution or an ill-judged policy unwilling to expose themselves to the odium of resisting the general current of feeling have betrayed by silence that Truth which they were unable not to perceive. Others, whose sentiments have weight in the community have been themselves the sincere dupes of .[1] Hence the voice of reason has been stifled and the Nation has been left unadmonished to travel on in one of the most degrading delusions that ever disparaged the understandings of an enlightened people.

To recal them from this dangerous error—to engage them to dismiss their prejudices & consult dispassionately their own good sense—to lead them to an appeal from their own enthusiasm to their reason and humanity would be the most important service that could be rendered to the UStates at the present juncture. The error entertained is not on a mere speculative question. The French Revolution is a political convulsion that in a great or less degree shakes the whole civilized world and it is of real consequence to the principles and of course to the happiness of a Nation to estimate it rightly.

ADf, Hamilton Papers, Library of Congress.

1. At this point H left a line blank in MS.

To George Washington

[Philadelphia, 1794] [1]

Mr Hamilton will with pleasure execute the commands of the President by the time appointed and have the honor of waiting upon him.

AL, Lloyd W. Smith Collection, Morristown National Historical Park, Morristown, New Jersey.

1. This letter is dated on the basis of an account for 1794 in George Washington's handwriting which is attached to the letter.

INDEX

COMPILED BY JEAN G. COOKE